**MATHEMATICAL METHODS IN THE SOCIAL AND MANAGERIAL SCIENCES**

# MATHEMATICAL METHODS IN THE SOCIAL AND MANAGERIAL SCIENCES

**PATRICK HAYES**

*Department of Mathematics*
*Carnegie-Mellon University*

**A Wiley-Interscience Publication**

**JOHN WILEY & SONS,**
**New York · London · Sydney · Toronto**

***Library of Congress Cataloging in Publication Data***

Hayes, Patrick, 1948–
Mathematical methods in the social and managerial sciences.

"A Wiley-interscience publication."
Includes bibliographical references.
1. Social sciences—Mathematical models. 2. Industrial management—Mathematical models. I. Title.
H61.H337 1975 300'.1'51 74-22361
ISBN 0-471-36490-8

Printed in the United States of America
10 9 8 7 6 5 4 3 2 1

*TO MY PARENTS*

# PREFACE

Traditionally, applications of mathematics have been restricted to the physical sciences. Even the flavor of courses ranging from calculus and differential equations to optimization and control theory has been related to chemistry, physics, and engineering. Mathematical theories in the social and managerial sciences have generally been neglected, perhaps in part because of a skepticism concerning their relative value. As a result, those with interests in the social and managerial sciences have frequently terminated their study of mathematics prematurely.

Recently, however, the mathematics curriculum has reflected a decidedly different attitude toward applications of mathematics in the social and managerial sciences. Mathematical methods have been recognized as providing a rational and systematic approach to solving many decision, allocation, and forecasting problems. For instance, our concern with social and economic change has led to the construction of many mathematical models that aid in predicting the effect of these changes, and our desire to make decisions that achieve the best results has even prompted the *development* of several optimization techniques. As a result, mathematics courses that prepare students to apply quantitative techniques in analyzing problems of the decision sciences have been introduced to the mathematics curriculum.

This book provides an introduction to applications and techniques of mathematics in the social and managerial sciences. Here mathematical models of problems from economics, psychology, sociology, and management science are formulated, and appropriate solution techniques are developed to solve them. The discussions presuppose relatively little mathematics and require no specialized knowledge of the social or managerial sciences.

No attempt is made in this volume, however, to cover every mathematical method of value in the social and managerial sciences. I have restricted the discussion to deterministic mathematics which rely upon the ideas and techniques of elementary calculus and matrix algebra. Specifically, topics from ordinary differential equations, convex analysis, convex programming, and geometric programming are included in the text; the discussions of each of these areas apply and reinforce methods of differentiation and integration of functions of one or several variables. For this reason topics such as difference equations, graph and network theory, numerical methods, and game theory are not considered here.

The text itself is divided into three parts—"Differential Equations in the Social and Managerial Sciences," "Convex Analysis in the Social and Managerial Sciences," and "Convex and Geometric Programming in Management Science"—and an appendix containing remedial material from the calculus of functions of several variables. Each of the topics presented in these parts is motivated by a mathematical problem of the social and managerial sciences. The approach is to first simplify the problem by making certain idealizations and by defining the essential variables. After assuming some relationship among these variables and formulating the corresponding equations, the equations are solved and other relations among the variables are derived. Whenever it is appropriate, these relations are interpreted to determine if the mathematical model reflects actual social or economic behavior. Finally, having introduced the reader to an appropriate application of mathematics in the decision sciences, the solution technique is generalized and illustrated further with numerical examples.

This approach provides an introduction to a variety of mathematical modeling techniques as well as to the methods of differential equations, convex analysis, and convex and geometric programming in an applied setting. For instance, the problems of personnel assignment and of voting distribution in the text illustrate two different techniques of formulating, solving, and analyzing mathematical models. In the former case, we proceed by defining a measure of an effective personnel assignment and use results of geometric programming to determine and analyze the optimal selection, while in the voting distribution model, we describe variations in the voting behavior of a population, use the methods of differential equations to predict the final voting distribution, and graphically analyze the stability of the system. In both problems, we have replaced a discrete process by a continuous one: that is, both the various possible personnel assignments and voting distributions change by discrete amounts but are treated as continuous. The actual discrete process is considered to be imbedded in the continuous one.

Thus, by discussing these problems and by doing the corresponding exercises the reader develops the techniques of constructing and analyzing mathematical models. Gradually, he develops the ability to eliminate the unnecessary details of the problem, simplify the essential information, and translate it into mathematical terms, recognizing similarities with other structures. The student realizes that the construction of a mathematical model is not unique and that, indeed, several models may prove useful in understanding some aspects of a problem.

These applications also provide the reader with a feeling and appreciation for the relationship between differential equations, convex analysis, or convex and geometric programming and the decision sciences. The reader not only develops an understanding of these mathematical topics but also a facility for using and interpreting these results in the social and managerial sciences.

In the first part, Differential Equations in the Social and Managerial Sciences, a development of the fundamental theory and techniques of ordinary differential equations is presented in such an applied setting. First-order equations are introduced by posing the questions of existence and uniqueness of solutions in the context of a sales–advertising problem. Explicit solution techniques for first-order equations are related to the applications as well as the fundamental theory by solving first-order initial-value problems; geometric methods are introduced to analyze solvable and "unsolvable" equations. In somewhat the same spirit, second-order linear equations and first-order linear systems with constant coefficients are treated in the remaining sections. Through applications in the social and managerial sciences the nature of these equations is discussed, followed by a treatment of the fundamental theory and appropriate solution techniques.

Although no prior knowledge of differential equations is assumed, both the examples and exercises require applications of numerous techniques of differentiation and integration of functions of one variable. A little matrix algebra is also used in the treatment of first-order linear systems. Throughout this part the proofs of theorems are in most cases omitted; generally, only those proofs demonstrating the value of the linear structure of equations are retained.

The notions of convexity and several of the modeling techniques introduced in the first part are extended into Part 2, Convex Analysis in the Social and Managerial Sciences. After defining the concept of a convex set, various convex structures are presented and discussed by considering their economic interpretation and significance in a linear production model. The properties of convex and concave functions are studied by means of models involving convex cost and concave utility functions. Lagrange multipliers are introduced to optimize convex or concave functions constrained by factors considered in several models.

Although much of this discussion is based upon geometric intuition, Part 2 contains many mathematical results. As in the previous part, these results are summarized in theorems. Proofs of most of these theorems have been retained to demonstrate the use of various definitions.

Much of this part and all of the last rely heavily on several geometric and topological notions in $\mathbb{R}^n$ as well as many techniques of differential calculus of functions of several variables. Consequently, a review of this material in the appendix prior to beginning this part may be advisable.

Many of the properties of convex sets and convex functions discussed in Part 2 are applied in the final chapter, Convex and Geometric Programming in Management Science. Here, using geometric and analytic properties of convex functions, the Kuhn–Tucker conditions of convex programming are developed. These conditions are then applied in developing duality theorems for convex programming and linear programming within an applied framework.

Although the techniques of geometric programming are developed from the arithmetic geometric mean inequality, the relationship between geometric and convex programming is emphasized throughout. In fact, the rather lengthy proof of the duality theorem of geometric programming is included to illustrate this application of the Kuhn–Tucker theory. After developing the remarkable technique of geometric programming, but noting its limitations, these ideas and methods are extended to solve other classes of optimization problems. These include problems of linear programming, exponential programming, reversed geometric programming, and parametric programming. Although basic notions of probability are used in two discussions in this part, their application is motivated by an intuitive discussion. Finally, topics of recent research in geometric programming, such as classification theory, vector valued criteria, and the harmonized geometric program, are introduced through a sequence of exercises.

Throughout this book, several conventions have been adopted. Beginning in Chapter 1, theorems, equations, tables, and figures are each numbered consecutively throughout the main text. In the appendix, the numbering system is separate and each number includes the prefix "A." Thus, for example, the fourth figure in the appendix is labeled Figure A4.

*Mathematical Methods in the Social and Managerial Sciences* developed from a course for students of applied mathematics, operations research, the social and managerial sciences, and related fields. At Carnegie-Mellon University this book has been the core of the two-semester applied mathematics sequence "Higher Mathematics in the Social and Managerial Sciences." Most of the students had completed only the traditional calculus sequence.

The book contains sufficient material to serve as the basis for a one-year course and for a variety of shorter courses and seminars in applied mathematics. For example, the third part, Convex and Geometric Programming in

Management Science, supplemented by a brief discussion of the properties of convex functions from Part 2, provides the structure for a one-semester applied nonlinear programming course. Furthermore, the second part, along with a discussion of convex programming and a brief introduction to constrained geometric programming from Part 3, may be used in an applied convex analysis course. Separately, Parts 1 and 2 provide the basis for mini-courses in applied mathematics; together they form an effective course in methods of applied mathematics. Naturally, the book also may be used as a reference for more traditional mathematics courses.

The development of this book would have been impossible without the aid of many individuals and institutions. First among these are the students who used the preliminary notes as a text in the "Higher Mathematics in the Social and Managerial Sciences" sequence at Carnegie-Mellon University. Throughout the development of this manuscript, they patiently tolerated the many difficulties and frequently contributed useful comments and criticisms. Without these students, this work, as well as my teaching experience at Carnegie-Mellon, would have been much less enjoyable.

I am especially appreciative of the stimulating encouragement of Professor Richard J. Duffin during the writing of this book. My interest in applied mathematics and my perception and appreciation of mathematical programming was greatly enhanced by Professor Duffin. I am indebted to Professor Albert A. Blank for his zealous interest and generous help in improving this book. Indeed, without his encouragement this work would not even have been published.

Sincere thanks also go to Professors Kenneth Kortanek and Charles Coffman for their many valuable suggestions and to my colleagues, Eugene McCarthy and Stephen Fesmire, for their help in teaching from preliminary versions of this work. I extend sincere gratitude to Edwin Mihallo, who offered much encouragement, assistance, and constructive criticism. My sister's help and enthusiastic interest in this project always will be appreciated. Throughout the development of this book, I spent many memorable and enjoyable moments with two very special friends, Sue and Ray Fretterd. I am deeply appreciative of their generous help, their continual encouragement, and, most important, their endless acts of friendship.

I wish to thank the National Defense Education Association for financial support and to acknowledge the Department of Mathematics at Carnegie-Mellon University for providing a stimulating environment for teaching.

Special thanks are extended to Miss Nancy Colmer for her considerate, prompt, and expert efforts in typing and retyping this manuscript. Finally, the consulting, editorial, and production staff of John Wiley and Sons has been most helpful and cooperative. I am particularly grateful to my delightful editor, Miss Beatrice Shube, for her editorial assistance was boundless.

PATRICK HAYES

*April 1974*

# CONTENTS

**MATHEMATICAL METHODS IN THE SOCIAL AND MANAGERIAL SCIENCES**

# PART 1

# DIFFERENTIAL EQUATIONS IN THE SOCIAL AND MANAGERIAL SCIENCES

# CHAPTER 1

# FIRST-ORDER EQUATIONS

## SALES AND ADVERTISING: THE FIRST-ORDER EQUATION

Many a mathematical description of social and economic change takes the form of an equation relating an unknown function of one variable and its derivatives. Such an equation is an *ordinary differential equation*. Ordinary differential equations are used in modeling such phenomena as the effect of political campaign efforts on voting distribution and the fluctuations of supply and demand with changes in price.

To illustrate the use of differential equations in the social and managerial sciences, we consider the mathematical problem of describing the variation in the sales of a product with different amounts of advertising expenditures. To simplify our model and yet exhibit the essential sales–advertising relationship let us first make several assumptions. Assume that sales is a function of advertising only and that in the absence of advertising there are no sales. Furthermore, assume that advertising merely obtains *new* customers from a finite population, so that increased customer usage of the product is neglected. We shall also ignore possible variations in the effectiveness of advertising dollars; that is, two advertising campaigns with identical total costs are assumed to be equally effective.

Sales generally would be expected to increase in response to increased advertising expenditures. However, although sales may rise very rapidly at first, they would eventually level off under our assumptions, despite the continuance of advertising. Since increased usage of the product is excluded, the limit of sales that can be captured by the product includes only sales to present customers and sales to those who will be attracted to the product as a result of advertising. Because there are fewer potential customers upon whom the advertising may be effective, the observed increase in sales per advertising dollar decreases as the level of advertising increases.

Now let us represent this marketing behavior by a differential equation. Denote the total sales by $S$, the advertising expenditure by $A$, and the

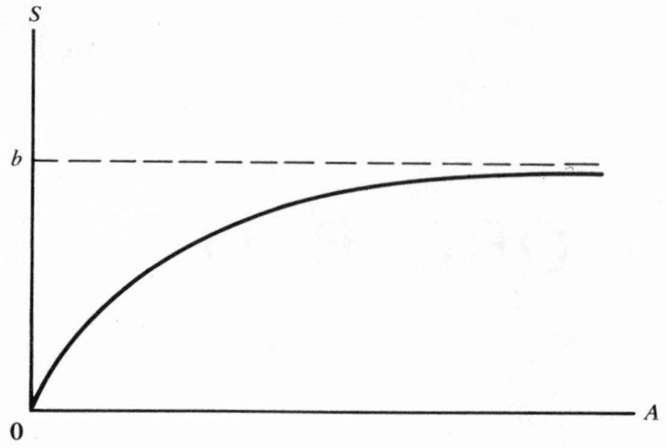


Figure 1

maximum market potential by $b$. Since sales are postulated to be an increasing function of advertising, we know $dS/dA > 0$. Initially, $S = 0$ when $A = 0$ by assumption. The rate of sales increase is most rapid for smaller advertising expenditures; that is, the first advertising expenditures are most effective because the total market $b$ is available. As sales approach the maximum market potential, $S \to b$, the rate of change in sales decreases; that is, $d^2S/dA^2 < 0$. Thus, $dS/dA$ is a function of the untapped market potential, $b - S$:

$$\frac{dS}{dA} = f(b - S)$$

(see Figure 1). The simplest function $f$ demonstrating the behavior that $dS/dA = f(b - S)$ is positive and decreases to zero as $S \to b$ is

$$f(b - S) = \alpha(b - S),$$

where $\alpha$ ($> 0$) is a constant. Therefore, under our assumptions, the simplest mathematical model describing the response of sales to advertising is given by the *first-order ordinary differential equation*

$$\frac{dS}{dA} = \alpha(b - S), \tag{1}$$

with the *initial condition*

$$S = 0 \quad \text{when} \quad A = 0. \tag{2}$$

Let us use this model to estimate the sales of a product when the advertising expenditure is $A^*$ dollars. First, we must find a function, $S(A)$, expressing the dependence of sales $S$ on advertising $A$ and "satisfying" the differential equation (1) and the initial condition (2) identically. That is,

$$\frac{dS(A)}{dA} = \alpha[b - S(A)]$$

$$S(0) = 0.$$

Such a function $S(A)$ is called a *solution* of (1) obeying initial conditions (2). If we can determine $S(A)$, the sales associated with an advertising expenditure $A^*$ is estimated to be $S(A^*)$.

However, does a solution $S(A)$ necessarily *exist*? Sales have been observed to vary with advertising. Therefore, if such a function does not exist, the assumptions of our mathematical model are inconsistent with experience. Furthermore, if a solution to (1) and (2) exists, is it *unique*? Having more than one level of sales corresponding to any advertising expenditure would not conform to observed marketing behavior. Finally, we are interested in the *sensitivity* of our solution to initial conditions. For instance, how would our sales–advertising relationship be effected if our initial sales were $S_0$, slightly greater than zero?

These questions demonstrate the need for a general existence and uniqueness theory, one applicable to a wide variety of problems involving differential equations. Hence, we begin our discussion of ordinary differential equations with a discussion of the fundamental theory.

## FUNDAMENTAL THEORY

An equation of the form

$$F(t, y, y') = 0,$$

where $y' = dy/dt$, is a *first-order differential equation*. First-order equations of the special forms

$$y' = p(t)y + q(t) \tag{3}$$

and

$$y' = g(t)h(y)$$

are particularly important in mathematical theories in the social and managerial sciences. We shall treat the fundamental theory of first-order equations for the general standard form

$$y' = f(t, y) \tag{4}$$

with an *initial condition* $y(t_0) = y_0$. A *solution* of (4) is any function $y = y(t)$ that, together with its derivative $y'(t)$, satisfies (4) identically. For example,

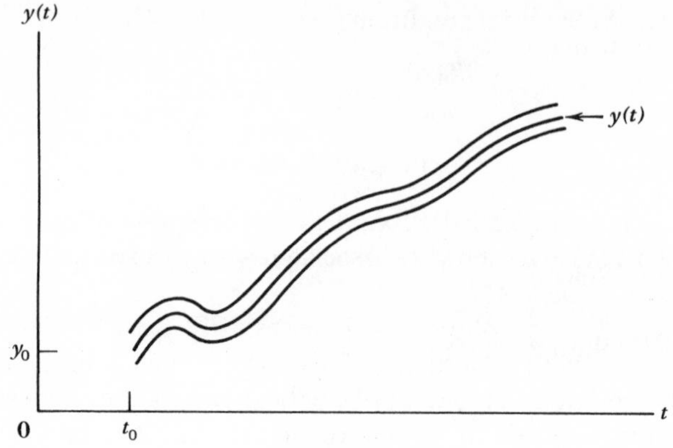


**Figure 2**

$e^t$ is a solution of

$$y' = y \tag{5}$$

for all $t$, because

$$(e^t)' = e^t.$$

For many first-order equations, such as (3), techniques have been developed to obtain formal solutions. Since solutions for these equations can be displayed, a general theorem asserting the existence of solutions is unnecessary. However, for other differential equations, solutions exist, but no manipulative procedure exists for exhibiting them.

The fundamental theory of first-order equations states that under certain conditions on $f(t, y)$ a *unique* solution of the *initial value problem*

$$y' = f(t, y)$$
$$y(t_0) = y_0$$

*exists* in some interval containing $t_0$. The fundamental theory also states that this unique solution *depends continuously* on the parameters $t_0$ and $y_0$; in other words, small changes in $t_0$ and $y_0$ result in solutions "close" to the original solution (see Figure 2).

The theorem summarizing these results is now stated:

THEOREM 1 If $f$ and $\partial f/\partial y$ are continuous in a rectangle $R: |t - t_0| \leq a$, $|y - y_0| \leq d$, then there is some interval $|t - t_0| \leq h \leq a$ in which there *exists* a *unique* solution $y(t)$ of the initial value problem

$$y' = f(t, y)$$
$$y(t_0) = y_0.$$

This unique solution is a *continuous function* of $t_0$ and $y_0$. ∎

To illustrate this theorem consider the initial value problem posed by our sales–advertising marketing model:

$$\frac{dy}{dt} = \alpha(b - y) \tag{6}$$

$$y(0) = 0 \tag{7}$$

($y = S$, $t = A$). Since $f(t, y) = \alpha(b - y)$ and $\partial f/\partial y = -\alpha$ are continuous on any rectangle $|t| \leq a$, $|y| \leq d$, Theorem 1 states that there *exists* a solution to (6) and (7). *All* solutions of (6) may be shown to be of the form

$$y(t) = ce^{-\alpha t} + b$$

for *any* real constant $c$. The initial condition (7) specifies a *single* value for $c$ and consequently a *unique* solution. Since

$$0 = y(0) = ce^{-\alpha 0} + b = c + b,$$

$c = -b$. Thus, the *unique* solution is

$$y(t) = b(1 - e^{-\alpha t}).$$

The continuous dependence of the solution on the initial data $y(0) = 0$ may be demonstrated by varying the initial condition. Consider the associated initial value problem

$$z' = \alpha(b - z) \tag{8}$$

$$z(0) = \epsilon \tag{9}$$

where $\epsilon$ ($> 0$) is "small." The unique solution of (8) and (9) is

$$z(t) = b(1 - e^{-\alpha t}) + \epsilon e^{-\alpha t}.$$

For $t$ satisfying $|t| \leq a$, we see that

$$|y(t) - z(t)| = |\epsilon e^{-\alpha t}| \leq \epsilon e^{\alpha a}$$

Thus, on any finite interval, $|y(t) - z(t)|$ is arbitrarily small if and only if $\epsilon = z(0) - y(0)$ is arbitrarily small. This means the solution $y(t)$ depends continuously on $y_0$, as shown in Figure 3. Similarly, $y(t)$ depends continuously on $t_0$.

Although several "stronger" existence and uniqueness theorems are known, Theorem 1 suffices for our purposes. We now proceed to examine several techniques for solving first-order equations.

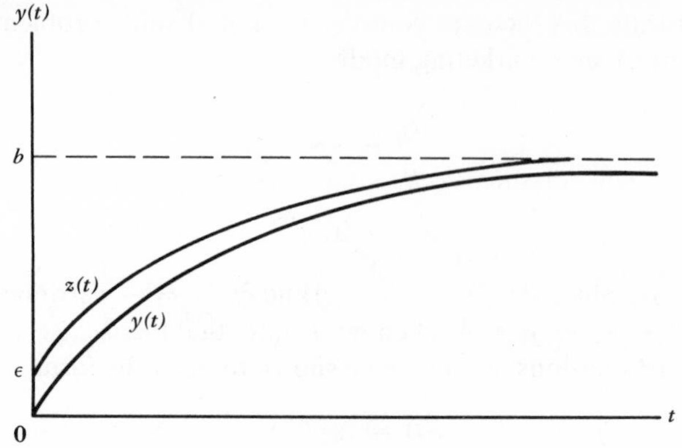


Figure 3

## THE ILLITERACY–LITERACY TRANSITION: LINEAR EQUATIONS

One of the fundamental problems of mathematical sociology is that of describing one-way social processes. One-way social processes include, for example, the transition from illiteracy to literacy or the transition from life to death. In general, such processes are characterized as having two states with a shift between states in only one possible direction (as from living to dead). In order to demonstrate the fundamental quality of the general one-way social-process model, we shall consider education as a one-way social process and mathematically describe the transition from an illiterate to a literate state.

In constructing a mathematical model of the illiterate–literate transition, we wish to describe the rate of transition and determine the number of individuals in either state at any time. In order to construct a mathematical model for this transition, we must make several simplifying assumptions. First, assume that we are dealing with a very large homogeneous population of fixed size $y_0$ all of whom are initially, at $t = 0$, illiterate. Second, let us consider education as the one-way social process that, operating over a period of time, transforms a person from a state of illiteracy to a state of literacy. Since educational facilities are improving through time, the shift rate from illiteracy to literacy depends upon the date at which people begin their education. Therefore, let us assume that the incremental rate of improvement in educational facilities is constant.

Because the population is assumed to be very large and homogeneous, it is reasonable to theorize that the rate of change of the number of illiterates with time is directly proportional to the number of illiterates. If $y$ denotes the number of illiterates at time $t$, then the ordinary differential equation

$$\frac{dy}{dt} = -ky$$

($k > 0$, a constant) mathematically describes this behavior. The constant $k$ may be interpreted as the illiteracy–literacy transition rate.

As was previously noted, this constant $k$ depends upon the rate of improvement of the educational facilities and the dates when the illiterates begin their education. The simplest such relationship is

$$k = \alpha\beta,$$

where $\alpha$ is the constant rate of improvement of the educational facilities and $\beta$ ($> 0$) is the *average* date on which the education for the initial group begins. Note that the transition rate $k$ increases if the average date $\beta$ increases; this reflects the effect of improved educational facilities.

Thus, we have modeled the illiteracy–literacy transition for a large illiterate, homogeneous population with the initial value problem

$$\frac{dy}{dt} = -ky \qquad (k = \alpha\beta) \tag{10}$$

$$y(0) = y_0. \tag{11}$$

Now we wish to use this model to determine actually the number of illiterates remaining in the population at any time $t$. That is, we wish to *solve* the initial value problem (10), (11).

Equation (10) can be solved by inspection. From elementary calculus we know the only function having a derivative that is a scalar multiple, $-k$, of the original function is of the form

$$y(t) = ce^{-kt} \qquad (k = \alpha\beta),$$

where $c$ is a constant. If the initial condition (11), $y(0) = y_0$, must be satisfied, $c = y_0$. Therefore, the solution of (10) and (11), the number of illiterates at time $t$, is

$$y(t) = y_0 e^{-kt} \qquad (k = \alpha\beta). \tag{12}$$

From this expression we see that as time passes, the number of illiterates decreases. This follows because as $t$ becomes large ($t \to \infty$),

$$e^{-kt} \to 0,$$

and hence, the number of illiterates tends to zero:

$$y(t) = y_0 e^{-kt} \to 0.$$

(see Figure 4).

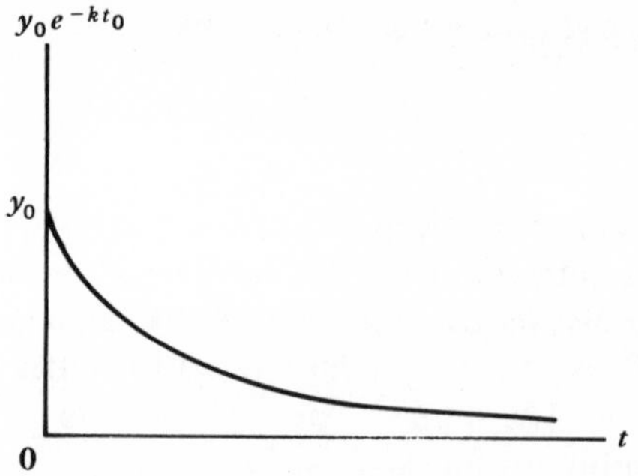


Figure 4

In a similar manner, observe that at any time $t_0$ the number of illiterates $y_0e^{-kt_0}$ also decreases as the rate of improvement in the educational facilities, $\alpha$, increases. That is, since $k = \alpha\beta$ increases as $\alpha$ increases for a constant $\beta$,

$$e^{-kt_0}$$

decreases. Hence, the number of illiterates at time $t_0$,

$$y_0e^{-kt_0},$$

decreases.

Finally, observe that substitution of (12) into (10) yields an expression for the rate of change in the number of illiterates at any time $t$,

$$\frac{dy}{dt} = -ky = -ky_0e^{-kt}.$$

Note that as time passes ($t \to \infty$), this rate of change in the number of illiterates increases to zero:

$$\frac{dy}{dt} \to 0.$$

How do variations in $\alpha$ effect this rate of change at a particular time $t_0$?

A more systematic technique for obtaining solutions of (10) or, equivalently,

$$y' + ky = 0 \tag{13}$$

would be the following. Notice that for any constant $k$, multiplication of (13) by $e^{kt}$ yields

$$e^{kt}y' + ke^{kt}y = 0,$$

the derivative of the product $e^{kt}y$. That is,

$$(e^{kt}y)' = 0.$$

Therefore, there is a constant $c$ such that

$$e^{kt}y = c$$

or

$$y = ce^{-kt}.$$

(The initial condition is now used to determine $c$.)

This procedure is also applicable to the more general equation

$$y' + ky = q(t), \tag{14}$$

where $q(t)$ is a continuous function on some interval. Multiplication in (14) by $e^{kt}$ gives

$$e^{kt}y' + ke^{kt}y = e^{kt}q(t). \tag{15}$$

The left side of (15) is the derivative of the product $e^{kt}y$ so that (15) is equivalent to

$$(ye^{kt})' = e^{kt}q(t). \tag{16}$$

The indefinite integral of (16) yields

$$e^{kt}y = \int e^{kt}q(t)\,dt + c$$

or

$$y(t) = e^{-kt}\int e^{kt}q(t)\,dt + ce^{-kt}$$

($c$ may be determined from the initial condition).

The general first-order *linear* equation

$$y' + p(t)y = q(t),$$

where $p(t)$ and $q(t)$ are continuous on some interval, also may be solved using this procedure. As in the case of equation (14) we wish to find a function $m(t)$ such that

$$m(t)[y' + p(t)y] = [m(t)y]' = m(t)q(t).$$

Observe that $m(t) = \exp[\int p(t)\,dt]$ is such a function:

$$\exp\left[\int p(t)\,dt\right]y' + p(t)\exp\left[\int p(t)\,dt\right]y = \left(\exp\left[\int p(t)\,dt\right]y\right)'.$$

Therefore,

$$\left(\exp\left[\int p(t)\,dt\right]y\right)' = \exp\left[\int p(t)\,dt\right]q(t). \tag{17}$$

Taking the indefinite integral of (17) we obtain

$$\exp\left[\int p(t)\,dt\right] y = \int \exp\left[\int p(t)\,dt\right] q(t)\,dt + c$$

or

$$y(t) = \exp\left[-\int p(t)\,dt\right]\int \exp\left[\int p(t)\,dt\right] q(t)\,dt + c\exp\left[-\int p(t)\,dt\right].$$

To illustrate this procedure, consider the following first-order linear initial value problem

$$y' + 2ty = 2t \tag{18}$$

$$y(0) = 7. \tag{19}$$

Multiplying (18) by $\exp(\int 2t\,dt)$, we obtain the left side of (18) in the form of the derivative of a product,

$$\exp\left[\int 2t\,dt\right] y' + 2t\exp\left[\int 2t\,dt\right] y = \left(\exp\left[\int 2t\,dt\right] y\right)'.$$

Thus, (18) becomes

$$(e^{t^2}y)' = 2te^{t^2}$$

and an integration gives

$$e^{t^2}y = \int 2te^{t^2}\,dt + c = e^{t^2} + c,$$

or

$$y(t) = 1 + ce^{-t^2}.$$

Since $y(0) = 1 + c = 7, c = 6$. Thus, the *unique* solution of the initial value problem (18), (19) is

$$y(t) = 6e^{-t^2} + 1.$$

As a second example, consider the first-order linear initial value problem

$$y' - y = 2te^t \tag{20}$$

$$y(0) = -1. \tag{21}$$

Multiplying (20) by $\exp(\int -1\,dt) = e^{-t}$, the left side of (20) is transformed into the derivative of a product,

$$e^{-t}y' - e^{-t}y = (e^{-t}y)'$$

and the right side becomes

$$(2te^t)(e^{-t}) = 2t.$$

Hence, equation (20) is equivalent to

$$(e^{-t}y)' = 2t. \tag{22}$$

By integrating (22) we find

$$e^{-t}y = t^2 + c$$

or

$$y = t^2e^t + ce^t.$$

Since $y(0) = 0 + c = -1, c = -1$. Thus, the *unique* solution of (20), (21) is

$$y(t) = t^2e^t - e^t.$$

The initial value problem

$$y' + \frac{1}{t}y = \frac{1}{t}, \qquad t > 0 \tag{23}$$

$$y(1) = -1 \tag{24}$$

provides a final illustration of this technique. Upon multiplying (23) by $\exp[\int (1/t)\,dt] = e^{\ln t} = t$, the left side of (23) becomes the derivative of a product,

$$ty' + y = (ty)',$$

and the right side equals

$$t\left(\frac{1}{t}\right) = 1.$$

Therefore, (23) is equivalent to

$$(ty)' = 1.$$

Integration of the latter expression yields

$$ty = t + c$$

or

$$y(t) = 1 + \frac{c}{t}.$$

Since $y(1) = 1 + (c/1) = -1$, $c = -2$, implying the *unique* solution of (23), (24) is

$$y(t) = 1 - \frac{2}{t}.$$

## THE SPREAD OF A RUMOR: SEPARABLE EQUATIONS

Mathematical models of the spread of a rumor are examples from a general class of social diffusion models. In these models of the spread of a rumor each individual in a group is characterized as knowing or not knowing the rumor. Complete diffusion of the rumor in this group of given size occurs when all individuals know the rumor.

One of the assumptions characterizing nearly all models of the spread of a rumor is that of a completely intermixed population. Without this assumption a serious bias may be introduced. For instance, if diffusion of the rumor begins with one person, then the person to whom he relates the rumor will not be a random person—this second person will usually be in contact with many of the same people as was the first person. The probable result of this is that as diffusion proceeds, the group that knows the rumor may be people who have many contacts with each other but few with the people who do not know the rumor. The rumor may die out.

We shall consider a model in which an unforgettable rumor spreads by contact between members of a community. We assume that no one enters or leaves this community; that is, for instance, there are no births or deaths. Ultimately, therefore, everyone in the community will hear the rumor.

In constructing a model to describe the rate with which the rumor spreads, suppose a single member of the community starts the rumor. Let $x$ denote the number of people who have not heard the rumor and let $y$ denote the number who have heard the rumor at any time $t$. The total population size is $x + y = n$. Let us assume that the entire population is subject to some process of homogeneous mixing. With this assumption, it is reasonable to assume that the rate at which the rumor spreads is proportional to the number of possible contacts in the community at any time $t$; that is, $dy/dt$ is proportional to $yx$. For $a > 0$ this process is described by the so-called *logistic differential equation*

$$\frac{dy}{dt} = axy = a(n - y)y \tag{25}$$

with the initial condition

$$y = 1 \quad \text{when} \quad t = 0. \tag{26}$$

The logistic equation (25) is an example of a *separable equation*. It is a first-order equation that can be reduced by algebraic manipulations to the form

$$y' = g(t)h(y), \tag{27}$$

where $g$ and $h$ are continuous in their domains. In the logistic equation

$$g(t) \equiv a \qquad \text{and} \qquad h(y) = y(n - y).$$

Separable equations may be solved by simple integrations. If (25) is put in the equivalent differential form

$$\frac{dy}{y(n - y)} = a\,dt, \tag{28}$$

we may solve (25) by integrating (28). The left side of (28) may be integrated by the technique of partial fractions:

$$\int \frac{dy}{y(n - y)} = \int \frac{1}{n}\frac{dy}{y} + \int \frac{1}{n}\frac{dy}{(n - y)} = \int a\,dt.$$

That is,

$$\frac{1}{n}(\ln y - \ln (n - y)) = at + c.$$

Solving for $y$ in terms of $t$, we obtain the solution:

$$y = \frac{n}{1 + e^{-n(at + c)}}.$$

Since $y(t)$ must satisfy $y(0) = 1$, $c = \ln (n - 1)$ and the *unique* solution of the initial value problem (25), (26) is

$$y = \frac{n}{1 + (n - 1)e^{-nat}}. \tag{29}$$

This represents the number of people who have heard the rumor at time $t$.

From this expression, we see that as time passes, the number of people who know the rumor approaches $n$. This follows, since as $t \to \infty$,

$$e^{-nat} \to 0$$

and consequently,

$$1 + (n - 1)e^{-nat} \to 1.$$

Thus, (29) shows that

$$y(t) \to n;$$

$y(t)$ approaches the size of the population.

Furthermore, the rate with which the rumor spreads tends to zero as time passes. This follows because as $t \to \infty$,

$$y - n \to 0,$$

and hence,

$$\frac{dy}{dt} = ay(y - n) \to 0.$$

How do $y(t)$ and $dy/dt$ vary with changes in the proportionality constant $a$ at a particular time $t_0$?

The general separation-of-variables technique is the same. Equation (27) may be put in the differential form

$$\frac{dy}{h(y)} = g(t)\,dt.$$

Integrating both sides of the latter equation, we obtain

$$\int \frac{dy}{h(y)} = \int g(t)\,dt + c. \tag{30}$$

Since $g$ and $h$ are continuous on their domains, the integrals in (30) exist. By evaluating these integrals, we obtain, perhaps in implicit form, the general solution of (27).

Let us consider a second separable equation,

$$y' = te^{-y}. \tag{31}$$

Here $g(t) = t$ and $h(y) = e^{-y}$. If (31) is put in differential form,

$$e^y\,dy = t\,dt, \tag{32}$$

we may integrate (32) to obtain the solution in *implicit form:*

$$e^y = \frac{t^2}{2} + c$$

for any constant $c$. Solving for $y$, we find

$$y = \ln\left(\frac{t^2}{2} + c\right).$$

The equation

$$y' = \frac{t}{y}e^{t^2 - y^2} \qquad (y \neq 0)$$

provides another illustration of the technique of separation of variables. Here $g(t) = te^{t^2}$ and $h(y) = e^{-y^2}/y$. This equation may be transformed into the differential form

$$e^{y^2}y\,dy = e^{t^2}t\,dt. \tag{33}$$

By integrating (33) we obtain the solution in *implicit form*,

$$e^{y^2} = e^{t^2} + c.$$

As a final example of the technique of separation of variables consider the initial value problem

(34) $$y' = \frac{\cos t}{3y^2 + e^y}$$

(35) $$y(0) = 0.$$

In this problem $g(t) = \cos t$ and $h(y) = 1/(3y^2 + e^y)$. The equivalent differential form of (34) is

(36) $$(3y^2 + e^y)\,dy = \cos t\,dt.$$

An integration of (36) yields the general form for all solutions in *implicit form*,

$$y^3 + e^y = \sin t + c.$$

Since $y(0) = 0$, $0^3 + 1 = \sin 0 + c$, implying $c = 1$ and the *unique* solution of (34), (35) is

$$y^3 + e^y = \sin t + 1.$$

## PRICE SPECULATION: GEOMETRIC ANALYSIS*

The response of consumer demand to alternative prices of a product is of interest in mathematical economics. The simplest mathematical models of this responsiveness have regarded prices as independent of time, but market prices for a commodity usually vary with time. Consequently, the demand for (and supply of) the commodity also changes with time, for whether the price is going up or down with time is an important factor in determining demand and supply.

In actual cases supply and demand are often not merely functions of price alone but are also stimulated or depressed by the fact that the price is rising or falling. For instance, business is usually good when prices are rising and usually not so good when prices are falling. The number of shirts, for example, that will be bought at $7 a piece will be greater if it is known that the price is increasing at a rate of 50¢ a week than if the price is supposed to be decreasing at a rate of 50¢ a week. In the former case, buyers will make purchases when prices are relatively low, while in the latter case buyers will wait until prices fall further before making purchases. This market behavior is known as the effect of *price speculation*.

Here we wish to incorporate the effect of speculation in a mathematical model describing the variation of market price as time passes. Our initial assumption is that the demand and supply are in equilibrium.

* Adapted from G. C. Evans, *Mathematical Introduction to Economics* (McGraw-Hill, New York, 1930). Used with permission.

The market behavior described above implies that demand and supply at time $t$ depend upon the price and the rate of change in the price (the speculative effect) at time $t$. Mathematically this implies the supply at time $t$, $s = s(t)$, and the demand at time $t$, $u = u(t)$, satisfy relationships of the form

$$s(t) = S\left(y(t), \frac{dy}{dt}\right)$$

and

$$u(t) = U\left(y(t), \frac{dy}{dt}\right),$$

where $y(t)$ is the price of the commodity at time $t$.

A measure of the responsiveness of demand to variations in the price, or the rate of change in price, is the partial derivative of $u = u(t)$ with respect to $y = y(t)$, or $w = dy/dt$. If, for instance, $w = dy/dt$ is held constant while the price level is increased by a small amount $\Delta y$, then the demand will vary by an amount $\Delta u$. The average variation in demand due to this price increase is

$$\frac{\Delta u}{\Delta y}; \tag{37}$$

the limiting value of (37) is

$$\frac{\partial u}{\partial y},$$

the *marginal demand with respect to price*. If demand increases with price increases, demand is an increasing function of price or

$$\frac{\partial u}{\partial y} > 0.$$

Likewise, if demand decreases as prices increase, demand is a decreasing function of price or

$$\frac{\partial u}{\partial y} < 0.$$

Similarly, we define the *marginal demand with respect to the rate of change in price* as

$$\frac{\partial u}{\partial w} \tag{38}$$

and analyze the sign of (38).

In this discussion, we assume that higher prices result in decreased demand; that is,

$$\frac{\partial u}{\partial y} < 0.$$

Furthermore we assume that demand increases when prices are rising; mathematically this means

$$\frac{\partial u}{\partial w} > 0$$

where $w = dy/dt$. That is, the faster prices rise as time passes, the greater the demand.

A simple, yet very reasonable, approximation of this market demand behavior is given by the linear function

$$u(t) = a_0 + a_1 y(t) + a_2 \frac{dy}{dt},$$

where $a_1 < 0$ and $a_2 > 0$. Note that $\partial u/\partial y < 0$ and $\partial u/\partial w > 0$ $(w = dy/dt)$.

Analogously, if supply is assumed to be an increasing function of price and an increasing function of the rate of price increase, $s(t)$ must satisfy

$$\frac{\partial s}{\partial y} > 0$$

and

$$\frac{\partial s}{\partial w} > 0,$$

where $w = dy/dt$. The linear function

$$s(t) = b_0 + b_1 y(t) + b_2 \frac{dy}{dt},$$

where $b_1 > 0$ and $b_2 > 0$, exhibits this behavior.

Under our assumptions that the supply balances the demand, we have

$$s(t) = u(t)$$

or, equivalently,

$$b_0 + b_1 y(t) + b_2 \frac{dy}{dt} = a_0 + a_1 y(t) + a_2 \frac{dy}{dt}.$$

If the initial price (at $t = 0$) of the commodity is $y_0$, we see after several algebraic manipulations that the price of the commodity at time $t$ must satisfy the initial value problem

$$\frac{dy}{dt} + \frac{b_1 - a_1}{b_2 - a_2} y = -\frac{b_0 - a_0}{b_2 - a_2} \tag{39}$$

$$y(0) = y_0. \tag{40}$$

Equation (39) is a first-order linear equation. Using an appropriate solution technique, we find as the solution of (39), (40)

(41) $$y(t) = y_1 + (y_0 - y_1)\exp\left[-\left(\frac{b_1 - a_1}{b_2 - a_2}\right)t\right],$$

where $y_1 = -(b_0 - a_0)/(b_1 - a_1)$. This solution provides a simple relationship between the price of a commodity and time under the assumptions of our model.

The particularly simple form of our speculative model (39), (40) and its solution (41) lends the model to further analysis. For instance equation (39) may be used to determine the market equilibrium price. The equilibrium price occurs whenever the price is stationary with respect to time; that is, $dy/dt = 0$. If $dy/dt = 0$ equation (39) implies that the equilibrium price is

$$y_1 = -\left(\frac{b_0 - a_0}{b_1 - a_1}\right).$$

The market behavior as time passes is also of interest. The market is said to be *stable* if the price tends to the equilibrium price as time lapses. Since the price of the commodity at time $t$ is given by (41) we see that the market stability depends upon the behavior of the exponential term. If

$$\frac{b_1 - a_1}{b_2 - a_2} > 0,$$

the market is *stable* because

$$\lim_{t\to\infty} y(t) = y_1.$$

(Recall $\lim_{x\to\infty} e^{-x} = 0$.) That is, as time goes on, the price moves to an equilibrium price. If, however,

$$\frac{b_1 - a_1}{b_2 - a_2} < 0,$$

the market is *unstable* because

(42) $$\begin{aligned} \lim_{t\to\infty} y(t) &= +\infty \qquad \text{when} \qquad y_0 - y_1 > 0 \\ &= -\infty \qquad \text{when} \qquad y_0 - y_1 < 0. \end{aligned}$$

(Recall $\lim_{x\to\infty} e^{x} = \infty$.) Unstable market behavior means that the price increases beyond the region where the linear forms for supply and demand are applicable.

The speculative model (39), (40) represents a practical theory if the changes in price are not too abrupt. Mathematically this means $dy/dt$ is small in numerical value. However, since it is desirable to consider very rapid changes of price, and even to allow $dy/dt$ to become infinite, this model is not sufficiently broad.

One technique for considering very rapid changes in price is to replace the term involving $dy/dt$ with one that behaves like it for small values of $dy/dt$ but that never becomes infinite as $dy/dt \to \infty$. Thus, demand $u$ cannot become infinite unless the price $y$ becomes infinite, which is absurd in reality. The function arctan $dy/dt$ behaves like $dy/dt$ for small values if its graph is chosen to pass through the origin. Furthermore, as $dy/dt \to \infty$, atctan $dy/dt$ remains finite because the values of arctan $dy/dt$ remain between $-\pi/2$ and $\pi/2$ (see Figure 5). In this case, demand and supply become

$$u(t) = a_0 + a_1 y(t) + a_2 \arctan \frac{dy}{dt}$$

and

$$s(t) = b_0 + b_1 y(t) + b_2 \arctan \frac{dy}{dt},$$

respectively.

Under our assumption that

$$s(t) = u(t),$$

we find that price satisfies the condition

$$\arctan \frac{dy}{dt} = -\frac{b_1 - a_1}{b_2 - a_2} y - \frac{b_0 - a_0}{b_2 - a_2}$$

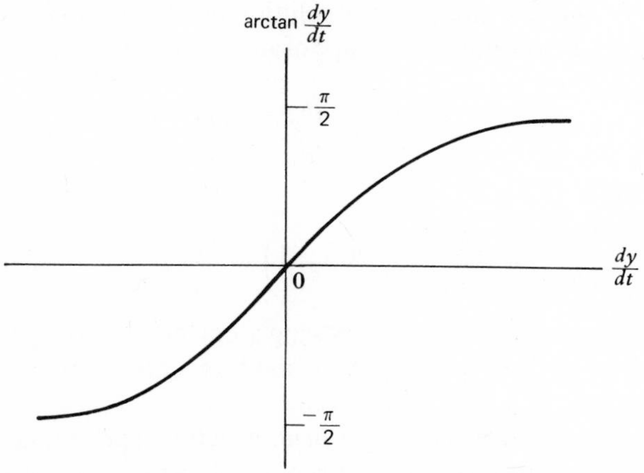


**Figure 5.** From *Mathematical Introduction to Economics* by G. C. Evans (McGraw Hill, New York, 1930). Used with permission.

or

$$\frac{dy}{dt} = \tan\left(-\frac{b_1 - a_1}{b_2 - a_2}y - \frac{b_0 - a_0}{b_2 - a_2}\right).$$

Note that because $|\arctan dy/dt| \leq \pi/2$, we must restrict $y$ to satisfy

$$\left|\frac{b_1 - a_1}{b_2 - a_2}y + \frac{b_0 - a_0}{b_2 - a_2}\right| \leq \frac{\pi}{2}.$$

With the initial condition that $y(0) = y_0$, we find that our price speculation model is

$$\text{(43)} \qquad \frac{dy}{dt} = \tan\left(-\frac{b_1 - a_1}{b_2 - a_2}y - \frac{b_0 - a_0}{b_2 - a_2}\right)$$

$$\text{(44)} \qquad y(0) = y_0.$$

Although this initial value problem may be solved explicitly, we may also use geometric methods to obtain information about the behavior of the solution of (43), (44).

The first-order equation

$$\text{(45)} \qquad \frac{dy}{dt} = \tan\left(-\frac{b_1 - a_1}{b_2 - a_2}y - \frac{b_0 - a_0}{b_2 - a_2}\right)$$

has an immediate geometric interpretation. For every point $(t, y)$ in the plane the value

$$\tan\left(-\frac{b_1 - a_1}{b_2 - a_2}y - \frac{b_0 - a_0}{b_2 - a_2}\right)$$

is the slope $dy/dt$ of the graph of any solution of equation (45) that takes the value $y$ at time $t$. For example, the slope of any solution curve passing through the point

$$p = \left(2, -\frac{(b_0 - a_0)}{(b_1 - a_1)}\right)$$

is 0, because at $p$,

$$\frac{dy}{dt} = \tan\left[\left(-\frac{b_1 - a_1}{b_2 - a_2}\right)\left(-\frac{b_0 - a_0}{b_1 - a_1}\right) - \frac{b_0 - a_0}{b_2 - a_2}\right] = \tan 0 = 0.$$

This is represented graphically by drawing a line of the corresponding slope at the point $p$ as in Figure 6. Any solution curve through the point $(2, -(b_0 - a_0)/(b_1 - a_1))$ has slope zero.

We say that (45) defines a *slope field*, which is represented graphically by drawing in the corresponding slopes at a large number of points. The result yields a clear impression of the general behavior of any solution curve, for any such curve must flow with the slope field. Since the solution is known

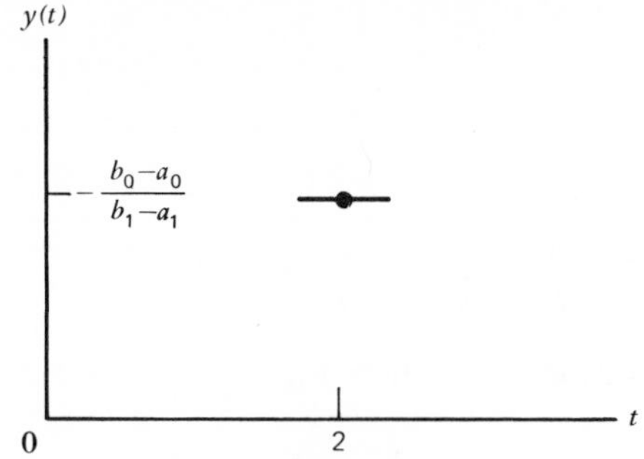


Figure 6

at the point $(0, y_0)$, we may sketch the curve through $(0, y_0)$ and follow the flow and so obtain a *reasonably accurate geometric description of the solution curve*.

Let us consider the slope field of

$$\frac{dy}{dt} = \tan\left[-\frac{(b_1 - a_1)y + b_0 - a_0}{b_2 - a_2}\right] \tag{45}$$

when $(b_1 - a_1)/(b_2 - a_2) > 0$. For the points $(t, -(b_0 - a_0)/(b_1 - a_1))$, $-\infty < t < \infty$,

$$\frac{dy}{dt} = \tan\left[-\frac{b_1 - a_1}{b_2 - a_2}\left(-\frac{b_0 - a_0}{b_1 - a_1}\right) - \frac{b_0 - a_0}{b_2 - a_2}\right] = \tan 0 = 0.$$

For the points $(t, y(t))$, where $y(t) > -(b_0 - a_0)/(b_1 - a_1)$,

$$\mu = -\frac{b_1 - a_1}{b_2 - a_2}y - \frac{b_0 - a_0}{b_2 - a_2} < \left(\frac{b_1 - a_1}{b_2 - a_2}\right)\left(\frac{b_0 - a_0}{b_1 - a_1}\right) - \frac{b_0 - a_0}{b_2 - a_2} = 0$$

and

$$\frac{dy}{dt} = \tan \mu < 0.$$

As $y(t)$ increases further above $-(b_0 - a_0)/(b_1 - a_1)$, $\mu$ tends to $-\pi/2$, the lower limit of $\mu$, and $dy/dt = \tan \mu$ tends to $-\infty$. Thus, the curve becomes steeper with negative slope, as illustrated in Figure 7.

For the points $(t, y(t))$, where $y(t) < -(b_0 - a_0)/(b_1 - a_1)$,

$$\mu = -\frac{b_1 - a_1}{b_2 - a_2}y - \frac{b_0 - a_0}{b_2 - a_2} > \left(\frac{b_1 - a_1}{b_2 - a_2}\right)\left(\frac{b_0 - a_0}{b_1 - a_1}\right) - \frac{b_0 - a_0}{b_2 - a_2} = 0$$

and

$$\frac{dy}{dt} = \tan \mu > 0.$$

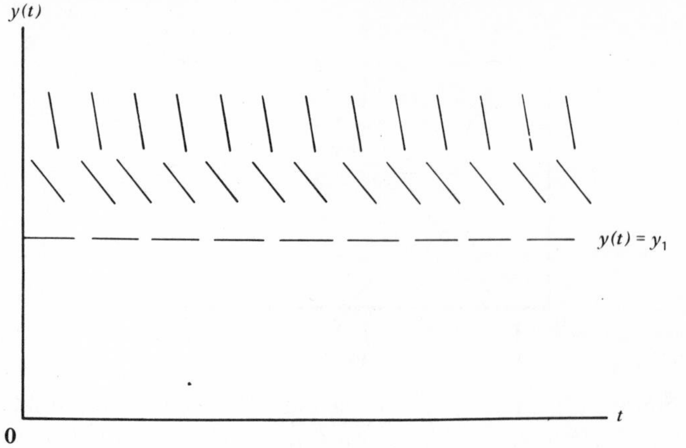


**Figure 7**

As $y(t)$ decreases further below $-(b_0 - a_0)/(b_1 - a_1)$, $\mu$ tends to $\pi/2$, the upper bound of $\mu$, and $dy/dt = \tan \mu$ tends to $+\infty$. Thus, the curve becomes steeper with positive slope and the completed slope field appears as in Figure 8.

Thus, depending on whether $y_0 > y_1 = -(b_0 - a_0)/(b_1 - a_1)$ or $y_0 < y_1$, a geometric description of the solution of (43), (44) lies above or below the line $y = y_1$. However, no matter what price $y_0$ we start from in the allowable range, we tend asymptotically toward the equilibrium price $y_1$. Hence, the market is *stable* when $(b_1 - a_1)/(b_2 - a_2) > 0$.

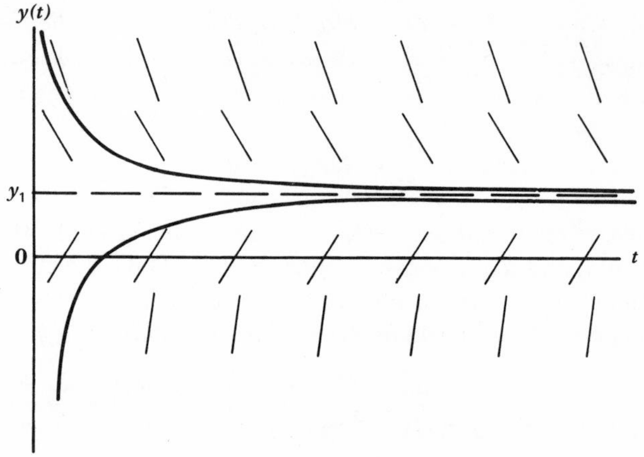


**Figure 8.** From *Mathematical Introduction to Economics* by G. C. Evans (McGraw Hill, New York, 1930). Used with permission.

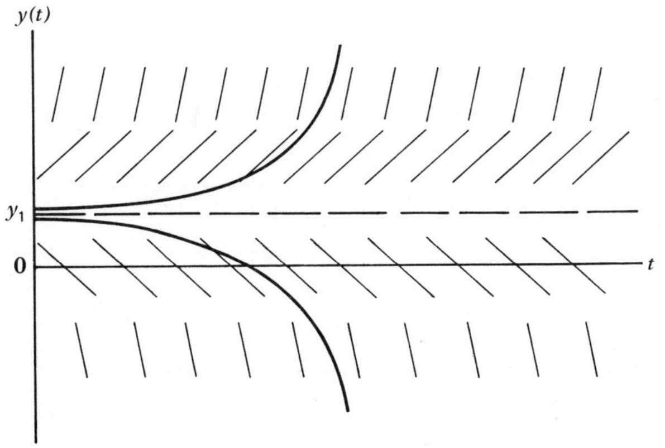


**Figure 9.** From *Mathematical Introduction to Economics* by G. C. Evans (McGraw Hill, New York, 1930). Used with permission.

A similar geometric analysis shows that the slope field of (43) when $(b_1 - a_1)/(b_2 - a_2) < 0$ appears as in Figure 9. From Figure 9 it is readily seen that no matter what price we start from, other than $y_0 = y_1$, the market is *unstable*. After a certain interval of time we come to a price $y^*$ for which $\mu = \pm\pi/2$ and $dy/dt = \tan(\pm\pi/2)$ is infinite. For $y \geq y^*$, the hypotheses of the problem no longer holds and new ones must be substituted.

The slope-field technique can be applied to the standard first-order equation

$$y' = f(t, y) \tag{46}$$

in exactly the same way. Equation (46) defines the slope of the solution curve at each point $(t, y)$ in the domain of $f(t, y)$. By sketching in a short linear element of slope $f(t, y)$ at each of a large number of points we obtain the *slope field*.

A somewhat more systematic method for representing slope fields is the *method of isoclines*, or *loci of equal slope*. In applying this technique, a specific value, say $r$, is assigned to the slope. The result is the equation $f(t, y) = r$, an *isocline*. Solving this equation yields the set of all points $(t, y)$ at which the solution curves have the assigned slope $r$. The solution curve may be determined by sketching in a curve that starts at an initial value $y(t_0) = y_0$ and crosses each isocline with the slope represented by that isocline.

For example, the isoclines of

$$\frac{dy}{dt} = \tan\left(-\frac{b_1 - a_1}{b_2 - a_2}y - \frac{b_0 - a_0}{b_2 - a_2}\right) \tag{45}$$

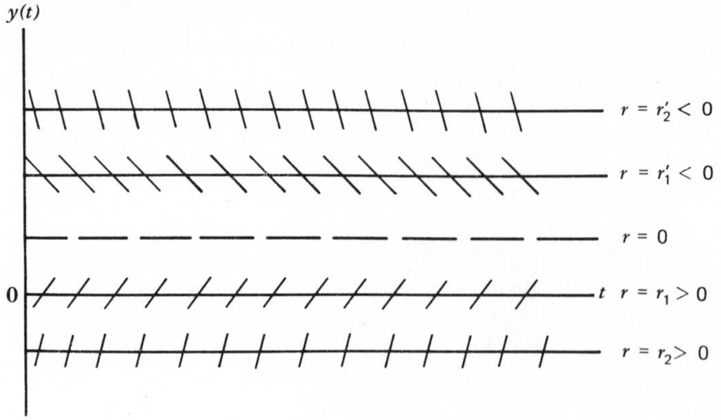


**Figure 10**

for $(b_1 - a_1)/(b_2 - a_2) > 0$ are the horizontal curves,

$$\tan\left(-\frac{b_1 - a_1}{b_2 - a_2}y - \frac{b_0 - a_0}{b_2 - a_2}\right) = r,$$

shown in Figure 10. The solution curve of (45) crosses each isocline with the indicated slope.

The curve $f(t, y) = 0$, the isocline of zero slope, is of particular importance. If $f$ is continuous, then the zero isocline divides the plane into regions in which the slopes are either all positive or all negative. Solutions must increase in the former region and decrease in the latter region.

To better illustrate the method of isoclines, consider the example

(47) $$y' = 1 - y.$$

The isoclines of (47) are the lines

$$r = 1 - y$$

or

$$y = 1 - r,$$

for $-\infty < t < \infty$. Note that the zero isocline is the line

$$y = 1.$$

The isoclines for $r = 1, r = 2, r = -1, r = -2$ are the lines $y = 0, y = -1, y = 2, y = 3$, respectively, as indicated in Figure 11. As shown in this figure, the solution curves cross each isocline with the indicated slope, "flowing" with the slope field.

A second example is provided by the nonlinear equation

(48) $$y' = t^2 + y^2.$$

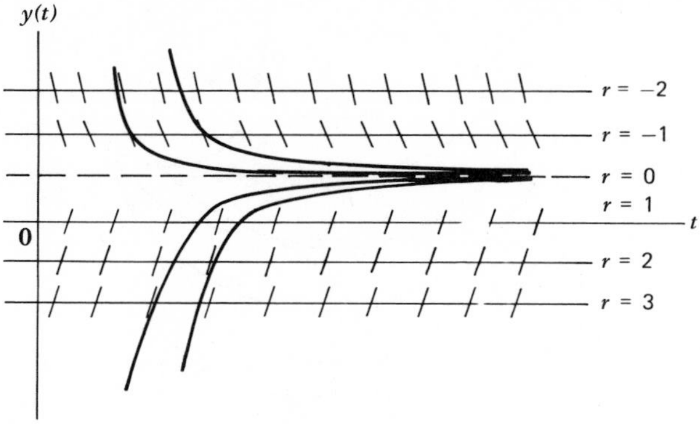


Figure 11

The isoclines of this equation are the curves described by

(49) $$r = t^2 + y^2,$$

the equation of a circle. Thus, the isoclines of (48) are circles; as the radius of the circle increases, the slope of any solution curves crossing the circle increases, as shown in Figure 12. Note that the zero isocline

$$0 = t^2 + y^2$$

is the point (0, 0).

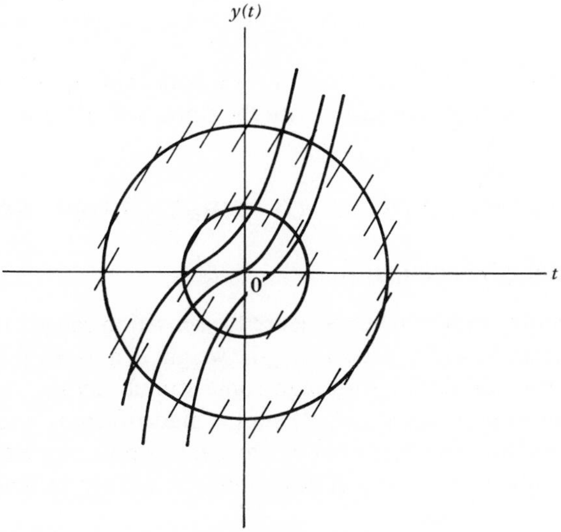


Figure 12

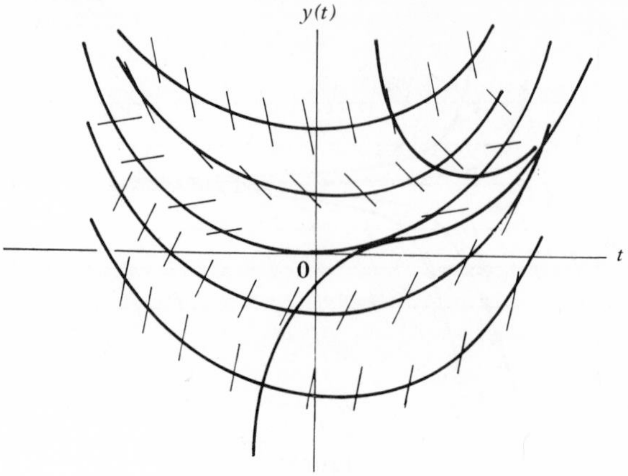


Figure 13

As a final illustration of the method of isoclines consider the example

(50) $$y' = -y + t^2.$$

The isoclines of (50) are the parabolas

$$r = -y + t^2$$

for $-\infty < t < \infty$. The zero isocline is

$$0 = -y + t^2$$

or

$$y = t^2$$

The isoclines for $r = 1, 2$ and $r = -1, -2$, appear in Figure 13. A graphical description of the solutions flows with the slope field as shown.

## FURTHER APPLICATIONS OF FIRST-ORDER EQUATIONS

### A Model of Perception

Many psychology experiments measure the sensation caused by a change in intensity of a stimulus. For instance, if the weight of a package is doubled, do we perceive it as doubled? Although some stimuli involve more than one variable, in most experiments an attempt is made to study one variable at a time with the other variables kept as constant as possible. Here we wish to construct a mathematical model describing the change in sensation caused by a one-variable stimulus.

Suppose $t$ denotes the magnitude of a stimulus. The variable $t$ may be measured in lumens for brightness or units of pounds for weight for instance. Let $y$ denote the magnitude of the sensation caused by the stimulus. This sensation may be measured in a variety of ways; for instance, $y$ may measure a verbal or physical reaction. Mathematically we may express the dependence of $y$ on $t$ as a functional relationship

$$y = f(t).$$

This relationship contains the hypothesis that for a given subject the sensation $y$ depends only on the stimulus $t$. That is, if the subject is exposed to the same stimulus on several occasions, the sensation will be the same each time. Moreover, $f$ is an increasing function, since the sensation increases when the stimulus increases. Furthermore, in most experiments $f$ is also continuous because a slight variation in the stimulus induces only a slight change in sensation. We wish to model this stimulus–sensation relationship and determine such a function $f$.

There are several theories relating the change in the stimulus to the corresponding change in sensation. One theory hypothesizes that for small changes in $t$, $\Delta t$, the *relative sensation*

$$\frac{\Delta y}{y}$$

is usually *proportional to the relative stimulus*

$$\frac{\Delta t}{t} \qquad (t \neq 0).$$

That is,

$$\frac{\Delta y}{y} = c\,\frac{\Delta t}{t}$$

or

$$\frac{\Delta y}{\Delta t} = \frac{c}{t}\,y,$$

where the constant $c$ ($> 0$) depends on the stimulus. In the limit, this becomes

$$\frac{dy}{dt} = \frac{c}{t}\,y \qquad (t \neq 0). \tag{51}$$

Equation (51) is easily solved using the technique of separation of variables. We obtain solutions of the form

$$y = kt^c \tag{52}$$

where $k$ is a constant. Equation (52) is known as *Stevens' law*.

The stimulus–sensation relationship (52) derived from our model is a

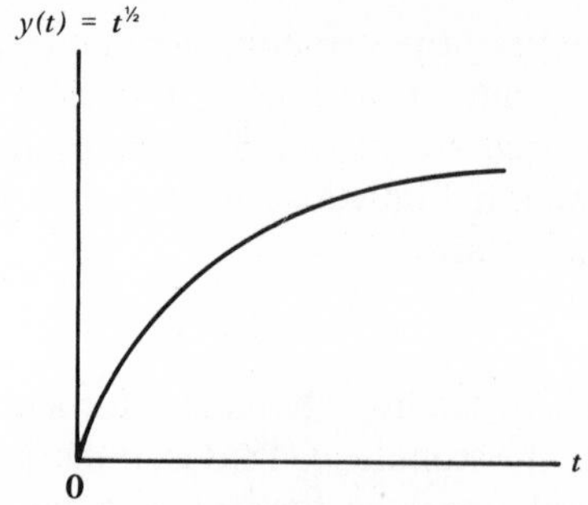


Figure 14

continuous function of $t$. Furthermore, since $k > 0$, $c > 0$, the measure of sensation $y$ increases as the measure of stimulus $t$ increases. The actual stimulus–sensation variations depend upon the values of $k$ and $c$. For instance, suppose $k = 1$ and $c = \frac{1}{2}$; then,

$$y = t^{1/2},$$

as shown in Figure 14. If the stimulus $t_0$ is quadrupled to $4t_0$, then the sensation only doubles; that is, it increases from

$$y_0 = t_0^{1/2}$$

to

$$y_0 = (4t_0)^{1/2} = 2t_0^{1/2}.$$

If, however,

$$y = t^2,$$

$k = 1$, $c = 2$, the sensation is 16 times as great when the stimulus is

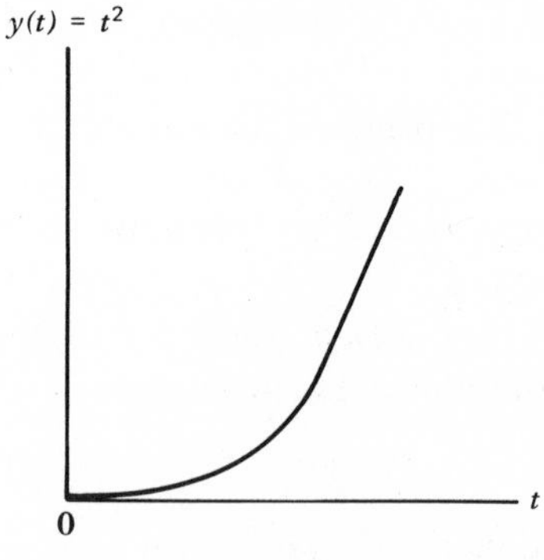


Figure 15

quadrupled. The sensation increases from

$$y = t_0^2$$

to

$$y = (4t_0)^2 = 16t_0^2.$$

(see Figure 15).

### A Model of Population Growth

In recent years many mathematical theories of population change have been developed. Although these theories are relatively simple, each putting the problem of overpopulation in precise terms, they are constructed with a variety of hypotheses and describe different aspects of population growth. For instance models have been constructed to describe the growth of populations by examining the size of various age groups or the male–female ratio. We shall construct the simplest type of growth model; we assume that the rate of change of the size of the population is proportional to the population size.

Before constructing our model let us make several simplifying assumptions. Suppose that the size of the population grows with a constant birthrate, $b$, and decreases with a constant death rate, $d$. Furthermore suppose that initially, at time $t = 0$, the size of the population is $y_0 > 0$. Finally, as previously stated, we assume that the rate of change of the size of the population is proportional to the population size.

Mathematically, the latter statement means

$$\frac{dy}{dt} = ky, \tag{53}$$

where $y$ is the population size at time $t$ and $k$ is a constant. In order to determine the form of the constant $k$, observe the following: If there are more deaths than births per unit time, $d > b$, the population size is decreasing. That is, $dy/dt < 0$ or, equivalently, $k < 0$. Similarly, if $d < b$, $y$ is increasing, $dy/dt > 0$, and $k > 0$. When there is one birth for each death, $b = d$, the population size is stationary. That is, $dy/dt = 0$, implying $k = 0$. Observe that with $k = b - d$, equation (53) exhibits this behavior.

Hence, our population growth model is given by

$$\frac{dy}{dt} = (b - d)y \tag{54}$$

$$y(0) = y_0. \tag{55}$$

Equation (54) is a first-order linear equation. The unique solution is readily seen to be

$$y(t) = y_0 e^{(b-d)t}. \tag{56}$$

From this expression for the size of the population at any time $t$, we see that the population becomes infinitely large as time passes if the birthrate exceeds the death rate. That is, if $b - d > 0$,

$$\lim_{t \to \infty} e^{(b-d)t} = \infty,$$

and consequently,

$$\lim_{t \to \infty} y(t) = \lim_{t \to \infty} y_0 e^{(b-d)t} = \infty.$$

Furthermore, since $dy/dt = (b - d)y = (b - d)y_0 e^{(b-d)t}$,

$$\lim_{t \to \infty} \frac{dy}{dt} = \infty;$$

the population increases at a greater rate as time passes.

Conversely, we see that if $b - d < 0$, the population diminishes to zero as time passes:

$$\lim_{t \to \infty} y(t) = \lim_{t \to \infty} y_0 e^{(b-d)t} = 0,$$

and

$$\lim_{t - \infty} \frac{dy}{dt} = \lim_{t \to \infty} (b - d) y_0 e^{(b-d)t} = 0.$$

Note, also, that according to our model if the initial population is zero ($y_0 = 0$), the population at any time $t$ remains zero. That is, if $y_0 = 0$, (56) implies

$$y(t) \equiv 0,$$

regardless of the relative size of $b$ and $d$, as expected.

## A Model of Price Adjustment

We now develop a simple model of a market for one commodity. We are interested in determining the equilibrium price (the price at which supply and demand are equal), as well as an expression for the price at any time $t$. Assume that demand and supply at a time $t$ are functions solely of the price of this commodity at time $t$. Demand $u$ is assumed to be a decreasing function of price $p$ ($du/dp < 0$) and supply $s$ is an increasing function of price ($ds/dp > 0$). In this model we express this behavior with the simplest functional relationships:

$$u(t) = a_0 + a_1 p(t) \tag{57}$$

$$s(t) = b_0 + b_1 p(t), \tag{58}$$

where $a_1 < 0$; $b_1 > 0$; and $u(t)$, $s(t)$, and $p(t)$ are the demand, supply, and price of the commodity, respectively, at time $t$.

Given these expressions for the supply and demand, we see that by setting $s(t) = u(t)$, the equilibrium price is

$$p_e = \frac{a_0 - b_0}{b_1 - a_1}.$$

Suppose, also, that a positive excess demand causes a rise in price and a negative excess demand causes a fall in price. A reasonable mathematical description of this behavior is given by

$$\frac{dp}{dt} = c[u(t) - s(t)], \tag{59}$$

where $c > 0$; that is, the rate of change of price is proportional to the difference between demand and supply. If $u(t) > s(t)$, prices are rising, $dp/dt > 0$; and if $u(t) < s(t)$, prices are falling, $dp/dt < 0$. Assume also that $p(0) = p_0$. Substituting (57) and (58) into (59) we have

$$\frac{dp}{dt} = c[a_0 - b_0 + (a_1 - b_1)p].$$

And after some algebraic manipulation, we find that the problem of finding an expression for the price as a function of time reduces to solving the initial value problem

$$\frac{dp}{dt} = c(a_1 - b_1)(p - p_e) \tag{60}$$

$$p(0) = p_0. \tag{61}$$

Equation (60) is a first-order linear ordinary differential equation possessing the unique solution

$$p(t) = p_e + (p_0 - p_e)e^{c(a_1 - b_1)t},$$

where, as above

$$p_e = \frac{a_0 - b_0}{b_1 - a_1}.$$

Note that since $c > 0$, $b_1 > 0$, $a_1 < 0$, we have $c(a_1 - b_1) < 0$, and hence,

$$\lim_{t \to \infty} e^{c(a_1 - b_1)t} = 0.$$

Therefore, since

$$\lim_{t \to \infty} p(t) = \lim_{t \to \infty} [p_e + (p_0 - p_e)e^{c(a_1 - b_1)t}],$$

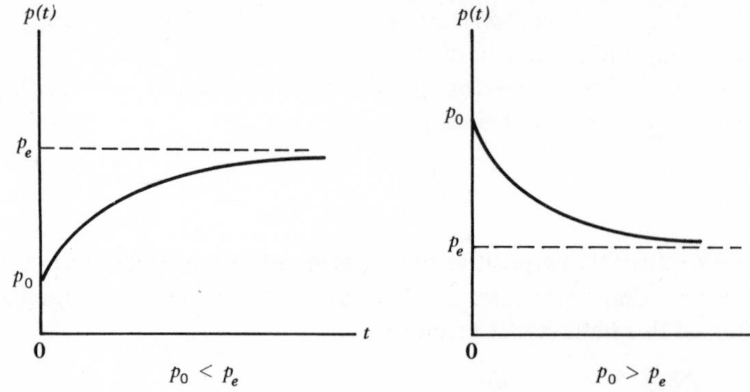


Figure 16

$p(t) \to p_e$ as $t \to \infty$; that is, the price tends to an *equilibrium* state in the limit, and therefore, the market is stable. Observe that this equilibrium condition holds regardless of whether $p_0 > p_e$ or $p_0 < p_e$, as shown in Figure 16.

## EXERCISES

1. Verify for each of the following that the given function is a solution of the differential equation:

(*a*) $y' + 2y = 0 \qquad y = 7e^{-2t}$

(*b*) $y' = 4(10 - y)y \qquad y = \dfrac{10}{1 + e^{-40t}}$

(*c*) $y' = te^{-y} \qquad y = \ln\left(\dfrac{t^2}{2} + 1\right)$

(*d*) $y' = 1 + 2ty \qquad y = e^{t^2}\displaystyle\int_0^t e^{-s^2}\,ds + e^{t^2}.$

2. Find solutions of the following:

(*a*) $y' = ty^{-2}$

(*b*) $y' = 5e^{t+y}$

(*c*) $y' = 4(y - 1)(y - 2)$

(*d*) $y' = \dfrac{(t^2 - 1)}{(y^2 - 1)}$

(*e*) $y' = y + ty + y^2 + ty^2$

(*f*) $(1 + e^t)yy' = e^{-y}e^t$

(*g*) $y' = \frac{t}{y} e^{t-y}$.

3. Solve the following initial value problems:

(*a*) $y' = \frac{1}{t}$ $\qquad y(1) = 2$

(*b*) $y' = -y \tan t$ $\qquad y(0) = 5$

(*c*) $y' = \dfrac{3t^2 + 4t + 2}{2(y - 1)}$ $\qquad y(0) = 3$

(*d*) $y' = -\csc y$ $\qquad y(0) = 0$

(*e*) $y' = (t \ln t)y$ $\qquad y(1) = 1$.

4. Show that by the change of variable $v = y/t$ the differential equation

$$ty' = te^{-(y/t)} + y$$

is transformed into the separable form

$$\frac{dv}{dt} = \frac{1}{t} e^v.$$

5. Show that by the change of variable $v = y/t$ the differential equation

$$y' = f\left(\frac{y}{t}\right)$$

may be transformed into the separable form

$$\frac{dv}{dt} = \frac{f(v) - v}{t}.$$

6. Solve the following initial value problems:

(*a*) $y' - ty = 0$ $\qquad y(0) = 1$

(*b*) $y' + \frac{1}{t}y = 1$ $\qquad y(1) = 1$

(*c*) $y' - 3y = e^t$ $\qquad y(0) = \frac{1}{2}$

(*d*) $y' + y = te^{-t} + 1$ $\qquad y(0) = 4$

(*e*) $y' + \frac{1}{t}y = t$ $\qquad y(1) = 1$.

7. (*a*) Show that if $z(t)$ is a solution of

(i) $$y' + p(t)y = 0,$$

then $cz(t)$ is also a solution of (i) for any constant $c$.

(*b*) Let $w(t)$ be a solution of

(ii) $$y' + p(t)y = q(t), \qquad q(t) \not\equiv 0.$$

Show that $cz(t) + w(t)$ is a solution of (ii) for any constant $c$.

8. Show that $z(t) = 1/t$ is a solution of

(iii) $$y' + y^2 = 0,$$

but $cz(t) = c/t$ is not a solution of (iii). Note that equation (iii) is a *nonlinear* equation.

9. By the method of isoclines, construct the slope fields of the following:

(*a*) $y' = y$

(*b*) $y' = y^4$

(*c*) $y' = \dfrac{t - y}{t}$

(*d*) $y' = t + 1$

(*e*) $y' = t(y - 1)$

(*f*) $y' = (y - 2)^2$.

10. In the illiteracy–literacy transition model, show that by substituting the expression for the number of illiterates at time $t$,

$$y(t) = y_0 e^{-kt},$$

into the right-hand side of equation (10),

$$\frac{dy}{dt} \to 0$$

as $\alpha \to \infty$.

11. (*a*) The victims of the communicable "balding-eagle" disease are characterized by permanent baldness. Construct a mathematical model describing the rate at which the disease spreads.

(*b*) How does this rate vary as $t \to \infty$?

(*c*) Suppose that one-fourth of the victims of the balding-eagle disease remove themselves from the population at every time $t$. How does this action affect the rate at which the disease spreads? Account for this behavior in your model.

12. The purchase of a Mercedes Benz can be conceived as a process consisting, in the simplest case, of two states separated by the act of buying—that is, owning and not owning. Construct a mathematical model describing the not-owning–owning transition.
13. Suppose the sales of a particular camera depend only on its price. Construct a mathematical model describing the variation in sales with respect to price.
14. A manufacturer of vacuum cleaners has decided to promote one of their new products in a certain community by initially demonstrating this vacuum cleaner to one-third of the population. This manufacturer assumes that these members will inform the remainder of the population of the new product. Develop a mathematical model that describes the rate at which news of this new product spreads.
15. Suppose a population growth model is formulated as

$$y' = (b - d)y^c$$
$$y(0) = y_0,$$

where $c$ is a positive constant and $y, b, d$ are as in the population growth model. Discuss the limiting value of $y(t)$ for each of the cases indicated in the table below.

| | $b - d > 0$ | $b - d < 0$ |
|---|---|---|
| $c = 1$ | $y \to \infty$ | $y \to 0$ |
| $0 < c < 1$ | | |
| $c > 1$ | | |

16. (*a*) Consider the *second*-order differential equation

(iv) $$y'' + y' = t + 1.$$

Show that by making the substitution

$$z(t) = y'(t)$$

equation (iv) is transformed into the first-order equation

(v) $$z' + z = t + 1.$$

(*b*) Show that by integrating solutions of (v) we obtain solutions of (iv).
(*c*) Generalize this technique to the second-order equation

$$f(t, y', y'') = 0.$$

17. Solve the following equations:

(*a*) $y'' - y' = 0$

(*b*) $y'' - 2y' = e^t$

(*c*) $y''y' = t.$

18. Suppose that in a stimulus–sensation experiment a change in the stimulus $\Delta t$ causes a change in the sensation $\Delta y$. The quantity $\Delta y$ is observed to be roughly proportional to the *relative* stimulus.
(*a*) Develop a mathematical model of this observation.
(*b*) From your model determine a stimulus–sensation relationship.
19. In the model of price adjustment, suppose that as time passes, demand fluctuates. Specifically, assume

$$u(t) = a_0 + a_1 p(t) + a_2 \sin ct,$$

where $a_0$ and $a_1$ are as in the model and $a_2 > 0$, $c > 0$.
(*a*) Determine an expression for $p(t)$ in this price adjustment model.
(*b*) Examine the behavior of $p(t)$ as $t \to \infty$.
20. Complete parts (*a*) and (*b*) of the previous problem when the demand in the model of price adjustment is a constant $u_0$.
21. The management of Rube's Bank and Trust Company wishes to improve customer service by reducing the average customer waiting time. However, it wishes to do this with the least cost. The additional money that the management is willing to spend to reduce the average waiting time by one unit depends upon the cost already incurred.
(*a*) Develop a mathematical model of this management problem.
(*b*) From your model derive an expression for cost as a function of waiting time.

## SOLUTIONS

2. (*a*) $\frac{y^3}{3} = \frac{t^2}{2} + c$ (implicit form)

(*b*) $y = -\ln(-5e^t - c)$

(*c*) $y = 1, y = 2, \frac{y-2}{y-1} = e^{4t+c}$ (implicit form)

(*d*) $\frac{y^3}{3} - y = \frac{t^3}{3} - t + c$ (implicit form)

(e) $\dfrac{y}{y+1} = \exp\left(\dfrac{t^2}{2} + t + c\right)$ (implicit form)

(f) $ye^y - e^y = \ln(1 + e^t) + c$ (implicit form)

(g) $ye^y - e^y = te^t - e^t + c$ (implicit form)

3. (a) $y = \ln t + 2$

(b) $y = 5\cos t$

(c) $y^2 - 2y = t^3 + 2t^2 + 2t + 3$ (implicit form)

(d) $\cos y = t + 1$ (implicit form)

(e) $y = \exp\left(\dfrac{t^2}{2}\ln t - \dfrac{t^2}{4} + \dfrac{1}{4}\right)$

6. (a) $y = e^{t^2/2}$

(b) $y = \dfrac{t}{2} + \dfrac{1}{2t}$

(c) $y = -\frac{1}{2}e^t + e^{3t}$

(d) $y = e^{-t}\dfrac{t^2}{2} + 1 + 3e^{-t}$

(e) $y = \dfrac{t^2}{3} + \dfrac{2}{3t}$

# CHAPTER 2

# SECOND-ORDER LINEAR EQUATIONS

## PRICE TRENDS: THE SECOND-ORDER LINEAR EQUATION

Buyers and sellers base their market behavior not only on the current price of a commodity but also on the prevailing price trend. The current price and the price-trend information are likely to lead purchasers and sellers to certain expectations regarding the price level in the future. Their expectations will, in turn, influence the quantities they demand and supply.

In our model of price speculation, we incorporated the effect of price trends by considering the demand and supply of a good as a function of price, $y(t)$, and the rate at which price changes, $dy/dt$. But a more accurate characterization of the effect of price trends would also consider whether the price is rising as well as whether the price is increasing at an increasing rate; that is, we should examine the effect of $d^2y/dt^2$ on demand, supply, and the price–time relationship.

The behavior of $d^2y/dt^2$ yields important information about the price–time relationship, known as the *price–time path*. If $d^2y/dt^2 > 0$, the price–time path is said to be *convex* and appears as in Figure 17. Whenever $d^2y/dt^2 < 0$, the price–time path is said to be *concave* and appears as in Figure 18. Thus, the sign of $dy^2/dt^2$ indicates the fluctuations in price as time passes. (Further characterizations of convexity appear in Part 2.)

The demand and supply of a commodity are also influenced by the *price acceleration*, $d^2y/dt^2$. For instance, the demand $u(t)$ varies according as the price is rising or falling at an increasing or decreasing rate at time $t$. We shall consider these four possibilities separately.

First, if the demand of a commodity at time $t$ is rising at an increasing rate, buyers would expect the price to continue to rise. Hence, they prefer to make their purchases while the price is still relatively low. Mathematically

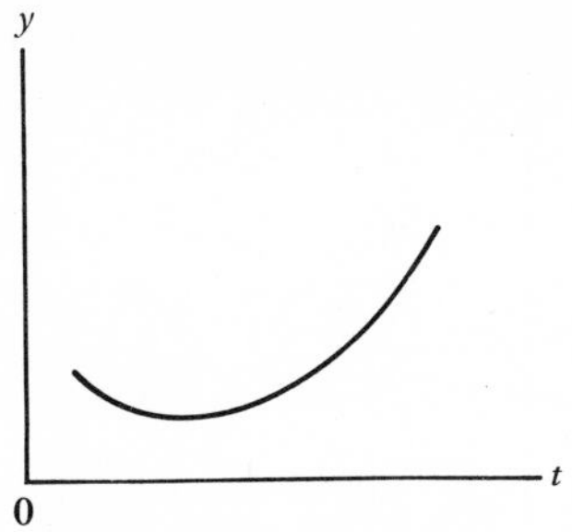


**Figure 17.** $d^2y/dt^2 > 0$.

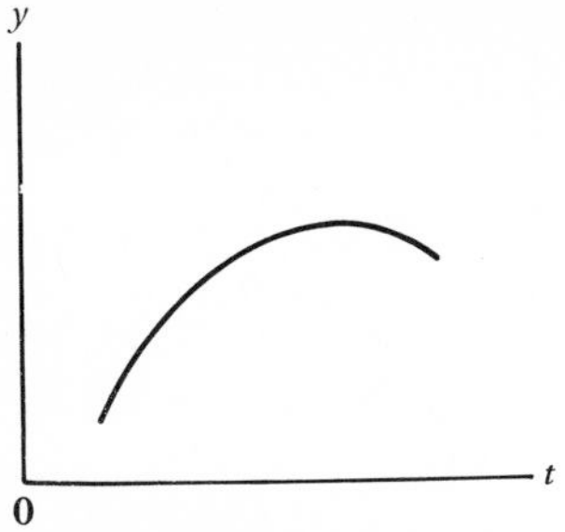


**Figure 18.** $d^2y/dt^2 < 0$.

a rising price means $dy/dt > 0$, and an increasing rate of rise means $d^2y/dt^2 > 0$ (see Figure 19). Thus, if $d^2y/dt^2 > 0$, the amount demanded increases.

Second, whenever the price is falling but the rate of decrease is slowing, buyers would expect the price eventually to ascend; hence, the amount demanded increases. A slowing rate of decrease is the same as a quickening rate of increase. Mathematically, falling prices mean $dy/dt < 0$, and a quickening rate of increase means $d^2y/dt^2 > 0$ (see Figure 20). Thus, in this case, $d^2y/dt^2 > 0$ implies that the amount demanded increases.

Third, if the price is rising but at a decreasing rate, buyers expect the price eventually to descend, and demand will then drop. Mathematically, rising prices, $dy/dt > 0$, at a decreasing rate means $d^2y/dt^2 < 0$ (see Figure 21). Thus, if $d^2y/dt^2 < 0$, the quantity demanded decreases.

Finally, demand would also decline when the price is falling and the rate of fall is increasing, because buyers would anticipate a further drop. An increasing rate of fall is, of course, the same as a decreasing rate of rise. Thus, in this case, $dy/dt < 0$ and $d^2y/dt^2 < 0$ (see Figure 22). Therefore, demand decreases whenever $d^2y/dt^2 < 0$.

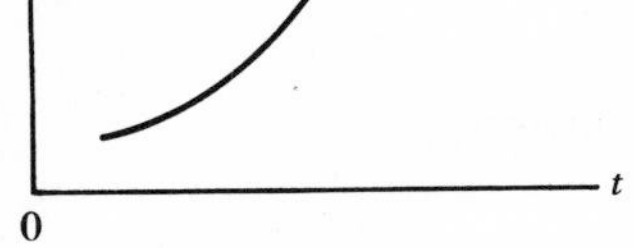


**Figure 19**

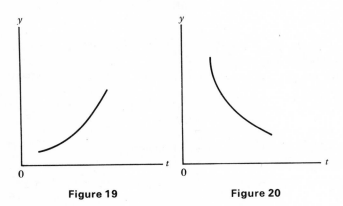

**Figure 20**

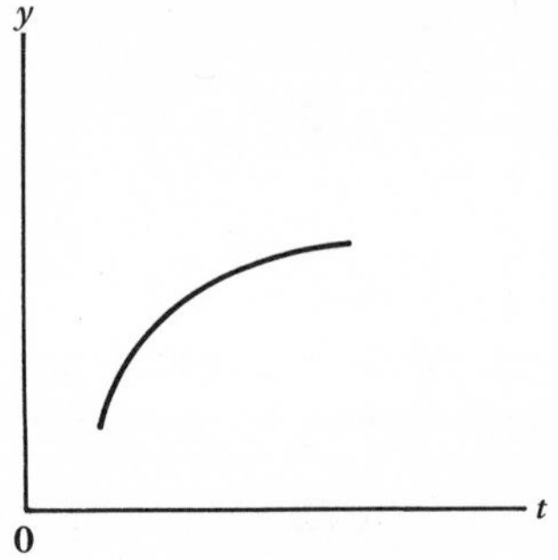


Figure 21

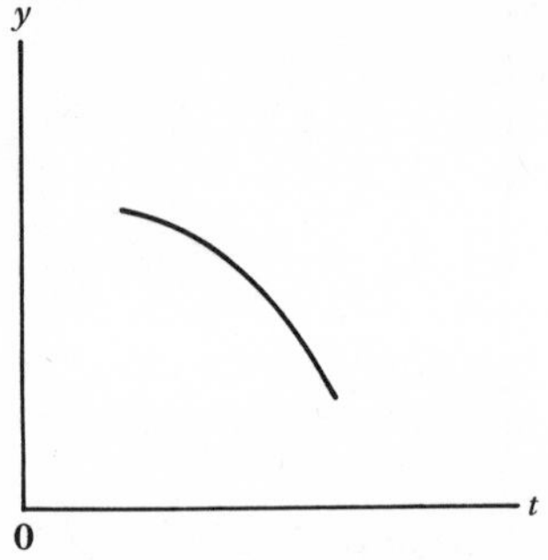


Figure 22

We can adapt our original price adjustment model to account for this additional price-trend information. Specifically, if we assume a linear relationship between $y(t)$, $dy/dt$, $d^2y/dt^2$; and demand, $u(t)$:

$$u(t) = a_0 + a_1 y(t) + a_2 \frac{dy}{dt} + a_3 \frac{d^2y}{dt^2}, \tag{62}$$

and if we choose appropriate constants, equation (62) will model the market behavior described above. Choose $a_0$, $a_1$, and $a_2$ as in the price speculation model and $a_3 > 0$. Note that since $a_3 > 0$, demand increases if prices are rising or falling at an increasing rate ($d^2y/dt^2 > 0$) as desired. Similarly, demand decreases if prices are rising or falling at a decreasing rate ($d^2y/dt^2 < 0$).

Analogously the suppliers' response to changes in price and the rate at which prices rise and fall may be modeled with the linear form

$$s(t) = b_0 + b_1 y(t) + b_2 \frac{dy}{dt} + b_3 \frac{d^2y}{dt^2}. \tag{63}$$

Here $b_1$ and $b_2$ are as before, $b_3 > 0$ ($b_3 \neq a_3$), and $b_0 < a_0$, the demand exceeds supply when $y \equiv 0$.

If the price is always at a level such that the market is cleared (i.e., there is equilibrium),

$$u(t) = s(t), \tag{64}$$

the price–time path satisfies the relationship

$$b_0 + b_1 y(t) + b_2 \frac{dy}{dt} + b_3 \frac{d^2y}{dt^2} = a_0 + a_1 y(t) + a_2 \frac{dy}{dt} + a_3 \frac{d^2y}{dt^2}.$$

This relationship can be compressed into the equation

$$\frac{d^2y}{dt^2} + \frac{b_2 - a_2}{b_3 - a_3}\frac{dy}{dt} + \frac{b_1 - a_1}{b_3 - a_3}y = -\frac{b_0 - a_0}{b_3 - a_3}. \tag{65}$$

This is a *second-order linear differential equation.*

Functions $y(t)$ "satisfying" equation (65) describe the price–time path for this price-trend model. The behavior of the price–time path depends crucially upon the relative size of the coefficients $a_i$, $b_i$, where $i = 0, 1, 2, 3$. For instance, if

$$0 > (b_2 - a_2)^2 - 4(b_3 - a_3)(b_1 - a_1),$$

it can be proved that the price–time path oscillates with decreasing amplitude, as shown in Figure 23. In this case the price–time path is referred to as *underdamped.*

However, if the reverse inequality holds,

$$(b_2 - a_2)^2 - 4(b_3 - a_3)(b_1 - a_1) > 0,$$

the price–time path tends to the equilibrium price

$$y_e = -\left(\frac{b_0 - a_0}{b_1 - a_1}\right)$$

as $t \to \infty$. In this case the price–time path is said to be *overdamped.* Depending upon the initial conditions, the price–time path appears as in Figure 24 or Figure 25.

Other behavior, such as the *oscillation* or *critical damping* illustrated in Figures 26 and 27, respectively, are also mathematically possible. Again, these characteristics depend upon the relative size of the constants $a_i$, $b_i$, where $i = 0, 1, 2, 3$.

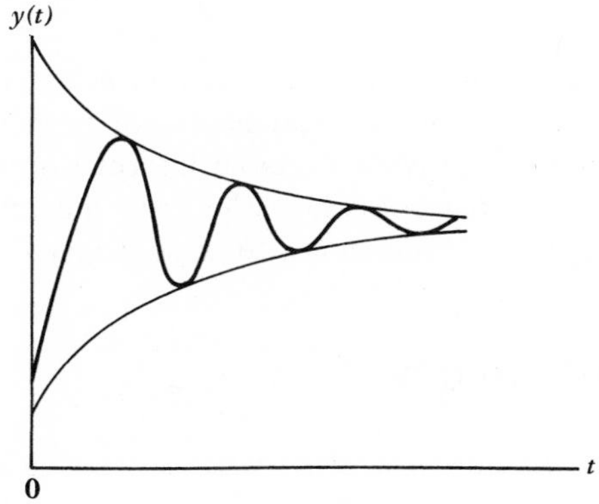


Figure 23

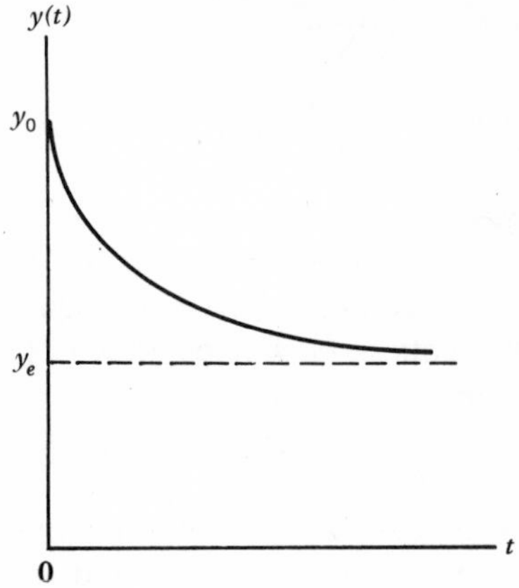


Figure 24

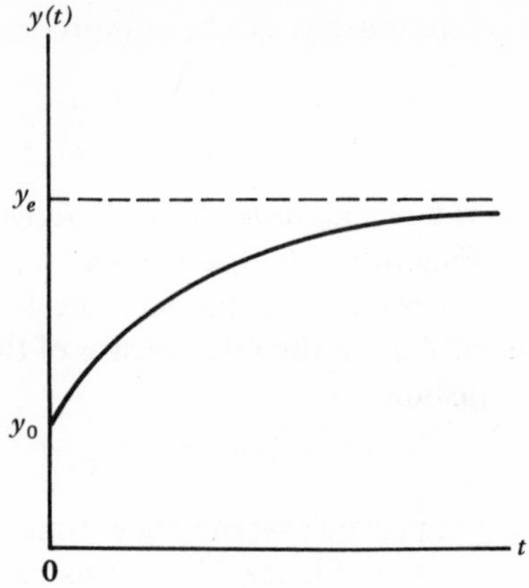


Figure 25

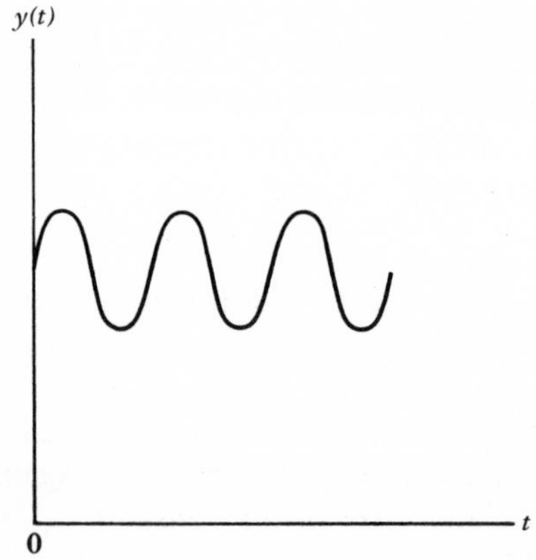


Figure 26

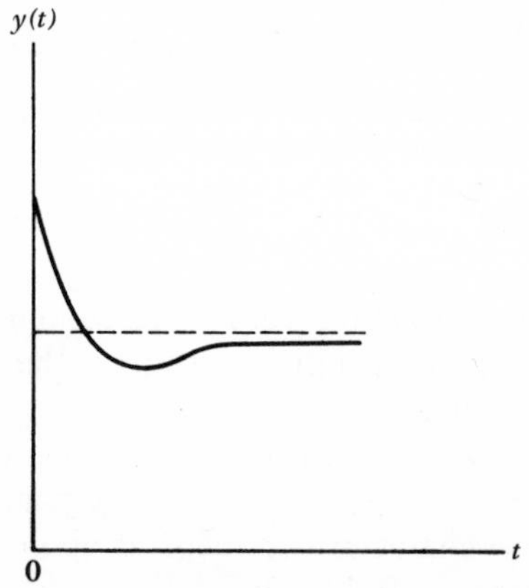


Figure 27

As this discussion demonstrates, second-order linear differential equations are important in mathematical theories of the social and managerial sciences. Their solutions provide valuable information concerning social and economic behavior. Hence, second-order linear differential equations are treated here; we begin our discussion with basic theory.

## FUNDAMENTAL THEORY

The general *second-order ordinary differential equation* is an equation of the form

$$F(t, y, y', y'') = 0.$$

The second-order *linear* equation is

(66) $$y'' + p(t)y' + q(t)y = r(t).$$

As with the general first-order equation the fundamental theory of the second-order linear equation asserts conditions that assure the existence of a unique function satisfying (66). Such functions are called *solutions*. We found that solutions of the first-order equation $y' = f(t, y)$ contain an arbitrary constant. By specifying an initial condition, we determined this constant and thus obtained a unique solution. We would expect solutions of the second-order linear equation to contain two arbitrary constants because, intuitively speaking, two integrations are required to find a solution. For example, the solution of

$$y'' = r(t)$$

is

$$y = c_1 + c_2 t + \int^t \left( \int^x r(s)\, ds \right) dx,$$

where $c_1$ and $c_2$ are arbitrary constants. In order to obtain a unique solution, we must specify two conditions,

(67) $$y(t_0) = y_0 \qquad \text{and} \qquad y'(t_0) = y_1.$$

These conditions are termed *initial conditions*. The initial conditions (67) specify a point through which a solution curve passes as well as the slope of the curve at this point.

The fundamental theory of second-order linear differential equations may be summarized in:

**THEOREM 2** If the functions $p$, $q$, and $r$ are continuous on the open interval $a < t < b$, then there exists one and only one function $y = y(t)$ satisfying the second-order linear differential equation (66),

$$y'' + p(t)y' + q(t)y = r(t),$$

on the interval $a < t < b$, and the initial conditions (67),

$$y(t_0) = y_0, \qquad y'(t_0) = y_1,$$

at a particular point $t_0$ in the interval. ▮

To illustrate this theorem, consider the initial value problem

(68) $$y'' + y = 0$$

(69) $$y(\pi) = -1, \qquad y'(\pi) = 0.$$

All solutions of (68) are of the form

$$y(t) = c_1 \sin t + c_2 \cos t,$$

where $c_1$ and $c_2$ are arbitrary constants. If the initial conditions are to be satisfied, we have

$$-1 = c_1 \sin \pi + c_2 \cos \pi$$
$$0 = c_1 \cos \pi - c_2 \sin \pi,$$

implying $c_1 = 0$ and $c_2 = 1$. Hence, the unique solution of (68), (69) is

$$y(t) = \cos t.$$

Although solutions of the linear second-order equation, (66), may not be readily determined, the structure of solutions can be easily investigated. Because (66) is linear, its solutions have several distinguishing properties. We first treat solutions of (66) without imposing initial conditions by considering the *homogeneous* equation

$$y'' + p(t)y' + q(t)y = 0, \tag{70}$$

where $p$ and $q$ are continuous on an open interval. Note that the term *homogeneous* refers to the fact that all terms are of the same order, in this case first order in $y$. The only constant with respect to $y$ with this property is zero; thus, the right side is zero.

The linear structure of (70) lends itself to a method of generating an infinite class of solutions from any two nontrivial solutions:

THEOREM 3 If $y_1$ and $y_2$ are solutions of the *linear homogeneous* equation (70), then

$$c_1y_1 + c_2y_2 \tag{71}$$

is also a solution for any constants $c_1$ and $c_2$.

PROOF

$$\begin{aligned}(c_1y_1 + c_2y_2)'' + p(t)(c_1y_1 + c_2y_2)' + q(t)(c_1y_1 + c_2y_2)\\ = c_1[y_1'' + p(t)y_1' + q(t)y_1] + c_2[y_2'' + p(t)y_2' + q(t)y_2]\\ = c_1(0) + c_2(0) = 0. \quad \blacksquare\end{aligned}$$

This is the basic *superposition principle;* namely, a *linear combination* $c_1y_1 + c_2y_2$ of solutions $y_1$ and $y_2$ to a second-order linear, homogeneous equation is also a solution.

The equation

$$y'' - y = 0 \tag{72}$$

with the solutions $y_1 = e^t$ and $y_2 = e^{-t}$ illustrates the value of Theorem 3. According to the theorem,

$$y = c_1e^t + c_2e^{-t}$$

is also a solution of (72) for any constants $c_1$ and $c_2$.

It must be noted that the principle of superposition depends crucially on the *linearity* of (70). For example, suppose that $y_1$ and $y_2$ are solutions of

$$y'' + 16y^2 = 0.$$

The linear combination $c_1y_1 + c_2y_2$ is not necessarily a solution, because

$$(c_1y_1 + c_2y_2)'' + 16(c_1y_1 + c_2y_2)^2 \neq c_1(y_1'' + 16y_1^2) + c_2(y_2'' + 16y_2^2).$$

The technique of generating solutions of (70) described by the principle of superposition prompts the question, Can *all possible* solutions be obtained as a linear combination of two arbitrary solutions? Indeed, if the two solutions $y_1$ and $y_2$ are "properly chosen," every solution is of the form

$$c_1y_1 + c_2y_2$$

for some constants $c_1$ and $c_2$.

In order to discuss the nature of these properly chosen solutions, we must introduce the notion of *linear independence*. Two functions $y_1$ and $y_2$ are said to be *linearly independent* on an interval if the expression

$$c_1y_1 + c_2y_2 = 0$$

implies $c_1 = 0$ and $c_2 = 0$. This means that neither function is a constant multiple of the other. For example, $y_1 = \sin t$ and $y_2 = \cos t$ are linearly independent because there does not exist a constant $d$ such that

$$\sin t = d \cos t.$$

However, the functions $y_1 = t$ and $y_2 = 2t$ are *linearly dependent* because $y_2 = 2y_1$; $y_2$ is a constant multiple of $y_1$.

Every linear, homogeneous second-order equation has a pair of linearly independent solutions. This is readily seen by considering the initial value problems

$$y'' + p(t)y' + q(t)y = 0$$

$$y(t_0) = 1, \qquad y'(t_0) = 0$$

and

$$y'' + p(t)y' + q(t)y = 0$$

$$y(t_0) = 0, \qquad y'(t_0) = 1$$

with unique solutions $y_1(t)$ and $y_2(t)$, respectively. Suppose that $y_1$ and $y_2$ satisfy

(73) $$c_1y_1(t) + c_2y_2(t) = 0;$$

then by differentiating (73) we obtain

(74) $$c_1y_1'(t) + c_2y_2'(t) = 0.$$

At the arbitrary initial point $t_0$, (73) implies $c_1 = 0$ and (74) implies $c_2 = 0$. Thus, $y_1$ and $y_2$ are linearly independent solutions of (70).

In general, it is an algebraic result that the system given by (73) and (74) has a solution $c_1, c_2$, *not both zero*, if and only if the determinant

$$W(y_1, y_2) = \begin{vmatrix} y_1(t_0) & y_2(t_0) \\ y_1'(t_0) & y_2'(t_0) \end{vmatrix} = 0$$

when evaluated at an arbitrary point $t_0$ in the interval of interest, $a < t < b$. Note also that if $c_1, c_2$ is a solution for $t = t_0$, then, by Theorem 3, $y(t) = c_1y_1(t) + c_2y_2(t)$ is a solution of (70). Since $y(t)$ clearly satisfies $y(t_0) = y'(t_0) = 0$, the uniqueness assertion of Theorem 2 implies that $y(t) = c_1y_1(t) + c_2y_2(t) = 0$ for all $t$. Hence, $W(y_1, y_2)(t_0) = 0$ if and only if $W(y_1, y_2)(t) = 0$ for all $t$ on the interval $a < t < b$. This means that $y_1$ and $y_2$ are linearly dependent on $a < t < b$ whenever $W(y_1, y_2)(t_0) = 0$ for some $t_0$ in $(a, b)$. The converse also may be proved. Thus, *any two solutions of* (70) *on* $a < t < b$ *are linearly dependent if and only if* $W(y_1, y_2)(t_0) = 0$ *for some* $t_0$ *in* $(a, b)$.

The latter statement gives a simple test for linear dependence of solutions of (70). For example, $y_1 = \sin t$ and $y_2 = \cos t$ are linearly independent solutions of $y'' + y = 0$ on $-\infty < t < \infty$ because

$$W(y_1, y_2) = \begin{vmatrix} \sin t & \cos t \\ \cos t & -\sin t \end{vmatrix} = -1 \neq 0.$$

Linearly independent solutions of (70) help us describe the structure of general solutions of (70):

**THEOREM 4** Every solution of

$$y'' + p(t)y' + q(t)y = 0 \tag{70}$$

has a *unique* expression as a linear combination of any two linearly independent solutions, $y_1$ and $y_2$.

**PROOF** Suppose $y(t)$ is an arbitrary solution. If there exists a unique set of constants $c_1$ and $c_2$ such that

$$\begin{aligned} y(t_0) &= c_1y_1(t_0) + c_2y_2(t_0), \\ y'(t_0) &= c_1y_1'(t_0) + c_2y_2'(t_0) \end{aligned} \tag{75}$$

for an arbitrary $t_0$, then by Theorem 2

$$y(t) = c_1y_1(t) + c_2y_2(t). \tag{76}$$

That is, equality (76) holds because the solutions $y(t)$ and $c_1y_1(t) + c_2y_2(t)$

satisfy the same initial conditions. Either unique constants $c_1$, $c_2$ satisfying equations (75) exist or there are numbers $b_1$ and $b_2$, not both zero, for which

$$b_1 y_1(t_0) + b_2 y_2(t_0) = 0,$$
$$b_1 y_1'(t_0) + b_2 y_2'(t_0) = 0.$$

This implies that the solution $u(t) = b_1 y_1(t) + b_2 y_2(t)$ satisfies $u(t_0) = 0$, $u'(t_0) = 0$. By uniqueness, $u(t) \equiv 0$. Therefore,

$$b_1 y_1(t) + b_2 y_2(t) \equiv 0,$$

which contradicts the linear independence of $y_1$ and $y_2$. ∎

The expression formed by taking a linear combination of any two linearly independent solutions $y_1$ and $y_2$ of (70),

$$c_1 y_1 + c_2 y_2,$$

is called the *general solution* of (70).

Theorem 4 implies that because $y_1 = \sin t$ and $y_2 = \cos t$ are two linearly independent solutions of

$$y'' + y = 0, \tag{77}$$

each solution of (77) may be expressed in the form

$$c_1 \sin t + c_2 \cos t,$$

for a unique set of constants $c_1$ and $c_2$.

Having discussed the structure of the general solution of the linear homogeneous equation (70) we now consider solutions of the associated linear, *nonhomogeneous** equation

$$y'' + p(t)y' + q(t)y = r(t), \tag{78}$$

where $p$, $q$, and $r \not\equiv 0$ are continuous. Suppose that a *particular solution* $y^*$ of (78) is known and that $y$ is *any other solution*. Then their difference,

$$y - y^*,$$

is a solution of the homogeneous equation (70) because

$$(y - y^*)'' + p(t)(y - y^*)' + q(t)(y - y^*)$$
$$= (y'' + py' + qy) - (y^{*''} + py^{*'} + qy^*) = r - r = 0.$$

Theorem 4 states that if $y_1$ and $y_2$ are two linearly independent solutions of

* Note that this equation is termed *nonhomogeneous* because the right side is of order 0 in $y$ rather than of order 1.

(70) there exists a unique set of constants $c_1$ and $c_2$ such that

$$y - y^* = c_1 y_1 + c_2 y_2.$$

In other words, since $y$ is an arbitrary solution, we have the following result:

THEOREM 5 Any solution $y(t)$ of the nonhomogeneous linear equation (78) can be expressed as

$$y(t) = y^*(t) + c_1 y_1(t) + c_2 y_2(t), \tag{79}$$

where $y^*$ is a particular solution of the nonhomogeneous equation (78) and $y_1$ and $y_2$ are linearly independent solutions of the corresponding homogeneous equation (70). ∎

Equation (79) is called the *general solution* of (78).

Thus, according to the theorem, we can find the general solution of a second-order nonhomogeneous linear differential equation by

1. determining the general solution of the associated homogeneous equation, and
2. determining a particular solution of the nonhomogeneous equation.

As an example, consider the linear nonhomogeneous equation

$$y'' + y = t. \tag{80}$$

A particular solution of (80) is seen to be $y^* = t$. Since the general solution of the associated homogeneous equation

$$y'' + y = 0$$

is $c_1 \sin t + c_2 \cos t$, Theorem 5 implies that the *general solution* of (80) is

$$y(t) = t + c_1 \sin t + c_2 \cos t.$$

Applications of second-order linear differential equations in the social and managerial sciences frequently involve equations with constant coefficients. That is, the functions $p(t)$ and $q(t)$ in (78) are constants. Theorem 2 guarantees the existence of solutions of second-order equations with constant coefficients on the interval $-\infty < t < \infty$ because $p(t)$ and $q(t)$ are constant and, hence, everywhere continuous.

We will proceed to investigate applications and solution techniques of second-order linear equations with constant coefficients.

## PHILLIPS' MULTIPLIER–ACCELERATOR EFFECT: NONHOMOGENEOUS EQUATIONS WITH CONSTANT COEFFICIENTS

The Keynesian national income model separates the national income into the three sections of consumption, investment, and government. Consumption and investment are internal to the fluctuations of the economy, while the government spending may be considered an external influence. For instance, while consumers with decreasing incomes will decrease their expenditures, and investors may follow a similar trend, government spending need not reflect the same trend.

Mathematically the Keynesian model states

$$Y = C + I + G,$$
$$C = dY,$$

where $Y$ is national output, $C$ is consumption, $I$ is investment, $G$ is government spending, and $d$ is the marginal propensity to consume. Whereas the first equation expresses the three divisions of national income, the second, known as the *multiplier effect*, states that individuals consume in proportion to their income. Keynes assumes further that the demand placed upon the economy, $D$, and the national output are in equilibrium:

$$D = C + I + G,$$

or

(81) $$D = (1 - s)Y + I + G,$$

where $s = 1 - d$ is the marginal propensity to save.

A change in national output must occur in order to meet this demand when investment and government spending are constant. However, this change cannot occur instantaneously, so that a time lag must be introduced into our analysis. The national output should increase as time passes ($dY/dt > 0$) if demand exceeds output ($D > Y$), and conversely, national output should decrease ($dY/dt < 0$) if demand is below output ($D < Y$). A simple mathematical description of this behavior is to assume the rate of change of output is proportional to the excess of demand over output:

(82) $$\frac{dY}{dt} = b(D - Y),$$

where $b$ ($>0$) is a constant. Combining (81) and (82), we see that

(83) $$\frac{dY}{dt} + bsY = b(I + G).$$

Now consider the investment sector when $C$ and $G$ are constant. The money of investment is used to produce goods in the future. Consequently, investment decisions are often based on changes in output pattern; these changes are extrapolated into the future. The *accelerator principle* incorporates this investment procedure into the Keynesian model by asserting that investment is proportional to the time rate of change of income

$$I(t) = a\frac{dY}{dt}.$$

The latter equation would accurately depict the level of investment if the economy could respond instantaneously to changes in output. However, the actual investment $I(t)$ does lag behind the induced investment $a(dY/dt)$. If the induced investment is greater than the actual investment $[a(dY/dt) > I(t)]$, then investment may be expected to increase as time passes $(dI/dt > 0)$. And conversely, investment decreases as time passes $(dI/dt < 0)$ if the induced investment is less than the actual investment $[a(dY/dt) < I(t)]$. A simple mathematical description of this behavior is given by

$$\frac{dI}{dt} = k\left(a\frac{dY}{dt} - I\right), \tag{84}$$

where $k\ (> 0)$ is a constant.

Now suppose that only government expenditures are required to remain constant, while *both* consumption and investment are permitted to vary. Then the time rate of change of investment, $dI/dt$, may be determined by solving (83) for $I$,

$$I = \frac{1}{b}Y' + sY - G, \tag{85}$$

and differentiating

$$\frac{dI}{dt} = \frac{1}{b}Y'' + sY'. \tag{86}$$

Upon combining (84) and (86) and performing several algebraic manipulations we find

$$Y'' + b(s - ka)Y' = -bkI. \tag{87}$$

Using (85) to replace $I = I(t)$ in (87) results in a second-order linear nonhomogeneous equation in $Y$ with constant coefficients:

$$Y'' + (bs - bka + k)Y' + skbY = kbG. \tag{88}$$

This differential equation models the changes in national output when only consumption and investment are permitted to change. The solution of (88) yields a relationship between the level of national output and time. The actual form of the solution depends intricately on the values of the constants $b$, $s$, $k$, $a$, and $G$, and hence, we shall only describe appropriate solution methods rather than attempt to find an explicit solution.

Recall that the procedure for finding the general solution of the second-order linear nonhomogeneous equation involves, first, determining the general solution of the corresponding homogeneous equation, and, second, determining a particular solution of the nonhomogeneous equation. We now develop solution techniques to complete these two steps.

### The Characteristic Equation

In attempting to solve the second-order linear homogeneous equation with constant coefficients,

(89) $$y'' + p_0 y' + q_0 y = 0,$$

it is wise to consider the analogous first-order equation

(90) $$y' + ky = 0.$$

Recall that all solutions of (90) have the form $ce^{-kt}$ because only the exponential function is a constant multiple of its derivative. Because the second-order equation (89) has only constant coefficients, it is natural to consider functions $y = y(t)$ such that $y$, $y'$, and $y''$ also differ only by constant multiples; one such function is the exponential function.

We shall try to find solutions of the form $y = e^{mt}$ for appropriate values of $m$. Upon substituting $y = e^{mt}$ into (89) we find

$$m^2 e^{mt} + p_0 m e^{mt} + q_0 e^{mt} = 0$$

or

$$e^{mt}(m^2 + p_0 m + q_0) = 0.$$

Since $e^{mt}$ never vanishes and the latter equation equals zero, we must have

(91) $$m^2 + p_0 m + q_0 = 0.$$

That is, *if m is a root of the quadratic equation* (91) *called the characteristic equation, then* $e^{mt}$ *is a solution of* (89).

The roots of (91) are given by

(92) $$m_1 = \frac{-p_0 + \sqrt{p_0^2 - 4q_0}}{2} \quad \text{and} \quad m_2 = \frac{-p_0 - \sqrt{p_0^2 - 4q_0}}{2}.$$

The form of the solutions of (89) depends upon the values of $m_1$ and $m_2$. And the values of $m_1$ and $m_2$ depend on the coefficients $p_0$ and $q_0$. To infer the behavior of solutions, we must examine three cases:

1. $p_0^2 - 4q_0 > 0$, so that (91) has real distinct roots.
2. $p_0^2 - 4q_0 = 0$, in which case (91) has real, equal roots.
3. $p_0^2 - 4q_0 < 0$, so that (91) has complex roots.

These three cases must be considered separately.

#### *Real and Distinct Roots*

Equations (92) yield two distinct real roots when $p_0^2 - 4q_0 > 0$. This implies

$$y_1 = e^{m_1 t} \quad \text{and} \quad y_2 = e^{m_2 t}$$

are solutions of (89). *Because* $y_1$ *and* $y_2$ *are linearly independent* $[W(y_1, y_2) \not\equiv 0]$, *the general solution of* (89) *in this case is*

$$c_1 e^{m_1 t} + c_2 e^{m_2 t}.$$

Consider, for example, the initial value problem

$$y'' + 2y' - 3y = 0$$
$$y(0) = 0, \qquad y'(0) = 4.$$

Substituting $y = e^{mt}$ leads to

$$m^2 + 2m - 3 = 0$$
$$(m + 3)(m - 1) = 0.$$

Hence, $m_1 = -3$, $m_2 = 1$. The general solution is

$$y(t) = c_1 e^{-3t} + c_2 e^t.$$

To satisfy the initial conditions at $t = 0$, the constants $c_1$ and $c_2$ must satisfy

$$y(0) = c_1 + c_2 = 0$$
$$y'(0) = -3c_1 + c_2 = 4;$$

hence, $c_1 = -1$ and $c_2 = 1$. Thus, the unique solution of this initial value problem is

$$-e^{-3t} + e^t.$$

### *Real and Equal Roots*

For $p_0^2 - 4q_0 = 0$, equations (92) yield equal real roots $m_1 = m_2 = -p_0/2$, and consequently, there is only one solution

(93) $$y = ce^{-(p_0/2)t}.$$

To obtain a second linearly independent solution assume that (89) has a solution of the form

$$y = z(t)e^{-(p_0/2)t}.$$

Therefore,

$$y' = z'e^{-(p_0/2)t} - \frac{p_0}{2} ze^{-(p_0/2)t},$$

$$y'' = \left(z'' - p_0 z' + \frac{p_0^2}{4} z\right)e^{-(p_0/2)t}.$$

If we substitute $y$, $y'$, and $y''$ into (89) and divide out the factor $e^{-(p_0/2)t}$, we find

$$\left(z'' - p_0 z' + \frac{p_0^2}{4} z\right) + p_0\left(z' - \frac{p_0}{2} z\right) + q_0 z = 0.$$

Upon collecting terms, we obtain

$$z'' - \left(\frac{p_0^2}{4} - q_0\right)z = 0.$$

The second term drops out because $p_0^2 - 4q_0 = 0$. Therefore,

$$z'' = 0,$$

implying

$$z(t) = d_1 + d_2 t,$$

where $d_1$ and $d_2$ are arbitrary constants. Thus, a second linearly independent solution of (89) when $p_0^2 - 4q_0 = 0$ is of the form

(94) $$(d_1 + d_2 t)e^{-(p_0/2)t}.$$

The sum of the two linearly independent solutions (93) and (94) yield the *general solution*

$$c_1 e^{-(p_0/2)t} + c_2 t e^{-(p_0/2)t}.$$

To illustrate this case, consider the initial value problem

$$y'' + 2y' + y = 0$$
$$y(0) = 2, \qquad y'(0) = 1.$$

The corresponding characteristic equation is

$$m^2 + 2m + 1 = 0$$
$$(m + 1)(m + 1) = 0,$$

implying $m = -1$ is a repeated root. According to the above discussion, the general solution is

$$y(t) = c_1 e^{-t} + c_2 t e^{-t}.$$

If the initial conditions at $t = 0$ are to be satisfied,

$$y(0) = c_1 = 2,$$
$$y'(0) = -c_1 + c_2 = 1,$$

or $c_1 = 2, c_2 = 3$. Hence, the unique solution of this initial value problem is

$$2e^{-t} + 3te^{-t}.$$

### *Complex Roots*

In the previous discussion the roots of the characteristic equation were real. If, however, $p_0^2 - 4q_0 < 0$ the roots

$$m_1 = \frac{-p_0 + \sqrt{p_0^2 - 4q_0}}{2} \qquad \text{and} \qquad m_2 = \frac{-p_0 - \sqrt{p_0^2 - 4q_0}}{2}$$

are complex. In fact, we see from equations (92) that these roots $m_1$ and $m_2$ are necessarily complex conjugate numbers,

$$m_1 = \alpha + i\beta, \qquad m_2 = \alpha - i\beta,$$

where $\alpha$ and $\beta$ are real, because $p_0$ and $q_0$ are real numbers. We now must investigate as to what meaning can be attached to the linearly independent solutions $e^{m_1 t}$, $e^{m_2 t}$ if $m_1$ and $m_2$ are complex.

Because $e^{(\alpha+i\beta)t}$ and $e^{(\alpha-i\beta)t}$ are linearly independent solutions, the general solution of (89) is the linear combination

$$c_1 e^{(\alpha+i\beta)t} + c_2 e^{(\alpha-i\beta)t}, \tag{95}$$

a complex-valued function. Since a complex-valued solution to a mathematical model in, say, economics, is not desirable, we wish to "extract" real-valued solutions from the complex-valued solution (95).

To obtain real-valued solutions from (95) we use Euler's formula (a derivation of which is given in many calculus texts):

$$e^{(\lambda+i\mu)t} = e^{\lambda t}(\cos \mu t + i \sin \mu t).$$

Using Euler's formula, the solutions of (89) may be put in the equivalent form

$$y_1 = e^{(\alpha+i\beta)t} = e^{\alpha t}(\cos \beta t + i \sin \beta t),$$
$$y_2 = e^{(\alpha-i\beta)t} = e^{\alpha t}(\cos \beta t - i \sin \beta t).$$

Since $y_1$ and $y_2$ are solutions of (89) Theorem 3 states that $y_1 - y_2$ and $y_1 + y_2$ are also solutions. Therefore,

$$\begin{aligned} y_1 - y_2 &= e^{\alpha t}(\cos \beta t + i \sin \beta t) - e^{\alpha t}(\cos \beta t - i \sin \beta t) \\ &= 2ie^{\alpha t} \sin \beta t \end{aligned}$$

and

$$\begin{aligned} y_1 + y_2 &= e^{\alpha t}(\cos \beta t + i \sin \beta t) + e^{\alpha t}(\cos \beta t - i \sin \beta t) \\ &= 2e^{\alpha t} \cos \beta t \end{aligned}$$

are solutions of (89). Since $(y_1 - y_2)/2i$ and $(y_1 + y_2)/2$ are solutions of (89) according to Theorem 3, the latter equations imply that

$$z_1 = e^{\alpha t} \cos \beta t \qquad \text{and} \qquad z_2 = e^{\alpha t} \sin \beta t$$

are two *real-valued* solutions of (89). Moreover, since $W(z_1, z_2) \neq 0$, it is readily seen that $z_1$ and $z_2$ are two linearly independent solutions of (89). Therefore, by Theorem 4 the *real-valued* function

$$c_1 e^{\alpha t} \cos \beta t + c_2 e^{\alpha t} \sin \beta t, \tag{96}$$

for arbitrary constants $c_1$ and $c_2$, is the general solution of (89).

To illustrate this technique, consider the initial value problem

$$
\begin{aligned}
&y'' + 2y' + 2y = 0 \\
&y(0) = 1, \qquad y'(0) = 2.
\end{aligned} \tag{97}
$$

Substituting $e^{mt}$ into (97) we find that the characteristic equation is

$$m^2 + 2m + 2 = 0.$$

The roots are $m_1 = -1 + i$ and $m_2 = -1 - i$. From (96) the general solution is seen to be

$$c_1 e^{-t} \cos t + c_2 e^{-t} \sin(-t).$$

To satisfy the initial conditions, we must have $c_1 = 1, c_2 = -3$; the unique solution is

$$e^{-t} \cos t - 3e^{-t} \sin(-t) = e^{-t} \cos t + 3e^{-t} \sin t.$$

## Undetermined Coefficients

One method of obtaining a particular solution for the nonhomogeneous second-order linear equation with constant coefficients,

$$y'' + p_0 y' + q_0 y = r(t), \tag{98}$$

is to "guess" the form of the solution. Frequently by examining the form of the nonhomogeneous term $r(t)$ we can make an intelligent guess as to the general form of the solution. Then we can find the solution in detail by substituting the guess into the differential equation. For instance, the equation

$$y'' + y' + 2y = 4$$

obviously has a particular solution that is a constant. Note that if $y = c$, a constant, then $y'' + y' = 0$; thus, $2y = 2c = 4$. Hence, $y^* = 2$ is a particular solution.

This technique for obtaining particular solutions, known as the method of *undetermined coefficients*, depends to a considerable extent on one's ability to recognize the general form of a particular solution. For equations with a completely arbitrary nonhomogeneous term $r(t)$, very little can be said about the solution. If, however, $r(t)$ is a polynomial, an exponential function, sinusoidal in behavior, or a sum, difference, or product of these types of functions, then a definite solution procedure may be developed. Here we consider these three types of functions separately.

### *r(t) a Polynomial*

To demonstrate the method of undetermined coefficients, consider the example

$$y'' + y' + y = t^2 + 2t - 1, \tag{99}$$

where $r(t)$ is a quadratic polynomial. Here we reason that if $y^*(t)$ is a polynomial of degree 2, then $y'' + y'$ is a polynomial of degree 1. Hence, $y'' + y' + y$ is a quadratic polynomial. Suppose that with constants $a$, $b$, and $c$,

$$y^*(t) = at^2 + bt + c. \tag{100}$$

The polynomial (100) is a solution if

$$(at^2 + bt + c)'' + (at^2 + bt + c)' + (at^2 + bt + c) = t^2 + 2t - 1.$$

Collecting like powers of $t$, we see that

$$at^2 + (2a + b)t + (2a + b + c) = t^2 + 2t - 1.$$

This equation holds when $a = 1$, $b = 0$, $c = -3$. Hence, $y^* = t^2 - 3$ is a particular solution of (99).

If, in the nonhomogeneous equation (98), $r(t)$ is a general polynomial of degree $n$ with real coefficients,

$$r(t) = p_n(t) = a_n t^n + a_{n-1} t^{n-1} + \cdots + a_0,$$

then it is reasonable to assume that a particular solution has the same form:

$$y^*(t) = A_n t^n + A_{n-1} t^{n-1} + \cdots + A_0. \tag{101}$$

We determine the coefficients $A_n, \ldots, A_0$ as in the example above, by substituting (101) into (98) and equating coefficients of like powers of $t$ to solve successively for $A_n, \ldots, A_0$.

The equation

$$y'' + 4y' = t^2 - t + 3 \tag{102}$$

illustrates a special problem in the undetermined coefficients procedure for $r(t) = p_n(t)$. If we assume $y^*$ is a second-degree polynomial, (102) will not be satisfied, because $y'' + 4y'$ will be a first-degree polynomial. Therefore, if $y'' + 4y'$ is to equal the quadratic $t^2 - t + 3$, we choose $y^*$ to be a third-degree polynomial of the form

$$y^*(t) = t(A_2 t^2 + A_1 t + A_0). \tag{103}$$

Similarly, to find a particular solution of

$$y'' = t^5 - 7t,$$

we assume

$$y^*(t) = t^2(A_5t^5 + \cdots + A_0) \tag{104}$$

so that $(y^*)''$ gives rise to a fifth-degree polynomial. Note that we do not introduce constant (linear) terms in (103) (104) because a constant (a linear expression) is a solution to the corresponding homogeneous equation, and thus, added terms of this form are not determined by $r(t)$.

In general, if $r(t) = p_n(t)$, the form of a particular solution is

$$y^*(t) = t^s(A_nt^n + \cdots + A_0),$$

where $s$ is the smallest nonnegative integer that will insure that no term of $y^*(t)$ is a solution of the corresponding homogeneous equation.

### *r(t) an Exponential*

A second illustration of the method of undetermined coefficients is provided by the equation

$$y'' + y' - 2y = 5e^{3t}. \tag{105}$$

A natural selection for a particular solution is

$$y^*(t) = Ae^{3t}. \tag{106}$$

All derivatives of $y^*(t) = Ae^{3t}$ are also exponential terms, and hence, the linear combination

$$(y^*)'' + (y^*)' - 2y^*$$

will be an exponential term. With the proper choice for the coefficient $A$, equation (105) will be satisfied. Substituting (106) into (105) yields

$$9Ae^{3t} + 3Ae^{3t} - 2Ae^{3t} = (9A + 3A - 2A)e^{3t} = 10Ae^{3t} = 5e^{3t},$$

implying $A = \frac{1}{2}$. Hence, a particular solution is

$$y^*(t) = \tfrac{1}{2}e^{3t}.$$

The technique for finding a particular solution of the more general equation

$$y'' + p_0y' + q_0y = ae^{\alpha t} \tag{107}$$

is similar. We seek a solution of the form $y^*(t) = Ae^{\alpha t}$. By substituting $y^*$ into (107), we determine that

$$A = \frac{a}{\alpha^2 + p_0\alpha + q_0}.$$

Therefore,

$$y^*(t) = \frac{a}{\alpha^2 + p_0\alpha + q_0}e^{\alpha t}. \tag{108}$$

Note that the denominator

$$p(\alpha) = \alpha^2 + p_0\alpha + q_0$$

is the characteristic equation of the associated homogeneous equation.

If $p(\alpha) = \alpha^2 + p_0\alpha + q_0 = 0$, equation (108) does not determine a particular solution. In this case, $\alpha$ is a root of the characteristic equation. Thus, $e^{\alpha t}$ is a solution of the corresponding homogeneous equation and cannot also be a solution of the nonhomogeneous equation. To find a particular solution when $p(\alpha) = 0$, we assume

(109) $$y^*(t) = Ate^{\alpha t}.$$

Substituting (109) into (107) and solving for $A$, we find

$$A = \frac{a}{2\alpha + p_0}$$

or

(110) $$y^*(t) = \frac{a}{2\alpha + p_0}\, te^{\alpha t}.$$

If the denominator of (110), $p'(\alpha) = 2\alpha + p_0 = 0$, then (110) is not a solution of (107). This means that $e^{\alpha t}$ and $te^{\alpha t}$ are both solutions of the homogeneous equation corresponding to (107). To find a particular solution when $p'(\alpha) = 0$, we assume

$$y^*(t) = At^2e^{\alpha t}.$$

Proceeding as before, we find that

$$y^*(t) = \frac{at^2e^{\alpha t}}{2}.$$

In general, if $r(t) = ce^{\alpha t}$, then $y^*(t) = At^se^{\alpha t}$, where $s$ is the smallest integer ($s = 0, 1, 2$) such that $y^*(t)$ is not a solution of the corresponding homogeneous equation.

To illustrate this case better, consider the example

(111) $$y'' - y' - 2y = -3e^{-t}.$$

Note that the characteristic equation of the corresponding homogeneous equation is

$$m^2 - m - 2 = (m - 2)(m + 1) = 0.$$

This implies that $e^{-t}$ is a solution of the homogeneous equation; we should not "guess" solutions of the form $Ae^{-t}$. We should seek a particular solution for (111) of the form

(112) $$y^*(t) = Ate^{-t}.$$

Substituting (112) into (111) and collecting like terms, we find $y^*(t) = te^{-t}$.

A second example is provided by the equation

$$y'' - 4y' + 4y = e^{2t}.$$

Note that the characteristic equation of the corresponding homogeneous equation is

$$m^2 - 4m + 4 = (m - 2)^2 = 0.$$

This implies that $e^{2t}$ and $te^{2t}$ are solutions of the homogeneous equation. Therefore, we should assume a particular solution of the form

$$y^*(t) = At^2e^{2t}.$$

Substituting $y^*(t)$ into the differential equation and collecting like terms, we find

$$y^*(t) = \tfrac{1}{2}t^2e^{2t}.$$

*$r(t)$ is Sinusoidal*

A third example of this process of judicious guessing is provided by

(113) $$y'' + 2y' - y = 2 \sin t.$$

There is little promise in trying a solution involving polynomials, exponential, or logarithmic terms. Indeed, any combination of these types of functions and their derivatives does not yield the desired $2 \sin t$ term. A reasonable guess is a solution of the form $y^*(t) = c_1 \sin t$. However, the $2(y^*)'$ term will place a troublesome $\cos t$ factor on the left. If we guess a solution of the form

(114) $$y^*(t) = c_1 \sin t + c_2 \cos t,$$

a proper choice for $c_1$ and $c_2$ may eliminate the $\cos t$ factors. With $y^*(t)$ as given by (114), we have

$$y^{*\prime}(t) = c_1 \cos t - c_2 \sin t,$$

$$y^{*\prime\prime}(t) = -c_1 \sin t - c_2 \cos t.$$

Substituting these terms into (113) and collecting terms yields

$$(-c_2 + 2c_1 - c_2) \cos t + (-c_1 - 2c_2 - c_1) \sin t = 2 \sin t.$$

This equation is satisfied if and only if

$$2c_1 - 2c_2 = 0,$$

$$-2c_1 - 2c_2 = 2.$$

Thus, $c_1 = -\tfrac{1}{2}$, $c_2 = -\tfrac{1}{2}$, and a particular solution of (113) is

$$y^*(t) = -\tfrac{1}{2} \sin t - \tfrac{1}{2} \cos t.$$

In general if the nonhomogeneous term $r(t)$ is sinusoidal—that is, $r(t)$ has the form $a_1 \cos b_1 t$ or $a_2 \sin b_2 t$—then the problem of finding a particular solution of, say,

$$y'' + p_0 y' + q_0 y = a \cos bt \tag{115}$$

can be reduced to the case where $r(t)$ is an exponential. This follows by noting that by Euler's formula

$$e^{ibt} = \cos bt + i \sin bt$$

and

$$e^{-ibt} = \cos bt - i \sin bt.$$

Hence,

$$\cos bt = \frac{e^{ibt} + e^{-ibt}}{2}.$$

Thus, equation (115) is equivalent to

$$y'' + p_0 y' + q_0 y = \frac{a}{2} e^{ibt} + \frac{a}{2} e^{-ibt}.$$

Here the nonhomogeneous term is the sum of exponentials. From our previous discussion we know that we should choose

$$y^*(t) = A_1 t^s e^{ibt} + A_2 t^s e^{-ibt}, \tag{116}$$

where $s$ is the smallest integer ($s = 0, 1, 2$) such that $y^*(t)$ is not a solution of the homogeneous equation. Note that we may use Euler's formula to put the particular solution (116) into the equivalent form

$$y^*(t) = B_1 t^s \cos bt + B_2 t^s \sin bt \tag{117}$$

for constants $B_1$ and $B_2$.

This technique also applies when $r(t) = a \sin bt$. Using Euler's formula we find that

$$\sin bt = \frac{e^{ibt} - e^{-ibt}}{2i}.$$

Then, with $s$ as above, we choose a particular solution to be

$$y^*(t) = A_1 t^s e^{ibt} + A_2 t^s e^{-ibt}, \tag{116}$$

which may be transformed into the equivalent form, (117).

Let us now consider the example

$$y'' + 4y = -4 \sin 2t. \tag{118}$$

Note that the characteristic equation of the homogeneous equation corresponding to (118) is

$$m^2 + 4 = (m - 2i)(m + 2i) = 0,$$

implying $e^{i2t}$ and $e^{-i2t}$ are solutions of the homogeneous equation. Therefore, according to equation (116), a particular solution is of the form

$$y^*(t) = A_1te^{i2t} + A_2te^{-i2t}$$

or, equivalently,

$$y^*(t) = B_1t\cos 2t + B_2t\sin 2t. \tag{119}$$

Substituting (119) into (118) gives

$$-4B_1\sin 2t + 4B_2\cos 2t = -4\sin 2t$$

or

$$B_1 = 1, \qquad B_2 = 0.$$

Therefore, a particular solution of (118) is

$$y^*(t) = t\cos 2t.$$

*Summary*

We may summarize these results in tabular form:

| $r(t)$ | $y^*(t)$ |
|---|---|
| $a_nt^n + a_{n-1}t^{n-1} + \cdots + a_0$ | $t^s(A_nt^n + \cdots + A_0)$ |
| $ae^{\alpha t}$ | $At^se^{\alpha t}$ |
| $a_1\sin b_1t$ or $a_1\cos b_1t$ | $t^s(B_1\sin b_1t + B_2\cos b_1t)$ |

In this table, $s$ is the smallest integer ($s = 0, 1, 2$) such that no term of $y^*(t)$ is a solution of the homogeneous equation.

The method of undetermined coefficients also applies when the nonhomogeneous term is a sum, difference, or product of the terms given above. If, for example,

$$r(t) = (t^2 + 4) - 9e^{-2t},$$

we would assume a solution of the form

$$y^*(t) = t^{s_1}(A_2t^2 + A_1t + A_0) + At^{s_2}e^{-2t}$$

with $s_1$ and $s_2$ chosen as is $s$ above. Similarly, if

$$r(t) = -6e^{3t}\sin 4t,$$

we would assume a solution of the form

$$y^*(t) = t^se^{3t}(B_1\cos 4t + B_2\sin 4t).$$

These results provide a technique for obtaining particular solutions for a large class of nonhomogeneous second-order linear equations with constant coefficients. To obtain a particular solution when the nonhomogeneous term involves other functions, such as ln $t$, or ratios of the above functions, other techniques must be employed. (For a discussion of such solution techniques, see W. E. Boyce and R. C. DiPrima, *Introduction to Differential Equations*, Wiley, 1970).

## A FURTHER APPLICATION OF SECOND-ORDER LINEAR EQUATIONS

### A Model of Price Adjustment with Stocks

Our model of price adjustment described the responsiveness of the supply and demand of a commodity with variations in its price as time passed. In that model the price at any time is set so that the demand clears the supply; either there are no stocks of the commodity or stocks are maintained at a constant level. Here we wish to extend this model of price speculation to account for changing stocks.

Although the buyers' demand for the commodity is realized in purchases, the suppliers' intentions are realized in sales to merchants who are assumed to hold stocks. The variations in price depend on how merchants set prices relative to stocks. We now revise our model and consider this third group, the merchants who hold stocks and make sales. For simplicity, merchants will be assumed to buy and sell the commodity at the same price and set prices according to the level of the stock.

Let us also assume that the stocks $q$ vary continuously over time as do the variations in demand $u$, supply $s$, and price $p$. If there is no time lag, stocks will increase with time if there is an excess supply and decrease if there is an excess demand. A plausible, yet simple, mathematical description of this behavior is

$$\frac{dq}{dt} = k(s - u), \tag{120}$$

where $k$ is a positive constant. Note that this relation says that the stock is increasing over time ($dq/dt > 0$) when there is an excess supply ($s > u$) and decreasing ($dq/dt < 0$) with an excess demand ($s < u$).

Furthermore, assume that the merchants set the price $p(t)$ at time $t$ so that the rate of increase is proportional to the amount by which stocks fall short of a given level $q_0$:

$$\frac{dp}{dt} = -m(q - q_0), \tag{121}$$

where $m > 0$ is a constant. From (121) we see that if $q > q_0$, prices are falling ($dp/dt < 0$); and if $q < q_0$, prices are increasing ($dp/dt > 0$).

Differentiating (121) yields the relationship

$$\frac{d^2p}{dt^2} = -m\frac{dq}{dt}; \tag{122}$$

the acceleration of the price increase is proportional to the rate of increase of stocks.

Combining (122) and (120), we see that

$$\frac{d^2p}{dt^2} = -mk(s - u) = mk(u - s). \tag{123}$$

Since we originally assumed that supply and demand satisfy linear relationships

$$u(t) = a_0 + a_1p(t),$$
$$s(t) = b_0 + b_1p(t),$$

where $a_1 < 0$ and $b_1 > 0$, we may substitute these functions into (123):

$$\frac{d^2p}{dt^2} - mk(a_1 - b_1)p = mk(a_0 - b_0).$$

Assuming that initially, at $t = 0$,

$$p(0) = p_0 \qquad \text{and} \qquad p'(0) = p_1,$$

this price-adjustment model accounting for the variations in stock is given by the initial value problem

$$p''(t) - k'(a_1 - b_1)p(t) = k'(a_0 - b_0), \tag{124}$$

$$p(0) = p_0, \qquad p'(0) = p_1, \tag{125}$$

where $k' = mk$. We shall assume, for convenience, that

$$p_0 > \left(\frac{a_0 - b_0}{a_1 - b_1}\right).$$

Equation (124) is a second-order linear nonhomogeneous equation with constant coefficients. A particular solution clearly is

$$-\left(\frac{a_0 - b_0}{a_1 - b_1}\right).$$

The general solution to the corresponding homogeneous equation is

$$c_1 \sin \alpha t + c_2 \cos \alpha t,$$

where $\alpha = [k'(b_1 - a_1)]^{1/2}$.

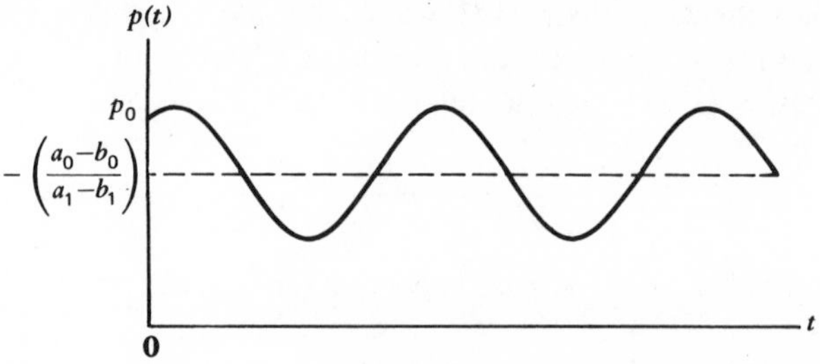


Figure 28

Hence, the general solution of (124) is

$$-\left(\frac{a_0 - b_0}{a_1 - b_1}\right) + c_1 \sin \alpha t + c_2 \cos \alpha t$$

and the unique solution satisfying the initial condition, (125), is

$$p(t) = -\left(\frac{a_0 - b_0}{a_1 - b_1}\right) + \frac{p_1}{\alpha} \sin \alpha t + \left(p_0 + \frac{a_0 - b_0}{a_1 - b_1}\right) \cos \alpha t.$$

$p(t)$ represents the time path of the price of the commodity in our model.

This price–time path is obviously oscillatory in behavior. As shown in Figure 28, $p(t)$ fluctuates about the value

$$-\left(\frac{a_0 - b_0}{a_1 - b_1}\right)$$

with period $2\pi$.

The maximum and minimum values of the price–time path occur at the critical points of $p(t)$; that is, maximizing and minimizing points of $p(t)$ satisfy

$$p'(t^*) = p_1 \cos \alpha t^* - \alpha\left(p_0 + \frac{a_0 - b_0}{a_1 - b_1}\right) \sin \alpha t^* = 0.$$

Equivalently, we can show that these points must satisfy

(126) $$\sin \alpha t^* = \pm\beta,$$

where

$$\beta = \left(\frac{p_1^2}{p_1^2 + \alpha^2[p_0 + (a_0 - b_0)/(a_1 - b_1)]^2}\right)^{1/2}.$$

By examining the sign of $p''(t)$ for points satisfying (126), we see that the maximum of $p(t)$ occurs at points $t_M$ satisfying

(127) $$\sin \alpha t_M = \beta,$$

and the minimum of $p(t)$ occurs at points $t_m$ satisfying

$$\sin \alpha t_m = -\beta. \tag{128}$$

Accordingly, the maximum value of $p(t)$ is

$$p(t_M) = -\left(\frac{a_0 - b_0}{a_1 - b_1}\right) + \frac{p_1}{\alpha}\beta + \left(p_0 + \frac{a_0 - b_0}{a_1 - b_1}\right)\sqrt{1 - \beta^2},$$

and the minimum value of $p(t)$ is

$$p(t_m) = -\left(\frac{a_0 - b_0}{a_1 - b_1}\right) - \frac{p_1}{\alpha}\beta - \left(p_0 + \frac{a_0 - b_0}{a_1 - b_1}\right)\sqrt{1 - \beta^2}.$$

The supply and demand functions also attain their extreme values at the points satisfying (127) and (128). Since the demand is given by

$$u(t) = a_0 + a_1 p(t),$$

the maximum and minimum demand occur at the critical points of $p(t)$,

$$u'(t) = a_1 p'(t) = 0.$$

That is, the extreme values of $u(t)$ occur when $p'(t) = 0$, or, equivalently, at points satisfying (127) and (128). Since $a_1 < 0$,

$$u''(t_M) = a_1 p''(t_M) \geq 0$$

and

$$u''(t_m) = a_1 p''(t_m) \leq 0;$$

demand is maximized at points satisfying (128) and minimized at points satisfying (127). In a similar manner, we can show that supply is maximized at points satisfying (127) and minimized at points satisfying (128).

## EXERCISES

1. [Kaplan, p. 467] Verify that $c_1 e^t + c_2 t^{-1}$ is the general solution of the homogeneous equation corresponding to

$$t(t + 1)y'' + (2 - t^2)y' - (2 + t)y = (t + 1)^2$$

and find the general solution. (*Hint*. Seek a particular solution of the form $At + B$.)

2. Find the general solution of

(*a*) $y'' - 4y = 0$

(*b*) $y'' + 16y' = 0$

(*c*) $y'' + y' + 7y = 0$.

3. Solve the initial value problems

(*a*) $y'' + y' - 3y = 0$

$y(0) = 0, \qquad y'(0) = 1$

(*b*) $y'' - 2y' + y = 0$

$y(0) = 1, \qquad y'(0) = 2.$

4. Find the general solution of

(*a*) $y'' - 3y' - 4y = 4t^2$

(*b*) $y'' - 3y' - 4y = e^{-t}$

(*c*) $y'' + 4y = te^t + \sin 2t$

(*d*) $y'' + y' + 4y = \sinh t \qquad \left(\sinh t = \dfrac{e^t - e^{-t}}{2}\right).$

5. Solve the initial value problems

(*a*) $y'' - 2y' + y = te^t + 4$

$y(0) = 1, \qquad y'(0) = 1$

(*b*) $y'' + 4y = t^2 + 3e^t$

$y(0) = 0, \qquad y'(0) = 2$

(*c*) $y'' - y' = e^t$

$y(0) = 0, \qquad y'(0) = 0$

(*d*) $y'' - y = t + e^t$

$y(0) = 0, \qquad y'(0) = 0$

(*e*) $y'' + 8y' - 9y = 20te^t + 12e^t$

$y(0) = 1, \qquad y'(0) = 0$

(*f*) $y'' + y = \dfrac{1}{1 + t} + (1 + t)\ln(1 + t) \qquad t > 0$

$y(0) = 0, \qquad y'(0) = 1$

(*g*) $y'' + y' - 2y = 2te^{t^2}(2t + 1)$

$y(0) = 0, \qquad y'(0) = 0$

(*h*) $y'' + y = 2\sin t + 4t\cos t$

$y(0) = 1, \qquad y'(0) = 0$

(*i*) $y'' - 2y' + y = -e^t \sin t$

$y(0) = 1, \qquad y'(0) = 0$

(*j*) $2y'' - y' - y = e^t\left(\frac{3t - 2}{t^2}\right) \qquad t > 0$

$y(1) = 0, \qquad y'(1) = 0$

(*k*) $y'' + 2y' + y = 4e^t + t + 2$

$y(0) = 0, \qquad y'(0) = 0$

(*l*) $y'' = t$

$y(0) = 0, \qquad y'(0) = 4$

(*m*) $y'' + y = \sin t$

$y(0) = 0, \qquad y'(0) = 1$

(*n*) $y'' + 4y' + 5y = 5$

$y(0) = 0, \qquad y'(0) = 1$

(*o*) $y'' + 4y' + 5y = 5$

$y(0) = 0, \qquad y'(0) = 0$

(*p*) $y'' + y' = t$

$y(0) = 0, \qquad y'(0) = 1$

(*q*) $y''' - 3y'' + 2y' = 0$

$y(0) = 0, \qquad y'(0) = 0, \qquad y''(0) = 1$

(*r*) $y''' = t$

$y(0) = 0, \qquad y'(0) = 0, \qquad y''(0) = 0.$

6. Suppose two twice-differentiable functions $y_1$ and $y_2$ are interrelated by the "system of differential equations"

$$y_1' = y_2 + 7$$
$$y_2' = y_1 + 2.$$

(*a*) Show that this system of differential equations is equivalent to the second-order linear differential equation

$$y_1'' - y_1 = 2.$$

(*Hint*. Differentiate the first equation with respect to $t$ and substitute in the second equation.)

(*b*) Determine functions $y_1$ and $y_2$ that satisfy this system.

7. Determine functions $y_1$ and $y_2$ that satisfy the following systems:

(*a*) $y_1' = y_2 + \sin t$

$y_2' = 7y_1 + t$

(*b*) $$y_1' = y_2 + 1$$
$$y_2' = y_1 + \cos e^t$$

(*c*) $$y_1' = y_1 + y_2$$
$$y_2' = y_1 + \sin t.$$

8. In attempting to determine new marketing methods for its products, the Suzy Doozy Company has attempted to forecast consumer buying behavior by analyzing the decision process of consumers. This company has determined that this decision process depends upon

   (i) the consumers' motivation toward the product
   (ii) the consumers' attitude toward the product
   (iii) the consumers' level of buying
   (iv) the firm's advertising expenditures for that product.

   The consumers' level of motivation and attitude toward the product may be quantified. Furthermore, the decision process of each group of consumers is characterized as follows: At any time $t$,

   (i) the rate of change of the consumers' attitude with respect to time depends upon the level of corporate advertising, the level of the consumers' attitude, and the level of buying at time $t$
   (ii) the level of the consumers' motivation and the level of consumers' attitude are proportional
   (iii) the rate of change of the level of buying depends upon the consumers' motivation and the level of buying at time $t$.

   Assuming a constant level of advertising expenditure,

   (*a*) Construct a mathematical model of this decision process.
   (*b*) From your model determine mathematical functions that describe the consumers' level of motivation, of attitude, and of buying at any time $t$.
   (*c*) Analyze the effect of variations of the parameters in your model on the level of buying at some time $t_0$.
   (*d*) From your model, determine conditions for unchanged levels of buying and of attitude.
   (*e*) Suppose the consumers' attitude level (buying level) is constant. From your model determine a mathematical description of the consumers' buying level (attitude level) at any time $t$.

9. In the model of price adjustment with stocks, analyze the effect of variations in $a_1$ and $b_1$ on the price–time path $p(t)$.

10. Determine a particular solution for each of the following:

(a) $y'' + \frac{1}{t}y' + y = -\frac{2}{t}\sin t - \frac{1}{t}\sin t \ln t \qquad t > 0$

(b) $y'' - \frac{\cos^2 t}{\sin t}y' - y = -e^{\cos t}\cos t \qquad 0 < t < \pi$

(c) $ty'' + y' - ty = e^t - t\ln t \qquad t > 0$

(d) $y'' + 2y = 2 - 2\cos^2 t + \cos t.$

## SOLUTIONS

2. (a) $y = c_1 e^{2t} + c_2 e^{-2t}$

(b) $y = c_1 + c_2 e^{-16t}$

(c) $y = c_1 e^{-(1/2)t}\cos \frac{3}{2}\sqrt{3}\,t + c_2 e^{-(1/2)t}\sin \frac{3}{2}\sqrt{3}\,t$

3. (a) $$y = \frac{1}{\sqrt{13}}\exp\left[\left(\frac{-1+\sqrt{13}}{2}\right)t\right] - \frac{1}{\sqrt{13}}\exp\left[\left(\frac{-1-\sqrt{13}}{2}\right)t\right]$$

(b) $y = e^t + te^t$

4. (a) $y = -t^2 + \frac{3}{2}t - \frac{13}{8} + c_1 e^{4t} + c_2 e^{-t}$

(b) $y = -\frac{1}{5}te^{-t} + c_1 e^{-t} + c_2 e^{4t}$

(c) $y = \frac{1}{5}te^t - \frac{2}{25}e^t - \frac{1}{4}t\cos 2t + c_1\cos 2t + c_2 \sin 2t$

(d) $y = \frac{1}{12}e^t - \frac{1}{8}e^{-t} + c_1 e^{-(1/2)t}\sin\frac{\sqrt{15}}{2}t + c_2 e^{-(1/2)t}\cos\frac{\sqrt{15}}{2}t$

5. (a) $y = \frac{1}{4}te^t - \frac{4}{3} + \frac{19}{48}e^{-3t} + \frac{93}{48}e^t$

(b) $y = \frac{1}{4}t^2 - \frac{1}{8} + \frac{3}{5}e^t - \frac{19}{40}\cos 2t + \frac{7}{10}\sin 2t$

(c) $y = 1 - e^t + te^t$

(d) $y = -t + \frac{1}{2}te^t + \frac{1}{4}e^t - \frac{1}{4}e^{-t}$

(e) $y = te^t(t+1) - \frac{131}{10}e^t + \frac{21}{10}e^{-9t}$

(f) $y = (t+1)\ln(t+1) + \sin t - \cos t$

(g) $y = e^{t^2} - \frac{1}{3}e^{-2t} - \frac{2}{3}e^t$

(h) $y = t^2 \sin t + \cos t - 6\sin t$

(*i*) $y = e^t \sin t + e^t - 2te^t$

(*j*) $y = -\frac{2}{3}e^t + \frac{2}{3}e^{-(1/2)(t-1)} + e^t \ln t$

(*k*) $y = t + e^t - e^{-t} - 3te^{-t}$

(*l*) $y = 4t + \frac{1}{6}t^3$

(*m*) $y = -\frac{1}{2}t \cos t - \frac{3}{2} \sin t$

(*n*) $y = e^{-2t}(-2 \cos t - 3 \sin t) + 2$

(*o*) $y = e^{-2t}(-2 \cos t - 4 \sin t) + 2$

(*p*) $y = \dfrac{t^2}{2} - t + 1 - e^{-t}$

(*q*) $y = \frac{1}{2} - e^t + \frac{1}{2}e^{2t}$

(*r*) $y = 0$

10\. (*a*) $y = \cos t \ln t$

(*b*) $y = e^{\cos t}$

(*c*) $y = e^t + \ln t$

(*d*) $y = \cos t + \sin^2 t$

# CHAPTER 3

# FIRST-ORDER LINEAR SYSTEMS

## THE MARRIAGE MODEL: THE FIRST-ORDER LINEAR SYSTEM*

The model of population dynamics developed in Chapter 1 was among the simplest such models. There we assumed that the rate of change of the size of the entire population is directly proportional to the population size. Mathematically we described this assumption with a simple first-order equation:

$$\frac{dy}{dt} = (b - d)y(t), \tag{129}$$

where $y(t)$ is the size of the population at time $t$ and $b$ and $d$ are the constant birth and death rates, respectively. The size of the population under this model was seen to be

$$y(t) = y_0 e^{(b-d)t},$$

$y_0$ being the initial population size.

In practice, a value that has been substituted for $b - d$ is the rate of natural increase for either sex. However, the corresponding data generated by this model has given no information about the trend in the sex ratio of males to females. Hence, to obtain information about the ratio of men to women, we must construct a population growth model that treats the number of single males, single females, and married couples separately.

Married couples and single persons of each sex constitute subpopulations of the total population of a community. These subpopulations are not

* Adapted from *An Introduction to the Mathematics of Population* by N. Keyfitz (Addison Wesley, Reading, Massachusetts, 1968). Used with permission.

closed; that is, for example, the subpopulation consisting of married persons generates (unmarried) children, and mortality among married people leaves widows and widowers, here treated as being single.

Consider the single-male population $M(t)$ at time $t$. The change in the number of unmarried males with time, $M'(t)$, depends on

1. the number of male deaths
2. the number of females marrying, each of whom takes one male out of $M(t)$
3. the number of new male babies born
4. the number of married women dying, each of whom releases one male into the ranks of the unmarried.

(For simplicity we shall assume that there are no divorces or separations.) As the number of male deaths increases and as the number of females marrying increases, the single-male population will decrease. As more male babies are born and more married women die, the number of single males will increase.

This behavior may be summarized mathematically by a simple linear relationship between $M'(t)$, $M(t)$, the number $F(t)$ of single females at time $t$, and the number $N(t)$ of married couples at time $t$. Assume a constant male death rate $d_m > 0$, a constant male birthrate $b_m^0 > 0$, a constant married female death rate of $d_f^0 > 0$, a constant fixed proportion $m > 0$ of single females marry, and $F(t) < M(t)$. If we assume for the moment that there are no male births and no married-female deaths, then the single-male population will decrease; that is, $M'(t) < 0$. There will only be single-male deaths and marriages. Furthermore, if we assume that the rate of change in the size of the single-male population at time $t$ due to single-male deaths and marriages is proportional to the size of the single-male population at time $t$ and single-female population at time $t$, respectively, then

$$M'(t) = -d_m M(t) - mF(t).$$

Note that the contribution due to marriage is proportional to $F(t)$ rather than $M(t)$, because $F(t) < M(t)$ by assumption. We can account for the increase in the size of the single-male population due to married-female deaths and male births in an analogous manner. We shall assume that the rate of change in the size of the single-male population at time $t$ due to married females dying and married couples having male babies is proportional to the number of married couples. Hence, the rate of change of the single-male population may be mathematically described as follows:

$$M'(t) = -d_m M(t) - mF(t) + (b_m^0 + d_f^0)N(t). \tag{130}$$

Similarly, we may describe the rate of change in the number of single females with time, $F'(t)$, and in the number of married couples with time, $N'(t)$:

$$F'(t) = -(d_f + m)F(t) + (b_f^0 + d_m^0)N(t), \tag{131}$$

$$N'(t) = mF(t) - (d_f^0 + d_m^0)N(t), \tag{132}$$

where $d_f$ ($> 0$) is the death rate of single females, $b_f^0$ ($> 0$) is the birthrate of females, and $d_m^0$ ($> 0$) is the death rate of married men.

Thus the relevant factors and interrelations in this population growth model are summarized by combining (130), (131), and (132) in the following system:

$$\begin{aligned} M'(t) &= -d_m M(t) - mF(t) + (b_m^0 + d_f^0)N(t) \\ F'(t) &= -(d_f + m)F(t) + (b_f^0 + d_m^0)N(t) \\ N'(t) &= mF(t) - (d_f^0 + d_m^0)N(t). \end{aligned} \tag{133}$$

System (133) is an example of a *first-order linear system of ordinary differential equations*. The theoretical basis of solution techniques for such linear systems is quite similar to that for second-order linear equations. As with second-order linear equations, an analysis of this system reveals that the behavior of a solution depends upon the relative size of the coefficients. Although this system is not solved, because of the numerous details, $F(t)$, $M(t)$, and $N(t)$ may, for instance, increase without bound or oscillate indefinitely. We now proceed to discuss the fundamental theory of first-order linear systems.

## FUNDAMENTAL THEORY

A system of ordinary differential equations for unknown functions $y_1$, $y_2, \ldots, y_n$ is called a *first-order system* if it has the form

$$\begin{aligned} \frac{dy_1}{dt} &= f_1(y_1, \ldots, y_n) \\ \frac{dy_2}{dt} &= f_2(y_1, \ldots, y_n) \\ &\vdots \\ \frac{dy_n}{dt} &= f_n(y_1, \ldots, y_n) \end{aligned}$$

where the functions $f_i$ are given. Note that the number of unknowns is the same as the number of equations and that no derivatives of order higher than 1 appear. A first-order system of the form:

$$\begin{aligned} y_1' &= a_{11}(t)y_1 + \cdots + a_{1n}(t)y_n + b_1(t) \\ &\ \ \vdots \qquad\qquad\qquad\qquad \vdots \qquad\quad \vdots \\ y_n' &= a_{1n}(t)y_1 + \cdots + a_{nn}(t)y_n + b_n(t), \end{aligned} \tag{134}$$

where the functions $a_{ij}(t)$ and $b_j(t)$ are given, is called a first-order *linear* system. The functions $a_{ij}(t)$ are called the *coefficients of the system* (134). If each of the functions $b_j(t)$ is the zero function, the system is said to be *homogeneous;* otherwise, it is *nonhomogeneous*.

An ordered set of functions $(y_1, \ldots, y_n)$ that satisfies system (134) on some interval $a < t < b$ is called a *solution* of the first-order linear system. Additional constraints on the solution of the form

$$y_1(t_0) = a_0, \ldots, y_n(t_0) = a_n \tag{135}$$

are called a set of *initial conditions* for the system (134), where $a < t_0 < b$. Together (134) and (135) are called an *initial value problem* (see Figure 29).

The fundamental theory of first-order systems closely parallels that of a single second-order linear equation. This is not surprising, because every second-order linear equation can be transformed into a first-order linear system. This fact follows by noting that with the substitution $v = y'$, the

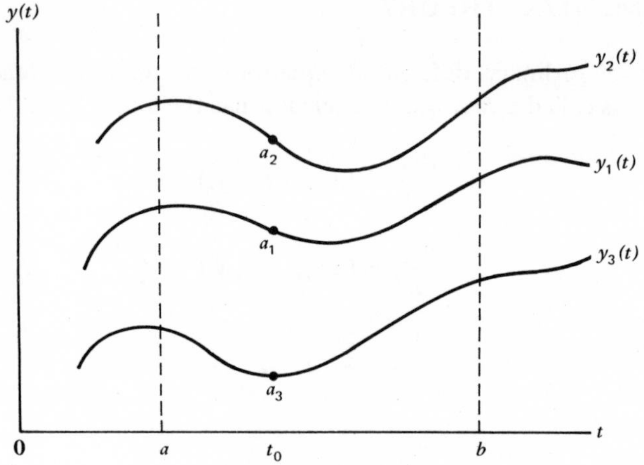


Figure 29

second-order linear equation

$$y'' = -p(t)y' - q(t)y + r(t)$$

is equivalent to the first-order linear system

$$v' = -p(t)v - q(t)y + r(t)$$
$$y' = v.$$

Analogous to the existence and uniqueness theorem for second-order linear equations, we have the following existence and uniqueness theorem for first-order linear systems.

**THEOREM 6** In an interval $a < t < b$ in which the coefficients

$$a_{11}(t), \ldots, a_{nn}(t)$$

and functions

$$b_1(t), \ldots, b_n(t)$$

of (134) are continuous there is a *unique* ordered set of functions $(y_1(t), \ldots, y_n(t))$ that satisfy (134) and the set of initial conditions

$$y_1(t_0) = a_1, \ldots, y_n(t_0) = a_n$$

at a point $t_0 \in (a, b)$. Moreover, these functions $y_1(t), \ldots, y_n(t)$ and their first derivatives are continuous in $(a, b)$. ▮

Thus, Theorem 6 guarantees the existence of a unique solution to an initial value problem like

$$y_1' = y_2 + 1$$
$$y_2' = y_1 + 1$$
$$y_1(0) = 1, \qquad y_2(0) = -1, \qquad -\infty < t < \infty.$$

The results and techniques to be developed will show that

$$(e^t + e^{-t} - 1, e^t - e^{-t} - 1)$$

is the unique solution of this initial value problem.

To simplify our discussion of first-order linear systems, we shall use matrix notation; that is, the functions $y_1, \ldots, y_n$ are considered components of a vector $\mathbf{y} = (y_1, \ldots, y_n)$ and the functions $b_1(t), \ldots, b_n(t)$ are considered components of a vector $\mathbf{b}(t)$. The functions $a_{11}(t), \ldots, a_{nn}(t)$ are entries in an $n \times n$ matrix $\mathbf{A}(t)$. Thus, system (134) may be written in matrix notation as:

(136) $$\mathbf{y}' = \mathbf{A}(t)\mathbf{y} + \mathbf{b}(t).$$

The notation

$$\mathbf{y}^k = (y_{k1}(t), \ldots, y_{kn}(t))$$

will be used to denote specific solutions of system (134).

In order to discuss the form of the general solution of (136), we examine the solution of the homogeneous system

$$\mathbf{y}' = \mathbf{A}(t)\mathbf{y}. \tag{137}$$

Just as solutions of the second-order linear homogeneous equation satisfy the *principle of superposition*, so do solutions of system (137):

THEOREM 7 If $\mathbf{y}^1(t)$ and $\mathbf{y}^2(t)$ are solutions of the system $\mathbf{y}' = \mathbf{A}(t)\mathbf{y}$, then the linear combination

$$c_1\mathbf{y}^1(t) + c_2\mathbf{y}^2(t)$$

is also a solution for any constants $c_1$ and $c_2$. ▮

This result is proved by differentiating $c_1\mathbf{y}^1 + c_2\mathbf{y}^2$ and using the fact that $\mathbf{y}^1$ and $\mathbf{y}^2$ satisfy (137).

As an example, it can be verified that two solutions of

$$\begin{aligned} y_1'(t) &= y_1(t) + y_2(t) \\ y_2'(t) &= 4y_1(t) + y_2(t) \end{aligned} \tag{138}$$

are

$$\mathbf{y}^1(t) = \begin{bmatrix} e^{3t} \\ 2e^{3t} \end{bmatrix} \quad \text{and} \quad \mathbf{y}^2(t) = \begin{bmatrix} e^{-t} \\ -2e^{-t} \end{bmatrix}. \tag{139}$$

According to Theorem 7,

$$\mathbf{y}(t) = c_1\begin{bmatrix} e^{3t} \\ 2e^{3t} \end{bmatrix} + c_2\begin{bmatrix} e^{-t} \\ -2e^{-t} \end{bmatrix}$$

is also a solution of (138) for arbitrary constants $c_1$ and $c_2$.

By repeated applications of Theorem 7, we may conclude that if $\mathbf{y}^1(t), \ldots, \mathbf{y}^k(t)$ are solutions of (137) then

$$\mathbf{y}(t) = c_1\mathbf{y}^1(t) + \cdots + c_k\mathbf{y}^k(t)$$

is also a solution of (137) for arbitrary constants $c_1, \ldots, c_k$. The question now arises whether all solutions can be obtained in this way. Recall that all solutions of the second-order linear homogeneous equation could be expressed as linear combinations of two linearly independent solutions. A similar result holds for linearly independent solutions of (137).

Before discussing this result, we must give an interpretation of linearly independent vector solutions. The concept of linearly independent vector-valued functions of one variable is essentially the same as that of linearly independent scalar functions of one variable. The vector functions $\mathbf{y}^1(t)$

and $\mathbf{y}^2(t)$ are said to be linearly independent for $a < t < b$ if

$$c_1\mathbf{y}^1(t) + c_2\mathbf{y}^2(t) = \mathbf{0} \tag{140}$$

implies $c_1 = c_2 = 0$.

For example, to see that $\mathbf{y}^1(t) = (e^{3t}, 2e^{3t})$ and $\mathbf{y}^2(t) = (e^{-t}, -2e^{-t})$, the solutions of (138), are linearly independent *for all t*, enter them in the expression (140):

$$c_1\begin{bmatrix} e^{3t} \\ 2e^{3t} \end{bmatrix} + c_2\begin{bmatrix} e^{-t} \\ -2e^{-t} \end{bmatrix} = \begin{bmatrix} 0 \\ 0 \end{bmatrix}. \tag{141}$$

If (141) is to hold for all $t$, then in particular it must hold for $t = 0$. At $t = 0$, (141) becomes

$$c_1\begin{pmatrix} 1 \\ 2 \end{pmatrix} + c_2\begin{pmatrix} 1 \\ -2 \end{pmatrix} = \begin{pmatrix} 0 \\ 0 \end{pmatrix}$$

or

$$\begin{aligned} c_1 + c_2 &= 0, \\ 2c_1 - 2c_2 &= 0. \end{aligned} \tag{142}$$

The only solution of (142) is $c_1 = c_2 = 0$. Hence, $\mathbf{y}^1(t) = (e^{3t}, 2e^{3t})$ and $\mathbf{y}^2(t) = (e^{-t}, -2e^{-t})$ are linearly independent for all $t$.

More generally, the vector-valued functions $\mathbf{y}^1(t), \ldots, \mathbf{y}^n(t)$ are linearly independent for $a < t < b$ if

$$c_1\mathbf{y}^1(t) + \cdots + c_n\mathbf{y}^n(t) = \mathbf{0}$$

implies $c_1 = c_2 = \cdots = c_n = 0$.

Now we state the desired result:

**THEOREM 8** If $\mathbf{y}^1(t), \ldots, \mathbf{y}^n(t)$ are linearly independent solutions of (137) for each point in the interval $a < t < b$, then each solution of (137) can be expressed uniquely as a linear combination

$$c_1\mathbf{y}^1(t) + \cdots + c_n\mathbf{y}^n(t). \quad \blacksquare \tag{143}$$

The expression (143) is called the *general solution* of (137).

According to Theorem 8, since $\mathbf{y}^1(t)$ and $\mathbf{y}^2(t)$ defined by (139) were seen to be linearly independent solutions of (138) each solution of system (138) may be expressed as

$$c_1\begin{bmatrix} e^{3t} \\ 2e^{3t} \end{bmatrix} + c_2\begin{bmatrix} e^{-t} \\ -2e^{-t} \end{bmatrix} \tag{144}$$

for a unique set of constants $c_1$ and $c_2$.

The general solution of the nonhomogeneous system (136) is also obtained in a manner similar to the procedure for finding the general solution of the second-order linear nonhomogeneous ordinary differential equation. Recall that the general solution of the second-order linear equation is of the form

$$z^*(t) + c_1 z_1(t) + c_2 z_2(t),$$

where $z^*(t)$ is a particular solution of the second-order linear equation and $z_1(t)$ and $z_2(t)$ are linearly independent solutions of the homogeneous equation. For first-order linear systems, we have:

THEOREM 9 If $\mathbf{y}^*(t)$ is a particular solution of

$$\mathbf{y}' = \mathbf{A}(t)\mathbf{y} + \mathbf{b}(t) \tag{136}$$

and $c_1\mathbf{y}^1(t) + \cdots + c_n\mathbf{y}^n(t)$ is the general solution of

$$\mathbf{y}' = \mathbf{A}(t)\mathbf{y}, \tag{137}$$

then

$$\mathbf{y}^*(t) + c_1\mathbf{y}^1(t) + \cdots + c_n\mathbf{y}^n(t) \tag{145}$$

is a solution of (136). ▮

Equation (145) is called the *general solution* of (136).

Theorem 9 indicates the procedure for finding the general solution of nonhomogeneous system (136). Specifically, we

1. determine the general solution of the homogeneous system, and
2. determine a particular solution of the nonhomogeneous system.

The sum of a particular solution of the nonhomogeneous system and the general solution of the homogeneous system is the general solution of the nonhomogeneous system.

To illustrate this theorem, consider the nonhomogeneous system

$$\begin{aligned} y_1' &= y_1 + y_2 + 1 \\ y_2' &= 4y_1 + y_2 - 1. \end{aligned} \tag{146}$$

It may be shown that $\mathbf{y}^*(t) = (\frac{2}{3}, -\frac{5}{3})$ is a particular solution of system (146). From Theorem 9 and (144) we conclude that the general solution of system (146) is

$$\begin{bmatrix} \frac{2}{3} \\ -\frac{5}{3} \end{bmatrix} + c_1 \begin{bmatrix} e^{3t} \\ 2e^{3t} \end{bmatrix} + c_2 \begin{bmatrix} e^{-t} \\ -2e^{-t} \end{bmatrix}$$

for arbitrary constants $c_1$ and $c_2$.

Elementary applications of first-order linear systems in the social and managerial sciences primarily involve equations with constant coefficients $a_{ij}(t)$ and constant nonhomogeneous terms $b_j(t)$. Therefore, we shall confine our study of first-order systems mainly to these.

## VOTING DISTRIBUTION: LINEAR HOMOGENEOUS SYSTEMS WITH CONSTANT COEFFICIENTS

Many individuals support a presidential candidate not because they have any firm conviction about their candidate but because the majority of the others with whom they come into contact support this candidate. There are of course all gradations from individuals who are guided only by their convictions to those who follow the lead of others. For instance, consider a situation in which the population of a community is composed of individuals who support and vote for a candidate only on their own initiative (type 1) and individuals who are strongly influenced by their fellow individuals and direct their support and votes exclusively according to what others do (type 2).

Suppose that the community has a very large population composed of individuals who are supporting one of two presidential candidates, Ben Dover or Art Gallery. Of these individuals let $x'_0$ be Ben Dover supporters of type 1; we refer to them as individuals $1_D$. Let $w'_0$ individuals be Art Gallery supporters of type 1; we refer to them as individuals $1_G$. We are interested in determining the voting behavior of the remaining individuals, all assumed to be of type 2.

In attempting to determine the voting behavior of an individual of type 2 let us assume that individuals of type 2 are more inclined to vote for either Dover or Gallery the more frequently he comes into contact with their respective type 1 supporters. Let each individual of type $1_D$ actively try to influence as many individuals of type 2 as possible by actually coming into contact with as many of them as he can. Then, denoting by $x$ the number of type 2 who are Dover supporters because they were influenced to do so by the individuals of type $1_D$, we see $x$ increases at a rate approximately proportional to $x'_0$. Let this proportionality coefficient be $a_0$, so that the total contribution of individuals of type $1_D$ to the increase of $x$ is $a_0 x'_0$.

The $x$ individuals who support Ben Dover also come into contact with other individuals of type 2 who have not yet decided to support Ben Dover. Therefore, they will also contribute to the rate of increase of $x$ in amount $ax$ ($a \neq a_0$).

Analogously, if there are $w$ individuals of type 2 who have been influenced to support Gallery through contact with other individuals of type 2, we find that the rate of increase of $w$ is proportional to $w'_0$ and $w$ by amounts $b'_0 w'_0$ and $b'w$, where $b'_0$ and $b'$ are constants.

If the population has only one alternative in their voting behavior, either Ben Dover or Art Gallery, then increases in $x$ are accompanied by decreases in $w$. Here we assume $w$ decreases by an amount $a'_0 x'_0 + a'x$. Conversely, increases in $w$ are assumed to be accompanied by decreases in $x$

by an amount $b_0 w'_0 + bw$. Thus, we have

$$\frac{dx}{dt} = a_0 x'_0 + ax - b_0 w'_0 - bw$$

and

$$\frac{dw}{dt} = b'_0 w'_0 + b'w - a'_0 x'_0 - a'x,$$

or, equivalently,

$$\text{(147)} \qquad \begin{aligned} \frac{dx}{dt} &= ax - bw + a_0 x'_0 - b_0 w'_0 \\ \frac{dw}{dt} &= -a'x + b'w - a'_0 x'_0 + b'_0 w'_0, \end{aligned}$$

where $a$, $a_0$, $a'$, $a'_0$, $b$, $b_0$, $b'$, $b'_0$ are positive constants. This linear, non-homogeneous system of ordinary differential equations with constant coefficients describes the variations in the number of Dover and Gallery supporters with time.

An analysis of this system provides information about the behavior of $x(t)$ and $w(t)$. For instance, by examining system (147), we see that when

$$ax > bw - a_0 x'_0 + b_0 w'_0,$$

$dx/dt > 0$; that is, $x(t)$, the number of supporters of Ben Dover, increases with time. Note that the converse is true when the reverse inequality holds. Similarly, system (147) shows that the number of Art Gallery's supporters increases when

$$b'w > a'x + a'_0 x'_0 - b'_0 w'_0.$$

A further analysis of this model yields conditions under which the voting distribution between Dover and Gallery is stable, or, equivalently, ultimately remains constant. Mathematically this means that the rates of change in $x(t)$ and $w(t)$ become zero. If we set the rates given by system (147) equal to zero, we obtain conditions that must be satisfied if stabilization is to occur:

$$\text{(148)} \qquad \begin{aligned} \frac{dx}{dt} &= ax - bw + a_0 x'_0 - b_0 w'_0 = 0 \\ \frac{dw}{dt} &= -a'x + b'w - a'_0 x'_0 + b'_0 w'_0 = 0. \end{aligned}$$

By rewriting system (148) we see that to achieve stability $x$ and $w$ must necessarily satisfy

$$\text{(149)} \qquad w = \frac{a}{b} x + \frac{a_0 x'_0 - b_0 w'_0}{b}$$

and

$$w = \frac{a'}{b'}x + \frac{a'_0 x'_0 - b'_0 w'_0}{b'}. \tag{150}$$

If $(x, w)$ lies on the straight line (149), $dx/dt = 0$, the voting distribution of Ben Dover's supporters is stable. Similarly, if $(x, w)$ lies on (150), $dw/dt = 0$, the voting distribution of Art Gallery's supporters is stable. Furthermore, if $(x, w)$ lies on both lines (149) and (150), this intersection is an equilibrium point $(x^*, w^*)$ for the voting distribution model. To see if the entire system is stable, we must determine whether an arbitrary voting distribution point $(x, w)$ approaches this equilibrium point.

To derive conditions that guarantee continued stabilization, we analyze system (149)–(150). Since the values of the constants in (149) and (150) have not been specified we proceed by making assumptions concerning their relative size.

Suppose the lines of stabilization, (149) and (150), appear as in Figure 30. That is, the slopes of (149) and (150) satisfy $a/b > a'/b'$, and the intercepts

$$\frac{a_0 x'_0 - b_0 w'_0}{b} \quad \text{and} \quad \frac{a'_0 x'_0 - b'_0 w'_0}{b'}$$

are positive.

If the initial voting distribution is the point $(x_0, w_0)$ shown in Figure 30, $(x_0, w_0)$ will not remain stationary, since the rates of change in $x$ and $w$ are nonzero here. Specifically, if the number of each candidate's supporters varies while the other's remains constant, the behavior is as shown in Figure 31, that is, if the initial number of Art Gallery supporters is $w_0$, the Ben Dover supporters will campaign to increase the number of his supporters to

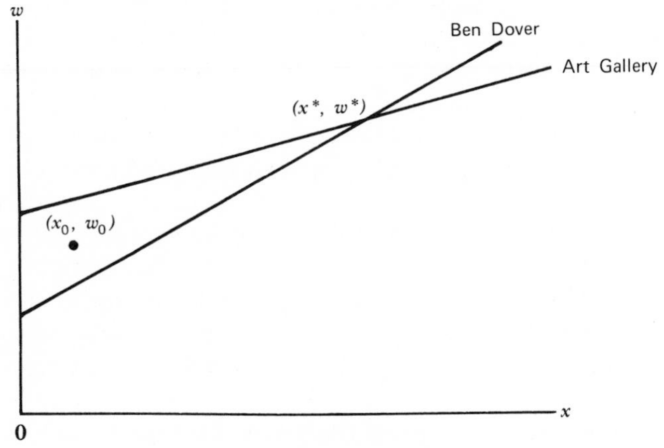


Figure 30

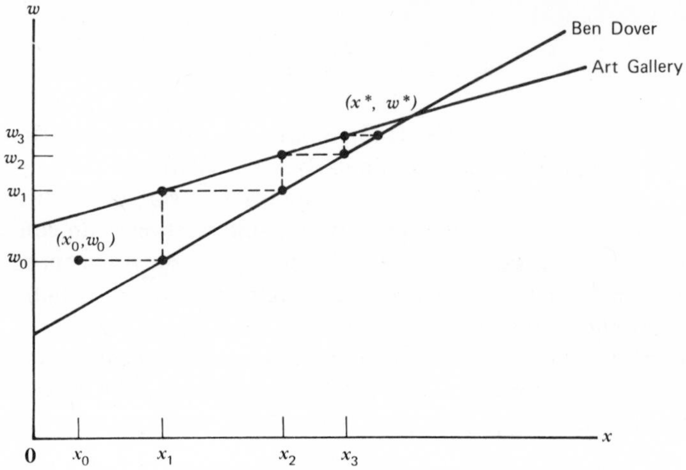


Figure 31

$x_1$ in order to remain on their line of stability. Now the Art Gallery supporters will increase the number of their campaigners to $w_1$ so as to operate on their line of stability. In order to operate on their line of stability, the number of Ben Dover supporters now increases to $x_2$. Continuing in this manner, it is readily seen that the points $(x_i, w_i)$ tend to the equilibrium point $(x^*, w^*)$; that is, the voting distribution of both candidates is ultimately stabilized. (Is this system still stable if a different initial voting distribution $(x_0, w_0)$ is chosen?)

If, however, the slopes of (149) and (150) satisfy the reverse inequality $a'/b' > a/b$, the system is not stable. In this case the lines of stability appear as in Figure 32. Again, if each candidate's supporters adjusts its effort while the other keeps his constant, the behavior is as shown in Figure 32.

To demonstrate the instability in this case suppose the initial voting distribution $(x_0, w_0)$ is as in Figure 32. To achieve stability on the Dover side, the number of Ben Dover supporters will be increased to $x_1$. Now the number of Art Gallery supporters will be increased to $w_1$ so as to remain on the Gallery line of stability. As this process continues the voting distribution tends away from the equilibrium point. Both the values of $x(t)$ and $w(t)$ increase indefinitely.

Note that if $(x_0, w_0)$ appears as in Figure 33 the voting distribution moves away from the equilibrium point in the opposite direction. As illustrated in Figure 33, ultimately Ben Dover will have no supporters of type 2.

Thus, through this technique of analysis we have determined conditions that provide a stable voting distribution as well as conditions resulting in an unstable voting distribution. (This type of analysis will also prove useful in our study of utility functions in Chapter 6.)

Actually determining an explicit solution for our voting distribution model (147) is a very tedious procedure, since the constants are not specified. However to illustrate one technique for solving (147), we simplify the system by assuming $a' = a$, $b' = b$, $a_0' = a_0$, and $b_0' = b_0$; thus,

$$\frac{dx}{dt} = ax - bw + a_0x_0' - b_0w_0'$$

$$\frac{dw}{dt} = -ax + bw + b_0w_0' - a_0x_0'.$$

From the fundamental theory we know that solutions of such linear, nonhomogeneous systems are the sum of a particular solution and the general solution of the corresponding homogeneous system. We proceed by first determining a particular solution.

In determining a particular solution of the second-order linear equation with constant coefficients and a constant nonhomogeneous term,

$$z'' + p_0z' + q_0z = r_0,$$

we saw that a reasonable "guess" is $z^*(t) = d$, a constant. Similarly, it is reasonable to assume that the particular solution of our system is a constant vector $(d_1, d_2)$. Upon substituting $x = d_1$ and $w = d_2$ into our linear system

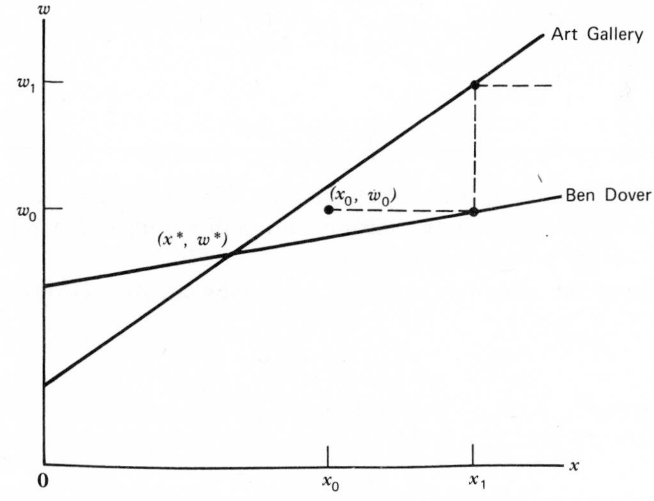


Figure 32

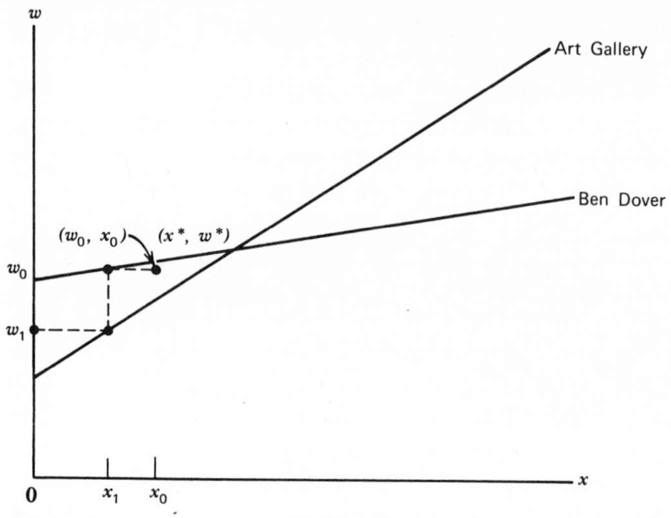


Figure 33

and solving for $d_1$ and $d_2$, we find that a particular solution is

$$\begin{bmatrix} d_1 \\ d_2 \end{bmatrix} = \begin{bmatrix} \dfrac{b - (a_0 x - b_0 w_0)}{a} \\ 1 \end{bmatrix}.$$

The corresponding homogeneous system

(151) $$\frac{dx}{dt} = ax - bw$$

(152) $$\frac{dw}{dt} = -ax + bw,$$

can be solved by the process of elimination. The dependent variable $w$ is eliminated and a second-order linear equation in $x$ is formed. Upon solving this equation for $x$ we can determine $w$.

We begin this elimination process by solving equation (151) for $w$,

(153) $$bw = ax - \frac{dx}{dt}.$$

Therefore,

(154) $$b\frac{dw}{dt} = a\frac{dx}{dt} - \frac{d^2x}{dt^2}.$$

After substituting (153) and (154) into (152) and performing several algebraic manipulations, we find

$$\frac{a}{b}\frac{dx}{dt} - \frac{1}{b}\frac{d^2x}{dt^2} = -\frac{dx}{dt}$$

or,

$$\frac{d^2x}{dt^2} - (a + b)\frac{dx}{dt} = 0.$$

The general solution of this second-order equation is

$$x(t) = c_1 + \frac{c_2}{a + b} e^{(a+b)t}$$

for constants $c_1$ and $c_2$. Equation (153) then implies

$$w(t) = c_1 \frac{a}{b} - \frac{c_2}{a + b} e^{(a+b)t}.$$

Thus, in vector notation, the general solution of the homogeneous system is

$$c_1 \begin{pmatrix} 1 \\ \dfrac{a}{b} \end{pmatrix} + c_2 \begin{pmatrix} \dfrac{1}{a+b} \\ -\dfrac{1}{a+b} \end{pmatrix} e^{(a+b)t}.$$

According to the fundamental theory, the general solution of the modified version of system (147) is the sum of the particular solution $(d_1, d_2)$ and the general solution of the homogeneous system

$$\begin{pmatrix} \dfrac{b - (a_0x'_0 - b_0w'_0)}{a} \\ 1 \end{pmatrix} + c_1 \begin{pmatrix} 1 \\ \dfrac{a}{b} \end{pmatrix} + c_2 \begin{pmatrix} \dfrac{1}{a+b} \\ -\dfrac{1}{a+b} \end{pmatrix} e^{(a+b)t}.$$

If this solution is to satisfy initial conditions, we can determine values for $c_1$ and $c_2$. For instance, if $(x(0), w(0)) = (1, 1)$, then

$$c_1 = \frac{b(a - b + a_0x'_0 - b_0w'_0)}{a(a + b)},$$

$$c_2 = a - b + a_0x'_0 - b_0w'_0.$$

The elimination process employed above provides a simple technique for solving systems with only two or three first-order equations. For large systems, however, we must apply other techniques; these techniques are considered now.

## The Homogeneous System

In this section we show how to construct the general solution of a first-order linear homogeneous system with constant real coefficients:

$$\mathbf{y}' = \mathbf{A}\mathbf{y}. \tag{155}$$

The procedure for constructing solutions of this general $n \times n$ system is best illustrated by first considering an example:

$$\mathbf{y}' = \begin{pmatrix} 2 & -1 \\ 3 & -2 \end{pmatrix}\mathbf{y}. \tag{156}$$

The algorithm for solving this example is analogous to our treatment of second-order linear homogeneous equations with constant coefficients:

$$z'' + p_0 z' + q_0 z = 0. \tag{157}$$

To solve the latter equation, we seek solutions of the general form $ce^{mt}$, where $c$ and $m$ are constants to be determined. To solve (156) we seek solutions of the form

$$\mathbf{y}(t) = \mathbf{v}e^{mt}, \tag{158}$$

where the constant $m$ and the constant vector $\mathbf{v} = (v_1, v_2)$ are to be determined. Substituting equation (158) for $\mathbf{y}(t)$ into system (156) leads to

$$m\begin{bmatrix} v_1 \\ v_2 \end{bmatrix} e^{mt} = \begin{bmatrix} 2 & -1 \\ 3 & -2 \end{bmatrix}\begin{bmatrix} v_1 \\ v_2 \end{bmatrix} e^{mt}.$$

Dividing out the scalar $e^{mt}$, we find

$$m\begin{bmatrix} v_1 \\ v_2 \end{bmatrix} = \begin{bmatrix} 2 & -1 \\ 3 & -2 \end{bmatrix}\begin{bmatrix} v_1 \\ v_2 \end{bmatrix}. \tag{159}$$

Equation (159) is equivalent to the scalar form

$$mv_1 = 2v_1 - v_2$$
$$mv_2 = 3v_1 - 2v_2$$

or

$$\begin{aligned} (m - 2)v_1 + v_2 &= 0, \\ -3v_1 + (m + 2)v_2 &= 0. \end{aligned} \tag{160}$$

The linear system (160) has a nontrivial solution $(v_1, v_2)$ if and only if the determinant of coefficients vanishes; that is,

$$\begin{vmatrix} m - 2 & 1 \\ -3 & m + 2 \end{vmatrix} = (m - 2)(m + 2) + 3 = m^2 - 1 = 0. \tag{161}$$

Thus, we see that $m$ must be a root of equation (161) called the *characteristic equation*. The roots are $m_1 = 1, m_2 = -1$.

Corresponding to each of these roots is a nontrivial solution $\mathbf{v} = (v_1, v_2)$ of the linear system (160). When $m = m_1 = 1$, the solution of system (160) is $\mathbf{v} = c_1(1, 1)$ for any constant $c_1$. Thus, the corresponding solution of (156) is

$$\mathbf{y}^1(t) = c_1\begin{pmatrix}1\\1\end{pmatrix}e^t. \tag{162}$$

For the root $m = m_2 = -1$, the solution of system (160) is $\mathbf{v} = c_2(1, 3)$. Thus, the corresponding solution of (156) is

$$\mathbf{y}^2(t) = c_2\begin{pmatrix}1\\3\end{pmatrix}e^{-t}. \tag{163}$$

Since $\mathbf{y}^1(t)$ and $\mathbf{y}^2(t)$ defined by (162) and (163), respectively, are linearly independent, the general solution of (156) is

$$c_1\begin{pmatrix}1\\1\end{pmatrix}e^t + c_2\begin{pmatrix}1\\3\end{pmatrix}e^{-t}.$$

The same procedure is used to solve the general linear homogeneous system with constant coefficients:

$$\mathbf{y}' = \mathbf{A}\mathbf{y} \tag{155}$$

where $\mathbf{A}$ is an $n \times n$ matrix of real coefficients and $\mathbf{y} = (y_1, \ldots, y_n)$. As in the preceding example, assuming a solution of the form

$$\mathbf{y} = \mathbf{v}e^{mt},$$

where $\mathbf{v} = (v_1, \ldots, v_n)$ is a vector of constants and $m$ is a constant, and substituting this expression into the general system (155), we obtain

$$m\mathbf{v}e^{mt} = \mathbf{A}\mathbf{v}e^{mt}.$$

Dividing out the scalar $e^{mt}$, we find

$$m\mathbf{v} = \mathbf{A}\mathbf{v}$$

or, equivalently,

$$(\mathbf{A} - m\mathbf{I})\mathbf{v} = \mathbf{0}, \tag{164}$$

where $\mathbf{I}$ is the identity matrix. As in the example, (164) has a nontrivial solution $\mathbf{v}$ if and only if

$$\det(\mathbf{A} - m\mathbf{I}) = 0. \tag{165}$$

Equation (165) is a polynomial of degree $n$ called the *characteristic equation.*

Having found a root $m^*$ of the characteristic equation, we may find a corresponding nontrivial solution $\mathbf{v}^* = (v_1^*, \ldots, v_n^*)$ of (164). Thus, the corresponding solution of (155) is

$$\mathbf{y}(t) = \mathbf{v}^* e^{m^* t}.$$

The roots $m_i$ ($i = 1, \ldots, n$) of the characteristic equation are called the *eigenvalues* of the coefficient matrix **A** and the corresponding vector solutions $\mathbf{v}^i$ ($i = 1, \ldots, n$) of (164) are called the corresponding *eigenvectors* of **A**. We have seen, for example, that $m_1 = 1$ is an eigenvalue of

$$\begin{pmatrix} 2 & -1 \\ 3 & -2 \end{pmatrix}$$

with corresponding eigenvector $\mathbf{v}^1 = c_1(1, 1)$, where $c_1$ is a constant.

From elementary algebra we know that the $n$ roots of the characteristic equation $\det(m\mathbf{I} - \mathbf{A}) = 0$ may be characterized as

1. distinct real eigenvalues of **A**,
2. complex eigenvalues of **A**,
3. repeated eigenvalues of **A**.

To complete our treatment of the linear homogeneous system with constant coefficients, we consider each of these cases separately.

### *Distinct Real Eigenvalues of* **A**

Let us consider an example where the eigenvalues are real and distinct:

$$\text{(166)} \qquad \mathbf{y}' = \begin{pmatrix} 3 & -2 \\ 2 & -2 \end{pmatrix} \mathbf{y}.$$

We seek solutions of the form $\mathbf{y}(t) = \mathbf{v}e^{mt}$, where $\mathbf{v} = (v_1, v_2)$. Substituting this expression into (166) leads us to

$$\text{(167)} \qquad \begin{aligned} (m - 3)v_1 + 2v_2 &= 0, \\ -2v_1 + (m + 2)v_2 &= 0. \end{aligned}$$

This system has a nontrivial solution $(v_1, v_2)$ if and only if

$$\begin{vmatrix} m - 3 & 2 \\ -2 & m + 2 \end{vmatrix} = (m + 1)(m - 2) = 0.$$

That is, we have the distinct eigenvalues $m_1 = -1$, $m_2 = 2$. By solving (167) with eigenvalues $m_1 = -1$, $m_2 = 2$, we see that the corresponding eigenvectors are

$$\mathbf{v}^1 = c_1\begin{pmatrix}1\\2\end{pmatrix} \quad \text{and} \quad \mathbf{v}^2 = c_2\begin{pmatrix}2\\1\end{pmatrix},$$

where $c_1$ and $c_2$ are constants. Hence, the corresponding solutions of system (166) are

$$(168) \qquad \mathbf{y}^1(t) = c_1\begin{pmatrix}1\\2\end{pmatrix}e^{-t} \quad \text{and} \quad \mathbf{y}^2(t) = c_2\begin{pmatrix}2\\1\end{pmatrix}e^{2t}$$

for constants $c_1$ and $c_2$.

It is readily shown that $\mathbf{y}^1(t)$ and $\mathbf{y}^2(t)$ defined by (168) are linearly independent. Hence, by Theorem 8, the general solution of (166) is

$$c_1\begin{pmatrix}1\\2\end{pmatrix}e^{-t} + c_2\begin{pmatrix}2\\1\end{pmatrix}e^{2t}$$

for constants $c_1$ and $c_2$.

The general solution of any system

$$(155) \qquad \mathbf{y}' = \mathbf{A}\mathbf{y}$$

with real, distinct eigenvalues is derived similarly. If the real eigenvalues of $\mathbf{A}$ are distinct, then corresponding to each $m_i$ ($i = 1, \ldots, n$) equation (164) determines (up to an arbitrary constant) the corresponding eigenvector $\mathbf{v}^i$. It can be shown that if the real eigenvalues of $\mathbf{A}$ are distinct, the corresponding eigenvectors are linearly independent. From this fact it is readily verified that the corresponding solutions

$$\mathbf{v}^i e^{m_i t},$$

where $i = 1, \ldots, n$, are linearly independent. Hence, using Theorem 8, we may summarize our results as follows:

THEOREM 10 If the real eigenvalues $m_1, \ldots, m_n$ of $\mathbf{A}$ are distinct with corresponding eigenvectors $\mathbf{v}^1, \ldots, \mathbf{v}^n$, then the solutions of $\mathbf{y}' = \mathbf{A}\mathbf{y}$,

$$\mathbf{v}^1 e^{m_1 t}, \ldots, \mathbf{v}^n e^{m_n t},$$

are linearly independent. The general solution of $\mathbf{y}' = \mathbf{A}\mathbf{y}$ is, therefore,

$$c_1\mathbf{v}^1 e^{m_1 t} + \cdots + c_n\mathbf{v}^n e^{m_n t},$$

where the $c_i$ are constants. ▮

### *Complex Eigenvalues of* **A**

Now consider an example of a linear system with complex eigenvalues:

$$\mathbf{y}' = \begin{bmatrix} 1 & 0 & 0 \\ 2 & 1 & -2 \\ 3 & 2 & 1 \end{bmatrix} \mathbf{y}.$$

By assuming solutions of the form $\mathbf{v}e^{mt}$ we find that the characteristic equation is:

$$(m - 1)[m - (1 + 2i)][m - (1 - 2i)] = 0.$$

Corresponding to the eigenvalues $m_1 = 1$, $m_2 = 1 + 2i$, and $m_3 = 1 - 2i$ are the eigenvectors $\mathbf{v}^1 = c_1(2, -3, 2)$, $\mathbf{v}^2 = c_2(0, i, 1)$, and $\mathbf{v}^3 = c_3(0, -i, 1)$, respectively. Note that the complex eigenvalues $m_2 = 1 + 2i$ and $m_3 = 1 - 2i$ are complex conjugates. Analogously, their respective eigenvectors are complex conjugate vectors $\mathbf{v}^2 = c_2(0, i, 1)$ and $\mathbf{v}^3 = c_3(0, -i, 1)$; that is, the respective components are complex conjugates.

Furthermore, the solutions corresponding to these complex eigenvalues,

$$\mathbf{y}^2(t) = c_2 \begin{bmatrix} 0 \\ i \\ 1 \end{bmatrix} e^{(1+2i)t} \quad \text{and} \quad \mathbf{y}^3(t) = c_3 \begin{bmatrix} 0 \\ -i \\ 1 \end{bmatrix} e^{(1-2i)t},$$

may be checked to be linearly independent.

Identical results hold for the general homogeneous system $\mathbf{y}' = \mathbf{A}\mathbf{y}$ with complex eigenvalues. Since the coefficients of the characteristic equation $\det(m\mathbf{I} - \mathbf{A}) = 0$ are real, complex roots occur in conjugate pairs. The corresponding eigenvectors also occur in conjugate pairs; the components are complex conjugates. Finally, we have the important result concerning the corresponding solutions of $\mathbf{y}' = \mathbf{A}\mathbf{y}$:

**THEOREM 11** If $m_1$ and $m_2$ are complex conjugate eigenvalues of **A** and if $\mathbf{v}^1$ and $\mathbf{v}^2$ are the corresponding eigenvectors, respectively, then the resulting solutions

$$\mathbf{v}^1 e^{m_1 t} \quad \text{and} \quad \mathbf{v}^2 e^{m_2 t}$$

of $\mathbf{y}' = \mathbf{A}\mathbf{y}$ are linearly independent. ▮

A second example of a system with complex eigenvalues is

$$\mathbf{y}' = \begin{pmatrix} 1 & -1 \\ 5 & -3 \end{pmatrix} \mathbf{y}. \tag{169}$$

By proceeding as explained above, we find that the eigenvalues of the coefficient matrix must satisfy

$$m^2 + 2m + 2 = 0.$$

That is, $m_1 = -1 + i$ and $m_2 = -1 - i$, complex conjugate pairs. The corresponding eigenvectors are

$$\mathbf{v}^1 = \begin{pmatrix} 1 \\ 2 - i \end{pmatrix} \quad \text{and} \quad \mathbf{v}^2 = \begin{pmatrix} 1 \\ 2 + i \end{pmatrix},$$

complex conjugate pairs. From Theorem 11 we know that the resulting solutions

$$\mathbf{y}^1(t) = \begin{pmatrix} 1 \\ 2 - i \end{pmatrix} e^{(-1+i)t} \quad \text{and} \quad \mathbf{y}^2(t) = \begin{pmatrix} 1 \\ 2 + i \end{pmatrix} e^{(-1-i)t}$$

are linearly independent. Hence, the general solution of (169) is

$$(170) \qquad c_1 \begin{pmatrix} 1 \\ 2 - i \end{pmatrix} e^{(-1+i)t} + c_2 \begin{pmatrix} 1 \\ 2 + i \end{pmatrix} e^{(-1-i)t},$$

for constants $c_1$ and $c_2$. The general solution, (170), may be converted to the real form by employing Euler's formula

$$e^{(\mu + i\lambda)t} = e^{\mu t}(\cos \lambda t + i \sin \lambda t).$$

Specifically, (170) becomes

$$b_1 e^{-t} \begin{pmatrix} \cos t \\ 2 \cos t + \sin t \end{pmatrix} + b_2 e^{-t} \begin{pmatrix} \sin t \\ 2 \sin t - \cos t \end{pmatrix}$$

for constants $b_1$ and $b_2$.

### *Repeated Eigenvalues of* **A**

We conclude our discussion of system (155) by considering the case when the eigenvalues of **A** have multiplicity $k > 1$; that is, the eigenvalues are repeated. In this case the corresponding eigenvectors may be either linearly independent or linearly dependent. And, further, when **A** is an $n \times n$ matrix of real entries and $n \geq 4$, the repeated eigenvalues may be real or complex.

When the eigenvectors corresponding to an eigenvalue of multiplicity $k > 1$ are linearly independent, we have the following result:

THEOREM 12 If $m_1$ is an eigenvalue of **A** with multiplicity $k > 1$ and the corresponding eigenvectors $\mathbf{v}^1, \ldots, \mathbf{v}^k$ are linearly independent, then

$$\mathbf{v}^1 e^{m_1 t}, \ldots, \mathbf{v}^k e^{m_1 t}$$

are $k$ linearly independent solutions of $\mathbf{y}' = \mathbf{A}\mathbf{y}$. ∎

To illustrate the case when an eigenvalue of **A** has multiplicity $k > 1$ and the eigenvectors are linearly independent consider the following example:

$$\begin{bmatrix} y_1 \\ y_2 \\ y_3 \end{bmatrix}' = \begin{bmatrix} 0 & 1 & 1 \\ 1 & 0 & 1 \\ 1 & 1 & 0 \end{bmatrix} \begin{bmatrix} y_1 \\ y_2 \\ y_3 \end{bmatrix}. \tag{171}$$

Assuming $\mathbf{y} = \mathbf{v}e^{mt}$, we obtain the set of algebraic equations

$$\begin{aligned} -mv_1 + v_2 + v_3 &= 0 \\ v_1 - mv_2 + v_3 &= 0 \\ v_1 + v_2 - mv_3 &= 0. \end{aligned} \tag{172}$$

This system has a nontrivial solution if and only if

$$\begin{vmatrix} -m & 1 & 1 \\ 1 & -m & 1 \\ 1 & 1 & -m \end{vmatrix} = -(m - 2)(m + 1)^2 = 0.$$

Hence, the eigenvalues of the coefficient matrix of (171) are $m_1 = -1$ (with multiplicity 2) and $m_2 = 2$. When $m_1 = -1$, system (172) reduces to

$$v_1 + v_2 + v_3 = 0.$$

The latter equation implies that any vector in the plane

$$(v_1, v_2, v_3) \cdot (1, 1, 1) = 0$$

is an eigenvector corresponding to $m_1 = -1$. To find two linearly independent eigenvectors, observe that if $v_1 = c_1$ and $v_2 = 0$, then $v_3 = -c_1$; and if $v_1 = 0$ and $v_2 = c_2$, then $v_3 = -c_2$. Thus,

$$c_1 \begin{bmatrix} 1 \\ 0 \\ -1 \end{bmatrix} \quad \text{and} \quad c_2 \begin{bmatrix} 0 \\ 1 \\ -1 \end{bmatrix}$$

are two linearly independent eigenvectors corresponding to $m_1 = -1$. The corresponding linearly independent solutions are

$$c_1 \begin{bmatrix} 1 \\ 0 \\ -1 \end{bmatrix} e^{-t} \quad \text{and} \quad c_2 \begin{bmatrix} 0 \\ 1 \\ -1 \end{bmatrix} e^{-t}.$$

Finally, for eigenvalue $m_2 = 2$, we obtain the eigenvector

$$c_3 \begin{bmatrix} 1 \\ 1 \\ 1 \end{bmatrix},$$

and hence a third linearly independent solution,

$$c_3 \begin{bmatrix} 1 \\ 1 \\ 1 \end{bmatrix} e^{2t}.$$

From Theorem 8 we see that the general solution to (171) is

$$\mathbf{y}(t) = c_1 \begin{bmatrix} 1 \\ 0 \\ -1 \end{bmatrix} e^{-t} + c_2 \begin{bmatrix} 0 \\ 1 \\ -1 \end{bmatrix} e^{-t} + c_3 \begin{bmatrix} 1 \\ 1 \\ 1 \end{bmatrix} e^{2t}.$$

The case when an eigenvalue $m$ of the matrix $\mathbf{A}$ has multiplicity $k > 1$ and the resulting eigenvectors are linearly dependent is quite different. In order to construct $k$ linearly independent solutions of

(155) $$\mathbf{y}' = \mathbf{A}\mathbf{y}$$

when the corresponding eigenvectors are linearly dependent, we seek solutions involving products of polynomials and exponential functions. To illustrate this solution technique, we shall consider an example.

The system

(173) $$\mathbf{y}' = \begin{pmatrix} 3 & -1 \\ 4 & -1 \end{pmatrix} \mathbf{y}$$

may be shown to have an eigenvalue $m_1 = 1$ of multiplicity 2. The only eigenvector corresponding to $m_1 = 1$ is $(1, 2)$. Drawing an analogy with the second-order linear homogeneous equation, we might expect a second linearly independent solution of the form

$$\mathbf{u}te^t,$$

where $\mathbf{u} = (u_1, u_2)$. However, the solution is more complicated. We must seek a solution of the form

(174) $$\mathbf{u}^1 te^t + \mathbf{u}^2 e^t,$$

where $\mathbf{u}^1 = (u_{11}, u_{12})$ and $\mathbf{u}^2 = (u_{21}, u_{22})$. Substituting expression (174) into system (173) gives

$$\mathbf{u}^1 te^t + (\mathbf{u}^1 + \mathbf{u}^2)e^t = \mathbf{A}(\mathbf{u}^1 te^t + \mathbf{u}^2 e^t), \tag{175}$$

where $\mathbf{A} = \begin{pmatrix} 3 & -1 \\ 4 & -1 \end{pmatrix}$. Equating the coefficients of $e^t$ and $te^t$ on each side of (175) gives the conditions

$$(\mathbf{I} - \mathbf{A})\mathbf{u}^1 = \mathbf{0} \tag{176}$$

and

$$(\mathbf{I} - \mathbf{A})\mathbf{u}^2 = -\mathbf{u}^1, \tag{177}$$

where $\mathbf{I}$ is the identity matrix. Solving (176) and (177) yields solutions

$$\mathbf{u}^1 = \begin{pmatrix} 1 \\ 2 \end{pmatrix} \quad \text{and} \quad \mathbf{u}^2 = \begin{pmatrix} 0 \\ -1 \end{pmatrix}.$$

Thus, a second (linearly independent) solution of (173) is

$$\begin{pmatrix} 1 \\ 2 \end{pmatrix} te^t + \begin{pmatrix} 0 \\ -1 \end{pmatrix} e^t.$$

Hence, the general solution of system (173) is

$$c_1 \begin{pmatrix} 1 \\ 2 \end{pmatrix} e^t + c_2 \begin{pmatrix} t \\ 2t - 1 \end{pmatrix} e^t.$$

A similar procedure is applied to more general problems. For instance, if the matrix $\mathbf{A}$ in (155) has an eigenvalue $m$ of multiplicity 3 and a single corresponding eigenvector $\mathbf{v}$, then we seek two additional linearly independent solutions of the forms

$$\mathbf{u}^1 te^{mt} + \mathbf{u}^2 e^{mt}$$

and

$$\mathbf{w}^1 \frac{t^2}{2!} e^{mt} + \mathbf{w}^2 te^{mt} + \mathbf{w}^3 e^{mt}.$$

Because of the obvious complexity and infrequent applicability of this solution technique, we shall not discuss it further. We now turn to a further application of first-order systems.

## A FURTHER APPLICATION OF FIRST-ORDER SYSTEMS

### Spread of a Disease

As an introduction to nonlinear systems of differential equations, let us consider a mathematical model that gives rise to such a system. Consider an epidemic model in which infection spreads by contact between the members of a community. Assume that the entire population is subject to some process of homogeneous mixing. At any time $t$ the community is comprised of $y_1$ susceptibles, $y_2$ infectives in circulation, and $y_3$ individuals who were isolated, dead, or recovered and immune. An additional assumption to be made is that the stock of susceptibles is continuously replenished. The simplest way to do this is to introduce a birthrate ($b \geq 0$). If the population is to remain stable, the arrival of new susceptibles must be balanced by an appropriately defined death rate. Therefore, let us assume that on the average the arrival of new susceptibles is just balanced by the deaths of infectives.

At any time $t$ the rate at which people die, become isolated, or become immune is dependent upon the number of infectives. A reasonable, yet simple, description of this relationship is

$$\frac{dy_3}{dt} = cy_2, \qquad c > 0;$$

that is, the death rate at time $t$ is directly proportional to the number of infectives at time $t$.

With the assumption that the entire population of the community is subject to some process of homogeneous mixing, it is reasonable to assume that at any time $t$ the rate at which the infection spreads ($dy_2/dt$) is proportional to the number of possible contacts in the community ($y_1y_2$). But further, the rate of infection ($dy_2/dt$) will increase or decrease as the death rate ($dy_3/dt$) decreases or increases. We may describe this behavior as

$$\frac{dy_2}{dt} = ay_1y_2 - \frac{dy_3}{dt}, \qquad a > 0,$$

or

$$\frac{dy_2}{dt} = ay_1y_2 - cy_2.$$

If we assume that at any time $t$ the rate of infection ($dy_2/dt$) is directly proportional to the number of possible contacts in the community ($y_1y_2$), then a reasonable dual assumption is that some "inverse" relationship holds between the rate at which individuals become susceptible ($dy_1/dt$) and ($y_1y_2$). This rate ($dy_1/dt$) is also a function of the birthrate ($b$). A simple, yet adequate, expression for $dy_1/dt$ that incorporates these assumptions is

$$\frac{dy_1}{dt} = -ay_1y_2 + b.$$

Thus, the relationships between the rates $dy_1/dt$, $dy_2/dt$, and $dy_3/dt$ in this model of the spread of infection is described by the *nonlinear* first-order system

$$\frac{dy_1}{dt} = -ay_1y_2 + b$$

$$\frac{dy_2}{dt} = ay_1y_2 - cy_2$$

$$\frac{dy_3}{dt} = cy_2.$$

This nonlinear system of differential equations is quite difficult to solve. Indeed, we shall not even attempt an analysis of this system; depending upon the size of the parameters, the solution may, for example, oscillate violently or tend toward a stable condition. (For a further discussion of a similar model, see Bailey.)

## EXERCISES

1. Show that $y(t) = (t, \ln t)$ is a solution of the following system on $[1, \infty)$:

$$y_1' = t^{-t}e^{y_1y_2}$$

$$y_2' = e^{y_2} + \frac{1}{y_1}\cos(t - y_1) - y_1.$$

2. Transform

$$y'' - ty = 0$$

into a $2 \times 2$ system of ordinary differential equations.

3. Obtain the general solution of each of the following:

(*a*)
$$\begin{aligned} y_1' &= y_1 + y_2 \\ y_2' &= 4y_1 + y_2 \end{aligned}$$

(*b*)
$$\begin{aligned} y_1' &= 4y_1 - 3y_2 \\ y_2' &= 8y_1 - 6y_2 \end{aligned}$$

(*c*)
$$\begin{aligned} y_1' &= 3y_1 - 2y_2 \\ y_2' &= 4y_1 - y_2 \end{aligned}$$

$$(d)\quad \begin{aligned} y_1' &= y_1 - y_2 \\ y_2' &= y_1 + 2y_2 + y_3 \\ y_3' &= -2y_1 + y_2 - y_3 \end{aligned}$$

$$(e)\quad \begin{aligned} y_1' &= 3y_1 + 2y_2 + 4y_3 \\ y_2' &= 2y_1 + 2y_3 \\ y_3' &= 4y_1 + 2y_2 + 3y_3 \end{aligned}$$

$$(f)\quad \begin{aligned} y_1' &= y_1 \\ y_2' &= 2y_2 \\ y_3' &= 3y_3 \end{aligned}$$

$$(g)\quad \begin{aligned} y_1' &= y_2 \\ y_2' &= y_3 \\ y_3' &= y_1 - y_2 + y_3 \end{aligned}$$

$$(h)\quad \begin{aligned} y_1' &= y_2 \\ y_2' &= -y_1 + 2y_2 \end{aligned}$$

$$(i)\quad \begin{aligned} y_1' &= y_1 - y_2 \\ y_2' &= y_1 + 3y_2 \end{aligned}$$

$$(j)\quad \begin{aligned} y_1' &= 6y_1 + 4y_2 + 8y_3 \\ y_2' &= 4y_1 + 4y_3 \\ y_3' &= 8y_1 + 4y_2 + 6y_3 \end{aligned}$$

$$(k)\quad \begin{aligned} y_1' &= y_1 \\ y_2' &= y_2 \end{aligned}$$

$$(l)\quad \begin{aligned} y_1' &= y_1 \\ y_2' &= y_2 \\ y_3' &= -y_3. \end{aligned}$$

4. The population of Herman, Wis., consists of individuals who oppose legalization of marijuana, individuals who favor legalization of marijuana, and individuals who have no opinion. A recent survey indicates that of the 40,000 residents of Herman, $x_0 = 731$ strongly favor legalization of marijuana, $y_0 = 2013$ strongly oppose legalization of marijuana, and the remainder have no opinion at the present time.

   We are interested in determining the future opinion of this remaining group so that we can predict the results of a future referendum on the issue. Let us assume that those who oppose or favor legalization of marijuana at the present will not change their opinion in the future.

Further assume that those who presently have no opinion on the marijuana issue will be inclined to oppose or favor legalization in the future the more frequently they come into contact with those individuals who presently oppose or favor legalization. Suppose those individuals with a definite opinion on the issue at present actively try to influence as many of the others as they can. Finally, assume that the population has only one alternative at the referendum; they must *either* oppose or favor legalization of marijuana.

Denote by $x$ the number of individuals who favor the legalization of marijuana at time $t$ but have no opinion at the present. Denote by $y$ the number of individuals who oppose legalization of marijuana at time $t$ but have no opinion at the present.

After making any additional assumptions that you feel are necessary, construct a mathematical model that describes the changes in $x$ and $y$ with time.

5. Suppose that the females of the world population were divided into two groups or subpopulations according to age. Let $A(t)$ be the number of females under or at age 13 at time $t$ and let $B(t)$ be the number of females over age 13 at time $t$. Assume that females under or at age 13 have zero rate of bearing children. After making any additional assumptions, construct a mathematical model describing the rate of change of the size of $A(t)$ and $B(t)$ with respect to time.
6. In recent years the members of the American Indian community in the southwestern city of El Sisson, N. Mex., have been victims of discrimination by other members of the population. Initially the Indian community consisted of $N$ individuals, only $x_0$ ($>1$) of whom expressed their discontent with the general population's acts of oppression. Initially one of these $x_0$ discontented Indians advocated violent reactions to the acts of the oppressors. The remainder of the population, $N - x_0$, initially appeared reluctant to express any discontent.

   The entire Indian community of El Sisson is characterized by a great deal of social interaction. The result has been an increase in the number of discontent Indians as well as an increase in the number of these discontent Indians who advocate violent reactions to their oppressors.

   Suppose that at any time $t$ the Indian population consists of $y$ individuals who have not expressed discontent with these acts of oppression and $x$ individuals who have expressed discontent either violently or nonviolently. We shall assume that there are no births or deaths in the community during the time period in question. After making any other necessary assumptions, construct a mathematical model that describes the rates at which the size of these two groups change. Also include in your model a mathematical description of the rate at which the number of discontent members advocating a violent response to oppression varies.

Exercises 7–12 are designed to introduce the reader to a geometrical technique for analyzing solutions of first-order systems of differential equations. In the initial discussion of this technique we analyze the following system:

$$\text{(i)} \qquad \begin{aligned} y_1' &= -y_1 - 2y_2 + 1 \\ y_2' &= 2y_1 \qquad\quad - 1; \end{aligned}$$

the methods are then extended by considering other examples.

At any time $t$ the state of this system is described by the values of $y_1$ and $y_2$. That is, to each state there corresponds a point in the $(y_1, y_2)$ plane. This plane is called the *phase plane*. Associated with each point in the phase plane is the direction in which the system will move. By joining these points in the indicated directions we form trajectories that indicate how the solutions of the system behave. In the following problem the phase plane for this system is developed; the phase plane is then used to analyze the qualitative behavior of solutions of (i).

7. (*a*) Show that $y_1' = 0$ and $y_2' = 0$ for points $(y_1, y_2)$ on the curves:

$$\text{(ii)} \qquad \begin{aligned} -y_1 - 2y_2 + 1 &= 0 \\ 2y_1 \qquad\quad - 1 &= 0, \end{aligned}$$

respectively. Show that the graphs of these curves appear as shown below.

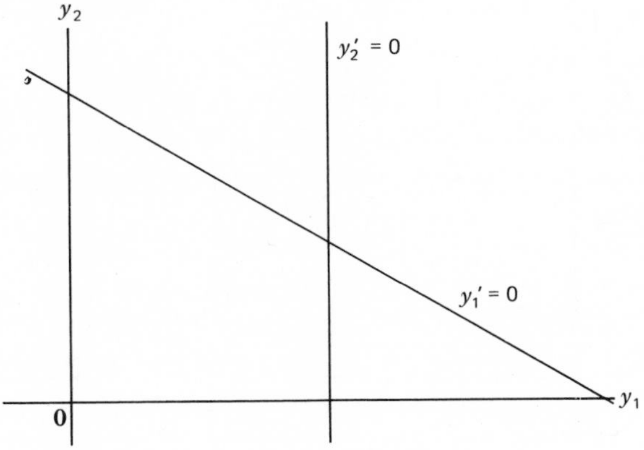

(*b*) Show that $(y_1^*, y_2^*) = (\frac{1}{2}, \frac{1}{4})$ is an equilibrium point of system (i).

(*c*) By analyzing systems (i) and (ii) show that for $y_1 > \frac{1}{2}$,

$$y_2' > 0,$$

and for $y_1 < \frac{1}{2}$,

$$y_2' < 0.$$

Thus, $y_2$ increases for $y_1 > \frac{1}{2}$ and $y_2$ decreases for $y_1 < \frac{1}{2}$, as indicated by the arrows in the figure below.

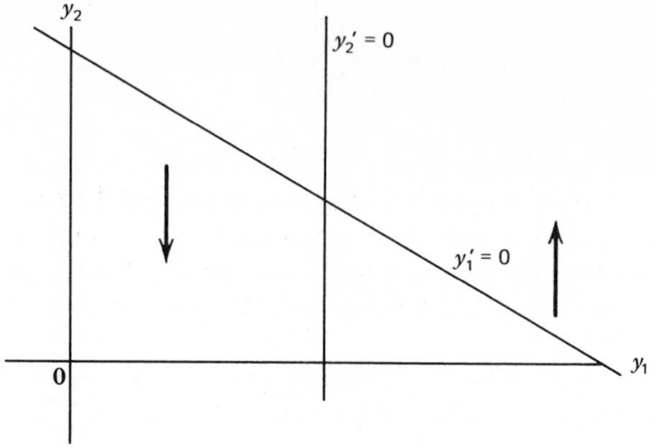


(*d*) In a similar manner show that for points $(y_1, y_2)$ below the line

$$-y_1 - 2y_2 + 1,$$

$$y_1' > 0,$$

and for points above this line,

$$y_1' < 0.$$

This behavior is indicated below.

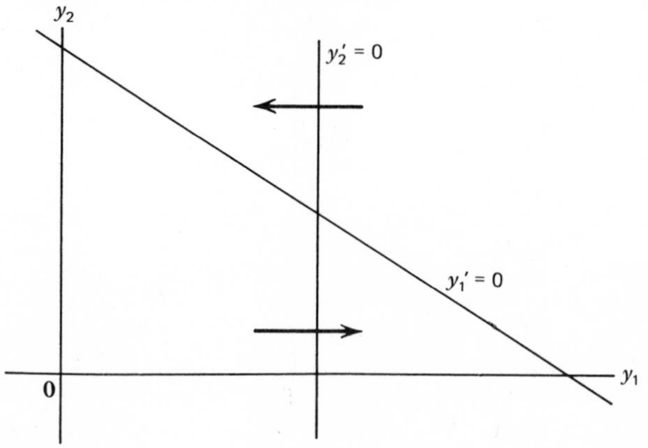

(e) Show that by plotting points on the phase plane the dynamics of the system appear as illustrated below.

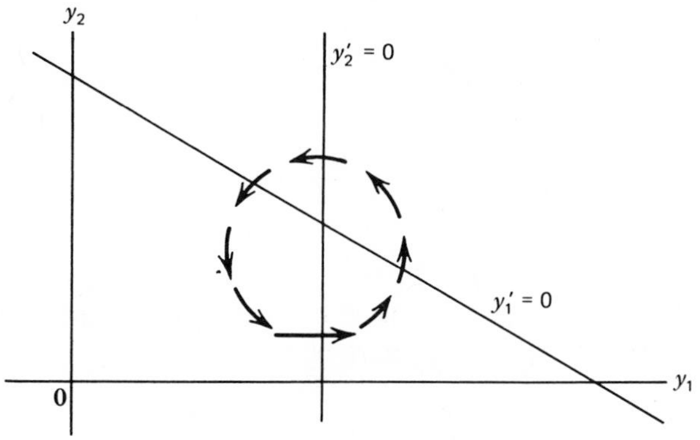


(f) Show that by joining these arrows a trajectory that "converges" to the equilibrium point is formed, as illustrated below.

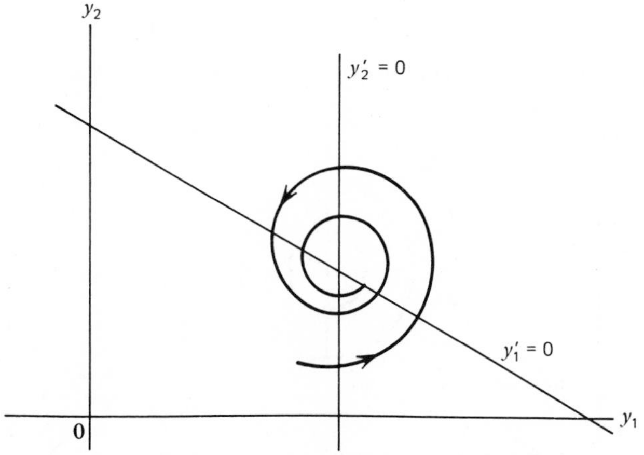


(g) Show that an analysis of the trajectory illustrated in part (f) indicates that the functions $y_1$ and $y_2$ oscillate with decreasing amplitude, as shown at the top of page 104.

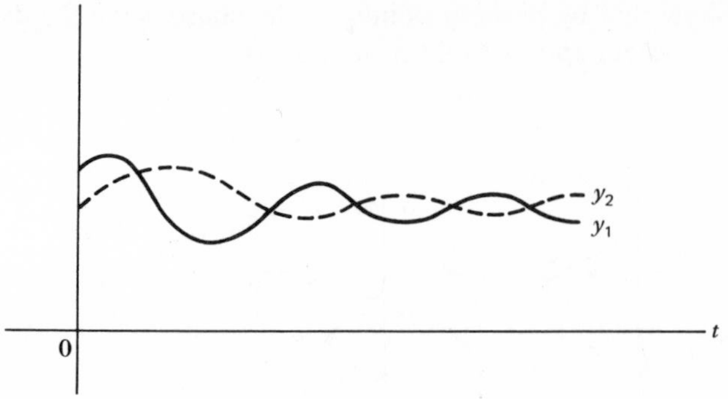


8. Analyze the behavior of $y_1$ and $y_2$ in the following systems by first forming the corresponding phase plane:

(*a*)
$$y_1' = 6y_2 - 1$$
$$y_2' = -y_1 - y_2 + 1$$

(*b*)
$$y_1' = -y_1y_2 - 2y_2^2 + y_2$$
$$y_2' = 2y_1^2 - y_1 \qquad (y_1 > 0,\ y_2 > 0).$$

9. (*a*) Show that the phase plane for the system

$$y_1' = -2y_2 + 1$$
$$y_2' = 2y_1 - 1$$

appears as shown below.

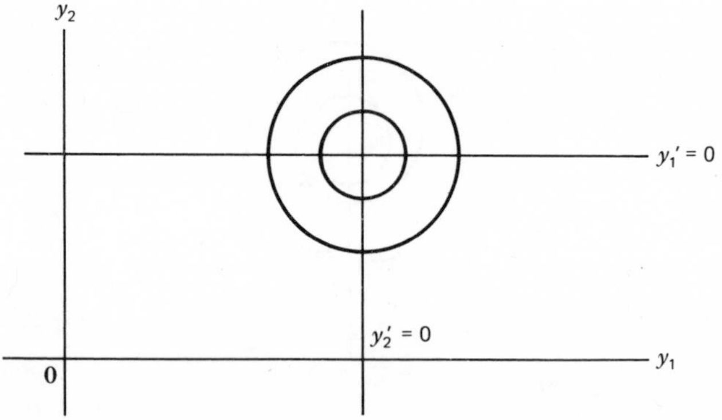


(*b*) Show that an analysis of this phase plane indicates that $y_1$ and $y_2$ oscillate with constant amplitudes.

(*c*) How do these amplitudes vary with the initial conditions? *Hint*.

Consider the relative location of the initial values and the equilibrium point.

10. (*a*) Show that the phase plane of the system:

$$y_1' = y_1 - y_2 + 1$$
$$y_2' = 2y_1 \qquad - 1$$

appears as shown below.

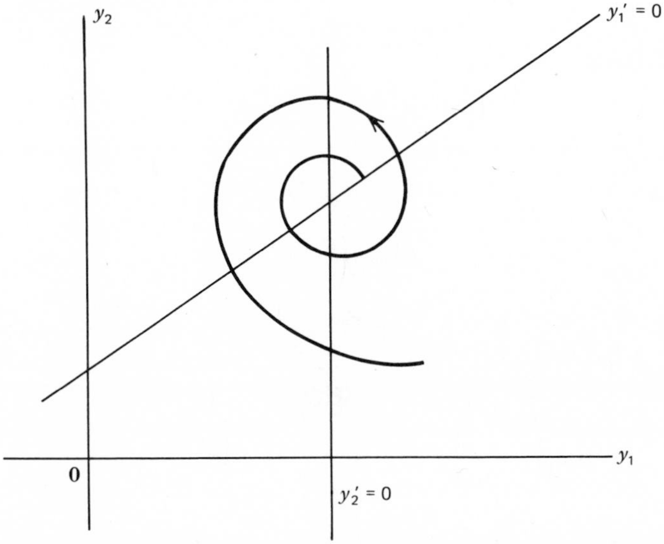


(*b*) Using this phase plane determine the qualitative behavior of $y_1$ and $y_2$.

11. Using the phase plane analyze the behavior of $y_1$ and $y_2$ in problem 3(*a*), (*b*), (*c*), (*h*), (*i*).

12. Using the phase plane analyze the behavior of $y_1$ and $y_2$ in the following nonlinear systems:

(*a*) $$y_1' = 6y_1 - 5y_1^2 - 7y_1y_2$$
$$y_2' = -2y_1 + y_1y_2$$

(*b*) $$y_1' = -y_2 + 1$$
$$y_2' = y_1y_2 - 1$$

(*c*) $$y_1' = y_1 - y_1^2 - 2y_1y_2$$
$$y_2' = y_2 - 7y_2^2/y_1 \qquad y_1 \neq 0$$

(*d*) $$y_1' = -y_2^2 + 1$$
$$y_2' = -y_1 + y_2 + 2.$$

13. Describe the variation in the size of the population of the country of East Norum by considering the variation in the size of only the female subpopulation and the male subpopulation. That is, after making any necessary assumptions, construct a system of ordinary differential equations that mathematically describes the rate of change of each of these subpopulations with respect to time. Under what conditions does the population remain stable?

## SOLUTIONS

2. $$\begin{aligned} y_1' &= \quad y_2 \\ y_2' &= ty_1 \end{aligned}$$

3. (a) $$\mathbf{y} = c_1\begin{pmatrix}1\\2\end{pmatrix}e^{3t} + c_2\begin{pmatrix}1\\-2\end{pmatrix}e^{-t}$$

(b) $$\mathbf{y} = c_1\begin{pmatrix}3\\4\end{pmatrix} + c_2\begin{pmatrix}1\\2\end{pmatrix}e^{-2t}$$

(c) $$\mathbf{y} = c_1\begin{pmatrix}\dfrac{1+i}{2}\\1\end{pmatrix}e^{(1+2i)t} + c_2\begin{pmatrix}\dfrac{1-i}{2}\\1\end{pmatrix}e^{(1-2i)t}$$

(d) $$\mathbf{y} = c_1\begin{pmatrix}1\\2\\-7\end{pmatrix}e^{-t} + c_2\begin{pmatrix}1\\-1\\-1\end{pmatrix}e^{2t} + c_3\begin{pmatrix}1\\0\\-1\end{pmatrix}e^{t}$$

(e) $$\mathbf{y} = c_1\begin{pmatrix}2\\1\\2\end{pmatrix}e^{8t} + c_2\begin{pmatrix}0\\2\\-1\end{pmatrix}e^{-t} + c_3\begin{pmatrix}1\\0\\-1\end{pmatrix}e^{-t}$$

(f) $$\mathbf{y} = c_1\begin{pmatrix}1\\0\\0\end{pmatrix}e^{t} + c_2\begin{pmatrix}0\\1\\0\end{pmatrix}e^{2t} + c_3\begin{pmatrix}0\\0\\1\end{pmatrix}e^{3t}$$

(g) $$\mathbf{y} = c_1\begin{pmatrix}1\\1\\1\end{pmatrix}e^{t} + c_2\begin{pmatrix}1\\i\\-1\end{pmatrix}e^{it} + c_3\begin{pmatrix}1\\-i\\-1\end{pmatrix}e^{-it}$$

(*h*) $$\mathbf{y} = c_1\begin{pmatrix}1\\1\end{pmatrix}e^t + c_2\left[\begin{pmatrix}1\\1\end{pmatrix}te^t + \begin{pmatrix}-1\\0\end{pmatrix}e^t\right]$$

(*i*) $$\mathbf{y} = c_1\begin{pmatrix}1\\-1\end{pmatrix}e^{2t} + c_2\left[\begin{pmatrix}1\\-1\end{pmatrix}te^{2t} + \begin{pmatrix}0\\1\end{pmatrix}e^{2t}\right]$$

(*j*) $$\mathbf{y} = c_1\begin{pmatrix}2\\1\\2\end{pmatrix}e^{16t} + c_2\begin{pmatrix}1\\0\\-1\end{pmatrix}e^{-2t} + c_3\begin{pmatrix}0\\2\\-1\end{pmatrix}e^{-2t}$$

(*k*) $$\mathbf{y} = c_1\begin{pmatrix}1\\0\end{pmatrix}e^t + c_2\begin{pmatrix}0\\1\end{pmatrix}e^t$$

(*l*) $$\mathbf{y} = c_1\begin{pmatrix}1\\0\\0\end{pmatrix}e^t + c_2\begin{pmatrix}0\\1\\0\end{pmatrix}e^t + c_3\begin{pmatrix}0\\0\\1\end{pmatrix}e^{-t}.$$

# PART 2

# CONVEX ANALYSIS IN THE SOCIAL AND MANAGERIAL SCIENCES

# CHAPTER 4

# PRELIMINARIES

## INTRODUCTION

Modern mathematical theories in the management sciences study economic systems by examining the mathematical properties imposed by the relevant economic laws. As we saw in the previous chapter, these properties often involve convexity. For instance, we saw that when prices are rising or falling with an increasing rate, the price–time path is convex. Furthermore, the law of diminishing returns in production also illustrates the convexity of some functional relationships.

Convex analysis has been an active area of research only in relatively modern times. This chapter combines results of convex analysis along with potential applications of these results in management science. It is hoped that with an understanding of these concepts and the fundamentals of economics, the reader will be prepared to study more-advanced economic models.

Much of this chapter requires an understanding of concepts and techniques beyond those utilized in our study of differential equations. For example, many algebraic and geometric notions from vector analysis are applied in our discussion of convex structures, and several properties of functions of several variables are used in the section on convex functions. These preliminary topics are treated in the Appendix. Here we begin with a discussion of convex sets.

## CONVEX SETS

The geometric "shape" of the set of solutions to a constrained optimization problem or of the consumption space of a set-theoretic economic model is a crucial characteristic of these problems. Frequently these sets are convex. This section treats properties of convex sets.

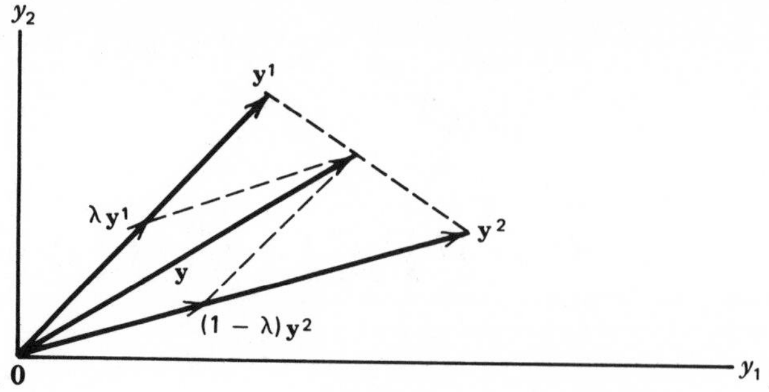


Figure 34

Before defining convexity, we introduce a concept that is fundamental to any discussion of convex analysis, that of a *convex combination* of vectors. A vector $\mathbf{y} \in \mathbb{R}^n$ is a convex combination of two vectors $\mathbf{y}^1$ and $\mathbf{y}^2$ in $\mathbb{R}^n$ if

$$\mathbf{y} = \lambda \mathbf{y}^1 + (1 - \lambda)\mathbf{y}^2,$$

where $0 \leq \lambda \leq 1$.

An example of this concept is the convex combination with $\lambda = \frac{5}{16}$ of the vectors $\mathbf{y}^1 = (1, 2)$ and $\mathbf{y}^2 = (3, 1)$:

$$\mathbf{y} = \tfrac{5}{16}\mathbf{y}^1 + \tfrac{11}{16}\mathbf{y}^2 = \tfrac{5}{16}(1, 2) + \tfrac{11}{16}(3, 1) = (\tfrac{19}{8}, \tfrac{21}{16}).$$

By varying $\lambda$ between 0 and 1, we readily see that the convex combinations $\mathbf{y} = \lambda \mathbf{y}^1 + (1 - \lambda)\mathbf{y}^2$ constitute the set of all points on the line segment joining $\mathbf{y}^1$ and $\mathbf{y}^2$ (see Figure 34).

Since the two scalar multiples in a convex combination are positive and add up to 1, it can be interpreted as a weighted average of the vectors $\mathbf{y}^1$ and $\mathbf{y}^2$.

More generally, we define a *convex combination* of any finite set of vectors. The vector $\mathbf{y} \in \mathbb{R}^n$ is a *convex combination* of the vectors $\mathbf{y}^1, \ldots, \mathbf{y}^k \in \mathbb{R}^n$ if

$$\mathbf{y} = \sum_{i=1}^{k} \lambda_i \mathbf{y}^i,$$

where $\lambda_i \geq 0$ and $\sum_{i=1}^{k} \lambda_i = 1$. For example, the vector $\mathbf{y} = (1, 2, 3)$ is a convex combination of the vectors $(-4, 0, 1)$, $(2, 1, 1)$, $(0, 1, 17)$, and $(8, 11, 1)$ because

$$(1, 2, 3) = \tfrac{1}{4}(-4, 0, 1) + \tfrac{1}{2}(2, 1, 1) + \tfrac{1}{8}(0, 1, 17) + \tfrac{1}{8}(8, 11, 1)$$

and $\frac{1}{4} + \frac{1}{2} + \frac{1}{8} + \frac{1}{8} = 1$.

A convex set may be defined in terms of the above definition. A set of vectors, $K \subset \mathbb{R}^n$, is *convex* if and only if for all $\mathbf{x}, \mathbf{y} \in K$ the convex combinations

$$\lambda\mathbf{x} + (1 - \lambda)\mathbf{y}$$

are elements of $K$ for $0 \le \lambda \le 1$. Geometrically this means that the segment joining any pair of points in $K$ lies entirely in $K$. For example, the set $K$ in Figure 35 is convex because any segment $\mathbf{xy}$ is contained entirely in $K$. The set $K'$ in Figure 36 is not convex, since the segment $\mathbf{xy}$ is not in $K'$. Note also that the empty set is convex.

Let us consider some further examples of convex sets. The set

$$K_1 = \{(y_1, y_2):(2, 1)\cdot(y_1, y_2) = 4\}$$

is a straight line in $\mathbb{R}^2$ (see Figure 37). To see that $K_1$ is convex, let $(y_1, y_2)$ and $(y_1', y_2')$ be any two elements of $K_1$ and consider $(y_1'', y_2'') = \lambda(y_1, y_2) + (1 - \lambda)(y_1', y_2')$, $0 \le \lambda \le 1$. Since

$$\begin{aligned}(2, 1)\cdot(y_1'', y_2'') &= \lambda(2, 1)\cdot(y_1, y_2) + (1 - \lambda)(2, 1)\cdot(y_1', y_2')\\ &= \lambda 4 + (1 - \lambda)4 = 4,\end{aligned}$$

$(y_1'', y_2'') \in K_1$ implying $K_1$ is a convex set.

As a second example, consider the set

$$K_2 = \{(y_1, y_2):(y_1, y_2)\cdot(2, 3) \le 4\}.$$

$K_2$ is pictured in Figure 38. To see that $K_2$ is convex take $(y_1, y_2)$ and $(y_1', y_2')$ in $K_2$ and consider the convex combination

$$(y_1'', y_2'') = \lambda(y_1, y_2) + (1 - \lambda)(y_1', y_2'),$$

$0 \le \lambda \le 1$. Since

$$\begin{aligned}(2, 3)\cdot(y_1'', y_2'') &= \lambda(2, 3)\cdot(y_1, y_2) + (1 - \lambda)(2, 3)\cdot(y_1', y_2')\\ &\le 4\lambda + 4(1 - \lambda) = 4,\end{aligned}$$

$(y_1'', y_2'') \in K_2$. Thus, $K_2$ is convex.

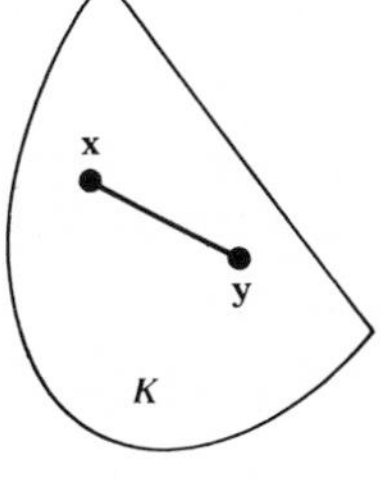


**Figure 35**

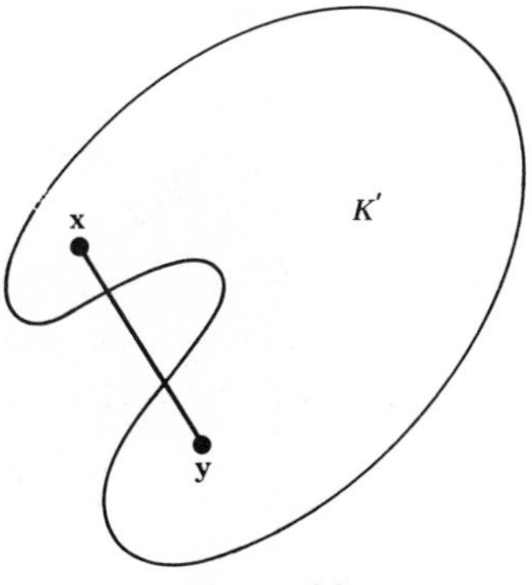


**Figure 36**

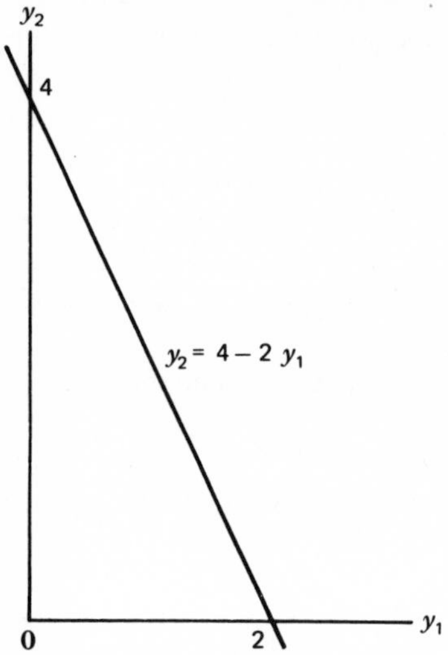


Figure 37

A final example is provided by the set

$$K_3 = \{(y_1, y_2, y_3):(1, 2, 3) \cdot (y_1, y_2, y_3) \leq 5\}.$$

$K_3$ consists of the points *on and below* the plane pictured in Figure 39. To see that $K_3$ is convex, suppose that $(y_1, y_2, y_3)$ and $(y_1', y_2', y_3')$ are arbitrary points in $K_3$ and consider the convex combinations

$$(y_1'', y_2'', y_3'') = \lambda(y_1, y_2, y_3) + (1 - \lambda)(y_1', y_2', y_3').$$

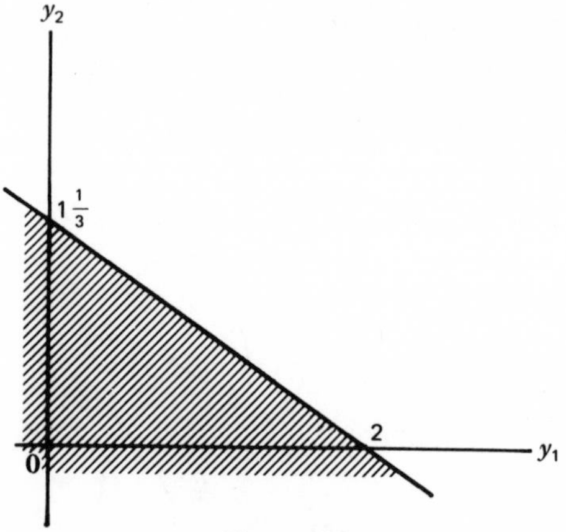


Figure 38

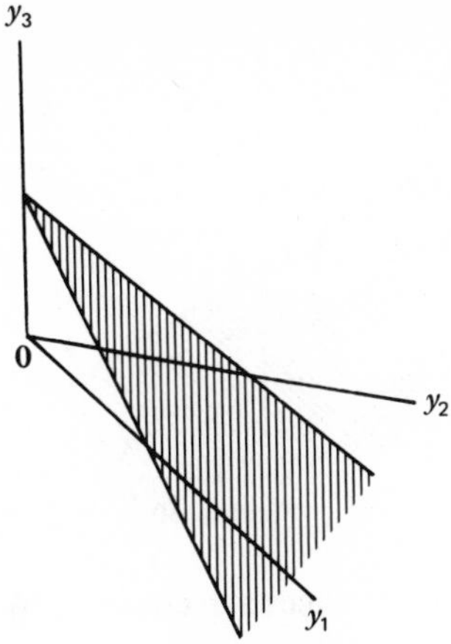


Figure 39

From

$$(1, 2, 3) \cdot (y_1'', y_2'', y_3'') = \lambda(1, 2, 3) \cdot (y_1, y_2, y_3) + (1 - \lambda)(1, 2, 3) \cdot (y_1', y_2', y_3')$$
$$\leq \lambda 4 + (1 - \lambda)4 = 4,$$

it follows that $(y_1'', y_2'', y_3'') \in K_3$. Therefore, $K_3$ is convex.

The sets $K_2$ and $K_3$ above are examples of *closed half spaces* in $\mathbb{R}^2$ and $\mathbb{R}^3$, respectively. More generally, a *closed half space* in $\mathbb{R}^n$ is a set of the form $\{\mathbf{y} : \mathbf{y} \cdot \mathbf{a} \leq b, \mathbf{y} \in \mathbb{R}^n\}$, where $\mathbf{a}$ is a constant vector in $\mathbb{R}^n$ and $b$ is a constant. (For convenience closed half spaces are frequently denoted in the abbreviated form $\mathbf{y} \cdot \mathbf{a} \leq b$ in the remaining discussion.)

Closed half spaces form an important class of convex sets:

**THEOREM 13** Closed half spaces are convex.

**PROOF** If $\mathbf{y}, \mathbf{y}' \in K$, a closed half space, then consider $\mathbf{y}'' = \lambda\mathbf{y} + (1 - \lambda)\mathbf{y}'$. Since

$$\mathbf{y}'' \cdot \mathbf{a} = \lambda\mathbf{y} \cdot \mathbf{a} + (1 - \lambda)\mathbf{y}' \cdot \mathbf{a} \leq \lambda b + (1 - \lambda)b = b,$$

$\mathbf{y}'' \in K$, implying $K$ is convex.

Similarly, we may define an *open half space* as a set of the form $\{\mathbf{y} : \mathbf{y} \cdot \mathbf{a} < b, \mathbf{y} \in \mathbb{R}^n\}$. As above, $\mathbf{a}$ is a constant vector in $\mathbb{R}^n$ and $b$ is a constant. For example, the set $K_4 = \{(y_1, y_2) : (y_1, y_2) \cdot (1, 2) < -1\}$ is an open half space. (see Figure 40):

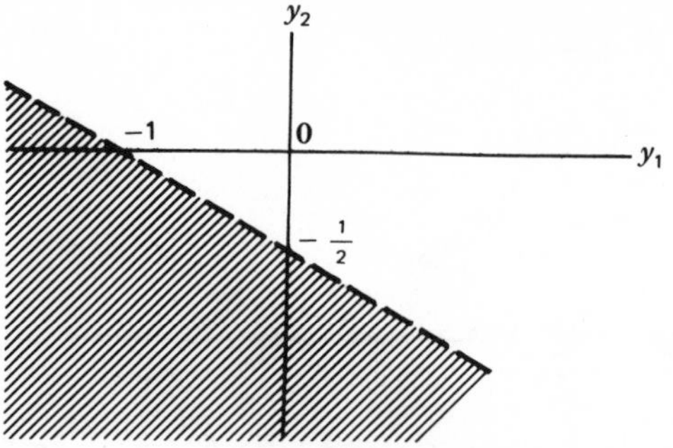


Figure 40

**THEOREM 14** Open half spaces are convex. ▮

The proof is essentially identical to that of Theorem 13.

Observe that the boundary of the open half space $\{\mathbf{y}:\mathbf{y}\cdot\mathbf{a} < b, \mathbf{y} \in \mathbb{R}^n\}$ is the set $H = \{\mathbf{y}:\mathbf{y}\cdot\mathbf{a} = b, \mathbf{y} \in \mathbb{R}^n\}$. The set $H$ is called a *hyperplane*. Thus, for instance, the boundary of $K_4$ above is the hyperplane

$$H_4 = \{(y_1, y_2):(y_1, y_2)\cdot(1, 2) = -1\}.$$

In $\mathbb{R}^2$ a hyperplane is a straight line. (For convenience hyperplanes are frequently denoted in the abbreviated form $\mathbf{y}\cdot\mathbf{a} = b$ in the remaining discussion.)

It is obvious that the straight line described by the hyperplane $H_4$ is convex, since a line segment connecting any two points on this line is in $H_4$. In general, we have the result:

**THEOREM 15** Hyperplanes are convex.

**PROOF** If $\mathbf{y}, \mathbf{y}' \in H$, a hyperplane, then consider the convex combination $\mathbf{y}'' = \lambda\mathbf{y} + (1 - \lambda)\mathbf{y}'$. Since

$$\mathbf{a}\cdot\mathbf{y}'' = \lambda\mathbf{a}\cdot\mathbf{y} + (1 - \lambda)\mathbf{a}\cdot\mathbf{y}' = \lambda b + (1 - \lambda)b = b,$$

$\mathbf{y}'' \in H$. Thus, $H$ is convex. ▮

Let us examine some of the properties of convex sets. As shown in Figure 41 convexity is preserved under set intersection.

**THEOREM 16** If $K_1$ and $K_2$ are convex sets in $\mathbb{R}^n$, their intersection is also a convex set in $\mathbb{R}^n$.

**PROOF** Suppose $\mathbf{y}, \mathbf{y}' \in K_1 \cap K_2$. Then $\mathbf{y}$ and $\mathbf{y}'$ both belong to $K_1$ and $K_2$. Because $K_1$ and $K_2$ are both convex, the segment joining $\mathbf{y}$ and $\mathbf{y}'$ must lie in both $K_1$ and $K_2$ and hence in their intersection; therefore, $K_1 \cap K_2$ is convex. ▮

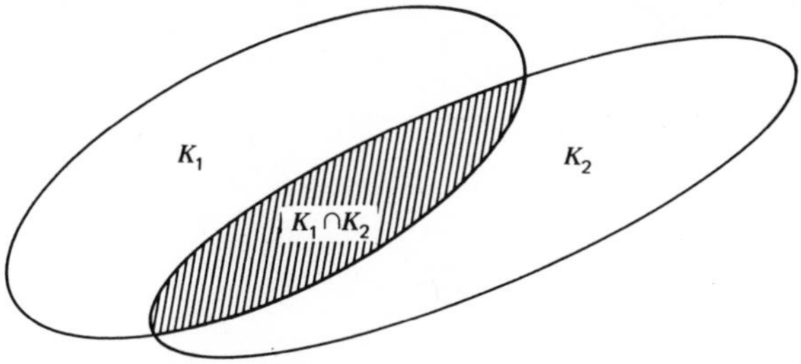


By induction one may prove the more general result:

**THEOREM 17** The intersection of a finite number of convex sets $K_1 \cap \cdots \cap K_m$ in $\mathbb{R}^n$ is convex. ▮

According to Theorem 16, for $K_1 = \{(y_1, y_2):(y_1, y_2) \cdot (2, 1) = 4\}$ and $K_2 = \{(y_1, y_2):(y_1, y_2) \cdot (2, 3) \leq 4\}$, the intersection

$$K_1 \cap K_2 = \{(y_1, y_2):(y_1, y_2) \cdot (2, 1) = 4 \text{ and } (y_1, y_2) \cdot (2, 3) \leq 4\}$$

is a convex set (see Figure 42).

Since Theorem 13 states that a closed half space is convex, it follows from Theorem 17 that the intersection of a finite number of closed half spaces is also convex. Actually, we could fortify this result to conclude that this intersection of closed half spaces is a closed convex set. (Similarly, the intersection of a finite number of open half spaces is a convex set.)

Convexity is also preserved under set addition; that is, the set constructed by forming all possible additions of vectors in a convex set $K_1$ with vectors in a convex set $K_2$,

$$\{\mathbf{y}^1 + \mathbf{y}^2 : \mathbf{y}^1 \in K_1, \mathbf{y}^2 \in K_2\},$$

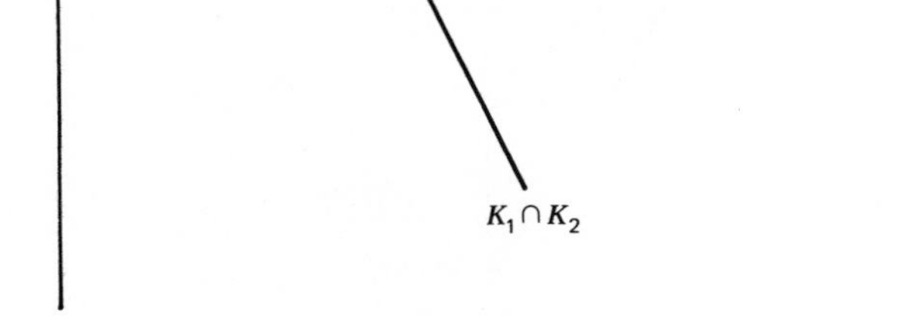

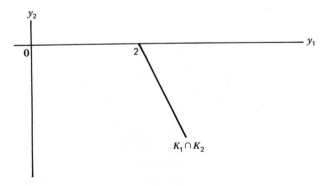

**Figure 42**

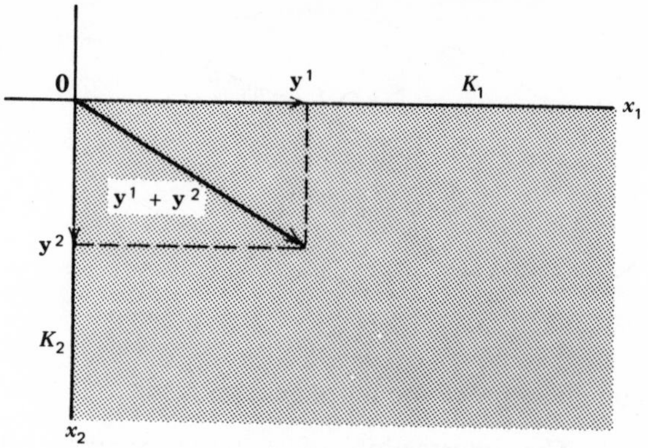


Figure 43

is convex. This set is denoted by

$$K_1 + K_2.$$

(Note that this definition is not equivalent to the union of two sets.)

For example, consider the convex sets

$$K_1 = \{(x_1, x_2) : x_1 \geq 0, x_2 = 0\}$$

and

$$K_2 = \{(x_1, x_2) : x_1 = 0, x_2 \leq 0\}.$$

The set $K_1 + K_2$ is the convex set constructed by forming the sums of each vector in $K_1$ with each vector in $K_2$. The set $K_1 + K_2$ is indicated by the shaded area in Figure 43.

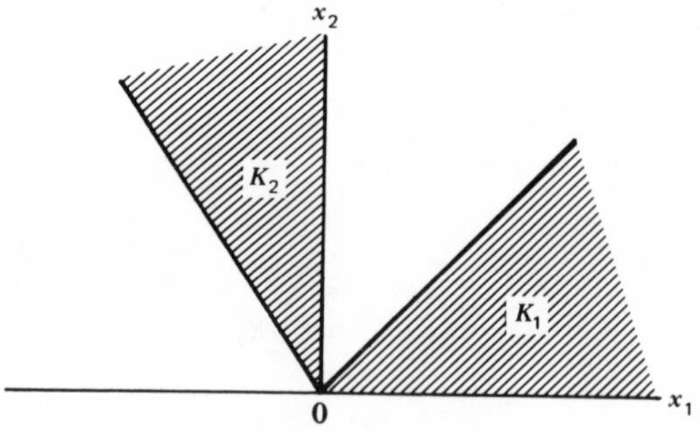


Figure 44

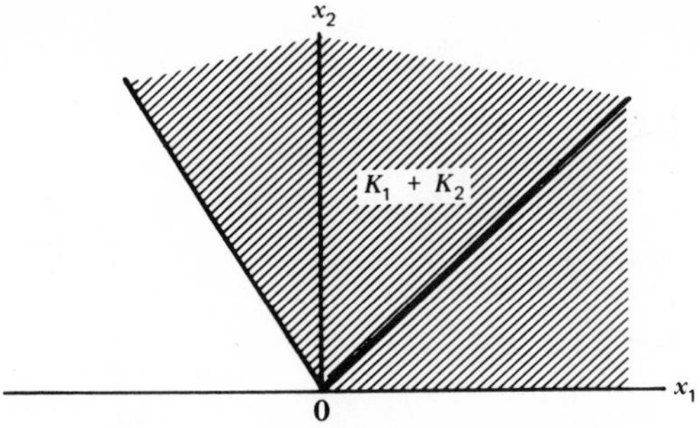


Figure 45

As a second illustration of the concept of set addition, consider the convex sets

$$K_1 = \{(x_1, x_2): x_1 - x_2 \leq 0, x_1 \geq 0\},$$
$$K_2 = \{(x_1, x_2): x_1 + x_2 \geq 0, x_2 \geq 0\}$$

shown in Figure 44. The sum of these two sets is the convex set $K_1 + K_2$ in Figure 45.

We summarize these results as a theorem:

**THEOREM 18** If $K_1$ and $K_2$ are convex sets in $\mathbb{R}^n$, then the set $K_1 + K_2$ is also a convex set.

**PROOF** Suppose $\mathbf{y}^1, \mathbf{y}^{1'} \in K_1$ and $\mathbf{y}^2, \mathbf{y}^{2'} \in K_2$, where $K_1$ and $K_2$ are convex sets. Then $\mathbf{y}^1 + \mathbf{y}^2, \mathbf{y}^{1'} + \mathbf{y}^{2'} \in K_1 + K_2$. Note that

$$\lambda(\mathbf{y}^1 + \mathbf{y}^2) + (1 - \lambda)(\mathbf{y}^{1'} + \mathbf{y}^{2'}) = \lambda\mathbf{y}^1 + (1 - \lambda)\mathbf{y}^{1'} + \lambda\mathbf{y}^2 + (1 - \lambda)\mathbf{y}^{2'}.$$

Since $\lambda\mathbf{y}^1 + (1 - \lambda)\mathbf{y}^{1'} \in K_1$ and $\lambda\mathbf{y}^2 + (1 - \lambda)\mathbf{y}^{2'} \in K_2$ their sum, above, is in $K_1 + K_2$, implying $K_1 + K_2$ is convex.

Our geometric intuition is that "expansions" and "contractions" of a convex set are still convex. For instance, consider the convex set $K$ in Figure 46. Its contraction $K_1$ has the same shape as $K$ and so must be convex also. Formally this implies convexity is preserved under scalar multiplication.

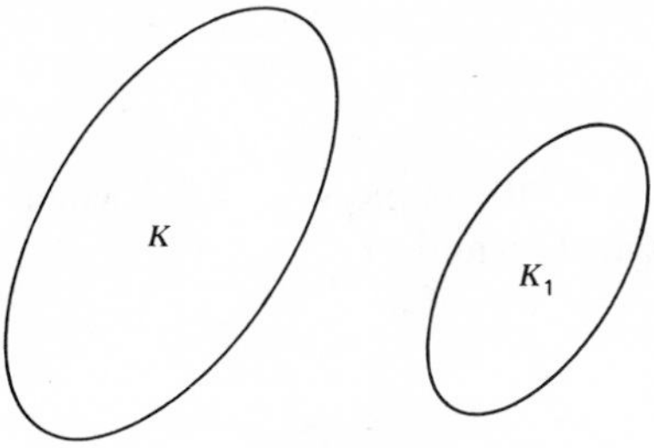


Figure 46

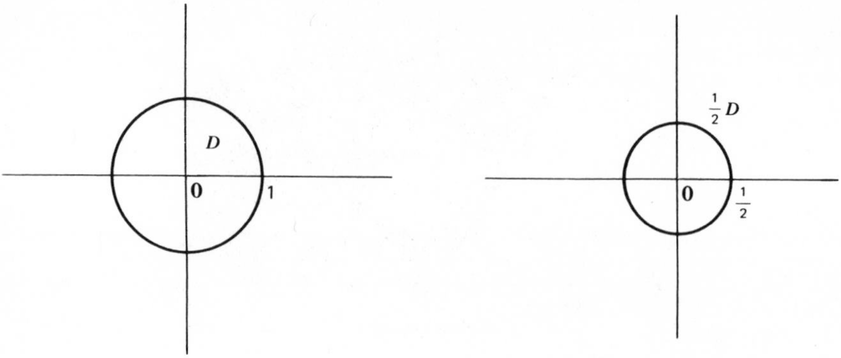


Figure 47.

**THEOREM 19** If $K$ is a convex set in $\mathbb{R}^n$, then $aK = \{a\mathbf{y}:\mathbf{y} \in K\}$, $a \geq 0$, is a convex set in $\mathbb{R}^n$.

**PROOF** Suppose $\mathbf{y}$ and $\mathbf{y}'$ are in the convex set $K \subset \mathbb{R}^n$. For $0 \leq \lambda \leq 1$ and $a \geq 0$,

$$\lambda a\mathbf{y} + (1 - \lambda)a\mathbf{y}' = a[\lambda\mathbf{y} + (1 - \lambda)\mathbf{y}'].$$

Since $\lambda\mathbf{y} + (1 - \lambda)\mathbf{y}' \in K$, $\lambda a\mathbf{y} + (1 - \lambda)a\mathbf{y}' \in aK$, which implies that $aK$ is convex. ▮

Theorem 19 implies that since the disk

$$D = \{(y_1, y_2): y_1^2 + y_2^2 \leq 1\}$$

is convex as it appears, the disk

$$\tfrac{1}{2}D = \{(\tfrac{1}{2}y_1, \tfrac{1}{2}y_2): y_1^2 + y_2^2 \leq 1\}$$

is also convex (see Figure 47).

## EXERCISES

1. Given the vectors $\mathbf{u} = (10, 6)$ and $\mathbf{v} = (4, 8)$, which of the following are convex combinations of $\mathbf{u}$ and $\mathbf{v}$?
   (*a*) (7, 7)
   (*b*) (6.2, 8.2)
   (*c*) (3.7).

2. Sketch a graph of each of the following sets and indicate whether the set is convex:

   (*a*) $\{(x_1, x_2): x_2 \geq e^{x_1}\}$

   (*b*) $\{(x_1, x_2): x_1^2 + x_2^2 \leq 16\}$

   (*c*) $\{(x_1, x_2): x_1 x_2 \geq 1, x_1 \geq 0, x_2 \geq 0\}$

   (*d*) $\{(x_1, x_2, x_3): x_1^2 + x_2^2 + x_3^2 \leq 7\}$

   (*e*) $\{(x_1, x_2): x_2 \geq |\sin x_1|\}$.

3. Give examples of each of the following:
   (*a*) A convex set in $\mathbb{R}^2$ whose complement is convex
   (*b*) A convex set in $\mathbb{R}^2$ whose complement is not convex
   (*c*) Two disjoint convex sets such that their union is a convex set
   (*d*) Two 3-dimensional convex sets such that their intersection is a 1-dimensional convex set.

4. Prove that each of the following is a convex set:

   (*a*) $\{(x_1, x_2): (x_1, x_2) \cdot (1, 2) \leq 3\}$

   (*b*) $\{(x_1, x_2): x_1 + 7x_2 \leq 9\}$

   (*c*) $\{(x_1, x_2, \ldots, x_n): (1, 1, \ldots, 1) \cdot (x_1, \ldots, x_n) \leq 9\}$

   (*d*) $\{(x_1, x_2, x_3): (3, 4, 7) \cdot (x_1, x_2, x_3) \leq 16, x_1 \geq 0, x_2 \geq 0, x_3 \geq 0\}$

   (*e*) $\{(x_1, x_2): x_1 - x_2 \geq 2, x_1 \geq 0, x_2 \geq 0, x_2 \leq 2\}$.

5. Indicate whether the following statements are true or false and explain your answer:
   (*a*) The empty set is a convex set.
   (*b*) The set containing exactly one point is a convex set.
   (*c*) Any set with a finite number of distinct points is a convex set.

6. Geometrically, the convex hull of a set $S$ is the smallest convex set containing $S$. What is the convex hull of the set shown below?

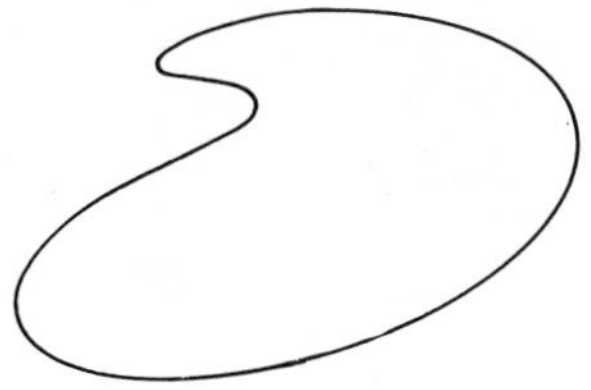

## SOLUTIONS

1. (*a*) (7, 7) $\lambda = \frac{1}{2}$.
2. *a*, *b*, *c*, *d* are convex; *e* is not convex.
3. (*a*) Halfplane
   (*b*) Disk
   (*c*) $\{x:x \geq 1\}$ and $\{x:x < 1\}$
   (*d*) Two "cones" intersecting along an "edge."
5. (*a*) True
   (*b*) True
   (*c*) False.

# CHAPTER 5

# CONVEX STRUCTURES

## A LINEAR PRODUCTION MODEL*

Industrial production may be described as a system for converting economic goods and services to products of increased utility. The production of commodities is organized into plants, coordinated aggregates of fixed equipment under common management. Within these plants production activities can be broken down into separate processes. For our purposes a production process means any specified treatment that brings materials closer to the final product. Processing does not necessarily imply a manufacturing activity; transportation, for instance, is also a process.

Inputs of a production process are the measurable quantities of economic goods and services consumed in the process. Common examples are labor, materials, energy, and the consumed machine time of the fixed equipment. However, different grades of raw material for different uses of fixed capital, for instance, should be regarded as different inputs. Various items of capital equipment as such are not considered inputs; buildings, for example, are productive only in an indirect sense. Factors that are not subject to the firm's control, such as weather, are not included as inputs in this analysis. Climatic conditions may affect the level of output in some processes by, for instance, restricting the water supply and, hence, may be considered a factor of production in a very broad sense.

Outputs are the economic goods produced by this process. Because outputs refer to particular processes rather than to the plant, an output may not be a finished product; an output of an intermediate process may be an input for a future stage in production. Waste products, as long as they are disposed of as worthless, do not count as outputs.

In a discussion of production processes, inputs and outputs—and hence costs and profits—are measured in market units per unit time; for

* Adapted from Danø.

example, fuel should be measured in tons of coal per month. This is because industrial engineers are concerned with the effect of increases in the quantities produced (or sold) *within a unit period of time* on costs. In choosing this unit period of time, we assume that the capacity of the plant is fixed, capacity being dependent on the number of plant or machine hours available per unit period.

Our analysis of production processes will treat short-run operations; that is, inputs and outputs refer to the same period. In a short-run analysis we also ignore the links between consecutive production periods. Nor shall we consider the proper timing of arrival of units requiring processing and the order in which the various jobs of processing are to be performed; these problems do not occur when only a single process is considered.

Having established the basic terminology of production models, let us attempt to describe a specific class of production processes in idealized form with a *linear production model*. The properties of a *linear production model* are implicit in the assumption of constant coefficients of production within each production activity. These production activities will be divisible and additive in terms of the time consumed, so that total output and inputs are linear functions of activity levels.

We shall deal with a process that produces only one commodity. Suppose this output can be produced in a finite number ($N$) of physically distinct subprocesses or activities each using wholly or partly the same inputs. Furthermore, assume each of the activities is characterized by constant coefficients of production and, consequently, constant returns to scale. In other words, there is a proportionality between the amounts of the inputs consumed in the process and the amount of the output produced. This is expressed formally by

$$v_{ik} = a_{ik}x_k \qquad (i = 1, \ldots, m;\ k = 1, \ldots, N) \tag{178}$$

where $v_{ik}$ is the amount of input $i$ required to produce $x_k$ units of the output in the $k$th subprocess and $a_{ik}$ is a constant. Note that the unit of $a_{ik}$ is the quotient of the units of the $i$th input and the units of the output. We assume that the activities can be applied simultaneously, so that total output becomes

$$x = \sum_{k=1}^{N} x_k \tag{179}$$

and the total amount of input $i$ required, $v_i$, is

$$v_i = \sum_{k=1}^{N} v_{ik} = \sum_{k=1}^{N} a_{ik}x_k \qquad (i = 1, \ldots, m). \tag{180}$$

Note that $v_i = \mathbf{v} \cdot \mathbf{e}_i$, where $\mathbf{v} = (v_1, \ldots, v_m) \in \mathbb{R}^m$ and $\mathbf{e}_i = (0, 0, \ldots, 1, 0, \ldots, 0) \in \mathbb{R}^m$ (a 1 in the $i$th position). The "activity levels" must be required to be nonnegative

$$x_k \geq 0 \qquad (k = 1, \ldots, N) \tag{181}$$

because negative output is nonsense. Similarly the amounts of each input must be nonnegative

$$0 \leq v_i = \mathbf{v} \cdot \mathbf{e}_i \qquad (i = 1, \ldots, m). \tag{182}$$

Finally, limitations of capacity and resources impose the constraints

$$\mathbf{e}_i \cdot \mathbf{v} = v_i \leq \bar{v}_i \qquad (i = 1, \ldots, m), \tag{183}$$

where $\bar{v}_i$ is the maximum amount of input $i$ available for the company of interest. Conditions (178)–(183) represent a *linear production model.*

To better illustrate the further discussion of linear production models, suppose a certain manufacturer can produce one particular output with either of two subprocesses. Each of the subprocesses uses the two inputs labor, $v_1$, and machine time, $v_2$, in some combination. Assume that the desired level of output is

$$x = x_1 + x_2, \tag{179'}$$

with the first and second subprocesses producing $x_1$ and $x_2$ units, respectively. Suppose also that activity 1 requires inputs

$$v_{11} = 2x_1, \qquad v_{21} = 6x_1, \tag{178'}$$

and activity 2 requires inputs

$$v_{12} = 4x_2, \qquad v_{22} = 2x_2. \tag{178'}$$

Hence, the total inputs demanded are given by

$$\begin{aligned} v_1 &= v_{11} + v_{12} = 2x_1 + 4x_2, \\ v_2 &= v_{21} + v_{22} = 6x_1 + 2x_2. \end{aligned} \tag{180'}$$

Suppose that limitations in capacity and resources impose the following constraints on the units of labor and machine time inputs:

$$v_1 \leq 200, \qquad v_2 \leq 100. \tag{183'}$$

Finally, the input levels and activity levels must satisfy nonnegativity conditions

$$0 \leq v_1, \qquad 0 \leq v_2, \tag{182'}$$

$$0 \leq x_1, \qquad 0 \leq x_2. \tag{181'}$$

The production model, (178)–(183), and consequently the example, (178′)–(183′), exhibits several economic properties because of its linear structure. In the following discussion we discover the economic characteristics of our model by examining its mathematical structure. Our discussion of the economic properties of this model, although somewhat elementary, is representative of the mathematical structure of more advanced set-theoretic economic models.

## THE TECHNOLOGY SET: A CONVEX CONE

The set of inputs $\mathbf{v} = (v_1, \ldots, v_m)$ that satisfy condition (180) of our linear production model for various output levels is called the *technology set*. Many important properties of a production technology are embodied in the structure of the corresponding technology set. Therefore, the study of a production technology from an economic point of view consists essentially of studying the structural characteristics of the corresponding technology set.

The technology set in our linear production model is a *convex cone*. Convex cones characterize the structure of many spaces used in set-theoretic economic models.

A set $C$ in $\mathbb{R}^n$ is called a *convex cone* if it is closed under the operations of addition and multiplication by nonnegative scalars; that is, if $\mathbf{x}, \mathbf{y} \in C$, then $\mathbf{x} + \mathbf{y} \in C$, and if $\mathbf{y} \in C$ and $\lambda \geq 0$, then $\lambda\mathbf{y} \in C$. Note that since $\lambda$ may equal zero, this definition implies that the zero vector, $\mathbf{0}$, is in any convex cone.

Before considering several specific examples of convex cones, note that this definition conforms to our geometric idea of an infinite cone. As is seen in Figure 48, if $\mathbf{y}$, $\mathbf{x}$ are in the cone, so is $\mathbf{y} + \mathbf{x}$. Likewise, positive multiples of $\mathbf{y}$ are in the cone (see Figure 49).

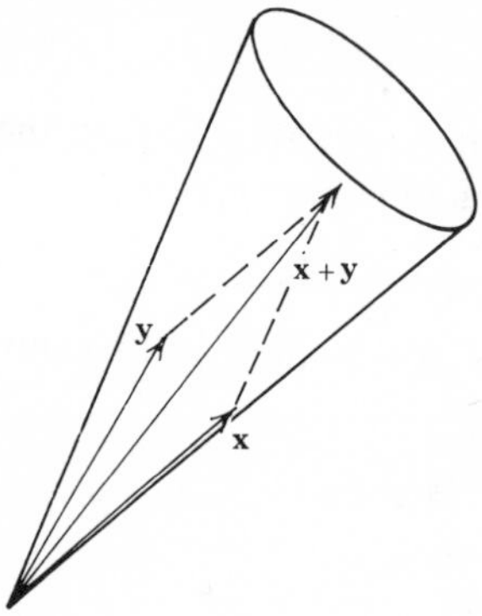


Figure 48

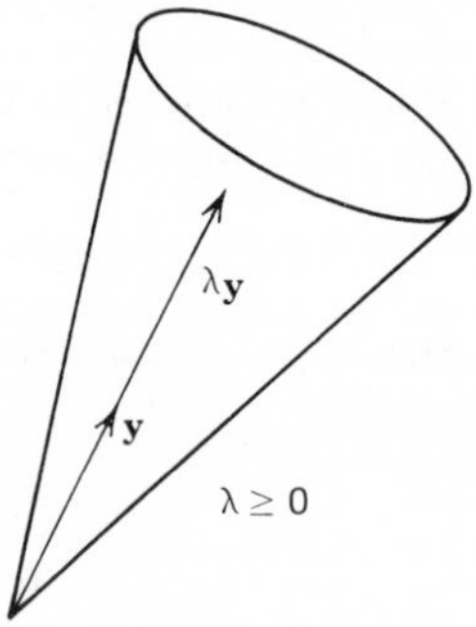


Figure 49

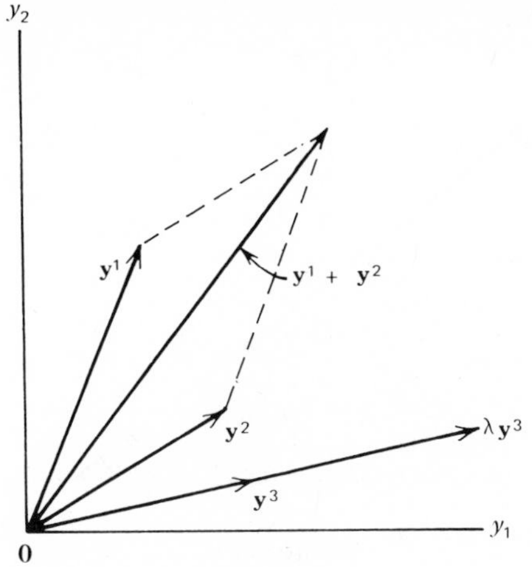


**Figure 50**

Let us consider several examples of convex cones. The set

$$C_1 = \{(y_1, y_2): y_1 \geq 0, y_2 \geq 0\}$$

is a convex cone. Graphically this is the first quadrant in $\mathbb{R}^2$ (see Figure 50). To see that $C_1$ is a convex cone, suppose that $\mathbf{y} = (y_1, y_2)$ and $\mathbf{y}' = (y_1', y_2') \in C_1$. Then $\mathbf{y} + \mathbf{y}' = (y_1 + y_1', y_2 + y_2') \in C_1$, since $y_1 + y_1' \geq 0$ and $y_2 + y_2' \geq 0$. Furthermore, if $\lambda \geq 0$, then $\lambda\mathbf{y} = (\lambda y_1, \lambda y_2) \in C_1$ since $\lambda y_1 \geq 0$ and $\lambda y_2 \geq 0$. More generally,

$$\{\mathbf{y} = (y_1, \ldots, y_n): y_1 \geq 0, \ldots, y_n \geq 0\}$$

is a convex cone; it is termed the *nonnegative orthant* of $\mathbb{R}^n$. (In $\mathbb{R}^2$ the nonnegative orthant is the first quadrant, $\{(y_1, y_2): y_1 \geq 0, y_2 \geq 0\}$.)

A second example is provided by the set

$$C_2 = \{(y_1, y_2): (y_1, y_2) \cdot (2, 3) \leq 0\}$$

(see Figure 51). To see that $C_2$ is a convex cone suppose $\mathbf{y} = (y_1, y_2)$ and $\mathbf{y}' = (y_1', y_2') \in C_2$. Then

$$\begin{aligned}(y_1 + y_1', y_2 + y_2') \cdot (2, 3) &= 2y_1 + 2y_1' + 3y_2 + 3y_2' \\ &= 2y_1 + 3y_2 + 2y_1' + 3y_2' \leq 0 + 0 \\ &= 0.\end{aligned}$$

Thus, $\mathbf{y} + \mathbf{y}' \in C_2$. If $\lambda \geq 0$, then $[\lambda(y_1, y_2)] \cdot (2, 3) = \lambda[(y_1, y_2) \cdot (2, 3)] \leq 0$, implying $\lambda\mathbf{y} \in C_2$. Therefore, $\mathbf{y} + \mathbf{y}'$ and $\lambda\mathbf{y}$ ($\lambda \geq 0$) are in $C_2$, implying that

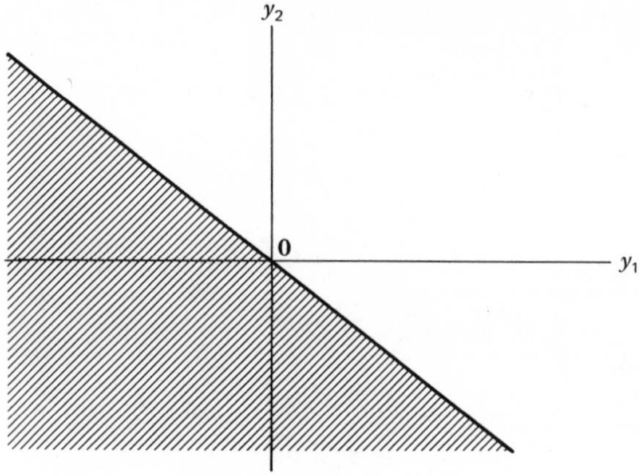


Figure 51

$C_2$ is a convex cone by definition. More generally, the half space

$$\{\mathbf{y} = (y_1, \ldots, y_n) : \mathbf{y} \cdot \mathbf{b} \leq 0\},$$

where **b** is a constant vector, is a convex cone.

The set

$$C_3 = \{\mathbf{y} = (y_1, y_2) : \mathbf{y} = \lambda(1, 2), \lambda \geq 0\}$$

is also a convex cone (see Figure 52). If $\mathbf{y} = (y_1, y_2)$ and $\mathbf{y}' = (y_1', y_2') \in C_3$, then $\mathbf{y} + \mathbf{y}' = \lambda(1, 2) + \lambda'(1, 2) = \lambda''(1, 2) \in C_3$. Further, $\lambda''\mathbf{y} = \lambda''\lambda(1, 2) = \lambda'''(1, 2) \in C_3$, $\lambda'' \geq 0$, $\lambda''' \geq 0$. Hence, because $\mathbf{y} + \mathbf{y}' \in C_3$ and $\lambda'''\mathbf{y} \in C_3$, $\lambda''' \geq 0$, $C_3$ is a convex cone. In general

$$\{\mathbf{y} = (y_1, \ldots, y_n) : \mathbf{y} = \lambda\mathbf{b}, \lambda \geq 0\},$$

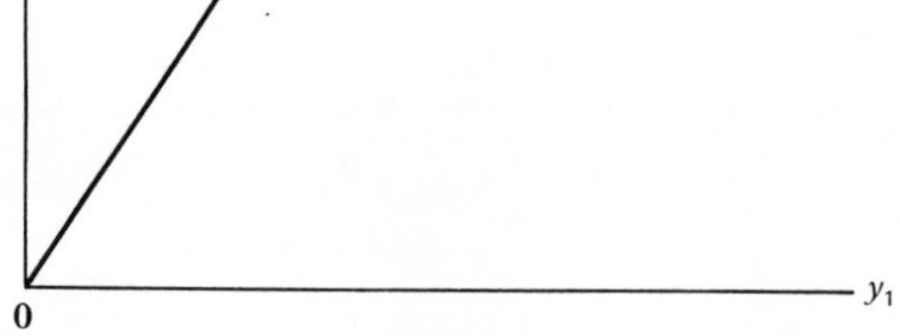

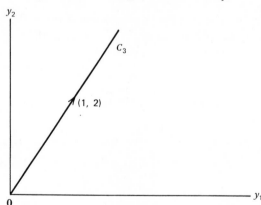

Figure 52

where **b** is a constant vector, is a convex cone and is denoted by (**b**). Sets of this form are called *half lines*.

As a special case of the general theorem for convex sets we have the following result:

**THEOREM 20** If $C_1$ and $C_2$ are convex cones, then

$$C_1 + C_2 = \{\mathbf{y} = \mathbf{y}^1 + \mathbf{y}^2 : \mathbf{y}^1 \in C_1, \mathbf{y}^2 \in C_2\}$$

and

$$C_1 \cap C_2 = \{\mathbf{y} : \mathbf{y} \in C_1, \mathbf{y} \in C_2\}$$

are convex cones. ▮

These operations on convex cones are illustrated in Figure 53.

Many applications of the concept of a convex cone are restricted to these cones "generated" by a finite number of half lines. This motivates the notion of a *finite cone*. A convex cone $C$ is called a *finite cone* if it is the sum of sets of the form $(\mathbf{b}) = \{\mathbf{y} : \mathbf{y} = \lambda \mathbf{b}, \lambda \geq 0\}$; that is,

$$C = (\mathbf{a}_1) + \cdots + (\mathbf{a}_n).$$

The vectors $\mathbf{a}_1, \ldots, \mathbf{a}_n$ are called generators of $C$. (Recall $(\mathbf{a}_i) = \{\mathbf{y} : \mathbf{y} = \lambda \mathbf{a}_i, \lambda \geq 0\}$.) The example,

$$C_1 = \{(y_1, y_2) : y_1 \geq 0, y_2 \geq 0\},$$

is a convex cone generated by (0, 1) and (1, 0). That is, $C_1$ has the form

$$\begin{aligned} C_1 &= ((0, 1)) + ((1, 0)) \\ &= \{\mathbf{y} = (y_1, y_2) : (y_1, y_2) = \lambda_1(0, 1) + \lambda_2(1, 0), \lambda_1 \geq 0, \lambda_2 \geq 0\}. \end{aligned}$$

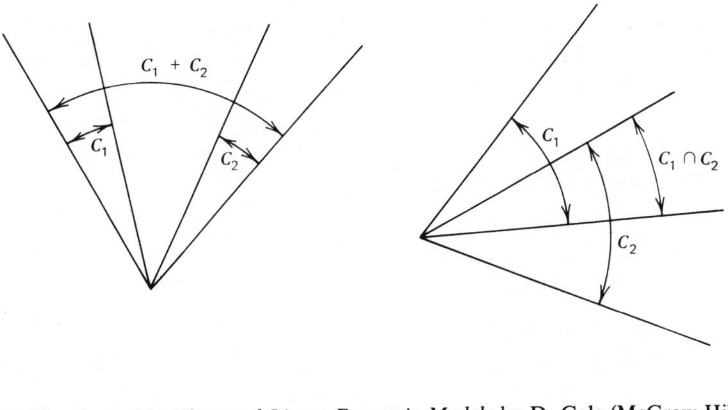


**Figure 53** From *The Theory of Linear Economic Models* by D. Gale (McGraw Hill, New York, 1960). Used with permission.

An equivalent description of the finite cone $C$ is

$$C = \{\mathbf{y}:\mathbf{y} = \mathbf{A}\mathbf{x}, \mathbf{x} \geq \mathbf{0}\},$$

where $\mathbf{A}$ is a matrix whose column vectors are the generators, $\mathbf{a}_i$ and $\mathbf{x}$ is a vector with positive real components. Thus, $C_1$, above, may be described as,

$$C_1 = \left\{\mathbf{y} = (y_1, y_2): \begin{pmatrix} y_1 \\ y_2 \end{pmatrix} = \begin{pmatrix} 0 & 1 \\ 1 & 0 \end{pmatrix}\begin{pmatrix} \lambda_1 \\ \lambda_2 \end{pmatrix}, \lambda_1 \geq 0, \lambda_2 \geq 0\right\}.$$

The technology set of our linear production model (178)–(183) is a convex cone. To see this, suppose $\mathbf{v} = (v_1, \ldots, v_m)$ and $\mathbf{v}^* = (v_1^*, \ldots, v_m^*)$ are points in the technology set corresponding to output levels $x = \sum_{k=1}^N x_k$ and $x^* = \sum_{k=1}^N x_k^*$, respectively. The point $\mathbf{v} + \mathbf{v}^*$ is also in the technology set; it corresponds to an output level $x + x^* = \sum_{k=1}^N (x_k + x_k^*)$, since

$$v_i + v_i^* = \sum_{k=1}^N a_{ik}x_k + \sum_{k=1}^N a_{ik}x_k^* = \sum_{k=1}^N a_{ik}(x_k + x_k^*),$$

$i = 1, \ldots, m$. Furthermore, the point $a\mathbf{v} = (av_1, \ldots, av_m)$ is also in the technology set for any constant $a \geq 0$; it corresponds to an output level $ax = \sum_{k=1}^N ax_k$ because

$$av_i = a\sum_{k=1}^N a_{ik}x_k = \sum_{k=1}^N a_{ik}ax_k,$$

$i = 1, \ldots, m$. Thus, the technology set is a convex cone because when $\mathbf{v}$ and $\mathbf{v}^*$ are in this set, $\mathbf{v} + \mathbf{v}^*$ and $a\mathbf{v}$, $a \geq 0$, are also in the technology set.

Our characterization of the technology set is extended upon noting that the technology set is a *finite cone*. This follows by noting that the technology set is generated by input vectors each corresponding to exclusive use of one of the $N$ activities to maintain the total output level $x$; that is, the $k$th generator is the vector $\mathbf{v}^{(k)} = (v_1^k, \ldots, v_m^k)$, $k = 1, \ldots, N$, with components

$$v_i^k = a_{ik}x \qquad (i = 1, \ldots, m).$$

To see that $\mathbf{v}^{(1)}, \ldots, \mathbf{v}^{(N)}$ are generators of the technology set, suppose that we are to maintain the output level

$$x = \sum_{k=1}^N x_k \qquad (x \neq 0) \tag{184}$$

corresponding to the input levels represented by the vector $(v_1, \ldots, v_m)$. Since (184) holds, so does

$$x = \sum_{k=1}^N \left(\frac{x_k}{x}\right)x.$$

Hence, $x = \sum_{k=1}^{N} \mu_k x$, where $\mu_k = x_k/x$ or equivalently $\mu_k x = x_k$. Therefore, for any vector $\mathbf{v} = (v_1, \ldots, v_m)$ in the technology set,

$$\mathbf{v} = \begin{pmatrix} v_1 \\ \cdot \\ \cdot \\ \cdot \\ v_m \end{pmatrix} = \sum_{k=1}^{N} \begin{pmatrix} a_{1k}x_k \\ \cdot \\ \cdot \\ \cdot \\ a_{mk}x_k \end{pmatrix} = \sum_{k=1}^{N} \begin{pmatrix} a_{1k}\mu_k x \\ \cdot \\ \cdot \\ \cdot \\ a_{mk}\mu_k x \end{pmatrix} = \sum_{k=1}^{N} \mu_k \begin{pmatrix} a_{1k}x \\ \cdot \\ \cdot \\ \cdot \\ a_{mk}x \end{pmatrix} = \sum_{k=1}^{N} \mu_k \mathbf{v}^{(k)}.$$

Since this arbitrary vector $\mathbf{v}$ in the technology set is expressed as the sum of half lines $(\mathbf{v}^{(i)})$

$$\mathbf{v} = (\mathbf{v}^{(1)}) + \cdots + (\mathbf{v}^{(N)})$$

we conclude that $\mathbf{v}^{(1)}, \ldots, \mathbf{v}^{(N)}$ generate the technology set.

*The law of constant returns to scale prevails in the linear production model* (178)–(183) *because the technology set is a convex cone*. That is, a proportional increase or decrease in inputs, $a\mathbf{v} = (av_1, \ldots, av_m)$, represented by a new point in the technology set, ensures a corresponding proportional increase or decrease of the output level by the same percentage, $ax = \sum_{k=1}^{N} ax_k$.

*External diseconomies are absent from this model because the technology set is convex*. A convex combination of two activities represents their simultaneous operation. If production at some output level is possible with any two original activities within the technology set, we can produce at least the same output by using no more than a weighted sum of the original inputs. Thus, for example, suppose 5000 straw baskets can be produced using two activities that require certain quantities of straw, labor, and a particular machine's time. Then, according to this model, 5000 baskets also may be manufactured using different levels of the same inputs; no additional machinery, for instance, is necessary to maintain this output level. This phenomenon is referred to as the absence of external diseconomies within the process for which this is the technology set.

The technology set for our example of a linear production model (178′)–(183′) is the finite convex cone generated by the two input vectors corresponding to exclusive use of only one of the two activities. If only activity 1 is utilized in producing the output, then the input vector $\mathbf{v}^{(1)} = (v_1, v_2)$ has components

(185)
$$\begin{aligned} v_1 &= 2x_1 + 4x_2 = 2x + 4(0) = 2x, \\ v_2 &= 6x_1 + 2x_2 = 6x + 2(0) = 6x; \end{aligned}$$

$\mathbf{v}^{(1)} = (2x, 6x)$. By solving for $x$ in (185), we see that exclusive use of the first

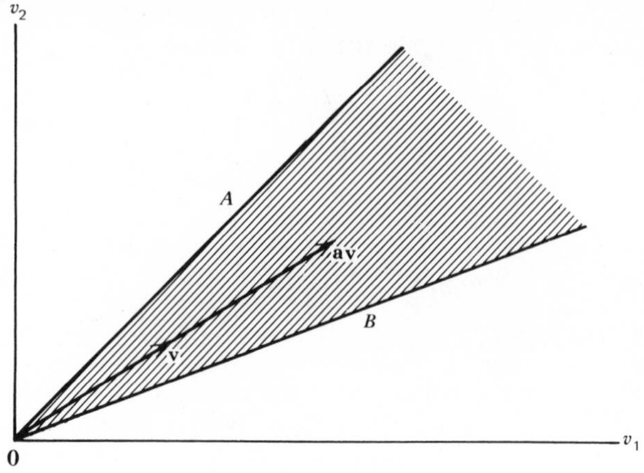


**Figure 54**

activity is represented by the expression $v_2 = 3v_1$. Geometrically this is the half line $A$ through the origin in Figure 54.

If only subprocess 2 is used in producing the output, then the input vector $\mathbf{v}^{(2)} = (v_1, v_2)$ has components

$$v_1 = 2x_1 + 4x_2 = 2(0) + 4x = 4x,$$
$$v_2 = 6x_1 + 2x_2 = 6(0) + 2x = 2x;$$

$\mathbf{v}^{(2)} = (4x, 2x)$. Proceeding as above, we see that the second activity is represented by the expression $v_2 = \frac{1}{2}v_1$. In Figure 54 this is half line $B$ through the origin.

Geometrically the technology set generated by $\mathbf{v}^{(1)}$ and $\mathbf{v}^{(2)}$ is the shaded area in Figure 54. Observe that constant returns to scale characterizes the model (178′)–(183′) because, as shown in Figure 54, if the input vector $\mathbf{v}$ is in the technology set, then so is $a\mathbf{v}$, $a \geq 0$. Note that if the input vector $\mathbf{v}$ corresponds to output level $x$, the new input vector $a\mathbf{v}$ corresponds to output level $ax$:

$$ax = ax_1 + ax_2.$$

Mathematically, multiplication of the input levels (and, therefore, the output level) by a number $a \geq 0$ is always possible. But some positive multiples are not technically possible; the capacity limitations, (183) place constraints on the process.

## ISOQUANTS: CONVEX HULLS

An arbitrary set $D$ in $\mathbb{R}^n$ need not be convex and therefore does not necessarily contain all the convex combinations of its points. However, one may expect

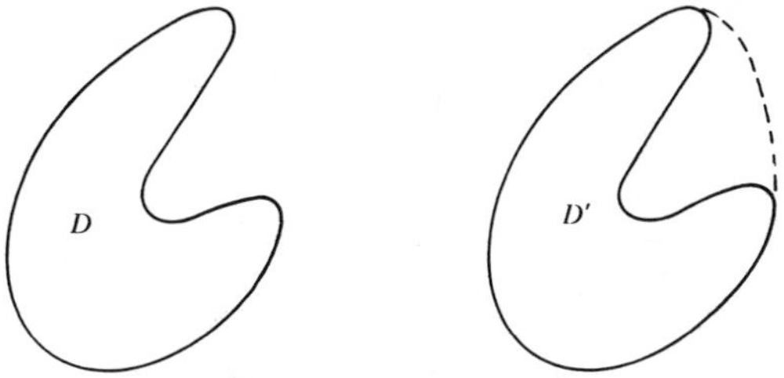


Figure 55

the existence of a smallest convex set containing $D$, which may be obtained by "filling in the hollows" of $D$. For instance, the set $D$ in Figure 55 is not convex but is contained in a convex set $D'$ ($D'$ is obviously the smallest convex set containing $D$). This motivates a formal definition. The smallest convex set containing a set $D$ in $\mathbb{R}^n$, in the sense of set theoretic inclusion, is termed the *convex hull* of $D$ and is indicated by $\langle D \rangle$.

As an example of a convex hull, suppose $D = \{(1, 0), (0, 3), (4, 2)\}$ is as shown in Figure 56. The smallest convex set containing $D$ is obviously the boundary and interior of the triangle with vertices $(1, 0)$, $(0, 3)$, $(4, 2)$ (see Figure 57).

In applications of convexity it is convenient to generate the convex hull of an arbitrary set $D$ as the set of all convex combinations of the points of $D$. Let $E$ be the set of all convex combinations of points of $D$. To see that $E = \langle D \rangle$, observe that $\langle D \rangle$ is by definition the smallest convex set containing $D$ and that $E$ also contains $D$; hence, $E \supset \langle D \rangle$. Furthermore, since $\langle D \rangle$ is a convex set, it contains all convex combinations of points of itself, and in particular, it contains all convex combinations of points of $D$; that is, $\langle D \rangle \supset E$. Thus, we have the following:

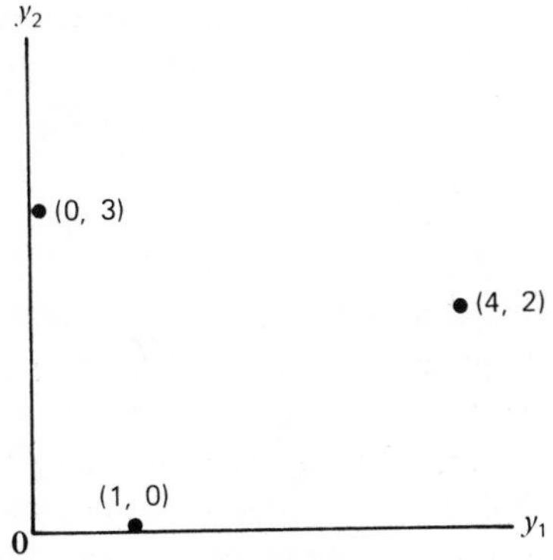


Figure 56

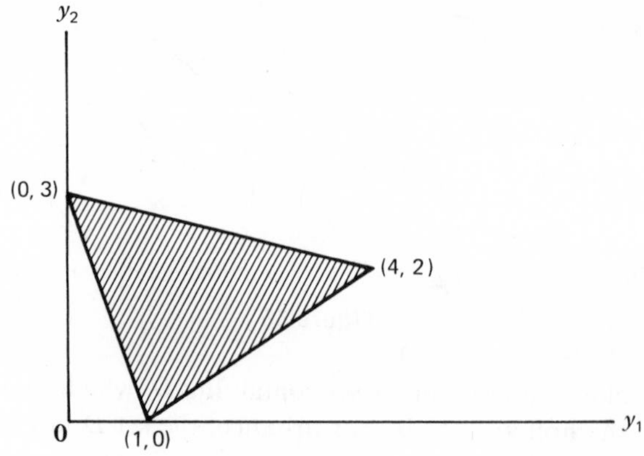


**Figure 57**

**THEOREM 21** $\langle D \rangle$ is equal to the set of all convex combinations of points of $D$. ▮

With Theorem 21, we may conclude, for instance, that any point in or on the triangle with vertices (1, 0), (0, 3), (4, 2) may be represented in the form

$$\lambda_1(1, 0) + \lambda_2(0, 3) + \lambda_3(4, 2),$$

where $\lambda_1 + \lambda_2 + \lambda_3 = 1, \lambda_1 \geq 0, \lambda_2 \geq 0, \lambda_3 \geq 0$.

In the special case that $D$ is convex, $D$ is itself the smallest convex set containing $D$. Formally we state, without proof, this result and its converse:

**THEOREM 22** If $D$ is any set in $\mathbb{R}^n$, then $D = \langle D \rangle$ if and only if $D$ is convex. ▮

*The linear production model* (178)–(183) *permits substitutions*. That is, the same total output can be produced by combinations of the $N$ (>1) activities. The "locus" of the input combinations capable of producing the same output level is a production *isoquant*. For a given output level $x = \bar{x}$, the production isoquant is defined in parametric form by

$$\left\{\mathbf{v} = (v_1, \ldots, v_m): v_i = \sum_{k=1}^{N} a_{ik}x_k, \sum_{k=1}^{N} x_k = \bar{x}, i = 1, \ldots, m\right\}.$$

Together with information concerning the combinations of inputs that correspond to constant expenditures, the information gathered from isoquants is used to determine a firm's optimal production decisions.

An isoquant of our linear production model (178)–(183) may be characterized as the *convex hull* of the set of input vectors corresponding to the use of one activity to produce $\bar{x}$ units of output. That is, the isoquant is $\langle \mathbf{v}^{(1)}, \ldots, \mathbf{v}^{(N)} \rangle$, where $\mathbf{v}^{(i)}$ is the input vector corresponding to exclusive use of the $i$th process to produce $\bar{x}$ units. The procedure for proving the latter statement is identical to the technique for showing that $\mathbf{v}^{(1)}, \ldots, \mathbf{v}^{(N)}$ generate the technology set because $0 \le \mu_i \le 1$. Thus, any input vector corresponding to $\bar{x}$ units of output may be expressed as some convex combination of the input vectors $\bar{\mathbf{v}}^{(1)}, \ldots, \bar{\mathbf{v}}^{(N)}$. This implies that the model (178)–(183) *permits substitutions;* that is, one convex combination of input vectors $\bar{\mathbf{v}}^{(1)}, \ldots, \bar{\mathbf{v}}^{(N)}$ capable of producing $\bar{x}$ units may be substituted for another convex combination of these input vectors corresponding to input level $\bar{x}$.

Consider the isoquants of example (178′)–(183′). If the vectors $\bar{\mathbf{v}}^{(1)}$ and $\bar{\mathbf{v}}^{(2)}$ correspond to exclusive use of the first and second subprocesses, respectively, to produce $\bar{x}$ units of output, then the corresponding isoquant is $\langle \bar{\mathbf{v}}^{(1)}, \bar{\mathbf{v}}^{(2)} \rangle$. That is, the $\bar{x}$-isoquant is the line connecting $\bar{\mathbf{v}}^{(1)}$ and $\bar{\mathbf{v}}^{(2)}$ in Figure 58—that is, all convex combinations of $\bar{\mathbf{v}}^{(1)}$ and $\bar{\mathbf{v}}^{(2)}$.

Note that if this process has three activities and the technology set is described by, say,

$$v_1 = 2x_1 + 4x_2 + x_3,$$
$$v_2 = 6x_1 + 2x_2 + x_3,$$

then use of the third activity alone ($x_1 = x_2 = 0$) corresponds to points along the half line $v_2 = v_1$. Suppose that $\bar{\mathbf{v}}^{(1)}$ and $\bar{\mathbf{v}}^{(2)}$ are as above and the vector $\bar{\mathbf{v}}^{(3)}$ corresponds to exclusive use of activity three to produce $\bar{x}$ units of output. In this case the $\bar{x}$-isoquant is $\langle \bar{\mathbf{v}}^{(1)}, \bar{\mathbf{v}}^{(2)}, \bar{\mathbf{v}}^{(3)} \rangle$. That is, the $\bar{x}$-isoquant is the triangle with vertices $\bar{\mathbf{v}}^{(1)}, \bar{\mathbf{v}}^{(2)}, \bar{\mathbf{v}}^{(3)}$ (see Figure 59).

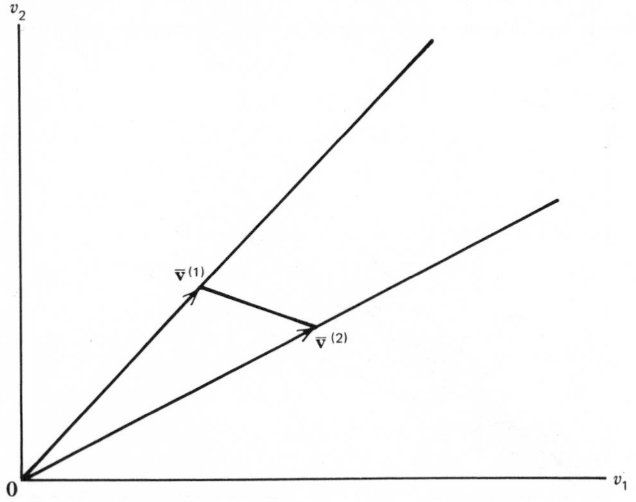


**Figure 58** From *Industrial Production Models: A Theoretical Study* by S. Danø (Springer-Verlag, New York, 1966). Used with permission.

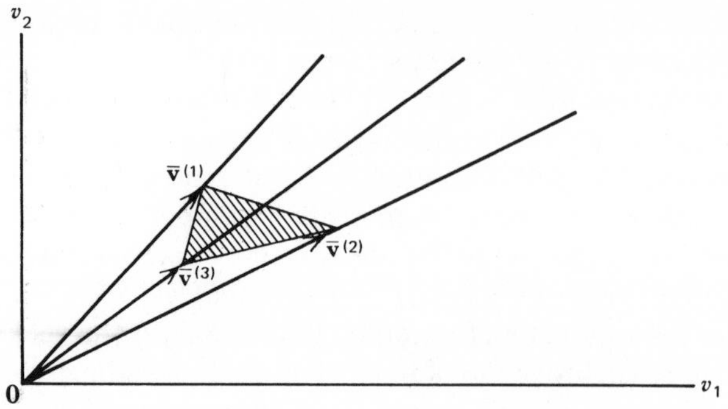


**Figure 59** From *Industrial Production Models: A Theoretical Study* by S. Danø (Springer-Verlag, New York, 1966). Used with permission.

Similarly, the isoquants of a linear production model of the type (178′)–(183′) with more than three activities, two inputs, and one output would be another polygonal figure bounded by "extreme activities," as $\bar{\mathbf{v}}^{(1)}$, $\bar{\mathbf{v}}^{(2)}$, $\bar{\mathbf{v}}^{(3)}$, and $\bar{\mathbf{v}}^{(4)}$ in Figure 60.

## THE FACTOR SPACE: A CONVEX POLYTOPE

A convex hull of a finite set is widely used in set-theoretic economic models. Here we shall see that the *factor space* of our linear production model, the set of inputs satisfying the capacity and resource limitations, (183),

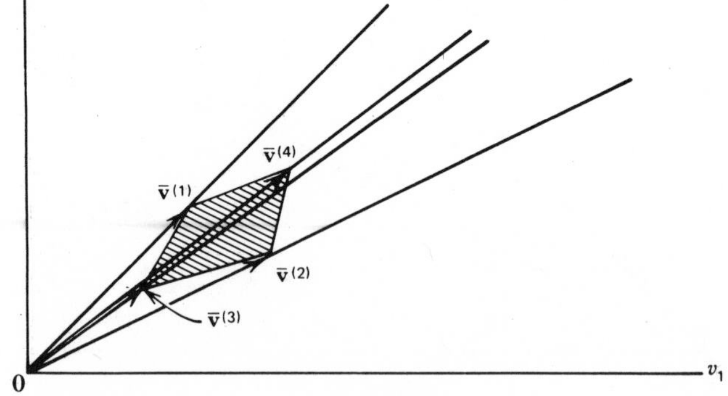


**Figure 60**

and the nonnegativity conditions, (182), may be characterized as the convex hull of a finite set of input vectors.

In our discussion of the convex hull of a finite set $D$, we make a convenient definition. If $D$ is a finite set in $\mathbb{R}^n$, $\langle D \rangle$ is called a *convex polytope*. (Note that the isoquants of our linear production model are actually convex polytopes because they are convex hulls of a finite set of input vectors.)

We next introduce the notion of an extreme point of a convex polytope. Consider the structure **ABCD** in Figure 61. Every point within this polygon or on its boundary can be expressed as a convex combination of some selected pair of points. All points of **AB** may be expressed as a convex combination of **A** and **B**. Similar statements are true of the other boundaries. Any interior point, such as **E**, can be expressed as a convex combination of **B** and a selected point, such as **F**. There are several points in this figure, however, that can be expressed only as a "degenerate" convex combination of pairs of points of **ABCD**. **A**, for example, may be expressed as

$$\mathbf{A} = \lambda \mathbf{y} + (1 - \lambda)\mathbf{y}' \qquad (0 < \lambda < 1),$$

but only for $\mathbf{y} = \mathbf{y}' = \mathbf{A}$. The same is true for **B, C,** and **D**. These four points are called *extreme points* of **ABCD**.

This example leads us to a general definition. A vector $\mathbf{y}$ in a convex set $K$ is called an *extreme point* of $K$ if, for any $\mathbf{y}', \mathbf{y}'' \in K$ and $0 < \lambda < 1$, $\mathbf{y} = \lambda\mathbf{y}' + (1 - \lambda)\mathbf{y}''$ implies $\mathbf{y} = \mathbf{y}' = \mathbf{y}''$. In geometric terms, an *extreme point of* $K$ is a point that is not an interior point of any segment of $K$.

Even if a convex set is bounded, it may not have any extreme points. For example, consider

$$\left\{(y_1, y_2): \frac{y_1^2}{2} + \frac{y_2^2}{4} < 1\right\};$$

this open set is the interior of the ellipse in Figure 62.

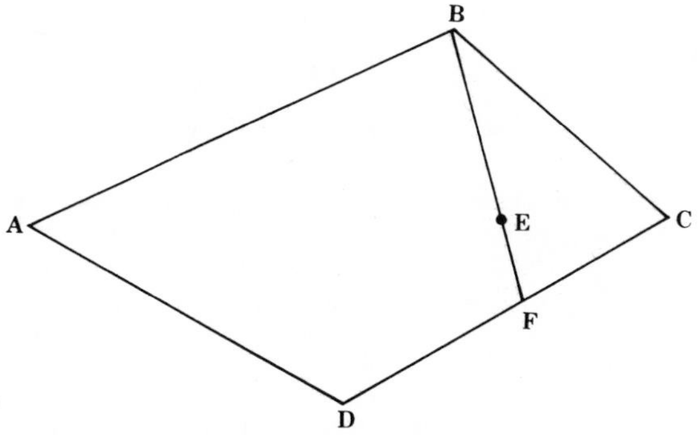


Figure 61

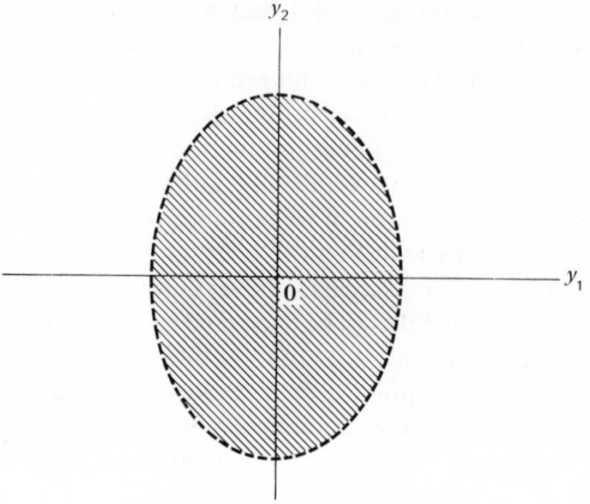


Figure 62

Polytopes may be characterized by their extreme points, as indicated by the following:

**THEOREM 23** If $K$ is a convex polytope and $\bar{K}$ is its set of extreme points, then $K = \langle \bar{K} \rangle$.

**PROOF** Let $K = \langle \mathbf{y}_1, \ldots, \mathbf{y}_n \rangle$. Then any extreme point of $K$ is one of the points $\mathbf{y}_i$ by the definition of vertex and convex hull. From among the set of $\mathbf{y}_i$ choose a subset with as few elements as possible whose convex hull is still $K$. Denote this set by $\{\mathbf{y}_1, \ldots, \mathbf{y}_m\}$. Each of these points is extreme. This follows because if, say, $\mathbf{y}_m = \lambda\mathbf{y} + (1 - \lambda)\mathbf{y}'$ and $0 < \lambda < 1$, we will show that $\mathbf{y} = \mathbf{y}' = \mathbf{y}_m$. Since $\mathbf{y} = \sum_{i=1}^m \lambda_i \mathbf{y}_i$ and $\mathbf{y}' = \sum_{i=1}^m \lambda_i' \mathbf{y}_i'$, we get $\mathbf{y}_m$ as a convex combination of the $\mathbf{y}_i$, $\mathbf{y}_m = \sum_{i=1}^m \mu_i \mathbf{y}_i$. If $\mu_m < 1$, we have

$$\mathbf{y}_m = \frac{1}{1 - \mu_m} \sum_{i=1}^{m-1} \mu_i \mathbf{y}_i,$$

contradicting the fact that $\{\mathbf{y}_1, \ldots, \mathbf{y}_m\}$ is the smallest set with convex hull $K$. If $\mu_m = 1$, then $\mu_i = 0$ for $i \neq m$ or

$$\lambda\lambda_i + (1 - \lambda)\lambda_i' = 0$$

for $i \neq m$, which means $\lambda_i = \lambda_i' = 0$ for $i \neq m$, so that $\mathbf{y} = \mathbf{y}' = \mathbf{y}_m$.

Another result that will prove useful in characterizing convex polytopes is the following, stated without proof:

**THEOREM 24** The intersection of a finite number of closed half spaces is a closed convex set having a finite number of extreme points. If this set is bounded, it is a convex polytope.

The number of extreme points in a convex set formed by intersecting a finite number of closed half spaces obviously can be large. The intersection of $k$ closed half spaces in $\mathbb{R}^n$ could form a convex set with as many as $k!/(k - n)!n!$ $(k \geq n)$ extreme points.

A particular class of polytopes with relatively few extreme points is the *simplex*. A simplex in $\mathbb{R}^n$ is the convex hull of any set of $n + 1$ points that do not all lie in one hyperplane in $\mathbb{R}^n$. In $\mathbb{R}^2$ a simplex consists of the convex hull of any three points that do not all lie in a line (see Figure 63). A simplex in $\mathbb{R}^3$ is the convex hull of four points that do not all lie in the same plane. Any three of these points must determine a plane; otherwise, they would be collinear and the four points coplanar. The fourth point must be outside this plane of the other three (see Figure 64).

The *factor space* of our linear production model includes all input combinations satisfying the capacity and resource limitations and the nonnegativity conditions. Note that for each $i$, $1 \leq i \leq m$, the capacity and resource limitations, (183), and nonnegativity requirement, (182), each are examples of closed half spaces. Specifically, the capacity and resource limitation and nonnegativity requirement are represented by the closed half spaces

$$L_i = \{\mathbf{v} : \mathbf{v} \cdot \mathbf{e}_i \leq \bar{v}_i, \mathbf{v} \in \mathbb{R}^m\} \tag{186}$$

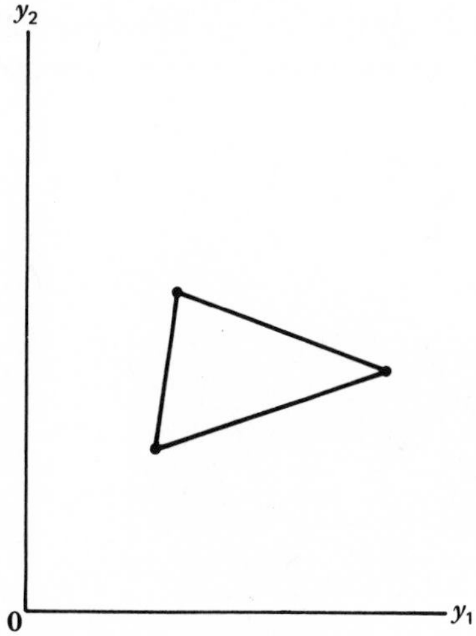


Figure 63

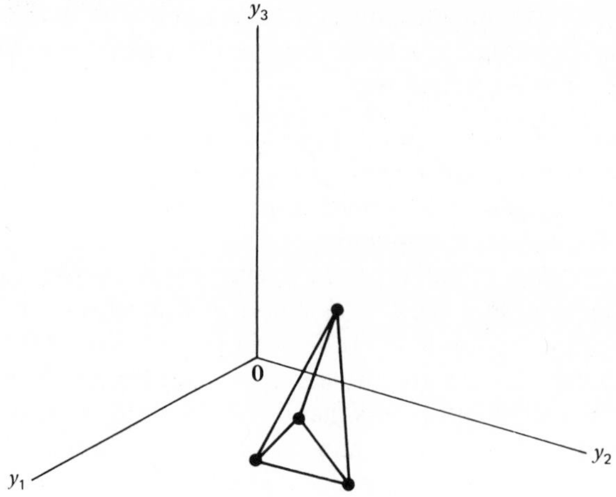


Figure 64

and

(187) $$N_i = \{\mathbf{v}: -\mathbf{v} \cdot \mathbf{e}_i \leq 0, \mathbf{v} \in \mathbb{R}^m\},$$

$i = 1, \ldots, m$, respectively. Since the factor space consists of all combinations of the $m$-inputs satisfying (186) and (187) for $i = 1, \ldots, m$, the factor space is actually the intersection of the $2m$ half spaces, $L_1, \ldots, L_m, N_1, \ldots, N_m$ defined above:

$$L_1 \cap \cdots \cap L_m \cap N_1 \cap \cdots \cap N_m.$$

According to Theorem 24 the intersection of a finite collection of closed half spaces is a closed convex set having a finite number of extreme points.

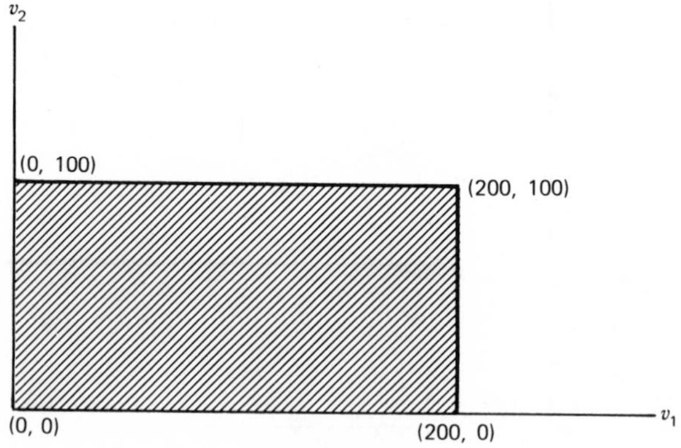


Figure 65

Further, since $0 \leq v_i \leq \bar{v}_i$ for $i = 1, \ldots, m$ the factor space is obviously a bounded set. Therefore, again by Theorem 24, the factor space may be characterized as a *convex polytope*.

In the example (178′)–(183′) the factor space is the intersection of half spaces

$$\{\mathbf{v}:\mathbf{v}\cdot\mathbf{e}_1 \leq 200\} \cap \{\mathbf{v}:\mathbf{v}\cdot\mathbf{e}_2 \leq 100\} \cap \{\mathbf{v}:-\mathbf{v}\cdot\mathbf{e}_1 \leq 0\} \cap \{\mathbf{v}:-\mathbf{v}\cdot\mathbf{e}_2 \leq 0\},$$

where $\mathbf{v} = (v_1, v_2) \in \mathbb{R}^2$. This factor space is shown in Figure 65. Observe that in this case the factor space is actually the convex polytope generated by the vectors (0, 0), (0, 100), (200, 100), and (200, 0).

## COST MINIMIZATION: SUPPORTING HYPERPLANES

Here we wish to discuss the notion of a supporting hyperplane of a convex structure and relate the associated results to a cost-minimization problem for our linear production model and to a geometrical study of the linear programming problem. Many of these theorems will be obvious in $\mathbb{R}^2$ and $\mathbb{R}^3$. Hence, we shall frequently rely on the reader's geometric intuition rather than state lengthy proofs. We begin by making a geometrical concept precise in $\mathbb{R}^n$.

An arbitrary set $S$ in $\mathbb{R}^n$ is said to be *contained on one side* of a hyperplane $\{\mathbf{y}:\mathbf{y}\cdot\mathbf{a} = b, \mathbf{y} \in \mathbb{R}^n\}$, if $\mathbf{y}\cdot\mathbf{a} \leq b$ for all $\mathbf{y} \in S$ or $\mathbf{y}\cdot\mathbf{a} \geq b$ for all $\mathbf{y} \in S$. In $\mathbb{R}^2$, this means that $S$ is on one side of a straight line, as shown in Figure 66. (The straight line may also include boundary points.)

If the set $S$ is *closed* and *convex* the hyperplane $\{\mathbf{y}:\mathbf{y}\cdot\mathbf{a} = b, \mathbf{y} \in \mathbb{R}^n\}$ may be chosen to pass through an arbitrary boundary point as well as entirely contain the set in one of the closed half spaces $\{\mathbf{y}:\mathbf{y}\cdot\mathbf{a} \leq b, \mathbf{y} \in \mathbb{R}^n\}$ or $\{\mathbf{y}:\mathbf{y}\cdot\mathbf{a} \geq b, \mathbf{y} \in \mathbb{R}^n\}$.

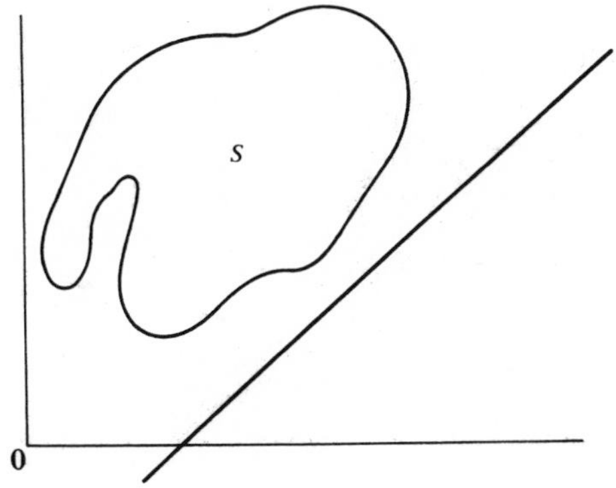


Figure 66

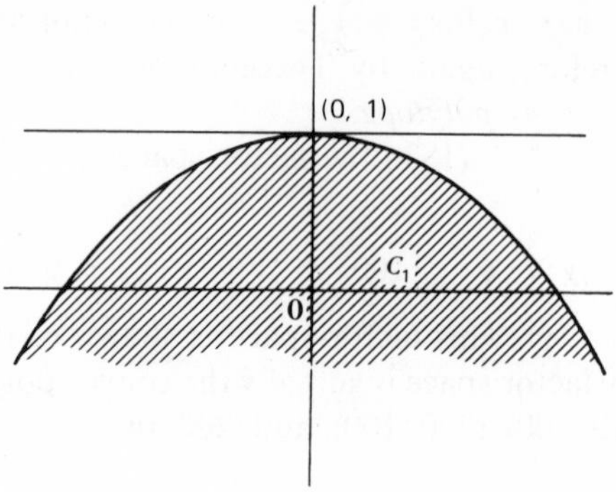


Figure 67

THEOREM 25 If $\bar{\mathbf{y}}$ is a boundary point of a closed convex set $C$, there exists a hyperplane, $\mathbf{y} \cdot \mathbf{a} = b$, that passes through $\bar{\mathbf{y}}$ and that has the property that all of $C$ is contained in one of the closed half spaces $\{\mathbf{y}:\mathbf{y} \cdot \mathbf{a} \geq b, \mathbf{y} \in \mathbb{R}^n\}$ or $\{\mathbf{y}:\mathbf{y} \cdot \mathbf{a} \leq b, \mathbf{y} \in \mathbb{R}^n\}$. ▮

Such a hyperplane is called a *supporting hyperplane of C at* $\bar{\mathbf{y}}$.

In Figure 67 the closed convex set $C_1$ has a supporting hyperplane at the boundary point (0, 1). (Note that $C_1$ is also unbounded.) The closed convex polytope $C_2$ in Figure 68 has supporting hyperplanes at the boundary points $(-1, -2)$ and (1, 1). A supporting hyperplane at (1, 1) lies along the edge of the polytope. Any supporting hyperplane meeting the interior of an edge of a polytope (i.e., along the intersection of two faces) will contain all

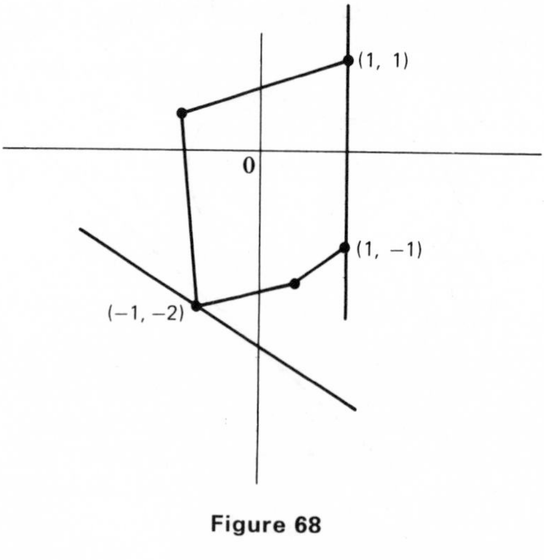


Figure 68

points on this edge. Note that supporting hyperplanes at a boundary point of a convex set need not be unique; for instance, there are infinitely many supporting hyperplanes of $C_2$ at $(-1, -2)$.

Observe that all of the supporting hyperplanes of $C_1$ and $C_2$ contain extreme points of the closed convex sets. In general, we have the result:

THEOREM 26 If $C$ is a closed convex set in $\mathbb{R}^n$ that is bounded from below (or above), then *every* supporting hyperplane of $C$ contains at least one extreme point of $C$. ▌

This result actually provides the basis of various numerical algorithms for solving linear programming problems and is fundamental to the following discussion of the cost minimization problem associated with our production model.

### Cost Minimization

Consider the problem of determining the amount of each of the $m$ inputs, $v_1, \ldots, v_m$, that minimizes the total cost of inputs and yet meets the input requirement necessary to produce $\bar{x}$ units of output. Mathematically this means that we wish to determine the input vector (or vectors) $\mathbf{v}^* = (v_1^*, \ldots, v_m^*)$ in the $\bar{x}$-isoquant $\langle \bar{\mathbf{v}}^{(1)}, \ldots, \bar{\mathbf{v}}^{(N)} \rangle$, of our linear production model (178)–(183), which minimizes the cost of inputs.

If the cost of one unit of the $i$th input is $c_i$, then the total cost of inputs associated with an input vector $\mathbf{v} = (v_1, \ldots, v_m)$ is given by

$$c_1 v_1 + \cdots + c_m v_m.$$

The total cost may also be expressed as the scalar product $\mathbf{c} \cdot \mathbf{v}$, where $\mathbf{c} = (c_1, \ldots, c_m)$. Suppose that the minimum total cost of inputs in the $\bar{x}$-isoquant is $M$ (i.e., $M = \mathbf{c} \cdot \mathbf{v}^*$). Then the minimum cost defines a *hyperplane*

$$\mathbf{c} \cdot \mathbf{v} = M. \tag{188}$$

Further, it may be proved that (188) is a *supporting hyperplane* of the $\bar{x}$-isoquant, $\langle \bar{\mathbf{v}}^{(1)}, \ldots, \bar{\mathbf{v}}^{(N)} \rangle$. Since $\langle \bar{\mathbf{v}}^{(1)}, \ldots, \bar{\mathbf{v}}^{(N)} \rangle$ is a (closed and bounded) convex polytope, Theorem 26 implies that the supporting hyperplane $M = \mathbf{c} \cdot \mathbf{v}$ contains at least one extreme point of $\langle \bar{\mathbf{v}}^{(1)}, \ldots, \bar{\mathbf{v}}^{(N)} \rangle$. That is, an input vector $\mathbf{v}^* = (v_1^*, \ldots, v_m^*)$ that is in the $\bar{x}$-isoquant and that minimizes the associated cost of inputs is an extreme point of $\langle \bar{\mathbf{v}}^{(1)}, \ldots, \bar{\mathbf{v}}^{(N)} \rangle$. Since the set of extreme points of the $\bar{x}$-isoquant is a finite subset of $\{\bar{\mathbf{v}}^{(1)}, \ldots, \bar{\mathbf{v}}^{(N)}\}$, $\mathbf{v}^* \in \{\bar{\mathbf{v}}^{(1)}, \ldots, \bar{\mathbf{v}}^{(N)}\}$; this greatly simplifies the problem: *to find* $\mathbf{v}^*$ *such that the cost is minimized,* $M = \mathbf{c} \cdot \mathbf{v}$, *we need only find the minimum of the costs,* $\mathbf{c} \cdot \bar{\mathbf{v}}^{(1)}, \ldots, \mathbf{c} \cdot \bar{\mathbf{v}}^{(N)}$.

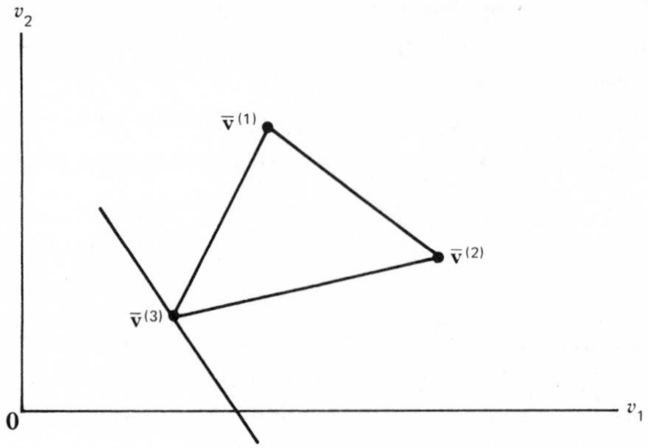


**Figure 69**

Suppose, for example, the isoquant for a two-input, three-activity linear production model is described parametrically by

$$\begin{aligned} v_1 &= 2x_1 + 4x_2 + x_3 \\ v_2 &= 6x_1 + 2x_2 + x_3 \\ \bar{x} &= x_1 + x_2 + x_3, \end{aligned}$$

where $\bar{x} = 3$. And suppose the total cost of inputs is given by $5v_1 + v_2$, or, equivalently, $\mathbf{c} \cdot \mathbf{v}$, where $\mathbf{c} = (5, 1)$ and $\mathbf{v} = (v_1, v_2)$. The input vectors corresponding to the exclusive use of a single activity to produce $\bar{x}$ units of output are given by

$$\bar{\mathbf{v}}^{(1)} = \begin{pmatrix} 2\bar{x} \\ 6\bar{x} \end{pmatrix} = \begin{pmatrix} 6 \\ 18 \end{pmatrix}, \bar{\mathbf{v}}^{(2)} = \begin{pmatrix} 4\bar{x} \\ 2\bar{x} \end{pmatrix} = \begin{pmatrix} 12 \\ 6 \end{pmatrix}, \bar{\mathbf{v}}^{(3)} = \begin{pmatrix} \bar{x} \\ \bar{x} \end{pmatrix} = \begin{pmatrix} 3 \\ 3 \end{pmatrix}.$$

Thus the $\bar{x}$-isoquant is $\langle \bar{\mathbf{v}}^{(1)}, \bar{\mathbf{v}}^{(2)}, \bar{\mathbf{v}}^{(3)} \rangle$ and the minimum cost of inputs is

$$\min \{\mathbf{c} \cdot \bar{\mathbf{v}}^{(1)} = 48, \mathbf{c} \cdot \bar{\mathbf{v}}^{(2)} = 66, \mathbf{c} \cdot \bar{\mathbf{v}}^{(3)} = 18\} = 18.$$

As shown in Figure 69, $(5, 1) \cdot (v_1, v_2) = 18$ is a supporting hyperplane of $\langle \bar{\mathbf{v}}^{(1)}, \bar{\mathbf{v}}^{(2)}, \bar{\mathbf{v}}^{(3)} \rangle$ through $\bar{\mathbf{v}}^{(3)}$.

## A Linear Programming Problem

The linear programming problem to be considered here is that of determining a vector $\mathbf{x} \in \mathbb{R}^n$ such that the value of the scalar product

$$\mathbf{a} \cdot \mathbf{x} \tag{189}$$

is minimized and such that $m$ inequality constraints

$$\mathbf{a}^1 \cdot \mathbf{x} \le b_1,$$

(190)
$$\vdots$$

$$\mathbf{a}^m \cdot \mathbf{x} \le b_m$$

are satisfied, where $\mathbf{a}, \mathbf{a}^1, \ldots, \mathbf{a}^m$ are vectors of constants in $\mathbb{R}^n$ and $b_1, \ldots, b_m$ are constants. $\mathbf{a} \cdot \mathbf{x}$ is called the *objective function* and the set of vectors $\mathbf{x} \in \mathbb{R}^n$ satisfying constraints (190) is called the *constraint set*.

Note that the constraint set of the general problem, (189) and (190), is a convex set. It is the intersection of $m$ closed half spaces, $\mathbf{a}^i \cdot \mathbf{x} \le b_i$, and consequently, by Theorem 24 the constraint set is a *closed convex set with a finite number of extreme points*. If the constraint set is bounded, it is actually a convex polytope, also by Theorem 24. The number of extreme points can be zero if the set is unbounded. For example, consider the infinite strip in the plane. (In this case the minimization problem need not be well posed.)

Before any further discussion of linear programming, consider an example of a linear programming problem:

(191) minimize $$(-3, 3) \cdot (x_1, x_2)$$

(192) subject to
$$(1, 1) \cdot (x_1, x_2) \le 3$$
$$(1, \tfrac{1}{4}) \cdot (x_1, x_2) \le 1$$
$$(-1, 0) \cdot (x_1, x_2) \le 0$$
$$(0, -1) \cdot (x_1, x_2) \le 0.$$

Here we must find a vector $\mathbf{x} = (x_1, x_2)$ such that $\mathbf{x}$ lies in the constraint set (192) and the objective function (191) is minimized. The constraint set in this example is the convex polytope with extreme points (0, 0), (1, 0), $(\frac{1}{3}, \frac{8}{3})$, and (0, 3) as shown in Figure 70.

Suppose that the minimum value of objective function (189) subject to constraints (190) is $M$. Then this minimum value of the objective function defines the *hyperplane*

(193) $$\mathbf{a} \cdot \mathbf{x} = M.$$

Furthermore, it can actually be proved that (193) is a *supporting hyperplane* of the constraint set of (189)–(190):

**THEOREM 27** If $M$ is the minimum value of the objective function $\mathbf{a} \cdot \mathbf{x}$ and $\mathbf{x}^*$ is the optimal solution (i.e., $M = \mathbf{a} \cdot \mathbf{x}^*$) to linear programming problem (189)–(190), then $M = \mathbf{a} \cdot \mathbf{x}$ is a supporting hyperplane of the convex set of solutions. ▮

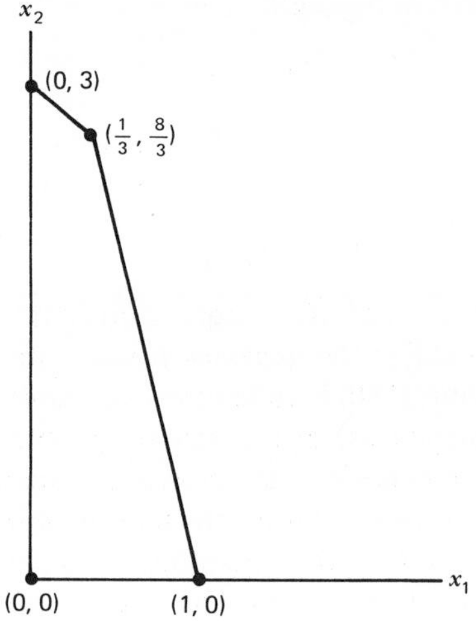


**Figure 70**

According to Theorem 26 the supporting hyperplane $M = \mathbf{a} \cdot \mathbf{x}$ contains at least one extreme point of the closed, convex constraint set. Thus, since all points of the supporting hyperplane $M = \mathbf{a} \cdot \mathbf{x}$ are optimal solutions of (189)–(190), *at least one* extreme point of the constraint set of solutions is optimal, provided that the objective function is not unbounded.

Therefore, to find the optimal solution and minimum value of linear programming problem (189)–(190), we need only compare the values of the objective function at the extreme points and show that the objective function is bounded below. This statement provides the fundamental idea of many numerical algorithms for solving linear programming problems.

In our example (191)–(192) the minimum value of $(-3, 3) \cdot (x_1, x_2)$ subject to constraints (192) occurs at one of the extreme points (0, 0), (1, 0), $(\frac{1}{3}, \frac{8}{3})$ or (0, 3). We compare the objective function values below:

| *Extreme point* | *Objective function value* |
|---|---|
| (0, 0) | 0 |
| (1, 0) | $-3$ |
| $(\frac{1}{3}, \frac{8}{3})$ | 7 |
| (0, 3) | 9 |

By comparing the values of the objective function in the above table we see that the minimum is $M = -3$. This implies that the supporting hyperplane $(-3, 3) \cdot (x_1, x_2) = -3$ must contain the extreme point (1, 0), as shown in Figure 71.

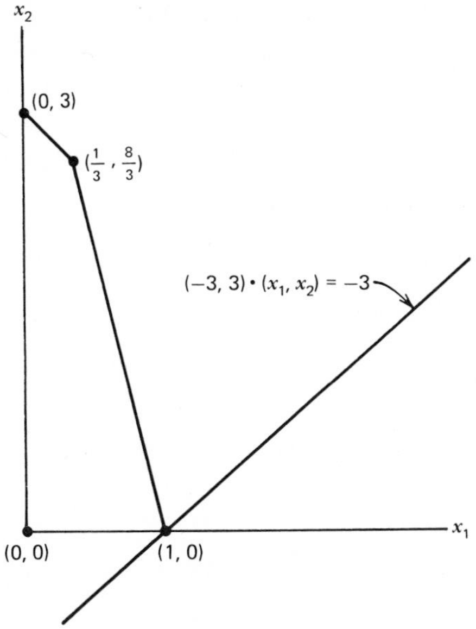


**Figure 71**

## EXERCISES

1. Identify the convex hull of each of the following sets:

   (*a*) $\{(x_1, x_2): x_1 = 1, x_2 = 1\}$

   (*b*) $\{(x_1, x_2): x_1 \geq 0, x_2 \geq 0, x_1 + x_2 \leq 2\}$

   (*c*) $\{(0, 0), (0, 1), (2, 2), (\frac{1}{2}, 7)\}$

   (*d*) $\{(x_1, x_2): x_1^2 + x_2^2 \leq 25, x_1x_2 \geq 1, x_1 \geq 0, x_2 \geq 0\}$

   (*e*) $\{(x_1, x_2): x_1^2 + x_2^2 < 1\}$.

2. Identify the extreme points of each of the following convex sets:

   (*a*) $\{(x_1, x_2): x_1 = 1, x_2 = 1\}$

   (*b*) $\{(x_1, x_2): x_1 \geq 0, x_2 \geq 0, x_1 + x_2 \leq 2\}$

   (*c*) $\{(x_1, x_2): x_1^2 + x_2^2 \leq 1\}$

   (*d*) $\{(x_1, x_2): x_1^2 + x_2^2 < 1\}$

   (*e*) $\{(x_1, x_2): x_1 = x_2, x_1 = -x_2\}$.

3. Give an example of each of the following:

   (*a*) A convex set with no extreme points

(*b*) A set that is identical to its convex hull
(*c*) A convex polytope with exactly two extreme points
(*d*) Two finite cones, the intersection of which contains only one point
(*e*) A bounded convex cone
(*f*) A convex polytope with exactly four extreme points.

4. Prove that each of the following is a convex cone:

(*a*) $\{(x_1, x_2):(x_1, x_2) \cdot (1, 1) = 0\}$

(*b*) $\{(x_1, x_2):(x_1, x_2) \cdot (3, 2) \leq 0\}$

(*c*) $\{(x_1, x_2):(x_1, x_2) \cdot (1, 2) \leq 0, (x_1, x_2) \cdot (1, -1) \leq 0\}$

(*d*) $\{(x_1, x_2):(x_1, x_2) \cdot (3, -1) = 0\}$.

5. Give a geometric interpretation of the following linear programming problem:

$$\begin{array}{ll} \text{minimize} & 10x_1 + 3x_2 \\ \text{subject to} & -\tfrac{1}{2}x_1 + x_2 \leq 5 \\ & x_1 \leq 3 \\ & -x_1 - x_2 \leq -6 \\ & -x_2 \leq 0 \\ & -x_1 \leq 0. \end{array}$$

6. Consider the two-activity, two-input linear production model. If the $\bar{x}$ isoquant for such a process has negative slope, as shown below, no point on the isoquant is *technically inefficient*. That is, $\bar{x}$ units of output can be produced with less of one input only by using more of the other.

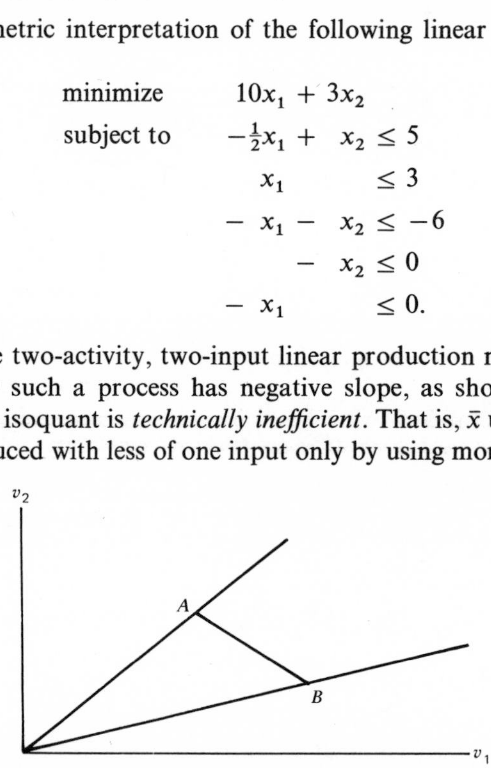


(*a*) Construct an example of a two-activity, two-input process in which no point on the $\bar{x}$ isoquant is technically inefficient.
(*b*) Give an economic interpretation of an isoquant with positive slope.
(*c*) Give an economic interpretation of an isoquant that is parallel to one of the axes.

7. If $c(\mathbf{v}) = c_1v_1 + \cdots + c_mv_m$ is the cost of inputs in our linear production model, the marginal cost of the $i$th input in our linear production model is given by $\partial c/\partial v_i$. Using this definition of marginal cost, show that the linear production model exhibits constant marginal costs.
8. An efficient point of the $\bar{x}$ isoquant of an $n$-activity ($n \geq 2$), $m$-input linear production model is a combination of at most $m$ activities. Construct a six-activity, two-input linear production model and determine the efficient points of the $\bar{x}$ isoquant.

## SOLUTIONS

1. The sets of parts $a, b, d, e$ are convex and, hence, identical to their convex hull. The convex hull of $c$ is the four-sided figure with extreme points $(0, 0), (0, 1), (2, 2), (\frac{1}{2}, 7)$.
2. (*a*) $(1, 1)$
   (*b*) $(0, 0), (0, 2), (2, 0)$
   (*c*) $\{(x_1, x_2): x_1^2 + x_2^2 = 1\}$
   (*d*) No extreme points
   (*e*) $(0, 0)$
3. (*a*) $\{(x_1, x_2): x_1^2 + x_2^2 < 1\}$
   (*b*) $\{(x_1, x_2): x_1^2 + x_2^2 < 1\}$
   (*c*) $\{x_1: -1 \leq x_1 \leq 1\}$
   (*d*) $\{(x_1, x_2): x_1 \geq 0, x_2 = 0\}, \{(x_1, x_2): x_1 = 0, x_2 \geq 0\}$
   (*e*) $\{(0, 0)\}$
   (*f*) Square

# CHAPTER 6

# CONVEX AND CONCAVE FUNCTIONS

## COST FUNCTIONS: THE CONVEXITY ASSUMPTION

In elementary calculus a twice differentiable function of a single variable, $f(x)$, is called *convex* whenever

$$\frac{d^2f}{dx^2} \geq 0.$$

That is, the graph of the function is U-shaped, as shown in Figure 72. Such functions frequently arise from common and realistic assumptions in mathematical formulations of problems in management science. For instance, consider the problem of determining a production and inventory policy for an industrial firm. The production level of a company's product must be chosen to minimize the production costs and the cost of storing the product prior to sales. For example, while we must consider the administrative, set up and input costs, we cannot neglect the cost of space, taxes, and insurance attributed to storage.

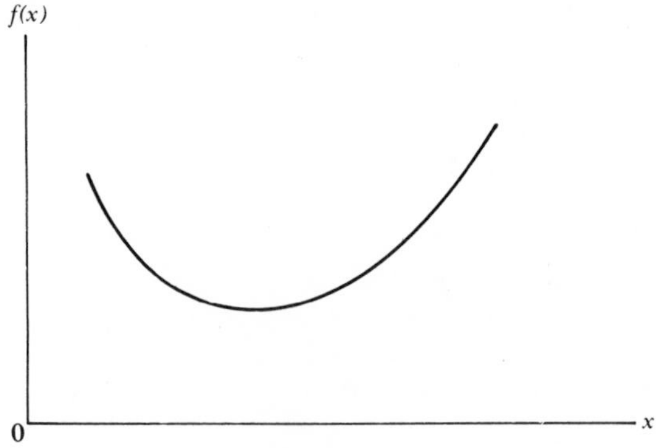


Figure 72

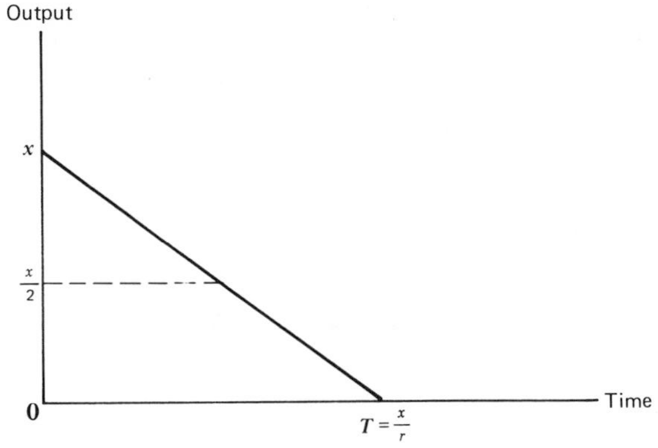


**Figure 73**

Suppose the cost of manufacturing an amount $x$ of the output can be represented by a twice differentiable function $p(x)$. If this production level $x$ is increased by an arbitrarily small amount $\Delta x$, then the cost will be increased by an amount $\Delta p$. The average cost of producing this additional amount is $\Delta p/\Delta x$, and the limiting value of this quotient is the derivative $dp/dx$. The function $dp/dx$ is defined to be the *marginal production cost*. The marginal production cost is sometimes assumed to be an increasing function; that is, the marginal production cost increases with each additional unit of output produced. Since $dp/dx$ is the marginal production cost, this means that increasing marginal production costs may be expressed as $d^2p/dx^2 > 0$. Thus, *the production function $p(x)$ with increasing marginal costs is a convex function.*

Consider now the storage cost associated with an output level of $x$ units. If the inventory of this product is depleted from $x$ to 0 at a constant rate $r$ over a period of time $T = x/r$, then the average inventory is $x/2$, as shown in Figure 73. Hence, the holding or storage cost is a function $\bar{h}(x/2) \equiv h(x)$. Again we assume $h(x)$ is twice differentiable. Proceeding as above, we define $dh/dx$ to be the *marginal holding cost*.

If there are several sources of limited storage with different unit costs available to the firm in this time period, it is optimal for the firm to use these sources in order of ascending marginal holding costs. Since $dh/dx$ is the marginal holding cost, increasing marginal holding costs are characterized by $d^2h/dx^2 > 0$. Therefore, *our holding cost $h(x)$ is also a convex function of $x$.*

Thus, since both the production and holding costs are characterized by the common and realistic assumption of increasing marginal costs, so is the total cost,

$$c(x) = p(x) + h(x).$$

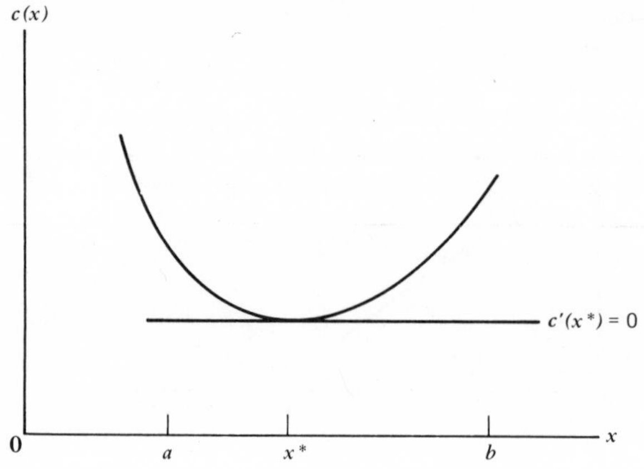


Figure 74

That is, $d^2c/dx^2 > 0$, implying *the total cost function is also a convex function.*

Convex cost functions such as $c(x)$ possess properties conducive to determining optimal policies for mathematical models in management science. Specifically, from elementary calculus we know that *any critical point of a convex function* $c(x)$ *on an open interval,* $a < x < b$, *is a minimizing point for* $c(x)$*;* that is, if a point $x^*$, $a < x^* < b$, satisfies $(dc/dx)(x^*) = 0$, $x^*$ is a minimizing point of $c(x)$ (see Figure 74). (Critical points of convex functions are never maxima, since $c''(x^*) \geq 0$.) Furthermore, an examination of a convex function, such as the convex function shown in Figure 74, indicates that it has a single minimum value; that is, $x^*$ is a global minimum of $c(x)$ on $a < x < b$. For functions, in general, as shown in Figure 75, a

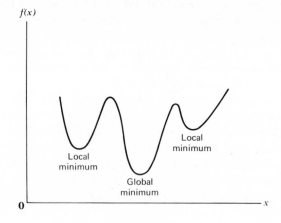

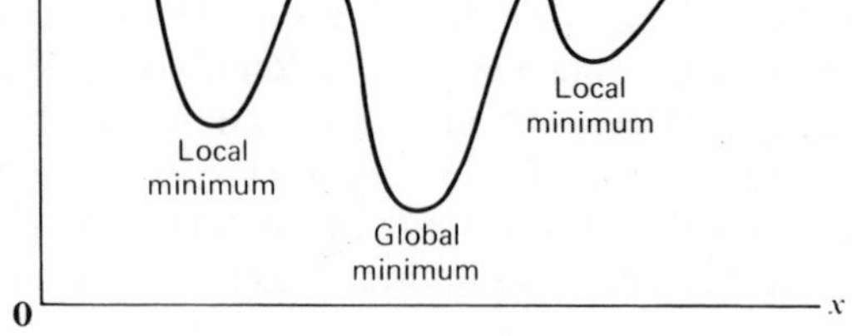


Figure 75

local minimum need not be a global minimum. But for convex functions it may be proved that *any local minimum is also a global minimum.*

Convex functions of two or more variables also frequently occur in mathematical modeling problems in management science. Convexity helps in the optimization of a function of several variables, as it does for one variable. Here we wish to develop several useful characterizations of convex functions of $n \geq 1$ independent variables. For illustrative purposes, in our study we frequently restrict $n$ to 1 or 2.

For convenience we write a function $f(x_1, \ldots, x_n)$ of $n \geq 1$ independent variables in the vector form, $f(\mathbf{x})$, where $\mathbf{x} = (x_1, \ldots, x_n) \in \mathbb{R}^n$. We now extend several familiar concepts to such functions. If $f(\mathbf{x})$ is defined on a set $K \subset \mathbb{R}^n$ and there exists a point $\mathbf{x}^* \in K$ such that $f(\mathbf{x}) \geq f(\mathbf{x}^*)$ for all $\mathbf{x} \in K$, $\mathbf{x}^*$ is called a *global minimizing point* of $f$ in $K$. If $f(\mathbf{x}) \geq f(\mathbf{x}^*)$ for all $\mathbf{x}$ in some neighborhood of $\mathbf{x}^* \in K$, $\mathbf{x}^*$ is called a *local minimizing point* of $f$ in $K$. The value $f(\mathbf{x}^*)$ is called, respectively, the corresponding *global* or corresponding *local* minimum. Similarly, if $f(\mathbf{x}^*) \geq f(\mathbf{x})$ for all $\mathbf{x} \in K$, $\mathbf{x}^*$ is called a *global maximizing point* of $f$ in $K$. If $f(\mathbf{x}^*) \geq f(\mathbf{x})$ for all $\mathbf{x}$ in a neighborhood of $\mathbf{x}^* \in K$, $\mathbf{x}^*$ is called a *local maximizing point* of $f$ in $K$. The value $f(\mathbf{x}^*)$ is called, respectively, the corresponding *global* or corresponding *local maximum.* (Occasionally in our discussion the term *local* is dropped for convenience, but the property under consideration holds locally.) Finally, a point $\mathbf{x}^*$ in the interior of $K$ such that $\nabla f(\mathbf{x}^*) = (\partial f/\partial x_1, \ldots, \partial f/\partial x_n)|_{\mathbf{x}=\mathbf{x}^*} = \mathbf{0}$ is called a *critical point* of $f$ in $K$.

Before imposing any differentiability conditions, we shall consider the general notion of a convex function of $n \geq 1$ independent variables. We define the family of convex functions in terms of convex sets. A function $f$ defined on a convex subset $K$ of $\mathbb{R}^n$ is said to be *convex* if $f$ satisfies the inequality

$$f[\lambda\mathbf{x} + (1 - \lambda)\mathbf{y}] \leq \lambda f(\mathbf{x}) + (1 - \lambda)f(\mathbf{y})$$

for all points $\mathbf{x}, \mathbf{y} \in K$, $0 \leq \lambda \leq 1$. A convex function is said to be *strictly convex* if the strict inequality

$$f[\lambda\mathbf{x} + (1 - \lambda)\mathbf{y}] < \lambda f(\mathbf{x}) + (1 - \lambda)f(\mathbf{y})$$

is satisfied when $\mathbf{x}, \mathbf{y} \in K$, $\mathbf{x} \neq \mathbf{y}$, $0 < \lambda < 1$.

The geometric interpretation of this definition for functions of a single variable is that the chord of the function connecting $f(\mathbf{x})$ and $f(\mathbf{y})$, $\lambda f(\mathbf{x}) + (1 - \lambda)f(\mathbf{y})$, $0 \leq \lambda \leq 1$, lies above or on the graph of the function, as shown in Figure 76.

A function may be convex on part of its domain but not in its entirety. For instance, consider $f(x) = \sin x$. We see from Figure 77 that $f(x)$ is not convex on all of $\mathbb{R}$ but is convex on the convex set $[\pi, 2\pi]$ because any chord lies above the graph of this function on this interval.

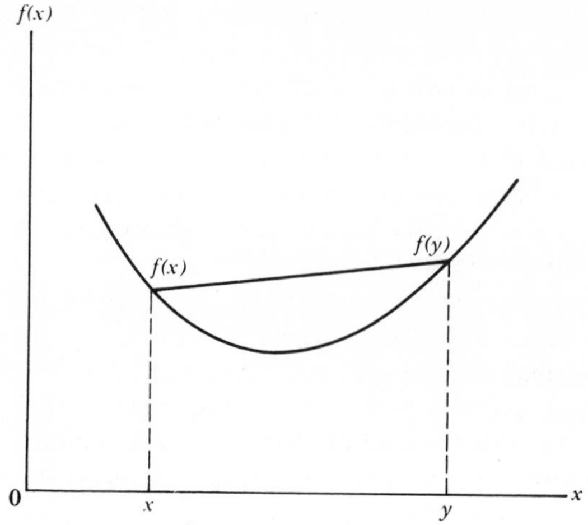


Figure 76

Using the geometric interpretation of the definition of convex functions, one can readily see by examining their graphs that $e^x$, $|x|$, and $x^2$ are examples of convex functions on all of $\mathbb{R}$ (see Figures 78–80.).

Proving that a function is convex by using the definition can be difficult. Consider, for example, $f(x) = x^2$ on the convex set $[-1, 1]$. We must show $[\lambda x_1 + (1 - \lambda)x_2]^2 \leq \lambda x_1^2 + (1 - \lambda)x_2^2$ for all $0 < \lambda < 1$ (the inequality clearly holds for $\lambda = 0$ and $\lambda = 1$). Squaring the left side and transposing terms yields

$$\lambda^2 x_1^2 - \lambda x_1^2 + (1 - \lambda)^2 x_2^2 - (1 - \lambda)x_2^2 + 2\lambda(1 - \lambda)x_1 x_2 \leq 0,$$

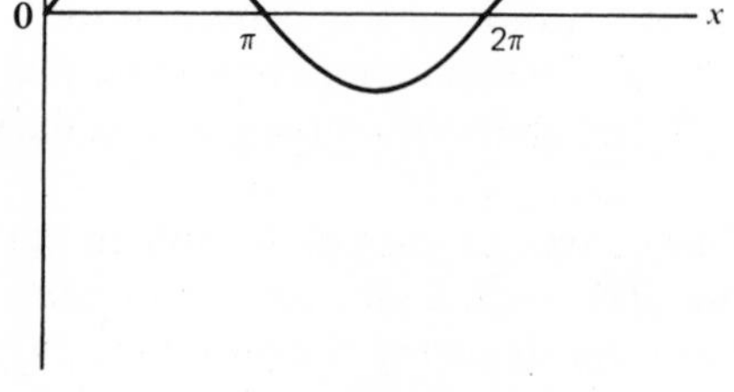

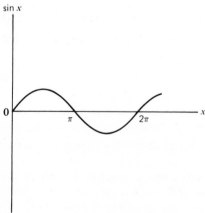

Figure 77

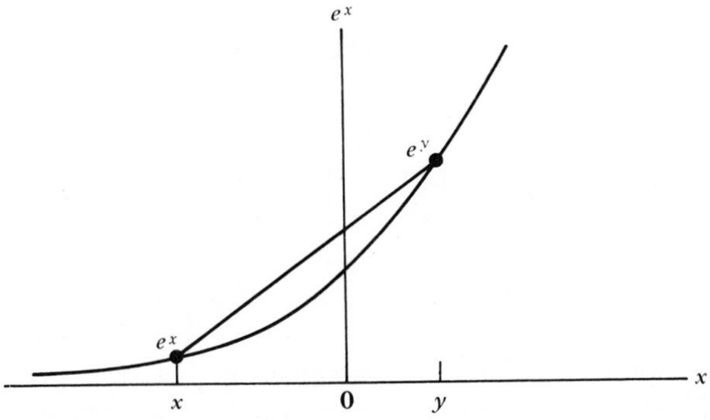


**Figure 78**

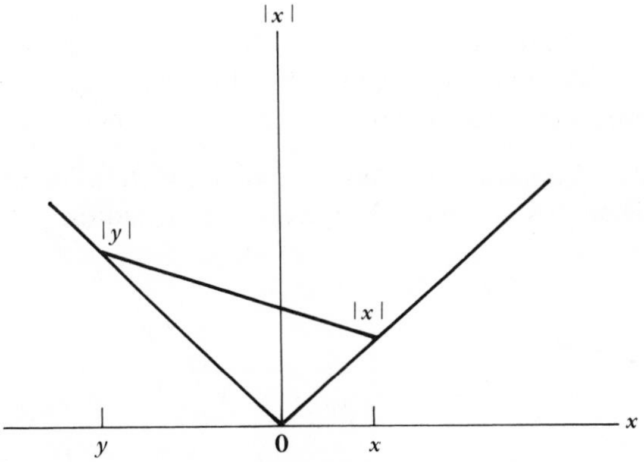


**Figure 79**

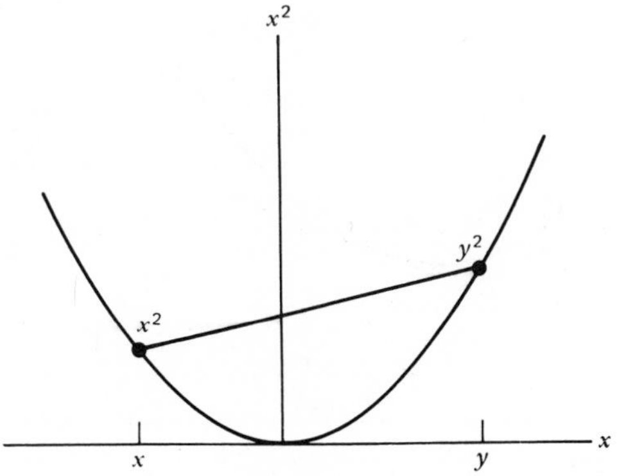


**Figure 80**

which may be written as

$$\lambda(\lambda - 1)x_1^2 - \lambda(1 - \lambda)x_2^2 + 2\lambda(1 - \lambda)x_1x_2 \leq 0$$

or

$$-\lambda(1 - \lambda)x_1^2 - \lambda(1 - \lambda)x_2^2 + 2\lambda(1 - \lambda)x_1x_2 \leq 0.$$

Multiplying both sides by $-1/\lambda(1 - \lambda) < 0$, we get $x_1^2 + x_2^2 - 2x_1x_2 \geq 0$ or $(x_1 - x_2)^2 \geq 0$. Consequently, $f$ is convex, and since the last inequality is strict whenever $x_1 \neq x_2$, $f$ is strictly convex.

Because of the obvious difficulty in applying this characterization of convex functions, we now proceed to develop other characterizations that are easier to apply. For instance, as shown in Figure 81, the graph of a continuously differentiable convex function of one variable $f(y)$ always lies above its tangent lines $f(x) + f'(x)(y - x)$; that is, for any $x$, $y$,

$$f(x) + f'(x)(y - x) \leq f(y).$$

Similarly, the graph of a continuously differentiable convex function of several variables always lies above its tangent planes, $f(\mathbf{x}) + \nabla f(\mathbf{x}) \cdot (\mathbf{y} - \mathbf{x})$. Accordingly, we have the following characterization of convexity:

**THEOREM 28** Suppose $f$ is a differentiable function on an open convex set $K \subset \mathbb{R}^n$. Then $f$ is a convex function on $K$ if and only if for all points $\mathbf{x}, \mathbf{y} \in K$,

$$f(\mathbf{x}) + \nabla f(\mathbf{x}) \cdot (\mathbf{y} - \mathbf{x}) \leq f(\mathbf{y}),$$

where

$$\nabla f(\mathbf{x}) = \left(\frac{\partial f}{\partial x_1}, \ldots, \frac{\partial f}{\partial x_n}\right).$$

**PROOF** Let $\mathbf{x}, \mathbf{y}$ be arbitrary points in $K$ and $0 < \lambda < 1$. Since $K$ is

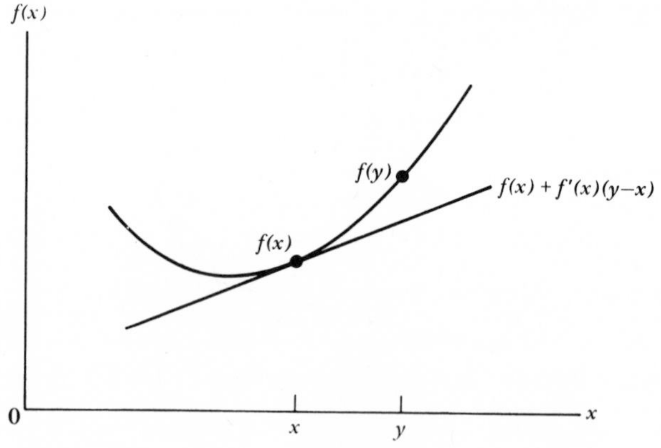


**Figure 81**

convex, $(1 - \lambda)\mathbf{x} + \lambda\mathbf{y} \in K$. Since $f$ is convex on $K$,

$$f[(1 - \lambda)\mathbf{x} + \lambda\mathbf{y}] \le (1 - \lambda)f(\mathbf{x}) + \lambda f(\mathbf{y}). \tag{194}$$

Rewriting the inequality and subtracting $\nabla f(\mathbf{x}) \cdot (\mathbf{y} - \mathbf{x})$ from both sides of expression (194), we obtain

$$\frac{f[(1 - \lambda)\mathbf{x} + \lambda\mathbf{y}] - f(\mathbf{x})}{\lambda} - \nabla f(\mathbf{x}) \cdot (\mathbf{y} - \mathbf{x}) \le f(\mathbf{y}) - f(\mathbf{x}) - \nabla f(\mathbf{x}) \cdot (\mathbf{y} - \mathbf{x}).$$

Since $f$ is differentiable at $\mathbf{x}$ the left side of this expression tends to 0 as $\lambda \to 0^+$. Thus,

$$0 \le f(\mathbf{y}) - f(\mathbf{x}) - \nabla f(\mathbf{x}) \cdot (\mathbf{y} - \mathbf{x}),$$

which is equivalent to the desired result. Now suppose

$$f(\mathbf{x}) + \nabla f(\mathbf{x}) \cdot (\mathbf{y} - \mathbf{x}) \le f(\mathbf{y}) \qquad \text{for all} \qquad \mathbf{x}, \mathbf{y} \in K. \tag{195}$$

Let $\mathbf{x}, \mathbf{y} \in K$ with $\mathbf{x} \neq \mathbf{y}$, and let $0 < \lambda < 1$. Set $\bar{\mathbf{x}} = \lambda\mathbf{y} + (1 - \lambda)\mathbf{x}$. Note that

$$\mathbf{x} = \bar{\mathbf{x}} - \frac{\lambda}{1 - \lambda}(\mathbf{y} - \bar{\mathbf{x}}).$$

Since expression (195) holds by hypothesis, we have

$$f(\mathbf{y}) \ge f(\bar{\mathbf{x}}) + \nabla f(\bar{\mathbf{x}}) \cdot (\mathbf{y} - \bar{\mathbf{x}}), \tag{196}$$

$$f(\mathbf{x}) \ge f(\bar{\mathbf{x}}) + \nabla f(\bar{\mathbf{x}}) \cdot (\mathbf{y} - \bar{\mathbf{x}})\left(\frac{-\lambda}{1 - \lambda}\right). \tag{197}$$

Multiplying expression (196) by $\lambda/(1 - \lambda)$ and adding it to expression (197), we obtain

$$\frac{\lambda}{1 - \lambda} f(\mathbf{y}) + f(\mathbf{x}) \ge \left(\frac{\lambda}{1 - \lambda} + 1\right) f(\bar{\mathbf{x}})$$

or

$$\lambda f(\mathbf{y}) + (1 - \lambda)f(\mathbf{x}) \ge f(\bar{\mathbf{x}}).$$

Hence, we have shown

$$\lambda f(\mathbf{y}) + (1 - \lambda)f(\mathbf{x}) \ge f[\lambda\mathbf{y} + (1 - \lambda)\mathbf{x}] \qquad \text{for} \qquad 0 < \lambda < 1.$$

This inequality holds trivially for $\lambda = 0$ or $\lambda = 1$. Therefore, $f$ is convex. ▮

An analogous result holds for strictly convex functions:

THEOREM 29 Let $f$ be a continuously differentiable function on an open convex set $K$. Then $f$ is strictly convex if and only if

$$f(\mathbf{y}) > f(\mathbf{x}) + \nabla f(\mathbf{x}) \cdot (\mathbf{y} - \mathbf{x}),$$

$(\mathbf{x} \neq \mathbf{y})$. ▮

Using Theorem 28, we prove that the function $f(x) = x^2$ is convex for all $x$. Since $(y - x)^2 \geq 0$, $y^2 \geq -x^2 + 2xy$ or $y^2 \geq x^2 + 2x(y - x)$. The latter is equivalent to $f(y) \geq f(x) + f'(x)(y - x)$, implying $f(x) = x^2$ is convex.

It is also relatively difficult to apply Theorem 28 in characterizing convex functions. We now proceed to indicate other characterizations that are easier to apply. For twice continuously differentiable functions of one variable, we have seen the following simple characterization of convexity:

**THEOREM 30** Suppose $f$ is a twice continuously differentiable function on the convex set $K$ in $\mathbb{R}$. Then $f$ is convex on $K$ if and only if $f''(x) \geq 0$ for all $x \in K$, and $f$ is strictly convex on $K$ if and only if $f''(x) > 0$ for all $x \in K$. ▮

The analogous result for functions of several variables is as follows:

**THEOREM 31** Suppose $f$ is a twice continuously differentiable function on an open convex set $K$ in $\mathbb{R}^n$. Then $f$ is convex on $K$ if and only if

$$\mathbf{y}^T \cdot \mathbf{H}(\mathbf{x})\mathbf{y} \geq 0$$

for all $\mathbf{y} \in \mathbb{R}^n$ and $\mathbf{x} \in K$, where

$$\mathbf{H}(\mathbf{x}) = \begin{pmatrix} f_{x_1x_1}(\mathbf{x}) & f_{x_1x_2}(\mathbf{x}) \cdots f_{x_1x_n}(\mathbf{x}) \\ \cdot & \cdot \\ \cdot & \cdot \\ \cdot & \cdot \\ f_{x_nx_1}(\mathbf{x}) & f_{x_nx_2}(\mathbf{x}) \cdots f_{x_nx_n}(\mathbf{x}) \end{pmatrix}. \quad ▮$$

(If inequality holds strictly in Theorem 31, we have strict convexity.)

For example, $f(x_1, x_2) = x_1^2 + x_2^2 + 7$ is convex on $\mathbb{R}^2$ because

$$(y_1, y_2) \cdot \begin{pmatrix} f_{x_1x_1} & f_{x_1x_2} \\ f_{x_2x_1} & f_{x_2x_2} \end{pmatrix} \begin{pmatrix} y_1 \\ y_2 \end{pmatrix} = (y_1, y_2) \cdot \begin{pmatrix} 2 & 0 \\ 0 & 2 \end{pmatrix} \begin{pmatrix} y_1 \\ y_2 \end{pmatrix} = 2y_1^2 + 2y_2^2 \geq 0,$$

for any $\mathbf{y} = (y_1, y_2) \in \mathbb{R}^2$.

The function $f(x_1, x_2, x_3) = -\ln x_1 - x_2 + e^{x_3}$ is convex on the convex set $\{(x_1, x_2, x_3) : x_1 > 0\}$ because

$$(y_1, y_2, y_3) \cdot \begin{pmatrix} \frac{1}{x_1^2} & 0 & 0 \\ 0 & 0 & 0 \\ 0 & 0 & e^{x_3} \end{pmatrix} \begin{pmatrix} y_1 \\ y_2 \\ y_3 \end{pmatrix} = \frac{y_1^2}{x_1^2} + y_3^2 e^{x_3} \geq 0.$$

As a third example, note that $f(x_1, x_2, x_3, x_4) = -\ln(x_1x_2x_3x_4)$ is convex on the open convex set $\{(x_1, x_2, x_3, x_4): x_i > 0, i = 1, 2, 3, 4\}$, since

$$(y_1, y_2, y_3, y_4) \cdot \begin{pmatrix} \frac{1}{x_1^2} & 0 & 0 & 0 \\ 0 & \frac{1}{x_2^2} & 0 & 0 \\ 0 & 0 & \frac{1}{x_3^2} & 0 \\ 0 & 0 & 0 & \frac{1}{x_4^2} \end{pmatrix} \begin{pmatrix} y_1 \\ y_2 \\ y_3 \\ y_4 \end{pmatrix}$$

$$= \frac{y_1^2}{x_1^2} + \frac{y_2^2}{x_2^2} + \frac{y_3^2}{x_3^2} + \frac{y_4^2}{x_4^2} \geq 0.$$

The function $f(x_1, x_2) = c_1x_1 + (c_2/x_1) + c_3x_2 + (c_4/x_2)$, $(c_i > 0, i = 1, 2, 3, 4)$ is convex on the open convex set $\{(x_1, x_2): x_1 > 0, x_2 > 0\}$ because

$$(y_1, y_2) \begin{pmatrix} \frac{2c_2}{x_1^3} & 0 \\ 0 & \frac{2c_4}{x_2^3} \end{pmatrix} \begin{pmatrix} y_1 \\ y_2 \end{pmatrix} = \frac{2c_2y_1^2}{x_1^3} + \frac{2c_4y_2^2}{x_2^3} \geq 0.$$

Observe that we may use Theorem 31 to conclude that functions of the form

$$f(\mathbf{x}) = a_0 + a_1x_1 + \cdots + a_nx_n,$$

defined on $\mathbb{R}^n$, are convex. This follows, since all entries of the corresponding matrix $\mathbf{H}(\mathbf{x})$ are identically zero, and thus,

$$\mathbf{y}^T \cdot \mathbf{H}(\mathbf{x})\mathbf{y} = 0.$$

Functions of this form are termed *affine functions.*

Frequently the "test" for convexity discussed in Theorem 31 is also very difficult to apply. As is demonstrated later in this chapter, convex functions are sometimes constructed from known convex functions and, in this manner, may be shown to be convex. Such constructions of convex functions are particularly apparent in applications involving convexity.

In addition to the family of convex functions, the class of *concave functions* is equally important in management science. Concave functions are also defined only for convex domains. A function $f$ defined on a convex

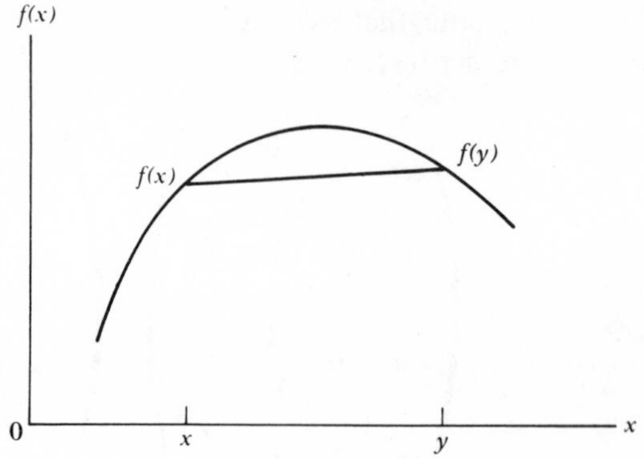


Figure 82

set $K \subset \mathbb{R}^n$ is said to be *concave* if $f$ satisfies the inequality

$$f(\lambda\mathbf{x} + (1 - \lambda)\mathbf{y}) \geq \lambda f(\mathbf{x}) + (1 - \lambda)f(\mathbf{y})$$

for all points $\mathbf{x}, \mathbf{y} \in K$, $0 \leq \lambda \leq 1$. A concave function is said to be *strictly concave* if

$$f[\lambda\mathbf{x} + (1 - \lambda)\mathbf{y}] > \lambda f(\mathbf{x}) + (1 - \lambda)f(\mathbf{y})$$

for any $\mathbf{x}, \mathbf{y} \in K$, $0 < \lambda < 1$.

For concave functions of one variable we may interpret this definition as stating that the chord of the graph always lies below or on the graph of the function (see Figure 82).

By examining their graphs we see that $\ln x$ and $-|x|$ are concave on $\mathbb{R}$ and that $\cos x$ is concave on $[-\pi/2, \pi/2]$ (see Figures 83–85).

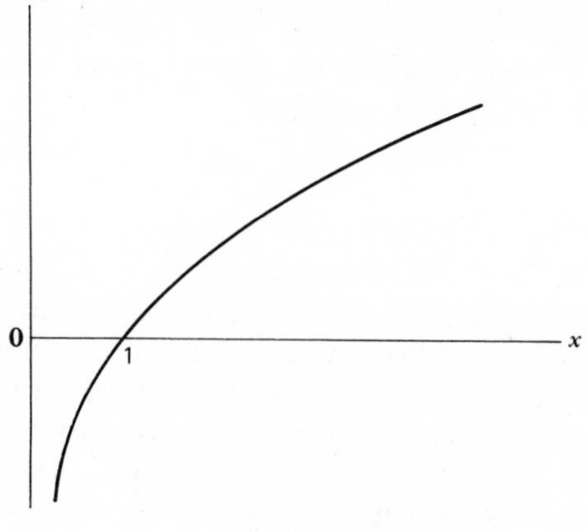


Figure 83

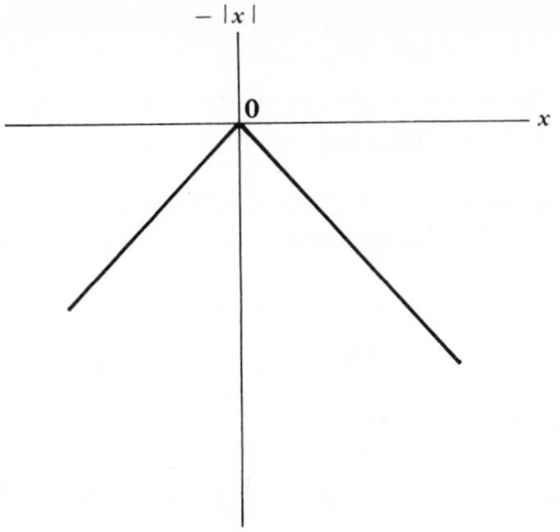


Figure 84

Observe that the definition for a concave function is obtained from the definition of a convex function by simply reversing the direction of the defining inequality. Intuitively a concave function of one variable may be obtained, for instance, by flipping a convex function of one variable over the $x$-axis—that is, by taking its negative. In fact, since

$$f[\lambda \mathbf{x} + (1 - \lambda)\mathbf{y}] \leq \lambda f(\mathbf{x}) + (1 - \lambda)f(\mathbf{y})$$

if and only if

$$-f[\lambda \mathbf{x} + (1 - \lambda)\mathbf{y}] \geq \lambda[-f(\mathbf{x})] + (1 - \lambda)[-f(\mathbf{y})]$$

for $\mathbf{x}$, $\mathbf{y}$ in a convex subset of $\mathbb{R}^n$, $0 \leq \lambda \leq 1$, we have the following result:

THEOREM 32 $f$ is a convex function on a convex set $K \subset \mathbb{R}^n$ if and only if $-f$ is a concave function on $K \subset \mathbb{R}^n$. ▮

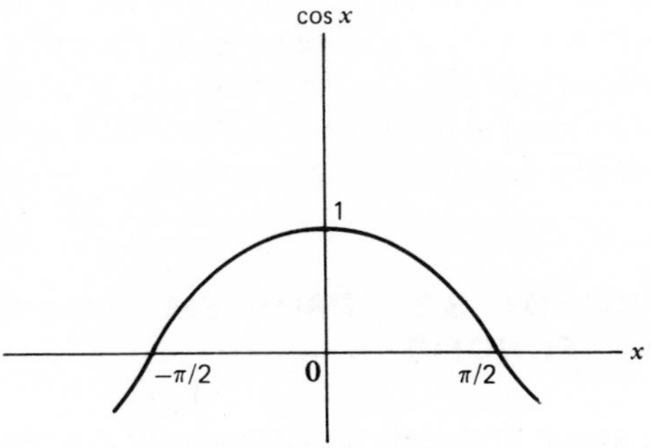


Figure 85

(Note that we have imposed no differentiability condition on $f$ in Theorem 32.)

Theorem 32 implies that each result for convex functions has an analog for concave functions. For instance, we have the following result:

**THEOREM 33** Suppose $f$ is a twice continuously differentiable function on a convex set $K \subset \mathbb{R}^n$. The function $f$ is concave on $K$ if and only if

$$\mathbf{y}^T \cdot \mathbf{H}(\mathbf{x})\mathbf{y} \leq 0$$

for all $\mathbf{y} \in \mathbb{R}^n$ and $\mathbf{x} \in K$, where $\mathbf{H}(\mathbf{x})$ is as in Theorem 31. ∎

From this result we see that

$$f(x_1, x_2) = \ln(1 + px_1 + qx_2) \qquad (p, q > 0)$$

is concave on the closed convex set $\{(x_1, x_2): x_1 \geq 0, x_2 \geq 0\}$ because

$$(y_1, y_2) \cdot \begin{pmatrix} \dfrac{-p^2}{(1 + px_1 + qx_2)^2} & \dfrac{-pq}{(1 + px_1 + qx_2)^2} \\ \dfrac{-pq}{(1 + px_1 + qx_2)^2} & \dfrac{-q^2}{(1 + px_1 + qx_2)^2} \end{pmatrix} \begin{pmatrix} y_1 \\ y_2 \end{pmatrix}$$

$$= \frac{-(py_1 + qy_2)^2}{(1 + px_1 + qx_2)^2} \leq 0.$$

Similarly, the analog of Theorem 28 is the following:

**THEOREM 34** Suppose $f$ is a continuously differentiable function on an open convex set $K \subset \mathbb{R}^n$. Then $f$ is concave on $K$ if and only if

$$f(\mathbf{y}) \leq f(\mathbf{x}) + \nabla f(\mathbf{x}) \cdot (\mathbf{y} - \mathbf{x})$$

for all $\mathbf{x}, \mathbf{y} \in K$. ∎

For functions of one variable on an interval $I$, this result states that the tangent to the curve $f(\mathbf{x})$ always lies above or on the curve for points in $I$.

Having developed several characterizations of convex and concave functions, we now proceed to investigate mathematical models characterized by convex and concave functional relationships.

## AN ECONOMIC LOT SIZE PROBLEM: MINIMIZING CONVEX COST FUNCTIONS

One of the fundamental problems of management science is that of determining inventory policies for industry. Perhaps the most common inventory problem is the economic lot size problem. It concerns the situation in which the stock levels are depleted with time and are then replenished by the arrival of new items.

In this economic lot size problem, assume our inventory consists of two products, $a$ and $b$, which are withdrawn continuously at a known constant rate $r$. Further, assuming the annual demand for each product is known, suppose that items are ordered in equal numbers several times a year and that, after the inventory is depleted, a new stock arrives instantaneously. Denote by $x_1$ the number of units of product $a$ and by $x_2$ the number of units of product $b$ to be ordered each time.

The costs to be considered here are the ordering and holding cost. If each product has an annual demand of $D$ units, then the number of times an order is to be placed is approximately $D/x_1$ for product $a$ and $D/x_2$ for product $b$. If the cost of a single order for product $a$ is $\alpha$ and for product $b$ is $\beta$, then the total ordering cost is

$$\alpha \frac{D}{x_1} + \beta \frac{D}{x_2}.$$

Assume the holding or storage cost for each unit of product $a$ is $\gamma$ and for each unit of product $b$ is also $\gamma$. Since the depletion is uniform, the average inventories are $x_1/2$ and $x_2/2$ (see Figure 86). Hence, the total average holding cost is

$$\gamma \frac{x_1}{2} + \gamma \frac{x_2}{2}.$$

Thus, the total cost function is the sum of the holding and ordering costs:

$$c(x_1, x_2) = \alpha \frac{D}{x_1} + \beta \frac{D}{x_2} + \gamma \frac{x_1}{2} + \gamma \frac{x_2}{2}, \tag{198}$$

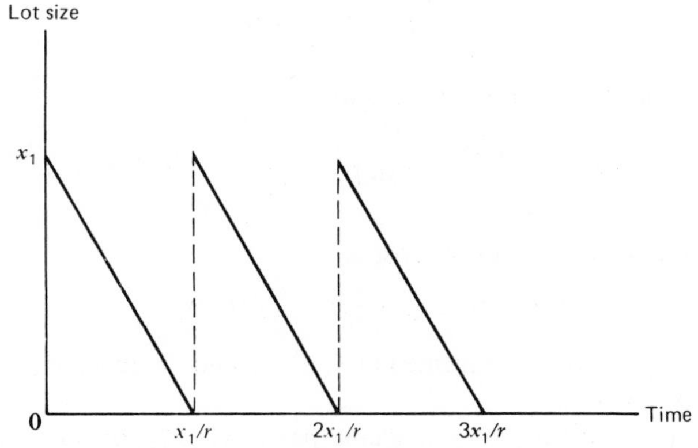


**Figure 86**

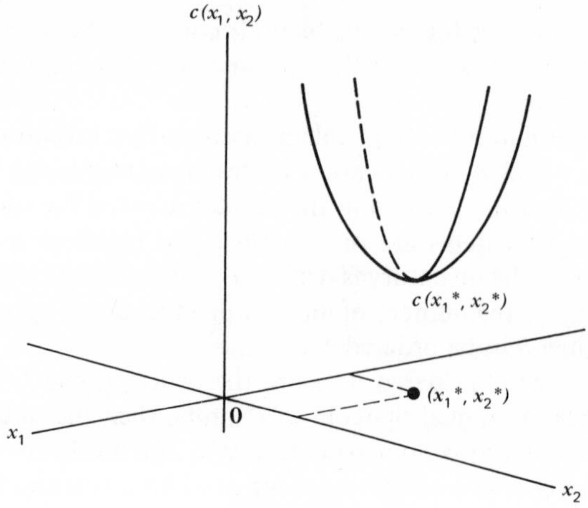


Figure 87

$x_1 > 0, x_2 > 0$. As we have seen in the previous section, $c(x_1, x_2)$ is a twice continuously differentiable convex function defined on the open convex set $K = \{(x_1, x_2): x_1 > 0, x_2 > 0\} \subset \mathbb{R}^2$.

The economic lot size problem is now to determine what size lots, $x_1$ and $x_2$, should be ordered to *minimize* the total cost, (198). From the graph of $c(x_1, x_2)$, shown in Figure 87, we see that the minimum of $c$ over $K$ obviously occurs for $x_1 = x_1^*$, $x_2 = x_2^*$ satisfying $\nabla c(x_1^*, x_2^*) = (\partial c/\partial x_1, \partial c/\partial x_2) = (0, 0)$. For other points $(x_1, x_2) \neq (x_1^*, x_2^*)$ in $K$, $c(x_1, x_2) > c(x_1^*, x_2^*)$. Therefore, the minimum of $c$ on $K$ occurs at the point satisfying

$$\frac{\partial c}{\partial x_1} = \frac{\gamma}{2} - \alpha \frac{D}{x_1^2} = 0,$$

$$\frac{\partial c}{\partial x_2} = \frac{\gamma}{2} - \beta \frac{D}{x_2^2} = 0.$$

That is, the optimal economic lot sizes are

$$x_1^* = \sqrt{\frac{2\alpha D}{\gamma}} \quad \text{and} \quad x_2^* = \sqrt{\frac{2\beta D}{\gamma}}$$

and the minimum total inventory cost is

$$c(x_1^*, x_2^*) = \sqrt{2\alpha\gamma D} + \sqrt{2\beta\gamma D}.$$

(How do variations in the parameters $\alpha$, $\beta$, $\gamma$, and $D$ affect the values of $x_1^*$, $x_2^*$, and $c(x_1^*, x_2^*)$?)

Thus, we determined the *minimizing point* $(x_1^*, x_2^*)$, of $c(x_1, x_2)$ on the open convex set $K \subset \mathbb{R}^2$ by just finding the critical point of $c(x_1, x_2)$ on $K$.

It was unnecessary to examine the signs of

$$\frac{\partial^2 c}{\partial x_1^2}\frac{\partial^2 c}{\partial x_2^2} - \left(\frac{\partial^2 c}{\partial x_1\,\partial x_2}\right)^2 \quad \text{and} \quad \frac{\partial^2 c}{\partial x_1^2} + \frac{\partial^2 c}{\partial x_2^2} \tag{199}$$

at a critical point $(x_1^*, x_2^*)$ as we must do to find the minimizing points of an arbitrary twice continuously differentiable function of two variables. This property is not unique to convex function (198). Observe that if $f$ is an arbitrary continuously differentiable convex function on an *open* convex set $K \subset \mathbb{R}^n$, Theorem 28 implies that

$$f(\mathbf{y}) \geq f(\mathbf{x}) + \nabla f(\mathbf{x}) \cdot (\mathbf{y} - \mathbf{x}) \tag{200}$$

for all $\mathbf{x}, \mathbf{y} \in K$. If for some $\mathbf{x} = \mathbf{x}^* \in K$, $\nabla f(\mathbf{x}^*) = \mathbf{0}$, then inequality (200) implies

$$f(\mathbf{y}) \geq f(\mathbf{x}^*)$$

for all $\mathbf{y} \in K$; that is, $\mathbf{x}^*$ is a minimizing point of $f$ on $K$. The reverse statement—if $\mathbf{x}^*$ is a minimizing point of $f$ on $K$, then $\nabla f(\mathbf{x}^*) = \mathbf{0}$—follows from the calculus. Therefore, we have the following important result:

**THEOREM 35** Suppose $f$ is a continuously differentiable convex function on an *open* convex set $K \subset \mathbb{R}^n$. Then $\mathbf{x}^* \in K$ is a minimizing point of $f$ on $K$ if and only if $\nabla f(\mathbf{x}^*) = \mathbf{0}$. ▮

Thus, in general, we need not investigate second-order conditions such as (199) to determine if a critical point of a convex function on an open convex set is a minimizing point.

The latter result implies that a convex function $f$ has a minimizing point $\mathbf{x}^*$ in the *interior* of a convex set $K \subset \mathbb{R}^n$ if and only if $\nabla f(\mathbf{x}^*) = \mathbf{0}$. Consider, for instance, the convex function

$$f(x_1, x_2) = x_1^2 + x_2^2 + 7$$

defined on the *closed* convex set $K = \{(x_1, x_2): x_1 \geq -1, x_2 \geq -2\}$. Here $f$ attains its minimum value at the point $(0, 0) \in K$, since $\nabla f(0, 0) = (0, 0)$ and $(0, 0)$ is in the *interior* of $K$.

We have seen that for convex functions of one variable, the local minimizing points are always global minimizing points. Convex functions of several variables also exhibit this somewhat remarkable and useful property.

**THEOREM 36** Each local minimizing point of a convex function on a convex set $K$ is also a global minimizing point of this convex function on $K$.

**PROOF** Suppose that $f$ is a convex function over a convex set $K$ and that $\mathbf{x}^*$ is a local minimizing point for $f$ over $K$; that is, $f(\mathbf{x}^*) \leq f(\mathbf{x})$ for $\mathbf{x}$ in a

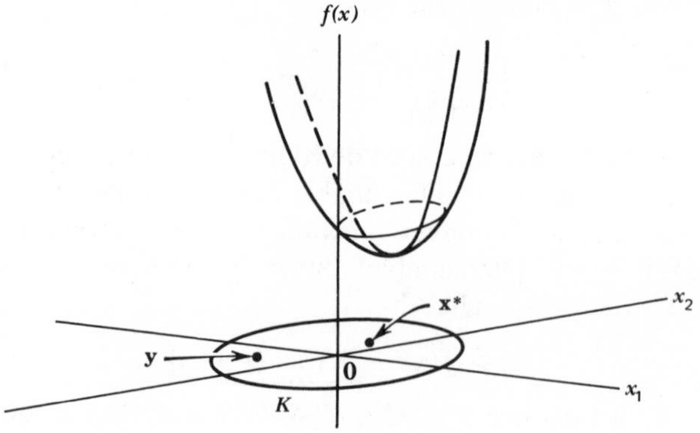


Figure 88

sufficiently small neighborhood $N$ of $\mathbf{x}^*$ contained in $K$ (see Figure 88). Given a point $\mathbf{y}$ in $K$, the point $(1 - s)\mathbf{x}^* + s\mathbf{y}$ is within $N$ when $1 > s\,(>0)$ is sufficiently small; this is true because $K$ is convex and $(1 - s)\mathbf{x}^* + s\mathbf{y} \to \mathbf{x}^*$ as $s \to 0$. Hence, since $\mathbf{x}^*$ is a local minimum,

$$f(\mathbf{x}^*) \leq f[(1 - s)\mathbf{x}^* + s\mathbf{y}].$$

But since $f$ is convex,

$$f[(1 - s)\mathbf{x}^* + s\mathbf{y}] \leq (1 - s)f(\mathbf{x}^*) + sf(\mathbf{y}).$$

Combining these two inequalities, we see that

$$f(\mathbf{x}^*) \leq (1 - s)f(\mathbf{x}^*) + sf(\mathbf{y})$$

or

$$sf(\mathbf{x}^*) \leq sf(\mathbf{y}).$$

Since $s > 0$, this implies

$$f(\mathbf{x}^*) \leq f(\mathbf{y}).$$

Because $\mathbf{y}$ is an arbitrary point of $K$, the latter inequality implies that the local minimizing point $\mathbf{x}^*$ is also a global minimizing point of $f$ over $K$.

(This result assures the absolute optimality of the stock level $x_1^*$, $x_2^*$ in our economic lot size model.)

Frequently, the minimizing point of a convex function defined on a closed convex set $K$ lies on the boundary of $K$. For instance, consider the convex function $f(x) = x^2$ defined on the closed convex set $\{x : 2 \leq x \leq 3\}$. As shown in Figure 89, the minimizing point $x^*$ is the boundary point $x^* = 2$, but $f'(x^*) \neq 0$. Minimization theorems dealing with these types of problems will be treated later in our study of convex programming.

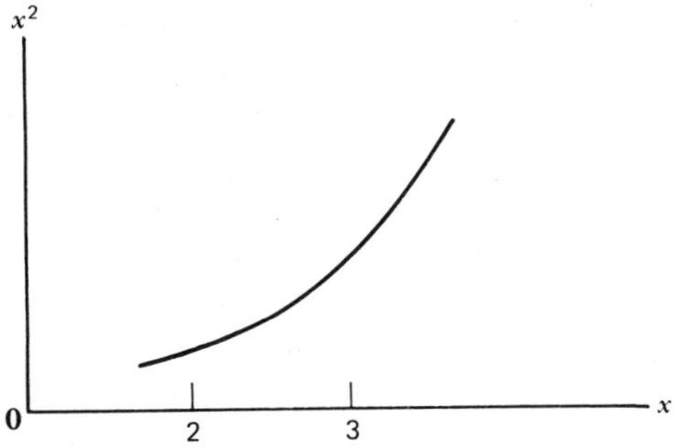


Figure 89

## A MODEL OF PSYCHOECONOMICS: MAXIMIZING CONCAVE UTILITY FUNCTIONS

As our previous discussion indicated, the structure and assumptions of many mathematical models in the social and managerial sciences result in functional relationships characterized by convexity. Similarly, concave functions are frequently employed in these mathematical models, particularly those describing a consumer's satisfaction. And, concavity, like convexity, is usually helpful in finding optimal solutions for the model. Here we construct an elementary mathematical model of psychoeconomics that gives rise to a *concave* utility function.

Consider a situation where two countries each produce a different good and each exchanges its product for an equal fraction of the other's product. Neither country exchanges its good with a third country. Each country wishes to choose a production level that maximizes its own satisfaction, but neither country responds to the needs of the other. When both countries are in equilibrium (i.e., both have maximized their satisfaction), neither country wishes to depart from this point by its own effort, because the result is an immediate decrease of its satisfaction. We shall construct a mathematical model of this situation and determine an equilibrium point as well as conditions under which one country may become parasitic on the other (i.e., cease to produce its product).

The fundamental problem in developing this mathematical model is that of constructing a measure of each country's satisfaction. For this purpose, we introduce the *utility function*. The utility function indicates the amount of satisfaction or utility each consumer receives from various amounts of different commodities. In our model the utility that each country derives depends both on the amounts of each good consumed and on its own efforts of production.

Each country would seem to receive "positive satisfaction" from consumption of both of the goods and "negative satisfaction" from their own efforts of production. Furthermore, another realistic assumption would seem to be diminishing marginal utility on the former; that is, each country's satisfaction with the total goods received will grow at a slower and slower rate with consumption of each successive unit of the goods.

The mathematical formulation of marginal utility is analogous to that of marginal cost. Suppose a country derives utility $u$ from consuming $x$ units of one of several products. If the amount consumed is increased by an arbitrarily small amount $\Delta x$, then the utility will be increased by an amount $\Delta u$. The average utility of consuming this additional amount is $\Delta u/\Delta x$. The limiting value of this quotient is $\partial u/\partial x$, defined to be the *marginal utility*. Since $\partial u/\partial x$ is the marginal utility, decreasing marginal utility means

$$\frac{\partial^2 u}{\partial x^2} < 0.$$

Let us now proceed to construct a utility function exhibiting these characteristics for each country.

In developing the utility function of each country, let us assume that country 1 and country 2 produce goods in amounts $x$ and $y$, respectively. Suppose that each country exchanges a fixed fraction $p$, $0 \leq p \leq 1$, of this good for an equal fraction of the other's. Hence, each country keeps a fraction $1 - p$ of his own good.

Consider the utility function $u_1 = u_1(x, y)$ for the first country. According to the preceding paragraph, country 1 receives $py$ units of the second country's product and keeps $(1 - p)x$ units of its own product. Hence, country 1 receives a total of $(1 - p)x + py$ units of goods. Since country 1 is assumed to derive "positive satisfaction" from consumption of these goods, the function $c_1$ measuring the satisfaction due to consumption must satisfy

$$c_1[(1 - p)x + py] > 0 \quad \text{for} \quad x > 0, y > 0, \tag{201}$$

and

$$c_1[(1 - p)x + py] = 0 \quad \text{for} \quad x = 0, y = 0. \tag{202}$$

Further, because we have assumed that $c_1$ exhibits diminishing marginal utility, we have

$$\frac{\partial^2 c_1}{\partial x^2} < 0 \quad \text{and} \quad \frac{\partial^2 c_1}{\partial y^2} < 0 \tag{203}$$

for $x > 0$, $y > 0$.

It is not difficult to construct functions satisfying properties (201)–(203). For example, the functions $\alpha\sqrt{(1 - p)x + py}$ and $\alpha \ln [1 + (1 - p)x + py]$,

$\alpha > 0$, satisfy all three. (Note that a 1 is added to the argument of ln so that when there is no production, $x = y = 0$, satisfaction is zero.) As we shall see below, the function

$$\alpha \ln [1 + (1 - p)x + py],$$

$\alpha > 0$, is chosen here as a measure of satisfaction derived from consumption, because it is better suited for the problem of maximizing satisfaction.

We also assumed that each country receives "negative satisfaction" from its efforts of production. Let us make the simplifying assumption that this negative satisfaction is proportional to the quantity produced. For country 1, the negative satisfaction derived from the effort involved in production is

$$-qx, \qquad q > 0.$$

Thus, the total satisfaction of the first country is measured by the utility function

$$u_1(x, y) = \ln [1 + (1 - p)x + py] - qx \tag{204}$$

for $x > 0$, $y > 0$. To guarantee the existence of a production level $x$ corresponding to maximum satisfaction, we assume $q \leq 1 - p$. Note that with $q > 0$, the first country's satisfaction may be negative for large values of $x$.

A similar analysis for country 2 yields the utility function

$$u_2(x, y) = \ln [1 + (1 - p)y + px] - qy \tag{205}$$

for $x > 0$, $y > 0$. Note that we have assumed that the negative satisfaction derived from the effort of production is given by the same proportion of output, $q$, as for country 1.

The concavity of the utility functions (204) and (205) on the open convex set $K = \{(x, y): x > 0, y > 0\}$ is easily verified. By examining the graphs of $u_1$ and $u_2$ on the open convex set $K$, we see that the maximum of each of these functions occurs at their critical points in $K$ (see Figure 90). Indeed, such a result holds for all continuously differentiable concave functions on an open convex set:

**THEOREM 37** Suppose $f$ is a continuously differentiable concave function on an open convex set $K \subset \mathbb{R}^n$. $\mathbf{x}^* \in K$ is a maximizing point of $f$ on $K$ if and only if $\nabla f(\mathbf{x}^*) = \mathbf{0}$. ▮

Moreover, in analogy to convex functions, we also have the following result characterizing the maximizing points:

**THEOREM 38** Each local maximizing point of a concave function on a convex set $K$ is also a global maximizing point of this concave function on $K$. ▮

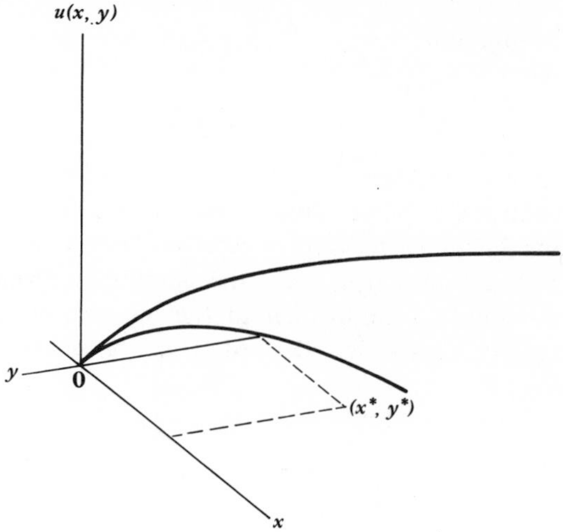


**Figure 90**

(The ideas of the proofs of Theorems 37 and 38 are similar to those of Theorems 35 and 36, respectively.)

Thus, according to Theorems 37 and 38 the global maximizing points of our utility functions $u_1$ and $u_2$ occur whenever

$$\frac{\partial u_1}{\partial x} = 0, \qquad \frac{\partial u_1}{\partial y} = 0$$

and

$$\frac{\partial u_2}{\partial x} = 0, \qquad \frac{\partial u_2}{\partial y} = 0,$$

respectively. Further, from these results we may conclude that the first and second countries may maximize their own satisfaction by determining $x$ and $y$ that satisfy

(206) $$\frac{\partial u_1}{\partial x} = \frac{1 - p}{1 + (1 - p)x + py} - q = 0$$

and

(207) $$\frac{\partial u_2}{\partial y} = \frac{1 - p}{1 + (1 - p)y + px} - q = 0,$$

$x > 0$, $y > 0$, respectively, for given levels of the other country's product.

Equations (206) and (207) define the lines of maximum satisfaction for countries 1 and 2, respectively.

Let us examine the "optimal lines" (206) and (207). These equations can be rewritten as

$$y = -\frac{(1-p)}{p}x + \frac{(1-p-q)}{pq}, \tag{206'}$$

and

$$y = -\frac{p}{1-p}x + \frac{(1-p-q)}{(1-p)q}. \tag{207'}$$

We see that the slopes of these optimal lines are $-[(1-p)/p]$ and $-[p/(1-p)]$, respectively. If $p \neq \frac{1}{2}$, an *equilibrium* occurs at the point of intersection of (206′) and (207′):

$$x^* = y^* = \frac{1-p}{q} - 1.$$

At this point, both countries have maximized their satisfaction. (If $p = \frac{1}{2}$, these optimal lines coincide, a case not considered here.)

Note that if $(1-p) > p$ (that is, $\frac{1}{2} > p$ and each country exports less than half of its product), these optimum lines appear as in Figure 91. If each country is allowed to adjust its effort, while the other keeps its constant, the behavior will be as shown in Figure 91. That is, if country 1 produces $x_1$ units, country 2 will produce $y_1$ units in order to be on country 2's optimum line. Then country 1 chooses to produce $x_2$ units to be on its optimum line.

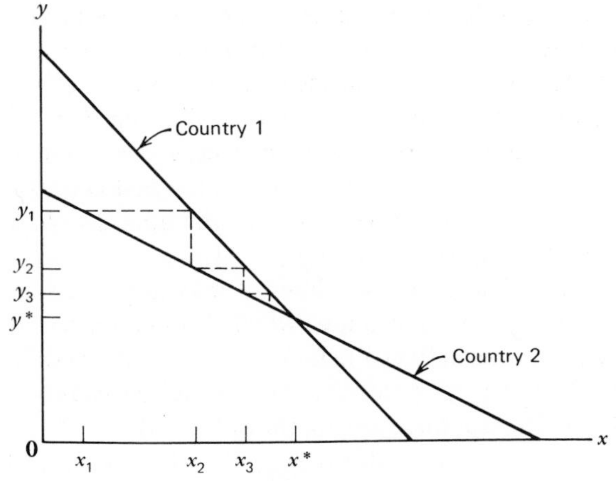


**Figure 91**

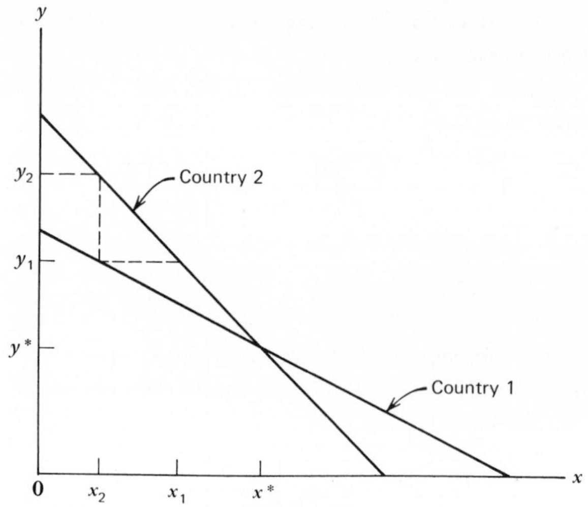


**Figure 92**

Country 2 responds by producing $y_2$ units so as to operate on its optimum line. As the process continues, it is readily seen that these points $(x_i, y_i)$ tend to the equilibrium point $(x^*, y^*)$; that is, both countries maximize their satisfaction.

However, if each country exports more of its product than it keeps, $p > 1 - p$ (or $p > \frac{1}{2}$), the optimum lines are as in Figure 92. Again, if each country is allowed to adjust its effort, while the other keeps its constant, the behavior will be as in Figure 92. If country 1 produces $x_1$ units, then country 2 will respond by producing $y_1$ so as to remain on its optimum curve. At this production level $y_1$, country 1 will produce $x_2$ units to remain on its optimum line. As this process continues, the production efforts of countries 1 and 2 $(x_i, y_i)$ will move away from the equilibrium $(x^*, y^*)$. Eventually this sequence of points will reach a point where $x = 0$ and $y > 0$ such as the point $(0, y_2)$ shown in Figure 92. That is, the first country will produce nothing and become parasitic. (Recall that the analysis of the voting distribution model of Chapter 3 is similar.)

Thus, we have determined the lines of maximum satisfaction for each country as well as a condition under which *both* countries simultaneously will maximize their satisfaction. Further, we have seen conditions where the efforts of each country to maximize its satisfaction causes a move away from equilibrium. Indeed, these are not the only conditions for an equilibrium or for a parasitic state; the reader is invited to find other such conditions. (For a further discussion of similar models see Luce.)

## PRODUCTION FUNCTIONS WITH BUDGET CONSTRAINTS: LAGRANGE MULTIPLIERS

Industrial production decisions depend crucially upon the relationship between the inputs and the output of a process. The present state of technology and the available capital equipment impose a set of technical relationships that restrict the output level produced by various amounts of the inputs. These technical relationships can be summarized by a *production function*. The problem of constructing and finding the optimum of such a production function while still meeting certain budgeting constraints is considered here.

Consider an industrial process in which an output is produced utilizing two inputs—say, for simplicity, labor and capital. Suppose $q$ denotes the amount of the output that the firm can produce if it uses $x_1$ units of labor and $x_2$ units of capital. We shall express this information mathematically by the short-run *production function*

$$q = f(x_1, x_2).$$

The production function states that more output cannot be produced unless more inputs are used and that the result of a decrease in input levels is a decrease in the output level. Further, the production function indicates how various amounts of labor and capital may be substituted for each other while maintaining a given output level.

If $q$ is the maximum output level corresponding to input levels $x_1$ and $x_2^0$, an arbitrarily small increase in the first input $\Delta x_1$ will cause the maximum output level to change by $\Delta q$. The average production increase caused by this increase $\Delta x_1$ is $\Delta q/\Delta x_1$. The limiting value of this quotient, $\partial q/\partial x_1$, is the *marginal productivity of the first input*. Similarly $\partial q/\partial x_2$ is the *marginal productivity of the second input*.

The standard assumption characterizing the production function is the law of diminishing marginal productivity or, more commonly, diminishing marginal returns in all of its inputs. The law of diminishing marginal productivity states that as equal increments of one input are added, the other input level being held constant, beyond some point the resulting increments of output will decrease. Note that we are assuming diminishing marginal productivity when the state of technology is held constant. Furthermore, there must be at least two inputs only one of which is varied at a time in discussing diminishing marginal returns. Mathematically diminishing marginal productivity means that beyond some point our production function satisfies

$$\frac{\partial^2 f}{\partial x_1^2} < 0 \quad \text{and} \quad \frac{\partial^2 f}{\partial x_2^2} < 0,$$

$x_1 > 0, x_2 > 0$.

The assumption of diminishing marginal productivity characterizes many production functions. Perhaps the best-known production function exhibiting diminishing marginal productivity is the Cobbs–Douglas function,

$$Ax_1^a x_2^{1-a}, \qquad x_1 > 0, x_2 > 0$$

where $A$ is a scaling factor and $0 \le a \le 1$.

Here we consider a relatively simple production function characterized by diminishing marginal productivity:

$$\begin{aligned} f(x_1, x_2) &= a_1 \ln (1 + x_1) + a_2 \ln (1 + x_2) \\ &= \ln (1 + x_1)^{a_1}(1 + x_2)^{a_2}, \end{aligned}$$

where $x_1 > 0$, $x_2 > 0$, and $a_1, a_2$ are positive constants. By Theorem 33 we see that $f$ is a concave function on the open convex set $K = \{(x_1, x_2): x_1 > 0, x_2 > 0\}$. Hence, by Theorems 37 and 38, if the global maximum of $f(x_1, x_2)$ exists on $K$, it occurs when

$$\text{(208)} \qquad \frac{\partial f}{\partial x_1} = 0 \quad \text{and} \quad \frac{\partial f}{\partial x_2} = 0.$$

That is, the output level $q$ will be maximized when the input levels $x_1^*$, $x_2^*$ satisfy conditions (208).

The problem of determining input levels that maximize the output is usually subject to constraints. For instance, suppose our production process is subject to a budgetary constraint. Assume that the total expenditures on labor and capital must be $M$ dollars. Thus, if the unit costs of labor and capital are $b_1$ and $b_2$, respectively, the input levels must satisfy the constraint

$$b_1x_1 + b_2x_2 = M,$$

or, equivalently,

$$b_1x_1 + b_2x_2 - M = 0.$$

Thus, our *constrained production maximization problem* is

$$\text{(209)} \qquad \begin{aligned} &\text{maximize} && f(x_1, x_2) = \ln (1 + x_1)^{a_1}(1 + x_2)^{a_2} \\ &\text{subject to} && b_1x_1 + b_2x_2 - M = 0, \end{aligned}$$

$x_1 > 0$, $x_2 > 0$. The solution of this production maximization problem has a simple geometric interpretation. The graph of the production function $\ln (1 + x_1)^{a_1}(1 + x_2)^{a_2}$ may be represented by contour lines, as shown in Figure 93. Each contour line, labeled $q_i$, $i = 0, 1, \ldots,$ represents a particular height of the production function surface. The contours

$$q_i = \ln (1 + x_1)^{a_1}(1 + x_2)^{a_2},$$

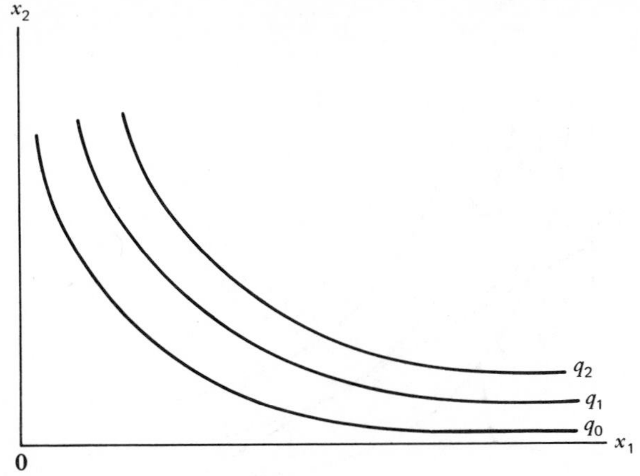


Figure 93

called *isoquant curves*, indicate all possible combinations of labor and capital that result in an output level $q_i$ ($q_0 < q_1 < q_2 < \cdots$). The budgetary constraint is also represented graphically by the straight line shown in Figure 94.

In Figure 95 we have superimposed the budgetary constraint curve and the isoquant curves. Our objective in the constrained maximization problem (209) is to determine inputs levels $(x_1^*, x_2^*)$ that lie on the budgetary constraint curve *and* on the isoquant curve corresponding to the *maximum* possible level of output. From Figure 95, we see that this point $(x_1^*, x_2^*)$ is

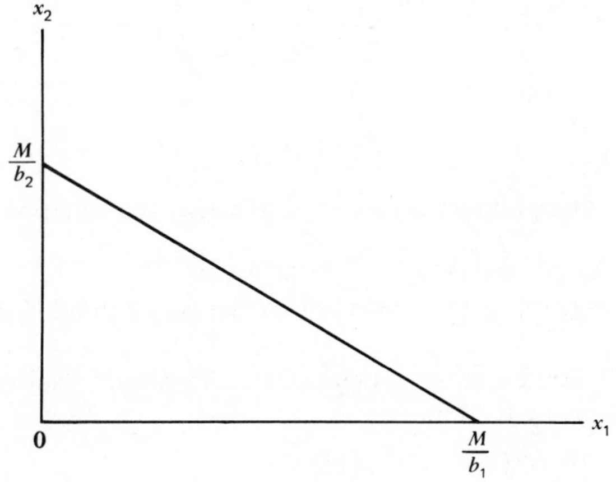


Figure 94

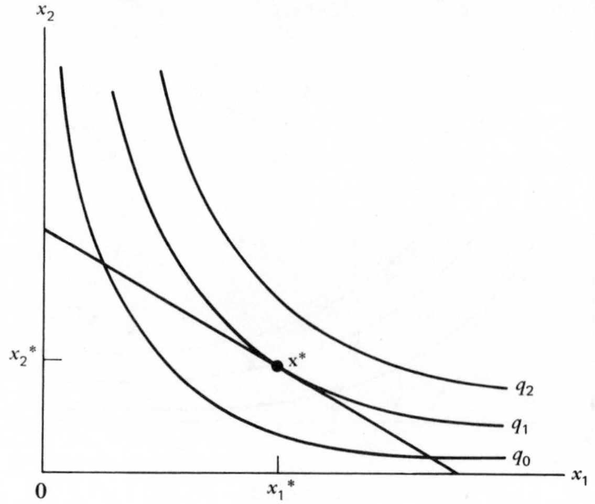


Figure 95

obviously the point of tangency between the budgetary constraint and the $q_1$ isoquant. This means that $x_1^*$ units of labor and $x_2^*$ units of capital satisfy the budgetary constraint and maximize the output level. It is obvious that since the isoquant curves do not intersect, any other point on the budgetary constraint curve lies on an isoquant corresponding to a lower level of output.

The classical technique for solving this constrained maximization problem is the method of Lagrange multipliers. In developing the method of Lagrange multipliers, we recall that the maximizing point $\mathbf{x}^* = (x_1^*, x_2^*)$ of $f(x_1, x_2) = \ln (1 + x_1)^{a_1}(1 + x_2)^{a_2}$ on the open convex set $K = \{(x_1, x_2): x_1 > 0, x_2 > 0\}$ clearly must satisfy the two equations

(210) $$\frac{\partial f}{\partial x_1} = 0$$

(211) $$\frac{\partial f}{\partial x_2} = 0.$$

But, the maximizing point $\mathbf{x}^*$ is restricted to satisfy the equation

(212) $$g(x_1, x_2) = b_1 x_1 + b_2 x_2 - M = 0.$$

Hence, equations (210) and (211) are not particularly helpful in determining $\mathbf{x}^*$.

To facilitate computation in determining $\mathbf{x}^*$, an artificial variable $\mu$ is introduced by forming the function

(213) $$\begin{aligned} L(x_1, x_2, \mu) &= f(x_1, x_2) + \mu[g(x_1, x_2)] \\ &= \ln (1 + x_1)^{a_1}(1 + x_2)^{a_2} + \mu(b_1 x_1 + b_2 x_2 - M). \end{aligned}$$

Observe that $f(x_1, x_2) \equiv L(x_1, x_2, \mu)$ for these values of $x_1$ and $x_2$ satisfying constraint (212), since

$$g(x_1, x_2) = b_1 x_1 + b_2 x_2 - M \equiv 0.$$

Hence, the values of $f(x_1, x_2)$ on the curve $g(x_1, x_2) = 0$ and the values of $L(x_1, x_2, \mu)$ are the same at the maximizing points of $L(x_1, x_2, \mu)$. Therefore, we proceed to find the maximizing points of $L(x_1, x_2, \mu)$ and thus determine the maximizing points of $f$ on $g = 0$.

A necessary condition for maximizing points $(x_1^*, x_2^*, \mu^*)$ of $L(x_1, x_2, \mu)$ is

$$\frac{\partial L}{\partial x_1} = 0, \qquad \frac{\partial L}{\partial x_2} = 0, \qquad \frac{\partial L}{\partial \mu} = 0.$$

That is, $x_1^*$, $x_2^*$, and $\mu^*$ must satisfy

$$\frac{\partial L}{\partial x_1} = \frac{\partial f}{\partial x_1} + \mu \frac{\partial g}{\partial x_1} = \frac{a_1}{1 + x_1} + \mu b_1 = 0,$$

$$\frac{\partial L}{\partial x_2} = \frac{\partial f}{\partial x_2} + \mu \frac{\partial g}{\partial x_2} = \frac{a_2}{1 + x_2} + \mu b_2 = 0,$$

$$\frac{\partial L}{\partial \mu} = g = b_1 x_1 + b_2 x_2 - M = 0.$$

By solving this system, we find

$$x_1^* = \frac{a_1 M + a_1 b_2 - a_2 b_1}{a_1 b_1 + a_2 b_1},$$

$$x_2^* = \frac{a_2 M + a_2 b_1 - a_1 b_2}{a_1 b_2 + a_2 b_2},$$

$$\mu^* = \frac{-(a_1 + a_2)}{M + b_1 + b_2}.$$

Since the maximizing points of $L(x_1, x_2, \mu)$ are the maximizing points of $f(x_1, x_2)$ on $g(x_1, x_2) = 0$, we conclude that $x_1^*, x_2^*$ are the maximizing points of $f(x_1, x_2)$ on $g(x_1, x_2) = 0$. That is, the input levels $x_1^*$ and $x_2^*$ maximize production and yet satisfy budgetary constraint (212). Correspondingly, the maximum value of our production function subject to the budgetary constraint is

$$f(x_1^*, x_2^*) = \ln \left(\frac{a_1(b_1 + b_2 + M)}{a_1 b_1 + a_2 b_1}\right)^{a_1} \left(\frac{a_2(b_1 + b_2 + M)}{a_1 b_2 + a_2 b_2}\right)^{a_2}.$$

It is interesting to examine the effect of variations in the total budget, $M$, on the maximum value of the production function, $f(x_1^*, x_2^*)$. One measure of the effect of perturbations in $M$ on $f(\mathbf{x}^*)$ is $(\partial f/\partial M)(\mathbf{x}^*)$. For instance, if $(\partial f/\partial M)(\mathbf{x}^*) > 0$, the production level $f(\mathbf{x}^*)$ increases with increases in the budget, while if $(\partial f/\partial M)(\mathbf{x}^*) < 0$, the value $f(\mathbf{x}^*)$ decreases with increases in $M$.

To obtain an expression for $(\partial f/\partial M)(\mathbf{x}^*)$, first note that according to the chain rule

(214) $$\frac{\partial f}{\partial M}(\mathbf{x}^*) = \frac{\partial f}{\partial x_1}(\mathbf{x}^*)\frac{\partial x_1}{\partial M} + \frac{\partial f}{\partial x_2}(\mathbf{x}^*)\frac{\partial x_2}{\partial M}.$$

Furthermore, at the optimum

(215) $$\frac{\partial L}{\partial x_1}(\mathbf{x}^*, \mu^*) = \frac{\partial f}{\partial x_1}(\mathbf{x}^*) + \mu^* \frac{\partial g}{\partial x_1}(\mathbf{x}^*) = 0$$

and

(216) $$\frac{\partial L}{\partial x_2}(\mathbf{x}^*, \mu^*) = \frac{\partial f}{\partial x_2}(\mathbf{x}^*) + \mu^* \frac{\partial g}{\partial x_2}(\mathbf{x}^*) = 0.$$

We may combine (214), (215), and (216) to conclude

$$\begin{aligned}\frac{\partial f}{\partial M}(\mathbf{x}^*) &= -\mu^* \frac{\partial g}{\partial x_1}(\mathbf{x}^*)\frac{\partial x_1}{\partial M} - \mu^* \frac{\partial g}{\partial x_2}(\mathbf{x}^*)\frac{\partial x_2}{\partial M}\\ &= -\mu^* \frac{\partial g}{\partial M}\\ &= \mu^*.\end{aligned}$$

Thus, $\mu^*$ represents the sensitivity of the maximum production with respect to variations in $M$. Intuitively, therefore, $\mu^*$ indicates the approximate variation in $f(\mathbf{x}^*)$ per unit increase in the budget.

Thus, by forming the function $L(x_1, x_2, \mu)$, called the Lagrangian, our constrained maximization problem (209) is transformed into the more familiar problem of maximizing an *unconstrained* function (213). Moreover, the result of introducing the Lagrange multiplier, $\mu$, is that we must solve three equations $\partial L/\partial x_1 = 0$, $\partial L/\partial x_2 = 0$, $\partial L/\partial \mu = 0$, in three unknowns $x_1$, $x_2$, and $\mu$, a problem more suited for computation.

Before generalizing this technique for finding maximizing and minimizing points of constrained functions, let us consider a second illustration of the method of Lagrange multipliers. Consider our economic lot size problem. Recall that in this inventory problem, we are to determine the amounts, $x_1^*$ and $x_2^*$, of the two products that minimize the convex holding and ordering cost function

$$c(x_1, x_2) = \alpha \frac{D}{x_1} + \beta \frac{D}{x_2} + \frac{\gamma x_1}{2} + \frac{\gamma x_2}{2}, \tag{217}$$

$x_1 > 0$, $x_2 > 0$. Suppose that a limitation is placed on the total number of units of storage space available. Assume $S$ units of space are available and that we wish all of it to be used. Assuming, for convenience, that one unit of either product requires one unit of space, this space limitation imposes the additional constraint

$$x_1 + x_2 = S,$$

or, equivalently,

$$x_1 + x_2 - S = 0. \tag{218}$$

Our problem of minimizing the total inventory and holding cost (217) while meeting the space constraint (218), is summarized in the following *constrained minimization problem:*

$$\begin{aligned} &\text{minimize} && \alpha \frac{D}{x_1} + \beta \frac{D}{x_2} + \frac{\gamma x_1}{2} + \frac{\gamma x_2}{2} \\ &\text{subject to} && x_1 + x_2 - S = 0. \end{aligned} \tag{219}$$

The geometric interpretation of this problem is similar to that for problem (209). We wish to determine a point $(x_1^*, x_2^*)$ on the space limitation curve, (218) minimizing the cost function, (217). As shown in Figure 96, $(x_1^*, x_2^*)$

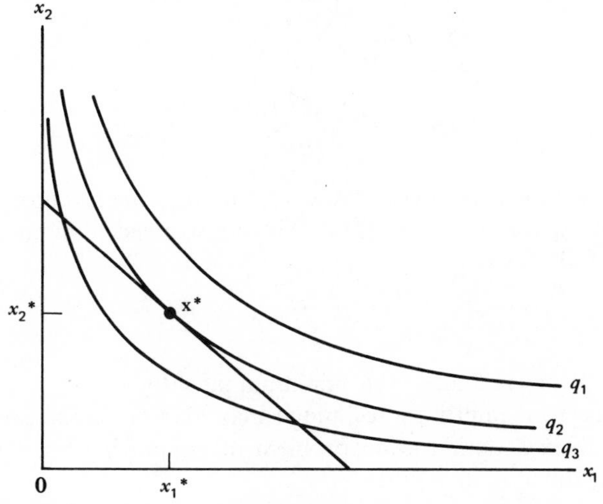


Figure 96

is a point of tangency between the space limitation curve, (218) and the *isocost curve* $q_2$. Note that because $c(x_1, x_2)$ is convex, $q_3 > q_2 > q_1 > \cdots$.

The constrained minimization problem (219) may be transformed into an equivalent unconstrained problem. By introducing the new variable $\mu$, we form the Lagrangian

$$L(x_1, x_2, \mu) = \alpha \frac{D}{x_1} + \beta \frac{D}{x_2} + \frac{\gamma x_1}{2} + \frac{\gamma x_2}{2} + \mu(x_1 + x_2 - S).$$

Since $x_1 + x_2 - S \equiv 0$, the value of $L$ and the values of $f$ satisfying the constraint (218) are the same. Hence, the value of $c(x_1, x_2)$ on the curve (218) is minimized at the minimizing points of $L$. The minimizing points of $L$ necessarily satisfy

$$\frac{\partial L}{\partial x_1} = -\frac{\alpha D}{x_1^2} + \frac{\gamma}{2} + \mu = 0,$$

$$\frac{\partial L}{\partial x_2} = -\frac{\beta D}{x_2^2} + \frac{\gamma}{2} + \mu = 0,$$

$$\frac{\partial L}{\partial \mu} = x_1 + x_2 - S = 0.$$

Solving this system, we find that the minimizing points of $L$, and thus of $c$, are

$$x_1^* = \frac{S}{(1 + \sqrt{\beta/\alpha})},$$

$$x_2^* = \frac{S\sqrt{\beta/\alpha}}{(1 + \sqrt{\beta/\alpha})},$$

$$\mu^* = \frac{\alpha D(1 + \sqrt{\beta/\alpha})^2}{S^2} - \frac{\gamma}{2}.$$

That is, the economic lot sizes $x_1^*$ and $x_2^*$ minimize the inventory cost while satisfying the space constraint (218). The constrained minimum inventory cost is therefore

$$c(x_1^*, x_2^*) = \frac{D}{S}(1 + \sqrt{\beta/\alpha})(\alpha + \sqrt{\alpha\beta}) + \gamma S.$$

How do variations in $S$ affect this minimum inventory cost?

The Lagrange multiplier technique may also be applied to the more general *constrained* optimization problem of minimizing (maximizing) the continuously differentiable function

$$f(\mathbf{x}), \qquad \mathbf{x} \in \mathbb{R}^n \tag{220}$$

subject to the $m$ equality constraints

$$g_1(\mathbf{x}) = 0$$
$$\vdots \qquad \qquad (221)$$
$$g_m(\mathbf{x}) = 0,$$

where $g_i(\mathbf{x}), i = 1, \ldots, m$, are continuously differentiable. As in the examples, we wish to transform this constrained optimization problem into an *unconstrained* optimization problem. We do so by introducing $m$ new variables $\mu_i$, $i = 1, \ldots, m$, each corresponding to one of the equality constraints, and by forming the Lagrangian

(222) $$L(\mathbf{x}, \boldsymbol{\mu}) = f(\mathbf{x}) + \mu_1 g_1(\mathbf{x}) + \cdots + \mu_m g_m(\mathbf{x}),$$

where $\boldsymbol{\mu} = (\mu_1, \ldots, \mu_m)$.

The values of $L(\mathbf{x}, \boldsymbol{\mu})$ and the values of $f(\mathbf{x})$ satisfying the $m$ equality constraints (221) are identical, since $g_1(\mathbf{x}) \equiv 0, \ldots, g_m(\mathbf{x}) \equiv 0$. Hence, the minimizing (maximizing) points of $f(\mathbf{x})$ on the curves $g_1(\mathbf{x}) = 0, \ldots, g_m(\mathbf{x}) = 0$ are identical to the minimizing (maximizing) points of $L$. Therefore, we consider the unconstrained optimization problem of minimizing (maximizing) $L(\mathbf{x}, \boldsymbol{\mu})$. A necessary condition for $(\mathbf{x}, \boldsymbol{\mu})$ to be a minimizing (maximizing) point $(\mathbf{x}^*, \boldsymbol{\mu}^*)$ of $L(\mathbf{x}, \boldsymbol{\mu})$ is that

(223)
$$\frac{\partial L}{\partial x_1}(\mathbf{x}^*, \boldsymbol{\mu}^*) = 0$$
$$\vdots$$
$$\frac{\partial L}{\partial x_n}(\mathbf{x}^*, \boldsymbol{\mu}^*) = 0$$
$$\frac{\partial L}{\partial \mu_1}(\mathbf{x}^*, \boldsymbol{\mu}^*) = g_1(\mathbf{x}^*) = 0$$
$$\vdots$$
$$\frac{\partial L}{\partial \mu_m}(\mathbf{x}^*, \boldsymbol{\mu}^*) = g_m(\mathbf{x}^*) = 0.$$

Thus, we must find $(\mathbf{x}^*, \boldsymbol{\mu}^*)$ satisfying system (223) in order to find minimizing (maximizing) points of $L$, and thus of problem (220)–(221).

The computational problem of determining $(\mathbf{x}^*, \boldsymbol{\mu}^*)$ satisfying the system (223) of $n + m$ equations in $n + m$ unknowns is usually quite difficult. There do not exist any simple algorithms for obtaining numerically all solutions of system (223). Conditions (223) are most useful when there is only one solution, and the solution may be obtained with relatively simple techniques.

We summarize the Lagrange multiplier technique as follows:

**THEOREM 39** If $\mathbf{x}^*$ is a minimizing (maximizing) point of the continuously differentiable function $f(\mathbf{x})$, $\mathbf{x} \in \mathbb{R}^n$, subject to the equality constraints (221), then $\mathbf{x}^*$ necessarily satisfies system (223). ▮

Sufficient conditions guaranteeing that $(\mathbf{x}^*, \boldsymbol{\mu}^*)$ is in fact a minimizing (maximizing) point of problem (220)–(221) are quite lengthy and are not discussed here.

To illustrate the technique of Lagrange multipliers, consider the following constrained minimization problem:

$$\text{(224)} \qquad \begin{aligned} &\text{minimize} && x_1^2 + x_2^2 \\ &\text{subject to} && x_1 + x_2 - 1 = 0. \end{aligned}$$

To solve this problem we transform (224) into an equivalent unconstrained minimization problem:

$$\text{(225)} \qquad \text{minimize} \quad L(\mathbf{x}, \boldsymbol{\mu}) = x_1^2 + x_2^2 + \mu(x_1 + x_2 - 1).$$

The Lagrangian is minimized when

$$\text{(226)} \qquad \frac{\partial L}{\partial x_1} = 2x_1 + \mu = 0,$$

$$\text{(227)} \qquad \frac{\partial L}{\partial x_2} = 2x_2 + \mu = 0,$$

$$\text{(228)} \qquad \frac{\partial L}{\partial \mu} = x_1 + x_2 - 1 = 0.$$

Equations (226) and (227) imply $x_1 = x_2$, and equation (228), in turn, implies $x_1 = x_2 = \frac{1}{2}$. Thus, from (226) and (227) we see that $\mu = -1$. Hence, problem (224) attains the minimum value $\frac{1}{2}$ at $x_1^* = \frac{1}{2}$, $x_2^* = \frac{1}{2}$.

As a second example, consider the following constrained maximization problem:

$$\text{(229)} \qquad \begin{aligned} &\text{maximize} && 2x_1x_2 \\ &\text{subject to} && x_1^2 + x_2^2 - 1 = 0 \\ & && x_1 - x_2 = 0. \end{aligned}$$

The equivalent unconstrained Lagrangian problem is formulated to solve (229):

$$\text{maximize} \qquad L(\mathbf{x}, \boldsymbol{\mu}) = 2x_1x_2 + \mu_1(x_1^2 + x_2^2 - 1) + \mu_2(x_1 - x_2).$$

At the maximum, we have

$$\frac{\partial L}{\partial x_1} = 2x_2 + 2\mu_1 x_1 + \mu_2 = 0, \tag{230}$$

$$\frac{\partial L}{\partial x_2} = 2x_1 + 2\mu_1 x_2 - \mu_2 = 0, \tag{231}$$

$$\frac{\partial L}{\partial \mu_1} = x_1^2 + x_2^2 - 1 = 0, \tag{232}$$

$$\frac{\partial L}{\partial \mu_2} = x_1 - x_2 = 0. \tag{233}$$

Since $x_1 = x_2$, according to (233), equation (232) implies $x_1 = \pm 1/\sqrt{2}$, $x_2 = \pm 1/\sqrt{2}$. With $x_1 = 1/\sqrt{2}, x_2 = 1/\sqrt{2}$ or $x_1 = -1/\sqrt{2}, x_2 = -1/\sqrt{2}$, equations (230) and (231) reduce to a linear system in $\mu_1$ and $\mu_2$. In either case $\mu_1 = -1$, $\mu_2 = 0$. Thus, problem (229) attains the maximum value 1 at $(1/\sqrt{2}, 1/\sqrt{2})$, and $(-1/\sqrt{2}, -1/\sqrt{2})$.

A more general Lagrange multiplier technique is applicable to problems involving the optimization of a continuously differentiable function subject to inequality constraints of the form $g(\mathbf{x}) \leq 0$. Problems of this type are considered in our study of convex programming.

## ADDITIONAL PROPERTIES OF CONVEX FUNCTIONS

Maximizing a convex function, or minimizing a concave function, over a convex set is a problem of somewhat less interest in economics and management science than the corresponding problem of minimizing a convex function or maximizing a concave function. Therefore, we shall indicate only two results related to the maximization of convex functions; analogous theorems exist for concave functions.

By considering several examples of convex functions of one variable, we see that on a closed and bounded interval one, or both, of the endpoints is a global maximizing point. For example, consider the convex function $f(x) = -\ln x$ on the closed and bounded interval $\frac{1}{2} \leq x \leq 4$ as shown in Figure 97. The global maximizing point of $f(x)$ is clearly the endpoint $x^* = \frac{1}{2}$. Similarly, the global maximum of $g(x) = x^2$ on the closed and

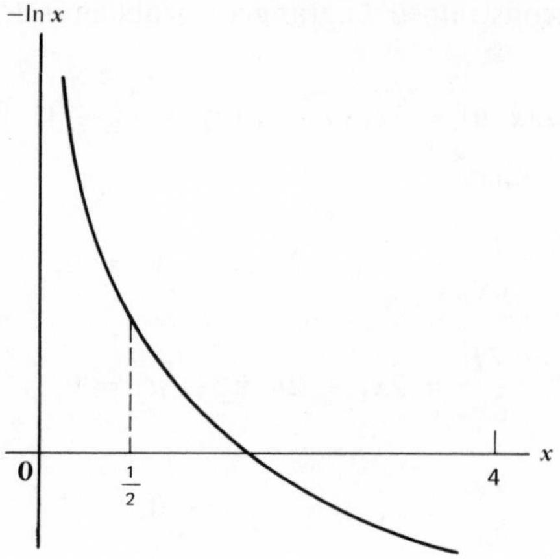


Figure 97

bounded interval $-1 \leq x \leq 1$ occurs at both endpoints $x^* = -1$, $y^* = 1$ (see Figure 98).

In general, for convex functions of one variable, we have the following result:

**THEOREM 40** The global maximizing point of a convex function $f(x)$ over a closed interval $a \leq x \leq b$ will either be $x = a$ or $x = b$ or both.

**PROOF** If $f(x)$ is an arbitrary linear or constant function, the theorem is obviously true (see Figure 99). Suppose $f(x)$ is convex with a minimum at $x^0$ within the interval $a \leq x^0 \leq b$, as shown in Figure 100; then as we

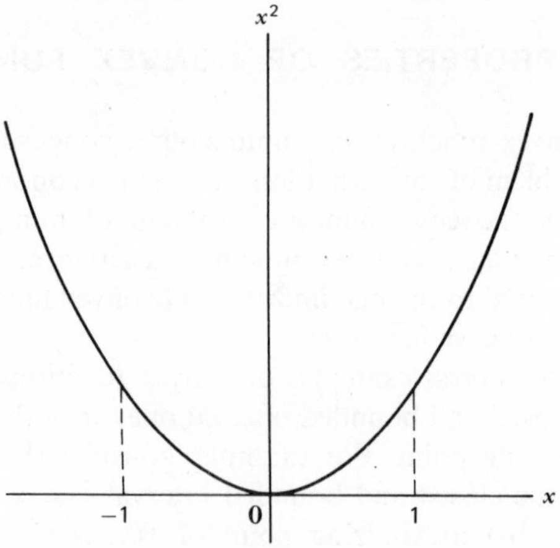


Figure 98

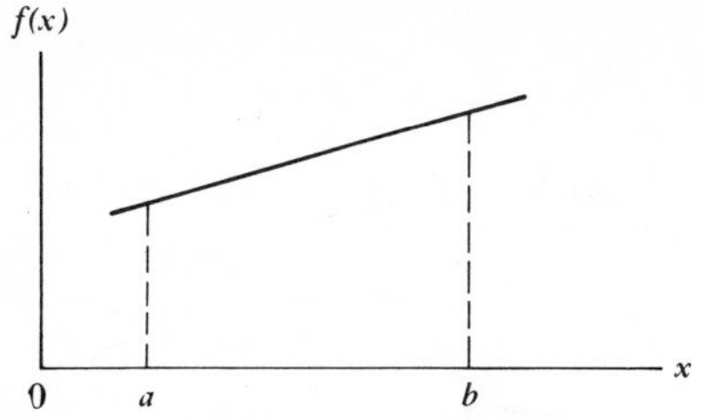


Figure 99

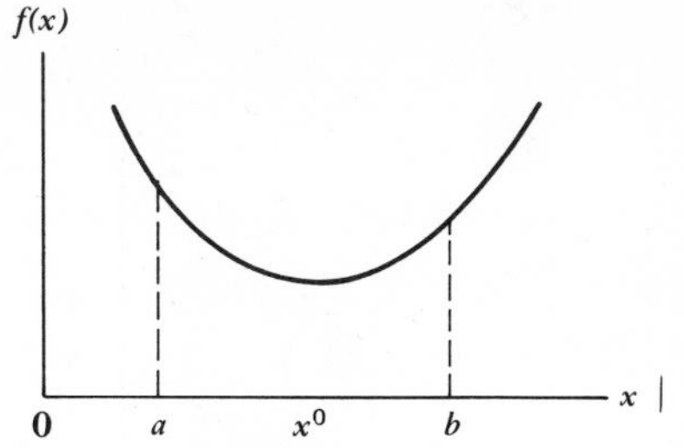


Figure 100

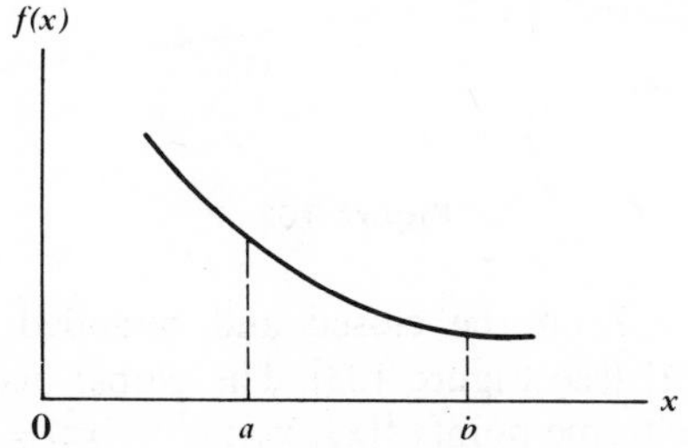


Figure 101

increase $x$, we cannot pass through a maximizing point for $x < b$ because otherwise $f(x)$ would not be convex on $a \leq x \leq b$. Similarly, as we decrease $x$, we cannot pass through a maximizing point for $a < x$, since otherwise $f(x)$ would not be convex. Therefore, the global maximizing point occurs at either $x = a$ or $x = b$ or both. If the minimizing point is at an endpoint, as shown in Figure 101, we cannot pass through a maximizing point until we reach the other endpoint, since $f(x)$ is convex on $a \leq x \leq b$. ▮

An analog to Theorem 40 for convex functions of several variables on a convex set is the following:

**THEOREM 41** If $f(\mathbf{x})$ is a convex function on a closed and bounded convex set $K \subset \mathbb{R}^n$, then one or more of the global maximizing points of $f$ on $K$ is an extreme point of $K$. ▮

Rather than discuss the proof of this result, let us consider several illustrative examples.

Consider the convex function $f(x_1, x_2) = e^{x_1}$ on the closed and bounded convex set $K_1 = \{(x_1, x_2): 0 \leq x_1 \leq 1, 0 \leq x_2 \leq 2\}$. As shown in Figure 102, the extreme points $(1, 0)$ and $(1, 2)$ are global maximizing points of $f$ on $K_1$.

A second illustration of Theorem 41 is provided by the convex function

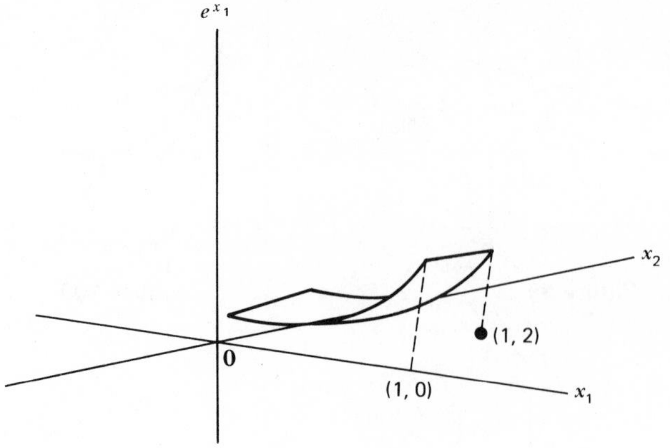


Figure 102

$g(x_1, x_2) = x_1^2 + x_2^2 + 7$ on the closed and bounded convex set $K_2 = \{(x_1, x_2): x_1^2 + x_2^2 \leq 2\}$ (see Figure 103). The global maximizing points of $g$ on $K_2$ is the set of extreme points $\{(x_1, x_2): x_1^2 + x_2^2 = 2\}$.

We now consider methods of generating convex functions from other convex functions. In applications, one often generates the functions of interest by combining functions exhibiting known properties such as convexity. Further, many of the results concerning generating convex functions will prove useful in our study of convex and geometric programming.

**THEOREM 42** If $g$ is a monotone nondecreasing convex function defined on $\mathbb{R}$ and if $f$ is a convex function defined on a convex set $K \subset \mathbb{R}^n$, then the composite function $g[f(\mathbf{x})]$ is a convex function on $K$.

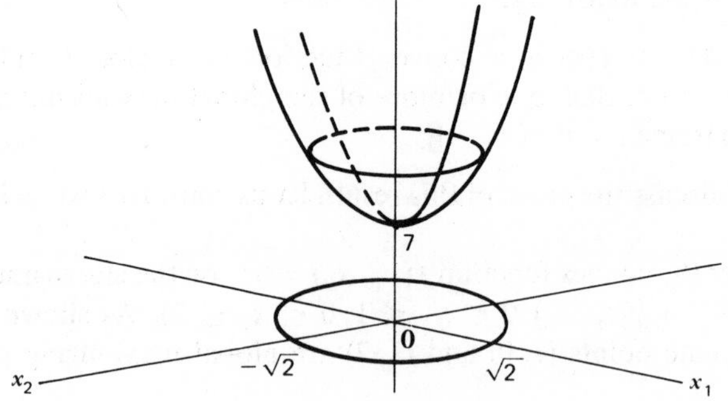


Figure 103

**PROOF** Suppose **x** and **y** are arbitrary points in $K$. Since $f$ is convex,

$$f[\lambda\mathbf{x} + (1 - \lambda)\mathbf{y}] \le \lambda f(\mathbf{x}) + (1 - \lambda)f(\mathbf{y}), \qquad 0 \le \lambda \le 1.$$

Because $g$ is monotone increasing and convex,

$$g(f[\lambda\mathbf{x} + (1 - \lambda)\mathbf{y}]) \le g[\lambda f(\mathbf{x}) + (1 - \lambda)f(\mathbf{y})]$$

and

$$g[\lambda f(\mathbf{x}) + (1 - \lambda)f(\mathbf{y})] \le \lambda g[f(\mathbf{x})] + (1 - \lambda)g[f(\mathbf{y})],$$

$0 \le \lambda \le 1$. Combining these inequalities, we have that $g(f)$ is convex,

$$g(f[\lambda\mathbf{x} + (1 - \lambda)\mathbf{y}]) \le \lambda g[f(\mathbf{x})] + (1 - \lambda)g[f(\mathbf{y})]. \quad \blacksquare$$

For example, consider the convex function $f(x_1, x_2) = x_1^2 + x_2^2 + 7$ on $\mathbb{R}^2$ and the convex function $g(y) = e^y$ on $\mathbb{R}$. From Theorem 42 we conclude that

$$g[f(x_1, x_2)] = e^{x_1^2 + x_2^2 + 7}$$

is convex.

Another method of generating convex functions from other convex functions is to consider positive linear combinations of convex functions:

**THEOREM 43** If the functions $f_i$ $(i = 1, \ldots, p)$ are convex on the same convex set $K$, then the linear combination

$$\sum_{i=1}^{p} c_i f_i(\mathbf{x})$$

is also a convex function on $K \subset \mathbb{R}^n$ when the constants $c_i \ge 0$.

**PROOF** Let **x** and **y** be arbitrary points of $K$. Since the $f_i$ are convex,

$$f_i[\lambda\mathbf{x} + (1 - \lambda)\mathbf{y}] \le \lambda f_i(\mathbf{x}) + (1 - \lambda)f_i(\mathbf{y}), \qquad 0 \le \lambda \le 1$$

$(i = 1, \ldots, p)$. Because the $c_i \ge 0$, we have

$$c_i f_i[\lambda\mathbf{x} + (1 - \lambda)\mathbf{y}] \le \lambda c_i f_i(\mathbf{x}) + (1 - \lambda)c_i f_i(\mathbf{y}),$$

$(i = 1, \ldots, p)$. Therefore,

$$\sum_{i=1}^{p} c_i f_i[\lambda\mathbf{x} + (1 - \lambda)\mathbf{y}] \le \lambda \sum_{i=1}^{p} c_i f_i(\mathbf{x}) + (1 - \lambda) \sum_{i=1}^{p} c_i f_i(\mathbf{y}),$$

which completes the proof. $\blacksquare$

To illustrate this theorem, note that since $e^x$, $|x|$, and $x^2 - 7x + 3$ are convex on $\mathbb{R}$, this theorem implies that

$$9e^x + 7\,|x| + 42(x^2 - 7x + 3)$$

is also convex on $\mathbb{R}$.

The preceding results provide methods for generating convex functions from other convex functions. We shall now see that convex sets may be generated from convex functions by placing certain inequality constraints on the convex functions.

**THEOREM 44** If $f$ is a convex function defined on a convex set $K \subset \mathbb{R}^n$ and $c$ is an arbitrary number, then all points $\mathbf{x} \in K$ that satisfy the inequality

$$f(\mathbf{x}) \leq c \tag{234}$$

form a convex (possibly empty) subset of $K$.

**PROOF** Suppose that $\mathbf{x}$ and $\mathbf{y}$ are arbitrary points of $K$ that satisfy (234). Since $f$ is convex,

$$f[\lambda\mathbf{x} + (1 - \lambda)\mathbf{y}] \leq \lambda f(\mathbf{x}) + (1 - \lambda)f(\mathbf{y}), \qquad 0 \leq \lambda \leq 1.$$

Note that $\lambda f(\mathbf{x}) + (1 - \lambda)f(\mathbf{y}) \leq \lambda c + (1 - \lambda)c = c$. Hence, each point $\lambda\mathbf{x} + (1 - \lambda)\mathbf{y}$ on the segment $\mathbf{xy}$ satisfies (234) when both $\mathbf{x}$ and $\mathbf{y}$ satisfy (234); that is, the set of points in $K$ satisfying (234) is convex. ∎

As an illustration of Theorem 44, consider the convex function $f(x_1, x_2) = x_1^2 + x_2^2 + 7$. If $f(x_1, x_2) \leq 9$, then $x_1^2 + x_2^2 + 7 \leq 9$ or $x_1^2 + x_2^2 \leq 2$. The latter inequality describes the interior and boundary of a circle of radius $\sqrt{2}$, a convex set (see Figure 104).

Theorem 44 is particularly important to our study of convex programming in Chapter 7. Frequently, the problem of minimizing a convex function $f(\mathbf{x})$ will be restricted by placing an inequality constraint on another convex function; that is, according to this result, the function $f(\mathbf{x})$ is restricted to a convex set.

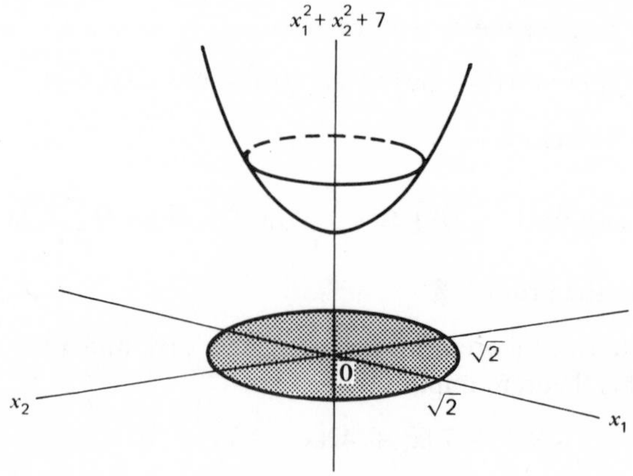


Figure 104

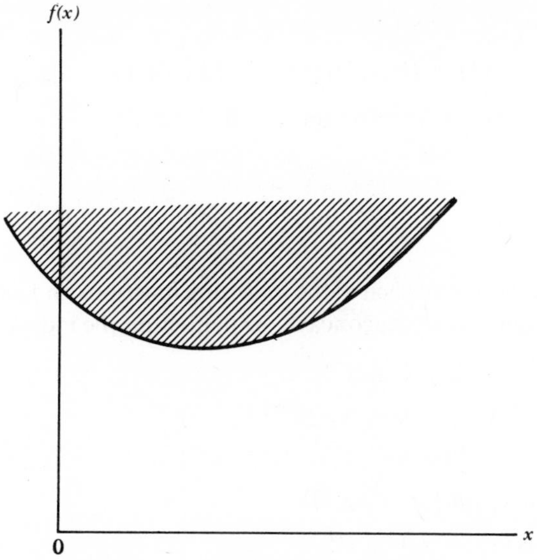


Figure 105

The following result appeals to the geometric properties of convex functions that generate convex sets. While discussing the definition of a convex function, we noted that the chord joining two points on the graph of a convex function always lies above the curve. Similarly, the line joining any two points on or above the curve also lies above the curve; intuitively, this defines a convex set (see Figure 105). Formally, we have the following result:

**THEOREM 45** A function $f$ defined on a convex set $K \subset \mathbb{R}^n$ is convex if and only if the set $F = \{(\mathbf{x}, z): z \geq f(\mathbf{x}), \mathbf{x} \in K\}$ is a convex set.

**PROOF** If $f$ is convex, then for $(\mathbf{x}^1, z^1) \in F$, $(\mathbf{x}^2, z^2) \in F$ we have $z^1 \geq f(\mathbf{x}^1)$, $z^2 \geq f(\mathbf{x}^2)$ and $\mathbf{x}^1, \mathbf{x}^2 \in K$. By definition of convexity of $f$,

$$\lambda z^1 + (1 - \lambda)z^2 \geq \lambda f(\mathbf{x}^1) + (1 - \lambda)f(\mathbf{x}^2) \geq f[\lambda \mathbf{x}^1 + (1 - \lambda)\mathbf{x}^2],$$

$0 \leq \lambda \leq 1$. Thus, we have

$$[\lambda \mathbf{x}^1 + (1 - \lambda)\mathbf{x}^2, \lambda z^1 + (1 - \lambda)z^2] = \lambda(\mathbf{x}^1, z^1) + (1 - \lambda)(\mathbf{x}^2, z^2) \in F,$$

implying $F$ is a convex set. Conversely, if $F$ is a convex set and $[\mathbf{x}^1, f(\mathbf{x}^1)] \in F$, $[\mathbf{x}^2, f(\mathbf{x}^2)] \in F$, then

$$\lambda[\mathbf{x}^1, f(\mathbf{x}^1)] + (1 - \lambda)[\mathbf{x}^2, f(\mathbf{x}^2)] \in F.$$

By the definition of the set $F$, we have

$$\lambda f(\mathbf{x}^1) + (1 - \lambda)f(\mathbf{x}^2) \geq f[\lambda \mathbf{x}^1 + (1 - \lambda)\mathbf{x}^2],$$

implying $f$ is a convex function on $K$. ▮

## EXERCISES

1. Sketch the graph of each of the following functions and indicate whether the function is convex, concave, or neither on the indicated convex set:

   (*a*) $x_1^{1/2}$ on $\{x_1 : 1 \leq x_1\}$
   (*b*) $e^{-x_1}$ on $\{x_1 : 0 \leq x_1 \leq 7\}$
   (*c*) $x_1^2 + x_2^2$ on $\{(x_1, x_2) : -1 \leq x_1 \leq 1, -1 \leq x_2 \leq 2\}$
   (*d*) $\sin x_1$ on $\{x_1 : x_1 \geq 0\}$
   (*e*) $\cos(x_1 + x_2)$ on $\mathbb{R}^2$.

2. Prove that each of the following functions is convex on the indicated convex set:

   (*a*) $-\ln(1 + x_1)$ on $\{x_1 : x_1 \geq 0\}$
   (*b*) $\sin x_1$ on $\{x_1 : \pi \leq x_1 \leq 2\pi\}$
   (*c*) $7e^{x_1} + x_1^2$ on $\{x_1 : 11 \leq x_1 \leq 19\}$
   (*d*) $x_1^2 + x_2^2$ on $\mathbb{R}^2$
   (*e*) $(x_1 - 2)^2 + x_2 - \ln(x_2^3)$ on $\{(x_1, x_2) : x_1 > 0, x_2 > 0\}$
   (*f*) $e^{x_1} + x_2^2$ on $\mathbb{R}^2$
   (*g*) $-\ln(x_1 x_2)^2$ on $\{(x_1, x_2) : x_1 \geq 1, x_2 \geq 1\}$
   (*h*) $(x_1 + x_2)^2$ on $\mathbb{R}^2$.

3. Prove each of the following:
   (*a*) The function

   $$x_1^{r_1} + x_2^{r_2} + x_3^{r_3}$$

   is convex on the interior of the positive orthant of $\mathbb{R}^3$ when $r_i > 1$, $i = 1, 2, 3$.
   (*b*) The function

   $$x_1^{r_1} + x_2^{r_2} + x_3^{r_3}$$

   is concave on the interior of the positive orthant of $\mathbb{R}^3$ when $0 < r_i < 1$, $i = 1, 2, 3$.
   (*c*) Any linear function is concave.

(*d*) If $f(\mathbf{x})$ is a convex function on $\mathbb{R}^n$, then $f(\mathbf{x} + \mathbf{a})$ is a convex function for any constant vector $\mathbf{a} \in \mathbb{R}^n$.

4. Is the product of two convex functions always a convex function? Why or why not?

5. Show that

$$16e^{-x_1+2x_2} + 7e^{4x_1-7x_2}$$

is a convex function on $\mathbb{R}^2$.

6. (*a*) Show that $e^{\omega^2}$ is a convex function on $\{\omega : \omega > 0\}$.

(*b*) Use part (*a*) to derive the inequality

$$\frac{x}{3} + \frac{2y}{3} \leq \ln\left(\tfrac{1}{3}e^{x^2} + \tfrac{2}{3}e^{y^2}\right),$$

$x > 0$, $y > 0$.

7. Classify the critical point or points of each of the following functions as global minimizing or maximizing points:

(*a*) $e^{x_1} - x_1 + x_2^2$ on $\mathbb{R}^2$

(*b*) $x_1^2 - 9x_1 + x_2^2 - 7$ on $\mathbb{R}^2$

(*c*) $-e^{x_1} + x_1 + \ln(x_2^3) - x_2$ on $\{(x_1, x_2) : x_2 > 0\}$

(*d*) $x_1^2 + (x_2 - 2)^2$ on $\mathbb{R}^2$

(*e*) $(x_1 - 1)^2 - \ln(x_2^3) + x_2$ on $\{(x_1, x_2) : x_1 > 0, x_2 > 0\}$.

8. To classify a critical point $\mathbf{x}^*$ of an arbitrary twice continuously differentiable function $f$ on $\mathbb{R}^2$, we must first calculate

$$A = \frac{\partial^2 f}{\partial x_1^2}(\mathbf{x}^*), \qquad C = \frac{\partial^2 f}{\partial x_2^2}(\mathbf{x}^*), \qquad B = \frac{\partial^2 f}{\partial x_1\, \partial x_2}(\mathbf{x}^*).$$

If $B^2 - AC < 0$ and $A + C < 0$, $\mathbf{x}^*$ is a *local* maximizing point. If $B^2 - AC < 0$ and $A + C > 0$, $\mathbf{x}^*$ is a *local* minimizing point. If $B^2 - AC > 0$, $\mathbf{x}^*$ is a saddle point. If $B^2 - AC = 0$, we may conclude nothing about the critical point $\mathbf{x}^*$. Using this test, classify the critical points of each of the following functions:

(*a*) $e^{-x_1^2 - x_2^2}$

(*b*) $\sin x_1 \left(\dfrac{e^{x_2} + e^{-x_2}}{2}\right)$

(*c*) $x_1^2 + x_2^2$

(*d*) $x_1^2 + x_2^2 - 2x_1x_2$

(*e*) $\dfrac{x_1}{x_1^2 + x_2^2}$.

9. Solve the following constrained minimization problems:

(*a*) minimize $2x_1 + 3x_2$
subject to $x_1^2 + x_2^2 = 1$

(*b*) minimize $x_1 x_2$
subject to $x_1^2 + x_2^2 = 1$

(*c*) minimize $x_1^2 + (x_2 - 2)^2$
subject to $x_1^2 - x_2^2 = 1$

(*d*) minimize $x_1 + 2x_2 + 4x_3$
subject to $x_1^2 + x_2^2 + x_3^2 = 7.$

10. Solve the following constrained maximization problems:

(*a*) maximize $x_1 x_2$
subject to $x_1^2 + x_2^2 = 1$

(*b*) maximize $x_1 x_2 x_3$
subject to $x_1^3 + x_2^3 + x_3^3 = 1$

(*c*) maximize $x_1 + 1 - 2x_2^2 x_1$
subject to $x_1 = 3.$

11. Find the point on the parabola $x_2 = x_1^2$ that is closest to $(0, -1)$.

12. [Curtis, p. 288]. Find the distance from the point (1, 1, 1) to the line that is the intersection of the planes defined by the equations

$$2x_1 + x_2 - x_3 = 1$$

and

$$x_1 - x_2 + x_3 = 2.$$

13. Find the dimensions of the open-top box that will have the greatest volume when the surface area is 3.

14. Determine the marginal costs in the economic lot size problem.

15. Suppose that the initial stock level $x_1$ of one of the products in the economic lot size problem is depleted at a constant rate of 0.5 per unit time. Although the stock is 0 after $x_1/0.5$ units of time, the continuing demand is backlogged. A replenishment order is placed after $y_1/0.5$ ($>x_1/0.5$) units of time. At this time an order of size $y_1$ arrives instantaneously to meet the backlogged demand and replenish the stock to $x_1$ units, as shown on page 193. These shortages in the first product cause a loss in revenue. Specifically these shortages represent a loss of goodwill, since consumers will be reluctant to do further business with the firm. Suppose the unit holding and ordering costs of the two products are as given in the economic lot size model and the unit shortage cost for the first product is $3 per item of unfilled demand per unit of time.

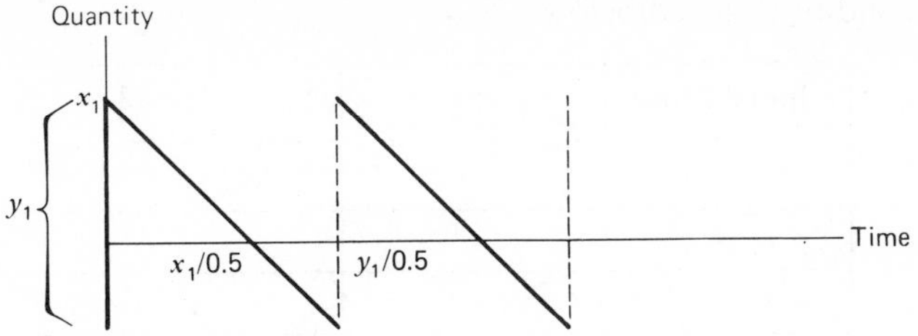


(*a*) Formulate the problem of minimizing the total holding, ordering, and shortage costs of this economic lot size problem.
(*b*) Determine $x_1^*$, $y_1^*$, and $x_2^*$.

16. Consider the utility function

$$u = u(x, y),$$

where $x$ and $y$ are the quantities of two commodities that are consumed. The locus of all points $(x, y)$ from which the same utility is derived is termed the *indifference curve*. Sketch the indifference curve for the following utility functions:

(*a*) $u(x, y) = xy$

(*b*) $u(x, y) = x^2y$

(*c*) $u(x, y) = y^2(1 + x)$

(*d*) $u(x, y) = \ln (1 + x + y)$.

17. The slope of an indifference curve, $dy/dx$, is the rate a consumer would be willing to substitute one commodity for the other to maintain a given level of utility. The quantity

$$-\frac{dy}{dx}$$

is termed the *marginal rate of substitution*.
(*a*) Determine the marginal rate of substitution for the utility functions in the previous problem.
(*b*) Show that for the utility function $u(x, y)$ the marginal rate of substitution is actually the ratio of the marginal utilities.

18. In the model of psychoeconomics it was determined that when $p < \frac{1}{2}$, the first country made the initial move, and each country desired to maximize its own satisfaction, the result is an equilibrium condition (indicated in the table below). Determine the resulting behavior when each of the countries attempts to maximize their own satisfaction under

the conditions listed below.

| Initial Move | $p < \frac{1}{2}$ | $p > \frac{1}{2}$ |
|---|---|---|
| $y_1 > y^*$ | | |
| $y_1 < y^*$ | | |
| $x_1 > x^*$ | | |
| $x_1 < x^*$ | Condition for equilibrium | First country becomes parasitic |

19. Suppose the utility functions of each country in the model of psycho-economics exhibit *increasing* marginal utility with respect to the consumption of either country's product.
    (*a*) Develop appropriate utility functions for each country.
    (*b*) Derive conditions under which each country maximizes its own satisfaction.
    (*c*) Determine conditions under which both countries simultaneously maximize their own satisfaction.
20. Determine the marginal productivities of the following production functions.

(*a*) $f(x_1, x_2) = 6x_1^{1/2}x_2^{1/2}$

(*b*) $f(x_1, x_2) = 7x_1 + 9x_2 + 3$

(*c*) $f(x_1, x_2) = 9x_1x_2^2 + x_1^2 + x_2$

(*d*) $f(x_1, x_2) = \dfrac{x_1^2 + x_2^2}{x_1x_2}, \qquad x_1 \neq 0, x_2 \neq 0$

(*e*) $f(x_1, x_2) = 7x_1^{1/8}x_2^{7/8}$

(*f*) $f(x_1, x_2) = \ln(1 + x_1)^{1/2} \ln(1 + x_2)^{1/2}$

(*g*) $f(x_1, x_2) = \dfrac{x_1x_2}{x_1 + x_2}$

(*h*) $f(x_1, x_2) = 6x_1^{3/4}x_2^{1/4}$.

21. Consider the production function

$$q = f(x_1, x_2).$$

The slope $dx_2/dx_1$ of the tangent at a point on an isoquant

$$q_i = f(x_1, x_2),$$

$i = 1, 2, \ldots$, ($q_i$ constants) is the rate at which $x_1$ may be substituted for $x_2$ to maintain output level $q_i$, $i = 1, 2, \ldots$. The quantity

$$-\frac{dx_2}{dx_1}$$

is defined as the *rate of technical substitution.* Determine the rate of technical substitution for each of the production functions in the previous problem.

22. Consider the production function

$$q = f(x_1, x_2).$$

If

$$f(ax_1, ax_2) = a^n f(x_1, x_2)$$

for any constant $a$, $f$ is said to be *homogeneous of degree n.*

(*a*) Show that the production function

$$f(x_1, x_2) = x_1^2 + 2x_1x_2 + 8x_2^2$$

is homogeneous of degree 2. *Hint:* Observe

$$f(ax_1, ax_2) = a^2x_1^2 + 2a^2x_1x_2 + 8a^2x_2^2$$
$$= a^2 f(x_1, x_2).$$

(*b*) Determine the degree of homogeneity of the following production functions:

(*i*) $f(x_1, x_2) = x_1^2 + x_2^2$

(*ii*) $f(x_1, x_2) = 6x_1 + 7x_2$

(*iii*) $f(x_1, x_2) = 7x_1^3 + x_1x_2^2 + 4x_2^3$

(*iv*) $f(x_1, x_2) = \dfrac{x_1^4 + 9x_1x_2^3 + x_1^3x_2}{x_1 + x_2}, \qquad x_1 \neq 0, x_2 \neq 0$

(*v*) $f(x_1, x_2) = \dfrac{x_1^2 + x_2^2}{9x_1x_2}, \qquad x_1 \neq 0, x_2 \neq 0.$

23. As indicated in the linear production model, the *returns to scale* of a production process indicate the change in output level with proportionate increases in all inputs. If the output increases by the same proportion as the inputs, the returns to scale are constant. If the output increases by a greater (smaller) proportion than inputs, returns to scale are increasing (decreasing).

(*a*) Show that the production process associated with the production function

$$f(x_1, x_2) = 6x_1 + 5x_2$$

exhibits constant returns to scale. Note that $f$ is homogeneous of degree 1. *Hint*. If the inputs are increased by a proportion $a$, then the output is given by

$$\begin{aligned} f(ax_1, ax_2) &= 6ax_1 + 5ax_2 \\ &= af(x_1, x_2). \end{aligned}$$

That is, the original output $f(x_1, x_2)$ is increased by the same proportion $a$.

(*b*) Show that the production process associated with the production function

$$f(x_1, x_2) = 6x_1^3 + x_2^3$$

exhibits increasing returns to scale. Note that $f$ is homogeneous of degree 3. *Hint*. If inputs are increased by a proportion $a$, then the corresponding output is

$$\begin{aligned} f(ax_1, ax_2) &= a^3x_1^3 + a^3x_2^3 \\ &= a^3f(x_1, x_2). \end{aligned}$$

Since $a > 1$, $a^3 > a$. Thus, the output increases by a proportion $a^3 > a$.

(*c*) Determine whether the production processes associated with the production functions in Problem 22(*b*) exhibit constant, increasing, or decreasing returns to scale.

24. Suppose the production function

$$q = f(x_1, x_2)$$

is a homogeneous production function of degree $n$.

(*a*) Show that if $n = 1$, then the associated production process exhibits constant returns to scale.

(*b*) Show that if $n > 1$ ($n < 1$), then the associated production process exhibits increasing (decreasing) returns to scale.

25. For a production function $f(x_1, x_2)$ that is homogeneous of degree $n$ and whose first partial derivatives exist, it is known that

$$x_1 \frac{\partial f}{\partial x_1} + x_2 \frac{\partial f}{\partial x_2} = nf(x_1, x_2).$$

This is *Euler's theorem*.

(*a*) Show that the production function

$$f(x_1, x_2) = x_1^2 + 2x_1x_2 + 8x_2^2,$$

homogeneous of degree 2, satisfies Euler's theorem. *Hint*. Observe that

$$x_1 \frac{\partial f}{\partial x_1} + x_2 \frac{\partial f}{\partial x_2} = x_1(2x_1 + 2x_2) + x_2(2x_1 + 16x_2)$$
$$= 2(x_1^2 + 2x_1x_2 + 8x_2^2)$$
$$= 2f(x_1, x_2).$$

(*b*) Show that the production functions in Problem 22(*b*) satisfy Euler's theorem.
(*c*) Prove Euler's theorem.

26. The theory of marginal productivity states that if each input costs the value of its marginal productivity and if total output is just used, then the value of the total output equals the total cost of inputs.
(*a*) Show that a production process associated with a production function, homogeneous of degree 1, demonstrates this theory. *Hint*. Note that the total output is $f(x_1, x_2)$ and that if each input is paid the value of its marginal productivity, then the total cost of inputs is

$$x_1 \frac{\partial f}{\partial x_1} + x_2 \frac{\partial f}{\partial x_2}.$$

Now use Euler's theorem.
(*b*) Show that if the production function is homogeneous of degree $n$ and each input is paid the value of its marginal productivity, then the total output exceeds (is less than) the total input cost for $n > 1$ ($n < 1$). *Hint*. Use Euler's theorem.

27. Consider a production process in which two inputs are used to produce a single output. Let $x_1$, $x_2$, denote the level of the first, second, input; let $c_1$, $c_2$, denote the unit cost of the first, second, input; and let $q$ denote the level of output production. The input–output level relationship for this process is described by the Cobbs–Douglas production function

$$q = Ax_1^a x_2^{1-a},$$

$A > 0, 0 < a < 1$.
(*a*) Formulate the problem of determining input levels that minimize the cost of inputs and yield $q_0$ units of output.
(*b*) Determine $x_1^*$ and $x_2^*$.
(*c*) Discuss the effect of variations in $a$, $c_1$, and $c_2$ on the minimum cost.

28. Suppose $p_1$ and $p_2$ are the respective prices of the first and second of two products. Furthermore, suppose that the demands of both products are functions of $p_1$ and $p_2$. That is, functions

$$u_1 = u_1(p_1, p_2)$$

and

$$u_2 = u_2(p_1, p_2)$$

represent the demands of the first and second products, respectively.

(*a*) These two products are said to be *complementary* when a decrease in the demand of one product due to an increase in its price leads to a decrease in the demand for the other. Formulate this definition mathematically.

(*b*) These two products are said to be *substitutes* when a decrease in the demand for one product due to an increase in its price leads to an increase in demand for the other. Formulate this definition mathematically.

(*c*) Show that the products with demand functions

$$u_1 = -p_1 + 7p_2 + 1$$
$$u_2 = 6p_1 - 8p_2 + 16$$

are *substitutes.*

(*d*) Show that the products with demand functions

$$u_1 = e^{-p_1} - \frac{1}{1 - p_2} \qquad p_1, p_2 > 1,$$

$$u_2 = -p_1 + e^{-p_2+1}$$

are *complementary*.

29. Consider the problem of minimizing

$$f(t) = t + t^{-c}$$

where $t > 0$ and $c$ is a positive parameter.

(*a*) Determine $t^*$, the minimizing point of $f(t)$, as a function of $c$.

(*b*) Show that the graph of $t^*(c)$ appears as shown below.

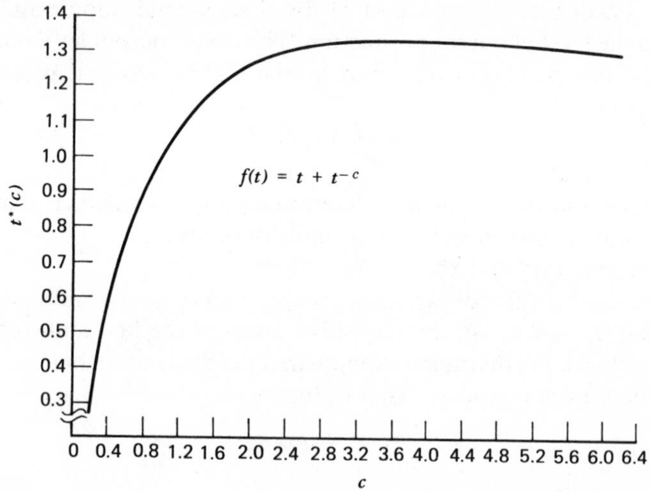

(*c*) Determine $M$, the minimum value of $f(t)$, as a function of $c$.
(*d*) Show that the graph of $M(c)$ appears as shown below.

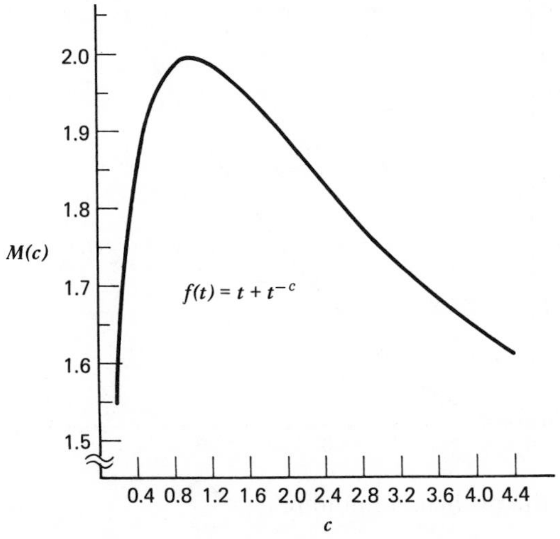


30. Consider the problem of minimizing

$$f(\mathbf{x}) = c^3e^{2x_1} + c^2e^{x_2} + ce^{-x_1-x_2}$$

where $c$ is a positive parameter.
(*a*) Determine $\mathbf{x}^* = (x_1^*, x_2^*)$, the minimizing point of $f(\mathbf{x})$, as a function of $c$.
(*b*) Show that the graphs of $x_1^*(c)$ and $x_2^*(c)$ appear as illustrated below.

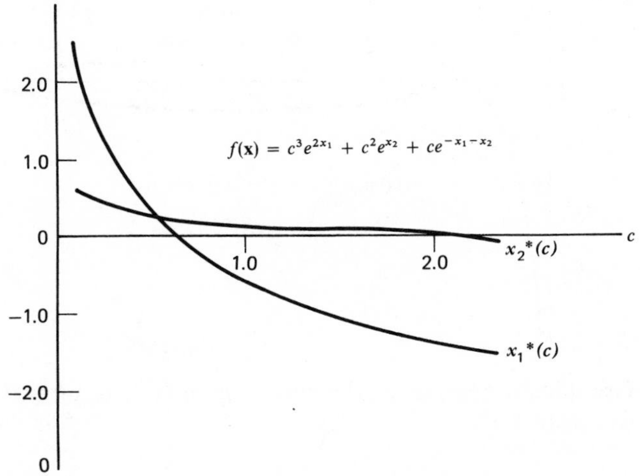

(*c*) Determine $M$, the minimum value of $f(\mathbf{x})$, as a function of $c$.
(*d*) Show that the graph of $M(c)$ appears as shown below.

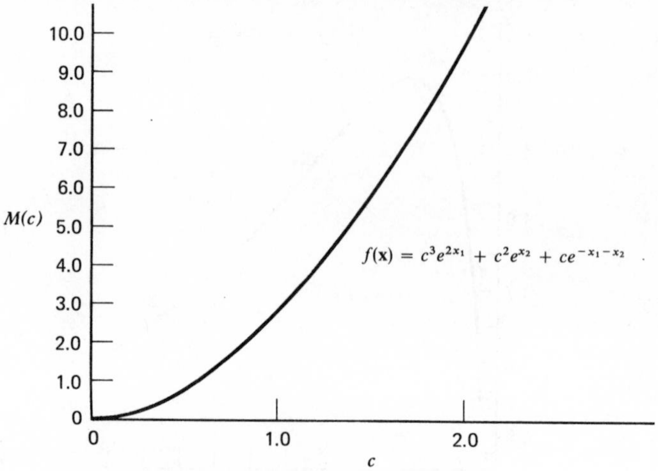


31. Consider the problem of minimizing

$$f(\mathbf{x}) = e^{cx_1} + e^{-2x_1 - cx_2} + e^{x_2}$$

where $c$ is a positive parameter.
(*a*) Determine $\mathbf{x}^* = (x_1^*, x_2^*)$, the minimizing point of $f(\mathbf{x})$, as a function of $c$.
(*b*) Show that the graphs of $x_1^*(c)$ and $x_2^*(c)$ appear as shown below.

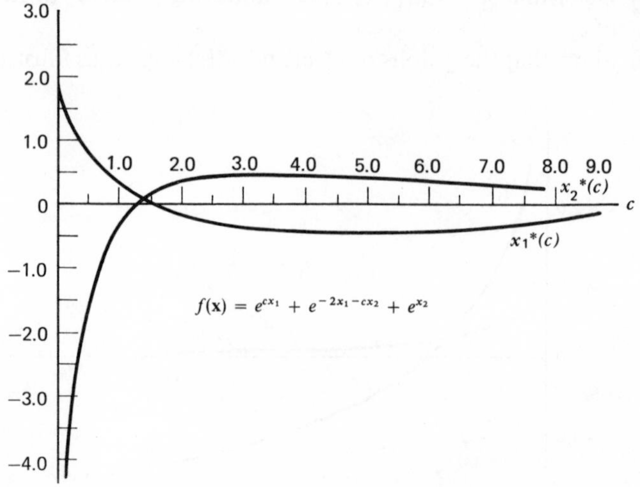


(*c*) Graphically analyze $M$, the minimum of $f(\mathbf{x})$, as a function of $c$.
32. Prove theorem 37.

33. Prove theorem 38.
34. Suppose a new employee has been assigned to do a single task on an assembly line. Initially, at $t = 1$, he requires $c$ minutes to complete the task. Gradually he learns the task and his completion times decrease.
  (*a*) Construct a twice continuously differentiable function $f(t)$ that describes this learning process.
  (*b*) Interpret the meaning of $df/dt$ and $d^2f/dt^2$ in this model.
  (*c*) What are the signs of $df/dt$ and $d^2f/dt^2$?

## SOLUTIONS

1. (*a*) Concave
  (*b*) Convex
  (*c*) Convex
  (*d*) Neither
  (*e*) Neither
4. No; consider the product of the convex functions $g(x) = x$ on $\mathbb{R}$ and $h(x) = x^2$ on $\mathbb{R}$
7. (*a*) Global minimizing point
  (*b*) Global minimizing point
  (*c*) Global maximizing point
  (*d*) Global minimizing point
  (*e*) Global minimizing point
8. (*a*) Local minimizing point
  (*b*) Saddle point
  (*c*) Local minimizing point
  (*d*) No conclusion
  (*e*) No critical points
9. (*a*) $x_1^* = -2/\sqrt{13},\ x_2^* = -3/\sqrt{13},\ \mu^* = \sqrt{13}/2$
  (*b*) $x_1^* = 1/\sqrt{2},\ x_2^* = -1/\sqrt{2},\ \mu^* = \frac{1}{2}$
  $x_1^* = -1/\sqrt{2},\ x_2^* = 1/\sqrt{2},\ \mu^* = \frac{1}{2}$
  (*c*) $x_1^* = \sqrt{2},\ x_2^* = 1,\ \mu^* = -1$
  $x_1^* = -\sqrt{2},\ x_2^* = 1,\ \mu^* = -1$
  (*d*) $x_1^* = -1/\sqrt{3},\ x_2^* = -2/\sqrt{3},\ x_3^* = -4/\sqrt{3},\ \mu^* = \sqrt{3}/2$
10. (*a*) $x_1^* = 1/\sqrt{2},\ x_2^* = 1/\sqrt{2},\ \mu^* = -\frac{1}{2}$
  $x_1^* = -1/\sqrt{2},\ x_2^* = -1/\sqrt{2},\ \mu^* = -\frac{1}{2}$
  (*b*) $x_1^* = x_2^* = x_3^* = (\frac{1}{3})^{1/3},\ \mu^* = -1$
  (*c*) $x_1^* = 3,\ x_2^* = 0,\ \mu^* = -1$
11. (0, 0)
12. $x_1^* = 1,\ x_2^* = \frac{1}{2},\ x_3^* = \frac{3}{2}$
13. $x_1^* = 1,\ x_2^* = 1,\ x_3^* = \frac{1}{2}$

# PART 3

# CONVEX AND GEOMETRIC PROGRAMMING IN MANAGEMENT SCIENCE

# CHAPTER 7

# CONVEX PROGRAMMING

## INTRODUCTION

Management scientists are making increased use of the techniques of modeling and optimization in the formulation and solution of industrial, governmental, and social decision problems. Many decisions are influenced by, first, constructing mathematical models of management systems; then, choosing a quantitative measure of the effectiveness of the system; and, finally, optimizing the effectiveness. These mathematical models must accurately describe the interaction of system variables as well as the competing influences and restrictions within the system. While the measure of system effectiveness often involves a value judgment, in most management systems this measure is either cost, profit, or efficiency. After developing a mathematical description of the system and determining a measure of the system effectiveness, the management scientist uses optimization techniques to determine the values of system variables yielding optimum effectiveness.

An illustration of this decision-making process is the problem of determining the lot size of a good that will meet the anticipated demand for the good. One measure of the effectiveness of this decision is provided by the total cost of ordering and storing the product until it is sold. The optimal decision chooses the lot size that minimizes the total cost. This inventory system may be operated by ordering the total anticipated demand in one or two large orders. Although this small number of orders certainly lowers the ordering cost, holding costs increase because this large lot size requires more storage space. On the other hand, if many orders of reduced size are placed, the storage cost decreases but additional ordering costs are introduced. Thus, an optimizing technique must determine the lot size that minimizes the total cost in the presence of these two competing costs and any additional restrictions.

Frequently the assumptions and structure of the mathematical formulation of these management decision problems give rise to a convex programming problem. Convex programming provides a method for characterizing and identifying the minimizing points of a convex function that is restricted to a convex set. This is accomplished by examining a related optimization problem. Thus, while convex programming is used in the formulation of a wide class of decision problems, it also provides valuable quantitative information.

These mathematical results will prove useful in developing another optimization technique, geometric programming. With a simple change of variables, any prototypical geometric programming problem becomes a convex programming problem, and the associated results may be applied.

We now proceed to develop the theory and techniques of convex programming by means of mathematical models of several management decision problems.

## A REPLACEMENT PROBLEM: THE CONVEX PROGRAMMING PROBLEM

The deterioration of equipment represents a cost to the industrial firm. The costs associated with equipment degradation and deterioration are caused by a decline in machine service and value. The value decreases because of better substitutes or because of the high cost of the maintenance necessary to sustain a specified level of output. Therefore, such a firm requires a replacement policy that chooses between equipment replacement and continued maintenance while attempting to minimize the associated costs.

Equipment replacement is usually required for one of two reasons. In the first case a unit is replaced because of its failure. The replacement policy must determine whether to replace the units individually or collectively. If the decision is collective replacement, the decision must determine when to replace the units. The second reason for replacement of deteriorated equipment is the availability of improved equipment offering cheaper and faster service. The policy problem is, therefore, to choose the optimum point in time of cumulative usage to replace, as well as the best equipment to be purchased.

In formulating a replacement policy the total cost is usually composed of the operating inferiority and capital costs. The costs of operating equipment as it deteriorates are called *operating inferiority costs.* Although accounting systems seldom record operating inferiority costs, it is assumed that the cost of operating equipment increases as the equipment deteriorates. These increased costs are caused by a decline in operating performance as compared with the performance that is obtainable from an identical machine new. Furthermore, operating inferiority costs increase because of the obsolescense of equipment relative to new machinery; new machinery may perform the same function more economically.

The frequency with which equipment is replaced because of these operating inferiority costs also depends upon the cost of the equipment. Our model must therefore consider the *capital costs*, or the cost of purchasing equipment. Thus, in analyzing a replacement policy, we must choose between higher capital cost with less operating inferiority and lower capital cost with more operating inferiority.

In the replacement problem discussed here, we wish to determine the replacement intervals of each of two pieces of equipment that will minimize the associated average operating inferiority and capital costs. In discussing these costs, we shall assume that each year operating costs accumulate at a constant rate $c = \frac{1}{2}$ dollar per machine because of operating inferiority. Moreover, we shall assume that the acquisition cost of the first (second) piece of equipment is a known constant $A_1 = 100$ $(A_2 = 81)$ and the salvage value for each machine is 0. Finally suppose that the rate of return on capital investments within the firm is $r = 0.06$.

Since all salvage values are zero, the net cost of each piece of equipment is just the acquisition cost. Over a replacement interval of $x_1$ years the average cost of the first piece of equipment is

$$(235) \qquad \frac{A_1}{x_1} = \frac{100}{x_1},$$

and similarly, the average cost of the second piece of equipment over a replacement interval of $x_2$ years is

$$(236) \qquad \frac{A_2}{x_2} = \frac{81}{x_2}.$$

The total capital cost is not solely determined by the average acquisition cost. We must also consider the average cost of money over the replacement intervals. This cost is approximated by the expression

$$(237) \qquad r\frac{A_1}{2} + r\frac{A_2}{2} = 5.43.$$

Therefore, the total average capital cost is the sum of (235)–(237):

$$\frac{A_1}{x_1} + \frac{A_2}{x_2} + r\left(\frac{A_1}{2} + \frac{A_2}{2}\right) = \frac{100}{x_1} + \frac{81}{x_2} + 5.43.$$

Operating costs are assumed to increase at a constant rate, $c = \frac{1}{2}$, because of operating inferiority. Thus, the operating inferiority cost of the first year is $c$; the operating inferiority cost of the second year is $2c$; and more generally, the operating inferiority cost of the $k$th year is $kc$. Hence, the total operating inferiority cost associated with the first machine over a period of length $x_1$ is

$$c + 2c + \cdots + x_1 c.$$

The average operating cost for the first machine is

$$\frac{c + 2c + \cdots + x_1 c}{x_1} = \frac{c}{x_1}\left(\frac{x_1(x_1 + 1)}{2}\right) = \frac{c(x_1 + 1)}{2} = \frac{x_1 + 1}{4}. \tag{238}$$

Analogously, the average operating cost of the second machine over a period of length $x_2$ is

$$c\left(\frac{x_2 + 1}{2}\right) = \frac{x_2 + 1}{4}. \tag{239}$$

The total operating cost is the sum of (238) and (239):

$$c\left(\frac{x_1 + 1}{2}\right) + c\left(\frac{x_2 + 1}{2}\right) = \frac{x_1 + 1}{4} + \frac{x_2 + 1}{4}.$$

The total cost of replacement,

$$g_0(\mathbf{x}) = \frac{x_1 + 1}{4} + \frac{x_2 + 1}{4} + \frac{100}{x_1} + \frac{81}{x_2} + 5.43, \tag{240}$$

where $\mathbf{x} = (x_1, x_2)$, is a continuously differentiable convex function defined on $\mathbb{R}^2$. Therefore, because of this convexity characterization, the critical point $\mathbf{x}^* = (x_1^*, x_2^*)$ of $g_0(\mathbf{x})$ is the global minimizing point of $g_0(\mathbf{x})$; the replacement intervals $x_1^*$ and $x_2^*$ will minimize the associated replacement cost. Since the critical point $\mathbf{x}^*$ of $g_0(\mathbf{x})$ satisfies $\nabla g_0(\mathbf{x}^*) = 0$, or, equivalently,

$$\frac{\partial g_0}{\partial x_1} = \frac{1}{4} - \frac{100}{x_2^{*2}} = 0,$$

$$\frac{\partial g_0}{\partial x_2} = \frac{1}{4} - \frac{81}{x_2^{*2}} = 0,$$

we find the optimal replacement intervals are $x_1^* = 20$ and $x_2^* = 18$. Hence, the minimum replacement cost is $g_0(\mathbf{x}^*) = 24.93$.

Suppose, however, that certain budgetary constraints must be considered in formulating this replacement policy. Specifically, assume that the cost of replacing equipment constrains the sum of the lengths of the replacement intervals, $x_1 + x_2$, to be *at least* some constant $T\,(>0)$:

$$x_1 + x_2 \geq T.$$

This means that the problem of minimizing the total cost of replacement, (240) is the following *constrained* minimization problem:

$$\text{(241)}\qquad \begin{aligned} &\text{minimize} && g_0(\mathbf{x}) = \frac{x_1 + 1}{4} + \frac{x_2 + 1}{4} + \frac{100}{x_1} + \frac{81}{x_2} + 5.43 \\ &\text{subject to} && g_1(\mathbf{x}) = T - x_1 - x_2 \leq 0. \end{aligned}$$

Optimization problem (241) poses the problem of determining replacement intervals, $x_1^*$ and $x_2^*$, which not only minimize the total replacement cost, $g_0(\mathbf{x})$ but also satisfy the *inequality* constraint, $g_1(\mathbf{x}) \leq 0$; that is, we must determine the point $(x_1^*, x_2^*)$ that lies in the *convex set* $K = \{(x_1, x_2): T - x_1 - x_2 \leq 0\}$ and minimizes the *convex function* $g_0(\mathbf{x})$, a *convex programming problem*.

If the critical point of $g_0(\mathbf{x})$, $\mathbf{x}^* = (20, 18)$, is interior to $K$, then $\mathbf{x}^*$ is the minimizing point of the constrained problem (241). This fact follows from Theorem 35 which is restated here:

THEOREM 46 An interior point $\mathbf{x}^*$ of a convex set $K \subset \mathbb{R}^n$ is a minimizing point of a convex function $f(\mathbf{x})$ on $K$ if and only if $\mathbf{x}^*$ is a critical point of $f(\mathbf{x})$ on $K$. ∎

Suppose, for example, $T = 30$. Then $g_1(\mathbf{x}^*) = T - 20 - 18 = -8 < 0$, implying $\mathbf{x}^* \in K$, as shown in Figure 106. Since $\mathbf{x}^*$ is an interior point of $K$, by Theorem 46, $\mathbf{x}^*$ is the minimizing point of problem (241); that is, with $T = 30$, $x_1^* = 20$ and $x_2^* = 18$ are the optimal replacement intervals and the minimum replacement cost is $g_0(\mathbf{x}^*) = 24.93$.

According to Theorem 46, if the critical point of $g_0(\mathbf{x})$ is exterior to $K$, any minimizing point of $g_0(\mathbf{x})$ on $K$ must lie on the boundary of $K$. Suppose, for instance, $T = 57$. Then $g_1(\mathbf{x}^*) = T - 20 - 18 = 19 > 0$, implying $\mathbf{x}^* \notin K$, as shown in Figure 107. In this case the minimizing point is on the boundary of $K$, as Theorem 46 implies, and may be determined by examining the contours of $g_0(\mathbf{x})$ on $K$. Since $g_0(\mathbf{x})$ is a convex function, the contours of $g_0(\mathbf{x})$ appear as in Figure 108, with $q_1 < q_2 < q_3 < \cdots$. The point $\mathbf{x}^*$ in Figure 108 is obviously the minimizing point of $g_0(\mathbf{x})$ on $K$ because it lies in $K$ on the contour corresponding to the least replacement cost, $q_2$. It may be shown that the minimizing point is $\mathbf{x}^* = (30, 27)$; that is, the optimal replacement intervals are $x_1^* = 30$ and $x_2^* = 27$. The corresponding minimum cost is $g_0(\mathbf{x}^*) = q_2 = 26.51$. (For an analysis of the sensitivity of the minimum replacement cost to variations in $T$, see Exercise 15.)

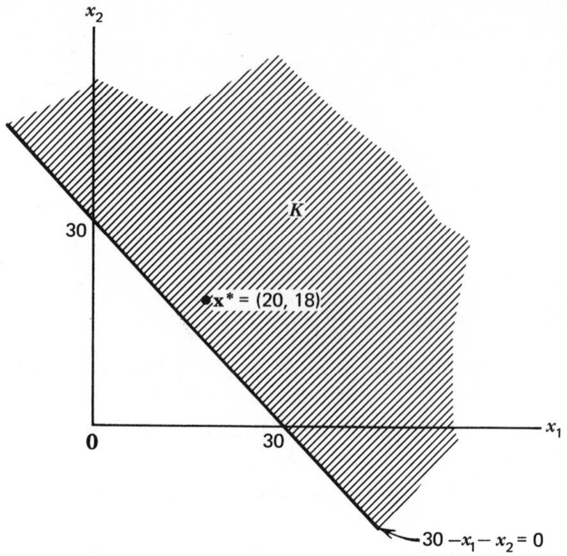


**Figure 106**

Neither of these techniques, however, provides a general characterization of the minimizing point $\mathbf{x}^*$ of problem (241). For instance, while $\mathbf{x}^* = (20, 18)$ is a critical point of $g_0(\mathbf{x})$ in the first case ($T = 30$), $\mathbf{x}^* = (30, 27)$ cannot be so characterized in the second case ($T = 57$). In *either* case, however, the minimizing point of (241) is a critical point of the associated Lagrangian function,

$$L(\mathbf{x}, \mu) = g_0(\mathbf{x}) + \mu g_1(\mathbf{x})$$

$$= \frac{x_1 + 1}{4} + \frac{x_2 + 1}{4} + \frac{100}{x_1} + \frac{81}{x_2} + 5.43 + \mu(T - x_1 - x_2),$$

for the appropriate choice of $\mu$. With $\mu = \mu' = 0$, $\mathbf{x}^* = (20, 18)$ is a critical point of $L(\mathbf{x}, \mu)$, and with $\mu = \mu' = \frac{5}{36}$, $\mathbf{x}^* = (30, 27)$ is a critical point of $L(\mathbf{x}, \mu)$. Hence, as one might expect, the Lagrangian function will prove useful in characterizing the minimizing points of convex programming problems.

Note also that in *either* case

$$\text{(242)} \qquad \mu' g_1(\mathbf{x}^*) = \mu'(T - x_1^* - x_2^*) = 0.$$

When $T = 30$, $T - x_1^* - x_2^* = 30 - 20 - 18 = -8$, but $\mu' = 0$. When $T = 57$, $\mu' = \frac{5}{36}$, but $T - x_1^* - x_2^* = 57 - 30 - 27 = 0$. Consequently, for the appropriate value of $\mu'$, the minimum replacement cost $g_0(\mathbf{x}^*)$

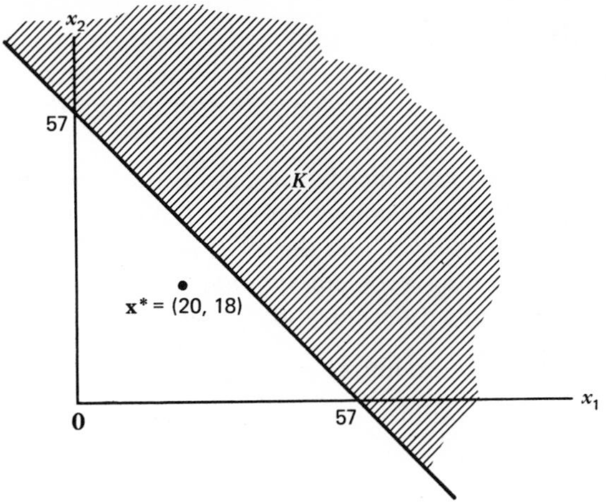


**Figure 107**

satisfies the relationship

$$L(\mathbf{x}^*, \mu') = g_0(\mathbf{x}^*).$$

As this replacement cost problem demonstrates, the Lagrangian function is useful in characterizing the minimizing points $\mathbf{x}^*$ of convex programming problems. Indeed, the central result of our discussion of convex programming states that a *nonnegative* Lagrange multiplier $\mu'$ exists such that

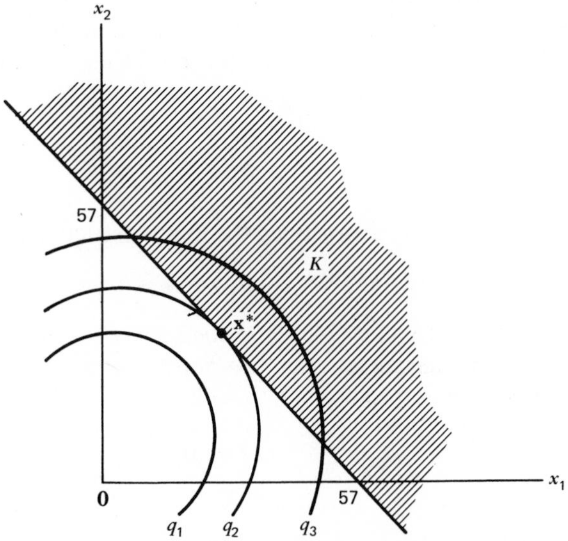


**Figure 108**

$(\mathbf{x}^*, \mu')$ is a critical point of $L(\mathbf{x}, \mu)$ and, moreover, condition (242) is satisfied. Having introduced some of the ideas of convex programming through the replacement cost problem, we now discuss the general convex programming problem.

The general *convex programming problem* is the problem of minimizing a convex function $g_0(\mathbf{x})$ over a convex set $K \subset \mathbb{R}^n$. The convex function $g_0(\mathbf{x})$ is termed the *objective function*, and the set $K$ is called the *constraint set*.

Convex programming problems in management science are usually formulated as a constrained optimization problem of the form

$$\begin{aligned} &\text{minimize} && g_0(\mathbf{x}) \\ &\text{subject to} && g_1(\mathbf{x}) \le 0 \\ & && \quad\vdots \\ & && g_p(\mathbf{x}) \le 0 \end{aligned} \tag{243}$$

where $g_k(\mathbf{x})$, $k = 0, 1, \ldots, p$, are convex on $\mathbb{R}^n$. In problem (243) the constraint set is specified by placing inequality constraints on convex functions. The set of points satisfying $g_k(\mathbf{x}) \le 0$ is convex because $g_k(\mathbf{x})$ is convex. It follows that the constraints $g_k(\mathbf{x}) \le 0$, $k = 1, \ldots, p$, are convex because the intersection of convex sets is convex. Note also that any inequality of the form $h(\mathbf{x}) \le c$, where $h(\mathbf{x})$ is convex on $\mathbb{R}^n$, may be put in the equivalent form $g(\mathbf{x}) \le 0$ by setting $g(\mathbf{x}) = h(\mathbf{x}) - c$.

The convex program (243) is said to be *consistent* if there is at least one point $\mathbf{x}'$ satisfying its constraints. The vector $\mathbf{x}'$ is termed a *feasible* point of (243). For instance, convex program (241) is consistent, since $\mathbf{x}' = (2T, 2T)$ satisfies its constraint:

$$g_1(\mathbf{x}') = T - x_1' - x_2' = -3T \le 0.$$

If there is at least one point $\mathbf{x}'$ satisfying the more restrictive condition

$$g_1(\mathbf{x}') < 0, \ldots, g_p(\mathbf{x}') < 0,$$

convex programming problem (243) is termed *superconsistent*. The superconsistent condition guarantees that the constraint set of (243) has an interior. Note that convex program (241) is also superconsistent, since

$$g_1(\mathbf{x}') = -3T < 0.$$

The minimizing point of a convex programming problem need not be unique nor necessarily exist. For example, while the constrained replacement cost problem has a unique minimizing point, the convex programming

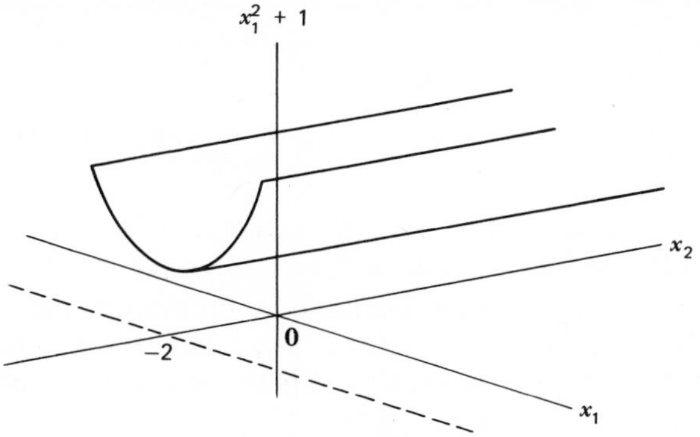


Figure 109

problem

(244)
$$\begin{array}{ll}\text{minimize} & x_1^2 + 1 \\ \text{subject to} & -x_2 - 2 \leq 0.\end{array}$$

has infinitely many minimizing points. This fact is readily seen by considering the graph of $x_1^2 + 1$ over the constraint set of (244) in Figure 109. Any point of the form $(0, x_2)$, $-2 \leq x_2$, is a minimizing point of convex program (244).

The convex programming problem

(245)
$$\begin{array}{ll}\text{minimize} & e^{x_1} \\ \text{subject to} & x_1 - 1 \leq 0\end{array}$$

has no minimizing point in the constraint set of (245). By considering the corresponding graph in Figure 110, we see that $e^{x_1}$ approaches the value zero as $x_1 \to -\infty$ but never attains it.

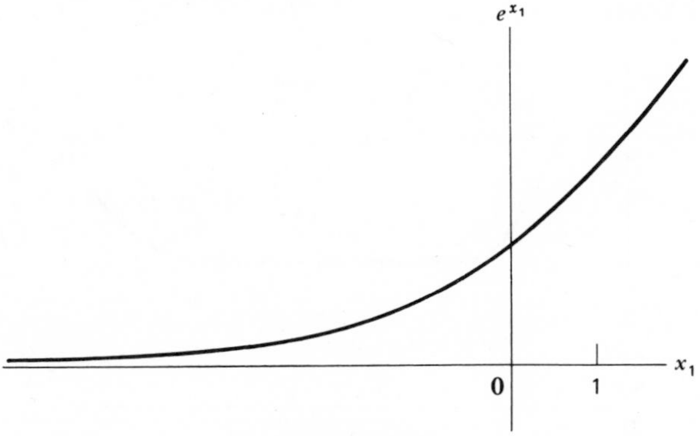


Figure 110

Observe that in problem (244) the set of minimizing points, $\{(x_1, x_2): x_1 = 0, -2 \leq x_2\}$, is a convex set. We have a similar characterization for the general convex programming problem:

**THEOREM 47** The set of minimizing points of a convex program is convex.

**PROOF** If a convex function $f$ has no minimum over a convex set $K$, the set of minimizing points is empty and, hence, convex. If $f$ has a minimum value $m$ on $K$, the set of minimizing points is the same as the set consisting of the intersection of $K$ with $\{\mathbf{x}: f(\mathbf{x}) \leq m\}$, a convex set. Since the intersection of convex sets is convex, this implies the set of minimizing points for a convex program is convex. ▮

Since the set of minimizing points of a convex program is itself convex, each point on any line segment within this set is a minimizing point when the endpoints are minimizing points. From this observation, we obtain the result:

**THEOREM 48** If the set of minimizing points for a convex program has at least two distinct points, it has an infinite number of points. ▮

In particular, consider the convex function defined on the convex set $[a, b]$ shown in Figure 111. The points $\mathbf{x}'$ and $\mathbf{x}''$ are both minimizing points and so is every point between them.

Although these results provide interesting information about the minimizing points of convex programming problems, they do not provide a useful means of identifying minimizing points. We now study a criterion that aids in identifying optimal points.

As our discussion of the replacement cost minimization problem demonstrated, the Lagrangian is useful in identifying the minimizing points

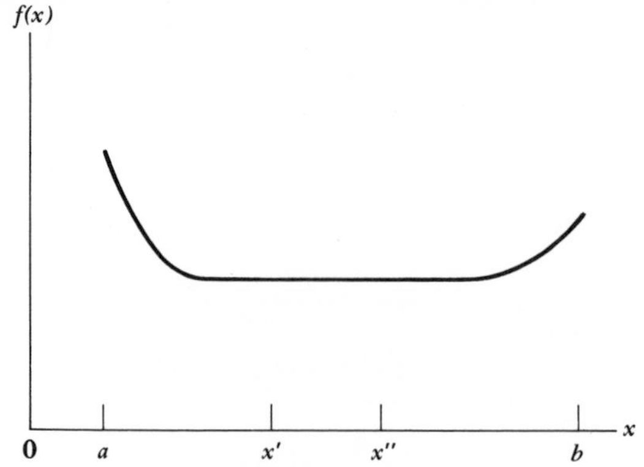


**Figure 111**

of a convex program. The following mathematical result, originating with H. W. Kuhn and A. W. Tucker, utilizes the Lagrangian of convex program (243)

$$L(\mathbf{x}, \boldsymbol{\mu}) = g_0(\mathbf{x}) + \sum_{k=1}^{p} \mu_k g_k(\mathbf{x}),$$

to identify the minimizing points of (243).

THEOREM 49 Suppose that convex programming problem (243) is *superconsistent* and that the convex functions $g_k(\mathbf{x})$, $k = 0, 1, \ldots, p$, have continuous first partial derivatives on $\mathbb{R}^n$. Then $\mathbf{x}^*$ in the constraint set of (243) is a minimizing point of (243) if and only if there exists *nonnegative* multipliers $\mu'_1, \ldots, \mu'_p$ satisfying

$$(246) \qquad \nabla_{\mathbf{x}} L(\mathbf{x}^*, \boldsymbol{\mu}') = \nabla g_0(\mathbf{x}^*) + \sum_{k=1}^{p} \mu'_k \nabla g_k(\mathbf{x}^*) = \mathbf{0},$$

$$\mu'_k g_k(\mathbf{x}^*) = 0, \qquad k = 1, \ldots, p.$$

PROOF Since the necessity of these conditions is quite difficult to prove, it is not proved here.

Suppose conditions (246) are satisfied and $\mathbf{x} \neq \mathbf{x}^*$ is in the constraint set of (243). Then, since $\mu'_k \geq 0$ and $g_k(\mathbf{x}) \leq 0$,

$$(247) \qquad g_0(\mathbf{x}) \geq g_0(\mathbf{x}) + \sum_{k=1}^{p} \mu'_k g_k(\mathbf{x}).$$

Since the functions $g_k(\mathbf{x})$, $k = 0, 1, \ldots, p$, are convex, they each satisfy the inequality

$$f(\mathbf{x}) \geq f(\mathbf{x}^*) + \nabla f(\mathbf{x}^*) \cdot (\mathbf{x} - \mathbf{x}^*).$$

The combination of these inequalities in (247) yields

$$\begin{aligned} g_0(\mathbf{x}) + \sum_{k=1}^{p} \mu'_k g_k(\mathbf{x}) &\geq g_0(\mathbf{x}^*) + \nabla g_0(\mathbf{x}^*) \cdot (\mathbf{x} - \mathbf{x}^*) \\ &\quad + \sum_{k=1}^{p} \mu'_k [g_k(\mathbf{x}^*) + \nabla g_k(\mathbf{x}^*) \cdot (\mathbf{x} - \mathbf{x}^*)] \\ &\geq g_0(\mathbf{x}^*) + \sum_{k=1}^{p} \mu'_k g_k(\mathbf{x}^*) \\ &\quad + [\nabla g_0(\mathbf{x}^*) + \sum_{k=1}^{p} \mu'_k \nabla g_k(\mathbf{x}^*)] \cdot (\mathbf{x} - \mathbf{x}^*). \end{aligned}$$

But according to the theorem, $\mu_k' g_k(\mathbf{x}^*) = 0$ and $\nabla_{\mathbf{x}} L(\mathbf{x}^*, \boldsymbol{\mu}') = \mathbf{0}$, which implies

$$g_0(\mathbf{x}) + \sum_{k=1}^{p} \mu_k' g_k(\mathbf{x}) \geq g_0(\mathbf{x}^*).$$

The combination of this inequality with (247) yields

$$g_0(\mathbf{x}) \geq g_0(\mathbf{x}^*).$$

Thus, $\mathbf{x}^*$ is a minimizing point of (243). ▮

Note that since $\mu_k' g_k(\mathbf{x}^*) = 0$, $k = 1, \ldots, p$,

$$L(\mathbf{x}^*, \boldsymbol{\mu}') = g_0(\mathbf{x}^*).$$

The Kuhn–Tucker theorem is *not* valid without the hypothesis that the convex programming program (243) is superconsistent. Consider, for example, the following convex programming problem:

$$\begin{aligned} &\text{minimize} && x \\ &\text{subject to} && x^2 \leq 0. \end{aligned}$$

This program is not superconsistent; zero is the only point in the constraint set. Thus, the minimum value of this problem must be attained at $x^* = 0$. However, the associated Lagrangian,

$$L(x, \mu) = x + \mu x^2,$$

has no critical point for $\mu \geq 0$ and $x^* = 0$:

$$\frac{\partial L}{\partial x} = 1 + 2\mu x^* \neq 0.$$

This violates the conclusion of Theorem 49.

According to the Kuhn–Tucker theorem, there exist multipliers $\mu_k' \geq 0$ $(k = 1, \ldots, p)$ such that the "complementary slackness condition"

$$\mu_k' g_k(\mathbf{x}^*) = 0,$$

where $k = 1, \ldots, p$, holds at the minimizing point $\mathbf{x}^*$. Thus, when the multiplier $\mu_k'$ is positive, the $k$th constraint is *active*,

$$g_k(\mathbf{x}^*) = 0.$$

That is, it exerts an influence on the constrained minimum. However, when the $k$th constraint is *inactive*, or exerts no influence on the constrained minimum of $g_0(\mathbf{x})$,

$$g_k(\mathbf{x}^*) < 0,$$

the multiplier $\mu_k'$ must be zero.

Consider, for example, the following superconsistent convex programming problem:

$$\begin{aligned} &\text{minimize} && g_0(\mathbf{x}) = x_1^2 + x_2^2 \\ &\text{subject to} && g_1(\mathbf{x}) = x_1 - 1 \le 0. \end{aligned}$$

Since the critical point $\mathbf{x}^* = (0, 0)$ of $g_0(\mathbf{x})$ is interior to the constraint set of this convex programming problem, $\mathbf{x}^*$ is the minimizing point. Thus, since the constraint is inactive at $\mathbf{x}^*, g_1(\mathbf{x}^*) = -1 < 0$, the "complementary slackness condition"

$$\mu_1' g_1(\mathbf{x}^*) = 0$$

only holds for $\mu_1' = 0$. Note also that $\mathbf{x}^* = (0, 0)$ and $\mu_1' = 0$ satisfy the other Kuhn–Tucker condition for a minimizing point; that is, with $\mathbf{x} = \mathbf{x}^* = (0, 0)$ and $\mu_1 = \mu_1' = 0$,

$$L(\mathbf{x}, \mu) = x_1^2 + x_2^2 + \mu_1(x_1 - 1),$$

and

$$\frac{\partial L}{\partial x_1} = 2x_1 + \mu_1 = 0,$$

$$\frac{\partial L}{\partial x_2} = 2x_2 = 0.$$

Consider a second illustration of the Kuhn–Tucker theorem. This theorem may be used to determine the minimizing point $\mathbf{x}^*$ of the following superconsistent convex programming problem

(248)
$$\begin{aligned} &\text{minimize} && g_0(\mathbf{x}) = 2x_1^2 + x_2^2 \\ &\text{subject to} && g_1(\mathbf{x}) = 1 + x_1^2 - x_2 \le 0. \end{aligned}$$

The associated Lagrangian is $L(\mathbf{x}, \mu) = 2x_1^2 + x_2^2 + \mu_1(1 + x_1^2 - x_2)$. According to Theorem 49, $\mathbf{x}^*$ is a minimizing point of (248) if and only if there exists $\mu_1' \ge 0$ such that

(249)
$$\frac{\partial L}{\partial x_1} = 4x_1^* + 2\mu_1' x_1^* = 0,$$

(250)
$$\frac{\partial L}{\partial x_2} = 2x_2^* - \mu_1' = 0,$$

(251)
$$\mu_1'(1 + x_1^{*2} - x_2^*) = 0.$$

Thus, we must solve this nonlinear system of equations to determine the minimizing point $\mathbf{x}^*$. In solving this system, observe that for $\mu_1' \ge 0$ equation (249) is only satisfied by $x_1^* = 0$. With $x_1^* = 0$ (251) is satisfied by setting

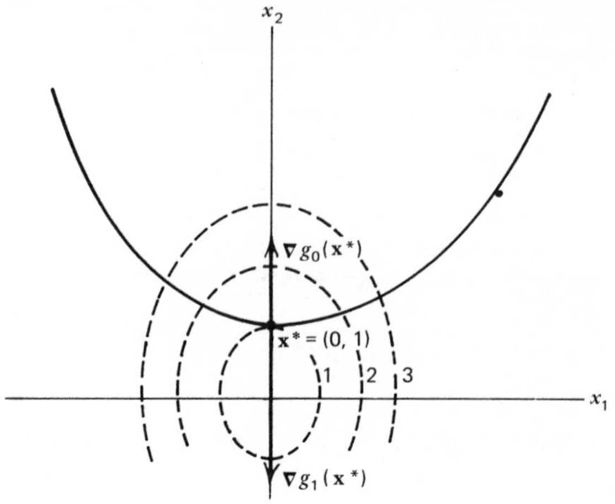


**Figure 112**

$x_2^* = 1$. If $x_2^* = 1$, equation (250) implies $\mu_1' = 2\ (>0)$. Thus, according to Theorem 49, since $\mathbf{x}^* = (0, 1)$ and $\mu_1' = 2$ is a solution of system (249)–(251), $\mathbf{x}^* = (0, 1)$ is a minimizing point of (248). Note that the minimum value of (248) is $g_0(\mathbf{x}^*) = 1$.

Geometrically, $\mathbf{x}^* = (0, 1)$ is readily seen to be the minimizing point of (248) by examining the contour lines of $g_0(\mathbf{x}) = 2x_1^2 + x_2^2$ in the constraint set of (248). From Figure 112 it is seen that the contour corresponding to the least value of $g_0(\mathbf{x})$ on $K$ is $\{\mathbf{x}: g_0(\mathbf{x}) = 1\}$. The value 1 is attained in $K$ at the point $\mathbf{x}^* = (0, 1)$. Note further that at the minimizing point $\nabla g_0(\mathbf{x}^*) = (0, 2)$ and $\nabla g_1(\mathbf{x}^*) = (0, -1)$; that is,

$$\nabla g_0(\mathbf{x}^*) = -2\nabla g_1(\mathbf{x}^*),$$

$$\nabla_{\mathbf{x}} L(\mathbf{x}^*, \mu') = \nabla g_0(\mathbf{x}^*) + 2\nabla g_1(\mathbf{x}^*) = \mathbf{0}.$$

The superconsistent convex programming problem

$$\begin{aligned} \text{minimize} \quad & g_0(\mathbf{x}) = -\ln x_1 + x_1 + x_2 \\ \text{subject to} \quad & g_1(\mathbf{x}) = -x_1 + 1 \le 0 \\ & g_2(\mathbf{x}) = -x_2 + 1 \le 0 \end{aligned}$$

provides a third illustration of the Kuhn–Tucker theorem. The associated Lagrangian is

$$L(\mathbf{x}, \boldsymbol{\mu}) = -\ln x_1 + x_1 + x_2 + \mu_1(-x_1 + 1) + \mu_2(-x_2 + 1).$$

A point $\mathbf{x}^*$ is a minimizing point of this convex programming problem if and only if there exist $\mu_1' \geq 0$ and $\mu_2' \geq 0$ such that

$$\frac{\partial L}{\partial x_1} = -\frac{1}{x_1^*} + 1 - \mu_1' = 0,$$

$$\frac{\partial L}{\partial x_2} = 1 - \mu_2' = 0,$$

$$\mu_1'(-x_1^* + 1) = 0,$$

$$\mu_2'(-x_2^* + 1) = 0.$$

First, note that $\partial L/\partial x_2 = 0$ implies that $\mu_2' = 1$ and, thus, $\mu_2'(-x_2^* + 1) = 0$ only when $x_2^* = 1$. The remaining conditions are clearly satisfied with $x_1^* = 1$ and $\mu_1' = 0$. Therefore, $\mathbf{x}^* = (1, 1)$ is the minimizing point of this problem and $g_0(\mathbf{x}^*) = 2$ is the minimum value.

As a final application of the Kuhn–Tucker theorem consider the following superconsistent convex programming problem:

$$\text{(252)} \qquad \begin{aligned} &\text{minimize} && e^{-x_1 - x_2} \\ &\text{subject to} && e^{x_1} + e^{x_2} - 20 \leq 0 \\ & && -x_1 \leq 0. \end{aligned}$$

The associated Lagrangian is

$$L(\mathbf{x}, \boldsymbol{\mu}) = e^{-x_1 - x_2} + \mu_1(e^{x_1} + e^{x_2} - 20) + \mu_2(-x_1).$$

According to the Kuhn–Tucker theorem, a point $\mathbf{x}^*$ is a minimizing point of (252) if and only if there exist $\mu_1' \geq 0$ and $\mu_2' \geq 0$ satisfying

$$\text{(253)} \qquad \frac{\partial L}{\partial x_1} = -e^{-x_1^* - x_2^*} + \mu_1' e^{x_1^*} - \mu_2' = 0,$$

$$\text{(254)} \qquad \frac{\partial L}{\partial x_2} = -e^{-x_1^* - x_2^*} + \mu_1' e^{x_2^*} = 0,$$

$$\text{(255)} \qquad \mu_1'(e^{x_1^*} + e^{x_2^*} - 20) = 0,$$

$$\mu_2'(-x_1^*) = 0.$$

Observe that if the second constraint of (252) is inactive—that is, $\mu_2' = 0$—(253) implies

$$\mu_1' = e^{-2x_1^* - x_2^*},$$

while (254) implies

$$\mu_1' = e^{-x_1^* - 2x_2^*}.$$

These relations imply that $\mu_1' > 0$ and that $x_1^* = x_2^*$. But if $\mu_1' > 0$, the first constraint of (252) must be active,

(256) $$e^{x_1^*} + e^{x_2^*} - 20 = 0.$$

Since $x_1^* = x_2^*$, it follows from (256) that $x_1^* = \ln 10$, $x_2^* = \ln 10$. With this choice of $x_1^*$ and $x_2^*$, $\mu_1' = \frac{1}{1000}$ according to (253) and (254). Thus, with $\mu_1' = \frac{1}{1000}$ and $\mu_2' = 0$, the Kuhn–Tucker theorem implies $\mathbf{x}^* = (\ln 10, \ln 10)$ is a minimizing point of convex programming problem (252). The minimum value of (252) is $g_0(\mathbf{x}^*) = \frac{1}{100}$.

The optimality conditions (246) of the Kuhn–Tucker theorem also have a geometric interpretation. Geometrically, the Kuhn–Tucker theorem states that the directional derivative of the objective function $g_0(\mathbf{x})$, in the direction of a movement *within* the constraint set, indicates a decrease in the value of $g_0(\mathbf{x})$. Suppose, for instance, only one constraint is active at $\mathbf{x}^*$,

$$g_1(\mathbf{x}^*) = 0,$$

and a tiny movement *within* the constraint set in the direction $\mathbf{v}'$, as shown in Figure 113, is considered. We show geometrically that such movements move us closer to $\mathbf{x}^*$.

At any point $\mathbf{x}'$ in the constraint set the vectors $\nabla g_0(\mathbf{x}')$ and $\nabla g_1(\mathbf{x}')$ point in the direction of steepest ascent of $g_0(\mathbf{x}')$ and $g_1(\mathbf{x}')$, respectively. Here we assume the vectors $\nabla g_0(\mathbf{x}')$ and $\nabla g_1(\mathbf{x}')$ are as shown in Figure 113.

From Figure 113 it is evident that we remain in the constraint set after a tiny movement away from $\mathbf{x}'$ in the direction $\mathbf{v}'$ whenever

(257) $$\frac{\pi}{2} < \varphi \leq \pi.$$

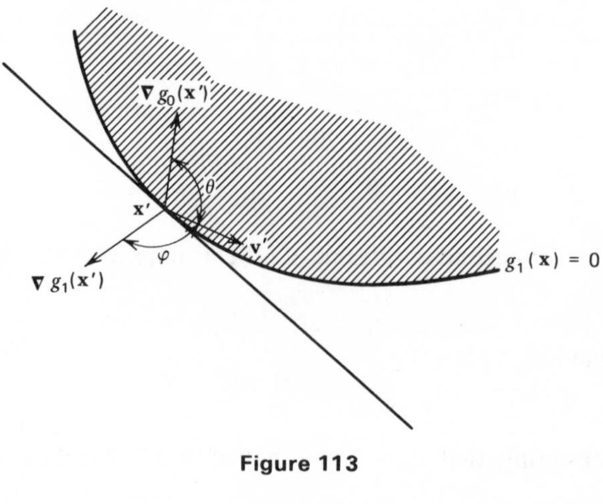


Figure 113

Since $\cos\varphi < 0$ for $\pi/2 < \varphi \leq \pi$ and since

$$\nabla g_1(\mathbf{x}') \cdot \mathbf{v}' = \|\nabla g_1(\mathbf{x}')\| \; \|\mathbf{v}'\| \cos\varphi,$$

condition (257) is equivalent to stating that we remain within the constraint set after such a movement whenever

$$\nabla g_1(\mathbf{x}') \cdot \mathbf{v}' \leq 0.$$

A tiny movement away from $\mathbf{x}'$ in the direction $\mathbf{v}'$ *within* the constraint set also reduces the value of $g_0(\mathbf{x})$ whenever

$$g_0(\mathbf{x}' + h'\mathbf{v}') < g_0(\mathbf{x}'),$$

or

$$g_0(\mathbf{x}' + h'\mathbf{v}') - g_0(\mathbf{x}') < 0. \tag{258}$$

Since, according to the definition of the directional derivative,

$$\nabla g_0(\mathbf{x}') \cdot \mathbf{v}' \approx \frac{g_0(\mathbf{x}' + h'\mathbf{v}') - g_0(\mathbf{x}')}{h'}, \tag{259}$$

for small values of $h'$ ($\geq 0$), condition (258) is equivalent to requiring

$$\nabla g_0(\mathbf{x}') \cdot \mathbf{v}' \leq 0.$$

The latter condition is equivalent to requiring $\pi/2 \leq \theta \leq \pi$ in Figure 113, since

$$\nabla g_0(\mathbf{x}') \cdot \mathbf{v}' = \|\nabla g_0(\mathbf{x}')\| \; \|\mathbf{v}'\| \cos\theta.$$

Thus, after a tiny movement away from $\mathbf{x}'$ in a direction $\mathbf{v}'$ we remain in the constraint set whenever

$$\nabla g_1(\mathbf{x}') \cdot \mathbf{v}' \leq 0,$$

and we reduce the value of $g_0(\mathbf{x})$ whenever

$$\nabla g_0(\mathbf{x}') \cdot \mathbf{v}' \leq 0.$$

Suppose that after such a movement we are at a point $\mathbf{x}'' = \mathbf{x}' + h'\mathbf{v}'$ within the constraint set. A tiny movement away from $\mathbf{x}''$ in the direction $\mathbf{v}''$, shown in Figure 114, will further reduce the constrained value of $g_0(\mathbf{x})$ if $\nabla g_0(\mathbf{x}'') \cdot \mathbf{v}'' \leq 0$ whenever $\nabla g_1(\mathbf{x}'') \cdot \mathbf{v}'' \leq 0$. This process is repeated at the new point $\mathbf{x}''' = \mathbf{x}'' + h''\mathbf{v}''$ ($h'' \geq 0$).

Several repetitions of this process continue to reduce the constrained value of $g_0(\mathbf{x})$ until at a point $\mathbf{x}^*$,

$$\nabla g_0(\mathbf{x}^*) \cdot \mathbf{v} = 0,$$

as shown in Figure 115. At this point, the value of $g_0(\mathbf{x})$ cannot be reduced

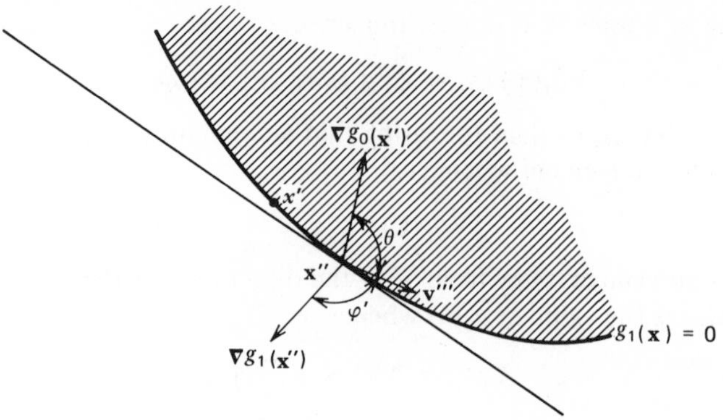


Figure 114

by a movement in any "feasible" direction **v**, because, according to (259),

$$g_0(\mathbf{x}^* + h\mathbf{v}) - g_0(\mathbf{x}^*) = 0$$

or

$$g_0(\mathbf{x}^* + h\mathbf{v}) = g_0(\mathbf{x}^*), \qquad (h \geq 0).$$

That is, $\mathbf{x}^*$ is a minimizing point of (243).

As illustrated in Figure 115, the vectors $\nabla g_0(\mathbf{x})$ and $\nabla g_1(\mathbf{x})$ are collinear at the minimizing point $\mathbf{x}^*$; that is, there exists a $\mu' \geq 0$ such that

$$-\nabla g_0(\mathbf{x}^*) = \mu' \nabla g_1(\mathbf{x}^*).$$

This condition is equivalent to stating that at the minimizing point $\mathbf{x}^*$, the negative of the gradient of $g_0(\mathbf{x})$, $-\nabla g_0(\mathbf{x}^*)$, lies in the cone generated by the vector $\nabla g_1(\mathbf{x}^*)$. If two constraints are active at $\mathbf{x}^*$,

$$g_1(\mathbf{x}^*) = 0, \qquad g_2(\mathbf{x}^*) = 0,$$

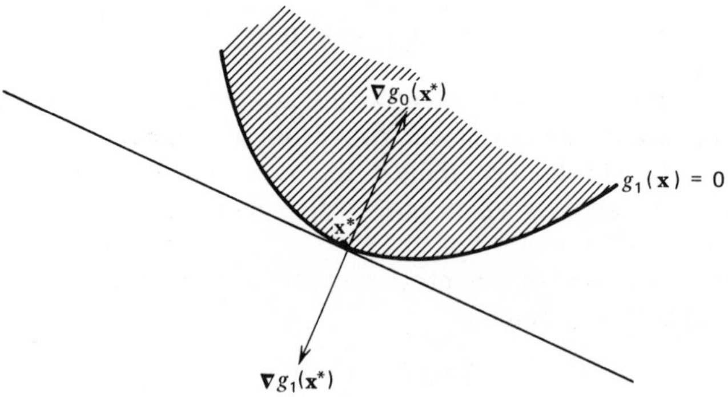


Figure 115

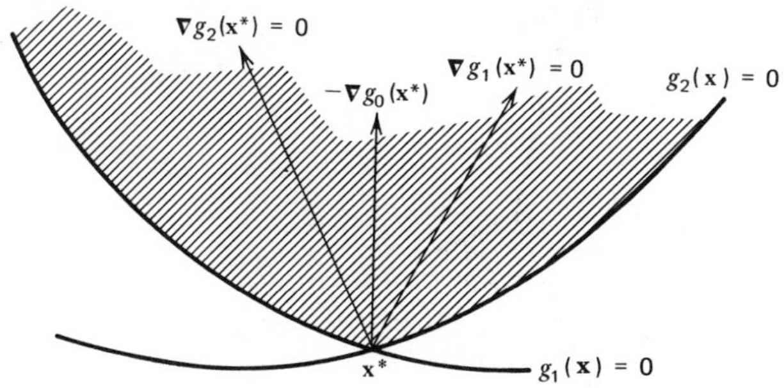


**Figure 116.** From *Nonlinear Programming: A Unified Approach* by W. Zangwill (Prentice Hall, Englewood Cliffs, New Jersey, 1969). Used with permission.

then a similar geometric analysis shows

$$-\nabla g_0(\mathbf{x}^*) = \mu_1' \nabla g_1(\mathbf{x}^*) + \mu_2' \nabla g_2(\mathbf{x}^*)$$

for some $\mu_1' \geq 0$ and $\mu_2' \geq 0$; that is, $-\nabla g_0(\mathbf{x}^*)$ is in the cone generated by the vectors $\nabla g_1(\mathbf{x}^*)$ and $\nabla g_2(\mathbf{x}^*)$, as illustrated in Figure 116.

More generally, the geometric interpretation of the Kuhn–Tucker condition

$$-\nabla g_0(\mathbf{x}^*) = \sum_{k=1}^{p} \mu_k' \nabla g_k(\mathbf{x}^*), \qquad \mu_k' \geq 0, \qquad k = 1, \ldots, p,$$

is that *at the minimizing point* $\mathbf{x}^*$ *the vector* $-\nabla g_0(\mathbf{x}^*)$ *lies in the cone generated by the gradient vectors of the active constraint functions at* $\mathbf{x}^*$.

This geometric analysis demonstrates the importance of the superconsistency condition in the Kuhn–Tucker theorem. From Figure 113 one can see intuitively that if the constraint set of (243) does not have an interior (i.e., (243) is not superconsistent), a feasible direction $\mathbf{v}$ does not necessarily exist; that is, a movement within the constraint set that decreases the value of $g_0(\mathbf{x})$ may not be possible.

In the special case when the constraint functions of (243) are linear, there is always such a feasible direction $\mathbf{v}$. For instance, if $g_1(\mathbf{x})$ is linear, as in Figure 117, the feasible direction $\mathbf{v}$ may always be taken to be along the curve $g_1(\mathbf{x}) = 0$, since along this curve

$$\nabla g_1(\mathbf{x}) \cdot \mathbf{v} = 0.$$

Therefore, intuitively, we see that if all the constraints of (243) are linear, the superconsistency restriction of the Kuhn–Tucker theorem may be removed. This fact is summarized in the following result:

**THEOREM 50** Suppose that in convex programming problem (243) the functions $g_1(\mathbf{x}), \ldots, g_p(\mathbf{x})$ are linear and $g_0(\mathbf{x})$ has continuous first partial

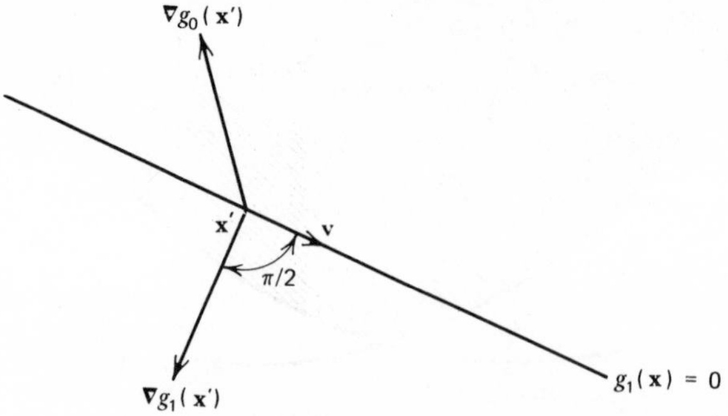


**Figure 117**

derivatives in $\mathbb{R}^n$. Then $\mathbf{x}^*$ is a minimizing point of (243) if and only if there exist nonnegative multipliers $\mu'_1, \ldots, \mu'_p$ such that

$$\nabla_{\mathbf{x}} L(\mathbf{x}^*, \boldsymbol{\mu}') = \nabla g_0(\mathbf{x}^*) + \sum_{k=1}^{p} \mu'_k \nabla g_k(\mathbf{x}^*) = \mathbf{0}$$

$$\mu'_k g_k(\mathbf{x}^*) = 0 \qquad (k = 1, \ldots, p). \quad \blacksquare$$

Thus, for example, although the following convex programming problem is not superconsistent, Theorem 50 may be applied to identify the minimizing points of (260):

$$\text{(260)} \qquad \begin{aligned} &\text{minimize} && g_0(\mathbf{x}) = x_1^2 + x_2 \\ &\text{subject to} && g_1(\mathbf{x}) = x_1 + x_2 - 1 \le 0 \\ &&& g_2(\mathbf{x}) = -x_1 - x_2 + 1 \le 0. \end{aligned}$$

With

$$L(\mathbf{x}, \boldsymbol{\mu}) = x_1^2 + x_2 + \mu_1(x_1 + x_2 - 1) + \mu_2(-x_1 - x_2 + 1)$$

as the associated Lagrangian, Theorem 50 states that $\mathbf{x}^* = (x_1^*, x_2^*)$ is a minimizing point of (260) if and only if there exist $\mu'_1 \ge 0, \mu'_2 \ge 0$ such that

$$\text{(261)} \qquad \frac{\partial L}{\partial x_1} = 2x_1^* + \mu'_1 - \mu'_2 = 0,$$

$$\text{(262)} \qquad \frac{\partial L}{\partial x_2} = 1 + \mu'_1 - \mu'_2 = 0,$$

$$\mu'_1(x_1^* + x_2^* - 1) = 0,$$

$$\mu'_2(-x_1^* - x_2^* + 1) = 0.$$

In solving this system, note that if both (261) and (262) are to be satisfied,

$x_1^* = \frac{1}{2}$. Given that (261) and (262) imply $\mu_1' = \mu_2' - 1$, the positivity of the multipliers is satisfied for $\mu_1' = 0$, $\mu_2' = 1$. With these values of $x_1^*$, $\mu_1'$, and $\mu_2'$, both complementary slackness conditions are satisfied with $x_2^* = \frac{1}{2}$. Hence, according to Theorem 50, the minimizing point of (260) is $\mathbf{x}^* = (\frac{1}{2}, \frac{1}{2})$ and the minimum value is $g_0(\mathbf{x}^*) = \frac{3}{4}$.

## COMPETITIVE INTERACTIONS: DUALITY IN CONVEX PROGRAMMING

The opposing goals of an industry and its marketplace result in a competitive interaction within an economy. While an industry attempts to minimize the costs of manufacturing its product, the market desires to maximize market revenue by adjusting the raw material prices paid by industry. These competing objectives cause price and production fluctuations within the economy and thus pose the problem of determining conditions for an economic competitive equilibrium: production costs are minimized, and market revenue is maximized. A mathematical formulation of these problems yields two interrelated optimization problems, the subject of this analysis.

The industry's objective of minimizing its cost of production may be represented as a convex programming problem. Suppose the industry produces $n$ products using $p$ raw materials. With the $i$th component of the vector $\mathbf{x} = (x_1, \ldots, x_n)$ representing the industry's production level for the $i$th product, the objective function of this programming problem, $g_0(\mathbf{x})$, is obviously the cost of operating at a level $\mathbf{x}$. This function is assumed to be convex.

Assume that the industry commences production with a quantity $r_k$, $k = 1, \ldots, p$, of raw material $k$ but, while operating at a level $\mathbf{x}$, uses an amount $h_k(\mathbf{x})$, $k = 1, \ldots, p$. The functions $h_k(\mathbf{x})$ are also assumed to be convex. Observe that the convex functions

$$g_k(\mathbf{x}) = h_k(\mathbf{x}) - r_k$$

represent excesses or shortages in raw materials. If $g_k(\mathbf{x}) > 0$, then initially there was a shortage of raw material $k$. Conversely, if $g_k(\mathbf{x}) < 0$, then an excess of raw material $k$ remains after production.

Thus, in producing these $n$ products, we wish to minimize the cost of raw materials and avoid insufficient amounts of the raw materials. Mathematically this means we wish to determine the minimizing points of the convex programming problem:

$$\begin{array}{lll} & \text{minimize} & g_0(\mathbf{x}) \\ & \text{subject to} & g_1(\mathbf{x}) \leq 0 \\ (263) & & \vdots \\ & & g_p(\mathbf{x}) \leq 0. \end{array}$$

The net revenue received by the market depends upon the shortages and excesses of raw materials in the industry. Suppose $\mu_k \geq 0$ is the unit price at which raw material $k$ is purchased or sold at the market. If a shortage of raw material $k$ exists, $g_k(\mathbf{x}) > 0$, the industry operates at a level $\mathbf{x}$ by purchasing an amount $g_k(\mathbf{x})$ of raw material $k$ at total cost

$$\mu_k g_k(\mathbf{x}).$$

Conversely, if the industry has an excess of the $k$th raw material, $g_k(\mathbf{x}) < 0$, the industry can sell the excess back to the market at a cost of

$$\mu_k g_k(\mathbf{x}).$$

Thus, the *net* revenue received by the market includes the revenue received from the industry's initial purchases of raw materials, $g_0(\mathbf{x})$, plus the net revenue from either purchasing back excess raw materials or selling additional raw materials. This net revenue of the market, or the net production cost to the industry, is represented by the Lagrangian of convex programming problem (263),

$$L(\mathbf{x}, \boldsymbol{\mu}) = g_0(\mathbf{x}) + \sum_{k=1}^{p} \mu_k g_k(\mathbf{x}).$$

The industry wishes to adjust its operating level $\mathbf{x}$ so as to minimize the net cost $L(\mathbf{x}, \boldsymbol{\mu})$ for a given set of raw material costs; that is, given $\mu_1, \ldots, \mu_p$, the industry desires to operate at a level $\mathbf{x}^*$ that satisfies

$$\nabla_{\mathbf{x}} L(\mathbf{x}^*, \boldsymbol{\mu}) = \nabla g_0(\mathbf{x}^*) + \sum_{k=1}^{p} \mu_k \nabla g_k(\mathbf{x}^*) = \mathbf{0}.$$

These interrelated problems of minimizing the net production cost and maximizing net market revenue suggests that associated with the production cost minimization problem (263) is a dual mathematical programming problem. This dual mathematical programming problem is a mathematical formulation of this market's problem of adjusting the unit prices so as to maximize net revenue given that the industry desires to minimize net production costs:

(264)
$$\begin{aligned}
&\underset{\mu_1,\ldots,\mu_p}{\text{maximize}} && L(\mathbf{x}, \boldsymbol{\mu}) = g_0(\mathbf{x}) + \sum_{k=1}^{p} \mu_k g_k(\mathbf{x}) \\
&\text{subject to} && \nabla_x L(\mathbf{x}, \boldsymbol{\mu}) = \nabla g_0(\mathbf{x}) + \sum_{k=1}^{p} \mu_k \nabla g_k(\mathbf{x}) = \mathbf{0}, \\
& && \mu_k \geq 0 \quad (k = 1, \ldots, p).
\end{aligned}$$

(Note that $\mathbf{x}$ must lie in the constraint set of (263)).

The production cost minimization problem (263) and the net market revenue maximization problem (264) are dual in the sense of a "duality inequality." Specifically, for any $\mathbf{x}'$ and $\mathbf{x}''$ in the constraint set of (263) and any point $(\mathbf{x}'', \boldsymbol{\mu}'')$ satisfying the constraints of (264), we have the duality inequality,

(265)
$$g_0(\mathbf{x}') \geq L(\mathbf{x}'', \boldsymbol{\mu}'').$$

Inequality (265) states that the production cost always exceeds the market's net revenue. The validity of this inequality follows by exploiting the convexity of $g_0, g_1, \ldots, g_p$. For $\mathbf{x}'$, $(\mathbf{x}'', \boldsymbol{\mu}'')$ as above, first note that because $\mu_k'' g_k(\mathbf{x}') \leq 0$,

(266)
$$g_0(\mathbf{x}') \geq g_0(\mathbf{x}') + \sum_{k=1}^{p} \mu_k'' g_k(\mathbf{x}') = L(\mathbf{x}', \boldsymbol{\mu}'').$$

Since $L(\mathbf{x}', \boldsymbol{\mu}'')$ is convex,

$$g_0(\mathbf{x}') + \sum_{k=1}^{p} \mu_k'' g_k(\mathbf{x}') \geq g_0(\mathbf{x}'') + \sum_{k=1}^{p} \mu_k'' g_k(\mathbf{x}'') + \left[\nabla g_0(\mathbf{x}'') + \sum_{k=1}^{p} \mu_k'' \nabla g_k(\mathbf{x}'')\right] \cdot (\mathbf{x}' - \mathbf{x}'').$$

This inequality simplifies to

(267)
$$g_0(\mathbf{x}') + \sum_{k=1}^{p} \mu_k'' g_k(\mathbf{x}') \geq g_0(\mathbf{x}'') + \sum_{k=1}^{p} \mu_k'' g_k(\mathbf{x}'') = L(\mathbf{x}'', \boldsymbol{\mu}'')$$

because $(\mathbf{x}'', \boldsymbol{\mu}'')$ satisfies the constraint

$$\nabla g_0(\mathbf{x}'') + \sum_{k=1}^{p} \mu_k'' \nabla g_k(\mathbf{x}'') = \mathbf{0}.$$

The duality inequality (265) follows by combining inequalities (266) and (267).

Under certain conditions the net market revenue $L(\mathbf{x}, \boldsymbol{\mu})$ is identical to the industry's production cost $g_0(\mathbf{x})$:

$$g_0(\mathbf{x}^*) = L(\mathbf{x}^*, \boldsymbol{\mu}'). \tag{268}$$

This situation represents an economic competitive equilibrium, and this equilibrium results in a stable market; that is, under conditions (268), no variation in the unit prices can increase costs and no change in the operating level by industry can decrease net market revenue.

As the following result states, this economic competitive equilibrium actually occurs when $\mathbf{x}$ and $\mu_1, \ldots, \mu_p$ satisfy the Kuhn–Tucker conditions:

**THEOREM 51** Suppose that convex programming problem (263) is superconsistent and attains a minimum value $M$ at the point $\mathbf{x}^*$. Then the dual programming problem (264) attains its maximum $\overline{M}$ at the point $(\mathbf{x}^*, \boldsymbol{\mu}')$, which satisfies the Kuhn–Tucker conditions. Moreover, $M = \overline{M}$.

**PROOF** If $(\mathbf{x}'', \boldsymbol{\mu}'')$ satisfies the constraints of (264) and $\mathbf{x}''$ is in the constraint set of (263), then, since $L$ is convex, $L(\mathbf{x}'', \boldsymbol{\mu}'')$ is a minimum of $L$ as a function of $\mathbf{x}$; that is,

$$L(\mathbf{x}'', \boldsymbol{\mu}'') \le L(\mathbf{x}, \boldsymbol{\mu}'')$$

for any point $\mathbf{x}$. In particular, for $\mathbf{x} = \mathbf{x}^*$,

$$L(\mathbf{x}'', \boldsymbol{\mu}'') \le L(\mathbf{x}^*, \boldsymbol{\mu}'') = g_0(\mathbf{x}^*) + \sum_{k=1}^{p} \mu_k'' g_k(\mathbf{x}^*).$$

Since $g_k(\mathbf{x}^*) \le 0$, $k = 1, \ldots, p$, and $g_0(\mathbf{x}^*) = M$,

$$L(\mathbf{x}'', \boldsymbol{\mu}'') \le g_0(\mathbf{x}^*) = M.$$

Thus, the least upper bound of $L(\mathbf{x}, \boldsymbol{\mu})$ is $M$. According to the Kuhn–Tucker theorem there exists a $\boldsymbol{\mu}'$ such that $(\mathbf{x}^*, \boldsymbol{\mu}')$ satisfies the constraints of (264) and

$$L(\mathbf{x}^*, \boldsymbol{\mu}') = M.$$

Hence, $\overline{M} = M$. ▌

This duality theorem states that at the competitive equilibrium the Kuhn–Tucker conditions hold. The first Kuhn–Tucker condition,

$$\nabla g_0(\mathbf{x}^*) + \sum_{k=1}^{p} \mu_k' \, \nabla g_k(\mathbf{x}^*) = \mathbf{0},$$

states that at the optimum, the marginal production cost equals the industry's marginal revenue. This follows by noting that since $g_0(\mathbf{x})$ is the production cost,

$$\nabla g_0(\mathbf{x}) = \left(\frac{\partial g_0}{\partial x_1}, \ldots, \frac{\partial g_0}{\partial x_n}\right)$$

economically represents the marginal production costs. Similarly, since $-\sum_{k=1}^{p} \mu_k g_k(\mathbf{x})$ is interpreted as the industry's net revenue due to selling raw materials,

$$-\sum_{k=1}^{p} \mu_k \nabla g_k(\mathbf{x}) = -\sum_{k=1}^{p} \mu_k \left( \frac{\partial g_k}{\partial x_1}, \ldots, \frac{\partial g_k}{\partial x_n} \right)$$

economically represents the industry's marginal net revenue.

The Kuhn–Tucker conditions

$$\mu_k' g_k(\mathbf{x}^*) = 0 \tag{269}$$

($k = 1, \ldots, p$) also have an economic interpretation. Suppose that this complementary slackness condition is not satisfied at equilibrium, $g_k(\mathbf{x}^*) < 0$ and $\mu_k' > 0$. Since $\mu_k' > 0$, the market would be able to decrease $\mu_k'$ slightly to $\mu_k''$, implying

$$\mu_k' g_k(\mathbf{x}^*) < \mu_k'' g_k(\mathbf{x}^*).$$

But $g_k(\mathbf{x}^*) < 0$ represents an excess of raw material $k$ in the industry, and such an action reduces the industry's net cost. However, at equilibrium any decrease in cost is impossible. Thus, $\mu_k' g_k(\mathbf{x}^*) = 0$.

Note, further, that since (269) holds, there is no revenue obtained from selling excesses of a raw material; that is, if $g_k(\mathbf{x}^*) < 0$, then $\mu_k' = 0$. Actually, since $g_k(\mathbf{x}) \leq 0$ for $k = 1, \ldots, p$, the industry never purchases additional raw materials.

To complete our discussion of this model of competitive interactions, let us examine the sensitivity of $g_0(\mathbf{x}^*)$, the minimum cost of raw materials, to variations in the constraining quantities $r_1, \ldots, r_p$. For simplicity, suppose that at $\mathbf{x}^*$ only the first constraint is active; that is,

$$\begin{aligned}
g_1(\mathbf{x}^*) &= h_1(\mathbf{x}^*) - r_1 = 0 \\
g_2(\mathbf{x}^*) &= h_2(\mathbf{x}^*) - r_2 < 0 \\
&\;\;\vdots \qquad\qquad\quad \vdots \\
g_p(\mathbf{x}^*) &= h_p(\mathbf{x}^*) - r_p < 0.
\end{aligned}$$

In this case the sensitivity of $g_0(\mathbf{x}^*)$ to $r_2, \ldots, r_p$ is obviously zero, since the corresponding constraints have no effect on the objective function.

However, $g_0(\mathbf{x}^*)$ is sensitive to variations in $r_1$. As a measure of this sensitivity, we compute

$$\frac{\partial g_0(\mathbf{x}^*)}{\partial r_1}.$$

Using the chain rule, we see that

$$(270) \qquad \frac{\partial g_0(\mathbf{x}^*)}{\partial r_1} = \frac{\partial g_0(\mathbf{x}^*)}{\partial x_1}\frac{\partial x_1}{\partial r_1} + \cdots + \frac{\partial g_0(\mathbf{x}^*)}{\partial x_n}\frac{\partial x_n}{\partial r_1}$$

$$= \nabla g_0(\mathbf{x}^*) \cdot \mathbf{x}_{r_1},$$

where $\mathbf{x}_{r_1} = (\partial x_1/\partial r_1, \ldots, \partial x_n/\partial r_1)$. Furthermore, according to the Kuhn–Tucker theorem,

$$(271) \qquad \nabla g_0(\mathbf{x}^*) = -\sum_{k=1}^{p} \mu_k' \nabla g_k(\mathbf{x}^*).$$

Since the complementary slackness condition implies $\mu_2' = \cdots = \mu_p' = 0$, (271) reduces to

$$(272) \qquad \nabla g_0(\mathbf{x}^*) = -\mu_1' \nabla g_1(\mathbf{x}^*).$$

Thus, combining (270) and (272), we find

$$\frac{\partial g_0(\mathbf{x}^*)}{\partial r_1} = [-\mu_1' \nabla g_1(\mathbf{x}^*)] \cdot \mathbf{x}_{r_1}$$

$$= -\mu_1'[\nabla g_1(\mathbf{x}^*) \cdot \mathbf{x}_{r_1}].$$

Finally, since, by the chain rule,

$$\frac{\partial g_1(\mathbf{x}^*)}{\partial r_1} = \nabla g_1(\mathbf{x}^*) \cdot \mathbf{x}_{r_1},$$

we have

$$\frac{\partial g_0(\mathbf{x}^*)}{\partial r_1} = -\mu_1' \frac{\partial g_1(\mathbf{x}^*)}{\partial r_1}$$

$$= -\mu_1' \frac{\partial}{\partial r_1}[h_1(\mathbf{x}^*) - r_1]$$

$$= \mu_1'.$$

Thus, $\mu_1'$, the optimal price of the first raw material, is also the sensitivity coefficient of $g_0(\mathbf{x}^*)$ with respect to a small change in the constraining quantity $r_1$.

For any convex programming problem of the form (263), the related mathematical programming problem (264) is called the *Wolfe dual*. As was previously pointed out these programs are dual in the sense of duality inequality (265). Moreover, according to Theorem 51 the values of the two programs are equal, and thus, the duality inequality becomes an equality when $\mathbf{x}$ and $\boldsymbol{\mu}$ satisfy the Kuhn–Tucker conditions.

The duality inequality is of computational value in estimating the constrained minimum value of a convex programming problem. The duality inequality provides upper and lower bounds for the minimum $M$ of convex program (263). For any point $\mathbf{x}'$ in the constraint set of (263),

$$g_0(\mathbf{x}') \geq M,$$

and for any point $(\mathbf{x}'', \boldsymbol{\mu}'')$ satisfying the constraints of (264), with $\mathbf{x}''$ in the constraint set of (263), the duality inequality implies

$$M \geq L(\mathbf{x}'', \boldsymbol{\mu}'').$$

Thus, according to the duality inequality, the minimum value $M$ of (263) satisfies

$$g_0(\mathbf{x}') \geq M \geq L(\mathbf{x}'', \boldsymbol{\mu}'').$$

To illustrate this inequality consider the following convex programming problem:

$$\begin{array}{lll} & \text{minimize} & g_0(\mathbf{x}) = x_1 + x_2 - \ln(x_1 x_2) \\ (273) & \text{subject to} & g_1(\mathbf{x}) = -x_1 + 1 \leq 0 \\ & & g_2(\mathbf{x}) = -x_2 + 1 \leq 0. \end{array}$$

The Wolfe dual of (273) is

$$\begin{array}{lll} & \text{maximize} & L(\mathbf{x}, \boldsymbol{\mu}) = x_1 + x_2 - \ln(x_1 x_2) + \mu_1(-x_1 + 1) \\ & & \qquad + \mu_2(-x_2 + 1) \\ (274) & \text{subject to} & \dfrac{\partial L}{\partial x_1} = 1 - \dfrac{1}{x_1} - \mu_1 = 0 \\ & & \dfrac{\partial L}{\partial x_2} = 1 - \dfrac{1}{x_2} - \mu_2 = 0 \\ & & \mu_1 \geq 0, \quad \mu_2 \geq 0. \end{array}$$

Since $\mathbf{x}' = (1, 2)$ is in the constraint set of (273), we have the upper bound on the minimum $M$ of (273): $g_0(\mathbf{x}') = 3 - \ln 2 = 2.3069 \geq M$. Further, note that $(\mathbf{x}'', \boldsymbol{\mu}'') = (1, 1, 0, 0)$ satisfies the constraints of (274) and $\mathbf{x}''$ is in the constraint set of (273). Hence,

$$M \geq L(\mathbf{x}'', \boldsymbol{\mu}'') = 2.$$

Thus, we have bounded $M$ from above and below as

$$2.3069 \geq M \geq 2.$$

Note that since $\mathbf{x}^* = (1, 1)$, $\boldsymbol{\mu}' = (0, 0)$ satisfy the Kuhn–Tucker conditions, $\mathbf{x}^* = (1, 1)$ is the minimizing point of (273). Further, according to the duality theorem, $(\mathbf{x}^*, \boldsymbol{\mu}') = (1, 1, 0, 0)$ is the maximizing point of dual program (274):

$$g_0(\mathbf{x}^*) = L(\mathbf{x}^*, \boldsymbol{\mu}') = 2.$$

As a second illustration of the duality inequality, consider the following convex programming problem:

$$(275) \qquad \begin{array}{ll} \text{minimize} & g_0(\mathbf{x}) = 2x_1^2 + x_2^2 \\ \text{subject to} & g_1(\mathbf{x}) = -1 + x_1^2 - x_2 \leq 0. \end{array}$$

The Wolfe dual of (275) is

$$(276) \qquad \begin{array}{ll} \text{maximize} & L(\mathbf{x}, \mu) = 2x_1^2 + x_2^2 + \mu_1(-1 + x_1^2 - x_2) \\ \text{subject to} & \dfrac{\partial L}{\partial x_1} = 4x_1 + 2\mu_1 x_1 = 0 \\ & \dfrac{\partial L}{\partial x_2} = 2x_2 - \mu_1 = 0 \\ & \mu_1 \geq 0, \end{array}$$

Since $\mathbf{x}' = (0, 2)$ satisfies the constraints of (275), the minimum value $M$ of (275) is at most $g_0(\mathbf{x}') = 4$; that is, $4 \geq M$. Because $(\mathbf{x}'', \boldsymbol{\mu}'') = (0, 0, 0)$ satisfies the constraints of (276), and $\mathbf{x}'' = (0, 0)$ is in the constraint set of (275), the duality inequality implies that the minimum value of (275) is at least $L(\mathbf{x}'', \boldsymbol{\mu}'') = 0$; that is, $M \geq L(\mathbf{x}'', \mu'') = 0$. Therefore, the duality inequality has provided upper and lower bounds for $M$:

$$4 \geq M \geq 0.$$

Further, since $\mathbf{x}^* = (0, 0)$ and $\mu_1' = 0$ satisfy the Kuhn–Tucker conditions, $\mathbf{x}^* = (0, 0)$ is a minimizing point of (275). And, according to the duality theorem, $(\mathbf{x}^*, \mu') = (0, 0, 0)$ is a maximizing point of dual program (276):

$$g_0(\mathbf{x}^*) = L(\mathbf{x}^*, \mu') = 0.$$

## A PRODUCTION SCHEDULING PROBLEM: DUALITY IN LINEAR PROGRAMMING

Mathematical analyses of production scheduling problems usually seek to determine the sequence of production lots that minimize the total elapsed production time and, thus, the associated costs. Typically, production scheduling problems concern the sequencing of jobs over a series of machines or the designing of an assembly line so as to minimize processing time.

**Table 1**

| | Product | |
|---|---|---|
| Period | $X$ | $Y$ |
| 1 | 320 | 240 |
| 2 | 400 | 285 |
| 3 | 360 | 420 |

Because of the complexity of these problems, systematic techniques for solving production scheduling problems have developed from necessity. The small problem of sequencing four jobs that each require processing time on five machines in no particular order involves $(4!)^5$, or 7,962,624, different sequences. If certain jobs must be processed on the machines in a particular order, this number is reduced; but the problem of determining the optimal sequence is complicated further. Thus, any procedure that determines the optimal solution of such a problem without testing all possible feasible solutions is of value.

The production scheduling problem discussed here is the problem of scheduling production overtime. Suppose a firm must allocate an available number of regular and overtime working hours in each of three periods so as to meet certain contracted deliveries and to minimize the cost of its operation. In particular, assume that in each production period the firm has contracted to produce and deliver each of two products, $X$ and $Y$, in the quantities indicated in Table 1.

Suppose, further, that during each production period there are 150 h of regular working time and 50 h of more expensive overtime available. If $\frac{1}{4}$ of an hour is necessary to produce each unit of product $X$ and $\frac{1}{3}$ of an hour for one unit of product $Y$, then the production time requirements are as indicated in Table 2.

By comparing the required and available production times in Table 2, we see that while the time requirements of period 3 exceed the time available

**Table 2**

| | Production Times | | | |
|---|---|---|---|---|
| Period | For $X$ | For $Y$ | Total Required | Total Available |
| 1 | $\frac{1}{4}(320)$ | $\frac{1}{3}(240)$ | 160 | 200 |
| 2 | $\frac{1}{4}(400)$ | $\frac{1}{3}(285)$ | 195 | 200 |
| 3 | $\frac{1}{4}(360)$ | $\frac{1}{3}(420)$ | 230 | 200 |

by 30 h, the total accumulated supply of excess production time, 45 h, is greater than 30. Hence, a feasible solution to this problem exists. Obviously, however, the demand of period 3 is met only by producing an excess in a previous period and storing it. Since a backlogging of demand is not permitted, the optimal solution of our production scheduling problem must therefore determine the production lots of $X$ and $Y$ that minimize the associated inventory cost as well as production costs.

In developing this model, we use the notation $x_{ij}$ ($\geq 0$) to denote the amount of product $X$ produced in period $i$ using regular working hours to satisfy the demand of period $j$. Similarly, $\bar{x}_{ij}$ ($\geq 0$) denotes the amount of product $X$ produced in period $i$ using overtime hours to satisfy demand in period $j$. Here $i, j = 1, 2, 3$. The notation $y_{ij}$ ($\geq 0$) and $\bar{y}_{ij}$ ($\geq 0$) has an analogous interpretation for product $Y$. Note that $i \leq j$, since no backlogging is permitted.

The values of these variables must be chosen so that the corresponding production times do not exceed the available regular and overtime hours of production. In period 3 the regular time used to produce products $X$ and $Y$ for use in period 3 cannot exceed 150:

$$\tfrac{1}{4}x_{33} + \tfrac{1}{3}y_{33} \leq 150.$$

Similarly, the overtime used in period 3 must satisfy

$$\tfrac{1}{4}\bar{x}_{33} + \tfrac{1}{3}\bar{y}_{33} \leq 50.$$

Since the regular and overtime hours required in period 2 may be used to produce quantities of $X$ and $Y$ for consumption in periods 2 or 3, the corresponding working time constraints for period 2 are

$$\tfrac{1}{4}x_{22} + \tfrac{1}{4}x_{23} + \tfrac{1}{3}y_{22} + \tfrac{1}{3}y_{23} \leq 150,$$
$$\tfrac{1}{4}\bar{x}_{22} + \tfrac{1}{4}\bar{x}_{23} + \tfrac{1}{3}\bar{y}_{22} + \tfrac{1}{3}\bar{y}_{23} \leq 50.$$

Analogously, because the production time of period 1 may be used to produce quantities of $X$ and $Y$ for consumption in periods 1, 2, or 3, we have the constraints,

$$\tfrac{1}{4}x_{11} + \tfrac{1}{4}x_{12} + \tfrac{1}{4}x_{13} + \tfrac{1}{3}y_{11} + \tfrac{1}{3}y_{12} + \tfrac{1}{3}y_{13} \leq 150,$$
$$\tfrac{1}{4}\bar{x}_{11} + \tfrac{1}{4}\bar{x}_{12} + \tfrac{1}{4}\bar{x}_{13} + \tfrac{1}{3}\bar{y}_{11} + \tfrac{1}{3}\bar{y}_{12} + \tfrac{1}{3}\bar{y}_{13} \leq 50.$$

The production levels must also meet the demand of each period. For example, the quantities of $X$ and $Y$ produced using regular and overtime working hours in period 1 for consumption in period 1 must satisfy

$$x_{11} + \bar{x}_{11} \geq 320,$$
$$y_{11} + \bar{y}_{11} \geq 240,$$

respectively. The demand of period 2 is met either from production in period 2 or from the production in period 1 carried in inventory. Thus, we have

$$x_{12} + \bar{x}_{12} + x_{22} + \bar{x}_{22} \geq 400,$$
$$y_{12} + \bar{y}_{12} + y_{22} + \bar{y}_{22} \geq 285.$$

Similarly, since the demand of product 3 is met by production in period 3 or by production in period 1 or 2 carried in inventory, we have the demand constraints

$$x_{13} + \bar{x}_{13} + x_{23} + \bar{x}_{23} + x_{33} + \bar{x}_{33} \geq 360,$$
$$y_{13} + \bar{y}_{13} + y_{23} + \bar{y}_{23} + y_{33} + \bar{y}_{33} \geq 420.$$

Three cost components are considered in determining the total cost of this operation: the costs of regular working hours, of overtime working hours, and of storing accumulated production. Suppose the cost of regular time is \$3/h, overtime time is \$6/h, double the regular rate, and the storage cost is \$2 per unit per period. Then the total costs of regular and overtime working hours used in producing products $X$ and $Y$ for consumption in the same period are

(277) $$\sum_{i=1}^{3} 3(\tfrac{1}{4}x_{ii}) + \sum_{i=1}^{3} 6(\tfrac{1}{4}\bar{x}_{ii})$$

and

(278) $$\sum_{i=1}^{3} 3(\tfrac{1}{3}y_{ii}) + \sum_{i=1}^{3} 6(\tfrac{1}{3}\bar{y}_{ii}),$$

respectively.

The costs of regular and working hours used in producing $X$ and $Y$ in one period for consumption in the following period are

(279) $$\sum_{i=1}^{2} 3(\tfrac{1}{4}x_{ii+1}) + \sum_{i=1}^{2} 6(\tfrac{1}{4}\bar{x}_{ii+1})$$

and

(280) $$\sum_{i=1}^{2} 3(\tfrac{1}{3}y_{ii+1}) + \sum_{i=1}^{2} 6(\tfrac{1}{3}\bar{y}_{ii+1}),$$

respectively. In this case, the cost of storing the production for one period must also be considered:

(281) $$\sum_{i=1}^{2} 2(x_{ii+1} + \bar{x}_{ii+1} + y_{ii+1} + \bar{y}_{ii+1}).$$

Similarly, we must also consider the cost of producing goods in period 1 for consumption in period 3. The total cost of regular and overtime hours in this case is

(282) $$3(\tfrac{1}{4}x_{13} + \tfrac{1}{3}y_{13}) + 6(\tfrac{1}{4}\bar{x}_{13} + \tfrac{1}{3}\bar{y}_{13}),$$

and the total cost of storing this production for two periods is

(283) $$2(2x_{13} + 2y_{13} + 2\bar{x}_{13} + 2\bar{y}_{13}).$$

Thus, the sum of (277)–(283) represents the total cost of this production scheduling problem:

$$\begin{aligned} g_0(\mathbf{x}) = {} & 0.75(x_{11} + x_{22} + x_{33}) + 2.75(x_{12} + x_{23}) + 4.75x_{13} \\ & + 1.5(\bar{x}_{11} + \bar{x}_{22} + \bar{x}_{33}) + 3.5(\bar{x}_{12} + \bar{x}_{23}) + 5.5\bar{x}_{13} \\ & + (y_{11} + y_{22} + y_{33}) + 3(y_{12} + y_{23}) + 5y_{13} \\ & + 2(\bar{y}_{11} + \bar{y}_{22} + \bar{y}_{33}) + 4(\bar{y}_{12} + \bar{y}_{23}) + 6\bar{y}_{13}. \end{aligned}$$

The mathematical formulation of this problem of determining production levels that require at most a specified number of working hours and that satisfy certain levels of demand at minimum cost is the following convex programming problem:

(284)
$$\begin{aligned} &\text{minimize} \quad g_0(\mathbf{x}) \\ &\text{subject to} \quad -x_{ij} \le 0, \qquad i, j = 1, 2, 3, \\ &\tfrac{1}{4}x_{33} + \tfrac{1}{3}y_{33} - 150 \le 0 \\ &\tfrac{1}{4}\bar{x}_{33} + \tfrac{1}{3}\bar{y}_{33} - 50 \le 0 \\ &\tfrac{1}{4}x_{22} + \tfrac{1}{4}x_{23} + \tfrac{1}{3}y_{22} + \tfrac{1}{3}y_{23} - 150 \le 0 \\ &\tfrac{1}{4}\bar{x}_{22} + \tfrac{1}{4}\bar{x}_{23} + \tfrac{1}{3}\bar{y}_{22} + \tfrac{1}{3}\bar{y}_{23} - 50 \le 0 \\ &\tfrac{1}{4}x_{11} + \tfrac{1}{4}x_{12} + \tfrac{1}{4}x_{13} + \tfrac{1}{3}y_{11} \\ &\qquad + \tfrac{1}{3}y_{12} + \tfrac{1}{3}y_{13} - 150 \le 0 \\ &\tfrac{1}{4}\bar{x}_{11} + \tfrac{1}{4}\bar{x}_{12} + \tfrac{1}{4}\bar{x}_{13} + \tfrac{1}{3}\bar{y}_{11} \\ &\qquad + \tfrac{1}{3}\bar{y}_{12} + \tfrac{1}{3}\bar{y}_{13} - 50 \le 0 \\ &-x_{11} - \bar{x}_{11} + 320 \le 0 \\ &-y_{11} - \bar{y}_{11} + 240 \le 0 \\ &-x_{12} - \bar{x}_{12} - x_{22} - \bar{x}_{22} + 400 \le 0 \\ &-y_{12} - \bar{y}_{12} - y_{22} - \bar{y}_{22} + 285 \le 0 \\ &-x_{13} - \bar{x}_{13} - x_{23} - \bar{x}_{23} - x_{33} - \bar{x}_{33} + 360 \le 0 \\ &-y_{13} - \bar{y}_{13} - y_{23} - \bar{y}_{23} - y_{33} - \bar{y}_{33} + 420 \le 0. \end{aligned}$$

Because of the linear structure of the objective function and constraint functions of (284), this convex programming problem is called a *linear programming problem.*

Although this problem is not solved here, because of its complexity, many numerical algorithms have been developed specifically to solve linear programming problems. Among these is the *simplex method*. This technique is an algorithm that examines the extreme points of the polygonal constraint set of (284), searching for the minimizing point (for a further discussion of the simplex method, see Duffin, Peterson, and Zener).

The previously developed results of convex programming certainly apply to this particular class of convex programming problems. In particular we may use the Kuhn Tucker theorem of convex programming to develop a special duality theory of linear programming.

Consider the general *linear programming problem:*

$$\begin{aligned} &\text{minimize} && g_0(\mathbf{x}) = \sum_{i=1}^{n} b_i x_i \\ &\text{subject to} && g_1(\mathbf{x}) = c_1 - \sum_{i=1}^{n} a_{i1} x_i \le 0 \\ &&& \vdots \\ &&& g_p(\mathbf{x}) = c_p - \sum_{i=1}^{n} a_{ip} x_i \le 0. \end{aligned} \tag{285}$$

Observe that the objective and constraint functions are all linear and, hence, convex functions of $x_1, \ldots, x_n$.

To aid in the analysis of this problem we introduce a related or "dual" linear programming problem:

$$\begin{aligned} &\text{maximize} && \sum_{k=1}^{p} \mu_k c_k \\ &\text{subject to} && \mu_1 \ge 0, \ldots, \mu_p \ge 0 \\ &&& b_1 - \sum_{k=1}^{p} \mu_k a_{1k} = 0 \\ &&& \vdots \\ &&& b_n - \sum_{k=1}^{p} \mu_k a_{nk} = 0. \end{aligned} \tag{286}$$

Program (286) is called the *unsymmetrical dual linear programming problem.* Notice that program (286) is constructed from linear program (285). The constrained minimization problem in $x_1, \ldots, x_n$ is replaced by a constrained maximization problem in the *nonnegative* variables $\mu_1, \ldots, \mu_p$. Although linear program (285) has inequality constraints, the associated problem (286) has equality constraints. Furthermore, the roles of the constants $c_1, \ldots, c_p$ and $b_1, \ldots, b_n$ are interchanged. Note that the summations in (285) are taken over the rows of the matrix with elements $a_{ij}$, while the summations in (286) are taken over the columns of this matrix.

Programs (285) and (286) are "dual" in the sense of the inequality

$$\sum_{i=1}^{n} b_i x_i' \geq \sum_{k=1}^{p} \mu_k'' c_k \tag{287}$$

for $\mathbf{x}'$ and $\boldsymbol{\mu}''$ satisfying the constraints of (285) and (286), respectively.

The validity of this inequality follows by first observing that $b_i = \sum_{k=1}^{p} \mu_k'' a_{ik}$, $i = 1, \ldots, n$ for $\boldsymbol{\mu}''$ satisfying the constraints of (286). Thus,

$$\sum_{i=1}^{n} b_i x_i' = \sum_{i=1}^{n} \left( \sum_{k=1}^{p} \mu_k'' a_{ik} \right) x_i'. \tag{288}$$

Since

$$\sum_{i=1}^{n} \left( \sum_{k=1}^{p} \mu_k'' a_{ik} \right) x_i' = \sum_{k=1}^{p} \mu_k'' \left( \sum_{i=1}^{n} a_{ik} x_i' \right)$$

and

$$\sum_{i=1}^{n} a_{ik} x_i' \geq c_k, \qquad k = 1, \ldots, p,$$

(these are the constraints of (285)),

$$\sum_{k=1}^{p} \mu_k'' \left( \sum_{i=1}^{n} a_{ik} x_i' \right) \geq \sum_{k=1}^{p} \mu_k'' c_k. \tag{289}$$

Combining (289) and (288) we have the *duality inequality* of unsymmetrical linear programming:

$$\sum_{i=1}^{n} b_i x_i' \geq \sum_{k=1}^{p} \mu_k'' c_k.$$

This duality inequality provides upper and lower bounds for $M$, the minimum of linear program (285). This follows since for any point $x'$ in the constraint set of (285),

$$g_0(\mathbf{x}') \geq M,$$

and for any point $\boldsymbol{\mu}''$ satisfying the constraints of (286),

$$M \geq \sum_{k=1}^{p} \mu_k'' c_k.$$

Thus, according to the duality inequality, the minimum value satisfies

$$\sum_{i=1}^{n} b_i x_i' \geq M \geq \sum_{k=1}^{p} \mu_k'' c_k.$$

Under certain conditions the latter inequality actually becomes an equality and, thus, the solution of (286) aids in solving (285). These conditions are summarized in the unsymmetrical duality theory of linear programming:

THEOREM 52 If linear programming problem (285) has an optimal solution $\mathbf{x}^*$, then the unsymmetrical dual linear programming problem (286) has an optimal solution $\boldsymbol{\mu}'$. Moreover,

$$\sum_{i=1}^{n} b_i x_i^* = \sum_{k=1}^{p} c_k \mu_k'.$$

PROOF In proving this duality theorem, we apply the Kuhn–Tucker conditions of convex programming to (285). According to the Kuhn–Tucker theorem, if linear programming problem (285) has an optimal solution $\mathbf{x}^*$, then there exist $\mu_k' \geq 0$, $k = 1, \ldots, p$, satisfying

$$\nabla g_0(\mathbf{x}^*) + \sum_{k=1}^{p} \mu_k' \nabla g_k(\mathbf{x}^*) = \mathbf{0} \tag{290}$$

and

$$\mu_k' g_k(\mathbf{x}^*) = 0, \qquad k = 1, \ldots, p. \tag{291}$$

Condition (290) is equivalent to stating that $\boldsymbol{\mu}' = (\mu_1', \ldots, \mu_p')$ satisfies the constraints of (286),

$$\begin{aligned} b_1 - \sum_{k=1}^{p} \mu_k' a_{1k} &= 0 \\ &\ \ \vdots \\ b_n - \sum_{k=1}^{p} \mu_k' a_{nk} &= 0. \end{aligned} \tag{290'}$$

It is now proved that this vector $\boldsymbol{\mu}'$ is actually the maximizing vector of (286). With the linear structure of problems (285) and (286) the complementary slackness condition (291) states that

$$\begin{aligned} \mu'_1\left(c_1 - \sum_{i=1}^{n} a_{i1}x_i^*\right) &= 0 \\ &\vdots \\ \mu'_p\left(c_p - \sum_{i=1}^{n} a_{ip}x_i^*\right) &= 0. \end{aligned} \tag{291'}$$

Since conditions (291′) hold, observe that at $(\mathbf{x}^*, \boldsymbol{\mu}')$ the Lagrangian of (285) satisfies

$$L(\mathbf{x}^*, \boldsymbol{\mu}') = \sum_{i=1}^{n} b_i x_i^* + \sum_{k=1}^{p} \mu'_k\left(c_k - \sum_{i=1}^{n} a_{ik}x_i^*\right) = \sum_{i=1}^{n} b_i x_i^*. \tag{292}$$

But a rearrangement of the terms of the Lagrangian shows that

$$L(\mathbf{x}^*, \boldsymbol{\mu}') = \sum_{k=1}^{p} c_k \mu'_k + \sum_{i=1}^{n} x_i^*\left(b_i - \sum_{k=1}^{p} \mu'_k a_{ik}\right).$$

Since $\boldsymbol{\mu}'$ satisfies (290′), the latter implies

$$L(\mathbf{x}^*, \boldsymbol{\mu}') = \sum_{k=1}^{p} c_k \mu'_k. \tag{293}$$

Thus, together (292) and (293) yield

$$\sum_{i=1}^{n} b_i x_i^* = \sum_{k=1}^{p} c_k \mu'_k. \tag{294}$$

Since the duality inequality (287) states that

$$\sum_{i=1}^{n} b_i x_i \geq \sum_{k=1}^{p} c_k \mu_k$$

for *any* $\mathbf{x}$ and $\boldsymbol{\mu}$ satisfying the constraints of (285) and (286), respectively, (294) implies that $\boldsymbol{\mu}'$ must be the maximizing point of (286).

Although the converse of this theorem also holds, it is not proved here. ▮

The Wolfe duality theorem also may be used to prove this result; see exercise 17.

To illustrate this duality theorem, consider the following linear programming problem:

$$
(295) \qquad \begin{aligned} &\text{minimize} && 3x_1 + x_2 \\ &\text{subject to} && -x_2 \le 0 \\ &&& x_1 - x_2 \le 0 \\ &&& 1 - 3x_1 - x_2 \le 0. \end{aligned}
$$

The unsymmetrical dual of (295) is as follows:

$$
(296) \qquad \begin{aligned} &\text{maximize} && \mu_3 \\ &\text{subject to} && 3 + \mu_2 - 3\mu_3 = 0 \\ &&& 1 - \mu_1 - \mu_2 - \mu_3 = 0 \\ &&& \mu_1 \ge 0, \quad \mu_2 \ge 0, \quad \mu_3 \ge 0. \end{aligned}
$$

According to the duality inequality $M$, the minimum of (295) satisfies

$$
3x_1 + x_2 \ge M \ge \mu_3
$$

for $\mathbf{x}$ and $\boldsymbol{\mu}$ satisfying the constraints of (295) and (296), respectively. With $\mathbf{x} = (1, 1)$ and $\boldsymbol{\mu} = (0, 0, 1)$, the latter inequality gives the following bounds on the minimum $M$,

$$
4 \ge M \ge 1.
$$

By applying the Kuhn–Tucker conditions to (295), we find that the minimizing vector of (295) is $\mathbf{x}^* = (0, 1)$ and the minimum value is 1. Therefore, since (295) has an optimal solution, the duality theorem states that there also exists an optimal solution of the unsymmetrical dual (296). Moreover, according to the proof of this theorem, the vector $\boldsymbol{\mu}'$ satisfying the Kuhn–Tucker conditions is the optimal solution. With $\mathbf{x}^* = (0, 1)$, $\boldsymbol{\mu}' = (0, 0, 1)$ satisfies the Kuhn–Tucker conditions and, thus, is the maximizing vector. Therefore, maximum $\mu_3 = \mu_3' = 1$. Hence, as the duality theorem states, the values of (295) and (296) are equal.

## FORMULATING OPTIMIZATION PROBLEMS OF MANAGEMENT SCIENCE AS CONVEX PROGRAMMING PROBLEMS

### Facility Location

Problems concerned with supplying and servicing people in an optimal manner frequently arise in urban and public affairs. The location and construction of hospitals, post offices, fire stations, or production facilities are examples of such problems. In each of these problems the number, location, and capacity of the facilities that will satisfy the requirements of the population most economically must be determined.

The mathematical formulation of these facility location problems are frequently convex programming problems that pose many theoretical and computational difficulties. Hence, these problems are of theoretical, as well as practical, interest to the management scientist. To illustrate the ideas of such problems a somewhat simplified version of the facility location problem is formulated here.

Consider the problem of determining the optimal locations of two hospitals of equal capacity with respect to centers of dense patient population within a particular service area. These locations are considered optimal when the total patient traveling distance is minimized. To simplify this problem, we assume that the service area is geographically flat; therefore, we consider the problem of locating these two hospitals in two-dimensional Euclidean space.

Suppose that within this service area a population of 35,000 is concentrated in 25 zones of 75 people or more. These zones are indicated in Figure 118 by a dot in the service area; larger dots represent zones of denser population. The notation $c_i$ will represent the population of the $i$th population center ($i = 1, 2, \ldots, 25$). The location of each of the population centers has a coordinate representation; suppose the $i$th center is located at $(a_i, b_i)$, ($i = 1, 2, \ldots, 25$).

Thus, if $(x_1, y_1)$ denotes the unknown coordinates of the first hospital,

$$[(x_1 - a_i)^2 + (y_1 - b_i)^2]^{1/2}$$

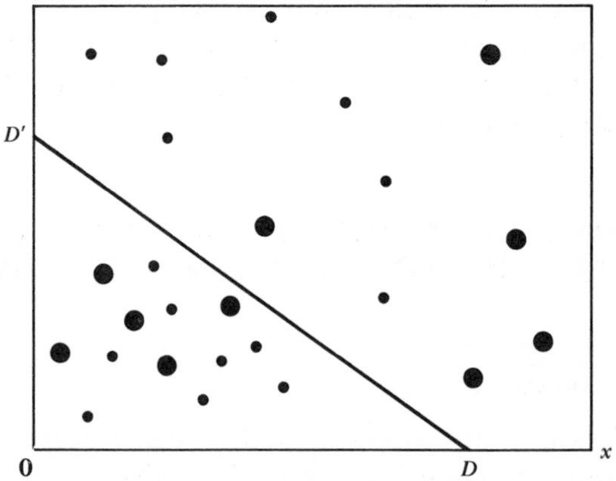


Figure 118

is the distance from the first hospital to the $i$th zone of population. Furthermore, since $c_i$ is the size of the $i$th population center,

$$c_i[(x_1 - a_i)^2 + (y_1 - b_i)^2]^{1/2}$$

is the total patient travel distance from the $i$th zone to the first hospital. Thus, the total patient straight line distance from all 25 zones of population to the first hospital is

$$\sum_{i=1}^{25} c_i[(x_1 - a_i)^2 + (y_1 - b_i)^2]^{1/2}. \tag{297}$$

Similarly, with $(x_2, y_2)$ denoting the coordinate location of the second hospital,

$$\sum_{i=1}^{25} c_i[(x_2 - a_i)^2 + (y_2 - b_i)^2]^{1/2} \tag{298}$$

is the total patient straight-line distance to the second hospital. The total patient straight-line travel distance to the two hospitals is the sum of (297) and (298):

$$\sum_{i=1}^{25} c_i[(x_1 - a_i)^2 + (y_1 - b_i)^2]^{1/2} + \sum_{i=1}^{25} c_i[(x_2 - a_i)^2 + (y_2 - b_i)^2]^{1/2}.$$

Let us assume that the second hospital is not to be located within the area of densest population. Specifically, assume the second hospital must be located above the straight line connecting $D$ and $D'$ in Figure 118:

$$y_2 \geq -\frac{D'}{D} x_2 + D'.$$

With these restrictions our hospital location problem may be formulated as a mathematical programming problem:

$$\begin{aligned}
\text{minimize} \quad & \sum_{i=1}^{25} c_i[(x_1 - a_i)^2 + (y_1 - b_i)^2]^{1/2} \\
& + \sum_{i=1}^{25} c_i[(x_2 - a_i)^2 + (y_2 - b_i)^2]^{1/2} \\
\text{subject to} \quad & -x_1 \leq 0, \qquad -y_1 \leq 0 \\
& -x_2 \leq 0, \qquad -y_2 \leq 0 \\
& -\frac{D'}{D} x_2 - y_2 + D' \leq 0.
\end{aligned} \tag{299}$$

Problem (299) is actually a convex programming problem. This follows because, as we will show, any function of the form

(300) $$f(\mathbf{z}) = [(x)^2 + (y)^2]^{1/2},$$

where $\mathbf{z} = (x, y)$, is convex. Since the objective function of (299) is a positive linear combination of such functions and since the constraint functions are also convex, (299) is a convex programming problem.

To prove that $f(\mathbf{z})$ is convex, we show

$$f[\lambda\mathbf{z} + (1 - \lambda)\mathbf{z}'] \leq \lambda f(\mathbf{z}) + (1 - \lambda)f(\mathbf{z}'), \qquad 0 \leq \lambda \leq 1,$$

by observing that

(301) $$f[\lambda\mathbf{z} + (1 - \lambda)\mathbf{z}'] - [\lambda f(\mathbf{z}) + (1 - \lambda)f(\mathbf{z}')]$$

is always negative. Here $\mathbf{z} = (x, y)$ and $\mathbf{z}' = (x', y')$. Since the sign of

(302) $$\begin{aligned}(f[\lambda\mathbf{z} + (1 - \lambda)\mathbf{z}'])^2 &- [\lambda f(\mathbf{z}) + (1 - \lambda)f(\mathbf{z}')]^2 \\ &= ([\lambda x + (1 - \lambda)x']^2 + [\lambda y + (1 - \lambda)y']^2) \\ &\quad - [\lambda(x^2 + y^2)^{1/2} + (1 - \lambda)(x'^2 + y'^2)^{1/2}]^2\end{aligned}$$

is the same as that of (301), we examine the sign of (302) for convenience. By expanding (302) and performing the indicated cancellations, we find (302) is equivalent to

(303) $$2\lambda(1 - \lambda)[(xx' + yy') - (x^2 + y^2)^{1/2}(x'^2 + y'^2)^{1/2}].$$

The negativity of (303) follows from first observing that since

(304) $$(yx' - y'x)^2 \geq 0,$$

the inequality

$$(yx')^2 + (y'x)^2 \geq 2(xx'yy')$$

follows by expanding the left side of (304). By adding $(xx')^2$ and $(yy')^2$ to both sides of the latter inequality, we find

$$(xx')^2 + (yx')^2 + (y'x)^2 + (yy')^2 \geq (xx')^2 + 2(xx'yy') + (yy')^2$$

or

(305) $$(x^2 + y^2)(x'^2 + y'^2) \geq (xx' + yy')^2.$$

After taking the square root of each side of (305), we find

$$(x^2 + y^2)^{1/2}(x'^2 + y'^2)^{1/2} \geq (xx' + yy').$$

The negativity of (303) and, consequently, the negativity of (301) follows from this inequality. Therefore,

$$f[\lambda \mathbf{z} + (1 - \lambda)\mathbf{z}'] \leq \lambda f(\mathbf{z}) + (1 - \lambda)f(\mathbf{z}')$$

for $\mathbf{z}, \mathbf{z}' \in \mathbb{R}^2$ or, equivalently, $f(\mathbf{z})$ is convex on $\mathbb{R}^2$.

The objective function of mathematical programming problem (299) is convex because it is a positive linear combination of convex functions of the form (300). Hence, the hospital location problem, (299), is a convex programming problem.

Convex programming problem (299) is not solved here because of the numerous computations. However, for a discussion of numerical techniques of convex programming, see texts such as *Optimization under Constraints* by Peter Whittle (Wiley-Interscience, 1971).

## EXERCISES

1. Determine the minimizing points and minimum values of the following problems:

(*a*) minimize $x_1^2 + x_2^2 - x_1 - x_2 + \frac{1}{2}$

subject to

$$\begin{aligned} x_1^2 + x_2^2 - 7 &\leq 9 \\ -x_1 \qquad\quad &\leq 0 \\ -x_2 \quad &\leq 0 \\ -x_1 - x_2 - 1 &\leq 7 \end{aligned}$$

(*b*) minimize $(x_1 - 2)^2 - \ln(x_2^3) + x_2$

subject to

$$\begin{aligned} x_1^2 + x_2^2 - 25 &\leq 0 \\ -x_1 \qquad\quad &\leq -1 \\ -x_2 \quad &\leq -1 \end{aligned}$$

(*c*) minimize $e^{(x_1 - 1)} + e^{(x_2 + 1)} - (x_1 + x_2)$

subject to

$$\begin{aligned} \frac{x_1^2}{2} + \frac{x_2^2}{4} &\leq 1 \\ 6e^{x_1} &\leq 662 \end{aligned}$$

(*d*) minimize $(x_1 - 1)^2 + x_2^2$

subject to

$$\begin{aligned} x_1 + x_2 &\leq 0 \\ x_1^2 - 4 &\leq 0 \end{aligned}$$

(*e*) minimize $-\ln(x_1 x_2) + x_1 + x_2$

subject to
$$-x_1 \le -1$$
$$-x_2 + 2 \le 0$$

(*f*) minimize $x_1^2 + (x_1 - 1)x_2 + 2$

subject to
$$-x_2 \le 0$$
$$-x_1 + 1 \le 0$$

(*g*) minimize $2x_1 - x_2$

subject to
$$x_2 - 2x_1 + 1 \le 0$$
$$x_1 + x_2 - 1 \le 0$$

(*h*) minimize $x_1^2 + x_2^2 - 2(x_1 + x_2 + 1)$

subject to
$$e^{-x_1} + e^{-x_2} \le 96$$
$$-x_1 \le 7$$

(*i*) minimize $-\ln(x_1 + x_2) + 12$

subject to
$$x_1 + x_2^2 - 71 \le 0$$
$$-x_1 \le 0$$
$$-x_2 \le 0$$

(*j*) minimize $x_1^2$

subject to
$$(x_1 - 1)(x_1 - 4) \le 0$$

(*k*) minimize $e^{-x_1 - x_2}$

subject to
$$e^{x_1} \le 10$$
$$e^{x_2} \le 10$$

(*l*) minimize $x_1^2 + x_2^2 - 2(2x_1 + x_2) + 5$

subject to
$$x_1^2 - x_2 \le 0$$
$$x_1 + x_2 - 2 \le 0$$

(*m*) minimize $e^{x_1} + x_2$

subject to
$$e^{-x_1} + x_2^2 - 1 \le 0$$
$$-x_2 \le 0$$

(*n*) minimize $-x_1 + x_2^2$

subject to
$$x_1 + x_2 - 1 \le 0.$$

2. Show that the Kuhn–Tucker theorem is not applicable to the following problem:

$$\begin{aligned} \text{minimize} \quad & e^{x_1} \\ \text{subject to} \quad & (x_1 - \pi)(x_1 - 2\pi) \le 0 \\ & -x_1 \le -2\pi. \end{aligned}$$

3. Use the duality inequality to obtain estimates of the minimum value of each of the programs in Problem 1.
4. Show that the optimization problem

$$\begin{aligned} \text{minimize} \quad & t_1^2 t_2^{-1/2} t_3^{1/3} \\ \text{subject to} \quad & t_1 > 0, \quad t_2 > 0, \quad t_3 > 0 \\ & t_1^{-1} t_2^{-3/4} t_3^{-2} \le 1 \\ & 9t_3 \le 1 \\ & \tfrac{6}{11} t_2^6 t_3^{-1} \le 1 \end{aligned}$$

is transformed into a convex programming problem under the change of variables

$$t_i = e^{z_i}, \qquad i = 1, 2, 3.$$

5. [Duffin, p. 72] A strictly convex function has no more than one minimizing point. If a differentiable convex function $f$ has only one minimizing point, does it follow that $f$ is strictly convex?
6. Formulate and solve the Wolfe dual of each of the convex programming problems in Problem 1.
7. Formulate the facility location problem (p. 241) when the second hospital is constrained to be built within a circular region of radius $r$ about the point $(D, D')$. Is this a convex programming problem?
8. (*a*) Formulate the facility location problem (p. 241) as a problem of finding the locations of two hospitals in three-dimensional Euclidean space that is optimal with respect to 25 zones of population.

   (*b*) Suppose the coordinates $(x_1, y_1, z_1)$ of one of the hospitals must satisfy

$$m_1 x_1 + m_2 y_1 + m_3 z_1 - D_1 \ge 0,$$

   where $m_i > 0$; $i = 1, 2, 3$; $D_1 > 0$. Geometrically interpret this constraint.
9. Formulate a mathematical programming problem that concerns the problem of locating $n$ warehouses so that the transportation cost to $m$ retailers is minimized. Adjust your model so that the $i$th warehouse is located within a straight-line distance $r$ of a point $x^i$, $i = 1, \ldots, n$.

10. Determine the optimizing points and optimal values of the following problems:

(*a*) maximize $-e^{x_1} - e^{x_2} + 1$
subject to $1 - x_1 - x_2 \leq 0$

(*b*) maximize $e^{(x_1/2)-3x_2}$
subject to $e^{x_1} + e^{-6x_2} \leq 2$

(*c*) maximize $2(2x_1 + x_2) - x_1^2 - x_2^2$
subject to
$$-x_1 - x_2 + 2 \geq 0$$
$$-x_1^2 + x_2 \geq 0.$$

11. Give examples of each of the following:
(*a*) A convex programming problem with no solution and an inconsistent Wolfe dual
(*b*) A convex programming problem that is inconsistent but with a Wolfe dual that has a solution
(*c*) A convex programming problem that is inconsistent and with a Wolfe dual that is inconsistent.

12. Solve the following optimization problem:

minimize $y_1^{-1}y_2^{-1}$
subject to $y_1 + y_2 \leq 100$

by transforming it into an equivalent convex programming problem with the change of variables $y_i = e^{z_i}$, $i = 1, 2$.

13. Formulate the unsymmetrical dual linear programming problem for the following:

minimize $4x_1 + 15x_2$
subject to
$$-2 + x_1 + x_2 \leq 0$$
$$-x_1 \leq 0$$
$$x_1 - x_2 \leq 0.$$

14. Solve the following optimization problem:

maximize $-2y_3$
subject to
$$-4 + y_1 - y_2 - y_3 = 0$$
$$-15 + y_2 - y_3 = 0$$
$$y_1 \geq 0, \quad y_2 \geq 0, \quad y_3 \geq 0.$$

15. Consider the replacement problem (241). Analyze the effect of variations in $T$ on $g_0(\mathbf{x}^*)$ by calculating

$$\frac{\partial g_0(\mathbf{x}^*)}{\partial T}.$$

16. Analyze the effect of variations in $A$ on the following convex programming problems:

(*a*) minimize $\quad -x_1 + x_2^2$

subject to $\quad x_1 + x_2 \le A$

(*b*) minimize $\quad e^{-x_1 - x_2}$

subject to $\quad e^{x_1} \le A$

$\quad e^{x_2} \le 10$

(*c*) minimize $\quad -\ln(x_1 + x_2) + 12$

subject to $\quad x_1 + x_2^2 - A \le 0$

$\quad -x_1 \le 0$

$\quad -x_2 \le 0.$

17. (*a*) Using the Wolfe duality theory of convex programming, derive the duality inequality of unsymmetrical linear programming.
(*b*) Using the Wolfe duality theory of convex programming, prove Theorem 52.

18. Consider the convex programming problem

$$\begin{aligned} \text{minimize} \quad & e^{-x} + e^{y} \\ \text{subject to} \quad & 6x - y \le G \end{aligned}$$

(*a*) Discuss the sensitivity of $M$, the minimum of this problem, to variations in the parameter $G$.
(*b*) Show that the graph of $M$ as a function of $G$ appears on the top of page 250.

19. Frequently, when the preliminary design of a management system is modeled as a constrained optimization problem, a function is constructed to analyze the sensitivity of the optimal value to variations in various parameters. Such a function is called a *policy function.** For example, suppose the Morrison Bank and Trust Company desires to improve customer service so as to minimize the average customer waiting time. The cost of this improved service, however, must not

* From C. Zener, *Engineering Design by Geometric Programming*, Wiley-Interscience, 1971, pp. 50–52.

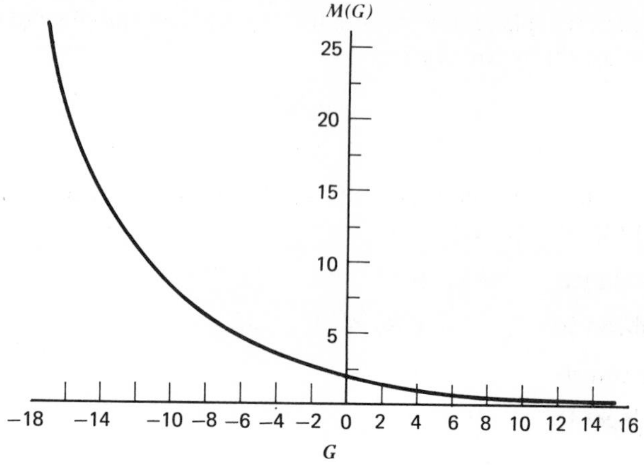


exceed some maximum acceptable cost $G_1$. Suppose this problem is modeled as follows:

$$G_0 = \text{minimize} \quad g_0(\mathbf{x})$$
$$\text{subject to} \quad g_1(\mathbf{x}) \le G_1,$$

where $g_0(\mathbf{x})$ is the average customer waiting time and $g_1(\mathbf{x})$ is the cost associated with achieving this improved service.

(*a*) Suppose that the policy function associated with this problem indicates that the minimum average waiting time varies with the maximum acceptable cost $G_1$ as illustrated below. By analyzing this curve, the Morrison Bank and Trust Company can estimate the maximum cost $G_1'$ associated with a waiting time $G_0'$. Furthermore, if several management consulting groups submit bids to help improve the system at Morrison so as to achieve waiting time $G_0'$, the

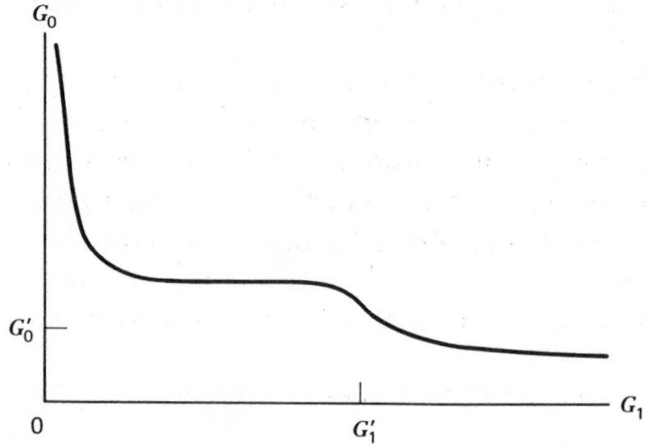

Morrison Bank and Trust Company will realize that bids exceeding $G_1'$ are not acceptable. Analyze this curve and suggest an operating point $(G_1', G_0')$ for this system.

(*b*) Consider the convex programming problem:

$$G_0 = \text{minimize} \quad e^{-x_1 + x_2}$$
$$\text{subject to} \quad \tfrac{1}{4}e^{-x_2} + e^{x_1} \leq G_1.$$

Show that

$$P(G_0, G_1) = G_0^{-1}G_1^{-2} = 1$$

is a policy function of this problem.

(*c*) Construct a policy function for the problem:

$$G_0 = \text{minimize} \quad -x_1 + x_2$$
$$\text{subject to} \quad e^{x_1} + x_2 \leq G_1.$$

20. Consider the convex programming problem

$$\text{(P)} \quad \begin{aligned} \text{minimize} \quad & g_0(\mathbf{x}) = x_1 + x_2^{-1} \\ \text{subject to} \quad & g_1(\mathbf{x}) = x_1^{-1} + x_2 - 1 \leq 0 \\ & g_2(\mathbf{x}) = -x_1 \leq 0 \\ & g_3(\mathbf{x}) = -x_2 \leq 0. \end{aligned}$$

(*a*) Show that the constrained values of $g_0(\mathbf{x})$ lie on or above the curve

$$f(x_2) = \frac{1}{x_2} + \frac{1}{1 - x_2}.$$

(*b*) Determine the minimum value and minimizing point of (P) from a sketch of $f(x_2)$.

(*c*) Show that the constrained values of the Wolf dual of (P) lie on or below the curve

$$l(\mu_1) = 4\mu_1^{1/2} - \mu_1.$$

(*d*) Sketch $l(\mu_1)$ and determine the maximum value of the Wolf dual. Note that the minimum value of (P) equals the maximum value of the Wolf dual as illustrated on page 252.

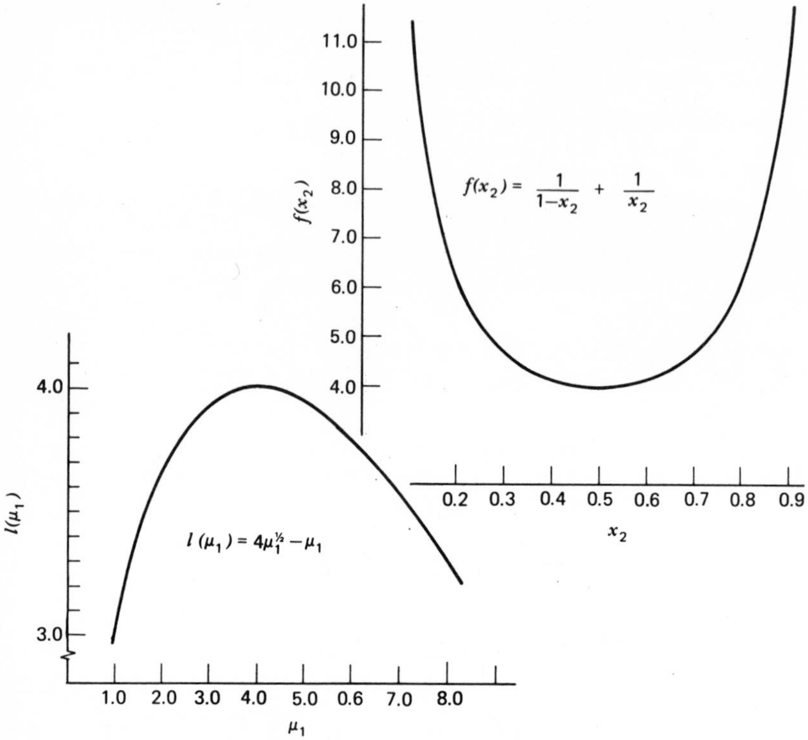


## SOLUTIONS

1. (*a*) $\mathbf{x}^* = (\frac{1}{2}, \frac{1}{2}), \boldsymbol{\mu}' = (0, 0, 0, 0), M = 0$

   (*b*) $\mathbf{x}^* = (2, 3), \boldsymbol{\mu}' = (0, 0, 0), M = 3 - 3 \ln 3$

   (*c*) $\mathbf{x}^* = (1, -1), \boldsymbol{\mu}' = (0, 0), M = 2$

   (*d*) $\mathbf{x}^* = (\frac{1}{2}, -\frac{1}{2}), \boldsymbol{\mu}' = (1, 0), M = \frac{1}{2}$

   (*e*) $\mathbf{x}^* = (1, 2), \boldsymbol{\mu}' = (0, \frac{1}{2}), M = 3 - \ln 2$

   (*f*) $\mathbf{x}^* = (1, 0), \boldsymbol{\mu}' = (0, 2), M = 3$

   (*g*) $\mathbf{x}^* = (\frac{2}{3}, \frac{1}{3}), \boldsymbol{\mu}' = (1, 1), M = 1$

   (*h*) $\mathbf{x}^* = (1, 1), \boldsymbol{\mu}' = (0, 0), M = -4$

   (*i*) $\mathbf{x}^* = (70\frac{3}{4}, \frac{1}{2}), \boldsymbol{\mu}' = (\frac{4}{285}, 0, 0), M = 12 - \ln (71\frac{1}{4})$

   (*j*) $x^* = 1, \mu' = \frac{2}{3}, M = 1$

(*k*) $\mathbf{x}^* = (\ln 10, \ln 10), \boldsymbol{\mu}' = (0.001, 0.001), M = 0.01$

(*l*) $\mathbf{x}^* = (1, 1), \boldsymbol{\mu}' = (\frac{2}{3}, \frac{2}{3}), M = 1$

(*m*) $\mathbf{x}^* = (0, 0), \boldsymbol{\mu}' = (1, 1), M = 1$

(*n*) $\mathbf{x}^* = (\frac{3}{2}, -\frac{1}{2}), \mu' = 1, M = -\frac{5}{4}$

2. This program is not superconsistent.
5. No; consider the function

$$f(x) = \begin{cases} x^2, & |x| \leq 1 \\ 2\,|x| - 1, & |x| \geq 1 \end{cases}$$

10. (*a*) $\mathbf{x}^* = (\frac{1}{2}, \frac{1}{2}), M = -e^{1/2} - e^{1/2} + 1$

(*b*) $\mathbf{x}^* = (0, 0), M = 1$

(*c*) $\mathbf{x}^* = (1, 1), M = 4$

12. $\mathbf{y}^* = (50, 50), M = \frac{1}{2500}$

# CHAPTER 8

# GEOMETRIC PROGRAMMING

## INTRODUCTION

Geometric programming provides a remarkable optimization technique for solving a wide class of design and decision problems. The mathematical formulation of these problems is characterized by the complicated nonlinear terms of generalized positive polynomials. But despite the complexity of these functions, the optimal value of such problems is frequently calculated with ease using the systematic techniques of geometric programming. Moreover, this optimal value is determined without first computing the values of the design or decision parameters.

The basis of this minimization technique is an "exploitation" of the properties of the classical arithmetic–geometric mean inequality. Using this inequality, we can develop a related or dual geometric programming problem, characterized by linear equality constraints. The constrained maximum of this dual problem is actually the minimum value of our original problem.

Geometric programming is a relatively new mathematical discipline. The fundamental work was done in the early 1960's by Richard Duffin and Clarence Zener, of Carnegie-Mellon University, and Duffin's student Elmor Peterson of Northwestern University. In 1961 Zener developed a technique for minimizing a particular type of cost function and Duffin generalized Zener's work. Together with Peterson, Duffin later developed the "duality theory" of geometric programming, while Zener continued to apply the theory and techniques of geometric programming in engineering design.

We begin our study of geometric programming with a discussion of the arithmetic–geometric mean inequality.

## PRELIMINARIES: THE ARITHMETIC–GEOMETRIC MEAN INEQUALITY

The techniques of geometric programming employ the classical arithmetic–geometric mean inequality to optimize a particular class of functions. This inequality states that the arithmetic mean is at least as great as the geometric mean.

In its simplest form, the arithmetic–geometric mean inequality is

$$\tfrac{1}{2}v_1 + \tfrac{1}{2}v_2 \geq v_1^{1/2}v_2^{1/2}, \tag{306}$$

where $v_1$ and $v_2$ are any nonnegative numbers. The left side of (306) is the arithmetic mean of $v_1$ and $v_2$ and the right side is the geometric mean of $v_1$ and $v_2$. To prove this inequality is correct, observe that since

$$(v_1 - v_2)^2 \geq 0,$$
$$v_1^2 - 2v_1v_2 + v_2^2 \geq 0.$$

By adding $4v_1v_2$ to both sides of this inequality, we find that

$$v_1^2 + 2v_1v_2 + v_2^2 \geq 4v_1v_2,$$

or, equivalently,

$$(v_1 + v_2)^2 \geq 4v_1v_2.$$

Taking the square root of both sides of the latter inequality yields (306). Note that (306) becomes an equality if and only if $v_1 = v_2$.

Inequality (306) may be used to derive a slightly more general form of the arithmetic–geometric mean inequality:

$$\tfrac{1}{4}v_1 + \tfrac{1}{4}v_2 + \tfrac{1}{4}v_3 + \tfrac{1}{4}v_4 \geq v_1^{1/4}v_2^{1/4}v_3^{1/4}v_4^{1/4}.$$

Observe that since

$$\tfrac{1}{4}v_1 + \tfrac{1}{4}v_2 + \tfrac{1}{4}v_3 + \tfrac{1}{4}v_4 = \frac{1}{2}\left(\frac{v_1 + v_2}{2}\right) + \frac{1}{2}\left(\frac{v_3 + v_4}{2}\right),$$

inequality (306) implies

$$\tfrac{1}{4}v_1 + \tfrac{1}{4}v_2 + \tfrac{1}{4}v_3 + \tfrac{1}{4}v_4 \geq \left(\frac{v_1 + v_2}{2}\right)^{1/2}\left(\frac{v_3 + v_4}{2}\right)^{1/2}. \tag{307}$$

Since, according to (306), $(v_1 + v_2)/2 \geq v_1^{1/2}v_2^{1/2}$ and $(v_3 + v_4)/2 \geq v_3^{1/2}v_4^{1/2}$, inequality (307) implies the desired result,

$$\tfrac{1}{4}v_1 + \tfrac{1}{4}v_2 + \tfrac{1}{4}v_3 + \tfrac{1}{4}v_4 \geq v_1^{1/4}v_2^{1/4}v_3^{1/4}v_4^{1/4}. \tag{308}$$

Again, this inequality becomes an equality if and only if $v_1 = v_2 = v_3 = v_4$.

Using the technique of backward induction, we may use (308) to prove

$$\tfrac{1}{3}v_1 + \tfrac{1}{3}v_2 + \tfrac{1}{3}v_3 \geq v_1^{1/3}v_2^{1/3}v_3^{1/3}.$$

Observe that with $v_4 = (v_1v_2v_3)^{1/3}$, inequality (308) implies

$$\tfrac{1}{4}v_1 + \tfrac{1}{4}v_2 + \tfrac{1}{4}v_3 + \tfrac{1}{4}(v_1v_2v_3)^{1/3} \geq v_1^{1/4}v_2^{1/4}v_3^{1/4}(v_1v_2v_3)^{1/12} = v_1^{1/3}v_2^{1/3}v_3^{1/3}.$$

After transposing the $v_4 = (v_1v_2v_3)^{1/3}$ term, we find

$$v_1 + v_2 + v_3 \geq 3v_1^{1/3}v_2^{1/3}v_3^{1/3},$$

or equivalently, we obtain the desired result,

$$\tfrac{1}{3}v_1 + \tfrac{1}{3}v_2 + \tfrac{1}{3}v_3 \geq v_1^{1/3}v_2^{1/3}v_3^{1/3}. \tag{309}$$

Equality holds here if and only if $v_1 = v_2 = v_3$.

Inequalities (308) and (309) may be used to derive certain weighted arithmetic–geometric mean inequalities. For example, suppose $v_2 = v_3$ in (309). Then (309) implies

$$\tfrac{1}{3}v_1 + \tfrac{2}{3}v_2 \geq v_1^{1/3}v_2^{2/3}.$$

The left side is the weighted arithmetic mean of $v_1$ and $v_2$, with weights $\frac{1}{3}$ and $\frac{2}{3}$, respectively, and the right side is the corresponding weighted geometric mean. Similarly, with $v_3 = v_4$, (308) implies the weighted arithmetic–geometric mean inequality

$$\tfrac{1}{4}v_1 + \tfrac{1}{4}v_2 + \tfrac{1}{2}v_3 \geq v_1^{1/4}v_2^{1/4}v_3^{1/2}.$$

The more general arithmetic–geometric mean inequality states that the weighted arithmetic mean is at least as great as the weighted geometric mean; that is, for $v_i \geq 0$, $\delta_i \geq 0$, $i = 1, \ldots, n$,

$$\delta_1 v_1 + \delta_2 v_2 + \cdots + \delta_n v_n \geq v_1^{\delta_1}v_2^{\delta_2} \cdots v_n^{\delta_n}, \tag{310}$$

where

$$\delta_1 + \delta_2 + \cdots + \delta_n = 1. \tag{311}$$

Here inequality (310) becomes an equality if and only if $v_1 = v_2 = \cdots = v_n$. Inequality (310) is called the *normalized* arithmetic–geometric mean inequality because the weights $\delta_i$ satisfy the normalization condition (311). The proof of the validity of inequality (310) is quite difficult and, hence, is not included in this discussion.

The minimization technique of geometric programming hinges on the arithmetic–geometric mean inequality. More specifically the duality theory of geometric programming depends on the following form of the arithmetic-geometric mean inequality,

(312) $$u_1 + u_2 + \cdots + u_n \geq \left(\frac{u_1}{\delta_1}\right)^{\delta_1} \cdots \left(\frac{u_n}{\delta_n}\right)^{\delta_n},$$

where $u_i \geq 0, \delta_i \geq 0, i = 1, \ldots, n$, and $\delta_1 + \cdots + \delta_n = 1$. This inequality is called the *geometric inequality*. With the change of variables $u_i = \delta_i v_i$, $i = 1, \ldots, n$, (312) is seen to be a consequence of (310). It can be proved that the geometric inequality becomes an equality if and only if

$$\delta_i\left(\sum_{i=1}^{n} u_i\right) = u_i, \qquad i = 1, \ldots, n.$$

In (312), $x^x$ and $x^{-x}$ are taken to be 1 when $x = 0$.

If the weights $\delta_i \geq 0$ do not satisfy the normalization condition (311), the geometric inequality takes the more general form

(313) $$(u_1 + \cdots + u_n)^{\lambda} \geq \left(\frac{u_1}{\delta_1}\right)^{\delta_1} \cdots \left(\frac{u_n}{\delta_n}\right)^{\delta_n} \lambda^{\lambda},$$

where $u_i \geq 0$, $\delta_i \geq 0$, $i = 1, \ldots, n$, and $\lambda = \delta_1 + \cdots + \delta_n$. Inequality (313) is called the *general geometric inequality*. As before, $x^x$ and $x^{-x}$ are taken to be 1 when $x = 0$. The general geometric inequality becomes an equality if and only if

$$\frac{\delta_i}{\lambda} = \frac{u_i}{\sum_{i=1}^{n} u_i}, \qquad i = 1, \ldots, n.$$

Using the general geometric inequality, it is easy to show that non-negative numbers $u_1, \ldots, u_n$ that satisfy

$$1 \geq u_1 + \cdots + u_n$$

also satisfy

(314) $$1 \geq (u_1 + \cdots + u_n)^{\lambda} \geq \left(\frac{u_1}{\delta_1}\right)^{\delta_1} \cdots \left(\frac{u_n}{\delta_n}\right)^{\delta_n} \lambda^{\lambda},$$

where $\delta_i \geq 0, i = 1, \ldots, n$, and $\lambda = \delta_1 + \cdots + \delta_n$. As above, $x^x = x^{-x} = 1$ when $x = 0$. Inequality (314) becomes an equality if and only if

$$\frac{\delta_i}{\lambda} = u_i, \qquad i = 1, \ldots, n.$$

This inequality is of particular value in our discussion of constrained geometric programming.

Before applying the geometric inequality in minimizing certain functions, we show that the geometric inequality may be employed to find lower bounds for these functions. For instance, the geometric inequality may be used to determine a lower bound for

$$g(t) = 4t^{-3} + \tfrac{3}{4}t \qquad (t > 0).$$

Application of (312) with $u_1 = 4t^{-3}$, $u_2 = \frac{3}{4}t$ and $\delta_1 = \frac{1}{4}$, $\delta_2 = \frac{3}{4}$, gives

$$4t^{-3} + \tfrac{3}{4}t \geq \left(\frac{4t^{-3}}{\frac{1}{4}}\right)^{1/4}\left(\frac{\frac{3}{4}t}{\frac{3}{4}}\right)^{3/4} = 2.$$

Thus, 2 is a lower bound for $g(t)$ when $t > 0$. Note that since $g(2) = 2$, 2 is actually the greatest lower bound of $g(t)$.

Similarly, the geometric inequality may be used to bound

$$g(\mathbf{t}) = \tfrac{1}{4}t_1^{-1} + 2t_2 + 4t_1t_2^{-2}, \qquad t_1 > 0, \qquad t_2 > 0.$$

With $u_1 = \frac{1}{4}t_1^{-1}$, $u_2 = 2t_2$, $u_3 = 4t_1t_2^{-2}$ and $\delta_1 = \frac{1}{4}$, $\delta_2 = \frac{1}{2}$, $\delta_3 = \frac{1}{4}$, the geometric inequality implies

$$\tfrac{1}{4}t_1^{-1} + 2t_2 + 4t_1t_2^{-2} \geq \left(\frac{\frac{1}{4}t_1^{-1}}{\frac{1}{4}}\right)^{1/4}\left(\frac{2t_2}{\frac{1}{2}}\right)^{1/2}\left(\frac{4t_1t_2^{-2}}{\frac{1}{4}}\right)^{1/4} = 4.$$

Thus, 4 is a lower bound for $g(\mathbf{t})$. Since $g(\frac{1}{4}, 1) = 4$, 4 is actually the greatest lower bound.

## A QUEUEING PROBLEM: THE UNCONSTRAINED GEOMETRIC PROGRAMMING PROBLEM

The flow of traffic along a turnpike is interrupted by waiting lines or queues forming at, for instance, toll gates. After the toll for these vehicles is collected, the flow of traffic resumes until a second toll gate causes a queue. When such a waiting line forms at a toll gate, the traveler incurs a cost because of the interruption of trip progress. Likewise, employing personnel and equipment to collect the tolls represents a cost to the government. Thus, such queueing systems pose the problem of determining the capacities of the toll gate or gates that will minimize the associated costs, given the arrival patterns. Here such a cost minimization problem is formulated and solved using the geometric inequality

Suppose that during the evening rush hour automobiles arrive at the waiting line at regular known intervals of length $b$ periods. The first arrival occurs at the beginning of the rush hour. The automobiles then proceed to one of two toll gates or service facilities on a first-come, first-served basis as shown in Figure 119. Each toll gate uses an identical technique for collecting tolls. If the service time, or the time required to collect the tolls, is equal to $t$

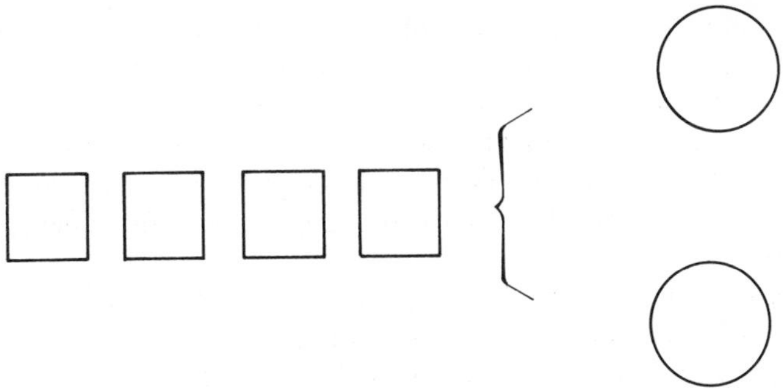


**Figure 119**

periods per automobile, then we must assume $t \leq 2b$. Otherwise, a waiting line will form and grow without bound.

When a vehicle joins the queue, a waiting cost is incurred. In this example, vehicles waiting in the queue incur a cost because of the interruption of trip progress. Our waiting cost per period is assumed to be the product of the average cost of waiting per vehicle per period, $c$, and the number of units waiting during each period, $t/b$. The waiting cost is therefore

$$u_1 = c\left(\frac{t}{b}\right).$$

Associated with each of the service facilities are the costs of overhead, maintenance, operation, capital investment, and personnel. Such costs are termed *service facility costs*. Here we assume that the service facility cost of *each* toll gate is the product of the cost of collecting the toll of one automobile, $d$, and the total number of units serviced during rush hour, $1/t$. Thus, the total service facility cost is

$$u_2 = 2d\left(\frac{1}{t}\right).$$

The total queueing system cost per period is the sum of the waiting and service facility costs,

$$(315) \qquad c\left(\frac{t}{b}\right) + 2d\left(\frac{1}{t}\right), \qquad t > 0.$$

In minimizing the total queueing system cost, note that the proportion of the total cost attributed to waiting costs may be reduced by installing additional equipment and personnel to collect tolls. This action will reduce the waiting lines and, consequently, the waiting line costs. However, in this case, the service facility cost component will increase. Conversely, providing a less expensive service facility results in higher waiting costs. Thus, we must determine a service time $t$ such that the relative contributions of the waiting cost and service facility cost to the total cost minimize the total queueing system cost. As an introduction to the technique of geometric programming, we employ the geometric inequality in minimizing the total queueing system cost (315).

By applying the geometric inequality to the total queueing system cost function (315) we obtain an estimate of the minimum cost. Specifically, since the waiting cost, $u_1$, and the service facility cost, $u_2$, are positive ($t > 0$), the geometric inequality,

$$u_1 + u_2 \geq \left(\frac{u_1}{\delta_1}\right)^{\delta_1}\left(\frac{u_2}{\delta_2}\right)^{\delta_2},$$

implies

$$g_0(t) = \frac{c}{b}\,t + \frac{2d}{t} \geq \left(\frac{(c/b)t}{\delta_1}\right)^{\delta_1}\left(\frac{2dt^{-1}}{\delta_2}\right)^{\delta_2} = V(\boldsymbol{\delta}, t), \tag{316}$$

where $\delta_1 \geq 0$, $\delta_2 \geq 0$, $\delta_1 + \delta_2 = 1$. In the attempt to minimize $g_0(t)$, this inequality suggests that we consider the dual program:

$$(\mathrm{D}_1')\qquad \begin{array}{ll} \text{maximize} & V(\boldsymbol{\delta}, t) \\ \text{subject to} & \delta_1 \geq 0, \quad \delta_2 \geq 0, \quad t > 0 \\ & \delta_1 + \delta_2 = 1. \end{array}$$

We expect the constrained maximum value of $V(\boldsymbol{\delta}, t)$ to provide a lower bound for $g_0(t)$. However, the maximum value of $(\mathrm{D}_1')$ depends on $t$ and hence will not provide a lower bound independent of $t$ for $g_0(t)$ or, in particular, the minimum of $g_0(t)$. By eliminating the dependence of $V(\boldsymbol{\delta}, t)$ on the variable $t$, we will obtain the desired lower bound.

The dependence of $V(\boldsymbol{\delta}, t)$ on $t$ may be eliminated by first observing that

$$V(\boldsymbol{\delta}, t) = \left(\frac{c/b}{\delta_1}\right)^{\delta_1}\left(\frac{2d}{\delta_2}\right)^{\delta_2} t^{\delta_1 - \delta_2}.$$

By imposing the additional condition

$$\delta_1 - \delta_2 = 0,$$

we eliminate the dependence of $V(\boldsymbol{\delta}, t)$ on $t$. Now the dual problem has an additional constraint but does not depend on the variable $t$:

$$(\mathrm{D}_1) \qquad \begin{aligned} &\text{maximize} && v(\boldsymbol{\delta}) = \left(\frac{c/b}{\delta_1}\right)^{\delta_1}\left(\frac{2d}{\delta_2}\right)^{\delta_2} \\ &\text{subject to} && \delta_1 \geq 0, \qquad \delta_2 \geq 0 \\ &&& \delta_1 + \delta_2 = 1 \\ &&& \delta_1 - \delta_2 = 0. \end{aligned}$$

Our duality inequality, (316) therefore reduces to

$$g_0(t) \geq v(\boldsymbol{\delta})$$

for $t > 0$ and $\boldsymbol{\delta} = (\delta_1, \delta_2)$ satisfying the constraints of $(\mathrm{D}_1)$. According to this inequality, the constrained function $v(\boldsymbol{\delta})$ provides a lower bound for $g_0(t)$ $(t > 0)$ and implies the existence of a greatest lower bound $M$ satisfying

$$g_0(t) \geq M \geq v(\boldsymbol{\delta}). \tag{317}$$

The value $M$ is also an upper bound for the constrained values of $v(\boldsymbol{\delta})$ and will be shown actually to be the least upper bound.

Intuitively, inequality (317) suggests that $g_0(t)$ and $v(\boldsymbol{\delta})$ will attain the common value $M$ when $g_0(t)$ is minimized and when we determine the constrained maximum of $v(\boldsymbol{\delta})$. This idea is indicative of the technique of unconstrained geometric programming; by solving the dual problem $(\mathrm{D}_1)$ we will obtain a value equal to the minimum queueing system cost $g_0(t)$.

Solving $(\mathrm{D}_1)$ is a relatively simple task. Observe that *only* the values $\delta_1^* = \frac{1}{2}$, $\delta_2^* = \frac{1}{2}$ satisfy the constraints of $(\mathrm{D}_1)$. Hence, the constrained maximum of $v(\boldsymbol{\delta})$ must be attained when $\delta_1^* = \frac{1}{2}$, $\delta_2^* = \frac{1}{2}$. Thus, since the constrained maximum value of $v(\boldsymbol{\delta})$ and the minimum total queueing system cost $g_0(t)$ are equal, we conclude that

$$\text{minimum } g_0(t) = v(\boldsymbol{\delta}^*) = \left(\frac{c/b}{\frac{1}{2}}\right)^{1/2}\left(\frac{2d}{\frac{1}{2}}\right)^{1/2} = 2\left(\frac{2cd}{b}\right)^{1/2}.$$

The minimum total queueing system cost has been obtained *without* first determining the optimal service time $t^*$. To determine $t^*$, we again employ the geometric inequality. Recall that according to the inequality

$$g_0(t^*) = v(\boldsymbol{\delta}^*) = 2\left(\frac{2cd}{b}\right)^{1/2}$$

if and only if

$$u_1 = \delta_1^* g_0(t^*) \qquad \text{and} \qquad u_2 = \delta_2^* g_0(t^*);$$

that is, if and only if

(318)
$$u_1 = \frac{c}{b}t^* = \frac{1}{2}\left[2\left(\frac{2cd}{b}\right)^{1/2}\right],$$
$$u_2 = \frac{2d}{t^*} = \frac{1}{2}\left[2\left(\frac{2cd}{b}\right)^{1/2}\right].$$

From (318) we determine that the optimal service time is

$$t^* = \left(\frac{2bd}{c}\right)^{1/2}.$$

The solution $\delta_1^* = \frac{1}{2}$, $\delta_2^* = \frac{1}{2}$ to dual program ($D_1$) provides more information and insight into our cost minimization problem. From (318) it is seen that $\delta_1^*$ indicates the relative contribution of the waiting cost to the minimum total cost; since $\delta_1^* = \frac{1}{2}$, the waiting cost is half of the minimum total cost. Analogously, because $\delta_2^* = \frac{1}{2}$, the relative contribution of the service facility cost to the minimum total cost is $\frac{1}{2}$. Furthermore, observe that these relative contributions to the minimum cost are independent of the factors $c$, $d$, and $b$. Regardless of how the values of $c$, $d$, and $b$ vary, the waiting and service facility costs each constitute half of the minimum.

This queueing system cost minimization problem illustrates the technique of unconstrained geometric programming; that is, first, by employing the geometric inequality, we formulate a dual program. Since the constrained maximum value of this dual program equals the minimum of $g_0(t)$, we solve the dual program. The solution of the dual program indicates the relative contribution of each term of $g_0(t)$ to the minimum of $g_0(t)$. Finally, we use the necessary and sufficient conditions for equality of the geometric inequality to determine the optimal value of $t$.

The general technique of geometric programming is similar. However, before analyzing the general unconstrained problem, we apply this technique to several other examples. Consider the following unconstrained minimization problem:

($P_2$) minimize $g_0(\mathbf{t}) = \frac{1}{6}t_1^{-2}t_2 + 2t_2 + \frac{1}{3}t_1t_2^{-2}$,

where $t_1 > 0$, $t_2 > 0$. Each of the terms $u_1 = \frac{1}{6}t_1^{-2}t_2$, $u_2 = 2t_2$, and $u_3 = \frac{1}{3}t_1t_2^{-2}$ of the function $g_0(\mathbf{t})$ is positive, so that we may apply the geometric inequality,

$$u_1 + u_2 + u_3 \geq \left(\frac{u_1}{\delta_1}\right)^{\delta_1}\left(\frac{u_2}{\delta_2}\right)^{\delta_2}\left(\frac{u_3}{\delta_3}\right)^{\delta_3},$$

$$\delta_1 \geq 0, \qquad \delta_2 \geq 0, \qquad \delta_3 \geq 0$$

$$\delta_1 + \delta_2 + \delta_3 = 1,$$

to conclude that

$$(319) \quad \tfrac{1}{6}t_1^{-2}t_2 + 2t_2 + \tfrac{1}{3}t_1t_2^{-2} \geq \left(\frac{\frac{1}{6}t_1^{-2}t_2}{\delta_1}\right)^{\delta_1}\left(\frac{2t_2}{\delta_2}\right)^{\delta_2}\left(\frac{\frac{1}{3}t_1t_2^{-2}}{\delta_3}\right)^{\delta_3},$$

$$\delta_1 \geq 0, \qquad \delta_2 \geq 0, \qquad \delta_3 \geq 0$$

$$\delta_1 + \delta_2 + \delta_3 = 1.$$

Inequality (319) suggests that the following dual problem

$$(\mathrm{D}_2') \quad \begin{array}{ll} \text{maximize} & V(\boldsymbol{\delta}, \mathbf{t}) = \left(\dfrac{\frac{1}{6}t_1^{-2}t_2}{\delta_1}\right)^{\delta_1}\left(\dfrac{2t_2}{\delta_2}\right)^{\delta_2}\left(\dfrac{\frac{1}{3}t_1t_2^{-2}}{\delta_3}\right)^{\delta_3} \\ \text{subject to} & \delta_1 \geq 0, \quad \delta_2 \geq 0, \quad \delta_3 \geq 0, \quad t_1 > 0, \quad t_2 > 0 \\ & \delta_1 + \delta_2 + \delta_3 = 1. \end{array}$$

may aid in bounding the minimum of $g_0(\mathbf{t})$ from below.

However, the constrained function $V(\boldsymbol{\delta}, \mathbf{t})$ will not provide a lower bound for $g_0(\mathbf{t})$ and the minimum of $g_0(\mathbf{t})$ unless we eliminate the dependence of $V(\boldsymbol{\delta}, \mathbf{t})$ on $\mathbf{t} = (t_1, t_2)$. This is readily accomplished by noting that since

$$V(\boldsymbol{\delta}, \mathbf{t}) = \left(\frac{\frac{1}{6}}{\delta_1}\right)^{\delta_1}\left(\frac{2}{\delta_2}\right)^{\delta_2}\left(\frac{\frac{1}{3}}{\delta_3}\right)^{\delta_3} t_1^{-2\delta_1+\delta_3} t_2^{\delta_1+\delta_2-2\delta_3},$$

the dependence of $V(\boldsymbol{\delta}, \mathbf{t})$ on $t_1$ and $t_2$ is eliminated by requiring

$$\begin{aligned} -2\delta_1 \qquad\quad + \delta_3 &= 0, \\ \delta_1 + \delta_2 - 2\delta_3 &= 0. \end{aligned}$$

Our dual problem is then as follows:

$$(\mathrm{D}_2) \quad \begin{array}{ll} \text{maximize} & v(\boldsymbol{\delta}) = \left(\dfrac{\frac{1}{6}}{\delta_1}\right)^{\delta_1}\left(\dfrac{2}{\delta_2}\right)^{\delta_2}\left(\dfrac{\frac{1}{3}}{\delta_3}\right)^{\delta_3} \\ \text{subject to} & \delta_1 \geq 0, \quad \delta_2 \geq 0, \quad \delta_3 \geq 0 \\ & \delta_1 + \delta_2 + \delta_3 = 1 \\ & -2\delta_1 \qquad\quad + \delta_3 = 0 \\ & \delta_1 + \delta_2 - 2\delta_3 = 0. \end{array}$$

The geometric inequality, (319), implies

$$g_0(\mathbf{t}) \geq M \geq v(\boldsymbol{\delta}),$$

for $\mathbf{t} > 0$ and $\boldsymbol{\delta}$ satisfying the constraints of $(\mathrm{D}_2)$. This inequality yields a lower bound, $v(\boldsymbol{\delta})$, for $M$, the minimum of $g_0(\mathbf{t})$. Since, at the optimum, $M$ equals the constrained maximum of $v(\boldsymbol{\delta})$, we must solve $(\mathrm{D}_2)$. The constraints of $(D_2)$ have the *unique* solution

(320) $$\delta_1^* = \tfrac{1}{6}, \qquad \delta_2^* = \tfrac{1}{2}, \qquad \delta_3^* = \tfrac{1}{3},$$

implying that the constrained maximum must be attained at this point; that is, the constrained maximum of $(D_2)$ is

$$v(\boldsymbol{\delta}^*) = \left(\frac{\frac{1}{6}}{\frac{1}{6}}\right)^{1/6}\left(\frac{2}{\frac{1}{2}}\right)^{1/2}\left(\frac{\frac{1}{3}}{\frac{1}{3}}\right)^{1/3} = 2.$$

Thus, the minimum of $g_0(\mathbf{t})$ is 2.

Further, from (320) we may conclude that the relative contribution of the first, second, and third terms of $g_0(\mathbf{t})$ to the minimum value are $\frac{1}{6}$, $\frac{1}{2}$, and $\frac{1}{3}$, respectively, independent of the coefficients of the terms of $g_0(\mathbf{t})$. The optimal values of $t_1$ and $t_2$ are determined by considering the conditions for equality of $g_0(\mathbf{t})$ and $v(\boldsymbol{\delta})$:

$$\tfrac{1}{6}t_1^{*-2}t_2^* = \tfrac{1}{6}2 = \tfrac{1}{3},$$
$$2t_2^* = \tfrac{1}{2}2 = 1,$$
$$\tfrac{1}{3}t_1^*t_2^{*-2} = \tfrac{1}{3}2 = \tfrac{2}{3}.$$

This system implies that the minimum value 2 is attained at

$$t_1^* = \tfrac{1}{2} \qquad \text{and} \qquad t_2^* = \tfrac{1}{2}.$$

As a final example, let us apply the technique of geometric programming to the following problem:

$(P_3)$ minimize $$g_0(\mathbf{t}) = \tfrac{1}{8}t_1t_2t_3 + \tfrac{3}{8}t_1^{-1} + \tfrac{1}{8}t_2^{-1} + \tfrac{1}{8}t_1^2t_3 + 4t_3^{-1},$$

where $t_1 > 0$, $t_2 > 0$, $t_3 > 0$. We may apply the geometric inequality to problem $(P_3)$ because each of the terms is positive:

$$\tfrac{1}{8}t_1t_2t_3 + \tfrac{3}{8}t_1^{-1} + \tfrac{1}{8}t_2^{-1} + \tfrac{1}{8}t_1^2t_3 + 4t_3^{-1}$$
$$\geq \left(\frac{\frac{1}{8}t_1t_2t_3}{\delta_1}\right)^{\delta_1}\left(\frac{\frac{3}{8}t_1^{-1}}{\delta_2}\right)^{\delta_2}\left(\frac{\frac{1}{8}t_2^{-1}}{\delta_3}\right)^{\delta_3}\left(\frac{\frac{1}{8}t_1^2t_3}{\delta_4}\right)^{\delta_4}\left(\frac{4t_3^{-1}}{\delta_5}\right)^{\delta_5} = V(\boldsymbol{\delta}, \mathbf{t}),$$
$$\delta_1 \geq 0, \quad \delta_2 \geq 0, \quad \delta_3 \geq 0, \quad \delta_4 \geq 0, \quad \delta_5 \geq 0$$
$$\delta_1 + \delta_2 + \delta_3 + \delta_4 + \delta_5 = 1.$$

This inequality suggests a dual problem associated with $(P_3)$:

maximize $V(\boldsymbol{\delta}, \mathbf{t})$

$(D_3')$ subject to $\delta_1 \geq 0, \ldots, \delta_5 \geq 0, \quad t_1 > 0, \quad t_2 > 0, \quad t_3 > 0$

$$\delta_1 + \delta_2 + \delta_3 + \delta_4 + \delta_5 = 1.$$

The values of the constrained function $V(\boldsymbol{\delta}, \mathbf{t})$ in $(\mathrm{D}_3')$ may be used as lower bounds for the minimum value of $g_0(\mathbf{t})$ by formulating $V(\boldsymbol{\delta}, \mathbf{t})$ as a function only of the $\delta_i$. This is accomplished by noting that since

$$V(\boldsymbol{\delta}, \mathbf{t}) = \left(\frac{\frac{1}{8}}{\delta_1}\right)^{\delta_1}\left(\frac{\frac{3}{8}}{\delta_2}\right)^{\delta_2}\left(\frac{\frac{1}{8}}{\delta_3}\right)^{\delta_3}\left(\frac{\frac{1}{8}}{\delta_4}\right)^{\delta_4}\left(\frac{4}{\delta_5}\right)^{\delta_5} t_1^{\delta_1-\delta_2+2\delta_4} t_2^{\delta_1-\delta_3} t_3^{\delta_1+\delta_4-\delta_5},$$

the dependence on $t_1, t_2, t_3$ is eliminated by requiring

$$\begin{aligned} \delta_1 - \delta_2 \qquad\quad + 2\delta_4 \qquad\quad &= 0 \\ \delta_1 \qquad - \delta_3 \qquad\qquad\qquad\quad &= 0 \\ \delta_1 \qquad\qquad\quad + \delta_4 - \delta_5 &= 0. \end{aligned}$$

Thus, problem $(\mathrm{D}_3')$ is transformed into the following dual problem:

$$\begin{aligned} &\text{maximize} && v(\boldsymbol{\delta}) = \left(\frac{\frac{1}{8}}{\delta_1}\right)^{\delta_1}\left(\frac{\frac{3}{8}}{\delta_2}\right)^{\delta_2}\left(\frac{\frac{1}{8}}{\delta_3}\right)^{\delta_3}\left(\frac{\frac{1}{8}}{\delta_4}\right)^{\delta_4}\left(\frac{4}{\delta_5}\right)^{\delta_5} \\ &\text{subject to} && \delta_1 \geq 0, \ldots, \delta_5 \geq 0 \\ (\mathrm{D}_3)\quad & && \delta_1 + \delta_2 + \delta_3 + \delta_4 + \delta_5 = 1 \\ & && \delta_1 - \delta_2 + 2\delta_4 = 0 \\ & && \delta_1 - \delta_3 = 0 \\ & && \delta_1 + \delta_4 - \delta_5 = 0. \end{aligned}$$

By the geometric inequality, the constrained values of $v(\boldsymbol{\delta})$ provide lower bounds for $M$, the minimum of $g_0(\mathbf{t})$. At the optimum, $M$ equals the constrained maximum of $v(\boldsymbol{\delta})$. Therefore, we solve $(\mathrm{D}_3)$.

Unlike the previous examples, the constraints of problem $(\mathrm{D}_3)$ *do not* have a unique solution. For instance, $\delta_1 = \frac{1}{8}$, $\delta_2 = \frac{3}{8}$, $\delta_3 = \frac{1}{8}$, $\delta_4 = \frac{1}{8}$, $\delta_5 = \frac{1}{4}$ and $\delta_1 = \frac{1}{6}$, $\delta_2 = \frac{1}{3}$, $\delta_3 = \frac{1}{6}$, $\delta_4 = \frac{1}{12}$, $\delta_5 = \frac{1}{4}$ are both solutions of the linear equality constraints of $(\mathrm{D}_3)$. Neither of these solutions necessarily yields the constrained maximum of $v(\boldsymbol{\delta})$. However, using these values of the $\delta_i$ $(i = 1, \ldots, 5)$ and the fact that, according to the geometric inequality, $M$ satisfies

$$g_0(\mathbf{t}) \geq M \geq v(\boldsymbol{\delta}) \tag{321}$$

for $\boldsymbol{\delta}$ satisfying the constraints of $(\mathrm{D}_3)$, we may estimate $M$. According to inequality (321), $v(\boldsymbol{\delta})$ evaluated at $\delta_1' = \frac{1}{8}$, $\delta_2' = \frac{3}{8}$, $\delta_3' = \frac{1}{8}$, $\delta_4' = \frac{1}{8}$, $\delta_5' = \frac{1}{4}$ provides a lower bound for $M$; that is, $M \geq 2 = v(\boldsymbol{\delta}')$. To obtain an upper bound for $M$ positive values of $t_1$, $t_2$, $t_3$ are substituted into $g_0(\mathbf{t})$. For instance, with $t_1' = 1$, $t_2' = 1$, $t_3' = 4$, inequality (321) implies $g_0(\mathbf{t}') = 2.5 \geq M$. Thus, although we were unable to obtain the minimum value $M$, we can estimate it as

$$2.5 \geq M \geq 2.$$

These examples reveal the advantages of the dual geometric program in certain minimization problems. Frequently, the minimum value is obtained immediately by solving the dual program, as examples ($P_1$) and ($P_2$) illustrated. Sometimes, as in problem ($P_3$), the dual program aids in approximating the minimum value. In discussing the dual for the general unconstrained geometric programming problem, we develop conditions assuring the existence of an optimal solution to the dual program for any well-posed unconstrained geometric programming problem.

All of the example geometric programming problems involve minimizing functions of the form

$$g_0(\mathbf{t}) = u_1 + \cdots + u_n,$$

where $u_i = c_i t_1^{a_{i1}} t_2^{a_{i2}} \cdots t_m^{a_{im}}$, the constants $c_i$ are *positive*, $a_{ij}$ are arbitrary real numbers, and $t_1 > 0, \ldots, t_m > 0$. Functions of this form are called *posynomials*.* The restriction that the coefficients $c_i$ be positive is fundamental to the use of geometric programming. As we shall see, without this restriction the terms $u_i$ are not necessarily positive and the geometric inequality cannot be applied.

The general unconstrained geometric programming problem is to minimize a posynomial,

$$\text{(P)} \qquad g_0(\mathbf{t}) = u_1 + u_2 + \cdots + u_n,$$

where $u_i = c_i t_1^{a_{i1}} t_2^{a_{i2}} \cdots t_m^{a_{im}}$, the constants $c_i$ are positive, and the $a_{ij}$ are arbitrary real constants. The *primal variables*, $t_1, t_2, \ldots, t_m$, are positive. Problem (P) is called the *primal* program and $g_0(\mathbf{t})$ is termed the *primal objective function*.

As in the examples, a dual geometric programming problem is formed by applying the geometric inequality to $g_0(\mathbf{t})$:

$$g_0(\mathbf{t}) \geq V(\boldsymbol{\delta}, \mathbf{t}) = \left(\frac{u_1}{\delta_1}\right)^{\delta_1} \left(\frac{u_2}{\delta_2}\right)^{\delta_2} \cdots \left(\frac{u_n}{\delta_n}\right)^{\delta_n},$$

$$\delta_1 \geq 0, \ldots, \delta_n \geq 0$$

$$\delta_1 + \cdots + \delta_n = 1.$$

Since

$$V(\boldsymbol{\delta}, \mathbf{t}) = \left(\frac{c_1}{\delta_1}\right)^{\delta_1} \cdots \left(\frac{c_n}{\delta_n}\right)^{\delta_n} t_1^{\sum_{i=1}^n a_{i1}\delta_i} \cdots t_m^{\sum_{i=1}^n a_{im}\delta_i},$$

* From Duffin, Peterson, and Zener.

the dependence of $V(\boldsymbol{\delta}, \mathbf{t})$ on $\mathbf{t}$ is eliminated by requiring

$$\sum_{i=1}^{n} a_{i1}\delta_i = 0$$
$$\vdots \qquad \vdots$$
$$\sum_{i=1}^{n} a_{im}\delta_i = 0.$$

Thus, our *dual program* is

(D) maximize $$v(\boldsymbol{\delta}) = \left(\frac{c_1}{\delta_1}\right)^{\delta_1} \cdots \left(\frac{c_n}{\delta_n}\right)^{\delta_n}$$

(322) subject to $$\delta_1 \geq 0, \ldots, \delta_n \geq 0$$

(323) $$\delta_1 + \delta_2 + \cdots + \delta_n = 1$$

(324) $$\sum_{i=1}^{n} a_{ij}\delta_i = 0, \qquad j = 1, \ldots, m.$$

We specify that $\delta_i^{\delta_i} = \delta_i^{-\delta_i} = 1$ for $\delta_i = 0$ in evaluating $v(\boldsymbol{\delta})$. The function $v(\boldsymbol{\delta})$ is called the *dual objective function* and the constraints (322)–(324) are termed *dual constraints*. Relation (322) is called the *positivity* condition, (323) constitutes the *normality* condition, and the set of linear equations (324) is called the *orthogonality condition*. Dual program (D) is said to be *consistent* when there exists a vector $\boldsymbol{\delta}' = (\delta_1', \ldots, \delta_n')$ satisfying the dual constraints; otherwise, (D) is said to be *inconsistent*.

As our examples have indicated, the basic technique of geometric programming for solving primal program (P) is to formulate and solve the dual program (D). Since we assumed that the constrained maximum value of the dual objective function equals the minimum of the primal objective function, program (P) is then solved. The conditions for equality of the geometric inequality provides a means of determining the optimal values of the primal variables. We now prove that it is always possible to satisfy the dual constraints corresponding to a well-posed unconstrained geometric programming problem and that, in general, the constrained maximum of the dual objective function equals the minimum of the primal objective function. This is the content of the following result:

THEOREM 53 If the primal objective function $g_0(\mathbf{t})$ in (P) attains a minimum value at a point $\mathbf{t}^* = (t_1^*, \ldots, t_m^*)$ with positive coordinates, then:

1. The corresponding dual program (D) is consistent and the dual objective function attains its constrained maximum value at a point $\boldsymbol{\delta}^*$ that satisfies the dual constraints.

2. The constrained maximum value of the dual objective function equals the minimum value of the primal objective function,

$$g_0(\mathbf{t}^*) = v(\boldsymbol{\delta}^*).$$

3. There is a maximizing vector $\boldsymbol{\delta}^*$ for dual program (D) whose components satisfy

$$\delta_i^* = \frac{u_i(\mathbf{t}^*)}{g_0(\mathbf{t}^*)}, \qquad i = 1, \ldots, n. \tag{325}$$

PROOF If $g_0(\mathbf{t})$ attains its minimum value at $\mathbf{t}^* = (t_1^*, \ldots, t_m^*)$, with positive components, $\mathbf{t}^*$ is a critical point of $g_0(\mathbf{t})$; that is,

$$0 = \frac{\partial g_0}{\partial t_j}(\mathbf{t}^*) = \sum_{i=1}^{n} \frac{\partial u_i}{\partial t_j}(\mathbf{t}^*)$$

$$= \sum_{i=1}^{n} a_{ij} c_i t_1^{*a_{i1}} \cdots t_j^{*a_{ij}-1} \cdots t_m^{*a_{im}},$$

$j = 1, \ldots, m$. By multiplying the $j$th equation by $t_j > 0$, we obtain the $m$ equations

$$0 = t_j \frac{\partial g_0}{\partial t_j}(\mathbf{t}^*) = \sum_{i=1}^{n} t_j \frac{\partial u_i}{\partial t_j}(\mathbf{t}^*) = \sum_{i=1}^{n} a_{ij} u_i(\mathbf{t}^*), \tag{326}$$

$j = 1, \ldots, m$. After dividing equations by $g_0(\mathbf{t}^*)$ $(>0)$, we find that

$$0 = \sum_{i=1}^{n} a_{ij} \frac{u_i(\mathbf{t}^*)}{g_0(\mathbf{t}^*)}, \tag{327}$$

$j = 1, \ldots, m$. By defining

$$\delta_i^* = \frac{u_i(\mathbf{t}^*)}{g_0(\mathbf{t}^*)} \qquad (>0), \tag{328}$$

$i = 1, \ldots, n$, we see that conditions (327) are precisely the orthogonality conditions,

$$0 = \sum_{i=1}^{n} a_{ij} \delta_i^*,$$

$j = 1, \ldots, m$. Moreover, this vector also satisfies the normality condition since

$$\delta_1^* + \cdots + \delta_n^* = \frac{u_1(\mathbf{t}^*)}{g_0(\mathbf{t}^*)} + \cdots + \frac{u_n(\mathbf{t}^*)}{g_0(\mathbf{t}^*)} = \frac{g_0(\mathbf{t}^*)}{g_0(\mathbf{t}^*)} = 1. \tag{329}$$

Thus, (D) is consistent because $\boldsymbol{\delta}^*$ satisfies the dual constraints.

To see that $\boldsymbol{\delta}^*$ is a maximizing vector of (D) first observe that since $\boldsymbol{\delta}^*$ satisfies the normality condition,

$$g_0(\mathbf{t}^*) = g_0(\mathbf{t}^*)^{\delta_1^* + \cdots + \delta_n^*} = (g_0^*)^{\delta_1^*} \cdots (g_0^*)^{\delta_n^*},$$

where $g_0^* = g_0(\mathbf{t}^*)$. But according to (328),

$$g_0(\mathbf{t}^*) = (g_0^*)^{\delta_1^*} \cdots (g_0^*)^{\delta_n^*} = \left(\frac{u_1(\mathbf{t}^*)}{\delta_1^*}\right)^{\delta_1^*} \cdots \left(\frac{u_n(\mathbf{t}^*)}{\delta_n^*}\right)^{\delta_n^*},$$

implying that

$$g_0(\mathbf{t}^*) = v(\boldsymbol{\delta}^*),$$

since $\boldsymbol{\delta}^*$ satisfies the orthogonality condition. This result, along with the geometric inequality

$$g_0(\mathbf{t}) \geq v(\boldsymbol{\delta}),$$

($\boldsymbol{\delta}$ satisfying the constraints of (D)) implies that the minimum value of the primal objective function equals the constrained maximum of the dual objective function.

This proves 1 and 2. To complete the proof observe that since $\boldsymbol{\delta}^*$ is a maximizing vector, 3 follows from relation (328). ∎

The results of the theorem are illustrated with another example:

$$(\mathrm{P}_4) \qquad \text{minimize} \quad g_0(\mathbf{t}) = 2t_1t_2^{-1} + 4t_2t_3^{-1} + t_1^{-2} + 4t_2^{-1/2}t_3$$
$$t_1 > 0, \qquad t_2 > 0, \qquad t_3 > 0.$$

According to part 1 of the theorem the corresponding dual program,

$$\text{maximize} \quad v(\boldsymbol{\delta}) = \left(\frac{2}{\delta_1}\right)^{\delta_1}\left(\frac{4}{\delta_2}\right)^{\delta_2}\left(\frac{1}{\delta_3}\right)^{\delta_3}\left(\frac{4}{\delta_4}\right)^{\delta_4}$$

$$(\mathrm{D}_4) \qquad \begin{aligned} \text{subject to} \quad & \delta_1 \geq 0, \quad \delta_2 \geq 0, \quad \delta_3 \geq 0, \quad \delta_4 \geq 0 \\ & \delta_1 + \delta_2 + \delta_3 + \delta_4 = 1 \\ & \delta_1 - 2\delta_3 = 0 \\ & -\delta_1 + \delta_2 - \tfrac{1}{2}\delta_4 = 0 \\ & -\delta_2 + \delta_4 = 0, \end{aligned}$$

attains its maximum value $v(\boldsymbol{\delta}^*)$ at a vector $\boldsymbol{\delta}^*$ satisfying the dual constraints. Since ($\mathrm{D}_3$) has the *unique* solution $\boldsymbol{\delta}^*$,

$$\delta_1^* = \tfrac{2}{11}, \qquad \delta_2^* = \tfrac{4}{11}, \qquad \delta_3^* = \tfrac{1}{11}, \qquad \delta_4^* = \tfrac{4}{11},$$

the maximum value of $v(\boldsymbol{\delta})$ is attained at $\boldsymbol{\delta}^*$ and equals 11. Moreover, by part 2 of the theorem the minimum value of the primal objective function also equals 11.

According to part 3 of Theorem 53, the dual variables $\delta_i^*$ indicate the relative contributions of the terms $u_i(\mathbf{t}^*)$ to the minimum value, $g_0(\mathbf{t}^*)$. Furthermore, the equations (325),

$$\begin{aligned}
\tfrac{2}{11}(11) &= u_1(\mathbf{t}^*) = 2t_1^* t_2^{*^{-1}}, \\
\tfrac{4}{11}(11) &= u_2(\mathbf{t}^*) = 4t_2^* t_3^{*^{-1}}, \\
\tfrac{1}{11}(11) &= u_3(\mathbf{t}^*) = t_1^{*^{-2}}, \\
\tfrac{4}{11}(11) &= u_4(\mathbf{t}^*) = 4t_2^{*^{-1/2}} t_3^*,
\end{aligned}$$

may be used to determine the optimal values of the primal variables. By taking the logarithm of these equations and letting $z_i = \ln t_i$, $i = 1, 2, 3$, we see that $t_1^*, t_2^*, t_3^*$ satisfy

$$\begin{aligned}
0 &= \quad z_1^* - z_2^*, \\
0 &= \qquad\qquad z_2^* - z_3^*, \\
0 &= -2z_1^*, \\
0 &= \qquad -\tfrac{1}{2}z_2^* + z_3^*.
\end{aligned}$$

This system has the unique solution $z_1^* = \ln 1$, $z_2^* = \ln 1$, $z_3^* = \ln 1$, implying $t_1^* = t_2^* = t_3^* = 1$.

As the examples illustrate, the dual program has a unique solution when the number of terms exceeds the number of variables by 1; that is, $n = m + 1$. In ($P_4$), for instance, there are four terms and three variables. When $n > m + 1$, as in ($P_3$), the solution to the dual problem is more difficult to determine and the difficulty increases as $n$ exceeds $m + 1$ by increasing amounts. Accordingly, we term

$$n - (m + 1)$$

the *degree of difficulty* of the geometric program. Thus, the degree of difficulty of ($P_3$) is 1 because there are five terms and three variables.

When the degree of difficulty of an unconstrained geometric programming problem is 0, the maximizing vector $\boldsymbol{\delta}^*$ of the dual does not depend on the posynomial coefficients, $c_i$. In this case the components of $\boldsymbol{\delta}^*$ yield global information about the minimum cost of a management system. For instance, the fact that the minimum value of the queueing system cost (315) is always proportional to the square root of the average waiting cost may be important in designing the queueing system. The dual maximizing vector $\boldsymbol{\delta}^*$, however, may depend on the posynomial coefficients $c_i$ when the degree of difficulty is nonzero.

This section has considered the techniques of unconstrained geometric programming problems. It is natural to extend these techniques to consider posynomial minimization problems with constraints. This is the subject of the following section.

## A PERSONNEL SELECTION PROBLEM: THE CONSTRAINED GEOMETRIC PROGRAMMING PROBLEM

Industrial firms are always confronted with the problem of selecting the best-qualified applicants to fill company positions. The cost of such personnel selection processes increases as finer selections are made. Consequently, the firm must develop a personnel selection process that meets certain requirements at minimum cost. Such a problem is formulated here as the problem of minimizing a posynomial subject to a posynomial inequality constraint, and the techniques of constrained geometric programming are applied to solve it.

Suppose an industrial psychology group of a computer corporation has decided to design a systematic selection procedure for hiring computer programmers. After studying the effectiveness of several experimental selection programs they decided to incorporate three selection processes in *series* to form their selection procedure. These three processes are interviewing applicants, testing applicants, and preliminary training of applicants. Each of these selection processes eliminates a certain fraction of the applicants for the available programming positions. The objective of these psychologists is to determine the fraction of applicants each of the processes should eliminate if at most a fraction $(1/c_4)$, $0 < 1/c_4 < 1$, of the original number of applicants are to remain for final consideration after passing through these three selection processes *and* the total cost of this selection procedure is to be minimized.

Suppose that after all of the applicants have been *interviewed* the personnel department decides to keep a fraction $0 < t_1 < 1$ of these applicants for testing. Cost data has indicated that the cost of interviewing applicants increases as the percent $t_1$ decreases. This is because the personnel department must spend more time establishing better interviewing techniques and evaluating the recommendations of the interviewers. We shall assume that the cost of the interviewing stage is represented by the function $c_1 t_1^{-1}$, $c_1 > 0$.

The second stage in the selection procedure, testing, is assumed to eliminate all but a fraction $0 < t_2 < 1$ of the applicants remaining after interviewing. Cost data has indicated that the cost of testing applicants increases as $t_2$ decreases. This is because more elaborate examinations must be developed if a finer selection is to be made at this stage. Assume that the cost of testing is represented by $c_2 t_2^{-1}$, $c_2 > 0$.

The third and final stage of the selection process involves preliminary training of those applicants remaining after interviewing and testing. Assume that a fraction $0 < t_3 < 1$ of these applicants remain for final consideration after this preliminary training period. Cost data has indicated that as more computer time (the primary cost of preliminary training) is rented, the average cost of computer time decreases. This means that as $t_3$ increases, the cost of preliminary training decreases. Assume that this cost function has the form $c_3 t_3^{-1}$, $c_3 > 0$.

The total cost of this selection procedure is given by the posynomial

$$g_0(\mathbf{t}) = c_1 t_1^{-1} + c_2 t_2^{-1} + c_3 t_3^{-1}.$$

While we wish to choose fractions $t_1^*$, $t_2^*$, $t_3^*$ that minimize the total cost $g_0(\mathbf{t})$, we must also determine fractions such that at most $0 < 1/c_4 < 1$ of the applicants remain for final consideration after completion of all three stages. Since the effect of process $i$ followed by process $j$ is that a fraction $t_i t_j$ of the original number of applicants remain, the latter statement implies

$$t_1 t_2 t_3 \le \frac{1}{c_4}$$

or, equivalently,

$$c_4 t_1 t_2 t_3 \le 1.$$

Thus, our constrained cost minimization problem is one of minimizing a posynomial subject to a posynomial constraint:

$$(\mathrm{P}_1) \qquad \begin{array}{ll} \text{minimize} & g_0(\mathbf{t}) = c_1 t_1^{-1} + c_2 t_2^{-1} + c_3 t_3^{-1} \\ \text{subject to} & t_1 > 0, \quad t_2 > 0, \quad t_3 > 0 \\ & g_1(\mathbf{t}) = c_4 t_1 t_2 t_3 \le 1. \end{array}$$

The geometric programming technique for solving this constrained minimization problem is identical to that for solving unconstrained posynomial minimization problems. Specifically, we formulate and solve a dual geometric programming problem; the maximum value of the dual problem equals the minimum of $(\mathrm{P}_1)$. We proceed as in the unconstrained problem and develop a dual problem from the geometric inequality,

$$(330) \qquad c_1 t_1^{-1} + c_2 t_2^{-1} + c_3 t_3^{-1} \ge \left(\frac{c_1 t_1^{-1}}{\delta_1}\right)^{\delta_1} \left(\frac{c_2 t_2^{-1}}{\delta_2}\right)^{\delta_2} \left(\frac{c_3 t_3^{-1}}{\delta_3}\right)^{\delta_3},$$

$$\delta_1 \ge 0, \qquad \delta_2 \ge 0, \qquad \delta_3 \ge 0$$

$$\delta_1 + \delta_2 + \delta_3 = 1.$$

But that procedure does not consider the constraint $g_1(\mathbf{t}) \le 1$. The appropriate technique is to obtain a second inequality by applying the general geometric inequality to $g_1(\mathbf{t})$ and then by combining these two relationships.

The application of the general geometric inequality to the constraint function, $c_4 t_1 t_2 t_3$, is trivial but illustrates the technique of constrained geometric programming. Specifically the general geometric inequality implies

$$(c_4 t_1 t_2 t_3)^{\delta_4} \geq \left(\frac{c_4 t_1 t_2 t_3}{\delta_4}\right)^{\delta_4} \delta_4^{\delta_4}, \qquad \delta_4 \geq 0. \tag{331}$$

(We do not use the normalized form of the geometric inequality, because, as we shall see, another normalization constraint would complicate the dual program.) If we combine inequality (331) and the constraint

$$1 \geq c_4 t_1 t_2 t_3,$$

we conclude that

$$1 = 1^{\delta_4} \geq \left(\frac{c_4 t_1 t_2 t_3}{\delta_4}\right)^{\delta_4} \delta_4^{\delta_4}, \qquad \delta_4 \geq 0. \tag{332}$$

Inequalities (330) and (332) provide the basis for formulating the dual geometric programming problem. By multiplying the geometric inequality (330) by the extreme sides of the constraint inequality (332), we find

$$\begin{aligned} (333) \quad g_0(\mathbf{t}) &= c_1 t_1^{-1} + c_2 t_2^{-1} + c_3 t_3^{-1} \\ &\geq \left(\frac{c_1 t_1^{-1}}{\delta_1}\right)^{\delta_1} \left(\frac{c_2 t_2^{-1}}{\delta_2}\right)^{\delta_2} \left(\frac{c_3 t_3^{-1}}{\delta_3}\right)^{\delta_3} \left(\frac{c_4 t_1 t_2 t_3}{\delta_4}\right)^{\delta_4} \delta_4^{\delta_4} = V(\boldsymbol{\delta}, \mathbf{t}), \\ &\quad \delta_1 \geq 0, \quad \delta_2 \geq 0, \quad \delta_3 \geq 0, \quad \delta_4 \geq 0 \\ &\quad \delta_1 + \delta_2 + \delta_3 = 1. \end{aligned}$$

This relationship suggests we solve the following dual program:

$$(\mathrm{D}_1') \quad \begin{array}{ll} \text{maximize} & V(\boldsymbol{\delta}, \mathbf{t}) \\ \text{subject to} & \delta_1 \geq 0, \quad \delta_2 \geq 0, \quad \delta_3 \geq 0, \quad \delta_4 \geq 0 \\ & t_1 > 0, \quad t_2 > 0, \quad t_3 > 0 \\ & \delta_1 + \delta_2 + \delta_3 = 1 \end{array}$$

in attempting to obtain an estimate of the constrained minimum value of $g_0(\mathbf{t})$. However, the maximum of $(\mathrm{D}_1')$ depends explicitly on the vector $\mathbf{t} = (t_1, t_2, t_3)$ and hence will not provide a lower bound for the constrained minimum of $g_0(\mathbf{t})$. By eliminating the dependence of $V(\boldsymbol{\delta}, \mathbf{t})$ on $\mathbf{t}$, we will obtain lower bounds for the constrained values of $g_0(\mathbf{t})$.

The variable **t** is eliminated by first observing that we may manipulate the function $V(\boldsymbol{\delta}, \mathbf{t})$ into the equivalent form

$$V(\boldsymbol{\delta}, \mathbf{t}) = \left(\frac{c_1}{\delta_1}\right)^{\delta_1}\left(\frac{c_2}{\delta_2}\right)^{\delta_2}\left(\frac{c_3}{\delta_3}\right)^{\delta_3}\left(\frac{c_4}{\delta_4}\right)^{\delta_4} \delta_4^{\delta_4} t_1^{-\delta_1+\delta_4} t_2^{-\delta_2+\delta_4} t_3^{-\delta_3+\delta_4}.$$

By requiring

$$\begin{aligned} -\delta_1 \qquad\qquad\qquad + \delta_4 &= 0, \\ -\delta_2 \qquad\quad + \delta_4 &= 0, \\ -\delta_3 + \delta_4 &= 0, \end{aligned}$$

the dependence of $V(\boldsymbol{\delta}, \mathbf{t})$ on **t** is eliminated. Hence, our dual program becomes as follows:

$$(\mathrm{D}_1) \qquad \begin{aligned} &\text{maximize} \quad v(\boldsymbol{\delta}) = \left(\frac{c_1}{\delta_1}\right)^{\delta_1}\left(\frac{c_2}{\delta_2}\right)^{\delta_2}\left(\frac{c_3}{\delta_3}\right)^{\delta_3}\left(\frac{c_4}{\delta_4}\right)^{\delta_4} \delta_4^{\delta_4} \\ &\text{subject to} \quad \delta_1 \geq 0, \quad \delta_2 \geq 0, \quad \delta_3 \geq 0, \quad \delta_4 \geq 0 \\ &\qquad \delta_1 + \delta_2 + \delta_3 = 1 \\ &\qquad -\delta_1 + \delta_4 = 0 \\ &\qquad -\delta_2 + \delta_4 = 0 \\ &\qquad -\delta_3 + \delta_4 = 0. \end{aligned}$$

The duality inequality, (333), now is

$$g_0(\mathbf{t}) \geq v(\boldsymbol{\delta}) \tag{334}$$

for **t** and **δ** satisfying the constraints of $(\mathrm{P}_1)$ and $(\mathrm{D}_1)$, respectively. This relation provides a lower bound, $v(\boldsymbol{\delta})$, for constrained values of $g_0(\mathbf{t})$ and implies the existence of a greatest lower bound, $M$, satisfying

$$g_0(\mathbf{t}) \geq M \geq v(\boldsymbol{\delta}). \tag{335}$$

Further, for these constrained values of **t** and **δ**, $M$ is an upper bound for $v(\boldsymbol{\delta})$ and, in particular, can be shown to be the least upper bound.

Intuitively, inequality (335) suggests that $g_0(\mathbf{t})$ and $v(\boldsymbol{\delta})$ will attain the common value $M$ when we determine the constrained minimum of $g_0(\mathbf{t})$ and the constrained maximum of $v(\boldsymbol{\delta})$. This is, indeed, the technique of constrained geometric programming; we determine the constrained minimum of problem $(\mathrm{P}_1)$ by finding the constrained maximum value of dual program $(\mathrm{D}_1)$.

The dual problem $(\mathrm{D}_1)$ has the unique solution $\delta_1^* = \frac{1}{3}$, $\delta_2^* = \frac{1}{3}$, $\delta_3^* = \frac{1}{3}$, $\delta_4^* = \frac{1}{3}$; and thus, the constrained maximum value of $v(\boldsymbol{\delta})$ must be attained at this point. The constrained maximum equals $v(\boldsymbol{\delta}^*) = 3(c_1c_2c_3c_4)^{1/3}$. Therefore, the minimum cost of this personnel selection process is

$$g_0(\mathbf{t}^*) = v(\boldsymbol{\delta}^*) = 3(c_1c_2c_3c_4)^{1/3}.$$

The solution of the dual program ($D_1$) yields additional information concerning the optimal solution of our personnel selection problem. The components of $\boldsymbol{\delta}^*$ corresponding to the terms of the cost function $g_0(\mathbf{t})$ indicate the relative contribution of interviewing, testing, and training to the minimum total cost. Since $\delta_1^* = \delta_2^* = \delta_3^* = \frac{1}{3}$, the cost of each of these processes is a third of the minimum total cost. Note that these proportions are independent of the cost coefficients $c_1$, $c_2$, $c_3$. Regardless of the variations in $c_1$, $c_2$, and $c_3$, the costs of interviewing, testing, and training each constitute a third of the minimum cost of personnel selection.

To determine the optimal values for $t_1, t_2, t_3$ observe that $g_0(\mathbf{t}^*) = v(\boldsymbol{\delta}^*)$ at the optimum. If $g_0(\mathbf{t}^*) = v(\boldsymbol{\delta}^*)$, then we must have equality in inequalities (330)–(332). The geometric inequality (330) is an equality if and only if

(336)
$$\begin{aligned} c_1 t_1^{*-1} &= \tfrac{1}{3}[3(c_1c_2c_3c_4)^{1/3}], \\ c_2 t_2^{*-1} &= \tfrac{1}{3}[3(c_1c_2c_3c_4)^{1/3}], \\ c_3 t_3^{*-1} &= \tfrac{1}{3}[3(c_1c_2c_3c_4)^{1/3}], \end{aligned}$$

and inequality (332) is an equality if and only if

(337)
$$c_4 t_1^* t_2^* t_3^* = \frac{\frac{1}{3}}{\frac{1}{3}} = 1.$$

From system (336) and (337) we determine that

$$t_1^* = \frac{c_1^{2/3}}{(c_2c_3c_4)^{1/3}}, \qquad t_2^* = \frac{c_2^{2/3}}{(c_1c_3c_4)^{1/3}}, \qquad t_3^* = \frac{c_3^{2/3}}{(c_1c_2c_4)^{1/3}}$$

are the values of $t_1$, $t_2$, and $t_3$ that minimize the cost of personnel selection. Thus, for example, at the optimum a fraction

$$t_1^* = \frac{c_1^{2/3}}{(c_2c_3c_4)^{1/3}}$$

of the original number of applicants will remain at the completion of the interviewing process. Note that at the completion of all three stages a fraction

$$t_1^* t_2^* t_3^* = \frac{1}{c_4}$$

of the applicants remains for final consideration.

The technique illustrated in this personnel selection problem and the general technique of constrained geometric programming are similar. By applying appropriate forms of the geometric inequality to the objective and constraint functions of our minimization problem, we formulate a dual problem. By maximizing the constrained dual objective function, we obtain the constrained minimum of our original geometric program.

Before discussing the general constrained geometric programming problem consider a second example:

$$(\mathrm{P}_2)\qquad \begin{array}{ll} \text{minimize} & g_0(\mathbf{t}) = 3t_1t_2^{-1} + \tfrac{1}{4}t_1^{-2}t_2t_3 \\ \text{subject to} & t_1 > 0, \quad t_2 > 0, \quad t_3 > 0 \\ & g_1(\mathbf{t}) = \tfrac{1}{4}t_1^{-1}t_3^{-1} + \tfrac{1}{2}t_2 \leq 1. \end{array}$$

As in the previous example, we wish to formulate and solve a dual program for $(\mathrm{P}_2)$. We proceed by applying the geometric inequality to $g_0(\mathbf{t})$,

$$g_0(\mathbf{t}) = 3t_1t_2^{-1} + \tfrac{1}{4}t_1^{-2}t_2t_3 \geq \left(\frac{3t_1t_2^{-1}}{\delta_1}\right)^{\delta_1}\left(\frac{\tfrac{1}{4}t_1^{-2}t_2t_3}{\delta_2}\right)^{\delta_2}, \tag{338}$$

$$\delta_1 \geq 0, \qquad \delta_2 \geq 0$$

$$\delta_1 + \delta_2 = 1,$$

and applying the general geometric inequality to $g_1(\mathbf{t})$,

$$\begin{aligned} [g_1(\mathbf{t})]^{\delta_3+\delta_4} &= (\tfrac{1}{4}t_1^{-1}t_3^{-1} + \tfrac{1}{2}t_2)^{\delta_3+\delta_4} \\ &\geq \left(\frac{\tfrac{1}{4}t_1^{-1}t_3^{-1}}{\delta_3}\right)^{\delta_3}\left(\frac{\tfrac{1}{2}t_2}{\delta_4}\right)^{\delta_4}(\delta_3+\delta_4)^{\delta_3+\delta_4}, \end{aligned} \tag{339}$$

$$\delta_3 \geq 0, \qquad \delta_4 \geq 0.$$

Since $1 \geq g_1(\mathbf{t})$ in program $(\mathrm{P}_2)$,

$$1 = 1^{\delta_3+\delta_4} \geq [g_1(\mathbf{t})]^{\delta_3+\delta_4}. \tag{340}$$

Together (339) and (340) imply

$$1 \geq \left(\frac{\tfrac{1}{4}t_1^{-1}t_3^{-1}}{\delta_3}\right)^{\delta_3}\left(\frac{\tfrac{1}{2}t_2}{\delta_4}\right)^{\delta_4}(\delta_3+\delta_4)^{\delta_3+\delta_4}. \tag{341}$$

In deriving the dual program inequalities (338) and (341) are combined. We multiply the two extreme sides of (341) by those of (338) to conclude

$$\begin{aligned} g_0(\mathbf{t}) &\geq \left(\frac{3t_1t_2^{-1}}{\delta_1}\right)^{\delta_1}\left(\frac{\tfrac{1}{4}t_1^{-2}t_2t_3}{\delta_2}\right)^{\delta_2}\left(\frac{\tfrac{1}{4}t_1^{-1}t_3^{-1}}{\delta_3}\right)^{\delta_3}\left(\frac{\tfrac{1}{2}t_2}{\delta_4}\right)^{\delta_4}(\delta_3+\delta_4)^{\delta_3+\delta_4} \\ &= V(\boldsymbol{\delta}, \mathbf{t}), \end{aligned} \tag{342}$$

where $\delta_1 \geq 0$, $\delta_2 \geq 0$, $\delta_3 \geq 0$, $\delta_4 \geq 0$, $\delta_1 + \delta_2 = 1$. As in the previous example, $V(\boldsymbol{\delta}, \mathbf{t})$ is transformed into a constrained function only of $\boldsymbol{\delta}$,

$$v(\boldsymbol{\delta}) = \left(\frac{3}{\delta_1}\right)^{\delta_1}\left(\frac{\frac{1}{4}}{\delta_2}\right)^{\delta_2}\left(\frac{\frac{1}{4}}{\delta_3}\right)^{\delta_3}\left(\frac{\frac{1}{2}}{\delta_4}\right)^{\delta_4}(\delta_3+\delta_4)^{\delta_3+\delta_4},$$

by requiring the sum of the respective exponents of $t_1$, $t_2$, and $t_3$ be zero; that is,

$$\begin{aligned} \delta_1 - 2\delta_2 - \delta_3 \qquad &= 0, \\ -\delta_1 + \delta_2 \qquad + \delta_4 &= 0, \\ \delta_2 - \delta_3 \qquad &= 0. \end{aligned}$$

Inequality (342) shows that the constrained function $v(\boldsymbol{\delta})$ provides a lower bound for the constrained function $g_0(\mathbf{t})$ and implies the existence of a greatest lower bound $M$ satisfying

$$g_0(\mathbf{t}) \geq M \geq v(\boldsymbol{\delta}).$$

Intuitively the latter duality inequality suggests that the common value $M$ is attained by the constrained minimum of $g_0(\mathbf{t})$ and the constrained maximum of $v(\boldsymbol{\delta})$, respectively. Therefore, we consider the following dual program:

$$\text{maximize} \quad v(\boldsymbol{\delta}) = \left(\frac{3}{\delta_1}\right)^{\delta_1}\left(\frac{\frac{1}{4}}{\delta_2}\right)^{\delta_2}\left(\frac{\frac{1}{4}}{\delta_3}\right)^{\delta_3}\left(\frac{\frac{1}{2}}{\delta_4}\right)^{\delta_4}(\delta_3 + \delta_4)^{\delta_3+\delta_4}$$

$$(\mathrm{D}_2) \quad \text{subject to} \quad \begin{aligned} &\delta_1 \geq 0, \quad \delta_2 \geq 0, \quad \delta_3 \geq 0, \quad \delta_4 \geq 0 \\ &\delta_1 + \delta_2 = 1 \\ &\delta_1 - 2\delta_2 - \delta_3 = 0 \\ &-\delta_1 + \delta_2 + \delta_4 = 0 \\ &\delta_2 - \delta_3 = 0. \end{aligned}$$

The linear constraints of dual program $(\mathrm{D}_2)$ have the *unique* solution $\delta_1^* = \frac{3}{4}$, $\delta_2^* = \frac{1}{4}$, $\delta_3^* = \frac{1}{4}$, $\delta_4^* = \frac{1}{2}$, and therefore, the maximum of $v(\boldsymbol{\delta})$ is attained here. The maximum of dual program $(\mathrm{D}_2)$, $v(\boldsymbol{\delta}^*)$, and hence the minimum of $(\mathrm{P}_2)$, $g_0(\mathbf{t}^*)$, is $3^{3/4}$. Note that since $\delta_1^* = \frac{3}{4}$ and $\delta_2^* = \frac{1}{4}$, the relative contribution of the first term of $g_0(\mathbf{t})$ to the minimum value is $\frac{3}{4}$, while the second term contributes only $\frac{1}{4}$ of the minimum. Further, these relative contributions are independent of the values of the posynomial coefficients.

The optimal values $t_1^*$, $t_2^*$, and $t_3^*$ are obtained by examining the necessary and sufficient condition for $g_0(\mathbf{t}^*) = v(\boldsymbol{\delta}^*)$. This equality holds when relations (338) and (341) are equalities. The geometric inequality (338) is an equality if and only if

$$(343) \qquad \begin{aligned} 3t_1^* t_2^{*-1} &= \tfrac{3}{4}(3^{3/4}), \\ \tfrac{1}{4}t_1^{*-2} t_2^* t_3^* &= \tfrac{1}{4}(3^{3/4}), \end{aligned}$$

and inequality (341) is an equality if and only if

$$(344)\qquad \begin{aligned} \tfrac{1}{4}t_1^{*-1}t_3^{*-1} &= \frac{\frac{1}{4}}{\frac{1}{4}+\frac{1}{2}} = \tfrac{1}{3}, \\ \tfrac{1}{2}t_2^{*} &= \frac{\frac{1}{2}}{\frac{1}{4}+\frac{1}{2}} = \tfrac{2}{3}. \end{aligned}$$

System (343) and (344) is easily reduced to a system of linear equations in the variables $\ln t_j$ $(j = 1, 2, 3)$, by taking the logarithm of both sides of the equations in (343) and (344),

$$\begin{aligned} \ln t_1^* - \ln t_2^* \qquad\qquad &= \ln \frac{3^{3/4}}{4} \\ -2\ln t_1^* + \ln t_2^* + \ln t_3^* &= \ln 3^{3/4} \\ -\ln t_1^* \qquad\qquad - \ln t_3^* &= \ln \tfrac{4}{3} \\ \ln t_2^* \qquad\qquad &= \ln \tfrac{4}{3}. \end{aligned}$$

By solving this system, we find that $\ln t_1^* = \ln 3^{-1/4}$, $\ln t_2^* = \ln \frac{4}{3}$, $\ln t_3^* = \ln (3^{5/4}/4)$ implying that $g_0(\mathbf{t})$ attains its constrained minimum at $t_1^* = 3^{-1/4}$, $t_2^* = \frac{4}{3}$, $t_3^* = 3^{5/4}/4$.

Both of these geometric programming problems, $(P_1)$ and $(P_2)$, have degree of difficulty zero; that is, the number of terms exceeds the number of variables by 1. In both $(P_1)$ and $(P_2)$ there are four terms and three variables. Their dual programs have a unique solution. In problems of higher degree of difficulty a solution of the dual problem is more difficult to determine.

Although techniques for solving geometric programming problems of nonzero degree of difficulty are discussed later, let us consider the following problem:

$$(P_3)\qquad \begin{aligned} &\text{minimize} && g_0(\mathbf{t}) = 3t_1t_2^{-1} + \tfrac{1}{4}t_1^{-2}t_2 \\ &\text{subject to} && t_1 > 0, \quad t_2 > 0 \\ &&& g_1(\mathbf{t}) = \tfrac{1}{4}t_1^{-1} + \tfrac{1}{2}t_2 \le 1. \end{aligned}$$

This is precisely the previous example with $t_3 = 1$. Note that since there are four terms and two variables, the degree of difficulty is 1. The corresponding dual program has no constraint corresponding to $t_3$:

$$(D_3)\qquad \begin{aligned} &\text{maximize} && v(\boldsymbol{\delta}) = \left(\frac{3}{\delta_1}\right)^{\delta_1}\left(\frac{\frac{1}{4}}{\delta_2}\right)^{\delta_2}\left(\frac{\frac{1}{4}}{\delta_3}\right)^{\delta_3}\left(\frac{\frac{1}{2}}{\delta_4}\right)^{\delta_4}(\delta_3+\delta_4)^{\delta_3+\delta_4} \\ &\text{subject to} && \delta_1 \ge 0, \quad \delta_2 \ge 0, \quad \delta_3 \ge 0, \quad \delta_4 \ge 0 \\ &&& \delta_1 + \delta_2 = 1 \\ &&& \delta_1 - 2\delta_2 - \delta_3 = 0 \\ &&& -\delta_1 + \delta_2 + \delta_4 = 0. \end{aligned}$$

Since the constraints of dual program $(D_3)$ cannot be solved uniquely the constrained maximum of $v(\boldsymbol{\delta})$, and hence, the constrained minimum of $g_0(\mathbf{t})$, $M$, is not easily determined. However, the corresponding duality inequality,

$$g_0(\mathbf{t}) \geq M \geq v(\boldsymbol{\delta})$$

may be used to bound $M$. For instance, since $\delta_1' = \frac{3}{4}$, $\delta_2' = \frac{1}{4}$, $\delta_3' = \frac{1}{4}$, $\delta_4' = \frac{1}{2}$ satisfies the constraints of $(D_3)$, $v(\boldsymbol{\delta}') = 3^{3/4}$ is a lower bound for $M$. Furthermore since $t_1' = 1$, $t_2' = 1$ satisfies the constraints of $(P_3)$ $g_0(\mathbf{t}') = \frac{13}{4}$ is an upper bound for $M$. Thus,

$$\tfrac{13}{4} \geq M \geq 3^{3/4}.$$

Better estimates of $M$ may be obtained by determining other points satisfying the constraints of $(P_3)$ and $(D_3)$.

The ideas and techniques illustrated in these examples are employed in discussing the solution of the general constrained geometric programming problem. As in the examples, the geometric inequality is utilized to formulate a dual program; the solution of the dual is the constrained minimum of our original geometric program. In general, however, we are not assured of the *existence* of a solution to the dual, and therefore, a general theorem of constrained geometric programming must be developed. To facilitate a discussion of this general theory, some terminology is introduced.

The general constrained geometric program is the problem of minimizing a posynomial subject to posynomial inequality constraints:

$$\text{(P)} \qquad \begin{aligned} \text{minimize} \quad & g_0(\mathbf{t}) = u_1 + \cdots + u_{n_0} \\ \text{subject to} \quad & t_1 > 0, \ldots, t_m > 0 \\ & g_1(\mathbf{t}) = u_{n_0+1} + \cdots + u_{n_1} \leq 1 \\ & g_2(\mathbf{t}) = u_{n_1+1} + \cdots + u_{n_2} \leq 1 \\ & \vdots \\ & g_p(\mathbf{t}) = u_{n_{p-1}+1} + \cdots + u_{n_p} \leq 1 \end{aligned}$$

where $u_i = c_i t_1^{a_{i1}} \cdots t_m^{a_{im}}$, $c_i > 0$, and $a_{ij}$ are arbitrary real numbers, $i = 1, \ldots, n$, $j = 1, \ldots, m$. Program (P) is called the *primal program*. The variables $t_1, \ldots, t_m$ are termed *primal variables*, the function $g_0(\mathbf{t})$ is called the *primal objective function*, and the constraints of (P) are called *primal constraints*. When a vector $\mathbf{t}' = (t_1', \ldots, t_m')$ satisfies the constraints of (P) the primal program is said to be *consistent*. Otherwise (P) is said to be *inconsistent*.

Just as was done in the examples, the dual program (D) of (P) is developed by applying the geometric inequality to the objective and constraint functions of (P). Since each term of the posynomial $g_0(\mathbf{t})$ is positive, we may apply the geometric inequality to obtain

$$g_0(\mathbf{t}) \geq \prod_{i=1}^{n_0} \left(\frac{u_i}{\delta_i}\right)^{\delta_i}, \tag{345}$$

where $\lambda_0(\boldsymbol{\delta}) = \delta_1 + \delta_2 + \cdots + \delta_{n_0} = 1$. Similarly, we apply the general geometric inequality to each of the constraint functions as

$$g_k(\mathbf{t})^{\lambda_k(\boldsymbol{\delta})} \geq \left[\prod_{i=n_{k-1}+1}^{n_k} \left(\frac{u_i}{\delta_i}\right)^{\delta_i}\right] \lambda_k(\boldsymbol{\delta})^{\lambda_k(\boldsymbol{\delta})}, \qquad n_p = n, \tag{346}$$

$\lambda_k(\boldsymbol{\delta}) = \delta_{n_{k-1}+1} + \cdots + \delta_{n_k}$, $k = 1, \ldots, p$. Since $\mathbf{t} = (t_1, \ldots, t_m)$ satisfies the constraints

$$1 \geq g_k(\mathbf{t}),$$

$k = 1, \ldots, p$, in program (P), $\mathbf{t}$ also satisfies

$$1 = 1^{\lambda_k(\boldsymbol{\delta})} \geq [g_k(\mathbf{t})]^{\lambda_k(\boldsymbol{\delta})}. \tag{347}$$

It is therefore a consequence of inequalities (346) and (347) that

$$1 \geq \left[\prod_{i=n_{k-1}+1}^{n_k} \left(\frac{u_i}{\delta_i}\right)^{\delta_i}\right] \lambda_k(\boldsymbol{\delta})^{\lambda_k(\boldsymbol{\delta})}, \tag{348}$$

$k = 1, \ldots, p$. Multiplication of (345) and inequalities (348) gives

$$g_0(\mathbf{t}) \geq \prod_{i=1}^{n} \left(\frac{u_i}{\delta_i}\right)^{\delta_i} \prod_{k=1}^{p} \lambda_k(\boldsymbol{\delta})^{\lambda_k(\boldsymbol{\delta})}, \tag{349}$$

where

$$\delta_1 + \delta_2 + \cdots + \delta_{n_0} = 1.$$

Since $(u_i/\delta_i)^{\delta_i} = (c_i/\delta_i)^{\delta_i} t_1^{a_{i1}\delta_i} \cdots t_m^{a_{im}\delta_i}$, an equivalent formulation of inequality (349) is

$$g_0(\mathbf{t}) \geq v(\boldsymbol{\delta}) t_1^{\sum_{i=1}^{n} a_{i1}\delta_i} \cdots t_m^{\sum_{i=1}^{n} a_{im}\delta_i}, \tag{350}$$

where

$$v(\boldsymbol{\delta}) = \prod_{i=1}^{n} \left(\frac{c_i}{\delta_i}\right)^{\delta_i} \prod_{k=1}^{p} \lambda_k(\boldsymbol{\delta})^{\lambda_k(\boldsymbol{\delta})}.$$

By requiring that the exponents of $t_j$ satisfy

$$\sum_{i=1}^{n} a_{ij}\delta_i = 0, \qquad j = 1, \ldots, m, \tag{351}$$

(350) reduces to the general duality inequality,

$$g_0(\mathbf{t}) \geq v(\boldsymbol{\delta}). \tag{352}$$

Moreover, just as in the examples, it can be shown that

$$g_0(\mathbf{t}) = v(\boldsymbol{\delta})$$

if and only if

$$\text{(353)} \qquad \delta_i = \frac{u_i}{g_0(\mathbf{t})}, \qquad i = 1, \ldots, n_0,$$

$$\delta_i = \lambda_k(\boldsymbol{\delta})u_i, \qquad i = n_{k-1} + 1, \ldots, n_k,$$

$$k = 1, \ldots, p.$$

This duality inequality and conditions (353) suggest that the problems of determining the constrained minimum of $g_0(\mathbf{t})$ in (P) and the maximum of $v(\boldsymbol{\delta})$ constrained by the condition, $\delta_1 + \cdots + \delta_{n_0} = 1$, and the conditions (351) are intimately related. Hence, we form the general *dual geometric programming problem:*

$$\text{(D)} \qquad \text{maximize} \qquad v(\boldsymbol{\delta}) = \left[\prod_{i=1}^{n}\left(\frac{c_i}{\delta_i}\right)^{\delta_i}\right]\prod_{k=1}^{p}\lambda_k(\boldsymbol{\delta})^{\lambda_k(\boldsymbol{\delta})}$$

$$\text{(354)} \qquad \text{subject to} \qquad \delta_1 \geq 0, \ldots, \delta_n \geq 0$$

$$\text{(355)} \qquad \sum_{i=1}^{n_0} \delta_i = 1$$

$$\text{(356)} \qquad \sum_{i=1}^{n} a_{ij}\delta_i = 0, \qquad j = 1, \ldots, m.$$

Here

$$\lambda_k(\boldsymbol{\delta}) = \sum_{i=n_{k-1}+1}^{n_k} \delta_i.$$

It is understood that $\delta_i^{\delta_i} = \delta_i^{-\delta_i} = 1$ for $\delta_i = 0$. The constraints of (D) are called the *dual constraints;* (354), (355), and (356) are known as the *positivity*, *normality*, and *orthogonality* conditions, respectively. When a vector $\boldsymbol{\delta}' = (\delta_1', \ldots, \delta_n')$ satisfies the dual constraints dual program, (D) is said to be *consistent;* otherwise, (D) is said to be *inconsistent*. The product function $v(\boldsymbol{\delta})$ is called the *dual objective function* and $\delta_1, \ldots, \delta_n$ are *dual variables*.

The dual program of (P) is readily formed by associating a dual variable $\delta_i$ with the $i$th term $u_i$ of the primal program (P). Each of the terms $\lambda_k(\boldsymbol{\delta})$ is the sum of the $\delta_i$ corresponding to the $k$th constraint. (Notice that no such factor corresponding to $g_0(\mathbf{t})$ appears in the dual objective function, because $\lambda_0(\boldsymbol{\delta}) = \delta_1 + \cdots + \delta_{n_0} = 1$.) The factors $c_i$ in the dual objective function are the coefficients of the posynomials in (P), and $a_{ij}$ is the exponent of $t_j$ in the $i$th term $u_i$. The coefficients of the $j$th orthogonality constraint are the exponents of $t_j$ in the primal program.

The duality inequality (352) relates the primal program (P) and the dual program (D). Inequality (352) implies that if (P) and (D) are consistent, the constrained value $g_0(\mathbf{t}')$ is greater than, or equal to, the constrained value $v(\boldsymbol{\delta}')$. These values are, in fact, equal when the primal variables $\mathbf{t}^*$ and dual variables $\boldsymbol{\delta}^*$ satisfy (353). The computational significance of the latter statement is obvious; if we can determine $\mathbf{t}^*$ and $\boldsymbol{\delta}^*$ satisfying (353) we can determine the constrained minimum of $g_0(\mathbf{t})$ in (P) by solving the dual program (D). In general, however, we are not assured of the *existence* of a maximizing vector $\boldsymbol{\delta}^*$ for dual program (D). Hence, a duality theorem analogous to the duality theorem of unconstrained geometric programming guaranteeing the existence of $\boldsymbol{\delta}^*$ is necessary.

In discussing this duality theorem for the constrained geometric programming problem (P) it is convenient to transform (P) into an equivalent, yet more familiar, form. Here the primal geometric program is converted into a convex program by the transformation $t_i = e^{x_i}$ $(i = 1, \ldots, m)$. If (P) is considered as a convex programming problem, the properties of convex functions and the Kuhn–Tucker theorem may be applied.

The transformation $t_i = e^{x_i}$ $(i = 1, 2, \ldots, m)$ converts geometric programming problem (P) into an *equivalent* convex programming problem because of its monotonic properties. Associated with each value of $t_i$ is a unique value $x_i$; as $x_i$ increases, $t_i$ increases and vice versa. That is, one variable reflects the behavior of the other (see Figure 120).

Note that, in general, without this transformation the Kuhn–Tucker theorem may not be applied in discussing program (P) because not all posynomials are convex functions. For instance, consider the following geometric programming problem:

$$\text{minimize} \quad t^{1/2}$$

$$t > 0$$

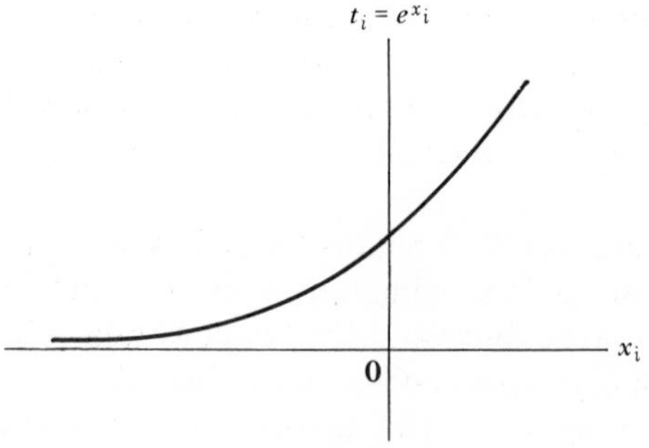


**Figure 120**

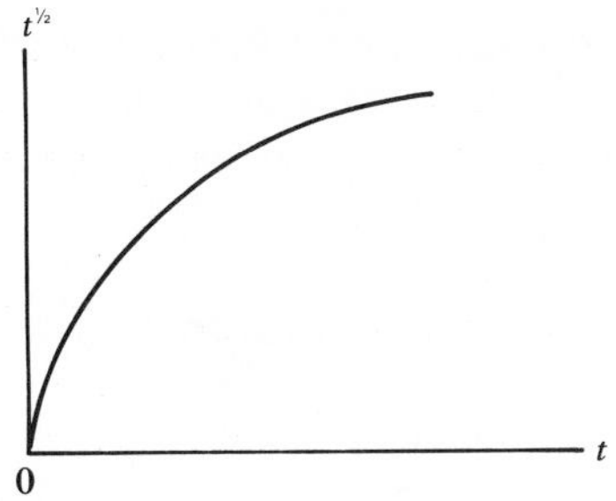


Figure 121

(see Figure 121). Although this is not a convex program in the variable $t$, it is a convex program in $x$ ($t = e^x$):

$$\text{minimize} \qquad e^{x/2}$$

Under this change of variables ($t_i = e^{x_i}$, $i = 1, 2, 3$) the geometric program

$$\begin{aligned} &\text{minimize} && g_0(\mathbf{t}) = 3t_1t_2^{-1} + \tfrac{1}{4}t_1^{-2}t_2t_3 \\ &\text{subject to} && t_1 > 0, \qquad t_2 > 0, \qquad t_3 > 0 \\ & && g_1(\mathbf{t}) = \tfrac{1}{4}t_1^{-2}t_3^{-1} + \tfrac{1}{2}t_2 \le 1 \end{aligned}$$

becomes the convex program

$$\begin{aligned} &\text{minimize} && g_0(\mathbf{x}) = 3e^{x_1 - x_2} + \tfrac{1}{4}e^{-2x_1 + x_2 + x_3} \\ &\text{subject to} && g_1(\mathbf{x}) - 1 = \tfrac{1}{4}e^{-2x_1 - x_3} + \tfrac{1}{2}e^{x_2} - 1 \le 0. \end{aligned}$$

Similarly, with $t_j = e^{x_j}$, $j = 1, \ldots, m$, the primal program (P) is transformed into the following equivalent convex program:

$$(\mathrm{P_x}) \qquad \begin{aligned} &\text{minimize} && g_0(\mathbf{x}) = \sum_{i=1}^{n_0} c_i e^{\sum_{j=1}^{m} a_{ij}x_j} \\ &\text{subject to} && g_1(\mathbf{x}) - 1 = \sum_{i=n_0+1}^{n_1} c_i e^{\sum_{j=1}^{m} a_{ij}x_j} - 1 \le 0 \\ & && \qquad \vdots \\ & && g_p(\mathbf{x}) - 1 = \sum_{i=n_{p-1}+1}^{n} c_i e^{\sum_{j=1}^{m} a_{ij}x_j} - 1 \le 0. \end{aligned}$$

Convex program ($\mathrm{P_x}$) is called the *transformed* program of (P). This transformation demonstrates the fact that geometric programming problems are actually a particular class of convex programs.

Having transformed primal program (P) into the equivalent convex program ($\mathrm{P_x}$), the technique of the proof of the duality theorem is to relate

($P_x$) to an unconstrained Lagrangian program and apply the Kuhn–Tucker theorem. Recall that to apply the Kuhn–Tucker theorem program ($P_x$) must be *superconsistent;* that is, there exists $\mathbf{x}'$ such that

$$g_k(\mathbf{x}') - 1 < 0, \qquad k = 1, \ldots, p.$$

Equivalently, (P) must be *superconsistent;* that is, there exists $\mathbf{t}'$ ($> 0$) such that

$$g_k(\mathbf{t}') < 1, \qquad k = 1, \ldots, p.$$

Therefore, we require (P) be *superconsistent* in the duality theorem.

We are now prepared to state and prove the duality theorem of constrained geometric programming:

THEOREM 54 Suppose that program (P) is superconsistent and that the objective function $g_0(\mathbf{t})$ attains its constrained minimum value at a point $\mathbf{t}^*$ that satisfies the constraints of (P). Then:

1. The corresponding dual program is consistent and the dual objective function attains its constrained maximum value at a point satisfying the dual constraints.
2. The constrained maximum value of the dual objective function equals the constrained minimum value of $g_0(\mathbf{t})$.
3. There are nonnegative Lagrange multipliers $\mu_k'$, $k = 1, \ldots, p$, such that

$$L(\mathbf{t}, \boldsymbol{\mu}) = g_0(\mathbf{t}) + \sum_{k=1}^{p} \mu_k[g_k(\mathbf{t}) - 1]$$

has a critical point at $(\mathbf{t}^*, \boldsymbol{\mu}')$. There is a maximizing vector $\boldsymbol{\delta}^*$ for the associated dual program with components

$$(357) \qquad \delta_i^* = \begin{cases} \dfrac{u_i^*}{g_0(\mathbf{t}^*)}, & i = 1, \ldots, n_0 \\ \lambda_k(\boldsymbol{\delta}^*)u_i^*, & i = n_{k-1} + 1, \ldots, n_k, \\ & k = 1, \ldots, p, \end{cases}$$

and

$$\lambda_k(\boldsymbol{\delta}^*) = \frac{\mu_k'}{g_0(\mathbf{t}^*)}.$$

PROOF If (P) is superconsistent, then ($P_x$) is obviously superconsistent. Furthermore, if $g_0(\mathbf{t})$ attains its constrained minimum value at $\mathbf{t}^*$, $g_0(\mathbf{x})$ attains its constrained minimum value at $\mathbf{x}^*$ where $t_j^* = e^{x_j^*}, j = 1, \ldots, m$. The Kuhn–Tucker theorem now may be applied to convex program ($P_x$) to conclude that there exists $\mu_k' \geq 0$, $k = 1, \ldots, p$, such that the associated

Lagrangian

$$L(\mathbf{x}, \boldsymbol{\mu}) = g_0(\mathbf{x}) + \sum_{k=1}^{p} \mu_k[g_k(\mathbf{x}) - 1]$$

has an unconstrained minimum at $(\mathbf{x}^*, \boldsymbol{\mu}')$. Thus,

(358) $$\frac{\partial L}{\partial x_j}(\mathbf{x}^*, \boldsymbol{\mu}') = 0,$$

$j = 1, \ldots, m$.

Observe that since $t_j = e^{x_j}$, expression (358) equals

$$\frac{\partial L}{\partial x_j} = \frac{\partial L}{\partial t_j}\frac{\partial t_j}{\partial x_j} = \frac{\partial L}{\partial t_j}\frac{\partial e^{x_j}}{\partial x_j} = \frac{\partial L}{\partial t_j} e^{x_j} = 0$$

by the chain rule. Since $e^{x_j} > 0, j = 1, \ldots, m$,

$$\frac{\partial L}{\partial x_j}(\mathbf{x}^*, \boldsymbol{\mu}') = 0$$

implies

$$\frac{\partial L}{\partial t_j}(\mathbf{t}^*, \boldsymbol{\mu}') = 0,$$

$j = 1, \ldots, m$.

The latter is equivalent to

$$t_j^* \frac{\partial L}{\partial t_j}(\mathbf{t}^*, \boldsymbol{\mu}') = 0$$

or

(359) $$t_j^* \frac{\partial g_0}{\partial t_j}(\mathbf{t}^*) + \sum_{k=1}^{p} \mu_k' t_j^* \frac{\partial g_k}{\partial t_j}(\mathbf{t}^*) = 0,$$

$j = 1, \ldots, m$. Since

$$g_k(\mathbf{t}) = \sum_{i=n_{k-1}+1}^{n_k} c_i t_1^{a_{i1}} \cdots t_m^{a_{im}},$$

$k = 0, 1, \ldots, p$, we have

$$t_j^* \frac{\partial g_k}{\partial t_j}(\mathbf{t}^*) = \sum_{i=n_{k-1}+1}^{n_k} a_{ij} u_i(\mathbf{t}^*),$$

where $u_i(\mathbf{t}) = c_i t_1^{a_{i1}} \cdots t_m^{a_{im}}$. In the case $p = 2$, for example, (359) becomes

$$t_j^* \frac{\partial L}{\partial t_j}(\mathbf{t}^*, \boldsymbol{\mu}') = \sum_{i=1}^{n_0} a_{ij} u_i^* + \sum_{i=n_0+1}^{n_1} \mu_1' a_{ij} u_i^* + \sum_{i=n_1+1}^{n_2} \mu_2' a_{ij} u_i^* = 0$$

where $u_i^* = u_i(\mathbf{t}^*)$. Dividing the latter expression by the posynomial

$$g_0(\mathbf{t}^*) = \sum_{i=1}^{n_0} u_i^* > 0,$$

we have

$$(360) \qquad \frac{t_j^* \dfrac{\partial L}{\partial t_j}(\mathbf{t}^*, \boldsymbol{\mu}')}{g_0(\mathbf{t}^*)} = \sum_{i=1}^{n_0} a_{ij} \frac{u_i^*}{g_0(\mathbf{t}^*)} + \sum_{i=n_0+1}^{n_1} a_{ij} \frac{\mu_1' u_i^*}{g_0(\mathbf{t}^*)} + \sum_{i=n_1+1}^{n_2} a_{ij} \frac{\mu_2' u_i^*}{g_0(\mathbf{t}^*)} = 0.$$

A similar expression holds when $p$ is arbitrary.

Expression (360) implies that the vector $\boldsymbol{\delta}^* = (\delta_1^*, \ldots, \delta_n^*)$ with nonnegative components

$$(361) \qquad \delta_i^* = \begin{cases} \dfrac{u_i^*}{g_0(\mathbf{t}^*)} & (> 0) \quad i = 1, \ldots, n_0 \\ \dfrac{\mu_k' u_i^*}{g_0(\mathbf{t}^*)} & (> 0) \quad i = n_{k-1} + 1, \ldots, n_k, \\ & \qquad\qquad k = 1, \ldots, p, \end{cases}$$

satisfies the *orthogonality* condition of the dual program (D). Note also that

$$\sum_{i=1}^{n_0} \delta_i^* = \sum_{i=1}^{n_0} \frac{u_i^*}{g_0(\mathbf{t}^*)} = \frac{1}{g_0(\mathbf{t}^*)} \sum_{i=1}^{n_0} u_i^* = \frac{1}{g_0(\mathbf{t}^*)} g_0(\mathbf{t}^*) = 1;$$

that is, $\boldsymbol{\delta}^*$ also satisfies the normality condition of (D). Thus, $\boldsymbol{\delta}^*$ satisfies the normality, orthogonality, and positivity conditions of the dual, implying the dual is *consistent*. Further, since

$$\lambda_k(\boldsymbol{\delta}^*) = \delta_{n_{k-1}+1}^* + \cdots + \delta_{n_k}^* = \frac{\mu_k' g_k(\mathbf{t}^*)}{g_0(\mathbf{t}^*)},$$

$k = 1, \ldots, p$, and $\mu_k'[g_k(\mathbf{t}^*) - 1] = \mu_k'[g_k(\mathbf{x}^*) - 1] = 0$, according to the Kuhn–Tucker theorem, we have

$$(362) \qquad \lambda_k(\boldsymbol{\delta}^*) = \frac{\mu_k'}{g_0(\mathbf{t}^*)}.$$

Together (361) and (362) imply

$$(363) \qquad \delta_i^* = \begin{cases} \dfrac{u_i^*}{g_0(\mathbf{t}^*)} & (> 0) \quad i = 1, \ldots, n_0 \\ \lambda_k(\boldsymbol{\delta}^*) u_i^* & (> 0) \quad i = n_{k-1} + 1, \ldots, n_k, \\ & \qquad\qquad k = 1, \ldots, p. \end{cases}$$

Having established (363) it follows from (353) that

$$g_0(\mathbf{t}^*) = v(\boldsymbol{\delta}^*).$$

The duality inequality (352) implies $\boldsymbol{\delta}^*$ is a maximizing vector of (D), establishing (1)–(3) of the theorem. ▮

As the examples have indicated, relation (357) of this duality theorem provides a method for finding a minimizing vector $\mathbf{t}^*$ from the maximizing vector $\boldsymbol{\delta}^*$. By taking the logarithm of both sides of the equations in (357), we see that (357) is reduced to a system of linear equations in the unknowns $\ln t_j^*, j = 1, \ldots, m$. We solve for $\ln t_j^*$ and then determine $t_j^*$.

This duality theorem of geometric programming provides a necessary condition for primal program (P) to attain a constrained minimum. A sufficient condition has also been proved by Duffin, Peterson, and Zener; we state it here without proof:

**THEOREM 55** If primal program (P) is consistent and if there is a point $\boldsymbol{\delta}'$ with *positive* components that satisfies the constraints of (D), the primal objective function $g_0(\mathbf{t})$ attains its constrained minimum value at a point $\mathbf{t}^*$ that satisfies the constraints of (P). ▮

To illustrate the ideas of our duality theorem, let us consider the following example:

$$(\mathrm{P}_4)\qquad \begin{aligned} &\text{minimize} && g_0(\mathbf{t}) = 9t_1t_2t_3^{-1} \\ &\text{subject to} && t_1 > 0, \quad t_2 > 0, \quad t_3 > 0 \\ & && g_1(\mathbf{t}) = \tfrac{1}{2}t_1^{-1}t_2^{-1} + t_2^{-1}t_3 \le 1 \\ & && g_2(\mathbf{t}) = \tfrac{1}{2}t_1^{-1}t_3 \le 1. \end{aligned}$$

The dual geometric programming problem of $(\mathrm{P}_4)$ is formed by letting one dual variable correspond to each term of $(\mathrm{P}_4)$:

$$(\mathrm{D}_4)\qquad \begin{aligned} &\text{maximize} && v(\boldsymbol{\delta}) = \left(\frac{9}{\delta_1}\right)^{\delta_1}\left(\frac{\frac{1}{2}}{\delta_2}\right)^{\delta_2}\left(\frac{1}{\delta_3}\right)^{\delta_3}\left(\frac{\frac{1}{2}}{\delta_4}\right)^{\delta_4}(\delta_2+\delta_3)^{\delta_2+\delta_3}\delta_4^{\delta_4} \\ &\text{subject to} && \delta_1 \ge 0, \quad \delta_2 \ge 0, \quad \delta_3 \ge 0, \quad \delta_4 \ge 0 \\ & && \delta_1 = 1 \\ & && \delta_1 - \delta_2 - \delta_4 = 0 \\ & && \delta_1 - \delta_2 - \delta_3 = 0 \\ & && -\delta_1 + \delta_3 + \delta_4 = 0. \end{aligned}$$

Note that the terms $\lambda_1(\boldsymbol{\delta}) = \delta_2 + \delta_3$ and $\lambda_2(\boldsymbol{\delta}) = \delta_4$ are the sums of the dual variables corresponding to the first and second constraints, respectively. Since this example has degree of difficulty 0, the constraints of the dual program has a unique solution:

$$\delta_1^* = 1, \qquad \delta_2^* = \tfrac{1}{2}, \qquad \delta_3^* = \tfrac{1}{2}, \qquad \delta_4^* = \tfrac{1}{2}.$$

Note that $v(\boldsymbol{\delta}^*) = 9$.

We use the duality theorem to conclude that the minimum of $g_0(\mathbf{t})$ is $g_0(\mathbf{t}^*) = 9$. To do so, we must show that $g_0(\mathbf{t})$ does attain its constrained minimum in ($P_4$) and that problem ($P_4$) is superconsistent. First, since each component of the vector $\boldsymbol{\delta}^* = (1, \frac{1}{2}, \frac{1}{2}, \frac{1}{2})$ is positive and since the point $\mathbf{t}' = (1, 1, \frac{1}{4})$ satisfies the constraints of ($P_4$), Theorem 55 implies that $g_0(\mathbf{t}) = 9t_1t_2t_3^{-1}$ in ($P_4$), does attain its constrained minimum. Next, note that ($P_4$) is superconsistent, because $g_1(\mathbf{t}') = \frac{3}{4} < 1$ and $g_2(\mathbf{t}') = \frac{1}{8} < 1$. Therefore, according to the duality theorem, program ($D_3$) attains its constrained maximum, $v(\boldsymbol{\delta}^*)$, and $g_0(\mathbf{t}^*) = v(\boldsymbol{\delta}^*)$. Hence, since $\boldsymbol{\delta}^* = (1, \frac{1}{2}, \frac{1}{2}, \frac{1}{2})$ is the unique solution of the dual constraints, it is the maximizing vector and $v(\boldsymbol{\delta}^*) = 9 = g_0(\mathbf{t}^*)$. Thus, the constrained minimum value of ($P_4$) is 9.

Since a maximizing vector $\boldsymbol{\delta}^*$ has been determined, conditions (357) may be employed to determine $\mathbf{t}^*$. Relations (357) imply

$$\delta_1^* = 1 = \frac{9t_1^*t_2^*t_3^{*^{-1}}}{9},$$

(364)

$$\begin{aligned}
\delta_2^* &= \tfrac{1}{2} = (\tfrac{1}{2} + \tfrac{1}{2})(\tfrac{1}{2}t_1^{*^{-1}}t_2^{*^{-1}}),\\
\delta_3^* &= \tfrac{1}{2} = (\tfrac{1}{2} + \tfrac{1}{2})(t_2^{*^{-1}}t_3^*),\\
\delta_4^* &= \tfrac{1}{2} = (\tfrac{1}{2})(\tfrac{1}{2}t_1^{*^{-1}}t_3^*).
\end{aligned}$$

To obtain values $t_1^*, t_2^*, t_3^*$, we take logarithms of both sides of system (364):

$$\begin{aligned}
0 &= \ln t_1^* + \ln t_2^* - \ln t_3^*\\
0 &= -\ln t_1^* - \ln t_2^*\\
\ln \tfrac{1}{2} &= -\ln t_2^* + \ln t_3^*\\
\ln 2 &= -\ln t_1^* + \ln t_3^*.
\end{aligned}$$

This system has the unique solution $\ln t_1^* = \ln \frac{1}{2}$, $\ln t_2^* = \ln 2$, $\ln t_3^* = 0$, implying that $g_0(\mathbf{t})$ attains its constrained minimum at $t_1^* = \frac{1}{2}, t_2^* = 2, t_3^* = 1$.

The techniques of geometric programming clearly exploit the structure of a class of parametric optimization problems. The duality theory of geometric programming, which relies on the posynomial form of the objective and constraint functions, provides additional insight and computational advantages in solving these optimization problems. This theory formulates an associated or dual optimization problem with linear equality constraints. Such constraints provide a computational advantage over working with the nonlinear inequality constraints of the primal. When the number of terms exceeds the number of variables by 1, or the degree of difficulty is 0, these linear constraints yield only one solution to the dual problem. There are also computational advantages in solving the dual of geometric programming problems of nonzero degree of difficulty; these are discussed later.

The most important computational advantage resulting from the duality theory of geometric programming is the equality of the constrained minimum of $g_0(\mathbf{t})$ and the constrained maximum of $v(\boldsymbol{\delta})$. Suppose an iteration scheme, for instance, is constructed to minimize $g_0(\mathbf{t})$ and maximize $v(\boldsymbol{\delta})$. After each iteration the resulting value of $g_0(\mathbf{t})$ yields an upper bound on the minimum value of $g_0(\mathbf{t})$, $M$, while the resulting value of $v(\boldsymbol{\delta})$ gives a lower bound for $M$. Thus, $M$ can be approximated with known accuracy after each iteration.

The ideas and techniques of this section have been restricted to a particular class of problems—geometric programming problems. However, many of these results may be applied to other types of optimization problems by transforming these optimization problems into geometric programming problems. This is the subject of the next chapter.

## EXERCISES

1. Determine the arithmetic (geometric) mean of

$$v_1 = 2, \qquad v_2 = 2, \qquad v_3 = 16, \qquad v_4 = 1$$

with the respective weights

$$\delta_1 = \tfrac{1}{4}, \qquad \delta_2 = \tfrac{1}{4}, \qquad \delta_3 = \tfrac{1}{8}, \qquad \delta_4 = \tfrac{3}{8}.$$

2. (*a*) Show that 4 is a lower bound for the function

$$2t + \frac{2}{t}, \qquad t > 0.$$

(*b*) Use part *a* to show that of all rectangles of area 1, the square has the smallest perimeter.

3. Suppose $u_1, \ldots, u_n$ are arbitrary positive numbers and $\delta_1, \ldots, \delta_n$ are positive numbers satisfying

$$\delta_1 + \delta_2 + \cdots + \delta_n = 1.$$

Show that if $u_1 = u_2 = \cdots = u_n$, the arithmetic-mean–geometric-mean inequality,

$$\delta_1 u_1 + \delta_2 u_2 + \cdots + \delta_n u_n \geq u_1^{\delta_1} u_2^{\delta_2} \cdots u_n^{\delta_n},$$

becomes an equality.

4. Show that the inequality

$$\frac{(u_1 + u_2 + \cdots + u_8)}{8} \geq (u_1 u_2 \cdots u_8)^{1/8}$$

for all $u_i > 0$, $i = 1, \ldots, 8$, implies that

$$\frac{(u_1 + u_2 + \cdots + u_7)}{7} \geq (u_1 u_2 \cdots u_7)^{1/7}.$$

5. [Duffin, p. 4] Use the inequality

$$u_1 + u_2 + u_3 \geq \left(\frac{u_1}{\frac{1}{4}}\right)^{1/4} \left(\frac{u_2}{\frac{1}{4}}\right)^{1/4} \left(\frac{u_3}{\frac{1}{2}}\right)^{1/2}$$

to show that 8 is a lower bound for the function

$$g_0(\mathbf{t}) = 4t_1 + t_1 t_2^{-2} + 4t_1^{-1} t_2,$$

$t_1 > 0, \quad t_2 > 0.$

6. Show that if $a_2 \geq a_1$, $b_2 \geq b_1$, then

$$a_1 b_1 + a_2 b_2 \geq a_1 b_2 + a_2 b_1.$$

*Hint*. Note that $(a_1 - a_2)(b_1 - b_2) \geq 0$.

7. Suppose that $r > 0$, $s > 0$ satisfy $1/r + 1/s = 1$. Show that if $u_1 > 0$ and $u_2 > 0$, then

$$\frac{u_1^r}{r} + \frac{u_2^s}{s} \geq u_1 u_2.$$

8. Use the inequality

$$u_1 + u_2 + u_3 + u_4 \geq \left(\frac{u_1}{\frac{1}{5}}\right)^{1/5} \left(\frac{u_2}{\frac{1}{5}}\right)^{1/5} \left(\frac{u_3}{\frac{1}{5}}\right)^{1/5} \left(\frac{u_4}{\frac{2}{5}}\right)^{2/5}$$

to obtain a lower bound for the function

$$g_0(\mathbf{t}) = t_1 t_2^{-2} + t_3 + t_1^{-1} t_3 + 2t_2 t_3^{-1},$$

$t_1 > 0, \quad t_2 > 0, \quad t_3 > 0.$

9. Use the inequality

$$u_1 + u_2 + u_3 + u_4 + u_5 \geq \left(\frac{u_1}{\frac{3}{7}}\right)^{3/7} \left(\frac{u_2}{\frac{1}{7}}\right)^{1/7} \left(\frac{u_3}{\frac{1}{7}}\right)^{1/7} \left(\frac{u_4}{\frac{1}{7}}\right)^{1/7} \left(\frac{u_5}{\frac{1}{7}}\right)^{1/7}$$

to obtain a lower bound for the function

$$g_0(\mathbf{t}) = 3t_3^{-1} t_4 + t_1 + t_2 t_4^{-2} + t_2^{-1} t_4^{-1} + t_1^{-1} t_3^3,$$

$t_1 > 0, \quad t_2 > 0, \quad t_3 > 0, \quad t_4 > 0.$

10. Use the inequality

$$\tfrac{1}{4}u_1 + \tfrac{1}{4}u_2 + \tfrac{1}{4}u_3 + \tfrac{1}{4}u_4 \geq u_1^{1/4} u_2^{1/4} u_3^{1/4} u_4^{1/4}$$

to prove the inequalities,

$$\tfrac{1}{4}u_1 + \tfrac{3}{4}u_2 \geq u_1^{1/4}u_2^{3/4},$$

and

$$\tfrac{1}{4}u_1 + \tfrac{1}{4}u_2 + \tfrac{1}{2}u_3 \geq u_1^{1/4}u_2^{1/4}u_3^{1/2}.$$

11. Show that if

$$\frac{a_1 + a_2 + a_3 + \cdots + a_n}{n} \geq (a_1 a_2 \cdots a_n)^{1/n}$$

holds for $n$ and $a_1 \geq 0, \ldots, a_n \geq 0$, then

$$\frac{b_1 + b_2 + \cdots + b_{n-1}}{n-1} \geq (b_1 b_2 \cdots b_{n-1})^{1/(n-1)}$$

holds for $n - 1$ and $b_1 \geq 0, \ldots, b_{n-1} \geq 0$. *Hint*. Set

$$a_1 = b_1, \ldots, a_{n-1} = b_{n-1}, \qquad a_n = \frac{b_1 + \cdots + b_{n-1}}{n-1}.$$

12. Determine the minimum value and the minimizing point $\mathbf{t}^*$ of each of the following geometric programming problems:

(*a*) minimize $4t^{10} + 3t^{-10/3}$
$t > 0$

(*b*) minimize $\tfrac{3}{5}t^6 + \tfrac{2}{5}t^{-9}$
$t > 0$

(*c*) minimize $3t_1t_2^{-1} + t_2 + 4t_2^{-1}t_3 + t_1^{-1}t_2t_3^{-1}$
$t_1 > 0, \quad t_2 > 0, \quad t_3 > 0$

(*d*) minimize $4t_1 + 2t_1t_2^{-2} + 4t_1^{-1}t_2$
$t_1 > 0, \quad t_2 > 0$

(*e*) minimize $t_1t_2^{-2} + t_3 + 2t_2t_3^{-1} + t_1^{-1}t_3$
$t_1 > 0, \quad t_2 > 0, \quad t_3 > 0$

(*f*) minimize $t_1^{-1}t_3^3 + t_2^{-1}t_4^{-1} + 3t_3^{-1}t_4 + t_2t_4^{-2} + t_1$
$t_1 > 0, \quad t_2 > 0, \quad t_3 > 0, \quad t_4 > 0$

(*g*) minimize $7t_1^{\pi}t_2^{-e} + 18t_2 + \tfrac{1}{2}t_1^{-1}$
$t_1 > 0, \quad t_2 > 0$

(*h*) minimize $t_1t_2^2t_3^3t_4^4t_5^5 + 5t_5^{-1} + 4t_4^{-1} + 3t_3^{-1} + 2t_2^{-1} + t_1^{-1}$
$t_1 > 0, \quad t_2 > 0, \quad t_3 > 0, \quad t_4 > 0,$
$t_5 > 0$

(*i*) minimize $4t_1^3 + 8t_1^{-1}t_2 + 3t_2^{-4} + 4t_1^{-1}t_2$

$t_1 > 0, \quad t_2 > 0$

(*j*) minimize $t_1^{-1}t_3 + t_1^{-1}t_2 + t_2^{-1}t_3^{-1} + 2t_1$

$t_1 > 0, \quad t_2 > 0, \quad t_3 > 0$

(*k*) minimize $5t_2t_3^2 + t_1^{-1}t_2^2t_3^{-2} + 33t_2^{-43/31}t_3^{1/31} + t_1^{19/26}t_3^{27/26}$

$t_1 > 0, \quad t_2 > 0, \quad t_3 > 0$

(*l*) minimize $17t_1t_2^{3/2} + 3t_1^{-1} + t_1^2t_2^{-2}$

$t_1 > 0, \quad t_2 > 0$

(*m*) minimize $5t_1^{-2}t_2^8 + 42t_2^{-1} + 2t_1^5t_2$

$t_1 > 0, \quad t_2 > 0$

(*n*) minimize $2t_3^{-1} + 3t_1^3t_2^2t_3 + 4t_2^{-1} + 5t_1^{-3}$

$t_1 > 0, \quad t_2 > 0, \quad t_3 > 0.$

13. [Duffin, p. 5] (*a*) Solve the following geometric programming problem:

$$\text{minimize} \quad 40t_1^{-1}t_2^{-1}t_3^{-1} + 40t_2t_3 + 20t_1t_3 + 10t_1t_2$$
$$t_1 > 0, \quad t_2 > 0, \quad t_3 > 0.$$

(*b*) Use part *a* to estimate the following:

$$\text{minimize} \quad 40t_1^{-1}t_2^{-1} + 40t_2 + 20t_1 + 10t_1t_2$$
$$t_1 > 0, \quad t_2 > 0.$$

(*c*) What are the degrees of difficulty of the programs in parts *a* and *b*?
(*d*) What is the relative contribution of each of the terms in part *a* to the minimum value?

14. In the queueing system model, suppose the average cost of waiting per vehicle per period, $c$, is reduced to the value $c/4$. How does this reduction in $c$ affect the total queueing system cost?
15. Formulate the queueing system model with an arbitrary, but constant, number of service facilities. Solve your cost minimization problem using geometric programming.
16. (*a*) Formulate the dual program of the following:

$$\text{minimize} \quad t_1^{-1}t_2 + \tfrac{1}{2}t_2 + \tfrac{1}{2}t_2^{-1} + t_1$$
$$t_1 > 0, \quad t_2 > 0.$$

(*b*) What is the degree of difficulty of the program in part *a*?
(*c*) Express the dual objective function as a function only of $\delta_4$.
(*d*) Indicate how you would determine the maximum of $v(\delta_4)$.

17. (*a*) Using geometric programming, determine the economic lot size of a good that will satisfy the known annual demand for the good and minimize the associated ordering and holding costs. Assume the following:
    (*i*) The annual demand is known to be $d$.
    (*ii*) The cost of ordering is a constant $b$ per order.
    (*iii*) The holding cost is a constant $h$ per unit per year.
    (*iv*) The stock is depleted at a constant rate, $a$.
    (*v*) The stock is replenished instantaneously when stock is zero; there are no shortages.
    (*b*) In your economic lot size model, what are the relative contributions of the ordering and holding cost to the minimum total cost?
    (*c*) Suppose the unit holding cost is reduced to $h/16$ per unit per year. How does this action affect the minimum inventory cost?
18. (*a*) What is the degree of difficulty of the following geometric programming problem:

$$\text{minimize} \quad 8t^{-2} + 2t + 3t^2$$
$$t > 0.$$

    (*b*) Formulate the dual of the program in part *a*.
    (*c*) Show that the dual program may be formulated as follows:

$$\text{maximize} \quad \left(\frac{8}{\delta_1}\right)^{\delta_1}\left(\frac{1}{1-2\delta_1}\right)^{(2-4\delta_1)}\left(\frac{1}{\delta_1-\frac{1}{3}}\right)^{(3\delta_1-1)}$$
$$\delta_1 \geq 0.$$

19. Show that the geometric programming problem

$$\text{minimize} \quad 2t_3^{-1} + 3t_1^3t_2^2t_3 + 4t_2^{-1} + 5t_1^{-3}$$
$$t_1 > 0, \qquad t_2 > 0, \qquad t_3 > 0,$$

may be transformed into an equivalent convex programming problem by the transformation

$$t_i = e^{x_i}, \qquad i = 1, 2, 3.$$

20. Determine the minimum value and minimizing point $\mathbf{t}^*$ of each of the following constrained geometric programming problems:

(*a*) minimize $\quad t_1^{-1/2}t_2^3$

subject to $\quad t_1 > 0, \qquad t_2 > 0$

$$\tfrac{1}{2}t_1 + \tfrac{1}{3}t_2^{-9} \leq 1$$

(b) minimize $40t_1t_2 + 20t_2t_3$

subject to $t_1 > 0, \quad t_2 > 0, \quad t_3 > 0$

$\frac{1}{5}t_1t_2^{-1/2} + \frac{3}{5}t_1^{-1}t_3^{-1/3} \le 1$

(c) minimize $5t_1t_2^{-1}t_3^2$

subject to $t_1 > 0, \quad t_2 > 0, \quad t_3 > 0$

$t_1^3t_2t_3^{-1} \le 1$

$t_1^{-2} + t_2^{-1/2} \le 1$

(d) minimize $t_1^{-1/2}t_2^{1/8} + t_1^{1/4}t_2^{-1/2}t_3^{1/2}$

subject to $t_1 > 0, \quad t_2 > 0, \quad t_3 > 0$

$\frac{4}{5}t_1^{1/2}t_2^{2/3}t_3^{-1} + \frac{2}{3}t_1^{1/3}t_2t_3^{-1} \le 1$

(e) minimize $t_1^3t_2^{-1/2}t_3^{1/3}$

subject to $t_1 > 0, \quad t_2 > 0, \quad t_3 > 0$

$9t_2^6t_3^{-1} \le 1$

$\frac{1}{4}t_3 \le 1$

$8t_1^{-1}t_2^{-3/4}t_3^{-2} \le 1$

(f) minimize $2t_1t_3^{-2} + 8t_1^{-1}t_2^4$

subject to $t_1 > 0, \quad t_2 > 0, \quad t_3 > 0$

$2t_2 + t_2^{-4}t_3 \le 1$

(g) minimize $t_1^{-2}t_4^8 + 2t_1t_3^3t_4^{-4}$

subject to $t_1 > 0, \quad t_2 > 0, \quad t_3 > 0, \quad t_4 > 0$

$\frac{1}{16}t_1^{-4}t_2^{-2}t_3^{16} + \frac{1}{8}t_1^5t_2t_3^{-8} + 3t_1^{-1}t_3^{-16/3} \le 1$

(h) minimize $t_1t_3$

subject to $t_1 > 0, \quad t_2 > 0, \quad t_3 > 0$

$3t_1^{-3}t_3^{-2} \le 1$

$4t_1^2t_2^{-2}t_3^3 \le 1$

$5t_1^{-1}t_2t_3^{-2} \le 1$

(i) minimize $t_1t_3^{\pi/(\pi-1)} + t_2^{-1}$

subject to $t_1 > 0, \quad t_2 > 0, \quad t_3 > 0$

$t_2t_3^{-\pi/(\pi-1)} \le 1$

$t_1^{-1/\pi} \le 1$

(*j*) minimize $7t_1t_2^{-1/2}$

subject to $t_1 > 0, \quad t_2 > 0, \quad t_3 > 0$

$$t_1^{-1/2}t_2^{1/2}t_3^{-1/4} \leq 1$$

$$8t_1^{-1/4}t_3^{1/2} + t_1^{-1/4}t_3^{-1/4} \leq 1$$

(*k*) minimize $t_1^{-1/3}t_2t_3^{-1}$

subject to $t_1 > 0, \quad t_2 > 0, \quad t_3 > 0, \quad t_4 > 0$

$$7t_1^{1/3}t_3t_4^{-1/2} + \tfrac{6}{5}t_1^{-2/3}t_4^{3/2} \leq 1$$

$$\tfrac{1}{9}t_1^{1/6}t_4^{-1/4} + \tfrac{2}{7}t_1^{1/2}t_2^{-1}t_4^{-3/4} \leq 1$$

(*l*) minimize $2t_1t_2^{-2/3}t_3^{-3}$

subject to $t_1 > 0, \quad t_2 > 0, \quad t_3 > 0$

$$\tfrac{1}{2}t_1^{-1}t_2 + \tfrac{1}{2}t_1^{-1}t_2^{-1/9}t_3 \leq 1$$

$$\tfrac{1}{2}t_1 \leq 1$$

(*m*) minimize $2t_1t_2^{-2/3}t_3^{-3}$

subject to $t_1 > 0, \quad t_2 > 0, \quad t_3 > 0$

$$\tfrac{1}{2}t_1^{-1}t_2 \leq 1$$

$$\tfrac{1}{2}t_1^{-1}t_2^{-1/9}t_3 \leq 1$$

$$\tfrac{1}{2}t_1 \leq 1$$

(*n*) minimize $\tfrac{1}{4}t_1^{-1}t_2^{-2}t_3 + \tfrac{3}{4}t_1^2t_2$

subject to $t_1 > 0, \quad t_2 > 0, \quad t_3 > 0$

$$\tfrac{1}{8}t_1^{-3}t_2^{-1}t_3^{-1} + \tfrac{1}{8}t_1^{-7}t_2^{-1}t_3^{-1} \leq 1.$$

21. Transform each of the following into equivalent convex programming problems and solve them using the Kuhn–Tucker theorem:

(*a*) minimize $9t_1t_2^{-2}t_3$

subject to $t_1 > 0, \quad t_2 > 0, \quad t_3 > 0$

$$\tfrac{1}{2}t_1^{-1}t_2 + \tfrac{1}{2}t_2^3 \leq 1$$

$$\tfrac{1}{2}t_1^{-1}t_3^{-2} \leq 1$$

(*b*) minimize $\tfrac{1}{2}t_1^{-3}t_3^{-1} + \tfrac{1}{2}t_2t_4^{-1/2}t_5$

subject to $t_1 > 0, \quad t_2 > 0, \quad t_3 > 0, \quad t_4 > 0,$

$t_5 > 0$

$$\tfrac{3}{2}t_1 + \tfrac{1}{4}t_2^{-2}t_4^2 \leq 1$$

$$t_4^{-1} \leq 1$$

$$\tfrac{1}{2}t_3t_5^{-1} \leq 1.$$

22. Solve problems 21*a* and 21*b* as geometric programming problems.
23. Consider the following problem:

$$\begin{aligned} &\text{minimize} && t_1 t_2^{-1} + t_1^{-1} \\ &\text{subject to} && t_1 > 0, \qquad t_2 > 0 \\ &&& t_1 t_2 + t_1 \le 1. \end{aligned}$$

(*a*) What is the degree of difficulty of this program?
(*b*) Is it superconsistent? Why or why not?
(*c*) Formulate the dual program.
(*d*) Show that the dual variables $\delta_1$, $\delta_2$, and $\delta_3$ may be expressed as functions of $\delta_4$.
(*e*) Show that this dual program may be reduced to an optimization problem in one variable, $\delta_4$.
(*f*) Indicate how you would solve the program in part *e*.

24. Consider the queueing system problem. Suppose that besides determining an optimal value for $t$, the number of service facilities is also a variable, $N$, to be determined. Suppose, also, that the labor unions require that there be at least two service facilities. Determine values for $t$ and $N$ that minimize the total queueing cost and satisfy the labor union constraint.
25. Solve the following problem:

$$\begin{aligned} &\text{maximize} && t_1 t_2 t_3 \\ &\text{subject to} && t_1 > 0, \qquad t_2 > 0, \qquad t_3 > 0 \\ &&& t_1^2 + t_2 + t_3^3 \le 1. \end{aligned}$$

26. Let $g(\mathbf{t})$ be a posynomial with a minimum value strictly greater than zero. Prove that the normality and orthogonality conditions can be satisfied.
27. Consider the following problem:

$$\begin{aligned} &\text{minimize} && At_1 + Bt_1^{-2} t_2^{-2} \\ &\text{subject to} && t_1 > 0, \qquad t_2 > 0 \\ &&& Ct_2^4 \le 1 \end{aligned}$$

where $A$, $B$, $C$ are *positive* constants.

(*a*) Formulate the dual geometric programming problem.
(*b*) Solve the above minimization problem.
(*c*) Suppose that $A$ is replaced by $\frac{1}{8}A$. How does this affect the minimum value?
(*d*) Suppose that $C$ is replaced by $\frac{1}{2}C$. Does this alteration affect the minimum value?

(*e*) What are the relative contributions of the first and second terms of the objective function to the minimum value of the objective function? Do these values depend on $A$ and $B$?

28. [Duffin, p. 14] Use geometric programming techniques to find two positive numbers $t_1$, $t_2$ whose *sum* is *not more than* 20 and whose product is as large as possible.

29. Consider the dual geometric programming problem corresponding to the following problem:

$$\begin{array}{ll} \text{minimize} & 2t_1 + 3t_2 + 4t_3 \\ \text{subject to} & t_1 > 0, \quad t_2 > 0, \quad t_3 > 0 \\ & 6t_1^{-1}t_2^{-2}t_3^{-3} \le 1 \\ & 7t_1^2 + 8t_2^2 \le 1. \end{array}$$

Show that the dual constraints form a convex set.

30. Determine the minimum value of the following problems:

(*a*) $$\begin{array}{ll} \text{minimize} & \tfrac{1}{3}t_1 + \tfrac{1}{5}t_1^{-2}t_2^{-2} + t_2^4 + 9 \\ & t_1 > 0, \quad t_2 > 0 \end{array}$$

(*b*) $$\begin{array}{ll} \text{minimize} & t_1 + \tfrac{2}{3}t_1^{-2}t_2^{-2} - 7 \\ \text{subject to} & t_1 > 0, \quad t_2 > 0 \\ & \tfrac{1}{9}t_2^4 \le \tfrac{2}{27}. \end{array}$$

31. Construct a problem of minimizing a posynomial subject to posynomial constraints that is *not* superconsistent.

32. The management science group of a Japanese industrial firm, Itsa Steel Company, has decided to design a waste water treatment plant at their Jeannette, Japan, facility. The plant design incorporates 16 water treatment processes in series. Each of the 16 processes removes a certain fraction of the sulfur present in the waste water. Their objective is to determine what percentage each of the 16 processes should eliminate if the final quality of the water is to meet certain standards and the operation is to take place at minimum cost. Construct and solve a geometric program that describes this constrained cost minimization problem.

33. [Zahradnik, p. 88] As director of research for the XYZ Company, it is your task to allocate this year's research budget of $50,000 between two existing projects. The total budget, however, need not be completely allocated. Since each project is partially dependent upon the information gained in the other project, it is essential that both projects be supported. The predicted return from these two projects is

$$t_1^3t_2^2,$$

where $t_i$ is the amount of money allocated to project $i$. For reasons of morale, it is important that project 1 receive no more than three times the amount allocated to project 2.

(*a*) Construct a geometric program that will aid in determining the maximum return.

(*b*) What is the degree of difficulty of your geometric programming problem?

34. [Duffin, p. 124] Devise a method to test the consistency of the posynomial constraints

$$\begin{aligned} g_1(\mathbf{t}) &\le 1 \\ g_2(\mathbf{t}) &\le 1 \\ \vdots\quad & \quad\vdots \\ g_p(\mathbf{t}) &\le 1. \end{aligned}$$

35. Show that the following problem

$$\begin{array}{ll} \text{minimize} & t_1^{-1}t_2 \\ \text{subject to} & t_1 > 0, \qquad t_2 > 0 \\ & t_1 + t_2 \le 1 \\ & \quad t_2^{-1} \le 1. \end{array}$$

is inconsistent.

36. Find the dimensions of the open-top box that will have the greatest volume when the surface area is at most 3.

37. Develop a computer program that does the following:

(*a*) Calculates the minimum value of constrained or unconstrained geometric programming problems of degree of difficulty zero

(*b*) Calculates the optimal values of the primal variables.

38. Use problem 20*m* to estimate the minimum value of the following geometric programming problem:

$$\begin{array}{ll} \text{minimize} & 2t_1t_2^{-2/3} \\ \text{subject to} & t_1 > 0, \qquad t_2 > 0 \\ & \tfrac{1}{2}t_1^{-1}t_2 \le 1 \\ & \tfrac{1}{2}t_1^{-1}t_2^{-1/9} \le 1 \\ & \tfrac{1}{2}t_1 \le 1. \end{array}$$

39. A furniture company's records reveal that the cost of furniture handled

in each of its warehouse districts depends primarily on

1. the volume of business passing through the warehouse, and
2. the area served by the warehouse.

Cost data has indicated the following:

1. The cost per dollar's worth of furniture distributed decreases as the volume of business increases. This follows, since labor has less idle time and the unit costs of overhead and supervision are lower.

2. The cost per dollar's worth of furniture distributed increases as the area served by the warehouse increases.

Given this information the company's management science group wishes to predict the cost of distributing goods as the volume handled in, and the area served by, each warehouse changes.

(*a*) Construct a cost function for this management system. Assume the following:

(*i*) Only the two factors considered above affect the cost.

(*ii*) The area is measured in square miles.

(*iii*) The volume of business is directly proportional to the area served.

(*iv*) The cost associated with the area served by the warehouse varies proportionally with the square root of the area.

(*v*) The cost associated with the sales volume varies in inverse proportion to the volume of business.

(*b*) Use geometric programming to determine the minimum cost of this management system and the optimal area to be served by the warehouse.

(*c*) Determine the relative contribution of each cost to the minimum cost.

40. Suppose that the total costs of ordering and holding a product of lot size $x$ are given by

$$c_1 x^{-1} \quad \text{and} \quad c_2 x^a,$$

respectively, where $c_1 > 0$, $c_2 > 0$, $a > 0$. The total inventory system cost is their sum,

$$c_1 x^{-1} + c_2 x^a.$$

(*a*) Show that if $a > 1$, the relative contribution of the ordering cost to the minimum cost exceeds the relative contribution of the holding cost to the minimum cost.

(*b*) Discuss the effect of variations in the value of $a$ on the minimum cost of this inventory system.

41. Consider an industrial process in which one product is manufactured utilizing two inputs, labor and capital. Suppose $q$ denotes the amount

of output that the firm can produce if it uses $x_1$ units of labor and $x_2$ units of capital. The relationship between the input levels, $x_1$ and $x_2$, and the output level, $q$, is expressed by the Cobbs–Douglas production function:

$$q = Ax_1^a x_2^{1-a},$$

$A > 0, 0 < a < 1$. Further, suppose the industrial production process is subject to a budgetary constraint. With labor and capital of unit costs, $b_1$ and $b_2$, respectively, assume that at most $M$ dollars may be spent on inputs.

(*a*) Formulate the problem of determining input levels that maximize output, while satisfying the budgetary constraint.

(*b*) Use geometric programming to determine the optimal input levels. *Hint*. minimize $q^{-1}$.

(*c*) Discuss the effect of the variations of $a$, $A$, $M$, $b_1$, and $b_2$ on the maximum output level.

(*d*) Discuss the effect of variations in $a$ on the optimal values of the dual variables.

42. Suppose the cost of a particular management system is given by

$$g(\mathbf{t}) = bt_1^{-b} + t_2 + bt_1^b t_2^{-1/b},$$

where $t_1 > 0$, $t_2 > 0$, and $b$ is a positive constant. Show that $M$, the minimum value of $g(\mathbf{t})$, increases as the value of $b$ increases. *Hint*. Show $dM/db > 0$.

43. Suppose a particular product is produced and held in inventory by the same company. During the production run, units of the product are continuously added to the inventory and, simultaneously, the inventory is being depleted. The rate of the production, $p$, exceeds the rate of inventory depletion, $r$. At the conclusion of the production run, the inventory continues to be depleted at the same rate $r$. When the inventory is completely depleted, a new production run is started. There are no shortages. This situation is illustrated below, where $t$ is

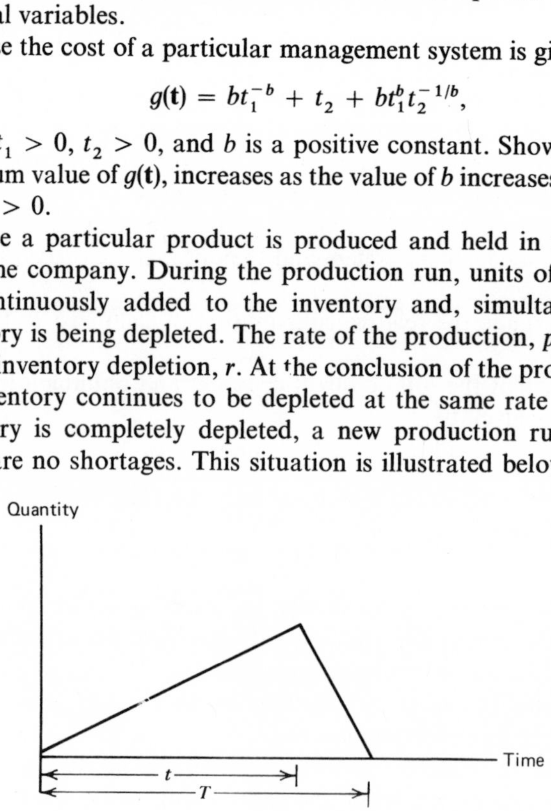

the time period of the production run and $T$ is the time between starts of production runs.

During the course of a year, $D$ units of the product must be produced to meet the annual demand. The costs of this system are the holding and production costs. Assuming the costs of each production run and of holding are constants per unit per year, use geometric programming to determine the minimum cost of this system.

44. (*a*) Consider the inventory control situation described in problem 17. Use geometric programming techniques to determine the economic lot sizes of $n$ goods, rather than one good, that minimize the total associated ordering and holding costs. Assume the following:

   (*i*) The annual demand of the $i$th good is $d_i$, $i = 1, \ldots, n$.

   (*ii*) The cost of placing one order is a constant $c$ per order, regardless of the product.

   (*iii*) The holding cost of the $i$th good is a constant $h_i$ per unit per year, $i = 1, \ldots, n$.

   (*iv*) The stock of the $i$th good is depleted at a constant rate $a_i$, $i = 1, \ldots, n$.

   (*v*) The stock of the $i$th good is replenished instantaneously when it is 0. There are no shortages.

   *Hint*. First determine conditions under which the total ordering cost is minimized.

   (*b*) What are the relative contributions of the total ordering and total holding costs to the minimum total cost?

45. Consider the following geometric programming problem:

$$\begin{aligned} \text{minimize} \quad & g_0(\mathbf{t}) = u_1 + u_2 \\ \text{subject to} \quad & t_1 > 0, \quad t_2 > 0, \quad t_3 > 0 \\ & g_1(\mathbf{t}) = u_3 + u_4 \leq G, \end{aligned}$$

where $u_i = c_i t_1^{a_{i1}} t_2^{a_{i2}} t_3^{a_{i3}}$, $c_i > 0$, $i = 1, 2, 3, 4$, and $G$ is a positive constant.

(*a*) Develop the dual geometric programming problem.

(*b*) Show that the minimum value of this problem is

$$g_0(\mathbf{t}^*) = \left(\frac{a_1}{\delta_1^*}\right)^{\delta_1^*} \cdots \left(\frac{a_4}{\delta_4^*}\right)^{\delta_4^*} \left(\frac{\lambda_1^*}{G}\right)^{\lambda_1^*},$$

where $\delta_1^*, \ldots, \delta_4^*$ is the optimal solution of the dual problem and $\lambda_1^* = \delta_3^* + \delta_4^*$.

(*c*) Show that

$$\lambda_1^* = -\left(\frac{\partial \ln g_0(\mathbf{t}^*)}{\partial \ln G}\right).$$

That is, $\lambda_1^*$ is the sensitivity coefficient of $g_0(\mathbf{t}^*)$ with respect to $G$.

(*d*) Suppose our geometric programming problem has only two variables, $t_1$ and $t_2$. Does $\lambda_1^*$ have a similar interpretation in this case?

(*e*) In the personnel selection problem, determine the sensitivity coefficient of $g_0(\mathbf{t}^*)$ with respect to $c_4$.

46. Consider the geometric programming problem

$$\begin{aligned} \text{minimize} \quad & g_0(\mathbf{t}) = \tfrac{1}{2}t_1 t_2^{-2} + \tfrac{9}{2}t_3^{-1} \\ \text{subject to} \quad & t_1 > 0, \quad t_2 > 0, \quad t_3 > 0 \\ & g_1(\mathbf{t}) = 3t_1^{-1}t_3 + t_2 \le G \end{aligned}$$

where $G$ is a positive constant. Show that the graph of the minimum of this problem as a function of $G$ appears as shown below.

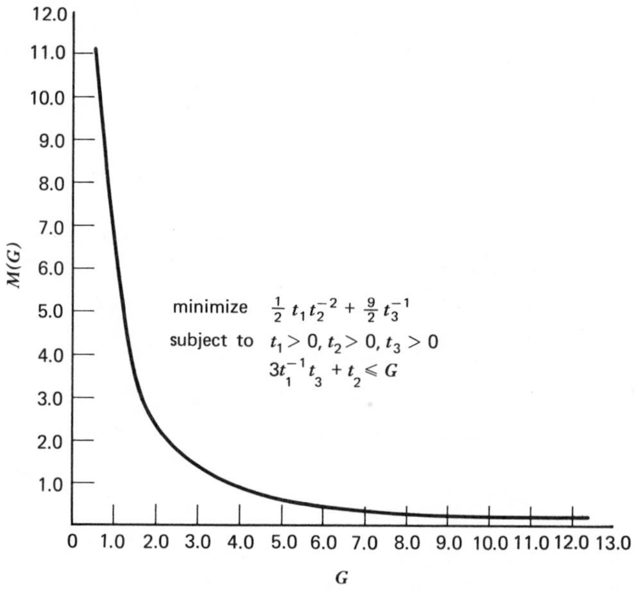


47. Consider the following unconstrained geometric programming problem:

$$\begin{aligned} \text{minimize} \quad & g_0(\mathbf{t}) = t_1^c + t_2 + t_1^{-2}t_2^{-c} \\ & t_1 > 0, \quad t_2 > 0, \end{aligned}$$

where $c$ is a positive parameter. Show that the graph of the minimum of $g_0(\mathbf{t})$ as a function of $c$ appears as illustrated on page 303.

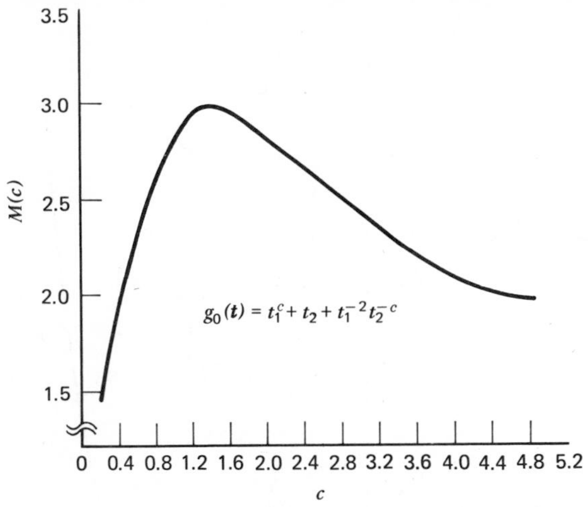


48. Consider the following geometric programming problem:

$$\text{(P)} \qquad \begin{array}{ll} \text{minimize} & g_0(\mathbf{t}) = t_1 + t_2^{-1} \\ \text{subject to} & t_1 > 0, \qquad t_2 > 0 \\ & g_1(\mathbf{t}) = t_1^{-1} + t_2 \le 1. \end{array}$$

(*a*) Show that the constrained values of $g_0(\mathbf{t})$ in (P) lie on or above the curve

$$f(t_2) = \frac{1}{1 - t_2} + \frac{1}{t_2}.$$

(*b*) Determine the minimum value and minimizing point of (P) from a sketch of $f(t_2)$.

(*c*) Show that the dual problem is equivalent to the problem

$$\text{(D}'\text{)} \qquad \text{maximize} \qquad v(\delta_1) = \left(\frac{1}{\delta_1}\right)^{2\delta_1}\left(\frac{1}{1 - \delta_1}\right)^{2(1-\delta_1)}$$

$$\delta_1 \ge 0.$$

(*d*) Sketch $v(\delta_1)$ and determine the maximum value of $v(\delta_1)$. Note that the minimum of (P) equals the maximum of (D′) as illustrated on page 304.

49. Consider the following geometric programming problem:

$$\text{(P)} \qquad \begin{array}{ll} \text{minimize} & g_0(\mathbf{t}) = 6t_1^{-1} + t_2^{-2} \\ \text{subject to} & t_1 > 0, \qquad t_2 > 0 \\ & g_1(\mathbf{t}) = t_1 + t_2 \le 1. \end{array}$$

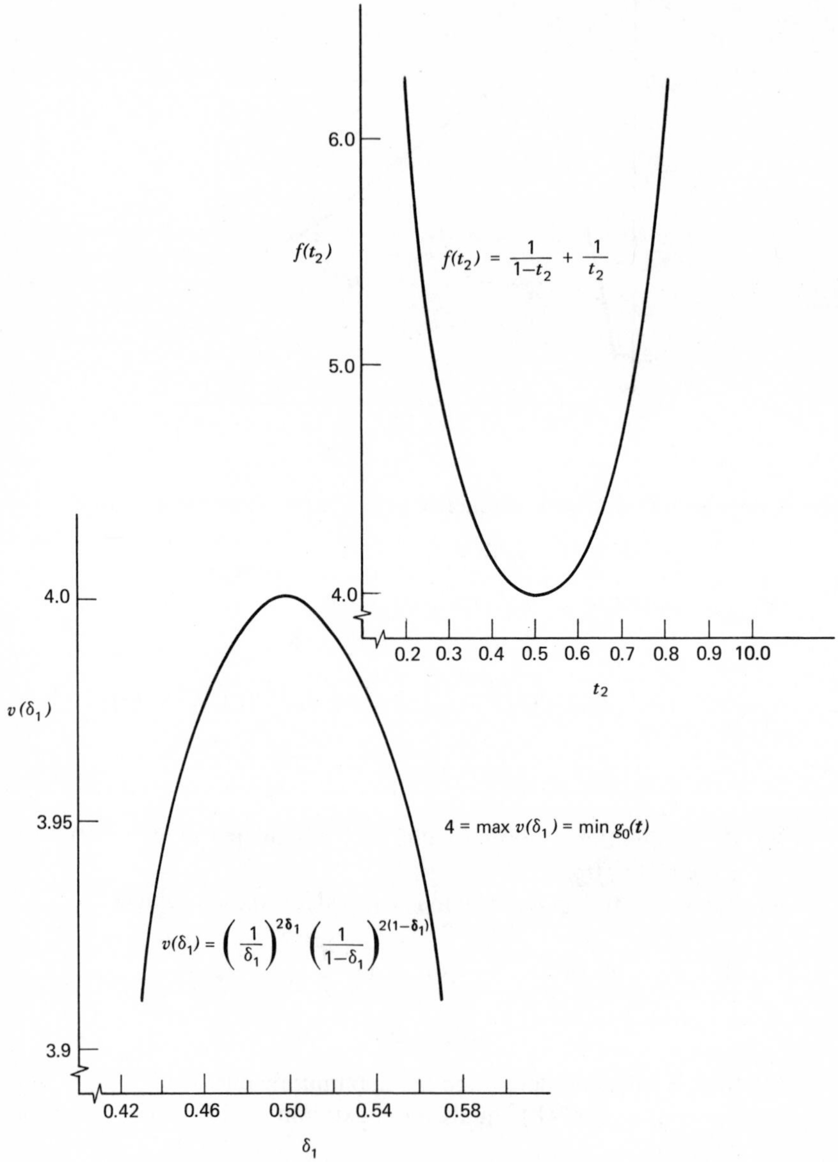

6.0
5.0
4.0
$f(t_2)$
$f(t_2) = \frac{1}{1-t_2} + \frac{1}{t_2}$
0.2 0.3 0.4 0.5 0.6 0.7 0.8 0.9 10.0
$t_2$
4.0
3.95
3.9
$v(\delta_1)$
$4 = \max v(\delta_1) = \min g_0(t)$
$v(\delta_1) = \left(\frac{1}{\delta_1}\right)^{2\delta_1} \left(\frac{1}{1-\delta_1}\right)^{2(1-\delta_1)}$
0.42 0.46 0.50 0.54 0.58
$\delta_1$

(*a*) Show that the constrained values of $g_0(\mathbf{t})$ in (P) lie on or above the curve

$$f(t_2) = \frac{1}{t_2^2} + \frac{6}{1 - t_2}.$$

(*b*) Determine the minimum value and minimizing point of (P) from a sketch of $f(t_2)$.

(*c*) Show that the dual problem is equivalent to the problem

$$\text{(D}'\text{)} \quad \text{maximize} \quad v(\delta_1) = \frac{2^{3\delta_1}3^{\delta_1}}{4}\left(\frac{1}{\delta_1}\right)^{2\delta_1}\left(\frac{1}{1-\delta_1}\right)^{3-3\delta_1}(2-\delta_1)^{(2-\delta_1)}$$

$$\delta_1 \geq 0$$

(*d*) Sketch $v(\delta_1)$ and determine the maximum value of $v(\delta_1)$. Note that the minimum of (P) equals the maximum of (D′) as illustrated on page 306.

50. Consider the following geometric programming problem:

$$\begin{aligned} &\text{minimize} && 10t_1^{-1/2}t_2^{-1}t_3^2t_4^{-1} \\ &\text{subject to} && t_1 > 0, \quad t_2 > 0, \quad t_3 > 0, \quad t_4 > 0 \\ &&& 4t_1t_3^{-3}t_4 + 3t_1^{-1/2}t_2^2t_3^{-8} \leq G_1 \\ &&& 2t_1^3t_2t_3^3t_4^6 + t_2t_3 \leq G_2 \end{aligned}$$

(*a*) Discuss the sensitivity of $M$, the minimum value of this problem, to variations in $G_1$ and $G_2$.

(*b*) Show that for $G_2 = 1, 2, 3, 4, 5$ the graphs of $M$ as a function of $G_1$ appear as shown on page 307.

51. (*a*) Suppose that an optimization problem associated with the preliminary design of a management system has been formulated as the geometric programming problem:

$$\begin{aligned} G_0 = &\text{ minimize} && g_0(\mathbf{t}) \\ &\text{subject to} && t_1 > 0, \ldots, t_m > 0 \\ &&& g_1(\mathbf{t}) \leq G_1 \\ &&& \vdots \qquad \vdots \\ &&& g_p(\mathbf{t}) \leq G_p \end{aligned}$$

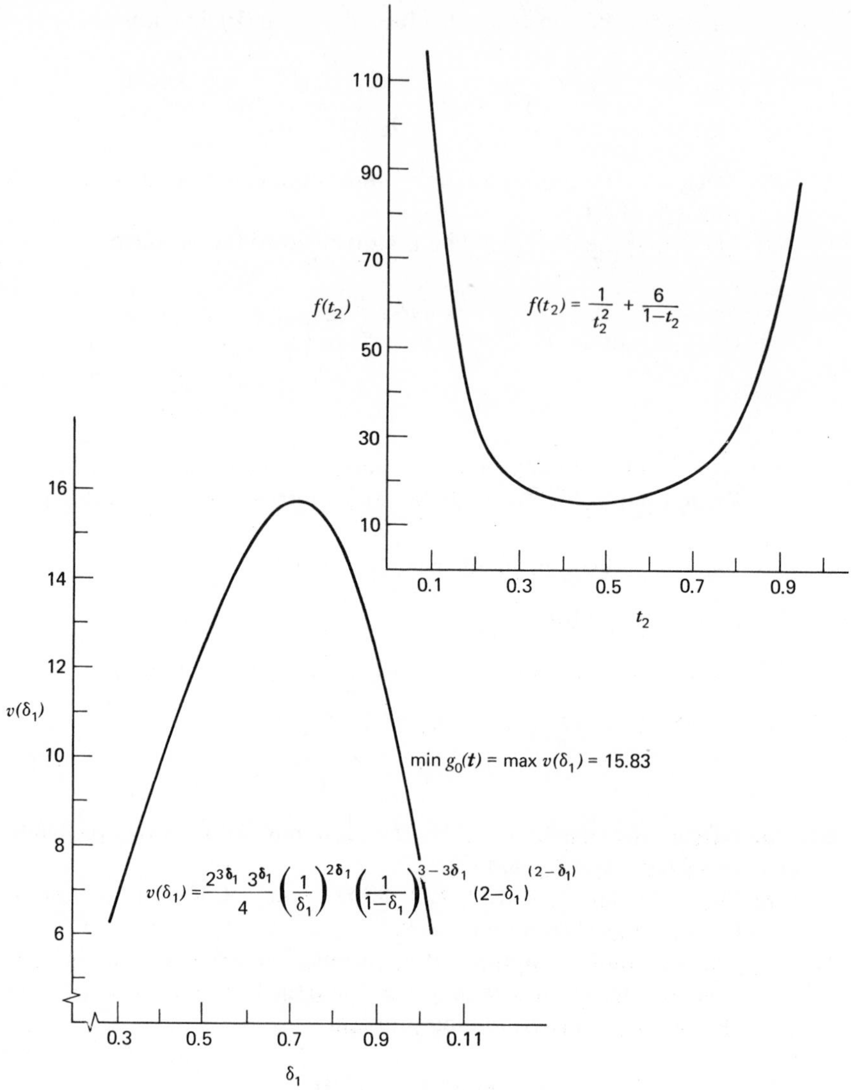


where $g_0(\mathbf{t}), \ldots, g_p(\mathbf{t})$ are posynomials and $G_1, \ldots, G_p$ are positive parameters. Construct a policy function (Exercise 19, Chapter 7),

$$P(G_0, G_1, \ldots, G_p) = 1$$

for this problem.

*Hint*. First construct the dual objective function with $\boldsymbol{\delta} = \boldsymbol{\delta}^*$.

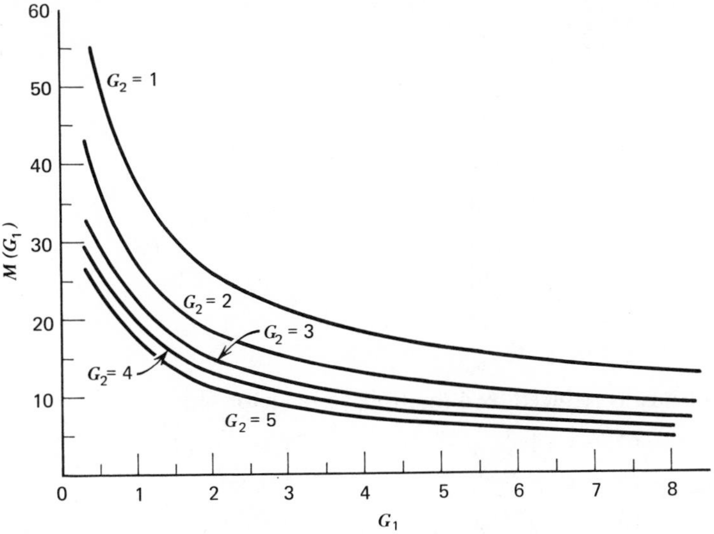


(b) Construct a policy function for the problem:

$$\begin{array}{ll} \text{minimize} & t_1 t_2 t_3 \\ \text{subject to} & t_1 > 0, \quad t_2 > 0, \quad t_3 > 0 \\ & t_1^{-1} + t_2^{-2} + t_3^{-3} \le G_1. \end{array}$$

Graphically analyze the sensitivity of $G_0$ to variations in $G_1$.

## SOLUTIONS

12. (a) $\delta^* = (\frac{1}{4}, \frac{3}{4})$

(b) $\delta^* = (\frac{3}{5}, \frac{2}{5})$

(c) $\delta^* = (\frac{1}{4}, \frac{1}{4}, \frac{1}{4}, \frac{1}{4})$

(d) $\delta^* = (\frac{1}{4}, \frac{1}{4}, \frac{1}{2})$

(e) $\delta^* = (\frac{1}{5}, \frac{1}{5}, \frac{2}{5}, \frac{1}{5})$

(f) $\delta^* = (\frac{1}{7}, \frac{1}{7}, \frac{3}{7}, \frac{1}{7}, \frac{1}{7})$

(g) $$\delta^* = \left(\frac{1}{1 + e + \pi}, \frac{e}{1 + e + \pi}, \frac{\pi}{1 + e + \pi}\right)$$

(h) $\delta^* = (\frac{1}{16}, \frac{5}{16}, \frac{4}{16}, \frac{3}{16}, \frac{2}{16}, \frac{1}{16})$

(i) $\delta^* = (\frac{4}{19}, \frac{12}{19}, \frac{3}{19})$

(j) $\delta^* = (\frac{1}{5}, \frac{1}{5}, \frac{1}{5}, \frac{2}{5})$

(*k*) $\delta^* = (\frac{5}{81}, \frac{19}{81}, \frac{31}{81}, \frac{26}{81})$

(*l*) $\delta^* = (\frac{4}{17}, \frac{10}{17}, \frac{3}{17})$

(*m*) $\delta^* = (\frac{5}{49}, \frac{42}{49}, \frac{2}{49})$

(*n*) $\delta^* = (\frac{1}{5}, \frac{1}{5}, \frac{2}{5}, \frac{1}{5})$

13. (*a*) $\delta^* = (\frac{2}{5}, \frac{1}{5}, \frac{1}{5}, \frac{1}{5})$

(*b*) $\delta^* = (\frac{2}{5}, \frac{1}{5}, \frac{1}{5}, \frac{1}{5})$, $\mathbf{t}' = (1, 1)$

$110 \geq M \geq 100$

(*c*) 0, 1

(*d*) $(\frac{2}{5}, \frac{1}{5}, \frac{1}{5}, \frac{1}{5})$

14. The cost is reduced by a multiplicative factor of $\frac{1}{2}$.

20. (*a*) $\delta^* = (1, \frac{1}{2}, \frac{1}{3})$

(*b*) $\delta^* = (\frac{1}{2}, \frac{1}{2}, 2, \frac{3}{2})$

(*c*) $\delta^* = (1, 2, \frac{7}{2}, 2)$

(*d*) $\delta^* = (\frac{20}{41}, \frac{21}{41}, \frac{15}{82}, \frac{3}{41})$

(*e*) $\delta^* = (1, \frac{1}{3}, 4, 2)$

(*f*) $\delta^* = (\frac{1}{2}, \frac{1}{2}, 2, 1)$

(*g*) $\delta^* = (\frac{1}{3}, \frac{2}{3}, \frac{1}{16}, \frac{1}{8}, \frac{3}{8})$

(*h*) $\delta^* = (1, \frac{1}{3}, \frac{1}{3}, \frac{2}{3})$

(*i*) $$\delta^* = \left(\frac{1}{\pi}, \frac{\pi - 1}{\pi}, \frac{\pi - 1}{\pi}, 1\right)$$

(*j*) $\delta^* = (1, 1, 1, 1)$

(*k*) $\delta^* = (1, 1, 1, 1, 1)$

(*l*) $\delta^* = (1, 1, 3, 3)$

(*m*) $\delta^* = (1, 1, 3, 3)$

(*n*) $\delta^* = (\frac{1}{4}, \frac{3}{4}, \frac{1}{8}, \frac{1}{8})$

22. (*a*) $\delta^* = (1, \frac{1}{2}, \frac{1}{2}, \frac{1}{2})$

(*b*) $\delta^* = (\frac{1}{2}, \frac{1}{2}, \frac{3}{2}, \frac{1}{4}, \frac{1}{4}, \frac{1}{2})$

26. $\mathbf{t}^* = (\sqrt{\frac{3}{11}}, \frac{6}{11}, \sqrt[3]{\frac{2}{11}})$

29. $\mathbf{t}^* = (10, 10)$

37. $\mathbf{t}^* = (1, 1, \frac{1}{2})$

39. $\delta' = (1, 1, 3, 3)$, $\mathbf{t}' = (1, 1, 1)$
$2 \geq M \geq \frac{1}{64}$

CHAPTER 9

# EXTENSIONS OF GEOMETRIC PROGRAMMING

## A MARKETING MIX PROBLEM: TRANSFORMING OPTIMIZATION PROBLEMS INTO GEOMETRIC PROGRAMMING PROBLEMS

The survival and growth of many industries is determined not only by their relative production and financial capabilities but also by their marketing decisions. Firms must provide customers with new products exhibiting a marginal utility greater than that of rival products. However, the development of new products is costly and risky; money may be spent finding new product ideas that are technically infeasible or commercially unsuccessful.

Therefore, management must decide which marketing variables most influence a customer's perceived utility and determine the *optimal mix* of these variables. For example, if price, quality, and advertising influence customers most, should a firm allocate its marketing dollars to lowering prices, increasing advertising, or increasing quality? Once management has decided on a *marketing mix*—that is, a combination of these marketing decision variables—estimates of the probable sales volume stimulated by this marketing mix, as well as the sales volume required to break even, are developed. The optimal marketing mix maximizes the difference between the stimulated sales and the break-even sales.

Here a mathematical model that relates the marketing decision variables of a particular company is constructed. The problem of maximizing the associated profits is transformed into a geometric program and the technique of geometric programming is used to determine the optimal marketing mix.

Suppose that the Mihallo Soap company is considering new grooming products for possible addition to the product line. Among these is a new hair conditioner. The company's marketing research group has found substantial and increasing interest in this type of product in the market.

The market research department has determined the sales response for this conditioner depends on its unit price, $P$; the advertising budget, $A$; and the salaries and commissions of salesmen, $S$. That is, the demand for this product, $Q$, may be represented by the functional relationship

$$Q = f(P, A, S).$$

Previous research indicated that the multiple exponential form of $f$ seems to be a plausible approximation in describing the marketing mix,

$$Q = kP^a A^b S^c,$$

where $k$ is a scale factor, $a$ is the price elasticity, $b$ is the advertising elasticity, and $c$ is the personal selling elasticity. In this example assume the demand is given by

$$Q = 10^8 \, P^{-3} A^{1/4} S^{1/6}.$$

This means that under constant conditions a 1% increase in advertising, $A$, (personal sales, $S$) increases unit demand by $\frac{1}{4}$ ($\frac{1}{6}$) of 1%. Similarly, a 1% reduction in price increases sales by 3%.

While determining the potential profitability of this new hair conditioner, thc production department has estimated the required investments for this new product. This group has estimated that $4,000 must be invested in new equipment and facilities and that this investment has an expected life of four years. Moreover, each year the additional overhead costs to cover rent, taxes, and executive salaries is approximately $2,100. These costs contribute to the *fixed* cost of the marketing system. Finally, the production department estimates that the new product would involve a direct labor and material cost of $10/bottle of hair conditioner. This $10/bottle is known as the unit variable cost.

This data may be used in computing how many bottles of hair conditioner must be sold to cover costs; that is, this data is used to determine the break-even sales volume. When the break-even sales volume, $Q_B$, is achieved, the total revenue equals the total cost. The total revenue is the product of the price, $P$, and the break-even sales volume, $Q_B$. The total cost is the fixed cost, $F$, plus the product of the unit variable cost, $V$, and the break even volume, $Q_B$; that is,

$$PQ_B = F + VQ_B$$

when the break-even sales volume is reached. Thus, from the latter expression we see the break-even sales volume is

$$Q_B = \frac{F}{P - V}.$$

We may express the break-even volume in terms of the marketing decision variables, $P$, $A$, and $S$. Since the unit variable cost $V$ is 10 and the fixed cost is the sum of the annual equipment depreciation, \$4,000/4; overhead, \$2,100; advertising, $A$; and personal selling, $S$, the break-even sales volume is

$$Q_B = \frac{1000 + 2100 + A + S}{P - 10}.$$

When expressions for the expected sales, $Q$, and the break-even sales volume, $Q_B$, have been determined, the profit level may be calculated for each marketing mix, $P$, $A$, $S$. One measure of the absolute profit expected from different marketing mixes is the product of the sales volume beyond the break even point, $Q - Q_B$, and the unit value, $P - V = P -$ \$10. That is, the absolute profit is

$$\begin{aligned} g(P, A, S) &= (P - 10)(Q - Q_B) \\ &= 10^8 P^{-2}A^{1/4}S^{1/6} - 10^9 P^{-3}A^{1/4}S^{1/6} - A - S - 3100. \end{aligned}$$

The problem of maximizing the profit function $g(P, A, S)$ is not a geometric programming problem. Indeed, $g(P, A, S)$ is not even a posynomial. But by introducing a new variable, we may transform the following profit maximization problem

$$\text{(365)} \qquad \text{maximize} \quad g(P, A, S) \qquad P > 0, \quad A > 0, \quad S > 0$$

into an equivalent geometric programming problem. (Observe that problem (365) is somewhat too complicated to solve using the techniques of calculus.) First note that $P^*$, $A^*$, and $S^*$ maximize $g(P, A, S)$ if and only if these values solve the following problem

$$\text{(366)} \quad \text{maximize} \quad 10^8 P^{-2}A^{1/4}S^{1/6} - 10^9 P^{-3}A^{1/4}S^{1/6} - A - S.$$

We shall work with problem (366). The geometric programming problem equivalent to (366) is formed by introducing a new positive variable $t_0$ satisfying,

$$\text{(367)} \qquad 10^8 P^{-2}A^{1/4}S^{1/6} - 10^9 P^{-3}A^{1/4}S^{1/6} - A - S \geq t_0.$$

If the variable $t_0$ is maximized subject to constraint (367), then according to inequality (367), the unconstrained profit function in (365) also will be maximized. That is, problem (366) is equivalent to the following:

$$\text{(368)}\quad \begin{array}{ll} \text{maximize} & t_0 \\ \text{subject to} & t_0 > 0, \quad P > 0, \quad A > 0, \quad S > 0 \\ & 10^8\, P^{-2}A^{1/4}S^{1/6} - 10^9\, P^{-3}A^{1/4}S^{1/6} - A - S \geq t_0. \end{array}$$

Note that maximum $t_0 - 3100 =$ maximum $g(P, A, S)$.

Since $t_0$ is maximized if and only if $t_0^{-1}$ is minimized, the constrained maximization problem (368) is equivalent to the following constrained minimization problem:

$$\text{(369)}\quad \begin{array}{ll} \text{minimize} & t_0^{-1} \\ \text{subject to} & t_0 > 0, \quad P > 0, \quad A > 0, \quad S > 0 \\ & 10^8\, P^{-2}A^{1/4}S^{1/6} - 10^9\, P^{-3}A^{1/4}S^{1/6} - A - S \geq t_0. \end{array}$$

Problem (369) may be formulated as a geometric program by observing that the constraint may be transformed into a prototype geometric programming constraint. By dividing the constraint inequality by $10^8\, P^{-2}A^{1/4}S^{1/6}$, the constraint becomes

$$1 - 10P^{-1} - 10^{-8}P^2A^{3/4}S^{-1/6} - 10^{-8}P^2A^{-1/4}S^{5/6} \geq 10^{-8}t_0P^2A^{-1/4}S^{-1/6},$$

or, equivalently,

$$1 \geq 10^{-8}t_0P^2A^{-1/4}S^{-1/6} + 10P^{-1} + 10^{-8}P^2A^{3/4}S^{-1/6} + 10^{-8}P^2A^{-1/4}S^{5/6}.$$

Thus, (366) is equivalent to the following constrained geometric programming problem of degree of difficulty 0:

$$\begin{array}{ll} \text{minimize} & t_0^{-1} \\ \text{subject to} & t_0 > 0, \quad P > 0, \quad A > 0, \quad S > 0 \\ & 10^{-8}t_0P^2A^{-1/4}S^{-1/6} + 10P^{-1} + 10^{-8}P^2A^{3/4}S^{-1/6} \\ & \qquad + 10^{-8}P^2A^{-1/4}S^{5/6} \leq 1. \end{array}$$

The dual geometric programming problem,

$$\begin{array}{ll} \text{maximize} & v(\boldsymbol{\delta}) = \left(\frac{1}{\delta_1}\right)^{\delta_1}\left(\frac{b}{\delta_2}\right)^{\delta_2}\left(\frac{10}{\delta_3}\right)^{\delta_3}\left(\frac{b}{\delta_4}\right)^{\delta_4}\left(\frac{b}{\delta_5}\right)^{\delta_5}(\delta_2 + \cdots + \delta_5)^{\delta_2+\cdots+\delta_5} \\ \text{subject to} & \delta_1 \geq 0, \ldots, \delta_5 \geq 0 \qquad (b = 10^{-8}) \\ & \delta_1 = 1 \\ & -\delta_1 + \delta_2 = 0 \\ & 2\delta_2 - \delta_3 + 2\delta_4 + 2\delta_5 = 0 \\ & -\tfrac{1}{4}\delta_2 + \tfrac{3}{4}\delta_4 - \tfrac{1}{4}\delta_5 = 0 \\ & -\tfrac{1}{6}\delta_2 - \tfrac{1}{6}\delta_4 + \tfrac{5}{6}\delta_5 = 0, \end{array}$$

has the unique solution $\delta_1^* = 1$, $\delta_2^* = 1$, $\delta_3^* = \frac{24}{7}$, $\delta_4^* = \frac{3}{7}$, $\delta_5^* = \frac{2}{7}$. The constrained minimum of $t_0^{-1}$ is $v(\boldsymbol{\delta}^*) = 0.70857 \times 10^{-8}$. The maximum profit is therefore $[1/v(\boldsymbol{\delta}^*)] - 3100 = 1411.255 \times 10^5$. Using condition 3 of the duality theorem of constrained geometric programming, we determine that the optimal marketing mix is

$$P^* = 15.0,$$
$$A^* = 604.837 \times 10^5,$$
$$S^* = 403.224 \times 10^5.$$

That is, these values represent the unit price of the hair conditioner, the associated advertising budget, and the salaries and commissions of salesmen that will maximize the expected profits. This marketing mix is used to determine whether this anticipated profit justifies development of this new hair conditioner. A more complicated mathematical model may be formulated to calculate the optimal marketing mix while incorporating the associated investment requirements as well as additional marketing variables.

The technique demonstrated in formulating maximization problem (365) as an equivalent geometric programming problem also may be applied to the following, more general problem:

$$\text{(370)} \qquad \text{maximize} \quad u(\mathbf{t}) - f(\mathbf{t}),$$

where $\mathbf{t} = (t_1, \ldots, t_m)$, $t_1 > 0, \ldots, t_m > 0$, $u$ is a single-term posynomial, $f$ is a posynomial, and $u - f > 0$. (In optimization problem (366), $u(\mathbf{t}) = 10^8 P^{-2} A^{1/4} S^{1/6}$ and $f(\mathbf{t}) = 10^9 P^{-3} A^{1/4} S^{1/6} + A + S$.) Note that $u - f$ is not a posynomial. By introducing a new positive variable $t_0$ satisfying

$$\text{(371)} \qquad u(\mathbf{t}) - f(\mathbf{t}) \geq t_0,$$

we see our maximization problem (370) is equivalent to the following:

$$\begin{aligned} &\text{maximize} && t_0 \\ &\text{subject to} && t_0 > 0,\ t_1 > 0, \ldots, t_m > 0 \\ &&& u(\mathbf{t}) - f(\mathbf{t}) \geq t_0. \end{aligned}$$

Observe that the latter problem is equivalent to determining the constrained minimum of $t_0^{-1}$:

$$\text{(372)} \qquad \begin{aligned} &\text{minimize} && t_0^{-1} \\ &\text{subject to} && t_0 > 0,\ t_1 > 0, \ldots, t_m > 0 \\ &&& u(\mathbf{t}) - f(\mathbf{t}) \geq t_0. \end{aligned}$$

If the constraint of (372) is transformed into the prototype form $g_1(\mathbf{t}) \leq 1$, where $g_1(\mathbf{t})$ is a posynomial, minimization problem (372) will be a constrained geometric programming problem. By transposing $f(\mathbf{t})$, the constraint becomes

$$u(\mathbf{t}) \geq t_0 + f(\mathbf{t}). \tag{373}$$

Since $u(\mathbf{t})$ is a *single*-term posynomial, we may divide both sides of (373) by $u(\mathbf{t})$ to obtain

$$1 \geq t_0[u(\mathbf{t})]^{-1} + [u(\mathbf{t})]^{-1}f(\mathbf{t}).$$

Thus, an equivalent formulation of problem (372), and consequently problem (370), is the following geometric programming problem:

$$\begin{array}{lll} & \text{minimize} & t_0^{-1} \\ (374) & \text{subject to} & t_0 > 0, t_1 > 0, \ldots, t_m > 0 \\ & & t_0[u(\mathbf{t})]^{-1} + [u(\mathbf{t})]^{-1}f(\mathbf{t}) \leq 1. \end{array}$$

The technique of geometric programming now may be applied to solve (374).

Let us consider a second optimization problem of this type:

$$\begin{array}{lll} (375) & \text{maximize} & t_1t_2 - 2t_1^2 - 3t_2^3 \\ & & t_1 > 0, \qquad t_2 > 0. \end{array}$$

Here $u(\mathbf{t}) = t_1t_2$ and $f(\mathbf{t}) = 2t_1^2 + 3t_2^3$. By introducing a positive variable $t_0$ satisfying

$$t_1t_2 - 2t_1^2 - 3t_2^3 \geq t_0$$

we see that (375) is equivalent to the following:

$$\begin{array}{lll} & \text{maximize} & t_0 \\ (376) & \text{subject to} & t_0 > 0, \qquad t_1 > 0, \qquad t_2 > 0 \\ & & t_1t_2 - 2t_1^2 - 3t_2^3 \geq t_0. \end{array}$$

The task of determining the constrained maximum of $t_0$ in the latter problem is equivalent to that of finding the constrained minimum of $t_0^{-1}$ in the following:

$$\begin{array}{ll} \text{minimize} & t_0^{-1} \\ \text{subject to} & t_0 > 0, \qquad t_1 > 0, \qquad t_2 > 0 \\ & t_1t_2 - 2t_1^2 - 3t_2^3 \geq t_0. \end{array}$$

By transforming the constraint into the prototype form, the result is a geometric programming problem of degree of difficulty 0:

$$\begin{array}{ll} \text{minimize} & t_0^{-1} \\ \text{subject to} & t_0 > 0, \qquad t_1 > 0, \qquad t_2 > 0 \\ & t_0t_1^{-1}t_2^{-1} + 2t_1t_2^{-1} + 3t_1^{-1}t_2^2 \leq 1. \end{array}$$

The dual geometric programming problem,

$$\text{maximize} \quad v(\boldsymbol{\delta}) = \left(\frac{1}{\delta_1}\right)^{\delta_1}\left(\frac{1}{\delta_2}\right)^{\delta_2}\left(\frac{2}{\delta_3}\right)^{\delta_3}\left(\frac{3}{\delta_4}\right)^{\delta_4}(\delta_2 + \delta_3 + \delta_4)^{\delta_2+\delta_3+\delta_4}$$

$$\begin{aligned} \text{subject to} \quad & \delta_1 \geq 0, \quad \delta_2 \geq 0, \quad \delta_3 \geq 0, \quad \delta_4 \geq 0 \\ & \delta_1 = 1 \\ & -\delta_1 + \delta_2 = 0 \\ & -\delta_2 + \delta_3 - \delta_4 = 0 \\ & -\delta_2 - \delta_3 + 2\delta_4 = 0, \end{aligned}$$

has the unique solution $\delta_1^* = 1$, $\delta_2^* = 1$, $\delta_3^* = 3$, $\delta_4^* = 2$. The maximum value is $v(\boldsymbol{\delta}^*) = (\frac{2}{3})6^6$. The constrained minimum value of $t_0^{-1}$ is therefore $v(\boldsymbol{\delta}^*) = (\frac{2}{3})6^6$. The constrained maximum value of $t_0$, and hence the maximum of (375), is $1/v(\boldsymbol{\delta}^*) = (\frac{3}{2})6^{-6}$.

Many other types of optimization problems may also be transformed into geometric programming problems using similar techniques. For example, consider the following problem:

$$\text{(377)} \qquad \text{minimize} \quad f(\mathbf{t}) + [p(\mathbf{t})]^a h(\mathbf{t}),$$

where $f, p$, and $h$ are posynomials; $\mathbf{t} = (t_1, \ldots, t_m)$; $t_1 > 0, \ldots, t_m > 0$; and $a > 0$. Unless $p(\mathbf{t})$ is a single-term posynomial, this may not even be a posynomial minimization problem. By introducing a new positive variable $t_0$ satisfying

$$p(\mathbf{t}) \leq t_0,$$

or, equivalently,

$$t_0^{-1}p(\mathbf{t}) \leq 1,$$

we may form a related problem:

$$\text{(378)} \qquad \begin{aligned} \text{minimize} \quad & f(\mathbf{t}) + t_0^a h(\mathbf{t}) \\ \text{subject to} \quad & t_0 > 0, t_1 > 0, \ldots, t_m > 0 \\ & t_0^{-1}p(\mathbf{t}) \leq 1. \end{aligned}$$

From the construction of this problem, we see that the problem of finding the unconstrained minimum of (377) is equivalent to determining the constrained minimum of geometric program (378). Moreover, the values are equal.

Let us consider an example of this type of optimization problem:

$$\text{(379)} \qquad \text{minimize} \quad 2t_1 + (\tfrac{1}{5}t_3^{-1} + \tfrac{1}{10}t_3^2)^{1/2}(2t_1^{-1}t_2 + t_2^{-2})$$

$$t_1 > 0, \qquad t_2 > 0, \qquad t_3 > 0.$$

By introducing a new positive variable $t_0$ satisfying

$$\tfrac{1}{5}t_3^{-1} + \tfrac{1}{10}t_3^2 \le t_0,$$

or, equivalently,

$$\tfrac{1}{5}t_3^{-1}t_0^{-1} + \tfrac{1}{10}t_3^2t_0^{-1} \le 1,$$

we see that determining the constrained minimum of the following problem:

$$\begin{array}{lll} & \text{minimize} & 2t_1 + t_0^{1/2}(2t_1^{-1}t_2 + t_2^{-2}) \\ (380) & \text{subject to} & t_0 > 0, \quad t_1 > 0, \quad t_2 > 0, \quad t_3 > 0 \\ & & \tfrac{1}{5}t_0^{-1}t_3^{-1} + \tfrac{1}{10}t_0^{-1}t_3^2 \le 1 \end{array}$$

is equivalent to solving (379).

By performing the indicated multiplication, problem (380) is transformed into a geometric programming problem of degree of difficulty 0:

$$\begin{array}{lll} & \text{minimize} & 2t_1 + 2t_0^{1/2}t_1^{-1}t_2 + t_0^{1/2}t_2^{-2} \\ (381) & \text{subject to} & t_0 > 0, \quad t_1 > 0, \quad t_2 > 0, \quad t_3 > 0 \\ & & \tfrac{1}{5}t_0^{-1}t_3^{-1} + \tfrac{1}{10}t_0^{-1}t_3^2 \le 1. \end{array}$$

The dual of this problem,

$$\text{maximize} \quad v(\boldsymbol{\delta}) = \left(\frac{2}{\delta_1}\right)^{\delta_1}\left(\frac{2}{\delta_2}\right)^{\delta_2}\left(\frac{1}{\delta_3}\right)^{\delta_3}\left(\frac{\frac{1}{5}}{\delta_4}\right)^{\delta_4}\left(\frac{\frac{1}{10}}{\delta_5}\right)^{\delta_5}(\delta_4 + \delta_5)^{\delta_4+\delta_5}$$

$$\begin{array}{ll} \text{subject to} & \delta_1 \ge 0, \quad \delta_2 \ge 0, \quad \delta_3 \ge 0, \quad \delta_4 \ge 0, \quad \delta_5 \ge 0 \\ & \delta_1 + \delta_2 + \delta_3 = 1 \\ & \delta_1 - \delta_2 = 0 \\ & \delta_2 - 2\delta_3 = 0 \\ & -\delta_4 + 2\delta_5 = 0 \\ & \tfrac{1}{2}\delta_2 + \tfrac{1}{2}\delta_3 - \delta_4 - \delta_5 = 0, \end{array}$$

has the unique solution $\delta_1^* = \tfrac{2}{5}$, $\delta_2^* = \tfrac{2}{5}$, $\delta_3^* = \tfrac{1}{5}$, $\delta_4^* = \tfrac{1}{5}$, $\delta_5^* = \tfrac{1}{10}$. The constrained maximum of the dual objective function, and, consequently the constrained minimum of problem (381), is $v(\boldsymbol{\delta}^*) = 5(\tfrac{3}{10})^{3/10}$. Since problems (381) and (379) are equivalent, the minimum of (379) is also $v(\boldsymbol{\delta}^*) = 5(\tfrac{3}{10})^{3/10}$.

The techniques used in solving optimization problem (377) may be extended to problems of the following, more general form:

$$(382) \qquad \text{minimize} \quad f(\mathbf{t}) + [p(\mathbf{t})]^a[h(\mathbf{t})]^b,$$

where $f$, $p$, and $h$ are posynomials; $\mathbf{t} = (t_1, \ldots, t_m)$; $t_1 > 0, \ldots, t_m > 0$; and $a > 0$, $b > 0$. While (382) may not be a geometric programming problem, we may transform it into one. By introducing two new positive variables $s$, $t_0$, satisfying

$$p(\mathbf{t}) \leq t_0,$$
$$h(\mathbf{t}) \leq s,$$

or, equivalently,

$$t_0^{-1}p(\mathbf{t}) \leq 1,$$
$$s^{-1}h(\mathbf{t}) \leq 1,$$

we formulate the related geometric programming problem:

$$\text{(383)} \qquad \begin{array}{ll} \text{minimize} & f(\mathbf{t}) + t_0^a s^b \\ \text{subject to} & s > 0, \quad t_0 > 0, t_1 > 0, \ldots, t_m > 0 \\ & t_0^{-1}p(\mathbf{t}) \leq 1 \\ & s^{-1}h(\mathbf{t}) \leq 1. \end{array}$$

Observe that according to the construction of geometric programming problem (383), the problem of determining the constrained minimum of (383) is equivalent to minimizing (382). Moreover, the constrained minimum value of (383) equals the minimum of problem (382).

To illustrate this technique, consider the following optimization problem

$$\text{(384)} \qquad \text{minimize} \quad t_1^2 + 6(\tfrac{2}{7}t_1^{-1}t_2 + \tfrac{1}{14}t_2^{-4})^{5/12}(\tfrac{2}{7}t_3^{-1} + \tfrac{1}{7}t_3^2)^{1/2}$$
$$t_1 > 0, \qquad t_2 > 0, \qquad t_3 > 0.$$

We formulate an equivalent geometric programming problem by introducing two new positive variables $s$, $t_0$ satisfying

$$\tfrac{2}{7}t_1^{-1}t_2 + \tfrac{1}{14}t_2^{-4} \leq t_0,$$
$$\tfrac{2}{7}t_3^{-1} + \tfrac{1}{7}t_3^2 \leq s.$$

or, equivalently,

$$\text{(385)} \qquad \begin{array}{c} \tfrac{2}{7}t_0^{-1}t_1^{-1}t_2 + \tfrac{1}{14}t_0^{-1}t_2^{-4} \leq 1, \\ \tfrac{2}{7}s^{-1}t_3^{-1} + \tfrac{1}{7}s^{-1}t_3^2 \leq 1. \end{array}$$

Now we formulate problem (384) as a geometric programming problem in the variables $t_1$, $t_2$, $t_3$, $t_0$, $s$ with constraints (385),

$$\text{(386)} \qquad \begin{array}{ll} \text{minimize} & t_1^2 + 6t_0^{5/12}s^{1/2} \\ \text{subject to} & t_0 > 0, \quad t_1 > 0, \quad t_2 > 0, \quad t_3 > 0, \quad s > 0 \\ & \tfrac{2}{7}s^{-1}t_3^{-1} + \tfrac{1}{7}s^{-1}t_3^2 \leq 1 \\ & \tfrac{2}{7}t_0^{-1}t_1^{-1}t_2 + \tfrac{1}{14}t_0^{-1}t_2^{-4} \leq 1. \end{array}$$

This geometric programming problem is of degree of difficulty 0.

Hence, its dual program, which follows, has a unique solution:

$$\text{maximize} \quad v(\boldsymbol{\delta}) = \left(\frac{1}{\delta_1}\right)^{\delta_1}\left(\frac{6}{\delta_2}\right)^{\delta_2}\left(\frac{\frac{2}{7}}{\delta_3}\right)^{\delta_3}\left(\frac{\frac{1}{7}}{\delta_4}\right)^{\delta_4}\left(\frac{\frac{2}{7}}{\delta_5}\right)^{\delta_5}\left(\frac{\frac{1}{14}}{\delta_6}\right)^{\delta_6} (\delta_3 + \delta_4)^{\delta_3+\delta_4}(\delta_5 + \delta_6)^{\delta_5+\delta_6}$$

(387)

$$\begin{aligned} \text{subject to} \quad & \delta_1 \geq 0, \ldots, \delta_6 \geq 0 \\ & \delta_1 + \delta_2 = 1 \\ & 2\delta_1 - \delta_5 = 0 \\ & \delta_5 - 4\delta_6 = 0 \\ & -\delta_3 + 2\delta_4 = 0 \\ & \tfrac{1}{2}\delta_2 - \delta_3 - \delta_4 = 0 \\ & \tfrac{5}{12}\delta_2 - \delta_5 - \delta_6 = 0. \end{aligned}$$

That solution is $\delta_1^* = \frac{1}{7}$, $\delta_2^* = \frac{6}{7}$, $\delta_3^* = \frac{2}{7}$, $\delta_4^* = \frac{1}{7}$, $\delta_5^* = \frac{2}{7}$, $\delta_6^* = \frac{1}{14}$. The constrained maximum of (387) and hence the minimum of (384), is $v(\boldsymbol{\delta}^*) = 7(\frac{3}{7})^{3/7}(\frac{5}{14})^{5/14}$.

The technique for transforming optimization problems (377) and (382) into equivalent geometric programming problems may also be applied to problems of the following form:

(388) $$\text{minimize} \quad f(\mathbf{t}) + \frac{p(\mathbf{t})}{[u(\mathbf{t}) - h(\mathbf{t})]^a}$$

where $f$, $p$, and $h$ are posynomials; $u$ is a single-term posynomial; $\mathbf{t} = (t_1, \ldots, t_m)$; $t_1 > 0, \ldots, t_m > 0$; and $a > 0$. After introducing a new variable $t_0$ ($>0$) that satisfies

(389) $$\frac{1}{u(\mathbf{t}) - h(\mathbf{t})} \leq \frac{1}{t_0},$$

or, equivalently,

(390) $$\frac{t_0}{u(\mathbf{t})} + \frac{h(\mathbf{t})}{u(\mathbf{t})} \leq 1,$$

consider the related geometric programming problem:

(391)

$$\begin{aligned} \text{minimize} \quad & f(\mathbf{t}) + \frac{p(\mathbf{t})}{t_0^a} \\ \text{subject to} \quad & t_0 > 0, t_1 > 0, \ldots, t_m > 0 \\ & \frac{t_0}{u(\mathbf{t})} + \frac{h(\mathbf{t})}{u(\mathbf{t})} \leq 1. \end{aligned}$$

(Note that (390) is a prototype constraint, since $u$ is a single-term posynomial.) Since $t_0$ satisfies inequality (390) minimization problem (388) is clearly equivalent to determining the constrained minimum of (391). Moreover the minimum of (388) equals the constrained minimum of (391).

Consider an example of this class of minimization problems:

$$\text{(392)} \qquad \text{minimize} \quad 2t_1 t_3^{-1} + \frac{8t_1^{-1}}{(t_2^{-1} - 4t_2^{-3}t_3 - t_2^{-1}t_3)}$$

$$t_1 > 0, \qquad t_2 > 0, \qquad t_3 > 0.$$

As in the previous examples, we may transform (392) into an equivalent geometric programming problem by introducing a new positive variable $t_0$. Specifically, we require that $t_0$ satisfy

$$\frac{1}{t_2^{-1} - 4t_2^{-3}t_3 - t_2^{-1}t_3} \le \frac{1}{t_0}.$$

Several algebraic manipulations show that the latter is equivalent to

$$t_0 \le t_2^{-1} - 4t_2^{-3}t_3 - t_2^{-1}t_3$$

or

$$t_0 t_2 + 4t_2^{-2}t_3 + t_3 \le 1.$$

Thus, associated with problem (392) is the following geometric programming problem:

$$\begin{array}{lll} & \text{minimize} & 2t_1 t_3^{-1} + 8t_1^{-1}t_0^{-1} \\ \text{(393)} & \text{subject to} & t_0 > 0, \quad t_1 > 0, \quad t_2 > 0, \quad t_3 > 0 \\ & & t_0 t_2 + 4t_2^{-2}t_3 + t_3 \le 1. \end{array}$$

Since this geometric programming problem has degree of difficulty 0, the dual problem, as follows, has a unique solution:

$$\text{maximize} \quad v(\boldsymbol{\delta}) = \left(\frac{2}{\delta_1}\right)^{\delta_1}\left(\frac{8}{\delta_2}\right)^{\delta_2}\left(\frac{1}{\delta_3}\right)^{\delta_3}\left(\frac{4}{\delta_4}\right)^{\delta_4}\left(\frac{1}{\delta_5}\right)^{\delta_5}(\delta_3 + \delta_4 + \delta_5)^{\delta_3+\delta_4+\delta_5}$$

$$\begin{array}{ll} \text{subject to} & \delta_1 \ge 0, \quad \delta_2 \ge 0, \quad \delta_3 \ge 0, \quad \delta_4 \ge 0, \quad \delta_5 \ge 0 \\ & \delta_1 + \delta_2 = 1 \\ & \delta_1 - \delta_2 = 0 \\ & \delta_3 - 2\delta_4 = 0 \\ & -\delta_1 + \delta_4 + \delta_5 = 0 \\ & -\delta_2 + \delta_3 = 0. \end{array}$$

The solution of the dual constraints is $\delta_1^* = \frac{1}{2}$, $\delta_2^* = \frac{1}{2}$, $\delta_3^* = \frac{1}{2}$, $\delta_4^* = \frac{1}{4}$,

$\delta_5^* = \frac{1}{4}$ and the constrained minimum value of problem (393), and thus (392) is $v(\boldsymbol{\delta}^*) = 32$.

As these examples illustrate, geometric programming has an intimate relationship with many classes of optimization problems. By introducing new variables, and thus additional constraints, these optimization problems are transformed into equivalent geometric programming problems. Further, as was demonstrated in the previous section, any geometric program belongs to the class of convex programs. This convex programming equivalence was achieved by the change of variables $t_j = e^{x_j}$, thus transforming each posynomial into a convex function.

We also wish to show that a particular class of geometric programming problems is equivalent to a class of linear programming problems. In certain instances a geometric programming problem may be solved more easily by considering its equivalent linear programming problem and vice versa.

The class of geometric programs to be considered are those of the form:

$$
\begin{aligned}
&\text{minimize} && u_0 \\
&\text{subject to} && t_1 > 0, \ldots, t_m > 0 \\
(394)\quad & && u_1 \le 1 \\
& && \vdots \\
& && u_n \le 1,
\end{aligned}
$$

where $u_i = c_i t_1^{a_{i1}} \cdots t_m^{a_{im}}$, $c_i > 0$, $i = 0, 1, \ldots, n$; that is, all posynomials are *monomials*. Program (394) will be shown to be equivalent to the general linear programming problem:

$$
\begin{aligned}
&\text{minimize} && P_0(\mathbf{x}) \\
&\text{subject to} && P_1(\mathbf{x}) \le 0 \\
(395)\quad & && \vdots \\
& && P_n(\mathbf{x}) \le 0,
\end{aligned}
$$

where $P_i(\mathbf{x}) = \sum_{j=1}^{m} a_{ij}x_j + C_i$, $C_i = \ln c_i$, $i = 0, 1, 2, \ldots, n$.

In order to better illustrate the technique involved in transforming program (394) into the equivalent form (395) we shall consider a special case of (394):

$$\text{(396)} \qquad \begin{array}{ll} \text{minimize} & c_0 t_1^{a_{01}} t_2^{a_{02}} \\ \text{subject to} & t_1 > 0, \qquad t_2 > 0 \\ & c_1 t_1^{a_{11}} t_2^{a_{12}} \leq 1 \\ & c_2 t_1^{a_{21}} t_2^{a_{22}} \leq 1. \end{array}$$

We have seen that the *one-to-one* transformation

$$t_j = e^{x_j}, \qquad j = 1, \ldots, m,$$

converts (396) into an equivalent convex program:

$$\text{(397)} \qquad \begin{array}{ll} \text{minimize} & c_0 e^{a_{01}x_1 + a_{02}x_2} \\ \text{subject to} & c_1 e^{a_{11}x_1 + a_{12}x_2} \leq 1 \\ & c_2 e^{a_{21}x_1 + a_{22}x_2} \leq 1. \end{array}$$

(Notice that there are no positivity constraints, because as $t_j$ varies over all positive values, $x_j$ varies from $-\infty$ to $\infty$.)

Observe that program (397) is "close" to a linear program, as the objective and constraint functions are just exponentials of linear functions. These exponential constraint functions are easily converted into linear constraints by using natural logarithms. Recall that $(0<)\ a_1 \leq a_2$ if and only if $\ln a_1 \leq \ln a_2$ because the natural logarithm is a monotone increasing function (see Figure 122). The latter fact may be applied to the constraints of (397) to conclude that these constraints are equivalent to

$$\ln c_1 + a_{11}x_1 + a_{12}x_2 \leq 0,$$
$$\ln c_2 + a_{21}x_1 + a_{22}x_2 \leq 0.$$

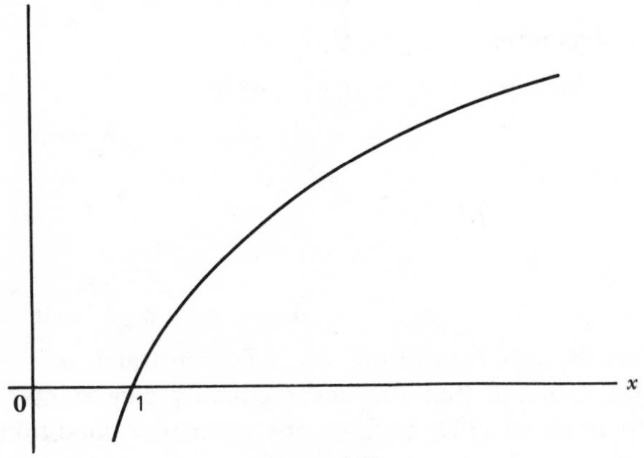


**Figure 122**

Similar reasoning applies to the objective function of (397). Since the natural logarithm is a monotone increasing function, $c_0 e^{a_{01}x_1 + a_{02}x_2}$ attains its constrained minimum if and only if

$$\ln (c_0 e^{a_{01}x_1 + a_{02}x_2}) = \ln c_0 + a_{01}x_1 + a_{02}x_2$$

attains its constrained minimum.

Therefore, problem (397), and thus geometric program (396), are equivalent to the following linear programming problem:

$$\begin{aligned} \text{minimize} \quad & a_{01}x_1 + a_{02}x_2 + C_0 \\ \text{subject to} \quad & a_{11}x_1 + a_{12}x_2 + C_1 \le 0 \\ & a_{21}x_1 + a_{22}x_2 + C_2 \le 0, \end{aligned}$$

where $C_i = \ln c_i$, $i = 0, 1, 2$. The procedure for converting the general problem (394) into the general form (395) is analogous.

The dual program of (394),

$$\begin{aligned} \text{maximize} \quad & \left(\frac{c_0}{\delta_0}\right)^{\delta_0} \left(\frac{c_1}{\delta_1}\right)^{\delta_1} \cdots \left(\frac{c_n}{\delta_n}\right)^{\delta_n} \delta_1^{\delta_1} \cdots \delta_n^{\delta_n} \\ \text{subject to} \quad & \delta_0 \ge 0, \delta_1 \ge 0, \ldots, \delta_n \ge 0 \\ & \delta_0 = 1 \\ (398) \qquad & a_{01}\delta_0 + a_{11}\delta_1 + \cdots + a_{n1}\delta_n = 0 \\ & \quad \vdots \\ & a_{0m}\delta_0 + a_{1m}\delta_1 + \cdots + a_{nm}\delta_n = 0, \end{aligned}$$

can be shown to be equivalent to the unsymmetrical dual of (395),

$$\begin{aligned} \text{maximize} \quad & C_0 + C_1\delta_1 + \cdots + C_n\delta_n \\ \text{subject to} \quad & \delta_1 \ge 0, \ldots, \delta_n \ge 0 \\ & a_{01} + a_{11}\delta_1 + \cdots + a_{n1}\delta_n = 0 \\ (399) \qquad & \quad \vdots \\ & a_{0m} + a_{1m}\delta_1 + \cdots + a_{nm}\delta_n = 0. \end{aligned}$$

The procedure for this transformation is demonstrated using the general problem (398). Observe that the linear equality constraints of (398) are equivalent to those of (399) because the normality condition is $\delta_0 = 1$. Further, since $\delta_0 = 1$ and the $\delta_i^{\delta_i}$ terms cancel in the numerator and denominator of the geometric dual objective function, the geometric dual objective function equals

$$c_0 \prod_{i=1}^{n} c_i^{\delta_i}. \tag{400}$$

Function (400) attains its constrained maximum if and only if

$$\ln\left(c_0 \prod_{i=1}^{n} c_i^{\delta_i}\right) = \ln c_0 + \sum_{i=1}^{n} (\ln c_i)\delta_i$$

attains its maximum subject to the same constraints. This follows from the monotonicity of the natural logarithm function. Hence, with $C_i = \ln c_i$, $i = 0, 1, \ldots, n$, program (398) is equivalent to the unsymmetrical dual of (395), where $C_i = \ln c_i$, $i = 0, 1, \ldots, n$.

As an illustration of this process consider the following geometric programming problem:

$$\begin{aligned} &\text{minimize} && t_1 t_3 \\ &\text{subject to} && t_1 > 0, \quad t_2 > 0, \quad t_3 > 0 \\ & && \tfrac{1}{2} t_1^{-1} t_2 t_3 \le 1 \\ & && \tfrac{3}{4} t_2^{-1} t_3 \le 1 \\ & && \tfrac{1}{4} t_2^{-1} t_3^{-3} \le 1. \end{aligned} \tag{401}$$

Note that (401) is of the form (394); the objective and constraint functions are single-term posynomials. Under the transformation $t_j = e^{x_j}$, $j = 1, 2, 3$, problem (401) is equivalent to the following convex programming problem:

$$\begin{aligned} &\text{minimize} && e^{x_1 + x_3} \\ &\text{subject to} && \tfrac{1}{2} e^{-x_1 + x_2 + x_3} \le 1 \\ & && \tfrac{3}{4} e^{-x_2 + x_3} \le 1 \\ & && \tfrac{1}{4} e^{-x_2 - 3x_3} \le 1. \end{aligned} \tag{402}$$

By taking the natural logarithm of both sides of the constraints of (402), we see that these constraints are equivalent to the linear constraints

$$\begin{aligned} \ln \tfrac{1}{2} - x_1 + x_2 + x_3 &\le 0, \\ \ln \tfrac{3}{4} \qquad - x_2 + x_3 &\le 0, \\ \ln \tfrac{1}{4} \qquad - x_2 - 3x_3 &\le 0. \end{aligned} \tag{403}$$

Since the natural logarithm function is monotone-increasing, determining the constrained minimum of $e^{x_1 + x_3}$ in (402) is equivalent to determining the constrained minimum of $\ln(e^{x_1 + x_3}) = x_1 + x_3$, a linear function. Thus, problem (402), and hence problem (401), is equivalent to the following linear programming problem:

$$\text{(404)}\qquad \begin{aligned} &\text{minimize} && x_1 + x_3 \\ &\text{subject to} && \ln \tfrac{1}{2} - x_1 + x_2 + x_3 \le 0 \\ &&& \ln \tfrac{3}{4} \quad - x_2 + x_3 \le 0 \\ &&& \ln \tfrac{1}{4} \quad - x_2 - 3x_3 \le 0. \end{aligned}$$

The dual of geometric program (401),

$$\text{(405)}\qquad \begin{aligned} &\text{maximize} && v(\boldsymbol{\delta}) = \left(\frac{1}{\delta_0}\right)^{\delta_0}\left(\frac{\frac{1}{2}}{\delta_1}\right)^{\delta_1}\left(\frac{\frac{3}{4}}{\delta_2}\right)^{\delta_2}\left(\frac{\frac{1}{4}}{\delta_3}\right)^{\delta_3} \delta_1^{\delta_1}\delta_2^{\delta_2}\delta_3^{\delta_3} \\ &\text{subject to} && \delta_0 \ge 0, \quad \delta_1 \ge 0, \quad \delta_2 \ge 0, \quad \delta_3 \ge 0 \\ &&& \delta_0 = 1 \\ &&& \delta_0 - \delta_1 = 0 \\ &&& \delta_1 - \delta_2 - \delta_3 = 0 \\ &&& \delta_0 + \delta_1 + \delta_2 - 3\delta_3 = 0, \end{aligned}$$

is seen to be equivalent to the unsymmetrical dual of (404),

$$\text{(406)}\qquad \begin{aligned} &\text{maximize} && (\ln \tfrac{1}{2})\delta_1 + (\ln \tfrac{3}{4})\delta_2 + (\ln \tfrac{1}{4})\delta_3 \\ &\text{subject to} && \delta_1 \ge 0, \quad \delta_2 \ge 0, \quad \delta_3 \ge 0 \\ &&& 1 - \delta_1 = 0 \\ &&& \delta_1 - \delta_2 - \delta_3 = 0 \\ &&& 1 + \delta_1 + \delta_2 - 3\delta_3 = 0. \end{aligned}$$

Since $\delta_0 = 1$ in (405), the constraints of (405) and (406) are identical. Furthermore, as explained above, determining the constrained maximum of $v(\boldsymbol{\delta})$ is equivalent to calculating the constrained maximum of $\ln v(\boldsymbol{\delta})$. Since

$$\ln v(\boldsymbol{\delta}) = \ln (\tfrac{1}{2})^{\delta_1}(\tfrac{3}{4})^{\delta_2}(\tfrac{1}{4})^{\delta_3} = (\ln \tfrac{1}{2})\delta_1 + (\ln \tfrac{3}{4})\delta_2 + (\ln \tfrac{1}{4})\delta_3,$$

problems (405) and (406) are equivalent.

Although we have only converted a particular class of geometric programming problems into an equivalent linear programming problem, it is readily seen that the inverse transformation $x_j = \ln t_j$, $C_j = \ln c_j$ converts an arbitrary primal linear programming problem into a primal geometric programming problem. Similarly, the unsymmetrical dual linear programming problem is equivalent to the dual geometric programming problem.

An arbitrary geometric programming problem may also be linearized. After approximating an arbitrary geometric programming problem with a geometric program of the form (394), we may convert any geometric program into a linear programming form by proceeding as above. The actual approximation procedure is discussed in a later section.

## A PERSONNEL ASSIGNMENT PROBLEM: EXPONENTIAL PROGRAMMING

The personnel assignment problem concerns the "best" assignment of a set of persons to a set of jobs. For example, suppose an industrial facility wishes to fill three positions each requiring different abilities and training. If three applicants of different abilities, training, and experience can be hired for identical salaries, their "value" to the company depends upon the one job to which each is assigned. Given measures of the "value" of each job to the company and of the "likelihood" that each of the three applicants will not succeed at each of the three jobs, we wish to determine which of the $3! = 6$ possible alternative assignments minimizes the anticipated lost value to the firm.

Suppose that a known constant $p$ $(0 \leq p \leq 1)$ indicates the likelihood that one of the applicants will fail on one of the jobs. If $p = 0$, there is no chance that the applicant will fail at the job. If $p = 1$, there is no possibility that the applicant will succeed at this particular job. As $p$ takes on increasing values between 0 and 1, the likelihood that the applicant will fail increases.

Assume, further, that this particular job is worth a constant $c$ dollars to the firm. The product

$$cp$$

is then a measure of the expected lost value of this personnel assignment. If there is no chance of the applicant succeeding on this job ($p = 1$), the expected lost value to the firm is $c$ dollars. However, as the probability of failure decreases ($p$ tends from 1 to 0), the expected lost value to the firm also decreases. If there is no chance of failure ($p = 0$) the expected lost value is 0.

Suppose an estimate of the probability that each of the three applicants will fail on each of the three jobs is as given in Table 3. Furthermore, assume

**Table 3**

| | Job | | |
|---|---|---|---|
| Applicant | 1 | 2 | 3 |
| 1 | 0.5 | 0.3 | 0.2 |
| 2 | 0.1 | 0.6 | 0.7 |
| 3 | 0.4 | 0.2 | 0.5 |

that the value of the first, second, and third jobs to the firm is 10, 10, and 7, respectively. These values are measured in thousands of dollars. The expected lost value to the firm is minimized by assigning applicant 1 to job 3, applicant 2 to job 1, and applicant 3 to job 2. Note that the expected lost value to the firm is

$$10(0.2) + 10(0.1) + 7(0.2) = 4.4$$

thousand dollars.

This example suggests a more general personnel assignment problem. Specifically, suppose that several applicants of each of two categories must be assigned to one of two jobs. We must determine the number of applicants of each category to assign to each of the jobs so that the expected lost value to the firm is minimized. Each applicant is assigned to one of two categories according to their abilities, education, and experience. Suppose the probabilities that any applicant of either category will fail at the first and second jobs is as given in Table 4.

Thus, for example, the likelihood that an applicant of category 1 will fail at the first job is 0.1353. More generally, suppose $x_{ij}$ represents the number of applicants of category $i$ assigned to the $j$th job. If $x_{11}$ applicants of type 1 are assigned to job 1, the likelihood that they will all fail is given by

$$(0.1353)^{x_{11}}.$$

As $x_{11}$ increases, the chance that all $x_{11}$ applicants of type 1 will fail at the first job decreases, as expected. Similarly, since the probability that one applicant of category 2 will fail at the first job is 0.6065, the likelihood that $x_{21}$ applicants of type 2 will fail at the first job is

$$(0.6065)^{x_{21}}.$$

Further, if these $x_{11}$ and $x_{21}$ applicants are simultaneously assigned to the first job, then a measure of the likelihood that all $x_{11} + x_{21}$ applicants will fail is

$$(0.1353)^{x_{11}}(0.6065)^{x_{21}}.$$

Again, as $x_{11}$ and $x_{21}$ increase, the probability that all $x_{11} + x_{21}$ applicants

**Table 4**

| | Job | |
|---|---|---|
| Applicant Category | 1 | 2 |
| 1 | 0.1353 | 0.2231 |
| 2 | 0.6065 | 0.4724 |

will fail decreases. Thus, if the value of this job to the firm is \$10,000, the expected lost value of this personnel assignment is

$$10^4(0.1353)^{x_{11}}(0.6065)^{x_{21}}. \tag{407}$$

Analogously, suppose that $x_{12}$ applicants of type 1 and $x_{22}$ applicants of type 2 are simultaneously assigned to the second job. The likelihood that all $x_{12} + x_{22}$ will fail is

$$(0.2231)^{x_{12}}(0.4724)^{x_{22}}.$$

And, further, if the second job has a value of \$15,000, the expected lost value of this personnel assignment to the firm is

$$(1.5 \times 10^4)(0.2231)^{x_{12}}(0.4724)^{x_{22}}. \tag{408}$$

The total expected lost value of this personnel assignment is the sum of (407) and (408)

$$10^4[(0.1353)^{x_{11}}(0.6065)^{x_{21}} + 1.5(0.2231)^{x_{12}}(0.4724)^{x_{22}}]. \tag{409}$$

The expected lost value (409) is obviously reduced as more applicants of each class are assigned to each job. That is, (409) decreases as the values of $x_{ij}$ $(i, j = 1, 2)$ are increased. Suppose, however, that at most 9 applicants of type 1 and at most 10 applicants of type 2 are assigned to these two jobs. Then, the values of $x_{ij}$ are restricted to satisfy

$$x_{11} + x_{12} \leq 9, \tag{410}$$

$$x_{21} + x_{22} \leq 10. \tag{411}$$

Furthermore, if labor union regulations require that the first job utilize at least 6 applicants, we have a third constraint,

$$x_{11} + x_{21} \geq 6. \tag{412}$$

Thus, our problem of determining values $x_{ij}$ that minimize the expected lost value (409) and satisfy restrictions (410)–(412) is the constrained optimization problem:

$$\begin{aligned} &\text{minimize} && 10^4[(0.1353)^{x_{11}}(0.6065)^{x_{21}} + 1.5(0.2231)^{x_{12}}(0.4724)^{x_{22}}] \\ &\text{subject to} && x_{11} + x_{12} \leq 9 \\ & && x_{21} + x_{22} \leq 10 \\ & && x_{11} + x_{21} \geq 6. \end{aligned} \tag{413}$$

Although (413) is not a geometric programming problem, with the simple change of variables

$$t_{ij} = e^{x_{ij}} \tag{414}$$

$(i, j = 1, 2)$, (413) may be transformed into an equivalent geometric program and solved accordingly. As we have seen, under this transformation, variations in the behavior of $x_{ij}$ are reflected by $t_{ij}$.

The term $10^4(0.1353)^{x_{11}}(0.6065)^{x_{21}}$ may be transformed into functions of $t_{11}$ and $t_{21}$ by first observing that

$$(0.1353)^{x_{11}} = e^{\ln(0.1353)^{x_{11}}} = e^{x_{11}\ln(0.1353)} = t_{11}^{\ln(0.1353)},$$

and

$$(0.6065)^{x_{21}} = e^{\ln(0.6065)^{x_{21}}} = e^{x_{21}\ln(0.6065)} = t_{21}^{\ln(0.6065)}.$$

Hence,

$$10^4(0.1353)^{x_{11}}(0.6065)^{x_{21}} = 10^4 t_{11}^{\ln(0.1353)} t_{21}^{\ln(0.6065)}.$$

Similarly,

$$(1.5 \times 10^4)(0.2231)^{x_{12}}(0.4724)^{x_{22}} = (1.5 \times 10^4) t_{12}^{\ln(0.2231)} t_{22}^{\ln(0.4724)}$$

Thus, the objective function of (413) is equivalent to the posynomial

$$(415) \quad 10^4 t_{11}^{\ln(0.1353)} t_{21}^{\ln(0.6065)} + (1.5 \times 10^4) t_{12}^{\ln(0.2231)} t_{22}^{\ln(0.4724)}$$
$$= 10^4 t_{11}^{-2} t_{21}^{-1/2} + (1.5 \times 10^4) t_{12}^{-3/2} t_{22}^{-3/4}$$

The constraints of (413) may be expressed as prototype geometric programming constraints under transformation (414). First, observe that since

$$t_{ij} = e^{x_{ij}},$$
$$x_{ij} = \ln t_{ij}.$$

Thus, constraint (410) is equivalent to

$$\ln t_{11} + \ln t_{12} \le 9,$$

and according to the logarithm addition rule,

$$(416) \qquad \ln t_{11} t_{12} \le 9.$$

Since the exponential function is monotone increasing inequality (416) holds if and only if

$$e^{\ln t_{11} t_{12}} \le e^9,$$

or

$$t_{11} t_{12} \le e^9.$$

Thus, constraint (410) is equivalent to the prototype geometric programming constraint

$$e^{-9} t_{11} t_{12} \le 1.$$

In a similar manner, we see that constraint (411) is equivalent to the prototype geometric programming constraint

$$e^{-10} t_{21} t_{22} \le 1.$$

With transformation (414) constraint (412) becomes

$$\ln t_{11} + \ln t_{21} \geq 6,$$

or, equivalently,

(417) $$\ln t_{11}t_{21} \geq 6.$$

Since the exponential function is monotone-increasing, inequality (417) holds if and only if

$$e^{\ln t_{11}t_{21}} \geq e^6,$$

or

(418) $$t_{11}t_{21} \geq e^6.$$

Multiplying both sides of (418) by $t_{11}^{-1}t_{21}^{-1}$, we see that (418) is equivalent to the prototype geometric programming constraint

$$e^6 t_{11}^{-1}t_{21}^{-1} \leq 1.$$

Thus, optimization problem (413) is equivalent to the constrained geometric program:

(419)
$$\begin{aligned} &\text{minimize} && 10^4 t_{11}^{-2} t_{21}^{-1/2} + (1.5 \times 10^4) t_{12}^{-3/2} t_{22}^{-3/4} \\ &\text{subject to} && t_{11} > 0, \quad t_{12} > 0, \quad t_{21} > 0, \quad t_{22} > 0 \\ & && e^{-9} t_{11} t_{12} \leq 1 \\ & && e^{-10} t_{21} t_{22} \leq 1 \\ & && e^6 t_{11}^{-1} t_{21}^{-1} \leq 1. \end{aligned}$$

Since (419) has five terms and four variables, the degree of difficulty is 0 and the dual program,

(420)
$$\begin{aligned} &\text{maximize} && \left(\frac{10^4}{\delta_1}\right)^{\delta_1} \left(\frac{1.5 \times 10^4}{\delta_2}\right)^{\delta_2} \left(\frac{e^{-9}}{\delta_3}\right)^{\delta_3} \left(\frac{e^{-10}}{\delta_4}\right)^{\delta_4} \left(\frac{e^6}{\delta_5}\right)^{\delta_5} \delta_3^{\delta_3} \delta_4^{\delta_4} \delta_5^{\delta_5} \\ &\text{subject to} && \delta_1 \geq 0, \quad \delta_2 \geq 0, \quad \delta_3 \geq 0, \quad \delta_4 \geq 0, \quad \delta_5 \geq 0 \\ & && \delta_1 + \delta_2 = 1 \\ & && -2\delta_1 + \delta_3 - \delta_5 = 0 \\ & && -\tfrac{1}{2}\delta_1 + \delta_4 - \delta_5 = 0 \\ & && -\tfrac{3}{2}\delta_2 + \delta_3 = 0 \\ & && -\tfrac{3}{4}\delta_2 + \delta_4 = 0, \end{aligned}$$

has a unique solution. The solution of the dual constraint is $\delta_1^* = \frac{1}{3}$, $\delta_2^* = \frac{2}{3}$, $\delta_3^* = 1$, $\delta_4^* = \frac{1}{2}$, $\delta_5^* = \frac{1}{3}$, and the minimum expected lost value to the firm is $M = 0.15216$.

Note that the values of $\delta_1^*$ and $\delta_2^*$ indicate the relative contribution of the costs of the first and second jobs, respectively, to the total expected lost value. Since $\delta_1^* = \frac{1}{3}$, the expected lost value of our personnel assignment attributed to the first job is $\frac{1}{3}M = \frac{1}{3}(0.15216) = 0.05072$. Similarly, since $\delta_2^* = \frac{2}{3}$, the expected lost value corresponding to the second job is $\frac{2}{3}M = \frac{2}{3}(0.15216) = 0.10144$. The values of $\delta_1^*$ and $\delta_2^*$ are dependent on the likelihoods of failure indicated in Table 4. Variations in these probabilities are reflected in the exponents of the cost function (415) and, consequently, in the coefficients of the dual constraints in (420). Accordingly, the optimal values of the dual variables may be affected.

In order to determine the optimal personnel assignment $x_{11}^*, x_{12}^*, x_{21}^*, x_{22}^*$ that minimizes the expected lost value, we must first determine $t_{11}^*, t_{12}^*, t_{21}^*, t_{22}^*$. According to the duality theory of geometric programming, $t_{11}^*, t_{12}^*, t_{21}^*, t_{22}^*$, must satisfy

$$\begin{aligned}
10^4 t_{11}^{*-2} t_{21}^{*-1/2} &= \tfrac{1}{3}(0.15216),\\
(1.5 \times 10^4) t_{12}^{*-3/2} t_{22}^{*-3/4} &= \tfrac{2}{3}(0.15216),\\
e^{-9} t_{11}^* t_{12}^* &= 1,\\
e^{-10} t_{21}^* t_{22}^* &= 1,\\
e^{6} t_{11}^{*-1} t_{21}^{*-1} &= 1.
\end{aligned}$$

Solving this system we find that $t_{11}^* = 0.9877$, $t_{21}^* = 408.4496$, $t_{12}^* = 8203.9300$, $t_{22}^* = 853.9270$. We now determine $x_{11}^*, x_{12}^*, x_{21}^*, x_{22}^*$ by inverting the transformation (414). That is, since

$$x_{ij} = \ln t_{ij},$$

$(i, j = 1, 2)$, $x_{11}^* = -0.0123$, $x_{21}^* = 6.0123$, $x_{12}^* = 9.0123$, $x_{22}^* = 3.9877$.

The optimal personnel assignment is obtained by rounding these values to the nearest integer value. Thus, the optimal personnel assignment is to assign 0 applicants of type 1 and 6 applicants of type 2 to the first job, and 9 applicants of type 1 and 4 applicants of type 2 to the second job. Moreover, the expected lost value of this personnel assignment is approximately \$0.15.

The technique used to solve this personnel assignment problem also applies to an entire class of optimization problems. However, before generalizing this method, consider a second example:

$$\text{(421)} \qquad \text{minimize} \quad 3^{x_1} + 2^{-x_2} + 3^{-x_1}2^{x_2}.$$

Under the transformation $t_i = e^{x_i}$, $i = 1, 2$, problem (421) may be transformed into a geometric programming problem. With this change of variables the terms $3^{x_1}$ and $2^{-x_2}$ become

$$3^{x_1} = e^{\ln 3^{x_1}} = e^{x_1 \ln 3} = t_1^{\ln 3}$$

and

$$2^{-x_2} = e^{\ln 2^{-x_2}} = e^{-x_2 \ln 2} = t_2^{-\ln 2},$$

respectively. Similarly, we find that

$$3^{-x_1}2^{x_2} = t_1^{-\ln 3}t_2^{\ln 2}.$$

Thus, optimization problem (421) is equivalent to the geometric programming problem:

(422) $$\text{minimize} \quad t_1^{\ln 3} + t_2^{-\ln 2} + t_1^{-\ln 3}t_2^{\ln 2}$$
$$t_1 > 0, \qquad t_2 > 0.$$

Since this geometric programming problem is of zero degree of difficulty, the dual program,

$$\text{maximize} \quad \left(\frac{1}{\delta_1}\right)^{\delta_1}\left(\frac{1}{\delta_2}\right)^{\delta_2}\left(\frac{1}{\delta_3}\right)^{\delta_3}$$

$$\begin{aligned} \text{subject to} \quad & \delta_1 \geq 0, \quad \delta_2 \geq 0, \quad \delta_3 \geq 0 \\ & \delta_1 + \delta_2 + \delta_3 = 1 \\ & \ln 3\delta_1 - \ln 3\delta_3 = 0 \\ & -\ln 2\delta_2 + \ln 2\delta_3 = 0, \end{aligned}$$

has a unique solution. Observe that since this unique solution is $\delta_1^* = \frac{1}{3}$, $\delta_2^* = \frac{1}{3}$, $\delta_3^* = \frac{1}{3}$, the minimum value of (422), and hence of (421), is $M = 3$.

In order to determine the optimal values of $x_1$ and $x_2$ in (421), we first calculate $t_1^*$ and $t_2^*$. According to the duality theory of geometric programming

$$t_1^{*\ln 3} = \delta_1^* M = \tfrac{1}{3}3 = 1$$

and

$$t_2^{*-\ln 2} = \delta_2^* M = \tfrac{1}{3}3 = 1.$$

Therefore, $t_1^* = 1$ and $t_2^* = 1$. Since $e^{x_i} = t_i, x_i = \ln t_i, i = 1, 2,$

$$x_1^* = \ln t_1^* = \ln 1 = 0$$

and

$$x_2^* = \ln t_2^* = \ln 1 = 0.$$

Hence, the optimum value of (421), $M = 3$, occurs when $x_1^* = 0$ and $x_2^* = 0$.

Consider a third illustration of this technique:

(423) $$\begin{aligned} \text{minimize} \quad & 3^{-x_1}2^{-x_2} \\ \text{subject to} \quad & (\tfrac{1}{2})9^{x_1} + (\tfrac{1}{2})4^{x_2} \leq 1. \end{aligned}$$

As in the previous example, optimization problem (423) may be transformed into an equivalent geometric programming problem under the change of variables $t_i = e^{x_i}$, $i = 1, 2$. With this transformation, we find that

$$\begin{aligned} 3^{-x_1}2^{-x_2} &= e^{\ln 3^{-x_1}}\, e^{\ln 2^{-x_2}} \\ &= e^{-x_1 \ln 3} e^{-x_2 \ln 2} \\ &= t_1^{-\ln 3} t_2^{-\ln 2}. \end{aligned}$$

Furthermore,

$$9^{x_1} = 3^{2x_1} = e^{\ln 3^{2x_1}} = e^{2x_1 \ln 3} = t_1^{2 \ln 3}$$

and

$$4^{x_2} = 2^{2x_2} = e^{\ln 2^{2x_2}} = e^{2x_2 \ln 2} = t_2^{2 \ln 2}.$$

Therefore, (423) is equivalent to the zero degree of difficulty geometric programming problem:

$$\text{(424)} \qquad \begin{aligned} &\text{minimize} && t_1^{-\ln 3} t_2^{-\ln 2} \\ &\text{subject to} && t_1 > 0, \quad t_2 > 0 \\ & && \tfrac{1}{2} t_1^{2 \ln 3} + \tfrac{1}{2} t_2^{2 \ln 2} \leq 1. \end{aligned}$$

The solution to the dual geometric programming problem,

$$\begin{aligned} &\text{maximize} && \left(\frac{1}{\delta_1}\right)^{\delta_1} \left(\frac{\frac{1}{2}}{\delta_2}\right)^{\delta_2} \left(\frac{\frac{1}{2}}{\delta_3}\right)^{\delta_3} (\delta_2 + \delta_3)^{\delta_2 + \delta_3} \\ &\text{subject to} && \delta_1 \geq 0, \quad \delta_2 \geq 0, \quad \delta_3 \geq 0 \\ & && \delta_1 = 1 \\ & && -\ln 3\delta_1 + 2 \ln 3\delta_2 = 0 \\ & && -\ln 2\delta_1 + 2 \ln 2\delta_3 = 0, \end{aligned}$$

is $\delta_1^* = 1$, $\delta_2^* = \frac{1}{2}$, $\delta_3^* = \frac{1}{2}$. The minimum value of (424), and thus (423), is $M = 1$.

As in the previous example, we calculate $x_1^*$ and $x_2^*$ by first determining $t_1^*$ and $t_2^*$. Since $t_1^*$ and $t_2^*$ satisfy

$$\frac{1}{2} t_1^{*2 \ln 3} = \frac{\delta_2^*}{\delta_2^* + \delta_3^*} = \frac{1}{2}$$

and

$$\frac{1}{2} t_2^{*2 \ln 2} = \frac{\delta_3^*}{\delta_2^* + \delta_3^*} = \frac{1}{2},$$

according to the duality theory of geometric programming, we find $t_1^* = 1$, $t_2^* = 1$. The optimal point of (423) is therefore $x_1^* = 0$, $x_2^* = 0$, since $t_1^* = e^{x_1^*}$ and $t_2^* = e^{x_2^*}$.

This technique also may be applied in solving the following, more general optimization problem:

$$\begin{aligned} &\text{minimize} && g_0(\mathbf{x}) \\ &\text{subject to} && g_1(\mathbf{x}) \le 1 \\ &&& \quad\vdots \\ &&& g_p(\mathbf{x}) \le 1, \end{aligned} \tag{425}$$

where $g_0(\mathbf{x}), g_1(\mathbf{x}), \ldots, g_p(\mathbf{x})$ are functions of the form

$$\sum_{i=1}^{n} c_i a_{i1}^{x_1} \cdot \ldots \cdot a_{im}^{x_m},$$

where $c_i \ge 0$; $a_{ik} \ge 0$; $i = 1, \ldots, n$; $k = 1, \ldots, m$. Optimization problems of this form are termed *exponential programming problems.*

Under the transformation $t_i = e^{x_i}$ these functions have the equivalent posynomial form

$$\sum_{i=1}^{n} c_i t_1^{\ln a_{i1}} \cdots t_m^{\ln a_{im}},$$

where $c_i \ge 0$; $a_{ik} \ge 0$; $i = 1, \ldots, n$; $k = 1, \ldots, m$. Now the techniques of geometric programming may be used to solve exponential program (425).

As a final example, consider this exponential programming problem:

$$\begin{aligned} &\text{minimize} && 3^{x_1 - 2x_3} + (\tfrac{1}{3})^{x_1} 2^{4x_2} \\ &\text{subject to} && \tfrac{2}{3}2^{x_2} + \tfrac{1}{3}2^{-4x_2}3^{x_3} \le 1. \end{aligned} \tag{426}$$

Under the change of variables $t_i = e^{x_i}$, $i = 1, 2, 3$, problem (426) is equivalent to the following geometric programming problem:

$$\begin{aligned} &\text{minimize} && t_1^{\ln 3} t_3^{-2\ln 3} + t_1^{-\ln 3} t_2^{4\ln 2} \\ &\text{subject to} && t_1 > 0, \quad t_2 > 0, \quad t_3 > 0 \\ &&& \tfrac{2}{3} t_2^{\ln 2} + \tfrac{1}{3} t_2^{-4\ln 2} t_3^{\ln 3} \le 1. \end{aligned} \tag{427}$$

The dual geometric programming problem,

$$\begin{aligned} &\text{maximize} && \left(\frac{1}{\delta_1}\right)^{\delta_1} \left(\frac{1}{\delta_2}\right)^{\delta_2} \left(\frac{\frac{2}{3}}{\delta_3}\right)^{\delta_3} \left(\frac{\frac{1}{3}}{\delta_4}\right)^{\delta_4} (\delta_3 + \delta_4)^{\delta_3 + \delta_4} \\ &\text{subject to} && \delta_1 \ge 0, \quad \delta_2 \ge 0, \quad \delta_3 \ge 0, \quad \delta_4 \ge 0 \\ &&& \delta_1 + \delta_2 = 1 \\ &&& \ln 3\delta_1 - \ln 3\delta_2 = 0 \\ &&& 4\ln 2\delta_2 + \ln 2\delta_3 - 4\ln 2\delta_4 = 0 \\ &&& -2\ln 3\delta_1 + \ln 3\delta_4 = 0, \end{aligned}$$

has the unique solution $\delta_1^* = \frac{1}{2}$, $\delta_2^* = \frac{1}{2}$, $\delta_3^* = 2$, $\delta_4^* = 1$. The optimal value of (427), and thus (426), is $M = 2$. By solving the duality conditions

$$t_1^{*\ln 3} t_3^{*-2\ln 3} = \delta_1^* M = \tfrac{1}{2}2 = 1$$

$$\frac{2}{3} t_2^{*\ln 2} = \frac{\delta_3^*}{\delta_3^* + \delta_4^*} = \frac{2}{3}$$

$$\frac{1}{3} t_2^{*-4\ln 2} t_3^{*\ln 3} = \frac{\delta_4^*}{\delta_3^* + \delta_4^*} = \frac{1}{3},$$

we find that $t_1^* = 1$, $t_2^* = 1$, $t_3^* = 1$, implying $x_1^* = 0$, $x_2^* = 0$, $x_3^* = 0$.

## AN INVENTORY CONTROL PROBLEM: THE CONDENSATION PROCEDURE

The maintenance and control of inventories of physical goods pose several problems for the industrial engineer. In every inventory control problem, decisions must be made regarding when an order should be placed and how much should be ordered. Indeed, depending upon the certainty of demand, such problems may become quite complicated. The simple problem of controlling the inventories of several items of known annual demand and constant rate of demand is discussed here.

Consider the problem of determining the lot sizes of two goods that will minimize the associated ordering and holding costs while satisfying certain warehouse space limitations. Suppose the annual demand for each product is 250 units and that the rate of demand is 0.2 per unit time. Thus, if the order size of product 1 is $t_1$ units and the stock is depleted at a constant rate 0.2, the stock of product 1 will be 0 after $t_1/0.2$ units of time (see Figure 123). Similarly, if $t_2$ is the lot size of product 2, this stock will be 0 after $t_2/0.2$ units of time. At these times, we shall assume lot size orders of size $t_1$ and

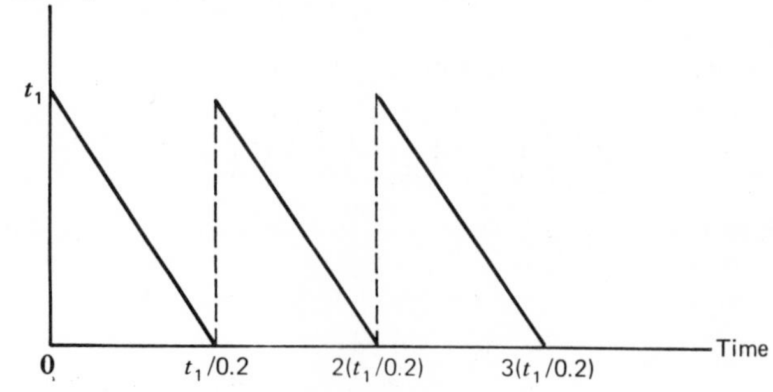


Figure 123

$t_2$, respectively, arrive instantaneously. Hence, there are no shortages of either product.

The problem of minimizing the total inventory cost involves determining lot sizes $t_1^*$ and $t_2^*$ that balance the contributions of the ordering and holding costs. The ordering cost of each product varies with the number of orders. Since 250 is the annual demand of product 1, $250/t_1$ is approximately the number of orders of product 1 per year. With 1.92 as the cost of a single order of product 1, $1.92(250/t_1) = 488/t_1$ is the annual ordering cost of product 1. Similarly, $250/t_2$ is approximately the number of orders of product 2 per year. If 2.00 is the cost of a single order of product 2, then $2.00(250/t_2) = 500/t_2$ is the annual ordering cost of product 2. Thus, the total annual ordering cost is

$$\frac{488}{t_1} + \frac{500}{t_2}. \tag{428}$$

The average annual holding cost depends upon the average size of the lot in storage. Since the inventories are depleted at a constant rate, the average inventories are $t_1/2$ and $t_2/2$. With unit storage costs of 2 and 1.90 for products 1 and 2, respectively, the average storage costs are $2(t_1/2) = t_1$ and $1.90(t_2/2) = 0.95t_2$. Therefore, the average annual holding cost is

$$t_1 + 0.95t_2. \tag{429}$$

The total inventory cost is the sum of (428) and (429),

$$g_0(\mathbf{t}) = t_1 + \frac{488}{t_1} + 0.95t_2 + \frac{500}{t_2}, \tag{430}$$

where $t_1 > 0$, $t_2 > 0$.

While lot sizes must be chosen to minimize (430), the storage space requirements of $t_1$ and $t_2$ must not exceed 30 units. Thus, if each unit of each product requires 1 unit of space, the space requirement, $t_1 + t_2$, must satisfy

$$t_1 + t_2 \leq 30. \tag{431}$$

Observe that the problem of determining lot sizes that minimize the total inventory cost (430) and yet satisfy the space constraint (431) may be formulated as a geometric programming problem. Specifically, our cost minimization problem is a geometric programming problem of degree of difficulty 3:

$$\begin{aligned} \text{minimize} \quad & t_1 + \frac{488}{t_1} + 0.95t_2 + \frac{500}{t_2} \\ \text{subject to} \quad & t_1 > 0, \qquad t_2 > 0 \\ & \tfrac{1}{30}t_1 + \tfrac{1}{30}t_2 \leq 1. \end{aligned} \tag{432}$$

The duality inequality of geometric programming may be used to estimate the minimum inventory system cost. By substituting the primal feasible vector $\mathbf{t}' = (12, 12)$ and the dual feasible vector $\boldsymbol{\delta}' = (\frac{1}{8}, \frac{3}{8}, \frac{1}{8}, \frac{3}{8}, \frac{1}{4}, \frac{1}{4})$, for instance, into the duality inequality,

$$g_0(\mathbf{t}) \geq M \geq v(\boldsymbol{\delta}),$$

the minimum cost $M$ is bounded as

$$105.75 \geq M \geq 94.34. \tag{433}$$

These bounds imply that the constrained minimum inventory system cost is 100.03 but with an error of 5.96%.

Although such conservative approximations are readily obtained, the actual minimum inventory system cost is difficult to determine, since geometric program (432) is of nonzero degree of difficulty. Therefore, the problem of solving this geometric programming problem would be greatly simplified by transforming (432) into an equivalent geometric programming problem of lower degree of difficulty. Although such a transformation is somewhat optimistic, (432) may be approximated by a family of geometric programs of a lower degree of difficulty. The minimum inventory cost is then estimated by the minimum values of each of the approximating geometric programming problems. As these approximations of (432) are improved, the corresponding estimates of the minimum inventory cost also improve. Note that, in particular, when the approximating geometric programs have degree of difficulty 0, the corresponding estimates of the minimum inventory cost are easily calculated.

Before constructing this family of approximating geometric programming problems, it is convenient to transform (432) into an equivalent form. By introducing a new positive variable $t_0$ satisfying

$$t_1 + \frac{488}{t_1} + 0.95t_2 + \frac{500}{t_2} \leq t_0,$$

(432) is transformed into the equivalent geometric program:

$$\begin{array}{lll} & \text{minimize} & g_0(\mathbf{t}) = t_0 \\ & \text{subject to} & t_0 > 0, \quad t_1 > 0, \quad t_2 > 0 \\ (434) & & g_1(\mathbf{t}) = \frac{1}{30}t_1 + \frac{1}{30}t_2 \leq 1 \\ & & g_1(\mathbf{t}) = t_0^{-1}t_1 + 488t_0^{-1}t_1^{-1} + 0.95t_0^{-1}t_2 \\ & & \qquad + 500t_0^{-1}t_2^{-1} \leq 1. \end{array}$$

The family of geometric programming problems that approximate (432) will also approximate this equivalent program. [Note that this transformation does not effect the degree of difficulty of (432).]

In developing these approximations of (434), we wish to construct geometric programs of degree of difficulty less than 3. One technique for constructing such geometric programs is to approximate, say, the four-term posynomial $g_2(\mathbf{t})$ by a posynomial $\bar{g}_2(\mathbf{t})$ with fewer terms. If, for example, $\bar{g}_2(\mathbf{t})$ has only three terms, the degree of difficulty of the approximating geometric program is $6 - (3 + 1) = 2$. Similarly, if $g_2(\mathbf{t})$ is approximated by a single-term posynomial, $\bar{g}_2(\mathbf{t})$, the degree of difficulty of the approximating geometric program is $4 - (3 + 1) = 0$; an approximating geometric program of degree of difficulty 0 is easily solved. This is the essence of our approximation technique; we wish to *condense* the posynomial $g_2(\mathbf{t})$ into an approximate posynomial $\bar{g}_2(\mathbf{t})$ with fewer terms. Program (434) is then approximated by a geometric program of reduced degree of difficulty.

Care must be taken in constructing the approximating geometric program:

(435)
$$\begin{aligned} &\text{minimize} && g_0(\mathbf{t}) = t_0 \\ &\text{subject to} && t_0 > 0, \qquad t_1 > 0, \qquad t_2 > 0 \\ & && g_1(\mathbf{t}) = \tfrac{1}{30}t_1 + \tfrac{1}{30}t_2 \le 1 \\ & && \bar{g}_2(\mathbf{t}) \le 1. \end{aligned}$$

The posynomial $\bar{g}_2(\mathbf{t})$ must be constructed so that the constraint set of (435) contains the constraint set of (434). That is, if $\mathbf{t}'$ satisfies the constraints of (434),

$$g_1(\mathbf{t}') \le 1, \qquad g_2(\mathbf{t}') \le 1,$$

then $\mathbf{t}'$ must satisfy the constraints of (435),

$$g_1(\mathbf{t}') \le 1, \qquad \bar{g}_2(\mathbf{t}') \le 1.$$

Otherwise, the constraint set of the approximating geometric program (435) may not contain the minimizing point $\mathbf{t}^*$ of (434).

Furthermore, at the minimizing point $\mathbf{t}^*$ the constraints of programs (434) and approximation (435) should be satisfied identically; that is,

$$g_2(\mathbf{t}^*) = \bar{g}_2(\mathbf{t}^*).$$

The actual construction of the condensed posynomial $\bar{g}_2(\mathbf{t})$ employs the geometric inequality. The geometric inequality states that

(436)
$$u_1 + u_2 + u_3 + u_4 \ge \left(\frac{u_1}{\epsilon_1}\right)^{\epsilon_1}\left(\frac{u_2}{\epsilon_2}\right)^{\epsilon_2}\left(\frac{u_3}{\epsilon_3}\right)^{\epsilon_3}\left(\frac{u_4}{\epsilon_4}\right)^{\epsilon_4},$$

where $u_i > 0, \epsilon_i \ge 0, i = 1, 2, 3, 4$ and $\sum_{i=1}^{4} \epsilon_i = 1$. Specifically, when (436) is applied to the posynomial $g_2(\mathbf{t})$, this inequality implies

(437) $$g_2(\mathbf{t}) = t_0^{-1}t_1 + 488t_0^{-1}t_1^{-1} + 0.95t_0^{-1}t_2 + 500t_0^{-1}t_2^{-1}$$
$$\geq \left(\frac{t_0^{-1}t_1}{\epsilon_1}\right)^{\epsilon_1}\left(\frac{488t_0^{-1}t_1^{-1}}{\epsilon_2}\right)^{\epsilon_2}\left(\frac{0.95t_0^{-1}t_2}{\epsilon_3}\right)^{\epsilon_3}\left(\frac{500t_0^{-1}t_2^{-1}}{\epsilon_4}\right)^{\epsilon_4}$$

for any choice of $\epsilon_i \geq 0$, $i = 1, 2, 3, 4$ satisfying $\sum_{i=1}^{4} \epsilon_i = 1$.

With the proper choice of weights $\epsilon_i$, the single-term posynomial

(438) $$\bar{g}_2(\mathbf{t}) = \left(\frac{t_0^{-1}t_1}{\epsilon_1}\right)^{\epsilon_1}\left(\frac{488t_0^{-1}t_1^{-1}}{\epsilon_2}\right)^{\epsilon_2}\left(\frac{0.95t_0^{-1}t_2}{\epsilon_3}\right)^{\epsilon_3}\left(\frac{500t_0^{-1}t_2^{-1}}{\epsilon_4}\right)^{\epsilon_4}$$

is a reasonable approximation of $g_2(\mathbf{t})$. Note that it is a consequence of the geometric inequality (437) that

$$\bar{g}_2(\mathbf{t}) \leq g_2(\mathbf{t}).$$

Thus, if $\mathbf{t}'$ satisfies $g_2(\mathbf{t}') \leq 1$, it also satisfies $\bar{g}_2(\mathbf{t}') \leq 1$ as desired. Observe that at the minimizing point $\mathbf{t}^*$ this approximation satisfies

$$g_2(\mathbf{t}^*) = \bar{g}_2(\mathbf{t}^*)$$

if the weights are chosen to be

(439) $$\epsilon_1^* = \frac{u_1^*}{g_2(\mathbf{t}^*)} = \frac{t_0^{*-1}t_1^*}{g_2(\mathbf{t}^*)}, \qquad \epsilon_2^* = \frac{u_2^*}{g_2(\mathbf{t}^*)} = \frac{488t_0^{*-1}t_1^{*-1}}{g_2(\mathbf{t}^*)},$$
$$\epsilon_3^* = \frac{u_3^*}{g_2(\mathbf{t}^*)} = \frac{0.95t_0^{*-1}t_2^*}{g_2(\mathbf{t}^*)}, \qquad \epsilon_4^* = \frac{u_4^*}{g_2(\mathbf{t}^*)} = \frac{500t_0^{*-1}t_2^{*-1}}{g_2(\mathbf{t}^*)}.$$

This fact follows from our preliminary discussion of the geometric inequality.

Hence, the minimum value of the corresponding condensed program of zero degree of difficulty,

($434_c(\epsilon)$)

minimize $\quad g_0(\mathbf{t}) = t_0$

subject to $\quad t_0 > 0, \quad t_1 > 0, \quad t_2 > 0$

$$g_1(\mathbf{t}) = \tfrac{1}{30}t_1 + \tfrac{1}{30}t_2 \leq 1$$

$$\bar{g}_2(\mathbf{t}) = \left(\frac{t_0^{-1}t_1}{\epsilon_1}\right)^{\epsilon_1}\left(\frac{488t_0^{-1}t_1^{-1}}{\epsilon_2}\right)^{\epsilon_2}\left(\frac{0.95t_0^{-1}t_2}{\epsilon_3}\right)^{\epsilon_3}\left(\frac{500t_0^{-1}t_2^{-1}}{\epsilon_4}\right)^{\epsilon_4} \leq 1$$

$$\epsilon_1 \geq 0, \quad \epsilon_2 \geq 0, \quad \epsilon_3 \geq 0, \quad \epsilon_4 \geq 0, \quad \sum_{i=1}^{4} \epsilon_i = 1,$$

approximates the constrained minimum inventory system cost for any choice of weights $\epsilon_i$. Intuitively, it is seen that better estimates of the minimum value of (434) are obtained if these weights indicate the relative contribution of each term of $g_2(\mathbf{t})$ to the minimum. In (434) the relative size of the coefficients of the terms of $g_2(\mathbf{t})$ seem to imply that the ordering cost terms contribute more to the minimum than the holding cost terms. Accordingly, the weights are chosen as

(440) $\epsilon_1^{(1)} = 0.05, \quad \epsilon_2^{(1)} = 0.45, \quad \epsilon_3^{(1)} = 0.05, \quad \epsilon_4^{(1)} = 0.45.$

With this choice of weights the minimum value of the condensed program $(434_c(\epsilon^1))$ is $\overline{M}_1 = 94.58333$. But according to estimate (433), $\overline{M}_1$ may not be a good approximation of the minimum inventory cost. Hence, a new choice of weights is desirable.

The conditions for equality of $g_2(\mathbf{t})$ and $\bar{g}_2(\mathbf{t})$ at $\mathbf{t}^*$ suggest that new weights should be chosen accordingly. That is, the weights should be given by (439) with $\mathbf{t}^* = \mathbf{t}^{(1)}$, the minimizing point of $(434_c(\epsilon^1))$. The point $\mathbf{t}^* = \mathbf{t}^{(1)}$ may be determined from conditions (357) of the duality theorem,

(441)
$$\tfrac{1}{30}t_1^* = \frac{\delta_2^*}{\delta_2^* + \delta_3^*},$$
$$\tfrac{1}{30}t_2^* = \frac{\delta_3^*}{\delta_2^* + \delta_3^*},$$

where $\delta_2^* = 0.4$ and $\delta_3^* = 0.4$ are solutions of the dual of the condensed program $(434_c(\epsilon^1))$. System (441) implies $\mathbf{t}^{(1)} = (t_1^{(1)}, t_2^{(1)}) = (15.0, 15.0)$. With $\mathbf{t}^* = \mathbf{t}^{(1)}$ the new weights are calculated using (439),

(442)
$$\epsilon_1^{(2)} = 0.1498160, \qquad \epsilon_2^{(2)} = 0.3420361,$$
$$\epsilon_3^{(2)} = 0.1577011, \qquad \epsilon_4^{(2)} = 0.3504467.$$

The minimum value of condensed program $(434_c(\epsilon^2))$ is $\overline{M}_2 = 95.11644$. According to (433), $\overline{M}_2$ is a more reasonable estimate of the minimum inventory system cost. Since the solution of the dual of program $(434_c(\epsilon^2))$ is $\delta_1^* = 1$, $\delta_2^* = 0.19222$, $\delta_3^* = 0.1927456$, $\delta_4^* = 1$, conditions (441) imply that the minimizing point of $(434_c(\epsilon^2))$ is $\mathbf{t}^{(2)} = (14.97953, 15.02048)$.

Using the minimizing point $\mathbf{t}^* = \mathbf{t}^{(2)}$, we may repeat this process to obtain a new estimate $\overline{M}_3$ of the minimum inventory system cost. By evaluating relations (439) at $\mathbf{t}^* = \mathbf{t}^{(2)}$, we find that the new weights are

$$\epsilon_1^{(3)} = 0.1496115, \qquad \epsilon_2^{(3)} = 0.3425034$$
$$\epsilon_3^{(3)} = 0.1579163, \qquad \epsilon_4^{(3)} = 0.3499688.$$

The minimum of the corresponding condensed program ($434_c(\epsilon^3)$) is $\overline{M}_3 =$ 95.11626. According to (441), this minimum is attained at $\mathbf{t}^{(3)} =$ (15.03271, 14.96729).

Observe that the absolute difference between the last two approximations, $\overline{M}_2$ and $\overline{M}_3$, is quite small. In fact, it is

$$|\overline{M}_2 - \overline{M}_3| = 0.0001831.$$

Intuitively this fact suggests that $\overline{M}_1, \overline{M}_2, \overline{M}_3$ are approaching a limit of approximately

$$M = 95.116.$$

This leads us to conclude that the minimum inventory system cost is approximately 95.12. Further, we may take the components of $\mathbf{t}^{(3)}$ as approximations of the optimal lot sizes, $t_1^*$ and $t_2^*$; that is, the lot sizes of the first and second products, which minimize the inventory system cost, are approximately 15.033 and 14.967, respectively.

To some extent, the rate of convergence of this algorithm depends upon our initial guess, $\epsilon_1^{(1)}, \epsilon_2^{(1)}, \epsilon_3^{(1)}, \epsilon_4^{(1)}$, of the weights. Intuitively we see that if the weights $\epsilon_i^{(1)}$ of each term $u_i(\mathbf{t})$ of $g_2(\mathbf{t})$ represent approximately the contribution of $u_i(\mathbf{t})$ to $g_2(\mathbf{t})$ at the minimum, the algorithm may converge more rapidly. In the inventory system problem the relative size of the coefficients of each term of $g_2(\mathbf{t})$ "implied" that the terms corresponding to ordering costs contributed much more to the minimum total cost than the terms corresponding to holding costs. Hence, the initial choice of weights (440) was made.

The condensation technique for the general geometric program is similar. Given the superconsistent geometric programming problem

$$\text{(P)}\qquad \begin{aligned} &\text{minimize} && g_0(\mathbf{t}) \\ &\text{subject to} && t_1 > 0, \ldots, t_m > 0 \\ &&& g_1(\mathbf{t}) \le 1 \\ &&& \vdots \\ &&& g_p(\mathbf{t}) \le 1, \end{aligned}$$

where

$$g_k(\mathbf{t}) = \sum_{i=n_{k-1}+1}^{n_k} c_i t_1^{a_{i1}} t_2^{a_{i2}} \cdots t_m^{a_{im}},$$

and a set of nonnegative weights $\epsilon_{n_{k-1}+1}, \ldots, \epsilon_{n_k}$ satisfying

$$\sum_{i=n_{k-1}+1}^{n_k} \epsilon_i = 1,$$

a *condensed geometric programming problem* is obtained by replacing $g_k(\mathbf{t})$ by

$$\bar{g}_k(\mathbf{t}) = \prod_{i=n_{k-1}+1}^{n_k} \left(\frac{u_i}{\epsilon_i}\right)^{\epsilon_i}.$$

Here the $u_i$ are the terms of $g_k(\mathbf{t})$. Hence,

$$\bar{g}_k(\mathbf{t}) = \bar{c}_k t_1^{\bar{a}_{k1}} \cdots t_m^{\bar{a}_{km}}$$

where

$$\bar{c}_k = \prod_{i=n_{k-1}+1}^{n_k} \left(\frac{c_i}{\epsilon_i}\right)^{\epsilon_i} \quad \text{and} \quad \bar{a}_{kj} = \sum_{i=n_{k-1}+1}^{n_k} \epsilon_i a_{ij},$$

$j = 1, \ldots, m$. For future reference, we write the condensed program as follows:

$$(\mathrm{P}_c(\epsilon)) \qquad \begin{array}{ll} \text{minimize} & g_0(\mathbf{t}) \\ \text{subject to} & t_1 > 0, \ldots, t_m > 0 \\ & g_1(\mathbf{t}) \le 1 \\ & \quad \vdots \\ & \bar{g}_k(\mathbf{t}) \le 1 \\ & \quad \vdots \\ & g_p(\mathbf{t}) \le 1. \end{array}$$

It is a direct consequence of the geometric inequality,

$$u_{n_{k-1}+1} + \cdots + u_{n_k} \ge \left(\frac{u_{n_{k-1}+1}}{\epsilon_{n_{k-1}+1}}\right)^{\epsilon_{n_{k-1}+1}} \cdots \left(\frac{u_{n_k}}{\epsilon_{n_k}}\right)^{\epsilon_{n_k}},$$

that

$$g_k(\mathbf{t}) \ge \bar{g}_k(\mathbf{t}).$$

Thus, if $\mathbf{t}'$ satisfies the constraints of (P), $\mathbf{t}'$ also satisfies the constraints of $(\mathrm{P}_c(\epsilon))$ because $g_k(\mathbf{t}') \le 1$ implies $\bar{g}_k(\mathbf{t}') \le 1$.

Further, since we have the implication

$$g_k(\mathbf{t}) \le 1 \rightarrow \bar{g}_k(\mathbf{t}) \le 1,$$

$M$, the minimum of (P), and $\overline{M}$, the minimum of $(\mathrm{P}_c(\epsilon))$, satisfy

$$M \ge \overline{M}.$$

That is, since the constraint set of (P) is contained in the constraint set of $(P_c(\epsilon))$, the minimum value of $(P_c(\epsilon))$ is at most $M$.

Thus, for any choice of nonnegative weights $\epsilon_i$ satisfying $\sum_{i=n_{k-1}+1}^{n_k} \epsilon_i = 1$, the minimum value of $(P_c(\epsilon))$ provides a lower bound for the minimum value of (P). As the following result states, with a prudent choice of weights $\epsilon_i$, the values $M$ and $\overline{M}$ are equal:

**THEOREM 56** Suppose (P) is superconsistent and attains its constrained minimum $M > 0$ at a point $\mathbf{t}^*$. If the weights of the condensed program $(P_c(\epsilon))$ are chosen as

(443)
$$\epsilon_i^* = \frac{u_i(\mathbf{t}^*)}{g_k(\mathbf{t}^*)},$$

$n_{k-1} + 1 \leq i \leq n_k$, then condensed program $(P_c(\epsilon))$ attains a minimum value $\overline{M}$ at $\mathbf{t}^*$. Moreover, $M = \overline{M}$. ▮

This result provides the basis for the condensation algorithm of geometric programming. As successively better approximations of the weights $\epsilon_i^*$ in (443) are developed, the minimum values of the corresponding condensed geometric programs converge to the value $M$. Suppose that condensed program $(P_c(\epsilon^1))$ is solved for an initial choice of weights $\epsilon_{n_{k-1}+1}^{(1)}, \ldots, \epsilon_{n_k}^{(1)}$ and that the minimizing point $\mathbf{t}^* = \mathbf{t}^{(1)} = (t_1^{(1)}, \ldots, t_m^{(1)})$ of $(P_c(\epsilon^1))$ is obtained by solving conditions (357) of the duality theorem:

(444)
$$u_i(\mathbf{t}^*) = \begin{cases} \delta_i^* g_0(\mathbf{t}^*), & i = 1, \ldots, n_0 \\ \dfrac{\delta_i^*}{\lambda_k(\boldsymbol{\delta}^*)}, & n_{k-1} + 1 \leq i \leq n_k, \\ & k = 1, \ldots, \mathrm{p}. \end{cases}$$

Having determined $\mathbf{t}^{(1)}$, we may assign the weights new values and repeat this process. As suggested by the theorem, we choose the new weights to be

$$\epsilon_i^{(2)} = \frac{u_i(\mathbf{t}^{(1)})}{g_k(\mathbf{t}^{(1)})}, \qquad i = n_{k-1} + 1, \ldots, n_k.$$

With these new weights program $(P_c(\epsilon^2))$ is solved and the value $\overline{M}_2$ is determined. Once again the duality conditions (444) are used to determine the minimizing point $\mathbf{t}^{(2)}$ and the relations

$$\epsilon_i^{(3)} = \frac{u_i(\mathbf{t}^{(2)})}{g_0(\mathbf{t}^{(2)})}, \qquad i = n_{k-1} + 1, \ldots, n_k,$$

are used to construct new weights. Upon determining the minimum $\overline{M}_3$ of $(P_c(\epsilon^3))$, we repeat this algorithm. The algorithm is terminated when

(445)
$$|\overline{M}_{k-1} - \overline{M}_k| < \epsilon,$$

for some predetermined small positive number $\epsilon$. Intuitively, condition (445) suggests that the sequence of minimum values $\overline{M}_1, \overline{M}_2, \overline{M}_3, \ldots$ converge to the minimum $M$. (A summary of the condensation procedure appears in Figure 124.)

In a similar manner these results and this algorithm apply when the geometric inequality is used to condense more than one posynomial $g_i(\mathbf{t})$ into single-term posynomials $\bar{g}_i(\mathbf{t})$. Likewise, this approximation technique applies when at least two terms are condensed into a single term.

To illustrate this algorithm better, consider a second example:

(446)
$$\begin{aligned} &\text{minimize} && g_0(\mathbf{t}) = 40t_1^{-1}t_2^{-1} + 20t_2 \\ &\text{subject to} && t_1 > 0, \quad t_2 > 0 \\ &&& g_1(\mathbf{t}) = 20t_1 + 10t_1t_2 \le 1. \end{aligned}$$

This geometric program of degree of difficulty $4 - (2 + 1) = 1$ may be approximated by a sequence of geometric programs of degree of difficulty 0:

(446$_c$($\epsilon$))
$$\begin{aligned} &\text{minimize} && g_0(\mathbf{t}) = 40t_1^{-1}t_2^{-1} + 20t_2 \\ &\text{subject to} && t_1 > 0, \quad t_2 > 0 \\ &&& \bar{g}_1(\mathbf{t}) = \left(\frac{20t_1}{\epsilon_1}\right)^{\epsilon_1}\left(\frac{10t_1t_2}{\epsilon_2}\right)^{\epsilon_2} \le 1 \\ &&& \epsilon_1 \ge 0, \quad \epsilon_2 \ge 0, \quad \epsilon_1 + \epsilon_2 = 1. \end{aligned}$$

Here the two-term constraint posynomial has been condensed to a single-term posynomial $\bar{g}_1(\mathbf{t})$. Initially with the weights $\epsilon_1^{(1)} = \frac{1}{3}$, $\epsilon_2^{(1)} = \frac{2}{3}$, the condensed program,

$$\begin{aligned} &\text{minimize} && g_0(\mathbf{t}) = 40t_1^{-1}t_2^{-1} + 20t_2 \\ &\text{subject to} && t_1 > 0, \quad t_2 > 0 \\ &&& \bar{g}_1(\mathbf{t}) = \left(\frac{20t_1}{\frac{1}{3}}\right)^{1/3}\left(\frac{10t_1t_2}{\frac{2}{3}}\right)^{2/3} \le 1, \end{aligned}$$

has the minimum value $\overline{M}_1 = 637.2947$. The dual variables have values $\delta_1^* = 0.75$, $\delta_2^* = 0.25$, $\delta_3^* = 0.75$. Upon solving the duality conditions,

(447)
$$\begin{aligned} 40t_1^{*-1}t_2^{*-1} &= \delta_1^* g_0(\mathbf{t}^*), \\ 20t_2^* &= \delta_2^* g_0(\mathbf{t}^*), \end{aligned}$$

we find that the minimizing vector is $\mathbf{t}^* = \mathbf{t}^{(1)} = (0.010558, 7.906286)$.

This information is used to assign new values to the weights so that the

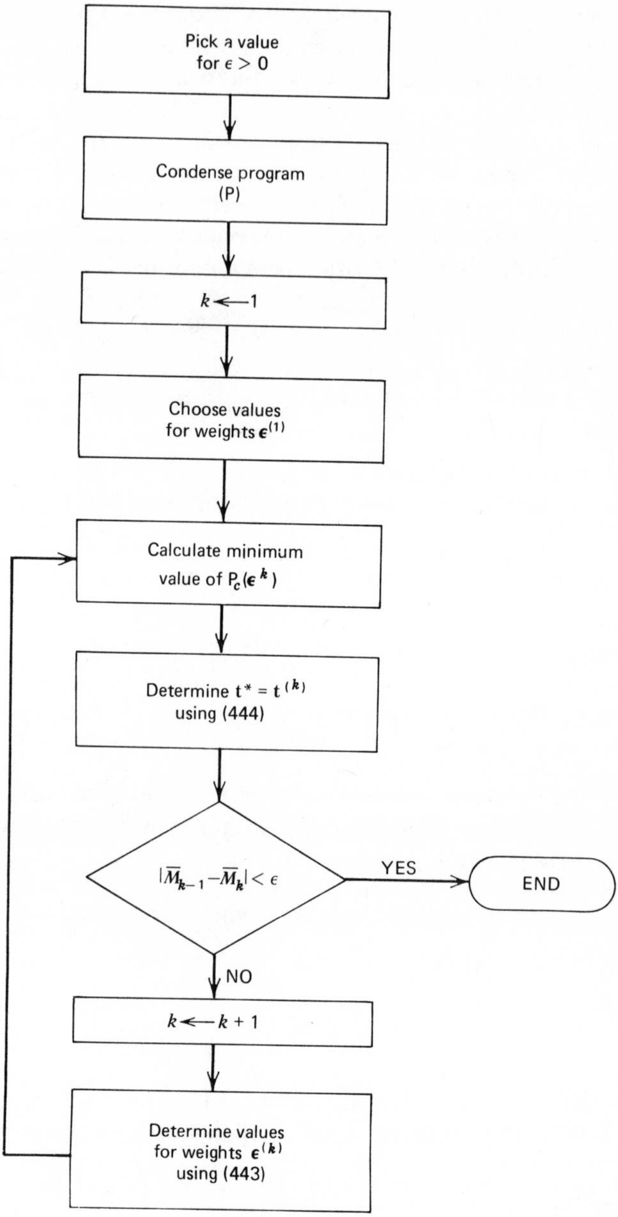
Pick a value for $\epsilon > 0$
Condense program (P)
$k \leftarrow 1$
Choose values for weights $\boldsymbol{\epsilon}^{(1)}$
Calculate minimum value of $P_c(\boldsymbol{\epsilon}^k)$
Determine $t^* = t^{(k)}$ using (444)
$|\overline{M}_{k-1} - \overline{M}_k| < \epsilon$
YES
END
NO
$k \leftarrow k + 1$
Determine values for weights $\boldsymbol{\epsilon}^{(k)}$ using (443)

**Figure 124**

process may be repeated. With

$$\epsilon_1^{(2)} = \left.\frac{20t_1}{20t_1 + 10t_1t_2}\right|_{\mathbf{t}^{(1)}} = 0.2018921,$$

$$\epsilon_2^{(2)} = \left.\frac{10t_1t_2}{20t_1 + 10t_1t_2}\right|_{\mathbf{t}^{(1)}} = 0.7981084,$$

we find that the minimum value of the condensed program is $\overline{M}_2 = 649.2808$. The solution of the dual program, $\delta_1^* = 0.8320217$, $\delta_2^* = 0.1679780$, $\delta_3^* = 0.8320222$, is used in (447) to calculate the minimizing point $\mathbf{t}^* = \mathbf{t}^{(2)} = (0.013578, 5.453245)$.

Having determined the minimizing vector $\mathbf{t}^{(2)}$ new values for the weights are calculated and the process is repeated. The process was terminated after 11 iterations when

$$|\overline{M}_{10} - \overline{M}_{11}| = 0.0007324 < 0.002.$$

Here $\overline{M}_{10} = 652.9805$ and $\overline{M}_{11} = 652.9812$. Hence, the minimum value of program (446) is approximately $M = 652.981$. This value is attained at $\mathbf{t}^* = (0.011997, 6.335470)$.

As a final example, consider the following geometric programming problem:

$$\text{(448)}\qquad \begin{aligned} &\text{minimize} && g_0(\mathbf{t}) = 6t_1^{-1} \\ &\text{subject to} && t_1 > 0, \quad t_2 > 0 \\ & && g_1(\mathbf{t}) = 6t_2^{-1} \leq 1 \\ & && g_2(\mathbf{t}) = t_1^2 + 0.01t_2 \leq 1. \end{aligned}$$

This geometric program of degree of difficulty $4 - (2 + 1) = 1$ may be approximated by a sequence of geometric programs of degree of difficulty 0:

$$\text{(448}_c(\boldsymbol{\epsilon})\text{)}\qquad \begin{aligned} &\text{minimize} && g_0(\mathbf{t}) = 6t_1^{-1} \\ &\text{subject to} && t_1 > 0, \quad t_2 > 0 \\ & && g_1(\mathbf{t}) = 6t_2^{-1} \leq 1 \\ & && \bar{g}_2(\mathbf{t}) = \left(\frac{t_1^2}{\epsilon_1}\right)^{\epsilon_1}\left(\frac{0.01t_2}{\epsilon_2}\right)^{\epsilon_2} \leq 1 \\ & && \epsilon_1 \geq 0, \quad \epsilon_2 \geq 0, \quad \epsilon_1 + \epsilon_2 = 1. \end{aligned}$$

Condensed program $(448_c(\boldsymbol{\epsilon}))$ is obtained from (448) by condensing the two-term constraint posynomial $g_2(\mathbf{t})$ into a single-term posynomial $\bar{g}_2(\mathbf{t})$. With the initial choice of weights $\epsilon_1^{(1)} = 0.95$ and $\epsilon_2^{(1)} = 0.05$, the minimum value of the condensed program,

$$
(448_c(\epsilon^1)) \qquad
\begin{aligned}
&\text{minimize} && g_0(\mathbf{t}) = 6t_1^{-1} \\
&\text{subject to} && t_1 > 0, \qquad t_2 > 0 \\
& && g_1(\mathbf{t}) = 6t_2^{-1} \le 1 \\
& && \bar{g}_2(\mathbf{t}) = \left(\frac{t_1^2}{0.95}\right)^{0.95}\left(\frac{0.01t_2}{0.05}\right)^{0.05} \le 1,
\end{aligned}
$$

is $\overline{M}_1 = 6.18547$. Using the solution of the dual geometric program, $\delta_1^* = 1.0$, $\delta_2^* = 0.0263158$, $\delta_3^* = 0.5263154$, the duality conditions,

$$
(449) \qquad
\begin{aligned}
6t_1^{*\,-1} &= \delta_1^* g_0(\mathbf{t}^*), \\
6t_2^{*\,-1} &= \frac{\delta_2^*}{\delta_2^*},
\end{aligned}
$$

implying the minimizing vector is $\mathbf{t}^* = \mathbf{t}^{(1)} = (0.9700152, 6.0000)$.

Using this point $\mathbf{t}^{(1)}$, new weights $\epsilon_1^{(2)}, \epsilon_2^{(2)}$ are calculated and the process is repeated. With

$$
\epsilon_1^{(2)} = \left.\frac{t_1^2}{t_1^2 + 0.01t_2}\right|_{\mathbf{t}^{(1)}} = 0.9982318,
$$

$$
\epsilon_2^{(2)} = \left.\frac{0.01t_2}{t_1^2 + 0.01t_2}\right|_{\mathbf{t}^{(1)}} = 0.0017682
$$

The minimum value of the corresponding condensed program is $\overline{M}_2 = 6.024024$. The solution of the dual program, $\delta_1^* = 1.0$, $\delta_2^* = 0.0008852491$, $\delta_3^* = 0.5008858$, is used in (449) to calculate $\mathbf{t}^* = \mathbf{t}^{(2)} = (0.9960037, 6.0000)$.

This process is repeated with the new weights:

$$
\epsilon_1^{(3)} = \left.\frac{t_1^2}{t_1^2 + 0.01t_2}\right|_{\mathbf{t}^{(2)}} = 0.9983227,
$$

$$
\epsilon_2^{(3)} = \left.\frac{0.01t_2}{t_1^2 + 0.01t_2}\right|_{\mathbf{t}^{(2)}} = 0.0016773.
$$

The minimum value of $(448_c(\epsilon^3))$ is calculated to be $\overline{M}_3 = 6.023097$ and the solution of the dual program is $\delta_1^* = 1.0$, $\delta_2^* = 0.0008400339$, $\delta_3^* = 0.5008401$. Conditions (449) imply the minimizing point of $(448_c(\epsilon^3))$ is $\mathbf{t}^* = \mathbf{t}^{(3)} = (0.9961652, 6.0000)$. Since

$$
|\overline{M}_2 - \overline{M}_3| = 0.0009766 < 0.002,
$$

the algorithm was terminated. Thus, the minimum value of (448) is approximately $M = 6.023$ and is attained at $\mathbf{t}^* = (0.9961652, 6.0000)$.

## SALES FORCE DECISIONS: APPROXIMATION TECHNIQUES

Marketing decisions must determine the mix of resources necessary to promote effectively company products to actual and potential buyers. Resources must be allocated among promotional elements, such as advertising and field selling, to optimize the calculated effect on the customers. Field selling, for instance, is usually a large element in marketing budgets, as it involves a sales force that travels to customers; that is, after resources are committed to field selling, an optimal sales force strategy must be developed. Sales force strategy factors such as the size of the sales force, sales efforts and calling policies for different types of customers, and salesman quotas and incentives are determined so as to maximize sales while satisfying budgetary constraints.

The problem of allocating sales effort between two types of customers is discussed here. Given an estimate of the sales response of direct customers and of wholesale customers, sales personnel must be distributed between these two groups so as to maximize the expected profit while satisfying budgetary constraints. In this analysis, sales territories are assumed to be specified and no competitive effects are considered. All salesmen are considered as equally effective and are paid identical salaries. All salesmen are assumed to sell the same products.

The profit function of this sales operation is dependent upon the returns from both direct and wholesale customers as well as the cost of maintaining salesmen in the field. If the annual salaries of these salesmen are assumed to equal 10,000 and if $t_1$ and $t_2$ are the number of salesmen serving direct and wholesale customers, respectively, then the total cost of maintaining salesmen in the field is

$$10^4(t_1 + t_2) \tag{450}$$

dollars. Suppose, however, that at most \$100,000 may be allocated to the salaries of salesmen. Then

$$10^4(t_1 + t_2) \leq 10^5$$

or, equivalently,

$$\tfrac{1}{10}t_1 + \tfrac{1}{10}t_2 \leq 1. \tag{451}$$

The profits also depend upon the quantities sold to wholesalers and those sold directly to customers. Let us assume that the sales response of each group of customers is of the form

$$q_i = s_i(1 - e^{-b_i t_i}),$$

where $q_i$ is the quantity sold to customers of type $i$, $s_i$ is the saturation level of sales to either customer, $b_i$ ($>0$) is a constant reflecting the sensitivity of sales to increases in $t_i$, and $i$ equals 1 (2) refers to direct (wholesale) sales. The relative sizes of $b_1$ and $b_2$ indicate the response of sales to the first few direct and wholesale salesmen, respectively. For instance, if $b_1 > b_2$, sales respond more rapidly to the first few direct salesmen than to the first few wholesale salesmen. Note that as the number of salesmen increases ($t_i \to \infty$), the quantity sold approaches the saturation level, since $e^{-b_i t_i} \to 0$. Furthermore, if $p_i$ represents the profit margin per product unit for the type $i$ customer,

$$p_i s_i(1 - e^{-b_i t_i}) \tag{452}$$

is the expected return from allocating $t_i$ salesmen to type $i$ customers ($i = 1, 2$). We shall assume that the constants $p_i$, $s_i$, and $b_i$ have the values indicated in Table 5.

The profit equation for this marketing model is the difference between the total return from sales and the cost of maintaining field salesmen:

(453)

$$P(\mathbf{t}) = (3.6 \times 10^5)(1 - e^{-0.2t_1}) + (2 \times 10^5)(1 - e^{-0.1t_2}) - 10^4(t_1 + t_2).$$

The problem of deciding upon a distribution of salesmen, $t_1$ and $t_2$, that maximizes profits (453) while satisfying budgetary constraints (451) poses the optimization problem:

$$\begin{aligned} &\text{maximize} && P(\mathbf{t}) = (3.6 \times 10^5)(1 - e^{-0.2t_1}) \\ & && \quad + 2 \times 10^5(1 - e^{-0.1t_2}) - 10^4(t_1 + t_2) \\ &\text{subject to} && t_1 > 0, \qquad t_2 > 0 \\ & && \tfrac{1}{10}t_1 + \tfrac{1}{10}t_2 \le 1. \end{aligned} \tag{454}$$

Although this profit maximization problem is not a geometric programming problem, it may be approximated by a sequence of geometric programming problems. Assuming that the profit function $P(\mathbf{t})$ remains positive, it may be approximated by a posynomial in the neighborhood of a point. In particular, if $P(\mathbf{t})$ is approximated by the single-term posynomial $ct_1^{a_1}t_2^{a_2}$ ($c$, $a_1$, $a_2$ constants), the optimal solution $\bar{\mathbf{t}}$ of (454) is determined

**Table 5**

| $i$ | $b_i$ | $p_i$ | $s_i$ |
|---|---|---|---|
| 1 | 0.20 | 4 | 90,000 |
| 2 | 0.10 | 5 | 40,000 |

approximately by solving the following:

$$\begin{array}{ll} \text{maximize} & c t_1^{a_1} t_2^{a_2} \\ \text{subject to} & t_1 > 0, \qquad t_2 > 0 \\ & \tfrac{1}{10} t_1 + \tfrac{1}{10} t_2 \le 1. \end{array}$$

Equivalently, $\bar{\mathbf{t}}$ is determined approximately by solving the geometric program of degree of difficulty 0:

$$\begin{array}{ll} \text{minimize} & \dfrac{1}{c} t_1^{-a_1} t_2^{-a_2} \\ \text{subject to} & t_1 > 0, \qquad t_2 > 0 \\ & \tfrac{1}{10} t_1 + \tfrac{1}{10} t_2 \le 1. \end{array}$$

There are several procedures for approximating $P(\mathbf{t})$ by a single-term posynomial $u(\mathbf{t})$ and the following technique is typical. First, observe that the positive monomial

$$u(\mathbf{t}) = c t_1^{a_1} t_2^{a_2}$$

has the equivalent form

$$u(\mathbf{t}) = \frac{c(t_1')^{a_1}(t_2')^{a_2}(t_1)^{a_1}(t_2)^{a_2}}{(t_1')^{a_1}(t_2')^{a_2}}$$

for $t_1' > 0, t_2' > 0$. Note that the latter expression is equivalent to

(455) $$u(\mathbf{t}) = u(\mathbf{t}')\left(\frac{t_1}{t_1'}\right)^{a_1}\left(\frac{t_2}{t_2'}\right)^{a_2}.$$

Once appropriate values of the exponents $a_1$ and $a_2$ are determined this form of the monomial $u(\mathbf{t})$ may be used to approximate $P(\mathbf{t})$ near $\mathbf{t}' = (t_1', t_2')$.

Values for the exponents are calculated by applying a particularly clever technique. First, observe that

$$\frac{\partial u}{\partial t_1} = a_1 u(\mathbf{t}') \frac{t_1^{a_1 - 1}}{(t_1')^{a_1}}\left(\frac{t_2}{t_2'}\right)^{a_2}.$$

Thus,

(456) $$t_1 \frac{\partial u}{\partial t_1} = a_1 u(\mathbf{t}')\left(\frac{t_1}{t_1'}\right)^{a_1}\left(\frac{t_2}{t_2'}\right)^{a_2}$$

for $t_1 > 0$. If this expression is evaluated at $\mathbf{t} = \mathbf{t}'$, the quotients on the right side of (456) cancel, yielding

$$t_1' \frac{\partial u}{\partial t_1}(\mathbf{t}') = a_1 u(\mathbf{t}').$$

This equation implies that the first exponent is

(457) $$a_1 = \frac{t'_1}{u(\mathbf{t}')}\frac{\partial u}{\partial t_1}(\mathbf{t}').$$

A similar process shows that the second exponent is

(458) $$a_2 = \frac{t'_2}{u(\mathbf{t}')}\frac{\partial u}{\partial t_2}(\mathbf{t}').$$

Expressions (455)–(458) are used to approximate $P(\mathbf{t})$ near an operating point $\mathbf{t}'$; that is,

$$P(\mathbf{t}) = P(\mathbf{t}')\left(\frac{t_1}{t'_1}\right)^{a_1}\left(\frac{t_2}{t'_2}\right)^{a_2}$$

where $a_1$ and $a_2$ are given by (457) and (458), respectively. Here, with $\mathbf{t}' = (t'_1, t'_2) = (3, 3)$, for example, the exponents are

(459) $$a_1 = \frac{t'_1[(7.2 \times 10^4)e^{-0.2t'_1} - 10^4]}{P(\mathbf{t}')} = 0.574$$

and

(460) $$a_2 = \frac{t'_2[(2 \times 10^4)e^{-0.1t'_2} - 10^4]}{P(\mathbf{t}')} = 0.094$$

Thus, with $P(\mathbf{t})$ approximated by a positive monomial, the optimal values of $t_1$ and $t_2$ in the profit maximization problem (454) are determined approximately by solving the geometric programming problem:

(461)

$$\text{minimize} \quad \left(\frac{1}{P(\mathbf{t}')}\right)\left(\frac{t_1}{t'_1}\right)^{-a_1}\left(\frac{t_2}{t'_2}\right)^{-a_2} = \frac{1}{154264.1}\left(\frac{t_1}{3}\right)^{-0.574}\left(\frac{t_2}{3}\right)^{-0.094}$$

$$\text{subject to} \quad t_1 > 0, \qquad t_2 > 0$$

$$\tfrac{1}{10}t_1 + \tfrac{1}{10}t_2 \leq 1.$$

Although this problem is not solved here because of the numerous computations, the duality theory of geometric programming may be applied to determine $\mathbf{t}^*$, the minimizing point of (461). The approximate number of salesmen that should serve direct and wholesale customers so as to maximize profits is derived by rounding the values of $t_1^*$ and $t_2^*$ to the nearest integer value. Obviously, we cannot distribute fractions of a salesman. The maximum profit of our sales decision model is calculated by inverting the minimum value of geometric programming problem (461).

Obviously these approximations of $t_1$ and $t_2$ are improved by refining the posynomial approximation. Thus, for instance, by estimating values

$t'_1$ and $t'_2$ that seem "near" the minimizing point $\bar{\mathbf{t}}$ of (454), the optimizing point of (461) will be a better approximation of $\bar{\mathbf{t}}$.

The method for improving the approximations of $P(\mathbf{t})$ near the optimum suggests an algorithm for obtaining improved estimates of $\bar{\mathbf{t}}$. Having solved problem (461) using the operating point $(t'_1, t'_2)$, we may use the duality theory to determine the optimal point $(t''_1, t''_2)$ of (461). Problem (461) is now resolved with the operating point $(t''_1, t''_2)$. The duality relationships yield a new, and hopefully better, approximation of the optimum point $\bar{\mathbf{t}}$. Geometric program (461) is resolved using this approximation of $\bar{\mathbf{t}}$ as the operating point. The successive solutions may provide better approximations of $\bar{\mathbf{t}}$.

The differentiable function $f(t_1, \ldots, t_m)$ may be approximated by a monomial near a point $\mathbf{t}' = (t'_1, \ldots, t'_m)$ in a similar manner (see Figure 125). First, observe that if $u(\mathbf{t})$ is a monomial,

$$u(\mathbf{t}) = c_1 t_1^{a_1} t_2^{a_2} \cdots t_m^{a_m}$$

and if $t'_1 > 0, \ldots, t'_m > 0$, then

$$u(\mathbf{t}) = \frac{c_1 (t'_1)^{a_1} \cdots (t'_m)^{a_m} t_1^{a_1} t_2^{a_2} \cdots t_m^{a_m}}{(t'_1)^{a_1} \cdots (t'_m)^{a_m}}. \tag{462}$$

The latter expression implies

$$u(\mathbf{t}) = u(\mathbf{t}') \left(\frac{t_1}{t'_1}\right)^{a_1} \cdots \left(\frac{t_m}{t'_m}\right)^{a_m}. \tag{463}$$

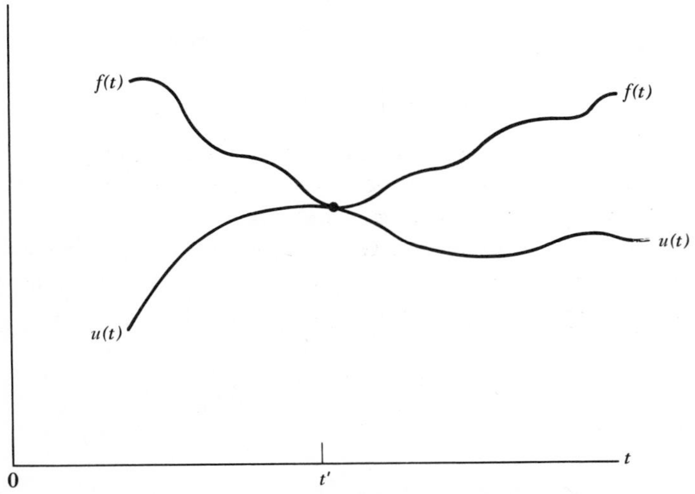


**Figure 125**

This form of the monomial $u(\mathbf{t})$ may be used to approximate $f(t_1, \ldots, t_m)$ for points $\mathbf{t}$ near $\mathbf{t}' = (t_1', \ldots, t_m')$ once the values of the exponents $a_1, \ldots, a_m$ have been calculated.

In determining $a_1, \ldots, a_m$ note that

$$\frac{\partial u}{\partial t_j} = a_j u(\mathbf{t}')\left(\frac{t_1}{t_1'}\right)^{a_1} \cdots \frac{(t_j)^{a_j - 1}}{(t_j')^{a_j}} \cdots \left(\frac{t_m}{t_m'}\right)^{a_m},$$

$j = 1, \ldots, m$. Therefore,

$$t_j \frac{\partial u}{\partial t_j} = a_j u(\mathbf{t}')\left(\frac{t_1}{t_1'}\right)^{a_1} \cdots \left(\frac{t_m}{t_m'}\right)^{a_m}$$

for any $t_j > 0$. If this expression is evaluated at $\mathbf{t}'$, the quotient terms of the right side cancel, yielding

$$t_j' \frac{\partial u}{\partial t_j}(\mathbf{t}') = a_j u(\mathbf{t}').$$

The values of the exponents are determined by solving for $a_j$,

(464) $$a_j = \frac{t_j'}{u(\mathbf{t}')} \frac{\partial u}{\partial t_j}(\mathbf{t}'), \qquad j = 1, \ldots, m.$$

The function $f(t_1, \ldots, t_m)$ may be approximated near $\mathbf{t}'$ by the monomial (463) with the exponents given by (464); that is,

$$f(\mathbf{t}) \sim f(\mathbf{t}')\left(\frac{t_1}{t_1'}\right)^{a_1} \cdots \left(\frac{t_m}{t_m'}\right)^{a_m},$$

where

$$a_j = \frac{t_j'}{f(\mathbf{t}')} \frac{\partial f}{\partial t_j}(\mathbf{t}'), \qquad j = 1, \ldots, m,$$

and $\mathbf{t} = (t_1, \ldots, t_m)$ is near $\mathbf{t}'$. This approximation is such that $f(\mathbf{t})$ and this approximating monomial have the same value and the same first partial derivatives at $\mathbf{t}'$. If $f$ is a positive function, this approximation is a posynomial.

This approximation technique is equivalent to approximating the function $\ln f(\mathbf{t})$ by the linear terms of a Taylor's series expansion in the variables $z_i = \ln(t_i/t_i')$ about $\mathbf{z}' = \mathbf{0}$; that is, since

$$\ln f(\mathbf{t}) \sim \ln\left[f(\mathbf{t}')\left(\frac{t_1}{t_1'}\right)^{a_1} \cdots \left(\frac{t_m}{t_m'}\right)^{a_m}\right]$$

or, equivalently,

$$\ln f(\mathbf{t}) \sim \ln f(\mathbf{t}') + a_1 \ln\left(\frac{t_1}{t_1'}\right) + \cdots + a_m \ln\left(\frac{t_m}{t_m'}\right),$$

this approximation is equivalent to

$$\ln f(\mathbf{t}) \sim \ln f(\mathbf{t}') + a_1 z_1 + a_2 z_2 + \cdots + a_m z_m,$$

where $z_j = \ln(t_j/t'_j)$, $j = 1, \ldots, m$. This is the truncated Taylor expansion of $f(\mathbf{t})$.

Before developing additional approximation methods, consider a second example of this posynomial approximation technique. The function

$$f(\mathbf{t}) = t_1 + \ln t_2^{-1}$$

may be approximated in a neighborhood of the point $\mathbf{t}' = (2, e)$ by a posynomial; that is, for $\mathbf{t}$ near $\mathbf{t}'$,

$$f(\mathbf{t}) \sim f(\mathbf{t}')\left(\frac{t_1}{t'_1}\right)^{a_1}\left(\frac{t_2}{t'_2}\right)^{a_2},$$

where $a_j = [t'_j/f(\mathbf{t}')](\partial f/\partial t_j)(\mathbf{t}')$, $j = 1, 2$. Since $t'_1 = 2$, $t'_2 = e$, $f(\mathbf{t}') = 1$, $a_1 = 2$, $a_2 = -1$,

$$f(\mathbf{t}) \sim \left(\frac{t_1}{2}\right)^2\left(\frac{t_2}{e}\right)^{-1} = \frac{e}{4}\, t_1^2 t_2^{-1} = u(\mathbf{t})$$

for $\mathbf{t}$ near $(2, e)$. The relative error of this approximation for points $\mathbf{t}$ near $\mathbf{t}'$ is given by $[f(\mathbf{t}) - u(\mathbf{t})]/f(\mathbf{t})$. Specific values of the relative error are listed in Table 6; note the increase in the relative error as the distance between $(t_1, t_2)$ and $(2, e)$ increases.

A second approximation method of geometric programming approximates a function as the *limit* of posynomials. Unlike the preceding posynomial approximation technique, this approximation may be made as accurate as desired (see Figure 126).

The function

$$f(\mathbf{t}) = \ln t_1^{1/2} t_2^{1/2},$$

for example, may be approximated as the limit of posynomials. First, observe that

$$\ln u = \int_1^u \frac{1}{x}\, dx,$$

where $u = t_1^{1/2} t_2^{1/2}$. Since $x^\epsilon$ is a uniform approximation to 1 on any interval for $x \geq 1$ and sufficiently small $\epsilon$ $(>0)$, $\ln u$ may be approximated by

$$\int_1^u \frac{x^\epsilon}{x}\, dx = \frac{u^\epsilon}{\epsilon} - \frac{1}{\epsilon}.$$

This approximation, the sum of the posynomial $u^\epsilon/\epsilon = (1/\epsilon) t_1^{\epsilon/2} t_2^{\epsilon/2}$ and a constant $-1/\epsilon$ is a uniform approximation on the given interval. The

Table 6

| $t_1$ | $t_2$ | Relative Error |
|---|---|---|
| 2.55999 | 3.27828 | 0.01031220 |
| 2.54000 | 3.25828 | 0.00972200 |
| 2.45999 | 3.17828 | 0.00746090 |
| 2.33999 | 3.05828 | 0.00444550 |
| 2.21999 | 2.93828 | 0.00203814 |
| 2.16000 | 2.87828 | 0.00113254 |
| 2.13999 | 2.85828 | 0.00087948 |
| 2.05999 | 2.77828 | 0.00017269 |
| 2.04000 | 2.75828 | 0.00007905 |
| 2.02000 | 2.73828 | 0.00002072 |
| 2.00000 | 2.71828 | 0.00000000 |
| 1.98000 | 2.69828 | 0.00002058 |
| 1.96000 | 2.67828 | 0.00008327 |
| 1.94000 | 2.65828 | 0.00019039 |
| 1.86000 | 2.57828 | 0.00110985 |
| 1.83999 | 2.55828 | 0.00147538 |
| 1.78000 | 2.49828 | 0.00294349 |
| 1.66000 | 2.37828 | 0.00785819 |
| 1.54000 | 2.25828 | 0.01616418 |
| 1.48000 | 2.19828 | 0.02194113 |
| 1.46000 | 2.17828 | 0.02414934 |

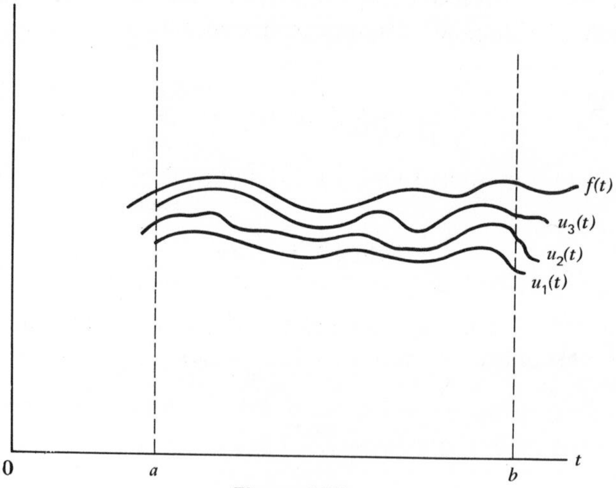


Figure 126

Table 7

| $t_1$ | $t_2$ | $\epsilon$ | Relative Error |
|---|---|---|---|
| 1.84999 | 1.84999 | 0.0001 | 0.0078569 |
| | | 0.0002 | 0.0001063 |
| | | 0.0003 | 0.0026891 |
| | | 0.0004 | 0.0001056 |
| 1.95000 | 1.95000 | 0.0001 | 0.0003848 |
| | | 0.0002 | 0.0003852 |
| | | 0.0003 | 0.0003843 |
| | | 0.0004 | 0.0003846 |
| 2.05000 | 2.05000 | 0.0001 | 0.0035996 |
| | | 0.0002 | 0.0036000 |
| | | 0.0003 | 0.0035992 |
| | | 0.0004 | 0.0027808 |
| 2.15000 | 2.15000 | 0.0001 | 0.0033025 |
| | | 0.0002 | 0.0033029 |
| | | 0.0003 | 0.0033021 |
| | | 0.0004 | 0.0018766 |
| 2.25000 | 2.25000 | 0.0001 | 0.0003785 |
| | | 0.0002 | 0.0003789 |
| | | 0.0003 | 0.0003780 |
| | | 0.0004 | 0.0003782 |

relative error of this approximation,

$$\frac{f(\mathbf{t}) - [(u^{\epsilon}/\epsilon) - (1/\epsilon)]}{f(\mathbf{t})}$$

is displayed in Table 7 for various values of $t_1$, $t_2$, and $\epsilon$.

With $\ln t_1^{1/2} t_2^{1/2}$ approximated by a sequence of posynomials, $(u^{\epsilon}/\epsilon) - (1/\epsilon)$, the optimization problem

(465) $$\text{minimize} \quad g(\mathbf{t}) = t_1^{-1} + t_2^{-1} + \ln t_1^{1/2} t_2^{1/2}$$
$$t_1 > 0, \qquad t_2 > 0,$$

for instance, may be transformed into a sequence of approximating geometric programming problems; that is, for $\epsilon$ ($>0$) sufficiently small, $g(\mathbf{t})$ may be approximated by the function

$$g_0(\mathbf{t}) = t_1^{-1} + t_2^{-1} + \frac{1}{\epsilon} t_1^{\epsilon/2} t_2^{\epsilon/2} - \frac{1}{\epsilon}.$$

The associated geometric programming problem is the following:

$$\text{(466)} \qquad \text{minimize} \quad t_1^{-1} + t_2^{-1} + \frac{1}{\epsilon} t_1^{\epsilon/2} t_2^{\epsilon/2}$$
$$t_1 > 0, \qquad t_2 > 0.$$

By adding $-1/\epsilon$ to the value of problem (466) an approximation of (465) is obtained.

Problem (466) is a geometric program of degree of difficulty 0. The dual problem has the unique solution

$$\delta_1 = \frac{\epsilon}{2(1+\epsilon)}, \qquad \delta_2 = \frac{\epsilon}{2(1+\epsilon)}, \qquad \delta_3 = \frac{1}{1+\epsilon}$$

and the value of (466) is

$$v' = \left(\frac{2(1+\epsilon)}{\epsilon}\right)^{\epsilon/(1+\epsilon)} \left(\frac{1+\epsilon}{\epsilon}\right)^{1/(1+\epsilon)} = 2^{\epsilon/(1+\epsilon)} \left(\frac{1+\epsilon}{\epsilon}\right).$$

From the duality theory of geometric programming, we see that the optimal point $\mathbf{t}^*$ of (466) satisfies

$$t_1^{*\,-1} = \delta_1 v' = \tfrac{1}{2} 2^{\epsilon/(1+\epsilon)} = 2^{-1/(1+\epsilon)},$$
$$t_2^{*\,-1} = \delta_2 v' = \tfrac{1}{2} 2^{\epsilon/(1+\epsilon)} = 2^{-1/(1+\epsilon)}.$$

These relations show that as $\epsilon \to 0$, $t_1^{*\,-1} \to \frac{1}{2}$, $t_2^{*\,-1} \to \frac{1}{2}$, or $(t_1^*, t_2^*) \to (2, 2)$, the minimizing point of (465). Furthermore, the minimum value of $g_0(\mathbf{t})$,

$$v' - \frac{1}{\epsilon} = 2^{\epsilon/(1+\epsilon)} \left(\frac{1}{\epsilon} + 1\right) - \frac{1}{\epsilon}$$
$$= \frac{1}{\epsilon} (2^{\epsilon/(1+\epsilon)} - 1) + 2^{\epsilon/(1+\epsilon)},$$

tends to $1 + \ln 2 = 1.6931$, the minimum value of $g(\mathbf{t})$, as $\epsilon \to 0$.

Thus, by decreasing $\epsilon$ ($>0$) the approximations of the minimum value of $g(\mathbf{t})$ improve. The minimum value and minimizing points of $g_0(\mathbf{t})$ are given in Table 8 for various values of $\epsilon$ ($>0$).

The technique for determining approximate solutions of

$$\text{minimize} \qquad f(\mathbf{t}) + \ln u(\mathbf{t})$$

where $f(\mathbf{t})$ is a posynomial, $u(\mathbf{t})$ is a single-term posynomial, and $\mathbf{t} = (t_1, \ldots, t_m)$, $t_1 > 0, \ldots, t_m > 0$, is similar. By using the approximation

$$\frac{u^\epsilon}{\epsilon} - \frac{1}{\epsilon}$$

**Table 8**

| $\epsilon$ | $g_0(\mathbf{t}^*)$ | $t_1^*$ | $t_2^*$ | Relative Error |
|---|---|---|---|---|
| 0.0001 | 1.753906 | 1.999848 | 1.999848 | −0.035885 |
| 0.0002 | 1.710938 | 1.999716 | 1.999716 | −0.010507 |
| 0.0003 | 1.703613 | 1.999577 | 1.999577 | −0.006182 |
| 0.0004 | 1.699951 | 1.999439 | 1.999439 | −0.004019 |

for ln $u$ with $\epsilon$ ($>0$), sufficiently small, this optimization problem is approximated by

$$\text{minimize} \qquad f(\mathbf{t}) + \frac{u^{\epsilon}}{\epsilon} - \frac{1}{\epsilon}.$$

The techniques of geometric programming may be used to solve the associated problem

$$\text{minimize} \qquad f(\mathbf{t}) + \frac{u^{\epsilon}}{\epsilon}.$$

Observe that the degree of difficulty of this geometric program is independent of $\epsilon$.

As a second illustration of these limiting techniques, consider the problem of approximating

$$g(\mathbf{t}) = \exp\,(t_1^{-2}t_2).$$

In approximating exponential functions, the limiting relation

$$e^u = \lim_{p\to\infty}\left(1 + \frac{u}{p}\right)^p,$$

where $u$ is a single-term posynomial, may be used; that is, for large values of $p$, $\exp\,(t_1^{-2}t_2)$ may be approximated by

$$h(\mathbf{t}) = \left(1 + \frac{t_1^{-2}t_2}{p}\right)^p.$$

The relative error $[g(\mathbf{t}) - h(\mathbf{t})]/g(\mathbf{t})$ of this approximation for various values of $t_1$, $t_2$, and $p$ is shown in Table 9.

This limiting approximation is useful in applying geometric programming techniques to solve optimization problems such as the following:

$$\begin{aligned} &\text{minimize} && g(\mathbf{t}) = 2t_1t_2^{-1}t_3^{-1} + 2e^{t_1^{-2}t_2} \\ (467)\qquad &\text{subject to} && t_1 > 0, \qquad t_2 > 0 \\ &&& \tfrac{1}{2}t_2^{1/2}t_3 \le 1. \end{aligned}$$

**Table 9**

| $t_1$ | $t_2$ | $p$ | Relative Error |
|---|---|---|---|
| 1.25000 | 2.75000 | 1000.0 | 0.0020142 |
| | | 2000.0 | 0.0021940 |
| | | 3000.0 | 0.0009854 |
| 1.50000 | 2.50000 | 1000.0 | 0.0006966 |
| | | 2000.0 | 0.0013408 |
| | | 3000.0 | 0.0012385 |
| 1.75000 | 2.25000 | 1000.0 | 0.0006335 |
| | | 2000.0 | 0.0004990 |
| | | 3000.0 | 0.0023585 |
| 2.00000 | 2.00000 | 1000.0 | 0.0003991 |
| | | 2000.0 | 0.0003372 |
| | | 3000.0 | 0.0022206 |
| 2.25000 | 1.75000 | 1000.0 | 0.0005082 |
| | | 2000.0 | 0.0004785 |
| | | 3000.0 | 0.0023731 |
| 2.50000 | 1.50000 | 1000.0 | 0.0006564 |
| | | 2000.0 | 0.0015941 |
| | | 3000.0 | 0.0025416 |
| 2.75000 | 1.25000 | 1000.0 | 0.0003177 |
| | | 2000.0 | 0.0012635 |
| | | 3000.0 | 0.0022133 |

For sufficiently large $p$, the function $g(\mathbf{t})$ is approximated by

$$2t_1t_2^{-1}t_3^{-1} + 2\left(1 + \frac{t_1^{-2}t_2}{p}\right)^p.$$

By introducing a new variable $t_0 \geq 1 + (t_1^{-2}t_2)/p$, $g(\mathbf{t})$ is replaced by the posynomial

$$g_0(\mathbf{t}) = 2t_1t_2^{-1}t_3^{-1} + 2t_0^p$$

with the additional constraint

$$t_0^{-1} + \frac{t_0^{-1}t_1^{-2}t_2}{p} \leq 1.$$

Thus, minimization problem (467) is approximated by the following geometric programming problem:

(468)
$$\begin{aligned} \text{minimize} \quad & 2t_1t_2^{-1}t_3^{-1} + 2t_0^p \\ \text{subject to} \quad & t_0 > 0, \quad t_1 > 0, \quad t_2 > 0 \\ & t_0^{-1} + \frac{t_0^{-1}t_1^{-2}t_2}{p} \leq 1 \\ & \tfrac{1}{2}t_2^{1/2}t_3 \leq 1. \end{aligned}$$

The value of (468) is an approximation of the value of (467).

The technique for approximating the more general optimization problem

(469) $$\text{minimize} \quad g(\mathbf{t}) = f(\mathbf{t}) + ce^u,$$

where $u$ is a single-term posynomial is similar. Again, the limiting relationship

$$e^u = \lim_{p\to\infty}\left(1 + \frac{u}{p}\right)^p$$

is used to approximate $e^u$ by $[1 + (u/p)]^p$ for sufficiently large $p$. To approximate (469) by a geometric programming problem, we introduce a new variable

(470) $$t_0 \geq 1 + \frac{u}{p}.$$

The function $g(\mathbf{t})$ is replaced by $f(\mathbf{t}) + ct_0^p$ with the additional constraint (470). Thus, minimization problem (469) is approximated by the following geometric programming problem:

(471)
$$\begin{aligned} \text{minimize} \quad & f(\mathbf{t}) + ct_0^p \\ \text{subject to} \quad & t_0^{-1} + \frac{t_0^{-1}u}{p} \leq 1. \end{aligned}$$

Note that the degree of difficulty of (470) is independent of $p$.

## FORMULATING OPTIMIZATION PROBLEMS OF MANAGEMENT SCIENCE AS GEOMETRIC PROGRAMMING PROBLEMS

### Maximizing Reliability by Redundancy in Industrial Production*

The problem of maximizing the probability of the successful operation of a production process is common in industrial engineering. In such problems

* Adapted from A. Federowicz and M. Mazumdar, "Use of Geometric Programming to Maximize Reliability Achieved by Redundancy," *Operations Research*, **16** (1968), 948–954.

we consider a machine that has several essential parts operating in series; successful operation of the production process depends upon successful operation of each of these distinct, vital components. If one component fails, then the entire machine collapses.

Since successful performance of the machine depends upon the successful performance of each of the vital components, we must stock additional units of each component. These additional components are to be used in case of process failure, thus maximizing the likelihood of successful operation. Therefore, our problem is to determine how many redundant units of each of the vital components should be purchased so as to maximize the reliability of the production process and yet satisfy certain budgetary constraints.

Suppose that our production process uses a machine with, say, three essential parts operating in series. Furthermore, suppose that the probability of failure of the $j$th component is represented by a known constant $q_j$ $(0 \leq q_j \leq 1)$. If $q_j = 0$, there is no chance of component $j$ failure; and if

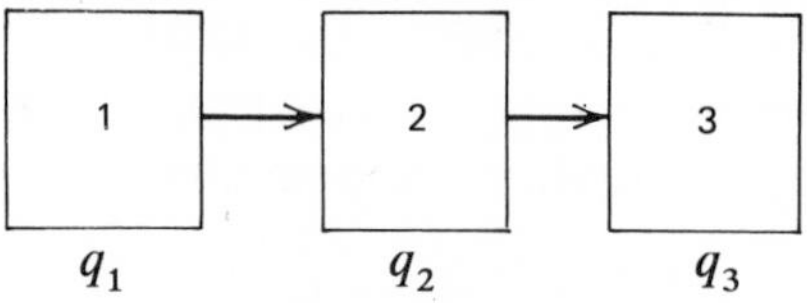


$q_j = 1$, there is no possibility that component $j$ will work properly. As $q_j$ takes values between 0 and 1, the likelihood of component $j$ failing varies. If $n_j$ units of component $j$ are available (including the one in the machine), then the possibility that all $n_j$ units of the $j$th component will fail is $q_j^{n_j}$. Correspondingly, with $n_j$ units of component $j$ available, the likelihood that component $j$ will not break is

$$1 - q_j^{n_j}.$$

As $n_j$ increases, and thus $q_j^{n_j}$ decreases, the likelihood that component $j$ will not break increases and vice versa. The operation of component $i$ is independent of the operation of component $j$ $(i \neq j)$.

Since the components work in series, the probability that component $i$ and component $j$ will work is

$$(1 - q_i^{n_i})(1 - q_j^{n_j}).$$

The probability of the production process being completely successful is

$$(472) \qquad (1 - q_1^{n_1})(1 - q_2^{n_2})(1 - q_3^{n_3}) = \prod_{j=1}^{3} (1 - q_j^{n_j}).$$

Obviously the probability of the production process being completely successful increases as more units of each of the three components are purchased. However, budgetary constraints limit the number of each of the three components that may be purchased and stored. In particular, suppose that at most $c_1$, $c_2$, and $c_3$ dollars may be allocated to the cost of purchasing, handling, and storing, respectively, these components. If $c_{1j}$, $c_{2j}$, and $c_{3j}$ denote the respective unit purchasing, handling, and storage costs associated with the $j$th component, then the following budgetary constraints must be satisfied:

$$\sum_{j=1}^{3} c_{ij} n_j \leq c_i, \qquad i = 1, 2, 3.$$

The problem of determining quantities $n_1$, $n_2$, $n_3$ that maximize the likelihood of successful operation of the production process may be expressed as a mathematical programming problem:

$$\begin{aligned} &\text{maximize} && \prod_{j=1}^{3} (1 - q_j^{n_j}) \\ (473) \qquad &\text{subject to} && n_1 > 0, \qquad n_2 > 0, \qquad n_3 > 0 \\ &&& \sum_{j=1}^{3} c_{ij} n_j \leq c_i, \qquad i = 1, 2, 3. \end{aligned}$$

By introducing several new variables, we obtain an equivalent geometric programming formulation of problem (473).

Specifically, we introduce new variables $x_j$ and $z_j$, $j = 1, 2, 3$, defined as

$$\begin{aligned} & x_j = e^{n_j}, \\ (474) \qquad & 1 - x_j^{\ln q_j} \geq z_j, \qquad j = 1, 2, 3. \end{aligned}$$

Note that with this change of variables, we have

$$\begin{aligned} (1 - q_j^{n_j}) &= [1 - \exp(\ln q_j^{n_j})] \\ &= [1 - \exp(n_j \ln q_j)] \\ &= (1 - x_j^{\ln q_j}) \geq z_j. \end{aligned}$$

Therefore, since $(1 - q_j^{n_j}) \geq z_j$,

$$\prod_{j=1}^{3} (1 - q_j^{n_j}) \geq \prod_{j=1}^{3} z_j.$$

Hence, maximizing (472) is equivalent to determining $z_j$ that maximize $\prod_{j=1}^{3} z_j$ or minimize $\prod_{j=1}^{3} z_j^{-1}$. Note that $\prod_{j=1}^{3} z_j^{-1}$ is a posynomial in the variables $z_j$, $j = 1, 2, 3$.

With these new variables the constraints of mathematical programming problem (473) become

$$\sum_{j=1}^{3} c_{ij} \ln x_j \le c_i, \qquad i = 1, 2, 3,$$

or, equivalently,

(475) $$\ln\left(\prod_{j=1}^{3} x_j^{c_{ij}}\right) \le c_i.$$

Since $a \le b$ implies $e^a \le e^b$, we see that (475) implies

$$\prod_{j=1}^{3} x_j^{c_{ij}} \le e^{c_i}$$

or

(476) $$e^{-c_i}\prod_{j=1}^{3} x_j^{c_{ij}} \le 1, \qquad i = 1, 2, 3.$$

Note that the constraint functions of (476) are posynomials.

Thus, by introducing several new variables, we see that optimization problem (473) may be transformed into an equivalent geometric programming problem:

$$\begin{aligned} &\text{minimize} && \prod_{j=1}^{3} z_j^{-1} \\ &\text{subject to} && x_j \ge 0, \quad z_j \ge 0, && j = 1, 2, 3 \\ &&& z_j + x_j^{\ln q_j} \le 1, && j = 1, 2, 3 \\ &&& e^{-c_i}\prod_{j=1}^{3} x_j^{c_{ij}} \le 1, && i = 1, 2, 3. \end{aligned}$$

### A Continuous Modular Design Problem*

The modular design problem of management science is the problem of assembling several combinations of a number of products in the most economic manner. For instance, suppose we wish to manufacture a variety of cosmetic kits, each consisting of an assortment of different cosmetics. The exact number of each cosmetic depends on the type of kit. In particular, suppose there are three different cosmetic kits and four types of cosmetics. The requirements of each kit are indicated in Table 10.

There are two options in producing these cosmetic kits: we can either supply each kit with precisely the required number of each cosmetic or we

* Adapted from U. Passy, "Modular Design: An Application of Structured Geometric Programming," *Operations Research*, **18** (1970), 441–453.

can supply a standard assortment of cosmetics and use one or more assortment per kit. In the first case, handling costs are high because three different assortments must be handled. In the second case, handling costs are reduced, but in some cases more than the required number of cosmetics will be supplied. Hence, a cost is incurred because of the waste or nonuse of some of the cosmetics in these standard assortments. For example, suppose the standard assortment consists of two units of each cosmetic. Since the second kit requires six units of cosmetic 4, three of the standard assortments are necessary to assemble this kit. But in this case, we incur a cost due to the waste of one unit of cosmetic 1, two units of cosmetic 2, and two units of cosmetic 3.

Thus, our modular design problem is to determine a standard assortment of each cosmetic that minimizes the waste and handling costs while meeting production requirements. Here we develop a geometric programming formulation of this problem.

Denote the entries of Table 10 by $r_{ij}$, the number of units of cosmetic $i$ required by kit $j$, where $i = 1, 2, 3, 4$ and $j = 1, 2, 3$. Suppose that the standard assortment consists of $s_i$ units of cosmetic $i$, where $i = 1, 2, 3, 4$, and that $m_j$ is the number of standard assortments supplied with kit $j$. Then the variables $s_i$ and $m_j$ must be chosen such that

$$s_i m_j \geq r_{ij}, \tag{477}$$

where $i = 1, 2, 3, 4$ and $j = 1, 2, 3$.

Let $c_i$ denote the cost of one unit of cosmetic $i$. Then the cost of $s_i$ units of cosmetic $i$ is $c_i s_i$ and the total cost of the four cosmetics in the assortment is

$$c_1 s_1 + c_2 s_2 + c_3 s_3 + c_4 s_4 .$$

Further, if a number $d_j$ of the $j$th kit are manufactured, then $d_j m_j$ is the number of standard assortments supplied in the $j$th kit. The total number

**Table 10**

| | Type of Kit | | |
|---|---|---|---|
| Type of Cosmetic | 1 | 2 | 3 |
| 1 | 4 | 5 | 1 |
| 2 | 6 | 4 | 5 |
| 3 | 5 | 4 | 4 |
| 4 | 2 | 6 | 2 |

of standard assortments is therefore

$$d_1m_1 + d_2m_2 + d_3m_3.$$

Note that $d_jm_j(c_1s_1 + \cdots + c_4s_4)$ is the cost of manufacturing $d_j$ units of the $j$th kit using $m_j$ units of the standard assortment. Therefore, the total cost of supplying cosmetic kits in standard assortments is proportional to

$$(d_1m_1 + d_2m_2 + d_3m_3)(c_1s_1 + c_2s_2 + c_3s_3 + c_4s_4). \tag{478}$$

Hence, our modular design problem is to determine the values $m_j$ ($j = 1, 2, 3$) and $s_i$ ($i = 1, 2, 3, 4$) that minimize the cost function (478) and yet satisfy constraints (477):

$$\begin{array}{lllll} \text{minimize} & (d_1m_1 + d_2m_2 + d_3m_3)(c_1s_1 + c_2s_2 + c_3s_3 + c_4s_4) & & \\ \text{subject to} & s_i > 0, & m_j > 0 & \\ & s_1m_1 \geq 4, & s_1m_2 \geq 5, & s_1m_3 \geq 1 \\ & s_2m_1 \geq 6, & s_2m_2 \geq 4, & s_2m_3 \geq 5 \\ & s_3m_1 \geq 5, & s_3m_2 \geq 4, & s_3m_3 \geq 4 \\ & s_4m_1 \geq 2, & s_4m_2 \geq 6, & s_4m_3 \geq 2. \end{array} \tag{479}$$

There are several techniques for transforming (479) into a prototype geometric programming problem. For example, if we perform the indicated multiplications in the objective function (478), the result is a posynomial consisting of 12 terms involving the products $s_im_j$, where $i = 1, 2, 3, 4$ and $j = 1, 2, 3$. The constraints

$$r_{ij} \leq s_im_j$$

are equivalent to the prototype constraints

$$r_{ij}s_i^{-1}m_j^{-1} \leq 1, \qquad i = 1, 2, 3, 4;\ j = 1, 2, 3, \tag{480}$$

since $s_i > 0$ and $m_j > 0$. The problem of minimizing this 12-term posynomial subject to constraints (480) is a geometric programming problem of degree of difficulty 17.

A second technique for transforming problem (479) into a geometric program is to introduce two new variables, $t_1$ ($>0$) and $t_2$ ($>0$), that satisfy

$$c_1s_1 + c_2s_2 + c_3s_3 + c_4s_4 \leq t_1,$$
$$d_1m_1 + d_2m_2 + d_3m_3 \leq t_2,$$

or, equivalently,

$$c_1s_1t_1^{-1} + c_2s_2t_1^{-1} + c_3s_3t_1^{-1} + c_4s_4t_1^{-1} \leq 1,$$
$$d_1m_1t_2^{-1} + d_2m_2t_2^{-1} + d_3m_3t_2^{-1} \leq 1.$$

These constraints, together with the prototype posynomial constraints (480), show that (479) may be transformed into an equivalent *geometric programming problem* of degree of difficulty 10:

$$
\begin{array}{ll}
\text{minimize} & t_1 t_2 \\
\text{subject to} & t_1 > 0, \quad t_2 > 0, \quad m_j > 0, \quad s_i > 0 \\
& c_1 s_1 t_1^{-1} + c_2 s_2 t_1^{-1} + c_3 s_3 t_1^{-1} + c_4 s_4 t_1^{-1} \le 1 \\
& d_1 m_1 t_2^{-1} + d_2 m_2 t_2^{-1} + d_3 m_3 t_2^{-1} \le 1 \\
& 4 s_1^{-1} m_1^{-1} \le 1, \quad 5 s_1^{-1} m_2^{-1} \le 1, \quad 1 s_1^{-1} m_3^{-1} \le 1 \\
& 6 s_2^{-1} m_1^{-1} \le 1, \quad 4 s_2^{-1} m_2^{-1} \le 1, \quad 5 s_2^{-1} m_3^{-1} \le 1 \\
& 5 s_3^{-1} m_1^{-1} \le 1, \quad 4 s_3^{-1} m_2^{-1} \le 1, \quad 4 s_3^{-1} m_3^{-1} \le 1 \\
& 2 s_4^{-1} m_1^{-1} \le 1, \quad 6 s_4^{-1} m_2^{-1} \le 1, \quad 2 s_4^{-1} m_3^{-1} \le 1.
\end{array}
$$

## EXERCISES

1. Determine the optimal value of each of the following optimization problems:

(*a*) minimize $t_1^2 + (t_2 + t_2^{-3})^{1/2} t_1^{-2} t_2$

$t_1 > 0, \quad t_2 > 0$

(*b*) minimize $2(t_1^2 + t_2^{-1})^{1/2} + 3 t_1^{-2} t_2^{1/2}$

$t_1 > 0, \quad t_2 > 0$

(*c*) minimize $41 t_1^{-1/2} t_2^{1/8} + 41(\frac{4}{5} t_1^{1/2} t_2^{2/3} + \frac{2}{5} t_1^{1/3} t_2)^{1/2} t_1^{1/4} t_2^{-1/2}$

$t_1 > 0, \quad t_2 > 0$

(*d*) maximize $8 t_1^{-4} t_2 t_3 - 9 t_2^2 t_3^2 - 10 t_2^3 t_3 - 12 t_1^{-5} t_2 t_3$

$t_1 > 0, \quad t_2 > 0, \quad t_3 > 0$

(*e*) maximize $(t_1 + t_1^{-1})^{-1/2} (t_2^2 + t_2^{-1})^{-1}$

$t_1 > 0, \quad t_2 > 0$

(*f*) maximize $-4 t_1^2 + 2 t_1 t_2 - 5 t_2^3$

$t_1 > 0, \quad t_2 > 0$

(*g*) minimize $4(25 t_1 t_3 + t_2^{-1} t_3^{-1})^{1/2} + \dfrac{1}{(t_1 - t_1^2 t_2)^2}$

$t_1 > 0, \quad t_2 > 0, \quad t_3 > 0$

(*h*) minimize $8 t_2 + (9 t_2^{-1} t_3 + 10 t_3^{-2})(t_1^{-1} + 2 t_1^2)^{1/2}$

$t_1 > 0, \quad t_2 > 0, \quad t_3 > 0$

(*i*) maximize $8(t_1^2 + t_2^{-1})^{-1/2}$

subject to $t_1 > 0, \quad t_2 > 0$

$9t_1^{-2}t_2^{1/2} \le 1$

(*j*) maximize $(t_1^{-1} + t_2^4)^{-17}$

subject to $t_1 > 0, \quad t_2 > 0$

$2t_1^2 t_2^{-1/2} \le 1$

(*k*) minimize $\frac{7}{16}t_1^{-1}t_2 + \frac{9}{16}t_1(t_2 - t_1^{-1}t_2^{-1})^{-1/2}$

$t_1 > 0, \quad t_2 > 0$

(*l*) minimize $3(t_1^2 + t_2^2)^{1/2} + \dfrac{1}{t_1^2 t_2}$

$t_1 > 0, \quad t_2 > 0$

(*m*) minimize $\frac{1}{2}(t_1 + t_1^{-1}t_2)^{3/2}(t_1^{-1} + t_2^{-1})$

$t_1 > 0, \quad t_2 > 0$

(*n*) maximize $t_1^{1/3}t_2 - t_1^{1/3}t_2^2 t_3^{-2} - t_1^{-2/3}t_2$

subject to $t_1 > 0, \quad t_2 > 0, \quad t_3 > 0$

$2t_1t_2t_3 \le 1$

(*o*) minimize $t_1^{-1}t_2^{-1/6} + 9t_1^2(t_2^8 + 7t_2^{-1})^{1/2}$

$t_1 > 0, \quad t_2 > 0$

(*p*) minimize $\dfrac{(t_1^{-2} + t_1^4 + t_1^4 t_2^3)^{1/2}}{6t_1t_2}$

$t_1 > 0, \quad t_2 > 0.$

2. Consider the problem

$$\text{minimize} \qquad f(\mathbf{t}) - u(\mathbf{t}),$$

where $\mathbf{t} = (t_1, \ldots, t_m)$; $t_j > 0$; $f(\mathbf{t})$ and $u(\mathbf{t})$ are posynomials; but $u(\mathbf{t})$ has only *one* term. Suppose also that this minimum value is known to be *negative*. Transform this minimization problem into an equivalent geometric programming problem.

3. Consider the problem

$$\text{minimize} \qquad f(\mathbf{t}) + \frac{g_1(\mathbf{t})}{[u_1(\mathbf{t}) - h_1(\mathbf{t})]^a} + \frac{g_2(\mathbf{t})}{[u_2(\mathbf{t}) - h_2(\mathbf{t})]^b},$$

where $f$, $g_1$, $g_2$, $h_1$, and $h_2$ are posynomials; $u_1$ and $u_2$ are one-term posynomials; $\mathbf{t} = (t_1, \ldots, t_m)$, $t_j > 0$; and $a > 0$, $b > 0$. Transform this minimization problem into an equivalent geometric programming problem.

4. A function $f(\mathbf{t}), \mathbf{t} \in \mathbb{R}^m, t_j > 0, j = 1, \ldots, m$, is called a *(posy) binomial** if it consists of the sum of two single-term posynomials; that is,

$$f(\mathbf{t}) = u_1(\mathbf{t}) + u_2(\mathbf{t}),$$

where

$$u_1(\mathbf{t}) = c_1 t_1^{a_{11}} t_2^{a_{12}} \cdots t_m^{a_{1m}}, \qquad c_1 > 0,$$

$$u_2(\mathbf{t}) = c_2 t_1^{a_{21}} t_2^{a_{22}} \cdots t_m^{a_{2m}}, \qquad c_2 > 0.$$

(*a*) Show that the unconstrained geometric programming problem

$$\text{minimize} \qquad g_0(\mathbf{t}) = u_1 + u_2 + u_3 + u_4,$$

where $u_i$ are single-term posynomials, may be transformed into an equivalent geometric programming problem of minimizing a (posy) binomial subject to (posy) binomial constraints.

(*b*) Repeat part *a* for the geometric programming problem

$$\text{minimize} \qquad g_0(\mathbf{t}) = u_1 + u_2 + u_3 + u_4 + u_5.$$

(*c*) Repeat part *a* for the following geometric programming problem:

$$\begin{aligned} &\text{minimize} && g_0(\mathbf{t}) = u_1 + u_2 + u_3 \\ &\text{subject to} && u_4 + u_5 + u_6 \le 1. \end{aligned}$$

5. Consider the problem

$$\begin{aligned} &\text{minimize} && 9(t_1 + t_2^{-1})^{3/4} + 8(t_1^2 - t_2^2)^{-2} \\ & && t_1 > 0, \qquad t_2 > 0 \end{aligned}$$

where $t_1 > t_2$.

(*a*) Transform this problem into an equivalent geometric programming problem.

(*b*) What is the degree of difficulty of the geometric programming problem in part *a*?

6. Consider the following problem:

$$\begin{aligned} &\text{minimize} && t_3^{17} \\ &\text{subject to} && t_1 > 0, \qquad t_2 > 0, \qquad t_3 > 0 \\ & && t_1^{-1} t_3^{-1} + t_2^4 t_3^{-1} \le 1 \\ & && t_1^{-2} t_2^{1/2} \ge 1. \end{aligned}$$

(*a*) Transform this problem into an equivalent prototype geometric programming problem.

(*b*) Find the constrained minimum value of this problem.

* From R. J. Duffin and E. L. Peterson, "The Proximity of (Algebraic) Geometric Programming to Linear Programming," Research Report 72-13, Department of Mathematics, Carnegie Mellon University, May 1972.

7. Transform the following problems into equivalent linear programming problems:

(*a*) minimize $t_1^2 t_2^{-1/2} t_3^{1/3}$

subject to $t_1 > 0, \quad t_2 > 0, \quad t_3 > 0$

$$9t_2^6 t_3^{-1} \le 1$$

$$\tfrac{1}{4}t_3 \le 1$$

$$8t_1^{-1} t_2^{-3/4} t_3^{-2} \le 1.$$

(*b*) maximize $\tfrac{1}{2}t_1^{-1} t_2^{2/3} t_3^3$

subject to $t_1 > 0, \quad t_2 > 0, \quad t_3 > 0$

$$\tfrac{1}{2}t_1^{-1} t_2 \le 1$$

$$\tfrac{1}{2}t_1^{-1} t_2^{-1/9} t_3 \le 1$$

$$2t_1^{-1} \ge 1.$$

8. Show that the dual geometric programming problem of program 7*a* above is equivalent to the unsymmetrical dual linear programming problem of the primal linear programming equivalent.

9. [Duffin, p. 122] Suppose $A$, $B$, $C$ are positive constants. Prove that

$$A - B - C \le \left(\frac{A}{p}\right)^p \left(\frac{q}{B}\right)^q \left(\frac{r}{C}\right)^r$$

for each set of positive numbers $p$, $q$, and $r$ satisfying the condition

$$p - q - r = 1.$$

*Hint*. Choose weights $\delta_1$, $\delta_2$, $\delta_3$, positive and summing to 1 in the inequality

$$T_1 + T_2 + T_3 \ge \left(\frac{T_1}{\delta_1}\right)^{\delta_1} \left(\frac{T_2}{\delta_2}\right)^{\delta_2} \left(\frac{T_3}{\delta_3}\right)^{\delta_3},$$

where $T_1 = (A/p)^p(q/B)^q(r/C)^r$, $T_2 = B$, $T_3 = C$.

10. Estimate the minimum value of the function

$$2t_1 t_3^{-1} + \frac{8t_1^{-1} + t_1}{(t_2^{-1} - 2t_2^{-3} t_3 - t_2^{-1} t_3^{-1})},$$

where $t_1 > 0$, $t_2 > 0$, $t_3 > 0$.

11. Determine the values of the following optimization problems:

(*a*) maximize $6t_1 t_2$

subject to $t_1 > 0, \quad t_2 > 0$

$$\frac{t_2}{t_1 t_2 + t_2^2} \ge 1$$

(*b*) minimize $t_1^{-2}t_2^{-2}$

subject to $t_1 > 0, \quad t_2 > 0$

$$t_1^{-1} - t_1^{-1}t_2 \geq 1$$

(*c*) minimize $6t_1 + 7t_2^{-1}t_3$

subject to $t_1 > 0, \quad t_2 > 0, \quad t_3 > 0$

$$1 + 2t_1t_2t_3 \leq 2t_1t_3$$

(*d*) maximize $8t_1^{-1}t_2t_3^{-2}$

subject to $t_1 > 0, \quad t_2 > 0, \quad t_3 > 0$

$$t_1^{-3}t_2^{-1}t_3 \geq 1$$

$$\frac{1}{t_2^{-1} - t_2^{-1/2}} \leq t_1^2$$

(*e*) minimize $5t_1^{-1}t_2^{-1}t_3^{-1} + t_3$

subject to $t_1 > 0, \quad t_2 > 0, \quad t_3 > 0$

$$1 + t_1^{-2}t_2 \leq t_1^{-2} - t_1^{-2}t_3^3.$$

12. Use the basic ideas of the condensation procedure to suggest an algorithm for approximating the value of the following:

$$\begin{aligned} &\text{minimize} && u_1 + u_2 + u_3 \\ &\text{subject to} && u_4 + u_5 \geq 1, \end{aligned}$$

where $u_1, u_2, u_3, u_4, u_5$ are single-term posynomials.

13. Consider the following optimization problem:

$$\begin{aligned} &\text{minimize} && u_1 + u_2 \\ &\text{subject to} && u_3 - u_4 \leq 1, \end{aligned}$$

where $u_1, u_2, u_3, u_4$ are single-term posynomials.

(*a*) Use the basic ideas of the condensation procedure to suggest an algorithm for approximating the value of this program by solving a sequence of geometric programming problems.

(*b*) Show that by introducing a new variable $t_0$ that satisfies

$$u_3 \leq t_0 \leq 1 + u_4,$$

this program is transformed into the following form:

$$\begin{aligned} &\text{minimize} && u_1 + u_2 \\ &\text{subject to} && t_0^{-1}u_3 \leq 1 \\ & && t_0^{-1} + t_0^{-1}u_4 \geq 1. \end{aligned}$$

(*c*) Is the algorithm of problem 12 applicable to this problem?

14. (*a*) Show that by introducing new variables

$$s \geq t_1 + 0.95t_2$$

and

$$t^{-1} \geq \frac{488}{t_1} + \frac{500}{t_2},$$

the inventory system cost minimization problem is transformed into the equivalent geometric programming problem:

$$\begin{array}{ll} \text{minimize} & s + t^{-1} \\ \text{subject to} & t_1 > 0, \quad t_2 > 0, \quad s > 0, \quad t > 0 \\ & \frac{1}{30}t_1 + \frac{1}{30}t_2 \leq 1 \\ & s^{-1}t_1 + 0.95s^{-1}t_2 \leq 1 \\ & 488tt_1^{-1} + 500tt_2^{-1} \leq 1. \end{array}$$

(*b*) Use the condensation procedure to approximate this geometric programming problem by a sequence of geometric programming problems of degree of difficulty 0.

15. Apply the condensation procedure to obtain estimates of the values of the following geometric programming problems:

(*a*)
$$\begin{array}{ll} \text{minimize} & 40t_1^{-1}t_2^{-1/2}t_3^{-1} + 20t_1t_3 + 20t_1t_2t_3 \\ \text{subject to} & t_1 > 0, \quad t_2 > 0, \quad t_3 > 0 \\ & \frac{4}{3}t_2^{1/2}t_3^{-1} + \frac{1}{3}t_1^{-2}t_2^{-2} \leq 1. \end{array}$$

(*b*)
$$\begin{array}{ll} \text{minimize} & 1000t_1 + (4 \times 10^9)t_1^{-1}t_2^{-1} + 9000t_1t_2 + (2.5 \times 10^5)t_2 \\ & t_1 > 0, \quad t_2 > 0. \end{array}$$

(*c*)
$$\begin{array}{ll} \text{minimize} & t_1^{1/2} + t_2^{-2} \\ \text{subject to} & t_1 > 0, \quad t_2 > 0, \quad t_3 > 0, \quad t_4 > 0 \\ & t_1^{-1}t_3 + t_1^{-1}t_4^{-1} \leq 1 \\ & t_2t_3^{-1} + t_2^{-1}t_4 \leq 1. \end{array}$$

16. (*a*) Use the ideas of problem 13 to transform the optimization problem

$$\begin{array}{ll} \text{minimize} & 40t_1^{-1}t_2^{-1}t_3^{-1} + 40t_2t_3 \\ \text{subject to} & t_1 > 0, \quad t_2 > 0, \quad t_3 > 0 \\ & \frac{1}{2}t_1t_3 + \frac{1}{4}t_1t_2 - \frac{1}{16}t_2t_3 \leq 1 \end{array}$$

into the problem

$$\begin{array}{ll} \text{minimize} & 40t_1^{-1}t_2^{-1}t_3^{-1} + 40t_2t_3 \\ \text{subject to} & t_1 > 0, \quad t_2 > 0, \quad t_3 > 0 \\ & \tfrac{1}{2}t_1t_3t_0^{-1} + \tfrac{1}{4}t_1t_2t_0^{-1} \leq 1 \\ & t_0^{-1} + \tfrac{1}{16}t_2t_3t_0^{-1} \geq 1. \end{array}$$

(*b*) Use the ideas of problem 12 to approximate the minimum value of the latter optimization problem.

17. Indicate how the condensation procedure might be applied to the following optimization problems:

(*a*) minimize $10t_1 + 6t_1^{-1}t_2^{-1} + 7t_2$
subject to $t_1 > 0, \quad t_2 > 0$
$t_1t_2 \geq 9$

(*b*) minimize $(t_1 + t_2^{-1})^{1/2} + (t_1 - t_2)^{-2}$
$t_1 > t_2 > 0$

(*c*) minimize $2t_1 + 5t_2 + 2t_3 + t_4$
subject to $t_1 > 0, \quad t_2 > 0, \quad t_3 > 0, \quad t_4 > 0$
$100t_1^{-1}t_2^{-1}t_3^{-1} \leq 1$
$t_1^{-2}t_4^{-2} + t_2^{-2}t_4^{-2} \leq 1.$

18. Approximate each of the following functions at the indicated point $\mathbf{t}'$ with a monomial:

(*a*) $e^t$, $\quad t' = 1$

(*b*) $\sin t$, $\quad t' = \dfrac{\pi}{4}$

(c) $t^2$, $\quad t' = 2$

(*d*) $e^{-t_1+t_2} + e^{t_2-1}$, $\quad \mathbf{t}' = (1, 1)$

(e) $t_1^{-1}t_2^3$, $\quad \mathbf{t}' = (1, 1)$

(*f*) $1 - \sin t$, $\quad t' = \dfrac{\pi}{4}$

(*g*) $\frac{1}{3}t_1 + \frac{1}{2}t_2$, $\quad \mathbf{t}' = (1, 1).$

19. [Duffin, p. 108] Approximate the function

$$h(\mathbf{t}) = t_1(e^{t_2-1} + t_1^2)^{1/2}$$

by fitting it with a single-term posynomial $u(\mathbf{t})$ at the operating point

$\mathbf{t}' = (1, 1)$. Compute the relative error

$$\frac{h(\mathbf{t}) - u(\mathbf{t})}{h(\mathbf{t})}$$

at the points $(1, \frac{1}{2})$, $(\frac{3}{2}, 1)$, $(1, \frac{3}{2})$, and $(\frac{1}{2}, 1)$.

20. Use a limiting technique to develop a class of approximating prototype geometric programming problem for each of the following optimization problems:

(*a*) minimize $\quad t_1^2 t_2^{-1} + 6e^{t_1^3 t_2^2}$

$\qquad t_1 > 0, \quad t_2 > 0$

(*b*) minimize $\quad \ln t$

subject to $\quad t > 0$

$\qquad t^{-1} \le 1$

(*c*) minimize $\quad 8t_1 t_2^{-1} + t_1^2 + \ln (t_1^{-3} t_2)$

$\qquad t_1 > 0, \quad t_2 > 0$

(*d*) minimize $\quad t^2 + \dfrac{3}{\ln t}$

subject to $\quad t > 0$

$\qquad t^{-1} \le 1.$

21. (*a*) Use a limiting technique to derive a posynomial approximation $u(\mathbf{t})$ for the function

$$f(\mathbf{t}) = \ln (6t_1^2 t_2^{\pi}).$$

(*b*) Show that the relative error

$$\frac{f(\mathbf{t}) - u(\mathbf{t})}{f(\mathbf{t})}$$

is as given on page 373 for the indicated points $(t_1, t_2)$ and the given values of $e$.

22. Suppose the function $f(\mathbf{t})$ is approximated by the single-term posynomial

$$f(\mathbf{t}')\left(\frac{t_1}{t'_1}\right)^{a_1} \cdots \left(\frac{t_m}{t'_m}\right)^{a_m}$$

where

$$a_j = \frac{t'_j}{f(\mathbf{t}')} \frac{\partial f}{\partial t_j}(\mathbf{t}'), \qquad j = 1, \ldots, m,$$

| $t_1$ | $t_2$ | $\epsilon$ | Relative Error |
|---|---|---|---|
| 2.5 | 1.75 | $0.79999 \times 10^{-5}$ | $0.1379193 \times 10^{-2}$ |
| 2.0 | 1.5 | $0.14000 \times 10^{-4}$ | $0.3225073 \times 10^{-2}$ |
| 2.0 | 1.5 | $0.15999 \times 10^{-4}$ | $0.9367172 \times 10^{-2}$ |
| 2.0 | 1.5 | $0.17999 \times 10^{-4}$ | $-0.2846974 \times 10^{-3}$ |
| 3.5 | 2.25 | $0.19999 \times 10^{-4}$ | $0.3591276 \times 10^{-2}$ |
| 3.5 | 2.25 | $0.23999 \times 10^{-4}$ | $0.1350855 \times 10^{-2}$ |
| 3.5 | 2.25 | $0.21999 \times 10^{-4}$ | $0.5873997 \times 10^{-2}$ |
| 3.0 | 2.0 | $0.20000 \times 10^{-5}$ | $0.6755245 \times 10^{-1}$ |
| 2.0 | 1.5 | $0.59999 \times 10^{-5}$ | $-0.1081401 \times 10^{-1}$ |

for points $\mathbf{t}$ near $\mathbf{t}' = (t'_1, \ldots, t'_m)$. Show that this approximation is such that $f$ and this posynomial have the same value and the same first partial derivatives at the point $\mathbf{t}'$.

23. Consider the following optimization problem:

$$\begin{aligned} \text{minimize} \quad & t_1^{-1} + t_2^{-1} + \ln t_1 t_2 \\ & t_1 > 0, \quad t_2 > 0. \end{aligned}$$

(*a*) Use a limiting technique to develop an associated approximating geometric programming problem.

(*b*) Show that the minimizing point of the approximating geometric programs tends to the minimizing point of this problem as $\epsilon \to 0$.

24. (*a*) Show that the optimization problem

$$\begin{aligned} \text{maximize} \quad & \exp(-t_1 t_2^2 t_3) \\ \text{subject to} \quad & t_1 > 0, \quad t_2 > 0, \quad t_3 > 0 \\ & t_1 t_3^{-1} + t_1^{-1} t_2^{-1} \leq 1 \end{aligned}$$

may be approximated by a sequence of geometric programming problems.

(*b*) Determine the optimal value of these geometric programming problems.

25. Use the technique of geometric programming to solve the following optimization problems:

(*a*) minimize $\quad (\frac{1}{2})^{x_1}(\frac{1}{3})^{x_2} + (\frac{1}{2})^{-x_1} + (\frac{1}{3})^{-x_2}$

(*b*) minimize $\quad 3^{x_1} + 3^{x_2} + 3^{x_3} + (\frac{1}{3})^{x_1+x_2+x_3}$

(c) minimize $\quad 2^{-x_1} + 4^{x_1}(\frac{1}{3})^{x_2} + 3^{x_2}$

(*d*) minimize $\quad (25)^{x_1}(\frac{1}{3})^{x_2} + 3^{x_2+2x_3} + 5^{-x_1}(\frac{1}{9})^{x_3} + 5^{-x_1}$

(*e*) minimize $2^{x_1+x_2-x_3}$

subject to $(\frac{1}{2})^{x_1+x_2} + 2^{-x_2+x_3} \leq 1$

$2^{-x_1+x_3} \leq 1$

(*f*) minimize $2^{x_1}3^{x_2}5^{x_3}$

subject to $(\frac{1}{8})^{x_1}(\frac{1}{9})^{x_2} \leq 1$

$4^{x_1}(\frac{1}{9})^{x_2}5^{3x_3} \leq 1$

$(\frac{1}{2})^{x_1}3^{x_2}(\frac{1}{25})^{x_3} \leq 1$

(*g*) minimize $3^{x_1-2x_3+1} + (\frac{1}{3})^{x_1}2^{4x_2+1}$

subject to $2^{x_2} + 2^{-4x_2}3^{x_3} \leq 1$

(*h*) minimize $(\frac{1}{2})^{x_1+x_3} + 2^{x_2+x_3}$

subject to $x_1 \geq 0$

$x_2 \leq 0$

(*i*) minimize $(\frac{1}{2})^{x_1}(\frac{1}{9})^{x_2} + (\frac{1}{4})^{x_1}(\frac{1}{3})^{x_2}$

subject to $x_1 + x_2 \geq 10.$

26. Suggest a technique for calculating approximations of the minimum value and minimizing point of an arbitrary superconsistent geometric programming problem by solving a sequence of linear programming problems.
27. Consider the more general personnel assignment problem of determining the assignment of $N$ applicants to $N$ jobs of known value to the firm that minimizes the expected lost value to the firm. Assume the following:
    (*a*) Each job must be filled by one and only one applicant.
    (*b*) Each of the $N$ applicants has been assigned to one, and only one, of $m$ categories according to abilities, education, and experiences. The $i$th personnel category contains only $c_i$ people, $i = 1, \ldots, m$.
    (*c*) Each of the $N$ jobs has been classified into one, and only one, of $n$ categories according to required ability and training. The $j$th job category contains only $b_j$ jobs, $j = 1, \ldots, n$.
    (*d*) The probability that any individual in the $i$th category will fail in the $j$th job are known constants, $p_{ij}$, where $i = 1, \ldots, m$ and $j = 1, \ldots, n$.

    Formulate the problem of minimizing the expected lost value to the firm as a constrained optimization problem. Transform this optimization problem into a geometric programming problem.

28. Suppose the demand for a product, $Q$, depends on its unit price, $P$; the advertising budget, $A$; and the salaries and commissions of salesmen, $S$, and may be represented by the multiple exponential function

$$Q = 10^8 P^{-3} A^{1/4} S^{1/6}.$$

Show that a 1% increase in the advertising expenditures increases the unit demand by approximately $\frac{1}{4}$ of 1%.

29. The Shumba Record Company has noted that the sales of record albums by the Tammies consists primarily of sales through the Shumba record catalog. Shumba has determined that the sales of these albums through a catalog fluctuates with the number of pages $P$ allocated to Tammies albums and with the total distribution quantity $Q$ of the catalog. The sales $S$ are related to the parameters $P$ and $Q$ by a multiple exponential function with scale factor 100 and page and distribution elasticities of $\frac{1}{2}$. The only cost to be considered in developing a section of this catalog for the Tammies is the $10 cost of designing each page. Further, the only restriction placed on planning this catalog is that the distribution quantity must not exceed $3 \times 10^4$. Given that the unit cost of a Tammies album is $10, formulate the problem of maximizing the net revenue from catalog sales of Tammies albums as a constrained optimization problem. Determine the optimal values of $P$ and $Q$.

30. Suppose the page elasticity in the previous problem is an unspecified constant $c$ $(0 < c < 1)$. Discuss the effect of variations in $c$ on the maximum net revenue received from catalog sales of Tammies albums.

Exercises 31–35 are designed to introduce the reader to geometric programming problems other than superconsistent geometric programs with a positive minimum examined in Chapter 8. In discussing this classification scheme of geometric programs, we consider the more general primal geometric program

$$\text{(P)} \qquad \begin{array}{ll} \text{infimum} & g_0(\mathbf{t}) \\ \text{subject to} & t_1 > 0, \ldots, t_m > 0 \\ & g_1(\mathbf{t}) \le 1, \ldots, g_p(\mathbf{t}) \le 1, \end{array}$$

where $g_k(\mathbf{t})$, $k = 0, 1, \ldots, p$ are as in (P) on page 279. Similarly, we consider the general dual geometric program (D) on page 281 with maximum $v(\boldsymbol{\delta})$ replaced by supremum $v(\boldsymbol{\delta})$.

The constrained infimum of (P) is the greatest lower bound of $g_0(\mathbf{t})$ subject to the constraints of (P). The constrained supremum of (D) is the least upper bound of $v(\boldsymbol{\delta})$ subject to the constraints of (D).

31. (*a*) Show that the value of the following geometric programming problem is 1:

$$\begin{aligned} &\text{infimum} && t_1 + t_2^2 \\ &\text{subject to} && t_1 > 0, \quad t_2 > 0 \\ &&& t_1^{-1} \le 1. \end{aligned}$$

(*b*) Show that the value of the following geometric programming problem is $\frac{1}{2}$:

$$\begin{aligned} &\text{infimum} && \tfrac{1}{2}t_1 + \tfrac{1}{2}t_2 \\ &\text{subject to} && t_1 > 0, \quad t_2 > 0 \\ &&& \tfrac{1}{4}t_1^{-1}t_2^{-1} \le 1. \end{aligned}$$

32. A geometric programming problem is said to be *subconsistent* if the constraints

$$t_1 > 0, \ldots, t_m > 0$$

and

$$\theta g_1(\mathbf{t}) \le 1, \ldots, \theta g_p(\mathbf{t}) \le 1$$

can be satisfied for each $\theta$ in the open interval (0, 1). Here, we term

$$\overline{M} = \lim_{\theta \to 1^-} (\text{infimum } \theta g_0(\mathbf{t}))$$

the *subinfimum* of (P).

(*a*) Show that the geometric programming problem

$$\begin{aligned} &\text{infimum} && t_1 + t_2 \\ &\text{subject to} && t_1 > 0, \quad t_2 > 0 \\ &&& t_1^{-1}t_2 \le 1 \\ &&& t_2 \le 1 \\ &&& t_1t_2^{-1} \le 1. \end{aligned}$$

is both consistent and subconsistent. Show that *every* consistent geometric programming problem is subconsistent.

(*b*) Show that although the geometric programming problem

$$\begin{aligned} &\text{infimum} && t_1^{-1} \\ &\text{subject to} && t_1 > 0, \quad t_2 > 0 \\ &&& t_1 + t_2 \le 1 \\ &&& t_2^{-1} \le 1. \end{aligned}$$

is inconsistent, it is subconsistent. Show that every inconsistent geometric programming problem is *not* subconsistent.

(*c*) Show that the geometric programming problem in problem 31*b* is superconsistent *and* subconsistent. Show that every superconsistent geometric program is subconsistent.

(*d*) Determine $\overline{M}$ in the previous sections of this problem.

33. A geometric program problem (P) is said to be *bounded* if and only if the constrained infimum of (P) is *positive*. Otherwise, (P) is said to be *unbounded*.

(*a*) Show that the geometric programming problem in 31*b* is bounded.

(*b*) Construct an example of an unbounded geometric programming problem.

34. A dual geometric programming problem is said to be *bounded* if and only if it is consistent and its constrained supremum is finite. Otherwise, (D) is said to be unbounded.

Classify the dual geometric programming problems of 31*b* and 32*b* as bounded or unbounded.

35. Every geometric programming problem may be classified into one of 18 states according to its consistency and boundedness characteristics. These 18 states are summarized in Table 11. However, Kortanek, Gochet, and Smeers have proved that of these 18 states, the only possible states are those indicated by an X in Table 11. Construct examples of each of these 7 possible states.

Exercises 36–47 are designed to introduce the reader to vector valued criteria in geometric programming. Although a specific class of problems is

**Table 11***

| | Primal | | | | | |
|---|---|---|---|---|---|---|
| | Subconsistent and Consistent | | Subconsistent and Inconsistent | | | Inconsistent |
| Dual | $\overline{M} > 0$ | $\overline{M} = 0$ | $0 < \overline{M} < \infty$ | $\overline{M} = 0$ | $\overline{M} = +\infty$ | |
| Consistent and bounded | × | | × | | | |
| Consistent and unbounded | | | | | × | × |
| Inconsistent | | × | | × | | × |

* From "On a classification theorem for Geometric Programming" by W. Gochet, K. Kortanek, and Y. Smeers, Management Science Research Report 250, Carnegie Mellon University, June, 1971.

considered in this development, the general vector valued criteria is characterized in a similar manner. Specifically consider the following problem:

The maintenance cost of the Ehret car wash center is dependent upon two variables, $t_1 > 0$ and $t_2 > 0$. The average customer waiting time at this car wash also is a function of these variables. Specifically, suppose that the cost of maintaining the car wash is

$$f_1(\mathbf{t}) = u_1 + u_2,$$

and the average customer waiting time is

$$f_2(\mathbf{t}) = u_3 + u_4,$$

where $u_i = c_i t_1^{a_{i1}} t_2^{a_{i2}}$, $c_i \geq 0$, $i = 1, 2, 3, 4$. Any decrease in the maintenance cost leads to greater profits and any decrease in the average waiting time leads to increased prestige for the firm. Consequently, the proprietor of the car wash wishes to minimize *both* this maintenance cost *and* the average customer waiting time.

The problem is summarized using vector notation:

$$\text{(V)} \qquad \text{minimize} \quad \begin{pmatrix} f_1(\mathbf{t}) \\ f_2(\mathbf{t}) \end{pmatrix}$$

$$t_1 > 0, \qquad t_2 > 0$$

Problem (V) is called a *vector geometric programming problem*. (It is considered in the remainder of this development.)

36. Suggest a definition for an "optimal" solution of problem (V).
37. A point $\mathbf{t}^0 = (t_1^0, t_2^0)$ is said to be an *efficient point* of (V) if $t_1^0 > 0$, $t_2^0 > 0$ and there exists no other point $\mathbf{t}$ such that

$$f_1(\mathbf{t}) < f_1(\mathbf{t}^0), \qquad f_2(\mathbf{t}) < f_2(\mathbf{t}^0),$$

and

$$f_1(\mathbf{t}) \neq f_1(\mathbf{t}^0), \qquad f_2(\mathbf{t}) \neq f_2(\mathbf{t}^0).$$

(*a*) Suggest an economic interpretation of an efficient point.
(*b*) Consider the vector geometric programming problem

$$\text{minimize} \begin{pmatrix} f_1(\mathbf{t}) \\ f_2(\mathbf{t}) \end{pmatrix} = \text{minimize} \begin{pmatrix} t_1 t_2^{-1} + t_1^{-1} t_2 \\ t_1 + t_1^{-1} \end{pmatrix}$$

$$t_1 > 0, \quad t_2 > 0 \qquad t_1 > 0, \quad t_2 > 0.$$

Show that $\mathbf{t}^0 = (1, 1)$ is an efficient point of this problem.

(*c*) Consider the vector geometric programming problem

$$\text{minimize} \quad \begin{pmatrix} t_1^{-1}t_2^3 + t_1^{1/2}t_2^{-3/2} \\ t_1 t_2^{-1/2} + t_1^{-2}t_2 \end{pmatrix}$$

$$t_1 > 0, \qquad t_2 > 0$$

Show that $\mathbf{t}^0 = (2^{4/15}, (\frac{1}{2})^{2/15})$ is an efficient point of this problem.

38. Information concerning the vector geometric programming problem (V) may be obtained by formulating and solving a related minimization problem with a single objective function. The following table suggests several approaches to such problems. (Case 5 is analyzed here.)

| Objective Function | Constraint |
|---|---|
| 1 Minimize maintenance cost | Waiting time bounded above by a maximum acceptable value |
| 2 Minimize average waiting time | Maintenance cost bounded above by a maximum acceptable value |
| 3 Minimize maintenance cost | Ignore waiting time |
| 4 Minimize average waiting time | Ignore maintenance cost |
| 5 Minimize a weighted mean of maintenance cost and waiting time | — |

Discuss the advantages and disadvantages of each approach.

39. Consider the optimization problem formed by minimizing an arithmetic mean of $f_1(\mathbf{t})$ and $f_2(\mathbf{t})$:

$$(\mathrm{V}(\boldsymbol{\beta})) \qquad \text{minimize} \quad \beta_1 f_1(\mathbf{t}) + \beta_2 f_2(\mathbf{t})$$

$$t_1 > 0, \qquad t_2 > 0$$

where $\beta_1 > 0$, $\beta_2 > 0$, $\beta_1 + \beta_2 = 1$. Problem $(\mathrm{V}(\boldsymbol{\beta}))$ is called an *arithmetic mean vector program*. Minimizing points of this problem aid in determining efficient points of (V).

(*a*) Is $(\mathrm{V}(\boldsymbol{\beta}))$ a geometric programming problem?

(*b*) Show that for fixed values of $\beta_1 > 0$, $\beta_2 > 0$, if $\mathbf{t}^0$ is a minimizing point of $(\mathrm{V}(\boldsymbol{\beta}))$, $\mathbf{t}^0$ is an efficient point of (V).

(*c*) Using this result determine an efficient point of

$$(\mathrm{V}_1) \qquad \text{minimize} \quad \begin{pmatrix} 8t_1^{-2}t_2^{-1} \\ 6t_1 + 4t_1^{-1}t_2 \end{pmatrix}$$
$$t_1 > 0, \qquad t_2 > 0$$

by solving the geometric program

$$(\mathrm{V}_1(\boldsymbol{\beta})) \qquad \text{minimize} \quad \beta_1(8t_1^{-2}t_2^{-1}) + \beta_2(6t_1 + 4t_1^{-1}t_2)$$
$$t_1 > 0, \qquad t_2 > 0$$

for particular values of $\beta_1$ and $\beta_2$.

(*d*) Determine an efficient point of

$$\text{minimize} \quad \begin{pmatrix} t_1t_2t_3 + t_3^{-1} \\ t_1^{-1}t_2 + t_1t_2^{-2}t_3^{-1} \end{pmatrix}$$
$$t_1 > 0, \qquad t_2 > 0, \qquad t_3 > 0$$

40. Show that the graph of $M$, the minimum of $(\mathrm{V}_1(\boldsymbol{\beta}))$ as a function of $\beta_1$, appears as shown below.

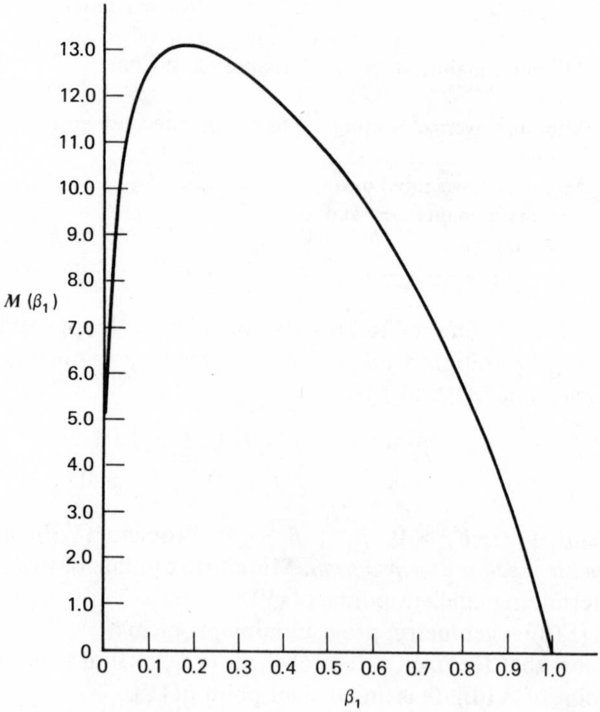

41. Consider the optimization problem formed by minimizing a geometric mean of $f_1(\mathbf{t})$ and $f_2(\mathbf{t})$:

$$(\bar{\mathrm{V}}'(\boldsymbol{\beta})) \qquad \text{maximize} \qquad (f_1(\mathbf{t}))^{\beta_1}(f_2(\mathbf{t}))^{\beta_2}$$
$$t_1 > 0, \qquad t_2 > 0$$
$$\beta_1 > 0, \qquad \beta_2 > 0, \qquad \beta_1 + \beta_2 = 1.$$

Problem $(\bar{\mathrm{V}}'(\boldsymbol{\beta}))$ is called the *geometric mean vector program.* The minimizing points of $(\bar{\mathrm{V}}'(\boldsymbol{\beta}))$ also aid in determining efficient points of (V).

(*a*) Is $(\bar{\mathrm{V}}'(\boldsymbol{\beta}))$ a geometric programming problem?

(*b*) Form the geometric mean vector program corresponding to the vector geometric programming problem:

$$(\mathrm{V}_2) \qquad \text{minimize} \qquad \begin{pmatrix} t_1^{-1}t_2^3 + t_1^{1/2}t_2^{-3/2} \\ t_1t_2^{-1/2} + t_1^{-2}t_2 \end{pmatrix}$$
$$t_1 > 0, \qquad t_2 > 0$$

(*c*) Show that for fixed $\beta_1 > 0$, $\beta_2 > 0$, if $\mathbf{t}^0$ is a minimizing point of $(\bar{\mathrm{V}}'(\boldsymbol{\beta}))$ then $\mathbf{t}^0$ is an efficient point of (V).*

42. (*a*) Show that $(\bar{\mathrm{V}}'(\boldsymbol{\beta}))$ is equivalent to the geometric programming problem

$$\begin{array}{lll} & \text{minimize} & s_1^{\beta_1}s_2^{\beta_2} \\ & \text{subject to} & t_1 > 0, \quad t_2 > 0, \quad s_1 > 0, \quad s_2 > 0 \\ (\bar{\mathrm{V}}(\boldsymbol{\beta})) & & s_1^{-1}f_1(\mathbf{t}) \le 1 \\ & & s_2^{-1}f_2(\mathbf{t}) \le 1 \\ & & \beta_1 > 0, \quad \beta_2 > 0, \quad \beta_1 + \beta_2 = 1. \end{array}$$

(*b*) Show that the geometric programming problem

$$\begin{array}{lll} & \text{minimize} & s_1^{\beta_1}s_2^{\beta_2} \\ & \text{subject to} & t_1 > 0, \quad t_2 > 0, \quad s_1 > 0, \quad s_2 > 0 \\ (\bar{\mathrm{V}}_2(\boldsymbol{\beta})) & & s_1^{-1}t_1^{-1}t_2^3 + s_1^{-1}t_1^{1/2}t_2^{-3/2} \le 1 \\ & & s_2^{-1}t_1t_2^{-1/2} + s_2^{-1}t_1^{-2}t_2 \le 1 \\ & & \beta_1 > 0, \quad \beta_2 > 0, \quad \beta_1 + \beta_2 = 1, \end{array}$$

is equivalent to the program formed in problem 41*b*.

43. (*a*) Show that for fixed values of $\beta_1 > 0$, $\beta_2 > 0$, if $\mathbf{t}^0$ is a minimizing point of $(\bar{\mathrm{V}}(\boldsymbol{\beta}))$ then $\mathbf{t}^0$ is an efficient point of (V).

* From L. Pascual and A. Ben-Israel, "Vector Valued Criteria in Geometric Programming," *Operations Research*, **19**, p. 98–104.

(*b*) Show that if the degree of difficulty of $(V(\boldsymbol{\beta}))$ is $n > 0$, then the degree of difficulty of $(\bar{V}(\boldsymbol{\beta}))$ is $n - 1$.
[Thus, when $n > 0$, $(\bar{V}(\boldsymbol{\beta}))$ is easier to solve than $(V(\boldsymbol{\beta}))$.]

(*c*) Use the result of part *a* to determine an efficient point of vector geometric program $(V_2)$ by solving geometric mean vector program $(\bar{V}_2(\boldsymbol{\beta}))$ for fixed values of $\beta_1 > 0$ and $\beta_2 > 0$.

44. (*a*) Using the result in problem 43*a* determine an efficient point of the vector geometric program

$$(V_3) \qquad \text{minimize} \quad \begin{pmatrix} t_1 t_2^{-1} + t_1^{-1} t_2 \\ 5t_1 + 5t_1^{-1} \end{pmatrix}.$$
$$t_1 > 0, \qquad t_2 > 0$$

(*b*) Show that the graph of $M$, the minimum of problem $(\bar{V}_3(\boldsymbol{\beta}))$, as a function of $\beta_1$ appears as shown below.

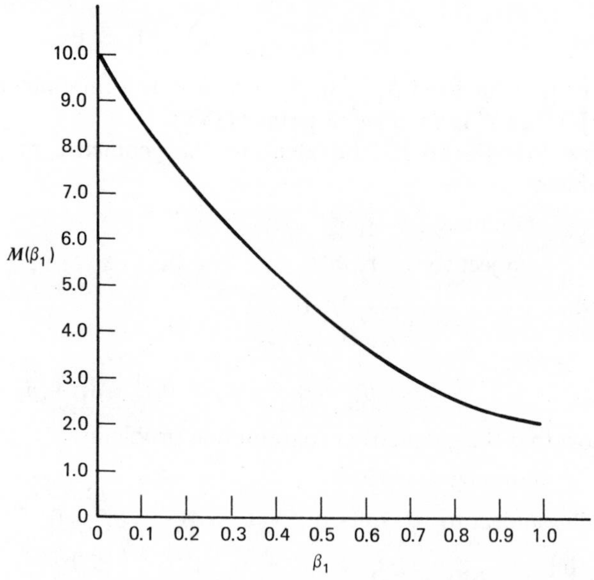


45. (*a*) Determine an efficient point of vector geometric program

$$(V_4) \qquad \text{minimize} \quad \begin{pmatrix} t_1^{-1} t_2^{3} + t_1^{1/2} t_2^{-3/2} \\ 8t_1 t_2^{-1/2} + 8t_1^{-2} t_2 \end{pmatrix}.$$
$$t_1 > 0, \qquad t_2 > 0$$

(*b*) Show that the graph of $M$, the minimum of problem $(\bar{\mathrm{V}}_4(\boldsymbol{\beta}))$, as a function of $\beta_1$ appears as shown below.

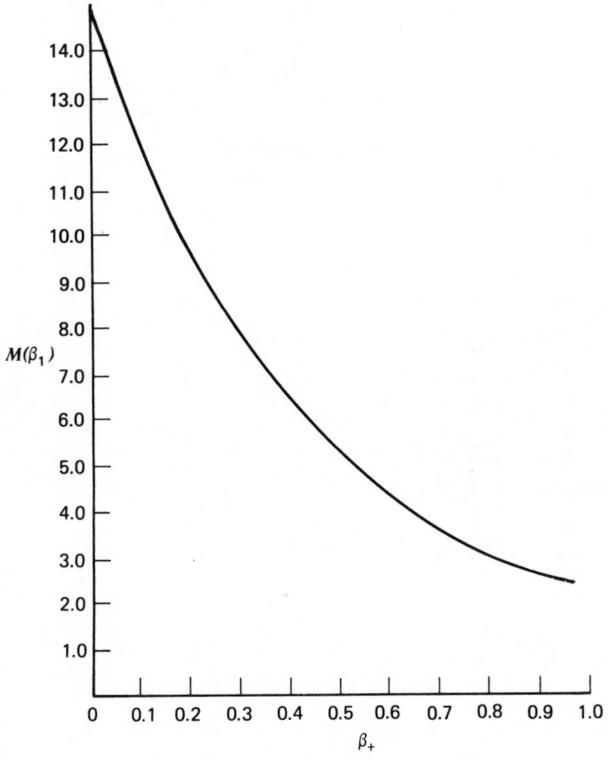


46. (*a*) Formulate the dual of $(\mathrm{V}(\boldsymbol{\beta}))$ and the dual of $(\bar{\mathrm{V}}(\boldsymbol{\beta}))$.
(*b*) Show that any feasible solution of the dual of $(\bar{\mathrm{V}}(\boldsymbol{\beta}))$ is also a feasible solution of the dual of $(\mathrm{V}(\boldsymbol{\beta}))$.
(*c*) Suppose that $\bar{v}(\boldsymbol{\delta})$ is the objective function of the dual of $(\bar{\mathrm{V}}(\boldsymbol{\beta}))$ and $v(\boldsymbol{\delta})$ is the objective function of the dual of $(\mathrm{V}(\boldsymbol{\beta}))$. Show that the optimal values of these dual problems satisfy

$$\text{maximum } \bar{v}(\boldsymbol{\delta}) \leq \text{maximum } v(\boldsymbol{\delta}).$$

47. Generalize the results of problems 39*b* and 43*a* to the vector geometric programming problem

$$\text{minimize} \quad \begin{pmatrix} f_1(\mathbf{t}) \\ \cdot \\ \cdot \\ \cdot \\ f_n(\mathbf{t}) \end{pmatrix},$$

$$t_1 > 0, \ldots, t_m > 0$$

where $f_i(\mathbf{t})$, $i = 1, \ldots, n$ are posynomials.

## SOLUTIONS

25. (*a*) $\delta^* = (\frac{1}{3}, \frac{1}{3}, \frac{1}{3})$
(*b*) $\delta^* = (\frac{1}{4}, \frac{1}{4}, \frac{1}{4}, \frac{1}{4})$
(*c*) $\delta^* = (\frac{1}{2}, \frac{1}{4}, \frac{1}{4})$
(*d*) $\delta^* = (\frac{1}{4}, \frac{1}{4}, \frac{1}{4}, \frac{1}{4})$
(*e*) $\delta^* = (1, \frac{1}{2}, \frac{1}{2}, \frac{1}{2})$
(*f*) $\delta^* = (1, \frac{1}{3}, \frac{1}{3}, \frac{2}{3})$
(*g*) $\delta^* = (\frac{1}{2}, \frac{1}{2}, 2, 1)$
(*h*) $\delta^* = (\frac{1}{2}, \frac{1}{2}, \frac{1}{2} \ln \frac{1}{2}, \frac{1}{2} \ln \frac{1}{2})$
(*i*) $\delta^* = (\frac{1}{2}, \frac{1}{2}, \frac{3}{2})$.

# CHAPTER 10

# REVERSED GEOMETRIC PROGRAMMING

## A CATALOG PLANNING PROBLEM: THE REVERSED GEOMETRIC PROGRAMMING PROBLEM*

Companies that advertise and sell products through a catalog must decide how to allocate space in the catalog for each merchandise line. Different allocations of space in the catalog may provide significantly different catalog sales. Hence, in order to obtain maximum benefit from the money spent on catalog advertising, the firm must first identify the market for each merchandise line, analyze historical sales data, and then plan the catalog accordingly. Decisions such as what merchandise lines to include in the catalog or how many pages of the catalog should be allocated to each line depend on being able to forecast the sales resulting from these decisions.

The planning of a catalog based on sales forecasts requires a merchandise line sales forecasting model. Historical sales data, such as the sensitivity of the sales of a line to the number of catalog pages devoted to that line, is necessary to develop such a model. Since the model should be relatively simple to apply, several simplifying assumptions must be made. The sales forecasts resulting from the model must then be evaluated in terms of these assumptions.

Here we develop a simple sales forecasting model for three lines of merchandise that are advertised in one catalog. The total sales of each line is assumed to depend only on the distribution quantity of the catalog, the number of catalog pages allocated to each of the three lines, and the number of items in each line. Other planning variables such as the catalog circulation

* From J. Dinkel and G. Kochenberger, "Applications of Geometric Programming in Marketing Decisions," Paper presented at the TIMS meeting, Houston, Texas, April 1972.

strategy, the number of warehouse outlets, and the number of color pages in the catalog are ignored. Although our objective is to determine the mix of these catalog variables that maximizes the resulting sales, our catalog planning model also considers budgetary restrictions.

Assume the sales of the $i$th merchandise line, $S_i$, is related to the planning parameters by an exponential expression

$$S_i = k_i Q^a P_i^{b_i} R_i^{c_i},$$

$i = 1, 2, 3$. Here $Q$ is the distribution quantity of the catalog, $P_i$ is the number of pages in the catalog devoted to the $i$th line, and $R_i$ is the number of items in the $i$th line. The constant $k_i$ is the ratio

$$\frac{\text{Average value of } S_i}{\text{Average value of } Q^a P_i^{b_i} R_i^{c_i}},$$

as determined from historical sales data. The exponents $a$, $b_i$, and $c_i$ are the elasticities of the distribution quantity, the number of pages, and the number of items in the $i$th line, respectively, also determined from historical data. These constants have the values given in Table 12. Thus, the total sales of the three merchandise lines is

$$\begin{aligned} (481) \quad S &= S_1 + S_2 + S_3 \\ &= 1.1Q^{0.51}P_1^{0.47}R_1^{0.24} + 0.9Q^{0.51}P_2^{0.53}R_2^{0.19} + 1.4Q^{0.51}P_3^{0.5}R_3^{0.21}. \end{aligned}$$

While we wish to maximize the total sales, (481), our catalog planning is constrained by budgetary, distribution, and total item restrictions. Suppose that the cost of developing and printing each page of the catalog for the first, second, and third lines is \$50, \$120, and \$85, respectively. If our development and printing budget cannot exceed \$10,000, then our catalog planning process is restricted by the constraint

$$50P_1 + 120P_2 + 85P_3 \leq 10^4$$

or

$$(482) \qquad 0.005P_1 + 0.012P_2 + 0.0085P_3 \leq 1.$$

Further, if at most 1000 catalogs may be distributed, we have the additional constraint

$$Q \leq 1000$$

or

$$(483) \qquad 0.001Q \leq 1.$$

**Table 12**

| $i$ | $k_i$ | $a$ | $b_i$ | $c_i$ |
|---|---|---|---|---|
| 1 | 1.1 | 0.51 | 0.47 | 0.24 |
| 2 | 0.9 | 0.51 | 0.53 | 0.19 |
| 3 | 1.4 | 0.51 | 0.50 | 0.21 |

Finally, suppose that among the three merchandise lines, a maximum of 500 items may be advertised. Then,

$$R_1 + R_2 + R_3 \leq 500$$

or

$$0.002R_1 + 0.002R_2 + 0.002R_3 \leq 1. \tag{484}$$

Thus, the problem of determining planning parameters $Q$, $P_i$, and $R_i$ that maximize the projected sales and yet satisfy the constraints of our problem, (482)–(484), may be summarized in the following optimization problem:

$$\begin{aligned} &\text{maximize} && f(\mathbf{t}) = 1.1Q^{0.51}P_1^{0.47}R_1^{0.24} + 0.9Q^{0.51}P_2^{0.53}R_2^{0.19} \\ &&& \qquad + 1.4Q^{0.51}P_3^{0.5}R_3^{0.21} \\ &\text{subject to} && Q > 0, \quad R_i > 0, \quad P_i > 0, \quad i = 1, 2, 3 \\ &&& 0.005P_1 + 0.012P_2 + 0.0085P_3 \leq 1 \\ &&& 0.001Q \leq 1 \\ &&& 0.002R_1 + 0.002R_2 + 0.002R_3 \leq 1, \end{aligned} \tag{485}$$

$\mathbf{t} = (Q, R_1, \ldots, P_3)$. (Note that the objective and constraint functions are all posynomials.)

This problem may be transposed into an equivalent minimization problem by introducing a new positive variable $t_0$ that satisfies

$$f(\mathbf{t}) \geq t_0 \tag{486}$$

or, equivalently,

$$t_0^{-1} f(\mathbf{t}) \geq 1. \tag{487}$$

Thus maximizing $t_0$ with constraint (487) and the constraints of (485) is identical to solving (485). The equivalent minimization problem is as follows:

$$\begin{aligned} &\text{minimize} && g_0(\mathbf{t}) = t_0^{-1} \\ &\text{subject to} && t_0 > 0, \quad Q > 0, \quad P_i > 0, \quad R_i > 0, \\ &&& \qquad\qquad\qquad\qquad i = 1, 2, 3 \\ &&& g_1(\mathbf{t}) = 0.005P_1 + 0.012P_2 + 0.0085P_3 \leq 1 \\ &&& g_2(\mathbf{t}) = 0.001Q \leq 1 \\ &&& g_3(\mathbf{t}) = 0.002R_1 + 0.002R_2 + 0.002R_3 \leq 1 \\ &&& g_4(\mathbf{t}) = 1.1t_0^{-1}Q^{0.51}P_1^{0.47}R_1^{0.24} \\ &&& \qquad + 0.9t_0^{-1}Q^{0.51}P_2^{0.53}R_2^{0.19} \\ &&& \qquad\qquad + 1.4t_0^{-1}Q^{0.51}P_3^{0.5}R_3^{0.21} \geq 1. \end{aligned} \tag{488}$$

Although the objective and constraint functions of (488) are posynomials, minimization problem (488) is not a prototype geometric programming problem, because the last constraint is reversed. Accordingly, (488) is called a reversed geometric programming problem. Observe that since (488) has 11 terms and 8 variables, reversed geometric program (488) has degree of difficulty 2.

One technique for determining a minimum value of (488) is to approximate this problem by a family of prototype geometric programming problems of lower degree of difficulty. If, for example, the reversed constraint

$$g_4(\mathbf{t}) \geq 1$$

is somehow replaced by a prototype constraint

$$\bar{g}_4(\mathbf{t}) \leq 1$$

with two fewer terms, the approximating geometric program will be a prototype geometric program of zero degree of difficulty. And approximating geometric programming problems of zero degree of difficulty are easily solved. This is the essence of our solution technique; we wish to replace the reversed constraint by a prototype constraint with fewer terms. The value of the resulting geometric program then approximates the value of the reversed geometric program.

The procedure for developing the approximating geometric program,

$$\begin{aligned}
&\text{minimize} && g_0(\mathbf{t}) = t_0^{-1} \\
&\text{subject to} && t_0 > 0, \quad Q > 0, \quad P_i > 0, \quad R_i > 0, \\
& && \qquad\qquad\qquad\qquad\qquad i = 1, 2, 3 \\
&(489) && g_1(\mathbf{t}) = 0.005P_1 + 0.012P_2 + 0.0085P_3 \leq 1 \\
& && g_2(\mathbf{t}) = 0.001Q \leq 1 \\
& && g_3(\mathbf{t}) = 0.002R_1 + 0.002R_2 + 0.002R_3 \leq 1 \\
& && \bar{g}_4(\mathbf{t}) \leq 1
\end{aligned}$$

employs the geometric inequality. Using this inequality, the posynomial $\bar{g}_4(\mathbf{t})$ is constructed such that if $\mathbf{t}'$ satisfies the constraints of (489),

$$g_1(\mathbf{t}') \leq 1, \qquad g_2(\mathbf{t}') \leq 1, \qquad g_3(\mathbf{t}') \leq 1, \qquad \bar{g}_4(\mathbf{t}') \leq 1,$$

then $\mathbf{t}'$ also satisfies the constraints of (488),

$$g_1(\mathbf{t}') \leq 1, \qquad g_2(\mathbf{t}') \leq 1, \qquad g_3(\mathbf{t}') \leq 1, \qquad g_4(\mathbf{t}') \geq 1.$$

With $u_1 = 1.1t_0^{-1}Q^{0.51}P_1^{0.47}R_1^{0.24}$, $u_2 = 0.9t_0^{-1}Q^{0.51}P_2^{0.53}R_2^{0.19}$, and $u_3 = 1.4t_0^{-1}Q^{0.51}P_3^{0.5}R_3^{0.21}$ the geometric inequality states that

(490) $$g_4(\mathbf{t}) = u_1 + u_2 + u_3 \geq \left(\frac{u_1}{\epsilon_1}\right)^{\epsilon_1}\left(\frac{u_2}{\epsilon_2}\right)^{\epsilon_2}\left(\frac{u_3}{\epsilon_3}\right)^{\epsilon_3},$$

where $\epsilon_i \geq 0$, $i = 1, 2, 3$ and $\sum_{i=1}^{3} \epsilon_i = 1$.

In constructing $\bar{g}_4$, first observe that if $\mathbf{t}'$ satisfies the prototype constraint

(491) $$\left(\frac{\epsilon_1}{u_1}\right)^{\epsilon_1}\left(\frac{\epsilon_2}{u_2}\right)^{\epsilon_2}\left(\frac{\epsilon_3}{u_3}\right)^{\epsilon_3} \leq 1,$$

then $\mathbf{t}'$ also satisfies the reversed constraint

(492) $$\left(\frac{u_1}{\epsilon_1}\right)^{\epsilon_1}\left(\frac{u_2}{\epsilon_2}\right)^{\epsilon_2}\left(\frac{u_3}{\epsilon_3}\right)^{\epsilon_3} \geq 1.$$

Furthermore, if $\mathbf{t}'$ satisfies (492), then, by (490), $\mathbf{t}'$ also satisfies

(493) $$g_4(\mathbf{t}) = u_1 + u_2 + u_3 \geq 1.$$

Thus, if $\mathbf{t}'$ satisfies prototype constraint (491) $\mathbf{t}'$ also satisfies the reversed constraint of reversed geometric programming problem (488). Accordingly, we replace the reversed constraint of (488) by the prototype constraint

$$\bar{g}_4(\mathbf{t}) = \left(\frac{\epsilon_1}{u_1}\right)^{\epsilon_1}\left(\frac{\epsilon_2}{u_2}\right)^{\epsilon_2}\left(\frac{\epsilon_3}{u_3}\right)^{\epsilon_3} \leq 1:$$

($488_R(\epsilon)$)

minimize $t_0^{-1}$

subject to
$$t_0 > 0, \quad Q > 0, \quad P_i > 0, \quad R_i > 0, \quad i = 1, 2, 3$$
$$g_1(\mathbf{t}) = 0.005P_1 + 0.012P_2 + 0.0085P_3 \leq 1$$
$$g_2(\mathbf{t}) = 0.001Q \leq 1$$
$$g_3(\mathbf{t}) = 0.002R_1 + 0.002R_2 + 0.002R_3 \leq 1$$
$$\bar{g}_4(\mathbf{t}) = \left(\frac{\epsilon_1}{1.1t_0^{-1}Q^{0.51}P_1^{0.47}R_1^{0.24}}\right)^{\epsilon_1}\left(\frac{\epsilon_2}{0.9t_0^{-1}Q^{0.51}P_2^{0.53}R_2^{0.19}}\right)^{\epsilon_2}\left(\frac{\epsilon_3}{1.4t_0^{-1}Q^{0.51}P_3^{0.5}R_3^{0.21}}\right)^{\epsilon_3} \leq 1$$
$$\epsilon_1 \geq 0, \quad \epsilon_2 \geq 0, \quad \epsilon_1 + \epsilon_2 = 1.$$

(Note that the degree of difficulty of ($488_R(\epsilon)$) is 0.) With the appropriate choice of weights $\epsilon_i$ the minimum value of ($488_R(\epsilon)$) approximates the minimum value of (488).

In choosing these weights, first observe that if $\mathbf{t}'$ is a point satisfying the constraints of (488), then $\mathbf{t}'$ is also a feasible solution of $(488_R(\epsilon))$ with the weights

$$\epsilon_i = \frac{u_i(\mathbf{t}')}{g_4(\mathbf{t}')}, \tag{494}$$

$i = 1, 2, 3$. This follows because with this choice of weights, the geometric inequality (490) becomes an equality,

$$g_4(\mathbf{t}') = \frac{1}{\bar{g}_4(\mathbf{t}')}.$$

Thus, if $g_4(\mathbf{t}') \geq 1$, then $1/\bar{g}_4(\mathbf{t}') \geq 1$ or $1 \geq \bar{g}_4(\mathbf{t}')$. In particular, if $\mathbf{t}' = \mathbf{t}^*$, a minimizing point of (488), then $\mathbf{t}^*$ is a feasible solution of $(488_R(\epsilon))$ with weights (494).

The algorithm suggested here for approximating the minimum of (488) by solving $(488_R(\epsilon))$ uses this choice of weights in a manner similar to the condensation procedure. After making an initial choice of weights $\epsilon_i^{(1)}$ $(i = 1, 2, 3)$, the minimum of program $(488_R(\epsilon^1))$, $\overline{M}_1$, is calculated. The duality conditions

$$u_i(\mathbf{t}^*) = \begin{cases} \delta_i^* g_0(\mathbf{t}^*), & i = 1 \\ \dfrac{\delta_i^*}{\lambda_k(\boldsymbol{\delta}^*)}, & i = n_{k-1} + 1, \ldots, n_k, \\ & k = 1, 2, 3, 4 \end{cases} \tag{495}$$

are used to determine a minimizing point $\mathbf{t}^* = \mathbf{t}^{(1)}$ of $(488_R(\epsilon^1))$. Now, using (494) with $\mathbf{t}' = \mathbf{t}^{(1)}$, new weights $\epsilon_i^{(2)}$ $(i = 1, 2, 3)$ are calculated. The minimum value of $(488_R(\epsilon^2))$, $\overline{M}_2$, is a second approximation of the minimum of (488), $M$. The duality conditions (495) are again used to calculate the corresponding minimizing point $\mathbf{t}^{(2)}$ and new weights $\epsilon_i^{(3)}$ are calculated with $\mathbf{t}' = \mathbf{t}^{(2)}$ in (494). The process is repeated. Just as in the condensation procedure, this algorithm is terminated when

$$|\overline{M}_{k-1} - \overline{M}_k| < \epsilon$$

for some predetermined small positive number $\epsilon$.

With the initial choice of weights,

$$\epsilon_1^{(1)} = \tfrac{1}{3}, \qquad \epsilon_2^{(1)} = \tfrac{1}{3}, \qquad \epsilon_3^{(1)} = \tfrac{1}{3},$$

Dinkel and Kochenberger found that this process converges after 15 iterations. With the values

$$\epsilon_1^{(15)} = 0.5162, \qquad \epsilon_2^{(15)} = 0.0514, \qquad \epsilon_3^{(15)} = 0.4322,$$

the minimum of $(488_R(\epsilon^{15}))$ and consequently the approximate minimum of (488) is 0.000413. The maximum sales is the inverse of this number, 2420.27.

Thus, given the sales forecasting equation, (481), as well as the constraints (482)–(484), the distribution quantity and the allocation of pages and merchandise that maximize sales are given in Table 13. An analysis of this model indicates that these values depend intricately on the elasticities and coefficients calculated from historical sales data for these particular lines of merchandise. As such the model in no way indicates which other lines would benefit most from catalog advertising. Thus, these values provide marketing information for a larger sales problem.

The procedure for solving the more general reversed geometric programming problem is similar. Given the reversed geometric programming problem,

$$
\text{(P)} \qquad
\begin{array}{ll}
\text{minimize} & g_0(\mathbf{t}) \\
\text{subject to} & t_1 > 0, \ldots, t_m > 0 \\
 & g_1(\mathbf{t}) \le 1 \\
 & \quad \vdots \quad \vdots \\
 & g_{p-1}(\mathbf{t}) \le 1 \\
 & g_p(\mathbf{t}) \ge 1,
\end{array}
$$

where the $g_k(\mathbf{t})$ are posynomials

$$\sum_{i=n_{k-1}+1}^{n_k} c_i t_1^{a_{i1}} \cdots t_m^{a_{im}},$$

and a set of nonnegative weights $\epsilon_{n_{p-1}+1}, \ldots, \epsilon_{n_p}$ satisfying

$$\sum_{i=n_{p-1}+1}^{n_p} \epsilon_i = 1,$$

an approximating geometric program is obtained by replacing $g_p(\mathbf{t}) \ge 1$ by

$$\bar{g}_p(\mathbf{t}) = \prod_{i=n_{p-1}+1}^{n_p} \left(\frac{\epsilon_i}{u_i}\right)^{\epsilon_i} \le 1.$$

**Table 13**

| $i$ | $Q$ | $P_i$ | $R_i$ |
|---|---|---|---|
| 1 | 1000 | 99.79 | 275.89 |
| 2 | 1000 | 4.70 | 21.91 |
| 3 | 1000 | 52.31 | 202.20 |

Here the $u_i$ are the terms of $g_p(\mathbf{t})$. Thus,

$$\bar{g}_p(\mathbf{t}) = \bar{c}_p t_1^{\bar{a}_{p1}} \cdots t_m^{\bar{a}_{pm}},$$

where

$$\bar{c}_p = \prod_{i=n_{p-1}+1}^{n_p} \left(\frac{\epsilon_i}{c_i}\right)^{\epsilon_i} \quad \text{and} \quad \bar{a}_{pj} = \sum_{i=n_{p-1}+1}^{n_p} \epsilon_i(-a_{ij}).$$

For future reference, we write the resulting approximating geometric programming problem as follows:

$$(\mathrm{P}_R(\epsilon)) \qquad \begin{aligned} &\text{minimize} && g_0(\mathbf{t}) \\ &\text{subject to} && t_1 > 0, \ldots, t_m > 0 \\ &&& g_1(\mathbf{t}) \le 1 \\ &&& \quad \vdots \\ &&& g_{p-1}(\mathbf{t}) \le 1 \\ &&& \bar{g}_p(\mathbf{t}) \le 1. \end{aligned}$$

It is a consequence of the geometric inequality

$$u_{n_{p-1}+1} + \cdots + u_{n_p} \ge \left(\frac{u_{n_{p-1}+1}}{\epsilon_{n_{p-1}+1}}\right)^{\epsilon_{n_{p-1}+1}} \cdots \left(\frac{u_{n_p}}{\epsilon_{n_p}}\right)^{\epsilon_{n_p}}$$

that

$$g_p(\mathbf{t}) \ge \frac{1}{\bar{g}_p(\mathbf{t})}.$$

Thus, if $\mathbf{t}'$ satisfies the constraint

$$1 \ge \bar{g}_p(\mathbf{t})$$

or

$$\frac{1}{\bar{g}_p(\mathbf{t})} \ge 1$$

in $(\mathrm{P}_R(\epsilon))$, then $\mathbf{t}'$ also satisfies the reversed constraint

$$g_p(\mathbf{t}) \ge 1.$$

Since we have the implication

$$\bar{g}_p(\mathbf{t}) \le 1 \rightarrow g_p(\mathbf{t}) \ge 1,$$

$\bar{M}$, the minimum of $(\mathrm{P}_R(\epsilon))$, and $M$, the minimum of (P) satisfy

$$\bar{M} \ge M.$$

That is, since the constraint set of $(\mathrm{P}_R(\epsilon))$ is contained in the constraint set of (P), the minimum of $(\mathrm{P}_R(\epsilon))$ is at least $M$.

As the following result indicates, with an appropriate choice of weights $\epsilon_i$ the values $M$ and $\overline{M}$ may become arbitrarily close:

THEOREM 57 If $\mathbf{t}'$ is a feasible solution to (P), then $\mathbf{t}'$ is a feasible solution to ($P_R(\epsilon)$) with weights

$$\epsilon_i = \frac{u_i(\mathbf{t}')}{g_p(\mathbf{t}')}, \qquad i = n_{p-1} + 1, \ldots, n_p, \tag{496}$$

and hence, the difference $\overline{M} - M$ can be made arbitrarily small.

PROOF Given $\mathbf{t}'$ ($>\mathbf{0}$) and the corresponding weights $\epsilon_i = u_i(\mathbf{t}')/g_p(\mathbf{t}')$, it follows from the geometric inequality that $g_p(\mathbf{t}') = (\bar{g}_p(\mathbf{t}'))^{-1}$. Since $g_p(\mathbf{t}') \geq 1$, it follows that $1 \geq \bar{g}_p(\mathbf{t}')$; $\mathbf{t}'$ is a feasible solution of $P_R(\epsilon)$). Hence, the fact that (P) and ($P_R(\epsilon)$) have the same objective function implies that $\overline{M} - M$ can be made arbitrarily small. ▮

This result provides the basis for our algorithm to solve certain reversed geometric programs. As successively better approximations of the weights $\epsilon_i$ in ($P_R(\epsilon)$) are developed, the minimum values of the corresponding approximate geometric programs converge to a minimum of (P).

If ($P_R(\epsilon^1)$) is solved for an initial choice of weights $\epsilon^{(1)}_{n_{p-1}+1}, \ldots, \epsilon^{(1)}_{n_p}$, an initial estimate $\overline{M}_1$ of (P) is obtained. The minimizing point of ($P_R(\epsilon^1)$), $\mathbf{t}^{(1)}$, may be calculated by solving conditions (357) of the duality theorem:

$$u_i(\mathbf{t}^*) = \begin{cases} \delta_i^* g_0(\mathbf{t}^*), & i = 1, \ldots, n_0 \\ \dfrac{\delta_i^*}{\lambda_k(\boldsymbol{\delta}^*)}, & n_{k-1} + 1 \leq i \leq n_k, \\ & k = 1, \ldots, p. \end{cases} \tag{497}$$

Using the point $\mathbf{t}^{(1)}$ the weights are assigned new values and the process is repeated. As suggested by the theorem, we choose the new weights to be

$$\epsilon_i^{(2)} = \frac{u_i(\mathbf{t}^{(1)})}{g_p(\mathbf{t}^{(1)})}, \qquad i = n_{p-1} + 1, \ldots, n_p.$$

With these new weights, program ($P_R(\epsilon^2)$) is solved and its value $\overline{M}_2$ is calculated. Once again the duality conditions (497) are used to determine the minimizing point $\mathbf{t}^{(2)}$ and the relations

$$\epsilon_i^{(3)} = \frac{u_i(\mathbf{t}^{(2)})}{g_p(\mathbf{t}^{(2)})}$$

are used to calculate new weights. After determining $\overline{M}_3$, the minimum of ($P_R(\epsilon^3)$), the process is repeated. This procedure is terminated when, for some $k$,

$$|\overline{M}_{k-1} - \overline{M}_k| < \epsilon,$$

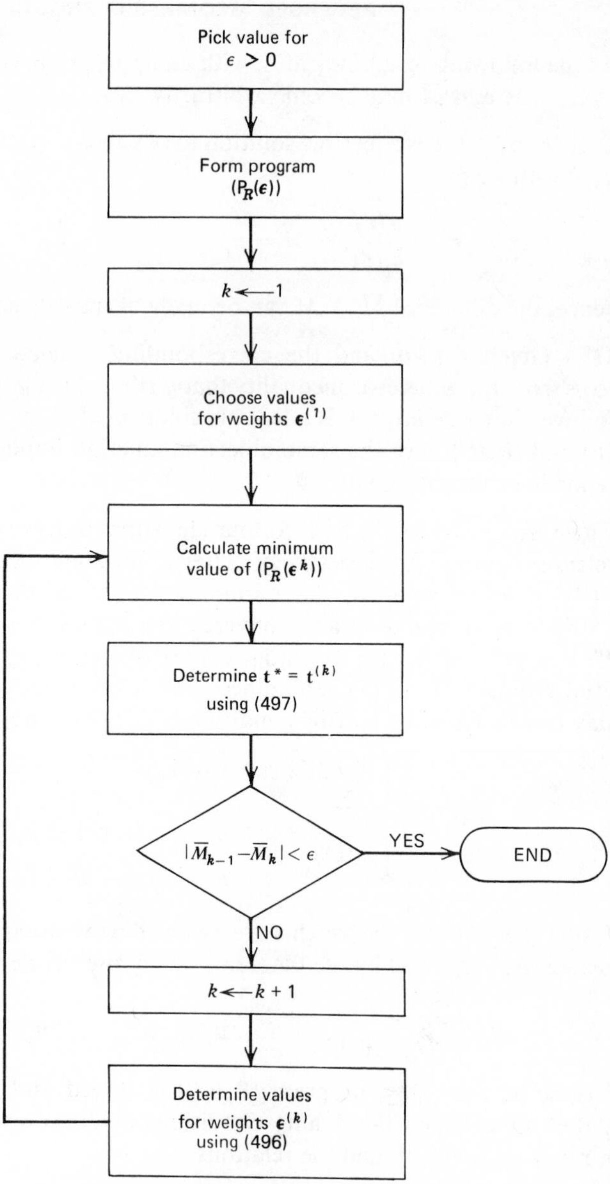
Pick value for
$\epsilon > 0$
Form program
$(P_R(\epsilon))$
$k \leftarrow 1$
Choose values
for weights $\epsilon^{(1)}$
Calculate minimum
value of $(P_R(\epsilon^k))$
Determine $t^* = t^{(k)}$
using (497)
$|\overline{M}_{k-1} - \overline{M}_k| < \epsilon$
YES
END
NO
$k \leftarrow k + 1$
Determine values
for weights $\epsilon^{(k)}$
using (496)

**Figure 127**

where $\epsilon$ is a predetermined small positive number. Intuitively the latter condition suggests that the sequence of minimum values $\overline{M}_1, \overline{M}_2, \overline{M}_3, \ldots$ converge to a minimum, $M$, of (P). (This algorithm is summarized in Figure 127.) In a similar manner this algorithm applies when more than one constraint is reversed.

It is a consequence of Theorem 57 that for each positive integer $k$, the optimal solution $\mathbf{t}^{(k)}$ to $(\mathrm{P}_R(\boldsymbol{\epsilon}^k))$ is also a feasible solution of program $(\mathrm{P}_R(\boldsymbol{\epsilon}^{k+1}))$; that is, $\mathbf{t}^{(k)}$ satisfies the constraints of $(\mathrm{P}_R(\boldsymbol{\epsilon}^{k+1}))$. This fact implies that

$$\overline{M}_1 \geq \overline{M}_2 \geq \overline{M}_3 \geq \cdots \geq M$$

because each program $(\mathrm{P}_R(\boldsymbol{\epsilon}^k))$ has the same objective function $g_0(\mathbf{t})$. Thus, the iterations $\overline{M}_k$ approach $M$ from above.

Although prototype geometric programs have the remarkable property that every constrained local minimum is also a global minimum, no such claim is made for reversed geometric programs. This follows because, unlike prototype geometric programs, the reversed geometric program is not equivalent to a convex program. Thus, this algorithm may compute a local minimum, or sometimes even an inflection point, of our reversed geometric programming problem.

To illustrate this algorithm better, consider the following reversed geometric programming problem:

$$\text{(498)}\quad \begin{aligned} &\text{minimize} && g_0(\mathbf{t}) = 300t_2^{-1} + t_2^{-1}t_3^2 + t_2^{-1}t_4^2 \\ &\text{subject to} && t_1 > 0, \quad t_2 > 0, \quad t_3 > 0, \quad t_4 > 0 \\ &&& g_1(\mathbf{t}) = t_1^{-1}t_2t_4^{-1} \leq 1 \\ &&& g_2(\mathbf{t}) = t_1^{-1} + t_1^{-1}t_3t_4^{-1} \geq 1. \end{aligned}$$

The reversed geometric program of degree of difficulty $6 - (4 + 1) = 1$ may be approximated by a family of geometric programs of degree of difficulty 0:

$$(498_R(\boldsymbol{\epsilon}))\quad \begin{aligned} &\text{minimize} && g_0(\mathbf{t}) = 300t_2^{-1} + t_2^{-1}t_3^2 + t_2^{-1}t_4^2 \\ &\text{subject to} && t_1 > 0, \quad t_2 > 0, \quad t_3 > 0, \quad t_4 > 0 \\ &&& g_1(\mathbf{t}) = t_1^{-1}t_2t_4^{-1} \leq 1 \\ &&& \bar{g}_2(\mathbf{t}) = \left(\frac{\epsilon_1}{t_1^{-1}}\right)^{\epsilon_1}\left(\frac{\epsilon_2}{t_1^{-1}t_3t_4^{-1}}\right)^{\epsilon_2} \leq 1 \\ &&& \epsilon_1 \geq 0, \quad \epsilon_2 \geq 0, \quad \epsilon_1 + \epsilon_2 = 1. \end{aligned}$$

The reversed constraint has been replaced by the single-term prototype constraint. With the initial choice of weights $\epsilon_1^{(1)} = 0.95$, $\epsilon_2^{(1)} = 0.05$, the approximating program $(498_R(\boldsymbol{\epsilon}^1))$ has the minimum value $\overline{M}_1 = 31.36772$.

The corresponding dual variables have values $\delta_1^* = 0.5$, $\delta_2^* = 0.025$, $\delta_3^* = 0.475$, $\delta_4^* = 1$, $\delta_5^* = 1$. By solving the system,

$$
\begin{aligned}
300t_2^{*^{-1}} &= \delta_1^* g_0(t^*), \\
t_2^{*^{-1}} t_3^{*^2} &= \delta_2^* g_0(t^*), \\
t_2^{*^{-1}} t_4^{*^2} &= \delta_3^* g_0(t^*), \\
t_1^{*^{-1}} t_2^* t_4^{*^{-1}} &= 1, \\
\epsilon_1^{\epsilon_1}\epsilon_2^{\epsilon_2} t_1^* t_3^{*^{-\epsilon_2}} t_4^{*^{\epsilon_2}} &= 1,
\end{aligned}
\tag{499}
$$

we find the minimizing vector is $\mathbf{t}^* = \mathbf{t}^{(1)} = (0.88251, 19.12793, 3.87298, 16.88193)$.

Using the point $\mathbf{t}' = \mathbf{t}^{(1)}$ in (496), new weights are calculated and the process is repeated. With

$$
\epsilon_1^{(2)} = \left.\frac{t_1^{-1}}{t_1^{-1} + t_1^{-1}t_3t_4^{-1}}\right|_{\mathbf{t}^{(1)}} = 0.8133956,
$$

$$
\epsilon_2^{(2)} = \left.\frac{t_1^{-1}t_3t_4^{-1}}{t_1^{-1} + t_1^{-1}t_3t_4^{-1}}\right|_{\mathbf{t}^{(1)}} = 0.1866056,
$$

the minimum value of $(498_R(\epsilon^2))$ is $\overline{M}_2 = 27.23235$. The solution of the dual program, $\delta_1^* = 0.5$, $\delta_2^* = 0.0933028$, $\delta_3^* = 0.4066978$, $\delta_4^* = 1$, $\delta_5^* = 1$, is used in (499) to calculate the minimizing point $\mathbf{t}^* = \mathbf{t}^{(2)} = (0.7088, 22.0326, 7.4821, 15.6211)$.

New weights $\epsilon_i^{(3)}$ are calculated using $\mathbf{t}' = \mathbf{t}^{(2)}$ and the process is repeated. After eight iterations, this process was terminated when

$$
|\overline{M}_7 - \overline{M}_8| = 0.00061 \le 0.002.
$$

Here $\overline{M}_7 = 24.49567$ and $\overline{M}_8 = 24.49506$. Hence, the minimum value of (498) is approximately $M = 24.495$. This value is attained at $\mathbf{t}^* = (0.5014, 24.4947, 12.2122, 12.2826)$.

As a second example, consider the reversed geometric program:

$$
\begin{aligned}
&\text{minimize} && g_0(\mathbf{t}) = 2t_1 + t_2^{-1} \\
&\text{subject to} && t_1 > 0, \quad t_2 > 0 \\
& && g_1(\mathbf{t}) = t_1^2 + t_2^{-1} \ge 1.
\end{aligned}
\tag{500}
$$

This reversed geometric programming problem of degree of difficulty $4 - (2 + 1) = 1$ may be approximated by a sequence of geometric programs of degree of difficulty 0:

$$
\begin{aligned}
&\text{minimize} && g_0(\mathbf{t}) = 2t_1 + t_2^{-1} \\
&\text{subject to} && t_1 > 0, \quad t_2 > 0 \\
& && \bar{g}_1(\mathbf{t}) = \left(\frac{\epsilon_1}{t_1^2}\right)^{\epsilon_1}\left(\frac{\epsilon_2}{t_2^{-1}}\right)^{\epsilon_2} \le 1 \\
& && \epsilon_1 \ge 0, \quad \epsilon_2 \ge 0, \quad \epsilon_1 + \epsilon_2 = 1.
\end{aligned}
\tag{$500_R(\epsilon)$}
$$

The reversed constraint of (500) has been replaced by the prototype constraint $\bar{g}_1(\mathbf{t}) \le 1$.

With the initial choice of weights $\epsilon_1^{(1)} = 0.05$, $\epsilon_2^{(1)} = 0.95$, the minimum value of the approximating program $(500_R(\boldsymbol{\epsilon}^1))$ is calculated to be $\overline{M}_1 = 1.210994$. Using the solution of the dual of $(500_R(\boldsymbol{\epsilon}^1))$, $\delta_1^* = 0.0952381$, $\delta_2^* = 0.9047625$, $\delta_3^* = 0.9523816$, the duality conditions,

$$(501) \qquad \begin{aligned} 2t_1^* &= \delta_1^* g_0(\mathbf{t}^*), \\ t_2^{*-1} &= \delta_2^* g_0(\mathbf{t}^*), \end{aligned}$$

imply the minimizing point is $\mathbf{t}^* = \mathbf{t}^{(1)} = (0.0576664, 0.9126909)$.

Using the point $\mathbf{t}' = \mathbf{t}^{(1)}$, new weights $\epsilon_1^{(2)}$, $\epsilon_2^{(2)}$ are calculated and the algorithm is repeated. With

$$\epsilon_1^{(2)} = \left.\frac{t_1^2}{t_1^2 + t_2^{-1}}\right|_{\mathbf{t}^{(1)}} = 0.0030259,$$

$$\epsilon_2^{(2)} = \left.\frac{t_2^{-1}}{t_1^2 + t_2^{-1}}\right|_{\mathbf{t}^{(1)}} = 0.9969755,$$

the minimum value of $(500_R(\boldsymbol{\epsilon}^2))$ is $\overline{M}_2 = 1.020731$. The solution of the dual program, $\delta_1^* = 0.0060335$, $\delta_2^* = 0.9939668$, $\delta_3^* = 0.9969822$, is used in (501) to determine that $\mathbf{t}^* = \mathbf{t}^{(2)} = (0.0030793, 0.9856371)$.

The algorithm is repeated with the new weights

$$\epsilon_1^{(3)} = \left.\frac{t_1^2}{t_1^2 + t_2^{-1}}\right|_{\mathbf{t}^{(2)}} = 0.0000093,$$

$$\epsilon_2^{(3)} = \left.\frac{t_2^{-1}}{t_1^2 + t_2^{-1}}\right|_{\mathbf{t}^{(2)}} = 0.9999924.$$

The minimum value of $(500_R(\boldsymbol{\epsilon}^3))$ is calculated to be $\overline{M}_3 = 1.000116$. Using the solution of the dual program, $\delta_1^* = 0.0000187$, $\delta_2^* = 0.9999819$, $\delta_3^* = 0.9999895$, in (501) we find that $\mathbf{t}^* = \mathbf{t}^{(2)} = (0.0000093, 0.9999027)$.

This process was terminated after a total of five iterations when

$$|\overline{M}_4 - \overline{M}_5| < 0.002$$

($\overline{M}_4 = 0.999999$, $\overline{M}_5 = 1.0$.) Thus, the minimum value of (500) is approximately $M = 1$ and is attained at $\mathbf{t}^* = (0.763 \times 10^{-20}, 1.0)$.

## INVENTORY CONTROL WITH SHORTAGES: THE SIGNOMIAL GEOMETRIC PROGRAMMING PROBLEM

The inventory problems discussed thus far have not accounted for possible shortages in the stock. When the stock of a commodity proves to be inadequate to meet the demand, a shortage cost is incurred. If the unsatisfied

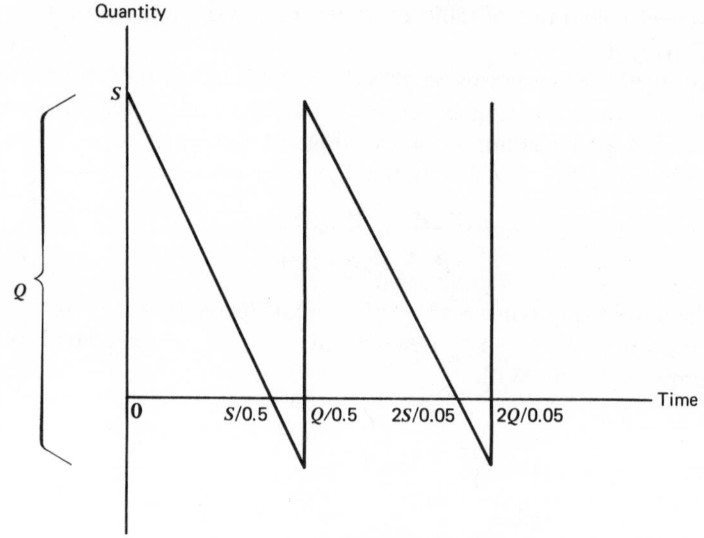


**Figure 128**

demand is lost, then the shortage cost is a loss of revenue. If this additional demand is met by a priority delivery, the shortage cost is the difference between the cost of a priority delivery and a routine shipment. Here a model is constructed in which the unsatisfied demand of one product is fulfilled by backlogging; that is, the demand is satisfied when the stock again becomes available. In this case the shortage cost represents a loss of goodwill; the consumers will be reluctant to do further business with the firm.

Suppose that the initial stock level, $S$, of our product is depleted at a constant rate of 0.5 per unit time. Although the stock is 0 after $S/0.5$ units of time, the continuing demand is backlogged. A replenishment order is placed after $Q/0.5$ ($\geq S/0.5$) units of time. At this time, an order of size $Q$ arrives instantaneously to meet the backlogged demand and replenish the stock to $S$ units (see Figure 128). Our objective is to determine the values $S^*$ and $Q^*$ that minimize the associated ordering, holding, and shortage costs.

Suppose that the ordering cost for each order of $Q$ units of the product is a linear function of $Q$,

$$600 + 0.1Q.$$

Note that larger orders are more expensive. During a period of length $Q/0.5$ the ordering cost per period is

$$\frac{600 + 0.1Q}{Q/0.5} = \frac{300}{Q} + 0.05. \tag{502}$$

Assume that the unit holding cost is $h = \$2$ per item per unit of time. Since the rate of demand is constant, the average inventory is $S/2$. Over a period of length $Q/0.5$ the inventory is positive for a fraction $S/Q$ of the time. Thus, in a period of length $Q/0.5$, $(S/Q)(S/2)$ is the average inventory and

$$h\left(\frac{S}{Q}\right)\left(\frac{S}{2}\right) = \frac{hS^2}{2Q} = \frac{S^2}{Q} \tag{503}$$

is the average inventory cost.

Similarly, suppose the unit shortage cost is $u = \$2$ per item of unfilled demand per unit of time. The average unfilled demand is $(Q - S)/2$. In a period of length $Q/0.5$ there is unfilled demand for a fraction $(Q - S)/Q$ of the time. Thus, in a period of length $Q/0.5$, $[(Q - S)/Q][(Q - S)/2]$ is the average unfilled demand and

$$u\left(\frac{Q - S}{Q}\right)\left(\frac{Q - S}{2}\right) = \frac{u(Q - S)^2}{2Q} = \frac{(Q - S)^2}{Q} \tag{504}$$

is the average inventory cost per period.

Hence, the total inventory system cost per unit time is the sum of the ordering, holding, and shortage costs per unit of time, (502)–(504),

$$g(\mathbf{t}) = \frac{300}{Q} + \frac{S^2}{Q} + \frac{(Q - S)^2}{Q} + 0.05, \tag{505}$$

$\mathbf{t} = (Q, S)$.

If $g(\mathbf{t})$ were a posynomial, the techniques of geometric programming could be applied to determine values $Q^*$ and $S^*$ that minimize the total cost. This problem, however, may be transformed into the problem of minimizing a constrained posynomial. By introducing a new positive variable $t_0$ that satisfies

$$Q - S \leq t_0$$

or

$$t_0^{-1}Q - t_0^{-1}S \leq 1, \tag{506}$$

we see that minimizing $g(\mathbf{t})$ is equivalent to solving the following constrained optimization problem:

$$\begin{aligned} &\text{minimize} && g_0(\mathbf{t}) = \frac{300}{Q} + \frac{S^2}{Q} + \frac{t_0^2}{Q} \\ &\text{subject to} && Q > 0, \quad S > 0, \quad t_0 > 0 \\ &&& t_0^{-1}Q - t_0^{-1}S \leq 1. \end{aligned} \tag{507}$$

Note that the constant 0.05 may be added to the constrained value of $g_0(\mathbf{t})$ to obtain the minimum of $g(\mathbf{t})$.

Although the objective function of (507) is a posynomial, the constraint function of (507), $t_0^{-1}Q - t_0^{-1}S$, is not. This constraint is neither a prototype or reversed posynomial constraint. However, by a simple transformation the constraint of (507) may be transformed into equivalent prototype and reversed constraints. Then the techniques of reversed geometric programming may be applied to solve (507). In developing this transformation, first observe that the constraint

(508) $$t_0^{-1}Q - t_0^{-1}S \le 1$$

is equivalent to

(509) $$t_0^{-1}Q \le 1 + t_0^{-1}S.$$

Thus, if we introduce a new positive variable $t_1$ satisfying

$$t_0^{-1}Q \le t_1 \le 1 + t_0^{-1}S$$

we see that (509), and thus (508), is equivalent to the constraint

$$t_1^{-1}t_0^{-1}Q \le 1 \le t_1^{-1} + t_1^{-1}t_0^{-1}S.$$

The latter constraint is equivalent to the prototype and reversed constraints

$$t_1^{-1}t_0^{-1}Q \le 1,$$
$$t_1^{-1} + t_1^{-1}t_0^{-1}S \ge 1.$$

Therefore, the constrained optimization problem (507) is equivalent to the reversed geometric programming problem,

$$\text{minimize} \quad g_0(\mathbf{t}) = \frac{300}{Q} + \frac{S^2}{Q} + \frac{t_0^2}{Q}$$

(510) $$\text{subject to} \quad t_0 > 0, \quad t_1 > 0, \quad Q > 0, \quad S > 0$$
$$t_1^{-1}t_0^{-1}Q \le 1$$
$$t_1^{-1} + t_1^{-1}t_0^{-1}S \ge 1.$$

Now the algorithm introduced in the preceding section may be applied to solve (510).

Reversed geometric program (510) is precisely problem (498) of the previous section with $t_1 = t_1$, $t_2 = Q$, $t_3 = S$, $t_4 = t_0$. We saw then that by applying the algorithm for reversed geometric programming, the optimal values of $Q$ and $S$ were approximately $Q^* = 24.49474$ and $S^* = 12.21218$. Thus, in order to minimize the inventory system cost, our initial stock should be $S^* = 12.21218$. Although stock is 0 after $S^*/0.5 = 24.42436$ units of time, the demand is backlogged. A replenishment order of size $Q^* = 24.49474$ is placed after $Q^*/0.5 = 48.98948$ units of time (see Figure

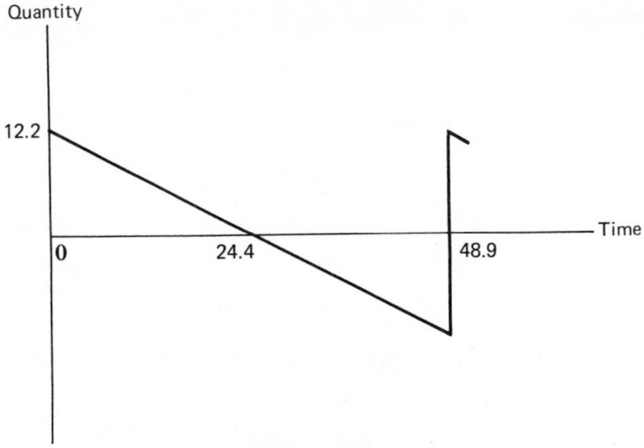


Figure 129

129). Note, further, that the minimum value of (510) is approximately 24.49, and therefore, the minimum total inventory system cost is approximately $24.49 + 0.05 = 24.54$.

The constraint function, $t_0^{-1}Q - t_0^{-1}S$, in (507) is a function of the form

$$f(\mathbf{t}) = \sum_{i=1}^{n} c_i t_1^{a_{i1}} \cdot \ldots \cdot t_m^{a_{im}},$$

where the *coefficients* $c_i$ and the exponents $a_{ij}$ are arbitrary real numbers and $t_1 > 0, \ldots, t_m > 0$. Functions of this form are called *signomials*.*

It is frequently convenient to arrange the terms of the signomial $f(\mathbf{t})$ so that the terms with positive coefficients appear first in the summation. Thus, $f(\mathbf{t})$ is either

(a) a posynomial,
(b) the negative of a posynomial, or
(c) the difference of two posynomials.

Just as the signomial constraint of (507) was transformed into the equivalent prototype and reversed posynomial constraints, a general signomial constraint

$$f(\mathbf{t}) \leq 1 \tag{511}$$

in a geometric programming problem may be transformed into equivalent prototype and reversed posynomial constraints. To prove this fact, we must consider the three possible forms of $f(\mathbf{t})$.

If $f(\mathbf{t})$ is a posynomial, then (511) is already a prototype constraint.

* From Duffin and Peterson (1973).

If $f(\mathbf{t})$ is the negative of a posynomial $g_1(\mathbf{t})$,

$$f(\mathbf{t}) = -g_1(\mathbf{t}),$$

then since $-g_1(\mathbf{t}) \leq 0$, the constraint

$$f(\mathbf{t}) = -g_1(\mathbf{t}) \leq 1$$

is always satisfied. Such a constraint may therefore be eliminated.

If the signomial $f(\mathbf{t})$ is the difference of two posynomials, $g_1(\mathbf{t})$ and $g_2(\mathbf{t})$,

$$f(\mathbf{t}) = g_1(\mathbf{t}) - g_2(\mathbf{t}),$$

then constraint (511) may be transformed into a prototype and a reversed constraint. As in problem (507), observe that

$$f(\mathbf{t}) = g_1(\mathbf{t}) - g_2(\mathbf{t}) \leq 1$$

is equivalent to

$$g_1(\mathbf{t}) \leq 1 + g_2(\mathbf{t}).$$

To form the prototype and reversed constraints, we first introduce a new positive variable $t_0$ satisfying

$$g_1(\mathbf{t}) \leq t_0 \leq 1 + g_2(\mathbf{t}). \tag{512}$$

By multiplying (512) by $t_0^{-1}$ ($>0$), we form the new inequalities,

$$t_0^{-1}g_1(\mathbf{t}) \leq 1 \leq t_0^{-1} + t_0^{-1}g_2(\mathbf{t}). \tag{513}$$

Inequalities (513) are clearly equivalent to the prototype and reversed constraints,

$$t_0^{-1}g_1(\mathbf{t}) \leq 1,$$
$$t_0^{-1} + t_0^{-1}g_2(\mathbf{t}) \geq 1,$$

respectively. Hence, any *signomial geometric programming problem* of the form,

$$\begin{aligned}
&\text{minimize} && g_0(\mathbf{t}) \\
&\text{subject to} && t_1 > 0, \ldots, t_m > 0 \\
& && f(\mathbf{t}) = g_1(\mathbf{t}) - g_2(\mathbf{t}) \leq 1 \\
& && g_3(\mathbf{t}) \leq 1 \\
& && \vdots \\
& && g_p(\mathbf{t}) \leq 1,
\end{aligned} \tag{514}$$

where the $g_k(\mathbf{t})$, $k = 0, 1, \ldots, p$ are posynomials, is equivalent to the reversed geometric programming problem:

$$
\begin{aligned}
&\text{minimize} && g_0(\mathbf{t}) \\
&\text{subject to} && t_0 > 0, t_1 > 0, \ldots, t_m > 0 \\
&&& t_0^{-1} g_1(\mathbf{t}) \le 1 \\
&&& t_0^{-1} + t_0^{-1} g_2(\mathbf{t}) \ge 1 \\
&&& g_3(\mathbf{t}) \le 1 \\
&&& \quad \cdot \quad \cdot \\
&&& \quad \cdot \quad \cdot \\
&&& \quad \cdot \quad \cdot \\
&&& g_p(\mathbf{t}) \le 1.
\end{aligned}
\tag{515}
$$

Thus, for example, the signomial geometric programming problem,

$$
\begin{aligned}
&\text{minimize} && g_0(\mathbf{t}) = 2t_1 t_2 + 3t_1^{-1} t_3 \\
&\text{subject to} && t_1 > 0, \quad t_2 > 0, \quad t_3 > 0 \\
&&& f(\mathbf{t}) = 2t_1^{-1} t_3^{-1} - 5t_2 t_3 - t_1^2 \le 1
\end{aligned}
\tag{516}
$$

may be transformed into an equivalent reversed geometric programming problem. The constraint of (516) is equivalent to

$$
2t_1^{-1} t_3^{-1} \le 1 + 5t_2 t_3 + t_1^2. \tag{517}
$$

By introducing a new positive variable $t_0$ that satisfies

$$
2t_1^{-1} t_3^{-1} \le t_0 \le 1 + 5t_2 t_3 + t_1^2,
$$

or

$$
2t_1^{-1} t_3^{-1} t_0^{-1} \le 1 \le t_0^{-1} + 5t_0^{-1} t_2 t_3 + t_0^{-1} t_1^2,
$$

(517) is seen to be equivalent to the constraints

$$
\begin{aligned}
2t_1^{-1} t_3^{-1} t_0^{-1} &\le 1, \\
t_0^{-1} + 5t_0^{-1} t_2 t_3 + t_0^{-1} t_1^2 &\ge 1.
\end{aligned}
$$

Hence, signomial geometric program (516) is equivalent to the following reversed geometric program:

$$
\begin{aligned}
&\text{minimize} && 2t_1 t_2 + 3t_1^{-1} t_3 \\
&\text{subject to} && t_1 > 0, \quad t_2 > 0, \quad t_3 > 0 \\
&&& 2t_0^{-1} t_1^{-1} t_3^{-1} \le 1 \\
&&& t_0^{-1} + 5t_0^{-1} t_2 t_3 + t_0^{-1} t_1^2 \ge 1.
\end{aligned}
$$

The *general signomial geometric programming problem* of minimizing a signomial $g(\mathbf{t})$ subject to signomial constraints of the form (511) also may be transformed into a reversed geometric programming problem. Since we have already seen that each signomial constraint of such problems may be formulated as prototype and reversed constraints, we need only consider the unconstrained signomial program:

$$\text{(518)} \qquad \text{minimize} \quad g(\mathbf{t}),$$

where $g(\mathbf{t})$ is a signomial.

The transformation used to formulate (518) as a reversed geometric programming problem depends upon the sign of the minimum of $g(\mathbf{t})$. If the minimum of $g(\mathbf{t})$ is *positive*, then problem (518) is equivalent to

$$\begin{array}{ll} \text{minimize} & s \\ \text{subject to} & s > 0, \quad t_1 > 0, \ldots, t_m > 0 \\ & g(\mathbf{t}) \leq s, \end{array}$$

or

$$\text{(519)} \qquad \begin{array}{ll} \text{minimize} & s \\ \text{subject to} & s > 0, \quad t_1 > 0, \ldots, t_m > 0 \\ & f(\mathbf{t}) = s^{-1}g(\mathbf{t}) \leq 1. \end{array}$$

In discussing (519), note that the constraint function $f(\mathbf{t})$ has two possible forms: either a posynomial or the difference between two posynomials. If $f(\mathbf{t}) = s^{-1}g(\mathbf{t})$ is a posynomial, then (519) is a prototype geometric programming problem. If $f(\mathbf{t})$ is the difference of two posynomials, $g_1(\mathbf{t}) - g_2(\mathbf{t})$, (519) is a signomial program of type (514) and may be transformed into a reversed geometric program of form (515).

To illustrate this technique, consider the signomial geometric program:

$$\text{(520)} \qquad \begin{array}{ll} \text{minimize} & g(\mathbf{t}) = t_1^2 t_2^{-2} + t_1 - t_2 \\ \text{subject to} & t_1 > 0, \quad t_2 > 0 \\ & t_1^{-1} t_2 \leq 1. \end{array}$$

Observe that the constraint of (520) implies $t_2 \leq t_1$ or $0 \leq t_1 - t_2$. Thus, $g(\mathbf{t}) = t_1^2 t_2^{-2} + t_1 - t_2 \geq t_1^2 t_2^{-2} \geq 1 > 0$, implying that the constrained values of $g(\mathbf{t})$ are positive. In particular, since the constrained minimum of (520) is positive, (520) is equivalent to

$$\begin{array}{ll} \text{minimize} & s \\ \text{subject to} & s > 0, \quad t_1 > 0, \quad t_2 > 0 \\ & t_1^{-1} t_2 \leq 1 \\ & t_1^2 t_2^{-2} + t_1 - t_2 \leq s, \end{array}$$

or

$$\text{(521)}\qquad \begin{aligned} &\text{minimize} && s \\ &\text{subject to} && s > 0, \quad t_1 > 0, \quad t_2 > 0 \\ &&& t_1^{-1}t_2 \leq 1 \\ &&& s^{-1}t_1^2t_2^{-2} + s^{-1}t_1 - s^{-1}t_2 \leq 1. \end{aligned}$$

Program (521) is a signomial program of type (514) and, as shown above, may be converted into an equivalent reversed program of form (515):

$$\begin{aligned} &\text{minimize} && s \\ &\text{subject to} && s > 0, \quad t_0 > 0, \quad t_1 > 0, \quad t_2 > 0 \\ &&& t_1^{-1}t_2 \leq 1 \\ &&& s^{-1}t_0^{-1}t_1^2t_2^{-2} + s^{-1}t_0^{-1}t_1 \leq 1 \\ &&& t_0^{-1} + t_0^{-1}s^{-1}t_2 \geq 1. \end{aligned}$$

If, however, the minimum of the signomial $g(\mathbf{t})$ in (518) is *negative*, a different technique is used to transform (518) into an equivalent reversed geometric programming problem. In this case, observe that problem (518) is equivalent to maximizing a positive parameter $s$ that satisfies $g(\mathbf{t}) + s \leq 0$; that is, (518) is equivalent to

$$\begin{aligned} &\text{maximize} && s \\ &\text{subject to} && s > 0, \quad t_1 > 0, \ldots, t_m > 0 \\ &&& f(\mathbf{t}) = g(\mathbf{t}) + s \leq 0, \end{aligned}$$

or

$$\text{(522)}\qquad \begin{aligned} &\text{minimize} && s^{-1} \\ &\text{subject to} && s > 0, \quad t_1 > 0, \ldots, t_m > 0 \\ &&& f(\mathbf{t}) = g(\mathbf{t}) + s \leq 0. \end{aligned}$$

The constraint function $f(\mathbf{t})$ may have two possible forms: either the negative of a posynomial or the difference between two posynomials. If $f(\mathbf{t}) = g(\mathbf{t}) + s$ is the negative of a posynomial, the constraint of (522) is always satisfied, and hence, the constraint can be ignored.

If $f(\mathbf{t}) = g(\mathbf{t}) + s$ is the difference of two posynomials, $g_1(\mathbf{t})$ and $g_2(\mathbf{t})$, then the constraint of (522) is

$$\text{(523)}\qquad f(\mathbf{t}) = g_1(\mathbf{t}) - g_2(\mathbf{t}) \leq 0.$$

The latter implies that

$$\text{(524)}\qquad g_1(\mathbf{t}) \leq g_2(\mathbf{t}).$$

By introducing a new positive variable $t_0$ that satisfies

$$g_1(\mathbf{t}) \le t_0 \le g_2(\mathbf{t}),$$

we see that (524) and thus (523), is equivalent to

$$t_0^{-1} g_1(\mathbf{t}) \le 1 \le t_0^{-1} g_2(\mathbf{t}).$$

This implies that constraint (523) is equivalent to the prototype and reversed constraints

$$t_0^{-1} g_1(\mathbf{t}) \le 1,$$
$$t_0^{-1} g_2(\mathbf{t}) \ge 1.$$

Hence, when $f(\mathbf{t})$ is the difference of two posynomials, $g_1(\mathbf{t}) - g_2(\mathbf{t})$, and the minimum of (518) is negative, (522), and thus signomial program (518), is equivalent to the following reversed geometric program:

$$\begin{aligned} &\text{minimize} && s^{-1} \\ &\text{subject to} && s > 0, \quad t_0 > 0, t_1 > 0, \ldots, t_m > 0 \\ &&& t_0^{-1} g_1(\mathbf{t}) \le 1 \\ &&& t_0^{-1} g_2(\mathbf{t}) \ge 1. \end{aligned}$$

To illustrate this procedure, consider the following signomial geometric program:

$$\begin{aligned} &\text{minimize} && t_1^2 - t_1 t_2 \\ &\text{subject to} && t_1 > 0, \quad t_2 > 0 \\ &&& t_1 t_2^{-1} \le 1. \end{aligned} \tag{525}$$

The constrained minimum of this program is negative. Hence, problem (525) is equivalent to

$$\begin{aligned} &\text{maximize} && s \\ &\text{subject to} && s > 0, \quad t_1 > 0, \quad t_2 > 0 \\ &&& t_1 t_2^{-1} \le 1 \\ &&& t_1^2 - t_1 t_2 + s \le 0, \end{aligned}$$

or

$$\begin{aligned} &\text{minimize} && s^{-1} \\ &\text{subject to} && s > 0, \quad t_1 > 0, \quad t_2 > 0 \\ &&& t_1 t_2^{-1} \le 1 \\ &&& t_1^2 + s - t_1 t_2 \le 0. \end{aligned} \tag{526}$$

Note that the second constraint of (526), the difference of two posynomials, is equivalent to

$$t_1^2 + s \leq t_1 t_2.$$

To transform the latter into prototype and reversed constraints, we introduce a new positive variable $t_0$ that satisfies

$$t_1^2 + s \leq t_0 \leq t_1 t_2$$

or

$$t_1^2 t_0^{-1} + s t_0^{-1} \leq 1 \leq t_0^{-1} t_1 t_2.$$

These inequalities are equivalent to

$$t_1^2 t_0^{-1} + s t_0^{-1} \leq 1,$$
$$t_0^{-1} t_1 t_2 \geq 1.$$

Thus, (525) is equivalent to the reversed geometric program:

$$\begin{aligned} \text{minimize} \quad & s^{-1} \\ \text{subject to} \quad & s > 0, \quad t_0 > 0, \quad t_1 > 0, \quad t_2 > 0 \\ & t_1 t_2^{-1} \leq 1 \\ & t_1^2 t_0^{-1} + s t_0^{-1} \leq 1 \\ & t_0^{-1} t_1 t_2 \geq 1. \end{aligned}$$

Note that by inverting the last constraint, this program becomes a prototype program.

## EXERCISES

1. Consider the following optimization problem:

$$\begin{aligned} \text{minimize} \quad & u_1 + u_2 \\ \text{subject to} \quad & \frac{u_3 - u_4}{u_5 - u_6} \leq 1, \end{aligned}$$

where $u_1, \ldots, u_6$ are single-term posynomials.

(*a*) Show that if $u_5 - u_6 > 0$, this problem may be transformed into the following problem:

$$\begin{aligned} \text{minimize} \quad & u_1 + u_2 \\ \text{subject to} \quad & \frac{u_3 + u_6}{u_4 + u_5} \leq 1. \end{aligned}$$

(*b*) Use the ideas presented in this chapter to suggest an algorithm for approximating the value of problem 1*a* by solving a sequence of geometric programming problems.

2. Consider the following optimization problem:

$$\text{(P)} \qquad \begin{array}{ll} \text{minimize} & g_0(\mathbf{t}) \\ \text{subject to} & g_1(\mathbf{t}) - g_2(\mathbf{t}) \le -1, \end{array}$$

where $g_0(\mathbf{t})$, $g_1(\mathbf{t})$, and $g_2(\mathbf{t})$ are posynomials. Show that (P) is equivalent to the following reversed geometric program:

$$\begin{array}{ll} \text{minimize} & g_0(\mathbf{t}) \\ \text{subject to} & t_0^{-1} + t_0^{-1} g_1(\mathbf{t}) \le 1 \\ & t_0^{-1} g_2(\mathbf{t}) \ge 1 \end{array}$$

where $t_0 > 0$.

3. Approximate the maximum value of the following:

$$\begin{array}{ll} \text{maximize} & t_1^{-1} \\ \text{subject to} & t_1 > 0, \qquad t_2 > 0 \\ & t_1 + t_2 \ge 1 \\ & t_1^2 t_2^{-1} + \frac{1}{4} t_2^{-1} \ge 1. \end{array}$$

4. Formulate and solve the replacement problem (with $T = 57$) as a reversed geometric programming problem.

5. Consider a production process in which two inputs are used to produce a single output. Let $x_1$, $x_2$ denote the level of the first and second inputs, respectively; let $c_1$, $c_2$ denote the unit cost of the first and second inputs, respectively; let $q$ denote the level of output. The input–output relationship is described by the Cobbs–Douglas production function

$$q = A x_1^a x_2^{1-a},$$

where $A > 0, 0 < a < 1$.

(*a*) Formulate the problem of determining input levels that minimize the cost of inputs and yield *at least* $q_0$ units of output as a reversed geometric program.

(*b*) Determine the minimum cost and optimal values of $x_1$ and $x_2$.

(*c*) Discuss the effect of variations in $c_1$ and $c_2$ on the minimum input cost.

(*d*) Discuss the effect of variations in $a$ on the relative contribution of each input cost to the total input cost.

Exercises 6–15 are designed to introduce the reader to another technique for solving reversed geometric programming problems. Although this discussion is restricted to the problem

$$\text{(P)} \qquad \begin{aligned} &\text{minimize} && g_0(\mathbf{t}) = u_1 + u_2 \\ &\text{subject to} && t_1 > 0, \qquad t_2 > 0 \\ &&& g_1(\mathbf{t}) = u_3 + u_4 \geq 1, \end{aligned}$$

where $u_i = c_i t_1^{a_{i1}} t_2^{a_{i2}}$, $c_i > 0$, $i = 1, 2, 3, 4$, a generalization of this technique to the general reversed geometric programming problem is straightforward.

6. Use the arithmetic–geometric inequality

$$(\tfrac{1}{2}x + \tfrac{1}{2}y) \geq x^{1/2}y^{1/2}$$
$$x > 0, \qquad y > 0$$

to conclude that

$$(\tfrac{1}{2}x + \tfrac{1}{2}y) \geq \left(\frac{1}{2x} + \frac{1}{2y}\right)^{-1}$$
$$x > 0, \qquad y > 0.$$

The latter inequality is an example of the *arithmetic–harmonic mean inequality*. *Hint*. Observe that

$$\left(\frac{1}{2x} + \frac{1}{2y}\right) \geq \left(\frac{1}{x}\right)^{1/2}\left(\frac{1}{y}\right)^{1/2},$$

and thus,

$$x^{1/2}y^{1/2} \geq \left(\frac{1}{2x} + \frac{1}{2y}\right)^{-1}.$$

7. Use the arithmetic geometric mean inequality

$$(\tfrac{1}{2}x + \tfrac{1}{3}y + \tfrac{1}{6}z) \geq x^{1/2}y^{1/3}z^{1/6}$$
$$x > 0, \qquad y > 0, \qquad z > 0,$$

to conclude that

$$(\tfrac{1}{2}x + \tfrac{1}{3}y + \tfrac{1}{6}z) \geq \left(\frac{1}{2x} + \frac{1}{3y} + \frac{1}{6z}\right)^{-1}$$
$$x > 0, \qquad y > 0, \qquad z > 0.$$

The latter inequality is an example of the *arithmetic–harmonic mean inequality*.

8. Use the arithmetic–geometric mean inequality

$$\alpha_1 v_1 + \alpha_2 v_2 \geq v_1^{\alpha_1} v_2^{\alpha_2}$$
$$v_1 > 0, \qquad v_2 > 0$$
$$\alpha_1 \geq 0, \qquad \alpha_2 \geq 0, \qquad \alpha_1 + \alpha_2 = 1$$

to conclude that

$$\alpha_1 v_1 + \alpha_2 v_2 \geq \left(\frac{\alpha_1}{v_1} + \frac{\alpha_2}{v_2}\right)^{-1}$$

$$v_1 > 0, \qquad v_2 > 0$$

$$\alpha_1 \geq 0, \qquad \alpha_2 \geq 0, \qquad \alpha_1 + \alpha_2 = 1.$$

This is an example of the *arithmetic–harmonic mean inequality*.

9. Use the arithmetic–harmonic mean inequality in problem 8 to conclude that

$$\frac{\alpha_1^2}{w_1} + \frac{\alpha_2^2}{w_2} \geq (w_1 + w_2)^{-1}$$

$$w_1 > 0, \qquad w_2 > 0$$

$$\alpha_1 \geq 0, \qquad \alpha_2 \geq 0, \qquad \alpha_1 + \alpha_2 = 1.$$

This is an example of the *harmonic inequality*. *Hint*. Make the substitutions

$$v_i = \frac{\alpha_i}{w_i}, \qquad i = 1, 2.$$

10. Show that if

$$\alpha_i = \frac{w_i}{w_1 + w_2}, \qquad i = 1, 2,$$

the harmonic inequality in problem 9 becomes an equality.

11. Use the harmonic inequality to conclude that if $\mathbf{t}'$ is a feasible solution of the prototype geometric programming problem

$$(\mathrm{P}_R(\boldsymbol{\alpha})) \qquad \begin{aligned} &\text{minimize} && g_0(\mathbf{t}) = u_1 + u_2 \\ &\text{subject to} && t_1 > 0, \quad t_2 > 0 \\ & && \bar{g}_1(\mathbf{t}) = \frac{\alpha_1^2}{u_3} + \frac{\alpha_2^2}{u_4} \leq 1 \\ & && \alpha_1 \geq 0, \quad \alpha_2 \geq 0, \quad \alpha_1 + \alpha_2 = 1 \end{aligned}$$

then $\mathbf{t}'$ is a feasible solution of the reversed geometric programming problem

$$(\mathrm{P}) \qquad \begin{aligned} &\text{minimize} && g_0(\mathbf{t}) = u_1 + u_2 \\ &\text{subject to} && t_1 > 0, \quad t_2 > 0 \\ & && g_1(\mathbf{t}) = u_3 + u_4 \geq 1, \end{aligned}$$

where $u_i = c_i t_1^{a_{i1}} t_2^{a_{i2}}$, $c_i > 0$, $i = 1, 2$. Program $(\mathrm{P}_R(\boldsymbol{\alpha}))$ is called the *harmonized geometric programming problem.** Note that since we have the implication

$$\bar{g}_1(\mathbf{t}) \leq 1 \rightarrow g_1(\mathbf{t}) \geq 1,$$

$\overline{M}$, the minimum of ($P_R(\boldsymbol{\alpha})$), and $M$, the minimum of (P), satisfy

$$\overline{M} \geq M.$$

12. Formulate the harmonized geometric programming program for the following reversed geometric programs:

(*a*) minimize $5t_1 + t_2^{-1}t_3$

subject to $t_1 > 0, \quad t_2 > 0, \quad t_3 > 0$

$\frac{1}{6}t_1^2t_3 + t_2^{-4} \geq 1$

(*b*) minimize $\frac{1}{9}t_1t_2^{-1} + t_3t_4^2$

subject to $t_1 > 0, \quad t_2 > 0, \quad t_3 > 0, \quad t_4 > 0$

$2t_4 + t_1^2t_2^{-1} + \frac{1}{3}t_3^2 \geq 1.$

13. Show that if $\mathbf{t}'$ is a feasible solution of (P) then $\mathbf{t}'$ is a feasible solution of ($P_R(\boldsymbol{\alpha})$) with weights

$$\alpha_i = \frac{u_i(\mathbf{t}')}{g_1(\mathbf{t}')}, \qquad i = 1, 2,$$

and hence, the difference $\overline{M} - M$ can be made arbitrarily small.

14. Use the result of problem 13 to suggest an algorithm that utilizes the harmonized geometric programming problem ($P_R(\boldsymbol{\alpha})$) to approximate the minimum of (P).
15. Use the suggested algorithm in problem 14 to solve problems 12*a* and 12*b*.
16. From past election results, incumbent Sen. May has determined that a portion of the votes he receives in the general election depends primarily on three variables. Specifically, the number of these votes he receives in the rural, urban, and suburban areas of his state depends upon the amount of money he spends on travel for personal appearances, salaries of staff members, and production of campaign literature in each of these areas. Assume the number of votes he receives in the $i$th area ($i = 1$, rural; $i = 2$, urban; $i = 3$, suburban) is proportional to

$$t_i^{a_i}s_i^{b_i}r_i^{c_i}$$

where $t_i$, $s_i$, and $r_i$ are the amounts spent on travel for personal appearances, salaries of staff members, and campaign literature, respectively.

* From Duffin and Peterson (1971).

($a_i$, $b_i$, $c_i$, $i = 1, 2, 3$ are constants.) Assume further that the total campaign expenditures for travel, staff members, and campaign literature are legally constrained not to exceed the amounts $T$, $S$, and $R$, respectively.

(*a*) Formulate the problem of maximizing this portion of the votes while meeting the campaign spending restrictions.

(*b*) Assign realistic values to the parameters of this optimization problem and use geometric programming techniques to solve it.

(*c*) Suppose that his campaign slogan, "May in November," prompts a negative reaction to Sen. May in the cities. Alter your optimization problem to account for the resulting voting behavior.

(*d*) Use geometric programming to solve the altered problem.

# APPENDIX TOPICS IN CALCULUS

## INTRODUCTION

Throughout this book an understanding of several mathematical concepts and techniques from the calculus of several variables is necessary. The following is a discussion of these preliminary topics. We proceed by first considering several algebraic, geometric, and topological notions and then relate them to the calculus.

## ALGEBRA AND GEOMETRY OF VECTORS IN $\mathbb{R}^n$

In analytic geometry the structures of the plane and space are studied by introducing the appropriate Cartesian coordinate system. In three space, for instance, this coordinate system consists of three perpendicular lines, or *axes*, marked with a scale used to identify points. To each point in the plane there corresponds an ordered pair of numbers, and to each point in space, an ordered triple of numbers.

The geometry of the plane, three space, and, indeed, spaces of higher dimensions may also be treated in terms of vectors. Here we introduce several of the algebraic and geometric properties of vectors necessary for an analysis of the geometry of convex structures. We begin by discussing a familiar set of vectors and later generalize the characteristics of this set.

The set of all ordered pairs of real numbers is called $\mathbb{R}^2$. An element or point $\mathbf{y} = (y_1, y_2)$ in $\mathbb{R}^2$ is called a *vector*. The numbers $y_1$ and $y_2$ are called the *first* and *second components*, respectively, of the vector $\mathbf{y}$. Examples of vectors in $\mathbb{R}^2$ are $(2, 1)$, $(0, -5)$, and $(\pi, \frac{1}{2})$. The term *ordered* means that we must distinguish between the first and second components of vectors. Two vectors $\mathbf{y} = (y_1, y_2)$ and $\mathbf{x} = (x_1, x_2)$ are equal if and only if $y_1 = x_1$ and $y_2 = x_2$. Thus, the vectors $(1, 4)$ and $(4, 1)$ are *not equal* because the respective components are not equal.

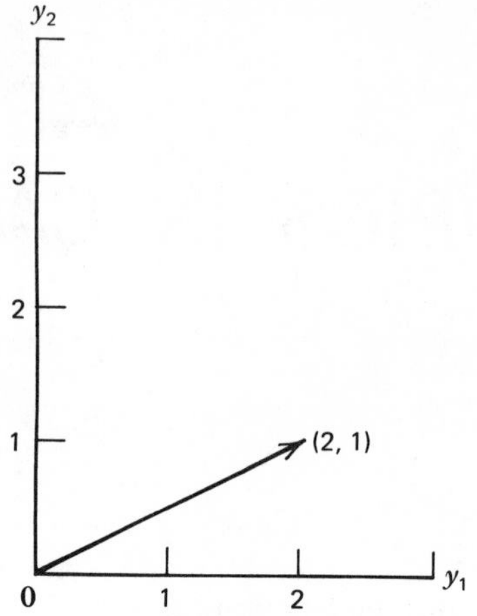


**Figure A1**

Geometrically, a vector $\mathbf{y} = (y_1, y_2)$ in $\mathbb{R}^2$ is represented in a Cartesian coordinate system by an arrow beginning at the origin and terminating at the point $(y_1, y_2)$. The vector (2, 1) is shown in Figure A1.

Just as for real numbers, we can define several algebraic operations for vectors in $\mathbb{R}^2$. If $\mathbf{x} = (x_1, x_2)$ and $\mathbf{y} = (y_1, y_2)$ are vectors in $\mathbb{R}^2$, we define the *vector sum*, denoted by $\mathbf{x} + \mathbf{y}$, to be the vector $(x_1 + y_1, x_2 + y_2)$ in $\mathbb{R}^2$; that is, the respective components of $\mathbf{x}$ and $\mathbf{y}$ are added to form the vector sum. For example, if $\mathbf{x} = (1, 7)$ and $\mathbf{y} = (2, 4)$ the vector sum is

$$\mathbf{x} + \mathbf{y} = (1, 7) + (2, 4) = (3, 11).$$

Vector addition may be viewed geometrically as shown in Figure A2. To add $\mathbf{x} = (1, 7)$ and $\mathbf{y} = (2, 4)$, we complete the parallelogram with sides $\mathbf{x}$ and $\mathbf{y}$. The vector $\mathbf{x} + \mathbf{y}$ is the diagonal of the parallelogram beginning at (0, 0).

This construction illustrates the fact that for any vectors $\mathbf{x}$ and $\mathbf{y}$, there is one, and only one, vector $\mathbf{z}$ such that $\mathbf{z} = \mathbf{x} + \mathbf{y}$. Accordingly, $\mathbf{y} = \mathbf{z} - \mathbf{x}$, thus providing a definition of vector subtraction.

Vector addition in $\mathbb{R}^2$ satisfies several properties:

$$\begin{aligned} \mathbf{x} + \mathbf{y} &= \mathbf{y} + \mathbf{x}, \\ \mathbf{x} + (\mathbf{y} + \mathbf{z}) &= (\mathbf{x} + \mathbf{y}) + \mathbf{z}, \\ \mathbf{x} + \mathbf{y} &= \mathbf{z} \quad \text{if and only if} \quad \mathbf{y} = \mathbf{z} - \mathbf{x}, \\ \mathbf{x} + \mathbf{0} &= \mathbf{x}, \\ \mathbf{x} - \mathbf{x} &= \mathbf{0}, \end{aligned} \tag{A1}$$

where $\mathbf{0}$ is the zero vector.

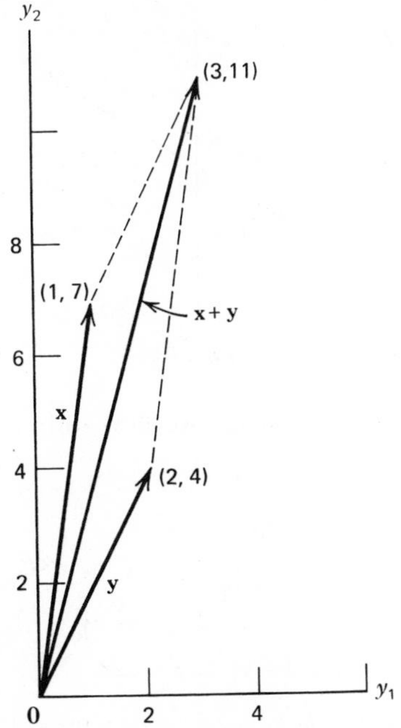


Figure A2

We can also define *scalar multiplication* of a vector $\mathbf{y} = (y_1, y_2) \in \mathbb{R}^2$ and a scalar $\alpha$. The product $\alpha\mathbf{y}$ is defined to be the vector $(\alpha y_1, \alpha y_2) \in \mathbb{R}^2$. For example, if $\mathbf{y} = (-1, 6)$ and $\alpha = 4$, then $\alpha\mathbf{y} = 4(-1, 6) = (-4, 24)$. Note that if $\alpha = 0$, $\alpha\mathbf{y} = (0, 0)$, the *zero vector*.

Geometrically, the product $\alpha\mathbf{y}$ is a vector that is collinear with $\mathbf{y}$. If $\alpha > 1$, the vector $\mathbf{y}$ is magnified (see Figure A3) and if $0 < \alpha < 1$, the vector $\mathbf{y}$ is contracted (see Figure A4). Note that when $\alpha < 0$, the direction of $\mathbf{y}$ is reversed (see Figure A5).

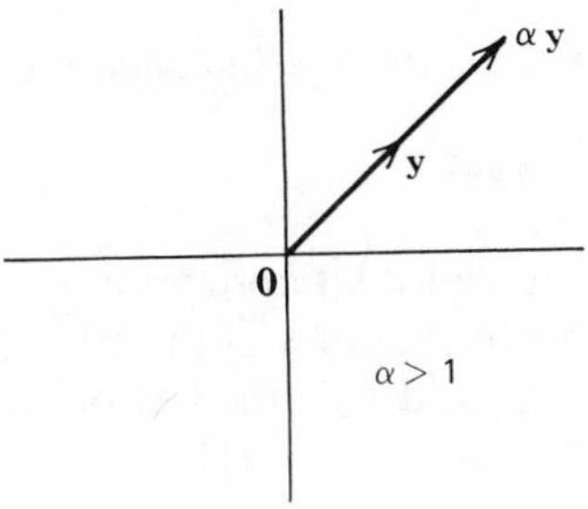


Figure A3

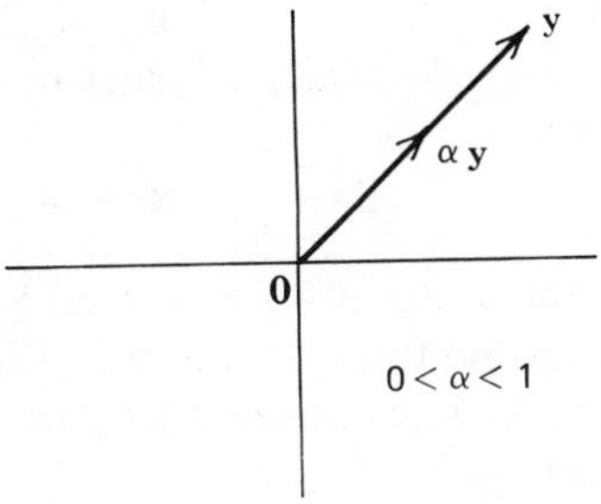


Figure A4

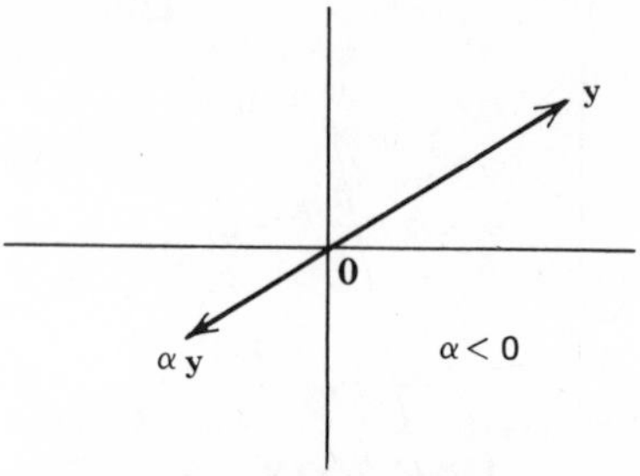


Figure A5

Scalar multiplication also satisfies several additional properties:

$$\begin{aligned} 1\mathbf{y} &= \mathbf{y}, \\ (\alpha\beta)\mathbf{y} &= \alpha(\beta\mathbf{y}), \\ (\alpha + \beta)\mathbf{y} &= \alpha\mathbf{y} + \beta\mathbf{y}, \\ \alpha(\mathbf{x} + \mathbf{y}) &= \alpha\mathbf{x} + \alpha\mathbf{y}, \\ \mathbf{x} + (-\mathbf{y}) &= \mathbf{x} - \mathbf{y}. \end{aligned} \tag{A2}$$

The definition of the *length*, or *norm*, of a vector in $\mathbb{R}^2$ is easily formulated. Consider the vector $\mathbf{y} = (y_1, y_2) \in \mathbb{R}^2$ shown in Figure A6. By the Pythagorean theorem, the length of $\mathbf{y}$, denoted by $\|\mathbf{y}\|$, is $\|\mathbf{y}\| = \sqrt{y_1^2 + y_2^2}$. Note that $\|\mathbf{y}\| \geq 0$ and, further, $\|\mathbf{y}\| = 0$ if and only if $\mathbf{y}$ is the zero vector.

Another important notion extensively used in our discussion of convex structures is that of the *scalar product* of two vectors. The *scalar product* of two vectors $\mathbf{x} = (x_1, x_2)$ and $\mathbf{y} = (y_1, y_2)$ in $\mathbb{R}^2$ is defined as

$$x_1y_1 + x_2y_2$$

and is denoted by $\mathbf{x} \cdot \mathbf{y}$. For instance, if $\mathbf{x} = (2, 3)$ and $\mathbf{y} = (-1, 4)$, the scalar product is the number

$$\mathbf{x} \cdot \mathbf{y} = (2)(-1) + (3)(4) = 10.$$

Note that the scalar product of a vector $\mathbf{x}$ with itself is the square of the norm of $\mathbf{x}$:

$$\mathbf{x} \cdot \mathbf{x} = x_1^2 + x_2^2 = \|\mathbf{x}\|^2.$$

The scalar product is readily given a geometric interpretation by considering the triangle shown in Figure A7. Since the sides of the triangle in Figure A7 have nonzero lengths $\|\mathbf{y}\|$, $\|\mathbf{x} - \mathbf{y}\|$, and $\|\mathbf{x}\|$, the law of cosines implies

$$\|\mathbf{x} - \mathbf{y}\|^2 = \|\mathbf{x}\|^2 + \|\mathbf{y}\|^2 - 2\,\|\mathbf{x}\|\,\|\mathbf{y}\|\cos\theta. \tag{A3}$$

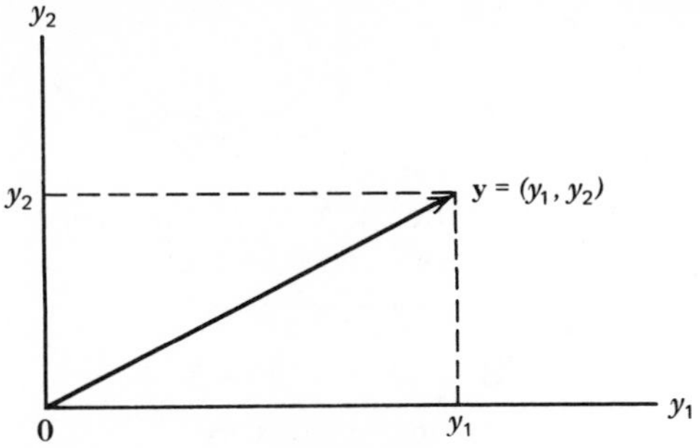


Figure A6

It is assumed that $0 \leq \theta \leq \pi$. With $\mathbf{x} = (x_1, x_2)$ and $\mathbf{y} = (y_1, y_2)$ an expansion of (A3) yields

$$\begin{aligned} 2\,\|\mathbf{x}\|\,\|\mathbf{y}\|\cos\theta &= \|\mathbf{x}\|^2 + \|\mathbf{y}\|^2 - \|\mathbf{x} - \mathbf{y}\|^2 \\ &= x_1^2 + x_2^2 + y_1^2 + y_2^2 - (x_1 - y_1)^2 - (x_2 - y_2)^2 \\ &= 2(x_1 y_1 + x_2 y_2) \\ &= 2(\mathbf{x} \cdot \mathbf{y}). \end{aligned}$$

Hence, $\mathbf{x} \cdot \mathbf{y} = \|\mathbf{x}\|\,\|\mathbf{y}\|\cos\theta$. Thus, the angle between the vectors $\mathbf{x}$ and $\mathbf{y}$ in $\mathbb{R}^2$ satisfies

$$\cos\theta = \frac{\mathbf{x} \cdot \mathbf{y}}{\|\mathbf{x}\|\,\|\mathbf{y}\|}.$$

If either $\mathbf{x}$ or $\mathbf{y}$ is the zero vector, the latter expression is not defined. Note that if $\mathbf{x} \cdot \mathbf{y} = 0$, $\theta = \pi/2$, implying that $\mathbf{x}$ and $\mathbf{y}$ are perpendicular.

As an example, note that the angle between $\mathbf{x} = (1, 1)$ and $\mathbf{y} = (0, 2)$

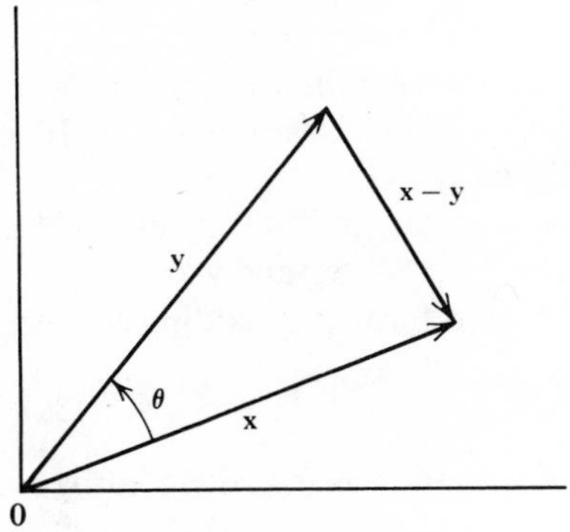


Figure A7

is $\pi/4$ since

$$\cos\theta = \frac{2}{2\sqrt{2}} = \frac{1}{\sqrt{2}}.$$

We now state without proof several of the properties of the *scalar product:*

$$\begin{aligned} \mathbf{x}\cdot\mathbf{y} &= \mathbf{y}\cdot\mathbf{x} \\ \mathbf{x}\cdot(\mathbf{y}+\mathbf{z}) &= \mathbf{x}\cdot\mathbf{y}+\mathbf{y}\cdot\mathbf{z} \\ \alpha\mathbf{x}\cdot\beta\mathbf{y} &= (\alpha\beta)\mathbf{x}\cdot\mathbf{y} \\ |\mathbf{x}\cdot\mathbf{y}| &\le \|\mathbf{x}\|\,\|\mathbf{y}\|. \end{aligned} \tag{A4}$$

The last property above is known as *Schwarz's inequality*.

The final concept to be introduced is *linear independence* of vectors in $\mathbb{R}^2$. Two vectors $\mathbf{y} = (y_1, y_2)$ and $\mathbf{x} = (x_1, x_2)$ are said to be *linearly independent* if

$$\alpha_1\mathbf{x} + \alpha_2\mathbf{y} = \mathbf{0}$$

holds only when the scalars $\alpha_1 = 0$ and $\alpha_2 = 0$. Otherwise, $\mathbf{x}$ and $\mathbf{y}$ are *linearly dependent*. Thus, $\mathbf{y} = (1, 1)$ and $\mathbf{x} = (1, 0)$ are examples of linearly independent vectors since if

$$\alpha_1\mathbf{x} + \alpha_2\mathbf{y} = \alpha_1(1, 0) + \alpha_2(1, 1) = (\alpha_1 + \alpha_2, \alpha_2) = (0, 0),$$

then $\alpha_1 = 0$ and $\alpha_2 = 0$. Note that if $\mathbf{x}$ and $\mathbf{y}$ are linearly dependent and $\mathbf{x} \neq \mathbf{0}$, $\mathbf{y}$ is a scalar multiple of $\mathbf{x}$; $\mathbf{x} = (1, 1)$ and $\mathbf{y} = (2, 2)$ are linearly dependent since $\mathbf{y} = 2\mathbf{x}$.

The concept of a vector in $\mathbb{R}^2$ and the associated algebraic operations may be generalized to an ordered $n$-tuple of real numbers, $(y_1, \ldots, y_n)$. The set denoted by $\mathbb{R}^n$, where $n$ is a positive integer, is the set of all ordered $n$-tuples of real numbers. An element or point of $\mathbb{R}^n$ is denoted by $\mathbf{y} = (y_1, \ldots, y_n)$ and is called a *vector*. As in $\mathbb{R}^2$ the term *ordered* means that the two vectors $\mathbf{y} = (y_1, \ldots, y_n)$ and $\mathbf{x} = (x_1, \ldots, x_n)$ are equal if and only if $x_1 = y_1, \ldots, x_n = y_n$. The real number $y_i$ is called the $i$th *component* of the vector $\mathbf{y} = (y_1, \ldots, y_n) \in \mathbb{R}^n$. The *zero vector* in $\mathbb{R}^n$ is the vector with all components identically zero.

Vector addition and scalar multiplication in $\mathbb{R}^n$ are defined as in $\mathbb{R}^2$. Consider the vectors $\mathbf{x} = (x_1, \ldots, x_n)$ and $\mathbf{y} = (y_1, \ldots, y_n)$ in $\mathbb{R}^n$. The vector sum $\mathbf{x} + \mathbf{y}$ of $\mathbf{x}$ and $\mathbf{y}$ in $\mathbb{R}^n$ is formed by adding corresponding components:

$$\mathbf{x} + \mathbf{y} = (x_1 + y_1, \ldots, x_n + y_n).$$

*Scalar multiplication* of $\mathbf{y}$ by the scalar $\alpha$, denoted by $\alpha\mathbf{y}$, is defined as

$$\alpha\mathbf{y} = (\alpha y_1, \ldots, \alpha y_n).$$

The vector sum and scalar multiplication in $\mathbb{R}^n$ also satisfy properties (A1) and (A2), respectively. Unless $n = 1, 2$, or 3, there is, of course, no geometric interpretations of these operations.

The *norm* of a vector $\mathbf{y} = (y_1, \ldots, y_n) \in \mathbb{R}^n$, denoted by $\|\mathbf{y}\|$, is readily generalized from $\mathbb{R}^2$:

$$\|\mathbf{y}\| = \sqrt{y_1^2 + \cdots + y_n^2}.$$

Note that $\|\mathbf{y}\| \geq 0$, and $\|\mathbf{y}\| = 0$ if and only if $\mathbf{y}$ is the zero vector. If $\|\mathbf{y}\| = 1$, $\mathbf{y}$ is called a *unit vector*.

The *scalar product* of vectors $\mathbf{x} = (x_1, \ldots, x_n)$ and $\mathbf{y} = (y_1, \ldots, y_n)$ in $\mathbb{R}^n$, denoted by $\mathbf{x} \cdot \mathbf{y}$, is the real number

$$\mathbf{x} \cdot \mathbf{y} = x_1 y_1 + \cdots + x_n y_n.$$

As in $\mathbb{R}^2$, if $\mathbf{x} = \mathbf{y}$,

$$\mathbf{x} \cdot \mathbf{x} = x_1^2 + \cdots + x_n^2 = \|\mathbf{x}\|^2.$$

The scalar product of vectors in $\mathbb{R}^n$ also satisfies properties (A4).

In $\mathbb{R}^n$ also, vectors may be characterized as being linearly independent or dependent. The vectors $\mathbf{y}^1, \ldots, \mathbf{y}^k$ in $\mathbb{R}^n$ are said to be *linearly independent* if

$$\alpha_1 \mathbf{y}^1 + \cdots + \alpha_k \mathbf{y}^k = \mathbf{0}$$

holds only when the scalars $\alpha_1, \ldots, \alpha_k$ satisfy $\alpha_1 = 0, \ldots, \alpha_k = 0$. Otherwise, $\mathbf{y}^1, \ldots, \mathbf{y}^k$ are *linearly dependent*.

For example, $\mathbf{y}^1 = (0, 1, 0, 1)$, $\mathbf{y}^2 = (2, 0, 0, 0)$, and $\mathbf{y}^3 = (0, 0, -1, 3)$ are linearly independent. If

$$\alpha_1(0, 1, 0, 1) + \alpha_2(2, 0, 0, 0) + \alpha_3(0, 0, -1, 3) = (0, 0, 0, 0),$$

then by adding corresponding components, we have

$$(2\alpha_2, \alpha_1, -\alpha_3, \alpha_1 + 3\alpha_3) = (0, 0, 0, 0),$$

which implies

$$\alpha_1 = 0, \qquad \alpha_2 = 0, \qquad \alpha_3 = 0.$$

The concept of *distance* between vectors or points in $\mathbb{R}^n$ is also important. The distance between vectors $\mathbf{x}$ and $\mathbf{y}$ in $\mathbb{R}^n$ is defined to be

$$d = \|\mathbf{x} - \mathbf{y}\| = \sqrt{(\mathbf{x} - \mathbf{y}) \cdot (\mathbf{x} - \mathbf{y})}.$$

If $\mathbf{x} = (x_1, \ldots, x_n)$ and $\mathbf{y} = (y_1, \ldots, y_n)$, then the distance between them is

$$d = [(x_1 - y_1)^2 + \cdots + (x_n - y_n)^2]^{1/2}.$$

Note that for $n = 2$ or $n = 3$ this is the Euclidean distance formula.

## TOPOLOGICAL NOTIONS ON $\mathbb{R}^n$

We shall consider the ideas of "nearness" and "inside" in relation to $\mathbb{R}^n$ and later employ them in our discussion of convex structures and convex functions. Elementary topological notions for $\mathbb{R}^n$ are presented now to give precision to these intuitive geometrical concepts.

The fundamental topological notion here is the concept of a *neighborhood*. The others are derived from it. A particular property is said to hold in a *neighborhood* of $\mathbf{y}^0 \in \mathbb{R}^n$ if it holds for all points within a specified distance of $\mathbf{y}^0$. Specifically a *neighborhood* of a point or vector $\mathbf{y}^0$ in $\mathbb{R}^n$ is a set of the form

$$N = \{\mathbf{y} : \|\mathbf{y} - \mathbf{y}^0\| < \epsilon\}.$$

In the set $\mathbb{R}^1$ a neighborhood of a point $\mathbf{y}^0$ is a symmetric interval centered at $\mathbf{y}^0$. In $\mathbb{R}^2$ a neighborhood of $\mathbf{y}^0 = (y_1^0, y_2^0)$ is the interior of the disk centered at $(y_1^0, y_2^0)$ (see Figure A8). In $\mathbb{R}^3$ a neighborhood of $\mathbf{y}^0 = (y_1^0, y_2^0, y_3^0)$ is the interior of the sphere centered at $\mathbf{y}^0$ (see Figure A9).

To be precise, the concept of a *neighborhood*, as defined above, should be called a *spherical neighborhood*. Although this is a special kind of neighborhood, it will suffice for our purposes.

Each point $\mathbf{y} \in \mathbb{R}^n$ is related in one of three ways to a set $S \subset \mathbb{R}^n$. The point $\mathbf{y}$ is *interior* to $S$ if and only if $S$ contains some neighborhood of $\mathbf{y}$. For example, in Figure A10 the points $\mathbf{y}^1$ and $\mathbf{y}^2$ are interior to $S$ because there exist neighborhoods $N_1$ and $N_2$ of $\mathbf{y}^1$ and $\mathbf{y}^2$, respectively, in $S$. The points $\mathbf{y}^3$ and $\mathbf{y}^4$ are not interior to $S$ because no such neighborhoods can be constructed entirely in $S$. Thus, an interior point is surrounded completely by points of $S$.

A point $\mathbf{y}$ is *exterior* to $S$ if and only if $\mathbf{y} \notin S$ and there is a neighborhood

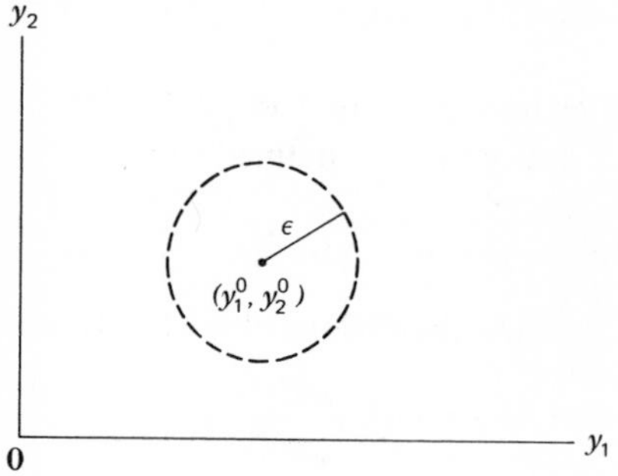


**Figure A8**

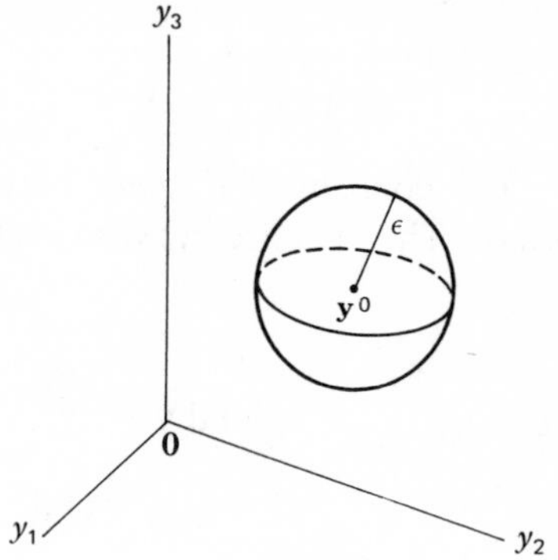


**Figure A9**

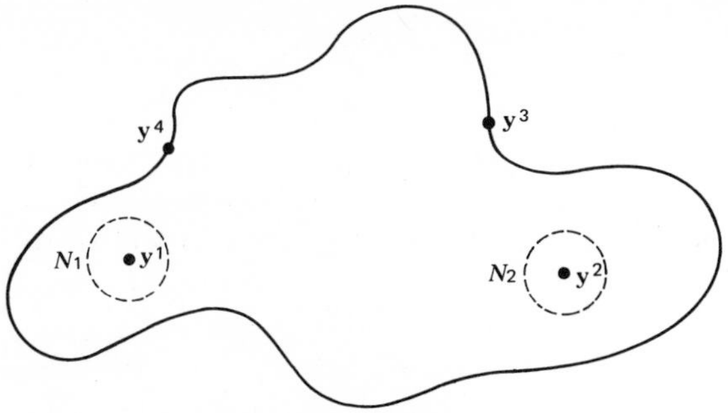


Figure A10

of $\mathbf{y}$ disjoint from $S$. As shown in Figure A11, $\mathbf{y}^5$ and $\mathbf{y}^6$ are exterior to $S$ because they can be contained in neighborhoods entirely outside the set.

Finally, $\mathbf{y} \in \mathbb{R}^n$ is a *boundary point* of $S \subset \mathbb{R}^n$ if and only if $\mathbf{y}$ is neither interior nor exterior to $S$. The set of all boundary points of a set $S$ is called its *boundary*. The points marked $\mathbf{y}^7$ and $\mathbf{y}^8$ in Figure A12 are boundary points of $S$. Neither of these points can be contained in a neighborhood entirely within or entirely outside $S$.

Having established these concepts, it is easy to define open and closed sets. A set $S$ is *open* if and only if every point $\mathbf{y}$ of $S$ is interior to $S$. Equivalently, an open set contains a neighborhood of each of its points. Thus, an open set contains no boundary points.

A set $S$ is *closed* if and only if every point that is not in $S$ is exterior to $S$. This definition implies $S$ is closed if and only if $S$ contains its boundary.

Consider several examples of sets that are open, sets that are closed, and sets that are neither open nor closed. The set

$$S_1 = \{(y_1, y_2): \tfrac{1}{2} < y_1 < 1, -1 < y_2 < -\tfrac{1}{2}\}$$

is open. $S_1$ is the inside of the square with dotted boundary shown in Figure

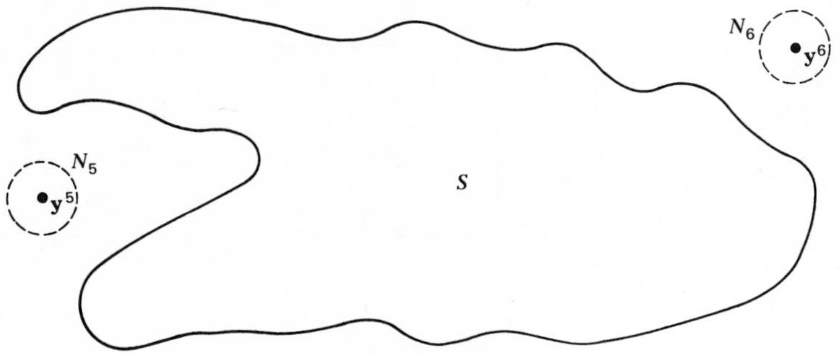


Figure A11

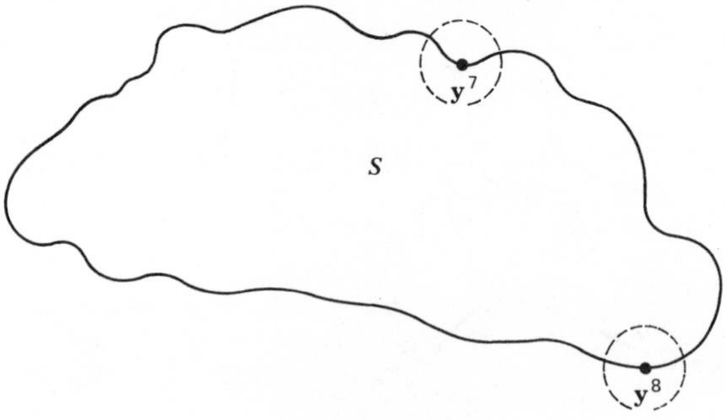


Figure A12

A13; it contains a neighborhood of each of its points. The set

$$S_2 = \{(y_1, y_2): \tfrac{1}{2} \le y_1 \le 1, -1 \le y_2 \le -\tfrac{1}{2}\}$$

is closed. It is the inside and *boundary* of the square in Figure A14. The set

$$S_3 = \{(y_1, y_2): \tfrac{1}{2} < y_1 < 1, -1 \le y_2 \le -\tfrac{1}{2}\}$$

is neither closed nor open. It is not closed, because it does not contain all of its boundary; it is not open, because it contains part of its boundary (see Figure A15).

The terms "bounded" and "unbounded" refer to the "geometric size" of a set $S$ in $\mathbb{R}^n$. A set $S \subset \mathbb{R}^n$ is said to be *bounded* if there exists a number $r$ such that $\|\mathbf{y}\| < r$ for every $\mathbf{y} \in S$. Geometrically, this means that the set $S$ can be contained in a "sphere" of radius $r$. For example, the set

$$S_4 = \{(y_1, y_2): 1 \le y_1 \le 2, 0 \le y_2 \le \tfrac{1}{3}\}$$

is bounded because it can be contained in a circle of radius $\frac{5}{2}$, as shown in

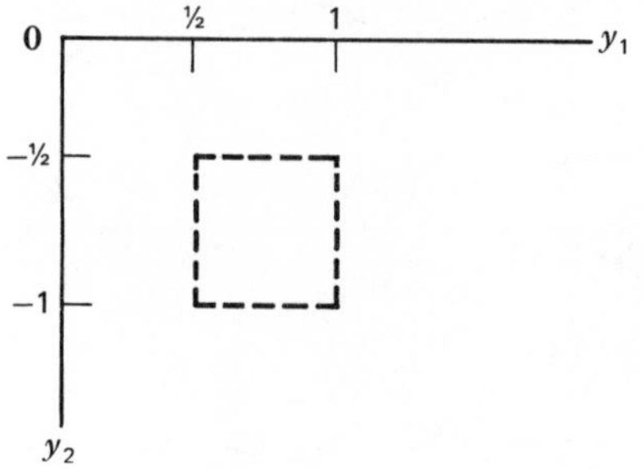


Figure A13

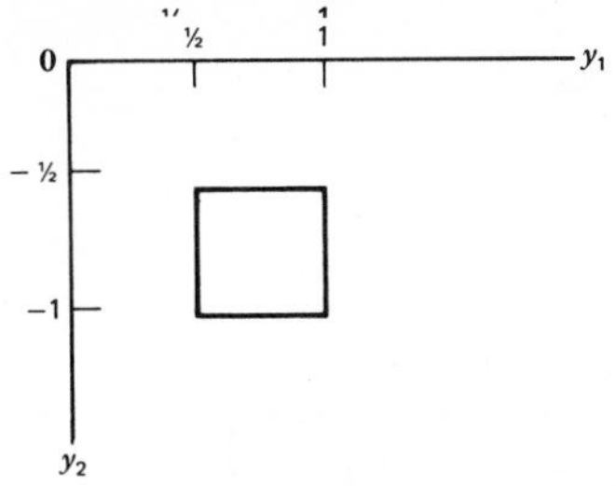


Figure A14

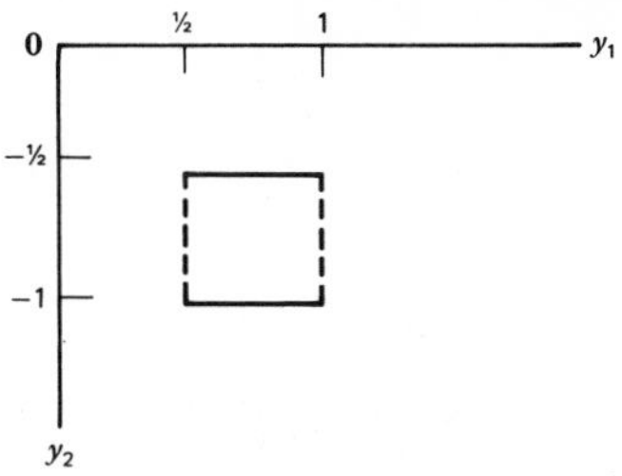


Figure A15

Figure A16. The set

$$S_5 = \{(y_1, y_2): 0 \le y_1, 0 \le y_2 \le 1\}$$

is unbounded because it cannot be contained in any circle, no matter how large (see Figure A17). More generally, a set $S$ is said to be *unbounded* if there exists no $r > 0$ such that $\|\mathbf{y}\| < r$ for all $\mathbf{y} \in S$.

Finally, a set $S \subset \mathbb{R}^n$ is said to be *bounded from below* if there exists a point $\mathbf{b} = (b_1, \ldots, b_n) \in \mathbb{R}^n$ with finite components such that for every $\mathbf{y} = (y_1, \ldots, y_n) \in S$, $y_i > b_i$, $i = 1, \ldots, n$. For example, the positive orthant, $\{(y_1, \ldots, y_n): y_i > 0, i = 1, \ldots, n\}$ is bounded from below, since $y_i > 0$, $i = 1, \ldots, n$. The $n$-dimensional open sphere

$$\left\{(y_1, \ldots, y_n): \sum_{i=1}^{n} y_i^2 < 1\right\}$$

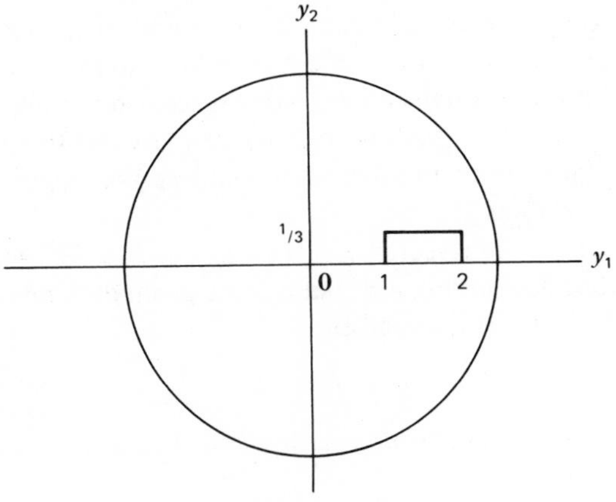


Figure A16

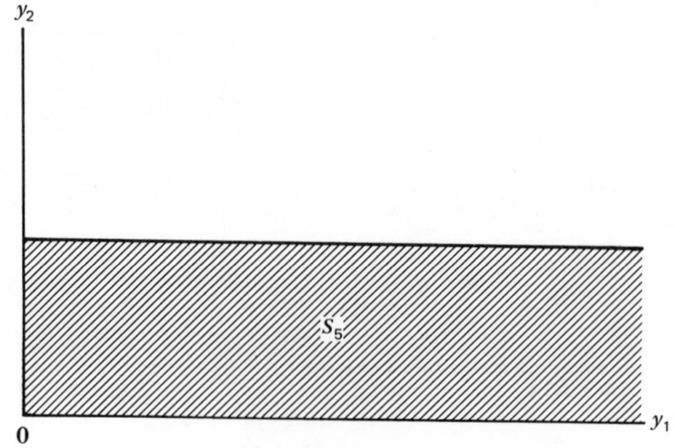


Figure A17

is bounded from below, since $y_i > -2$, $i = 1, \ldots, n$. An analogous definition holds if a set is *bounded from above*.

## DIFFERENTIAL CALCULUS OF FUNCTIONS OF SEVERAL VARIABLES

In many mathematical models the effect of variations in *several* independent parameters must be considered when representing a social or economic situation. For instance, the sales of a new appliance depend not only on the price of the product but also on factors such as the advertising expenditures and the availability of the product. Thus, the sales of this appliance are a function of several variables—price, advertising, and availability.

In this section properties of functions of several variables are examined. Concepts such as continuity and differentiability are extended to functions of several variables. Although much of this discussion is restricted to functions of two variables for illustrative purposes, the results are appropriate for functions of any finite number of variables. We begin by defining a function of two variables.

Suppose that to each vector $\mathbf{x} = (x_1, x_2)$ in $S \subset \mathbb{R}^2$ we can assign a real number $q$. The real number $q$ is said to be given as a *function of the two variables* $x_1$ and $x_2$ and is denoted by

$$q = f(x_1, x_2).$$

In vector notation, this functional relationship is simply

$$q = f(\mathbf{x}),$$

where $\mathbf{x} \in S$.

Thus, for example, the function

$$f(\mathbf{x}) = \sqrt{1 - x_1^2 - x_2^2}$$

assigns to each point $\mathbf{x} = (x_1, x_2)$ in the set

$$S = \{(x_1, x_2): x_1^2 + x_2^2 \le 1\} \subset \mathbb{R}^2$$

the real number

$$q = \sqrt{1 - x_1^2 - x_2^2}.$$

For instance, associated with the points $(-1, 0)$ and $(\frac{1}{2}, \frac{1}{2})$ in $S$ are the real numbers

$$q_1 = f(-1, 0) = \sqrt{1 - (-1)^2 - (0)^2} = 0$$

and

$$q_2 = f(\tfrac{1}{2}, \tfrac{1}{2}) = \sqrt{1 - (\tfrac{1}{2})^2 - (\tfrac{1}{2})^2} = \frac{\sqrt{2}}{2},$$

respectively. Note that no real number $q$ corresponds to points $\mathbf{x} \notin S$; for points not in $S$ the corresponding value is imaginary.

As a second example, consider the function

$$f(\mathbf{x}) = x_1^2 + x_2^2,$$

defined on $S = \mathbb{R}^2$. To each point $\mathbf{x} = (x_1, x_2) \in S$ corresponds a real number

$$q = x_1^2 + x_2^2.$$

For instance, associated with the points $(2, 5)$ and $(-1, 4)$ in $S$ are the real numbers

$$q_1 = 2^2 + 5^2 = 29$$

and

$$q_2 = (-1)^2 + (4)^2 = 17,$$

respectively.

Functions of two variables may be represented geometrically by the *method of contour lines*. A *contour line* is a set on which the function has a constant value $c$:

$$\{\mathbf{x} = (x_1, x_2): f(\mathbf{x}) = c\}.$$

Each point on the curve $f(\mathbf{x}) = c$ corresponds to the functional value $c$. By considering various values of $c$, we obtain several contour lines. An analysis of these contour lines yields information about the variation in $f(\mathbf{x})$ with changes in $x_1$ and $x_2$.

For example, the *contour lines* of the function

$$f(\mathbf{x}) = x_1^2 + x_2^2$$

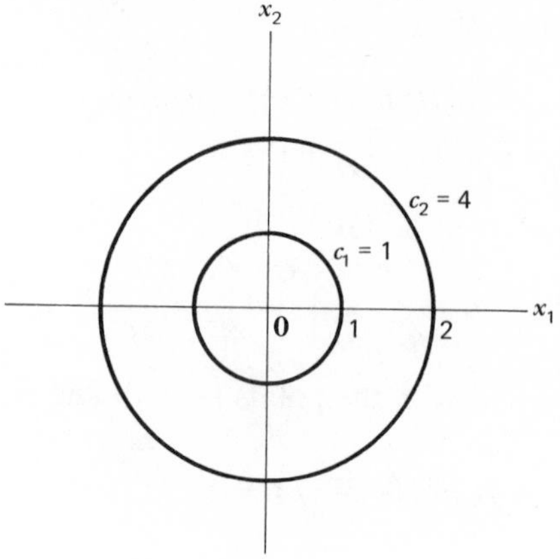


Figure A18

are sets of the form

$$\{\mathbf{x} = (x_1, x_2): x_1^2 + x_2^2 = c\},$$

where $c$ is some constant. Geometrically, this means the contour lines of $f(\mathbf{x})$ are circles with centers at the origin, as shown in Figure A18. The $c_0 = 0$ contour is the origin, (0, 0). The $c_1 = 1$ contour line is a circle of radius 1:

$$\{(x_1, x_2): x_1^2 + x_2^2 = 1\}.$$

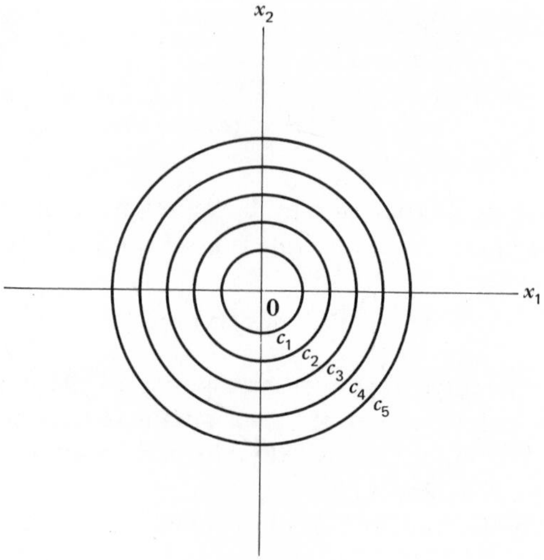


Figure A19

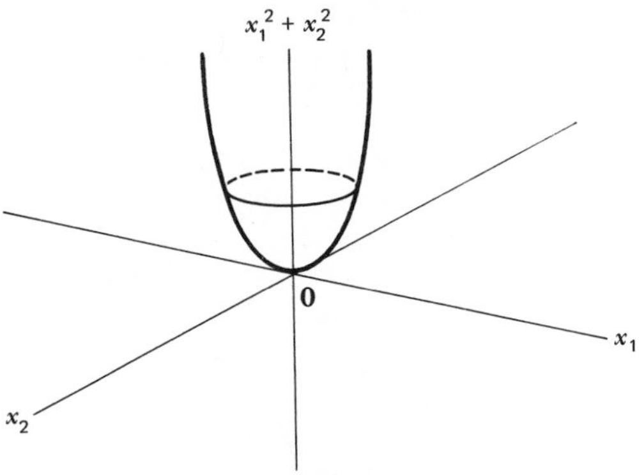


Figure A20

The $c_2 = 4$ contour line is a circle of radius 2:

$$\{(x_1, x_2): x_1^2 + x_2^2 = 4\}.$$

By continuing to plot the loci, $x_1^2 + x_2^2 = c_3$, $x_1^2 + x_2^2 = c_4$, . . . for various constants $c_3$, $c_4$, . . . , the contour lines provide a better understanding of the function $f(\mathbf{x}) = x_1^2 + x_2^2$. Specifically, as shown in Figure A19, the value of $f(\mathbf{x})$ at (0, 0) is 0 and increases as we move radially away from the origin in any direction.

With this information we may represent the function $f(\mathbf{x}) = x_1^2 + x_2^2$ by a surface in three-dimensional space. Each point $\mathbf{x} = (x_1, x_2)$ on the contour $\{\mathbf{x} = (x_1, x_2): x_1^2 + x_2^2 = c\}$ corresponds to a functional value $c$. If each of these points $(x_1, x_2, c)$ is plotted in three-dimensional space, the result is a circle of radius $\sqrt{c}$ that is $c$ units above the $x_1$ and $x_2$ plane. By considering all possible values of $c$, we obtain the surface shown in Figure A20.

As a second illustration of the method of contours, consider the function

$$f(\mathbf{x}) = x_1 x_2.$$

The contours of $f(\mathbf{x})$ are sets of the form

$$\{\mathbf{x} = (x_1, x_2): x_1 x_2 = c\},$$

where $c$ is a constant. The $c_1 = 1$ and $c_2 = -1$ contours are the sets

$$\{(x_1, x_2): x_1 x_2 = 1\}$$

and

$$\{(x_1, x_2): x_1 x_2 = -1\},$$

respectively. These are shown in Figure A21.

Continuing to plot more contour lines, we discover the contour lines

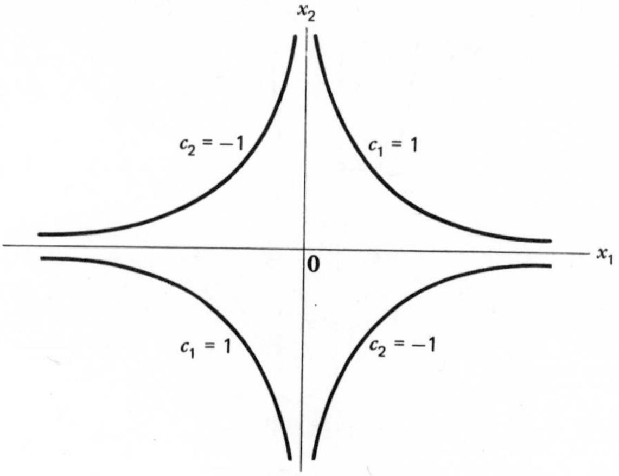


**Figure A21**

of $f(\mathbf{x}) = x_1x_2$ appear as in Figure A22. For points $\mathbf{x}$ in the first and third quadrants, the values of $f(\mathbf{x})$ are positive and increase as we move away from the axes. For points $\mathbf{x}$ in the second and fourth quadrants the values of $f(\mathbf{x})$ are negative and decrease as we move away from the axes. If for each contour the points $(x_1, x_2, c)$ are plotted in three-dimensional space, the function $f(\mathbf{x}) = x_1x_2$ is represented by the surface shown in Figure A23.

Contour lines also provide information about the "steepness" of the corresponding surfaces. The closer the contour lines of $f(\mathbf{x})$ appear, the more rapidly the values of $f(\mathbf{x})$ are changing. For instance, the distance between

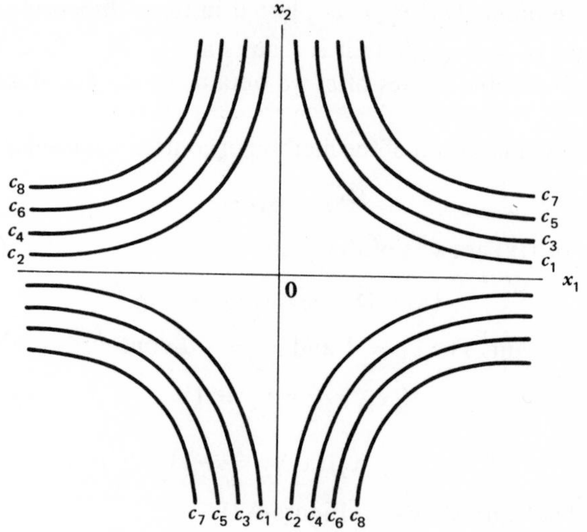


**Figure A22**

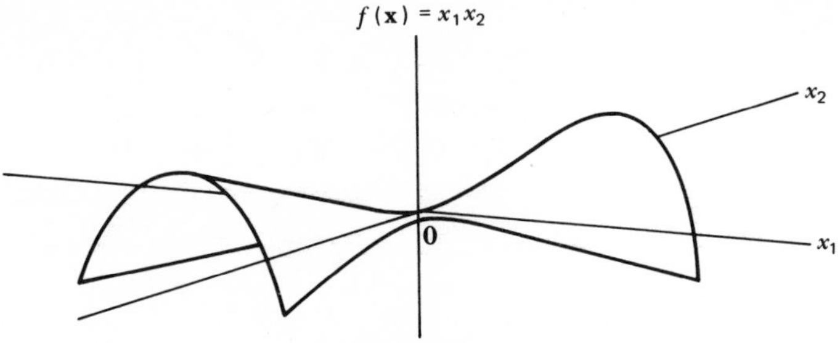


Figure A23

the contours of $f(\mathbf{x}) = x_1^2 + x_2^2$ decreases as we move away from the origin, implying that the values of $f(\mathbf{x})$ are increasing more rapidly.

## Limits and Continuity

Observe that any changes in the "height" of the surfaces in Figures A20 and A23 are gradual; that is, there are no sudden breaks or interruptions in the surfaces. Intuitively this suggests a characterization for continuous functions of two variables; specifically, there are no abrupt changes in the surface corresponding to a continuous function of two variables. Although this intuitive description may be of value, let us define precisely the notions of limit and continuity for functions of two variables.

Suppose $f(\mathbf{x})$ is defined on some open set $S \subset \mathbb{R}^2$, except possibly at $\mathbf{y}$, an interior or boundary point of $S$. Then the *limit* of $f(\mathbf{x})$ as $\mathbf{x}$ approaches $\mathbf{y}$ is $a$, written as

$$\lim_{\mathbf{x}\to\mathbf{y}} f(\mathbf{x}) = a,$$

if for any $\epsilon > 0$, there exists a $\delta > 0$ such that

$$|f(\mathbf{x}) - a| < \epsilon \qquad \text{whenever} \qquad \|\mathbf{x} - \mathbf{y}\| < \delta.$$

That is, if $\mathbf{x}$ is sufficiently close to (and not at) $\mathbf{y}$, the value of $f(\mathbf{x})$ is as close as desired to the limiting value $a$. Note that it is not necessary for the function to be defined at $\mathbf{y}$ in order for this limit to exist.

To illustrate this definition, consider the function

$$f(\mathbf{x}) = x_1^2 + x_2^2 + 1$$

on $S = \mathbb{R}^2$. The limit,

$$\lim_{\mathbf{x}\to\mathbf{0}} x_1^2 + x_2^2 + 1 = 1,$$

where $\mathbf{0} = (0, 0)$, is correct because for a given $\epsilon > 0$,

$$|x_1^2 + x_2^2 + 1 - 1| < \epsilon$$

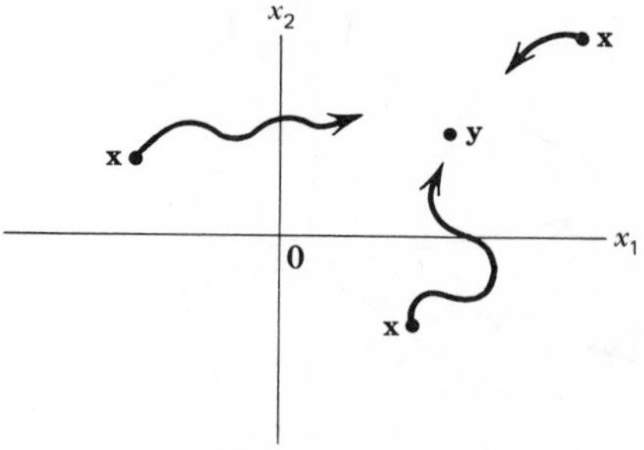


**Figure A24**

if $\|\mathbf{x} - \mathbf{0}\| < \delta$ whenever $\delta = \epsilon^{1/2}$. That is, with $\delta = \epsilon^{1/2}$,

$$\|\mathbf{x} - \mathbf{0}\| = [(x_1 - 0)^2 + (x_2 - 0)^2]^{1/2} = (x_1^2 + x_2^2)^{1/2} < \delta = \epsilon^{1/2},$$

or

$$(x_1^2 + x_2^2) < \epsilon.$$

Thus,

$$|f(\mathbf{x}) - 1| = |x_1^2 + x_2^2 + 1 - 1| = |x_1^2 + x_2^2| < \epsilon.$$

The definition of a continuous function of several variables may be expressed in terms of limits. Suppose a function $f(\mathbf{x})$ is defined on an open set $S \subset \mathbb{R}^2$.The function $f(\mathbf{x})$ is said to be *continuous at a point* $\mathbf{y} \in S$ if and only if

$$\lim_{\mathbf{x}\to\mathbf{y}} f(\mathbf{x}) = f(\mathbf{y}).$$

That is, as the point **x** approaches **y** *from any direction* (see Figure A24), the value $f(\mathbf{x})$ tends to the value $f(\mathbf{y})$. The function $f(\mathbf{x})$ is said to be *continuous on* $S$ if it is continuous at every point of $S$.

Thus, for instance,

$$f(\mathbf{x}) = 2x_1 + x_2$$

is continuous at $\mathbf{y} = (1, 2)$, since $f(\mathbf{y}) = 4$ and

$$\lim_{\mathbf{x}\to\mathbf{y}} f(\mathbf{x}) = \lim_{\mathbf{x}\to\mathbf{y}} 2x_1 + x_2 = 4 = f(\mathbf{y}).$$

Note that this limiting value is $f(\mathbf{y}) = 4$ regardless of the direction from which **x** approaches **y**.

The function

$$f(\mathbf{x}) = \frac{x_1^2 - x_2^2}{x_1^2 + x_2^2}$$

defined on $S = \mathbb{R}^2$, however, is not continuous at (0, 0). This is because as $\mathbf{x} = (x_1, x_2)$ approaches (0, 0) along the $x_2$-axis (with $x_1 \equiv 0$), $f(\mathbf{x})$ tends to

$-1$; but if $\mathbf{x} = (x_1, x_2)$ approaches $(0, 0)$ along the $x_1$-axis (with $x_2 \equiv 0$), $f(\mathbf{x})$ tends to 1. The limiting value depends upon the path along which $\mathbf{x}$ approaches $\mathbf{y}$.

Corresponding to the results for continuous functions of one variable, the following can be proved:

THEOREM A1 If $f(\mathbf{x})$ and $g(\mathbf{x})$ are continuous at a point $\mathbf{y} \in S \subset \mathbb{R}^2$, then $f(\mathbf{x}) + g(\mathbf{x})$, $f(\mathbf{x})g(\mathbf{x})$, and $f(\mathbf{x})/g(\mathbf{x})$, where $g(\mathbf{y}) \neq 0$, are continuous at $\mathbf{y}$. ▮

Furthermore, the elementary functions such as exponentials, logarithms, polynomials, and trigonometric functions are generally continuous, provided the logarithm of zero is not calculated and denominators are nonzero.

### The Directional Derivative

The concept of a "derivative" of a function of two variables involves examining the rate of change of a function *in a particular direction*. The rate of change of $f(\mathbf{x})$ at a point $\mathbf{y}$ depends not only on the point $\mathbf{y}$ but also on the direction in which the change is taking place.

Given a function $f(\mathbf{x}) = f(x_1, x_2)$ defined on an open set $S \subset \mathbb{R}^2$ and a (unit) vector $\mathbf{v}$ in $\mathbb{R}^2$, we consider values of $f(\mathbf{x})$ in the direction $\mathbf{v}$ along the line

$$\{\mathbf{x} = (x_1, x_2) : \mathbf{x} = \mathbf{y} + h\mathbf{v}, h \in \mathbb{R}, \mathbf{y} \in S\}$$

in $S$ (see Figure A25). The change in $f(\mathbf{x})$ from its value at $\mathbf{y}$ to its value at $\mathbf{y} + h\mathbf{v}$ is

$$f(\mathbf{y} + h\mathbf{v}) - f(\mathbf{y}).$$

Since $\mathbf{v}$ is a unit vector, the distance from $\mathbf{y}$ to $\mathbf{y} + h\mathbf{v}$ is $h$, and, therefore,

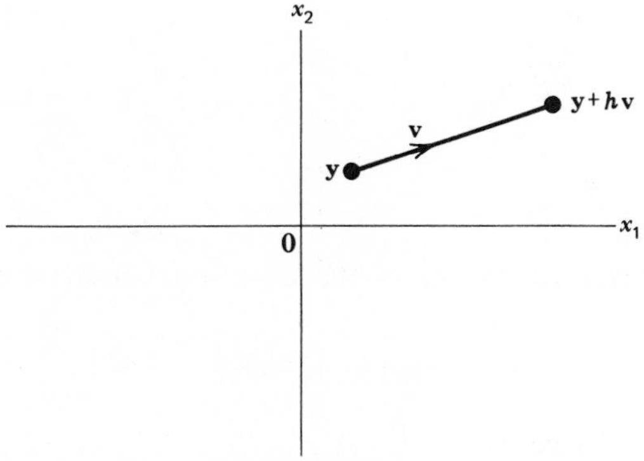


Figure A25

the average rate of change in $f(\mathbf{x})$ per unit distance is

$$\frac{f(\mathbf{y} + h\mathbf{v}) - f(\mathbf{y})}{h}. \tag{A5}$$

The instantaneous rate of change in the value of $f(\mathbf{x})$ at $\mathbf{y}$ in the direction $\mathbf{v}$ is, then, the limit of (A5):

$$\lim_{h \to 0} \frac{f(\mathbf{y} + h\mathbf{v}) - f(\mathbf{y})}{h}.$$

The latter quantity is called the *directional derivative* of $f(\mathbf{x})$ at $\mathbf{y}$ in the direction $\mathbf{v}$ and is denoted by

$$D_{\mathbf{v}} f(\mathbf{y}).$$

Thus, for example, the directional derivative of

$$f(\mathbf{x}) = x_1 + x_2$$

at $\mathbf{y} = (2, -1)$ in the direction $\mathbf{v} = (1/\sqrt{2}, 1/\sqrt{2})$ is

$$\begin{aligned}
D_{\mathbf{v}} f(\mathbf{y}) &= \lim_{h \to 0} \frac{f(\mathbf{y} + h\mathbf{v}) - f(\mathbf{y})}{h} \\
&= \lim_{h \to 0} \frac{y_1 + h(1/\sqrt{2}) + y_2 + h(1/\sqrt{2}) - y_1 - y_2}{h} \\
&= \lim_{h \to 0} \frac{2 + h(1/\sqrt{2}) - 1 + h(1/\sqrt{2}) - 2 + 1}{h} \\
&= \lim_{h \to 0} \frac{h}{h} \frac{2}{\sqrt{2}} \\
&= \frac{2}{\sqrt{2}}.
\end{aligned}$$

As a second illustration of the directional derivative, consider the function

$$f(\mathbf{x}) = x_1^2 + x_2^2.$$

The directional derivative of $f(\mathbf{x})$ at $\mathbf{y} = (2, -2)$ in the direction $\mathbf{v} = (1, 0)$

is given by

$$D_{\mathbf{v}}f(\mathbf{y}) = \lim_{h\to 0}\frac{f(\mathbf{y}+h\mathbf{v})-f(\mathbf{y})}{h}$$

$$= \lim_{h\to 0}\frac{(y_1+h)^2+y_2^2-y_1^2-y_2^2}{h}$$

(A6)
$$= \lim_{h\to 0}\frac{(2+h)^2+(-2)^2-(2)^2-(-2)^2}{h}$$

$$= \lim_{h\to 0}\frac{4h+h^2}{h}$$

$$= 4.$$

The directional derivative $D_{\mathbf{v}}f(\mathbf{y})$ has a geometric interpretation. Consider the curve cut out on the intersection of the surface of $f(\mathbf{x})$ and the plane through $\mathbf{y}$ in the direction $\mathbf{v}$, as shown in Figure A26. The directional derivative $D_{\mathbf{v}}f(\mathbf{y})$ is the slope of the tangent to this curve at $(\mathbf{y}, f(\mathbf{y}))$ (see Figure A27).

To illustrate this point, consider the directional derivative of $f(\mathbf{x}) = x_1^2 + x_2^2$ at $\mathbf{y} = (2, -2)$ in the direction $\mathbf{v} = (1, 0)$. As shown above in (A6), $D_{\mathbf{v}}f(\mathbf{y}) = 4$. Thus, the slope of the tangent at $(2, -2, 4)$ to the curve shown in Figure A28 is 4.

Of particular importance are the directional derivatives of a function of two variables in the directions $\mathbf{v} = (1, 0)$ and $\mathbf{v} = (0, 1)$—that is, along

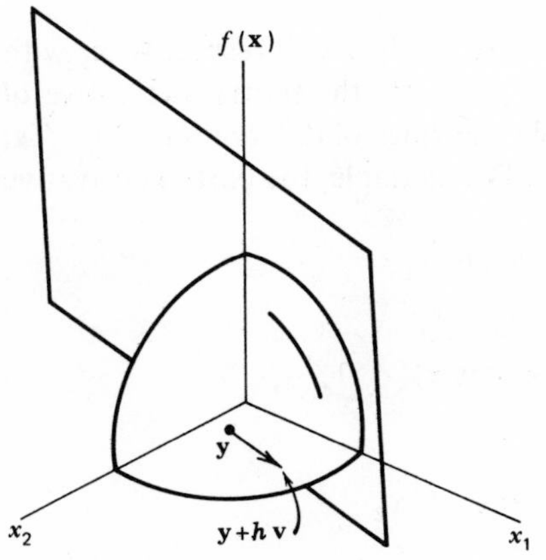

Figure A26

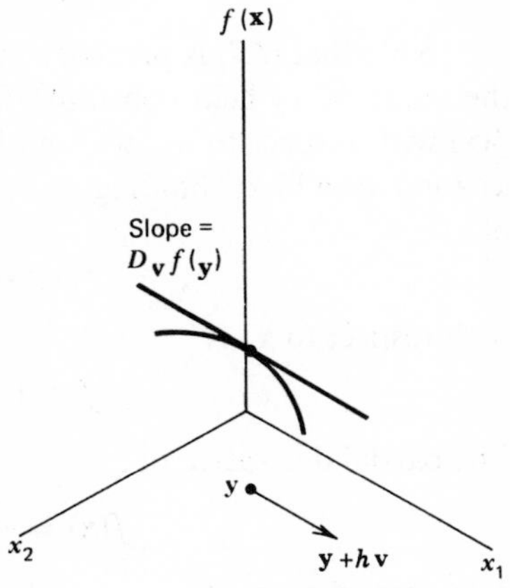

Figure A27

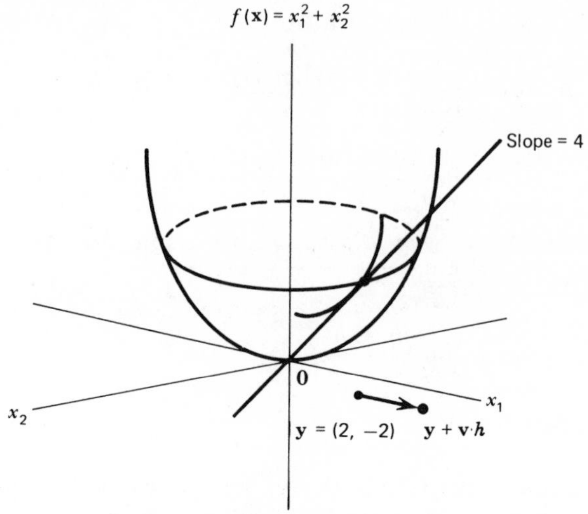


**Figure A28**

the $x_1$- and $x_2$-axes, respectively. Along the $x_1$-axis, in the direction $\mathbf{v} = (1, 0)$, the directional derivative of a function $f(\mathbf{x})$ at $\mathbf{y} = (y_1, y_2)$ is

$$\text{(A7)} \qquad \lim_{h \to 0} \frac{f(\mathbf{y} + h\mathbf{v}) - f(\mathbf{y})}{h} = \lim_{h \to 0} \frac{f(y_1 + h, y_2) - f(y_1, y_2)}{h}.$$

This quantity is called the *partial derivative of* $f(\mathbf{x})$ *with respect to* $x_1$ at $\mathbf{y}$ and is denoted by

$$f_{x_1}(\mathbf{y}) \qquad \text{or} \qquad \frac{\partial f}{\partial x_1}(\mathbf{y}).$$

Note that (A7) is precisely the derivative of $f(\mathbf{x})$ with respect to $x_1$ with the value of $x_2$ held constant. Thus, to calculate the partial derivative of $f(\mathbf{x})$ with respect to $x_1$, we simply apply the rules of differentiation to $f(\mathbf{x})$ as a function of $x_1$, holding $x_2$ constant. For example, the partial derivative of

$$f(\mathbf{x}) = x_1 x_2 + \sin x_1$$

with respect to $x_1$ is

$$f_{x_1}(\mathbf{x}) = x_2 + \cos x_1.$$

The partial derivative of

$$f(\mathbf{x}) = e^{2x_1} + x_1^2 x_2 + x_2$$

with respect to $x_1$ is

$$f_{x_1}(\mathbf{x}) = 2e^{2x_1} + 2x_1 x_2.$$

Similarly, the directional derivative of $f(\mathbf{x})$ at $\mathbf{y}$ in the direction $\mathbf{v} = (0, 1)$ is given by

$$\text{(A8)} \qquad \lim_{h \to 0} \frac{f(\mathbf{y} + h\mathbf{v}) - f(\mathbf{y})}{h} = \lim_{h \to 0} \frac{f(y_1, y_2 + h) - f(y_1, y_2)}{h}.$$

This quantity is termed the *partial derivative of* $f(\mathbf{x})$ *with respect to* $x_2$ at $\mathbf{y}$ and is denoted by

$$f_{x_2}(\mathbf{y}) \qquad \text{or} \qquad \frac{\partial f}{\partial x_2}(\mathbf{y}).$$

As (A8) implies, to partially differentiate with respect to $x_2$, we treat $x_1$ as a constant and apply the rules of differentiation to $f(\mathbf{x})$ as a function of $x_2$. Thus, the partial derivative of

$$f(\mathbf{x}) = e^{x_1} \sin x_2 + \ln x_2$$

with respect to $x_2$ is

$$f_{x_2}(\mathbf{x}) = e^{x_1} \cos x_2 + \frac{1}{x_2}.$$

The partial derivative of

$$f(\mathbf{x}) = e^{(x_1 + 1)x_2} + x_1^3$$

with respect to $x_2$ is given by

$$f_{x_2}(\mathbf{x}) = (x_1 + 1)e^{(x_1 + 1)x_2}.$$

The geometric interpretation of the partial derivative is, of course, similar to that of the more general directional derivative. Consider the curve on the intersection of the surface $f(\mathbf{x})$ and the plane through $\mathbf{y}$ in the direction $\mathbf{v} = (1, 0)$. The partial derivative $f_{x_1}(\mathbf{y})$ is the slope of the tangent to this curve at $(\mathbf{y}, f(\mathbf{y}))$ (see Figure A29). Likewise, $f_{x_2}(\mathbf{y})$ is the slope of the tangent to the curve at $(\mathbf{y}, f(\mathbf{y}))$ in the intersection of the surface $f(\mathbf{x})$ and the plane through $\mathbf{y}$ in the direction $\mathbf{v} = (0, 1)$ (see Figure A30). Note that the partial derivatives at a single point represent the slopes of different tangent lines and hence are not necessarily equal.

From this geometric interpretation of partial derivatives at a point $\mathbf{y}$, we see intuitively that if the surface is sufficiently smooth near $\mathbf{y}$ both partial derivatives exist; that is, at the point $\mathbf{y}$ there are tangent lines to the surface in the directions $\mathbf{v} = (1, 0)$ and $\mathbf{v} = (0, 1)$. Furthermore, since these two lines determine a plane, it is reasonable to conjecture that the equation of the plane containing the tangent lines at $(\mathbf{y}, f(\mathbf{y}))$ to *all* curves in the surface passing through $(\mathbf{y}, f(\mathbf{y}))$ may be characterized in terms of these partials. Such a plane is termed the *tangent plane* to the surface at $(\mathbf{y}, f(\mathbf{y}))$.

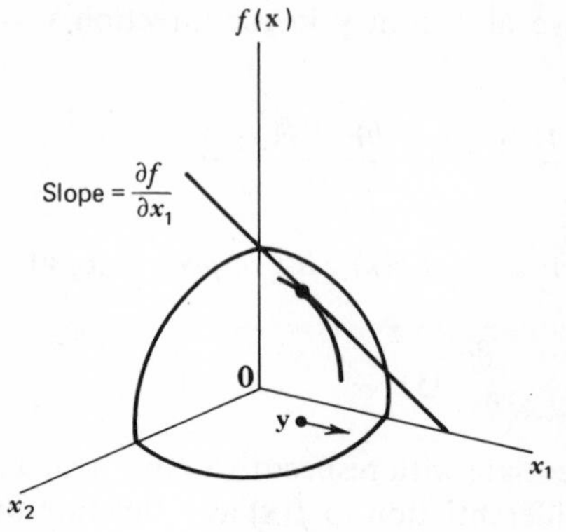


Figure A29

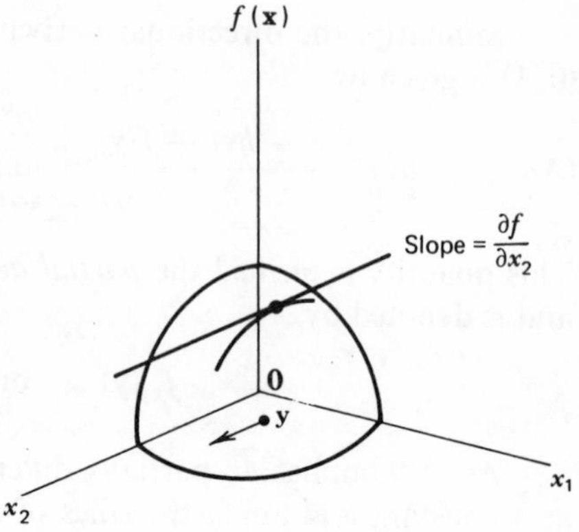


Figure A30

The equation of the tangent plane to the surface corresponding to $f(\mathbf{x})$ at the point $(\mathbf{y}, f(\mathbf{y}))$ has the form

$$\text{(A9)} \qquad A(x_1 - y_1) + B(x_2 - y_2) + C[f(\mathbf{x}) - f(\mathbf{y})] = 0,$$

for constants $A$, $B$, and $C$. And, as we shall show, these constants are, in fact, related to the partials of $f(\mathbf{x})$.

To determine this relationship, consider the curve cut out on the surface of $f(\mathbf{x})$ by the plane $x_2 = y_2$ through $(\mathbf{y}, f(\mathbf{y}))$ (see Figure A31). According to the geometric interpretation of the partial derivative, the tangent to the curve at $(\mathbf{y}, f(\mathbf{y}))$ has slope

$$f_{x_1}(\mathbf{y}).$$

As illustrated in Figure A31, this tangent line lies both in the plane $x_2 = y_2$

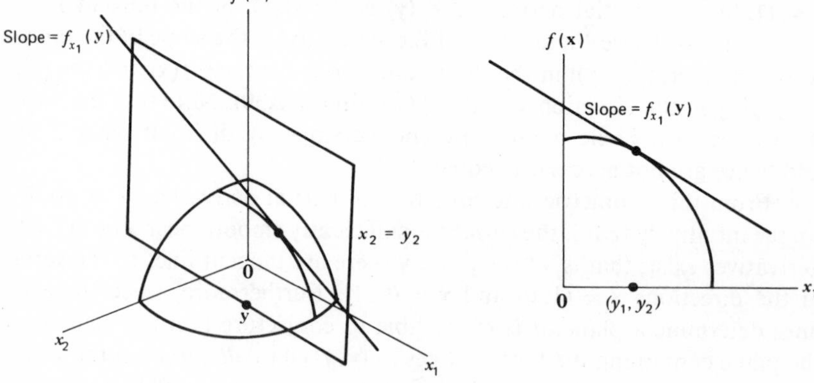


Figure A31

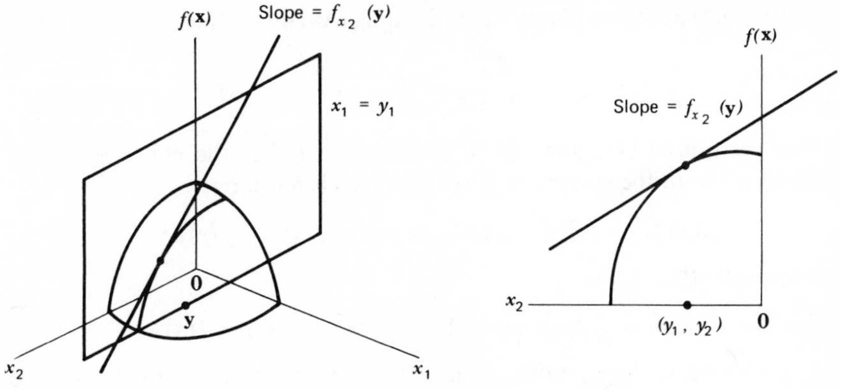


**Figure A32**

and the plane (A9). Equation (A9) implies that the equation of this tangent line in the $x_2 = y_2$ plane is

(A10) $$A(x_1 - y_1) + C[f(\mathbf{x}) - f(\mathbf{y})] = 0.$$

By differentiating (A10) with respect to $x_1$, we determine that the slope of this tangent line at $(\mathbf{y}, f(\mathbf{y}))$ is

(A11) $$f_{x_1}(\mathbf{y}) = -\frac{A}{C}.$$

Thus, we have determined a relationship between $A$, $C$, and $f_{x_1}(\mathbf{y})$.

In a similar manner, consider the curve cut out on the surface through $(\mathbf{y}, f(\mathbf{y}))$ by the plane $x_1 = y_1$ (see Figure A32). According to the geometric interpretation of the partial derivative, the tangent to this curve at $(\mathbf{y}, f(\mathbf{y}))$ has slope

$$f_{x_2}(\mathbf{y}).$$

As shown in Figure A32, this tangent line lies both in the plane (A9) and the plane $x_1 = y_1$. As above, (A9) implies that the equation of this tangent line is

(A12) $$B(x_2 - y_2) + C[f(\mathbf{x}) - f(\mathbf{y})] = 0.$$

By differentiating (A12) with respect to $x_2$, we determine that the slope of this tangent line at $(\mathbf{y}, f(\mathbf{y}))$ is

(A13) $$f_{x_2}(\mathbf{y}) = -\frac{B}{C},$$

thus relating $B$, $C$, and $f_{x_2}(\mathbf{y})$.

Now relationships (A11) and (A13) may be used in developing the equation of the tangent plane. First, dividing (A9) by $-C\,(\neq 0)$, (A9) becomes

$$-\frac{A}{C}(x_1 - y_1) - \frac{B}{C}(x_2 - y_2) - [f(\mathbf{x}) - f(\mathbf{y})] = 0.$$

Using relations (A11) and (A13), we determine that the equation of the tangent plane to the surface of $f(\mathbf{x})$ at $(\mathbf{y}, f(\mathbf{y}))$ is given by

$$f_{x_1}(\mathbf{y})(x_1 - y_1) + f_{x_2}(\mathbf{y})(x_2 - y_2) - [f(\mathbf{x}) - f(\mathbf{y})] = 0,$$

or, equivalently,

$$\text{(A14)} \qquad f(\mathbf{y}) + f_{x_1}(\mathbf{y})(x_1 - y_1) + f_{x_2}(\mathbf{y})(x_2 - y_2) = f(\mathbf{x}).$$

To illustrate the equation of the tangent plane, consider the tangent to the surface defined by

$$f(\mathbf{x}) = x_1^2 + x_2^2$$

at the point $\mathbf{y} = (1, 1)$. According to (A14), in order to form this equation, first we must determine the partial derivatives of $f(\mathbf{x})$,

$$f_{x_1}(\mathbf{x}) = 2x_1, \qquad f_{x_2}(\mathbf{x}) = 2x_2.$$

At the point $\mathbf{y} = (1, 1)$, these partials have the values

$$f_{x_1}(\mathbf{y}) = 2, \qquad f_{x_2}(\mathbf{y}) = 2.$$

Therefore, according to (A14), since $f(\mathbf{y}) = 2$, the equation of the tangent plane to this surface at $\mathbf{y} = (1, 1)$ is

$$2 + 2(x_1 - 1) + 2(x_2 - 1) = f(\mathbf{x}).$$

Consider a second example. We wish to determine the equation of the tangent plane to the surface given by

$$f(\mathbf{x}) = x_1x_2 + 1$$

at $\mathbf{y} = (-1, 0)$. In constructing this equation, we first determine the partials of $f(\mathbf{x})$,

$$f_{x_1}(\mathbf{x}) = x_2, \qquad f_{x_2}(\mathbf{x}) = x_1.$$

At $\mathbf{y} = (-1, 0)$ the partials have values

$$f_{x_1}(\mathbf{y}) = 0, \qquad f_{x_2}(\mathbf{y}) = -1.$$

Thus, by (A14), since $f(\mathbf{y}) = 1$, the equation of this tangent plane to the surface at $\mathbf{y} = (-1, 0)$ is given by

$$1 - x_2 = f(\mathbf{x}).$$

Vector notation provides an equivalent and more convenient formulation of the equation of a tangent plane. By forming the vector,

$$\mathbf{x} - \mathbf{y} = (x_1 - y_1, x_2 - y_2),$$

and the vector,

$$(f_{x_1}(\mathbf{y}), f_{x_2}(\mathbf{y})),$$

denoted by $\nabla f(\mathbf{y})$, we see that an equivalent formulation of (A14) is

(A15) $$f(\mathbf{y}) + \nabla f(\mathbf{y}) \cdot (\mathbf{x} - \mathbf{y}) = f(\mathbf{x}).$$

The vector of partial derivatives,

$$\nabla f(\mathbf{y}) = (f_{x_1}(\mathbf{y}), f_{x_2}(\mathbf{y})),$$

is known as the *gradient* of $f(\mathbf{x})$ at $\mathbf{y}$. The gradient of

$$f(\mathbf{x}) = \sin x_1 + e^{x_2} + 7,$$

for example, is the vector of partials,

$$\nabla f(\mathbf{x}) = (f_{x_1}(\mathbf{x}), f_{x_2}(\mathbf{x})) = (\cos x_1, e^{x_2}).$$

### Differentiability

The gradient and the directional derivative of a function are essential in defining the concept of a differentiable function of two variables. Specifically, a function $f(\mathbf{x}) = f(x_1, x_2)$ is said to be *differentiable at a point* $\mathbf{y}$ in an open set $S$ if

$$D_{\mathbf{v}}(\mathbf{y}) = \lim_{h \to 0} \frac{f(\mathbf{y} + h\mathbf{v}) - f(\mathbf{y})}{h} = \nabla f(\mathbf{y}) \cdot \mathbf{v}$$

for any unit vector $\mathbf{v}$. $f(\mathbf{x})$ is *differential on* $S$ if it is differentiable at every point of $S$.

For differentiable functions the gradient has a geometric interpretation. Specifically, *the gradient vector* $\nabla f(\mathbf{x})$ *is perpendicular to the tangent to each point on the contour lines of* $f(\mathbf{x})$ (see Figure A33). To see that this is true, consider a point $\mathbf{y}$ on the $c_1$ contour line. The directional derivative in the direction $\mathbf{v}$ of the tangent to this contour line is zero because $f(\mathbf{x})$ remains constant on the contour line. Hence, since $f(\mathbf{x})$ is differentiable,

$$D_{\mathbf{v}} f(\mathbf{y}) = 0 = \nabla f(\mathbf{y}) \cdot \mathbf{v},$$

implying $\nabla f(\mathbf{y})$ is perpendicular to $\mathbf{v}$.

*The direction of the gradient of a differentiable function* $f(\mathbf{x})$ *is the direction of steepest ascent of* $f(\mathbf{x})$. This is readily seen by noting that since

$$D_{\mathbf{v}} f(\mathbf{x}) = \nabla f(\mathbf{x}) \cdot \mathbf{v}$$

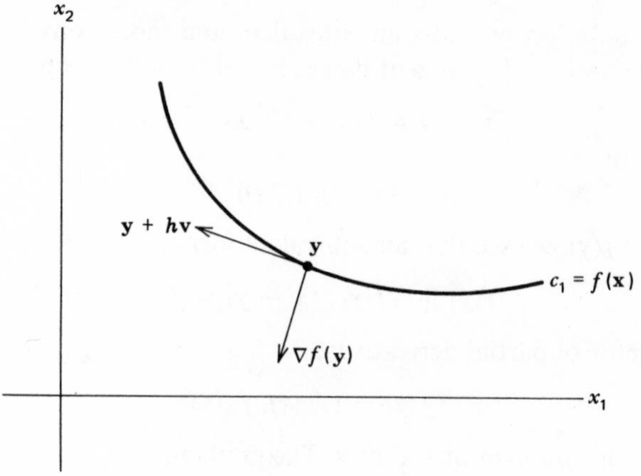


**Figure A33**

for a unit vector $\mathbf{v}$, we have

(A16) $$D_{\mathbf{v}} f(\mathbf{x}) = \|\nabla f(\mathbf{x})\| \, \|\mathbf{v}\| \cos \theta = \|\nabla f(\mathbf{x})\| \cos \theta.$$

Here $\theta$ is the angle between $\mathbf{v}$ and $\nabla f(\mathbf{x})$. The value of $f(\mathbf{x})$ changes most rapidly when $D_{\mathbf{v}} f(\mathbf{x})$ is maximized. According to (A16), $D_{\mathbf{v}} f(\mathbf{x})$ is maximized when $\cos \theta = 1$, that is, when $\mathbf{v}$ and $\nabla f(\mathbf{x})$ have the same direction. Thus, the direction of steepest ascent of $f(\mathbf{x})$ is the direction of $\nabla f(\mathbf{x})$.

### Higher-Order Partial Derivatives

Just as ordinary differentiation may be repeated several times, so can the process of partial differentiation. For instance, consider the function

(A17) $$f(\mathbf{x}) = \sin x_1^2 + 2x_2^2 + x_1 e^{x_2}.$$

The partial derivative of $f(\mathbf{x})$ with respect to $x_1$ is

(A18) $$f_{x_1}(\mathbf{x}) = 2x_1 \cos x_1^2 + e^{x_2}.$$

The second partial derivative of $f(\mathbf{x})$ with respect to $x_1$ is the partial derivative of (A18) with respect to $x_1$,

$$2 \cos x_1^2 - 4x_1^2 \sin x_1^2,$$

and is denoted by $f_{x_1x_1}(\mathbf{x})$.

Similarly, the second partial derivative of (A17) with respect to $x_2$ is the partial of $f_{x_2}(\mathbf{x})$ with respect to $x_2$. Since

$$f_{x_2}(\mathbf{x}) = 4x_2 + x_1 e^{x_2},$$

the second partial with respect to $x_2$ is

$$4 + x_1 e^{x_2}$$

and is denoted by $f_{x_2x_2}(\mathbf{x})$. Partial derivatives of higher order are calculated in a similar manner.

In an analogous way, we may define the mixed partials,

$$f_{x_1x_2}(\mathbf{x}) \qquad \text{and} \qquad f_{x_2x_1}(\mathbf{x}).$$

As expected $f_{x_1x_2}(\mathbf{x})$ is the partial of $f_{x_2}(\mathbf{x})$ with respect to $x_1$, and $f_{x_2x_1}(\mathbf{x})$ is the partial of $f_{x_1}(\mathbf{x})$ with respect to $x_2$.

To illustrate these mixed partials, consider the function (A17). The mixed partial $f_{x_2x_1}(\mathbf{x})$ is the partial of

$$f_{x_1}(\mathbf{x}) = 2x_1 \cos x_1^2 + e^{x_2}$$

with respect to $x_2$. Therefore,

$$f_{x_2x_1}(\mathbf{x}) = e^{x_2}.$$

The mixed partial $f_{x_1x_2}(\mathbf{x})$ is the partial of

$$f_{x_2}(\mathbf{x}) = 4x_2 + x_1 e^{x_2}$$

with respect to $x_1$. Hence,

$$f_{x_1x_2}(\mathbf{x}) = e^{x_2}.$$

Note in our example that

$$f_{x_1x_2}(\mathbf{x}) = f_{x_2x_1}(\mathbf{x});$$

this equality is not unique to our example. In general, we have the following result:

THEOREM A2 If $f(\mathbf{x})$ together with the partials

$$f_{x_1}(\mathbf{x}), \qquad f_{x_2}(\mathbf{x}), \qquad f_{x_1x_1}(\mathbf{x}), \qquad f_{x_2x_2}(\mathbf{x})$$

are continuous in a neighborhood of a point $\mathbf{y}$, then

$$f_{x_1x_2}(\mathbf{y}) = f_{x_2x_1}(\mathbf{y}). \quad ∎$$

### Functions of *n* Variables

The concepts of limit, continuity, and differentiability may be extended to functions of $n$ variables. Although functions of $n \geq 2$ variables cannot be represented by three-dimensional surfaces, their characteristics are similar to functions of two variables. We begin by defining a function of $n$ variables.

Suppose that to each point $\mathbf{x} = (x_1, \ldots, x_n) \in S \subset \mathbb{R}^n$ we can assign a real number $q$. The real number $q$ is said to be given as a *function of the $n$ variables* $x_1, \ldots, x_n$ and is denoted by

$$q = f(x_1, \ldots, x_n)$$

or, in vector notation,

$$q = f(\mathbf{x}).$$

If this function is defined on an open set $S \subset \mathbb{R}^n$, except possibly at an interior or boundary point $\mathbf{y}$ of $S$, we may define the notion of a limit of $f(\mathbf{x})$. The *limit* of $f(\mathbf{x})$ as $\mathbf{x}$ approaches $\mathbf{y}$ is $a$, written

$$\lim_{\mathbf{x} \to \mathbf{y}} f(\mathbf{x}) = a,$$

if for any $\epsilon > 0$, there exists $\delta > 0$ such that

$$|f(\mathbf{x}) - a| < \epsilon \quad \text{whenever} \quad \|\mathbf{x} - \mathbf{y}\| < \delta.$$

Just as for functions of two variables, this definition states that if $\mathbf{x}$ is sufficiently close to (but not at) $\mathbf{y}$, the value of $f(\mathbf{x})$ is as close as desired to the limiting value $a$.

From the definition of a limit, we define the concept of a continuous function of $n$ variables. Suppose a function $f(\mathbf{x})$ is defined on an open set $S \subset \mathbb{R}^n$. The function $f(\mathbf{x})$ is said to be *continuous at a point* $\mathbf{y} \in S$ if and only if

$$\lim_{\mathbf{x} \to \mathbf{y}} f(\mathbf{x}) = f(\mathbf{y}).$$

If $f(\mathbf{x})$ is continuous at every point of $S$, $f(\mathbf{x})$ is said to be *continuous on* $S$.

The concept of a directional derivative for a function of $n$ variables is defined in a manner similar to that of a function of two variables. Suppose $f(\mathbf{x})$ is defined on an open set $S \subset \mathbb{R}^n$. The *directional derivative* of $f(\mathbf{x})$ at a point $\mathbf{y} = (y_1, \ldots, y_n) \in S$ in the direction of a unit vector $\mathbf{v} \in \mathbb{R}^n$ is given by

$$\lim_{h \to 0} \frac{f(\mathbf{y} + h\mathbf{v}) - f(\mathbf{y})}{h}.$$

This quantity is denoted by $D_{\mathbf{v}} f(\mathbf{y})$.

The partial derivatives of a function of $n$ variables are special cases of the directional derivative. The partial derivative of $f(\mathbf{x})$ with respect to $x_i$ at a point $\mathbf{y} = (y_1, \ldots, y_n) \in S \subset \mathbb{R}^n$ is the directional derivative of $f(\mathbf{x})$ at $\mathbf{y}$ in the direction of $\mathbf{v} = (0, \ldots, 0, 1, 0, \ldots, 0)$. Here $\mathbf{v}$ has a 1 in the $i$th component; that is, the *partial derivative* of $f(\mathbf{x})$ with respect to $x_i$ at $\mathbf{y} \in \mathbb{R}^n$ is given by

$$\lim_{h \to 0} \frac{f(\mathbf{y} + h\mathbf{v}) - f(\mathbf{y})}{h} =$$

$$\lim_{h \to 0} \frac{f(y_1, \ldots, y_i + h, \ldots, y_n) - f(y_1, \ldots, y_n)}{h}$$

and is denoted by

$$f_{x_i}(\mathbf{y}) \qquad \text{or} \qquad \frac{\partial f}{\partial x_i}(\mathbf{y}).$$

As the definition implies, the partial derivative of $f(\mathbf{x})$ with respect to $x_i$ is obtained by differentiating $f(\mathbf{x})$ with respect to $x_i$, holding all other variables constant. Higher-order partials such as

$$f_{x_i x_i}(\mathbf{x})$$

and mixed partials

$$f_{x_i x_j}(\mathbf{x})$$

are defined just as for functions of two variables.

Having introduced the concept of a partial derivative for a function of $n$ variables, we define the gradient of these functions. The *gradient* of $f(\mathbf{x})$ at a point $\mathbf{y} \in S \subset \mathbb{R}^n$ is the vector of first partials of $f(\mathbf{x})$ at $\mathbf{y}$,

$$(f_{x_1}(\mathbf{y}), f_{x_2}(\mathbf{y}), \ldots, f_{x_n}(\mathbf{y})),$$

and is denoted by $\nabla f(\mathbf{y})$.

Finally, the concepts of the gradient and directional derivative are utilized to define a differentiable function of $n$ variables. The function $f(\mathbf{x})$ defined on an open set $S \subset \mathbb{R}^n$ is said to be *differentiable* at a point $\mathbf{y} \in S$ if

$$D_{\mathbf{v}} f(\mathbf{y}) = \nabla f(\mathbf{y}) \cdot \mathbf{v}$$

for any unit vector $\mathbf{v}$.

## EXERCISES

1. Let $\mathbf{x} = (7, 1)$, $\mathbf{y} = (2, -4)$, and $\mathbf{z} = (-1, 3)$. Determine each of the following and represent them graphically:

   (*a*) $9\mathbf{x}$

   (*b*) $\mathbf{x} + \mathbf{y}$

   (*c*) $\mathbf{x} - \mathbf{y}$

   (*d*) $7\mathbf{x} + 4\mathbf{y}$

   (*e*) $3\mathbf{x} + 0\mathbf{y}$

   (*f*) $6\mathbf{z} + \mathbf{0}$

   (*g*) $(\mathbf{x} - 4\mathbf{y}) + (3\mathbf{y} - \mathbf{z})$

   (*h*) $6[\mathbf{x} + (\mathbf{y} - 7\mathbf{z})]$.

2. Determine the norm of the following vectors:

(*a*) $\mathbf{x} = (-1, 2)$

(*b*) $\mathbf{x} = (1, -3)$

(*c*) $\mathbf{x} = (8, -1, 4)$

(*d*) $\mathbf{x} = (-2, 6, 10, 1)$.

3. Let $\mathbf{x} = (-1, 8)$ and $\mathbf{y} = (3, 4)$. Determine

(*a*) $\mathbf{x} \cdot \mathbf{y}$

(*b*) the angle between $\mathbf{x}$ and $\mathbf{y}$.

4. Let $\mathbf{x} = (0, -1, 4, -4)$ and $\mathbf{y} = (6, 6, -2, 3)$. Determine

(*a*) $\mathbf{x} \cdot \mathbf{y}$

(*b*) the angle between $\mathbf{x}$ and $\mathbf{y}$.

5. Show that $\mathbf{x} = (-1, 0)$ and $\mathbf{y} = (2, 2)$ are linearly independent vectors.
6. Determine whether the vectors $\mathbf{w} = (2, 3, -4, 5)$, $\mathbf{x} = (1, 0, 0, 0)$, $\mathbf{y} = (-1, 0, 0, 6)$, $\mathbf{z} = (0, -1, 2, -1)$ are linearly independent.
7. Sketch a graph of each of the following sets and classify each as open, closed, or neither:

(*a*) $\{(x_1, x_2): x_1^2 + x_2^2 \geq 1\}$

(*b*) $\{(x_1, x_2): x_1^2 + x_2^2 \leq 0\}$

(*c*) $\{(x_1, x_2): x_1 + x_2 > 0, x_1 - x_2 < 2\}$

(*d*) $\{(x_1, x_2): (x_1 - 1)^2 x_2^2 \geq 0\}$

(*e*) $\{(x_1, x_2): x_1 > 1, x_1 - x_2 < 0\}$.

8. (*a*) Show that the intersection of two open sets is open.
(*b*) Show that the union of two open sets is open.
9. Represent each of the following functions by drawing contour lines and sketching a surface in three-dimensional space:

(*a*) $f(\mathbf{x}) = x_1$

(*b*) $f(\mathbf{x}) = x_1 + x_2$

(*c*) $f(\mathbf{x}) = x_1^2 + x_2^2 + 3$

(*d*) $f(\mathbf{x}) = \sin(x_1 + x_2)$

(*e*) $f(\mathbf{x}) = x_1^2 - x_2^2$

(*f*) $f(\mathbf{x}) = e^{x_1} + x_2$

(*g*) $f(\mathbf{x}) = \sqrt{x_1^2 + x_2^2}$.

10. For each of the functions in problem 9 determine:

(*a*) the directional derivative at $\mathbf{y} = (1, 1)$ in the direction $\mathbf{v} = (1/\sqrt{3}, \sqrt{\frac{2}{3}})$;

(*b*) the partial derivatives $f_{x_1}(\mathbf{x})$ and $f_{x_2}(\mathbf{x})$;

(*c*) the second-order partial derivatives, $f_{x_1x_1}(\mathbf{x})$ and $f_{x_2x_2}(\mathbf{x})$;

(*d*) the mixed partial derivatives, $f_{x_1x_2}(\mathbf{x})$ and $f_{x_2x_1}(\mathbf{x})$;

(*e*) the gradient of $f(\mathbf{x})$ at (2, 4).

11. For each of the following, determine the equation of the tangent plane to the surface representation of $f(\mathbf{x})$ at the indicated point $(\mathbf{y}, f(\mathbf{y}))$.

(*a*) $f(\mathbf{x}) = x_1^2 - 2x_1x_2 + x_2^2$ (0, 4, 16)

(*b*) $f(\mathbf{x}) = \dfrac{x_1^2}{\sqrt{x_1^2 + x_2^2}}$ $(\sqrt{2}, \sqrt{2}, 1)$

(*c*) $f(\mathbf{x}) = \sin(x_1 + x_2)$ (0, 0, 0)

(*d*) $f(\mathbf{x}) = 4x_1 + 5x_2$ $(1, -1, -1)$

(*e*) $f(\mathbf{x}) = 4x_1^2 - 6x_2^2$ $(2, -1, 10)$.

12. Show that $f_{x_1x_1}(\mathbf{x}) = a^2 f_{x_2x_2}(\mathbf{x})$ for $f(\mathbf{x}) = (ax_1 + x_2)^2$, $f(\mathbf{x}) = \sin(ax_1 + x_2)$, and $f(\mathbf{x}) = e^{ax_1 + x_2}$.
13. Show that $f_{x_1x_1}(\mathbf{x}) + f_{x_2x_2}(\mathbf{x}) = 0$ for $f(\mathbf{x}) = \ln(x_1^2 + x_2^2)^{1/2}$.
14. Construct a method for determining the directional derivative of $f(\mathbf{x}) = \sin(x_1 + x_2)$ at the point $(1, -1)$ *in the direction of increasing* $x_1$ *on the curve* $x_2 = x_1^2$.
15. (*a*) Sketch the contour lines and surface for the function $f(\mathbf{x}) = |x_2|$, $\mathbf{x} \in \mathbb{R}^2$.

(*b*) Discuss the continuity and differentiability of $f(\mathbf{x})$.

# SELECTED REFERENCES


Allen, R. G. D., *Mathematical Economics*, Macmillan, London, 1957.

Bailey, N. T. J., *The Mathematical Approach to Biology and Medicine*, Wiley, New York, 1967.

Boyce, W. E. and DiPrima, R. C., *Elementary Differential Equations and Boundary Value Problems*, Wiley, New York, 1965.

Campbell, H. G., *An Introduction to Matrices, Vectors, and Linear Programming*, Appleton-Century-Crofts, New York, 1965.

Chiang, A. C., *Fundamental Methods of Mathematical Economics*, McGraw-Hill, New York, 1967.

Cohen, K. J. and Cyert, R. M., *Theory of the Firm: Resource Allocation in a Market Economy*, Prentice-Hall, Englewood Cliffs, N.J., 1965.

Coleman, J. S., *Introduction to Mathematical Sociology*, Collier-Macmillan, London, 1964.

Dantzig, G. B., *Linear Programming and Extensions*, Princeton University Press, Princeton, N.J., 1963.

Curtis, P. C., *Multivariate Calculus with Linear Algebra*, Wiley, New York, 1972.

Danø, S., *Industrial Production Models: A Theoretical Study*, Springer-Verlag, New York, 1966.

Duffin, R. J. and Peterson, E. L., "Geometric Programming with Signomials," *J. Optimization Theory Appl.*, **11** (1973), 3–35.

Duffin, R. J. and Peterson, E. L., "Reversed Geometric Programming Treated by Harmonic Means," Research Report 71–19, Dept. of Mathematics, Carnegie-Mellon Univ., March 1971.

Duffin, R. J., Peterson, E. L., and Zener, C., *Geometric Programming: Theory and Applications*, Wiley, New York, 1967.

Evans, G. C., *Mathematical Introduction to Economics*, McGraw-Hill, New York, 1930.

Gale, D., *The Theory of Linear Economic Models*, McGraw-Hill, New York, 1960.

Gass, S. I., *Linear Programming*, McGraw-Hill, New York, 1969.

Hanssmann, F., *Operations Research in Production and Inventory Control*, Wiley, New York, 1962.

Kaplan, W., *Advanced Calculus*, Addison-Wesley, Reading, Mass., 1959.

Kazarinoff, N. D., *Geometric Inequalities*, Random House, New York, 1961.

Keyfitz, N., *An Introduction to the Mathematics of Population*, Addison-Wesley, Reading, Mass., 1968.

Kotler, P., *Marketing Decisions Making: A Model Building Approach*, Holt, Rinehart, and Winston, New York, 1971.

Luce, R. N., Bush, R. R., and Galanter, E. (eds.), *Handbook of Mathematical Psychology*, Vol. II, Wiley, New York, 1963.

Moore, R. A., *Introduction to Differential Equations*, Allyn and Bacon, Boston, 1962.

Ritger, P. D. and Rose, N. J., *Differential Equations with Applications*, McGraw-Hill, New York, 1968.

Starr, M. K. and Miller, D. W., *Inventory Control: Theory and Practice*, Prentice Hall, Englewood Cliffs, N.J., 1962.

Simmonard, M., *Linear Programming*, Prentice-Hall, Englewood Cliffs, N.J., 1966.

Taha, H. M., *Operations Research: An Introduction*, Macmillan, New York, 1971.

Thomas, G., *Calculus and Analytic Geometry*, 4th ed., Addison-Wesley, Reading, Mass., 1969.

Wagner, H. M., *Principles of Operations Research, With Applications to Managerial Decisions*, Prentice-Hall, Englewood Cliffs, N.J., 1969.

Whittle, P., *Optimization Under Constraints*, Wiley, New York, 1971.

Wilde, D. J. and Beightler, C. S., *Foundations of Optimization*, Prentice-Hall, Englewood Cliffs, N.J., 1967.

Zahradnik, R. L., *Theory and Techniques of Optimization for Practicing Engineers*, Barnes and Noble, New York, 1971.

Zangwill, W. I., *Nonlinear Programming: A Unified Approach*, Prentice Hall, Englewood Cliffs, N.J., 1969.

Zener, C., *Engineering Design by Geometric Programming*, Wiley, New York, 1971.

# INDEX